2001

Encyclopedia of Postcolonial Studies

Edited by
JOHN C. HAWLEY

Emmanuel S. Nelson, Advisory Editor

GREENWOOD PRESS
Westport, Connecticut • London

Library of Congress Cataloging-in-Publication Data

Encyclopedia of postcolonial studies / edited by John C. Hawley.
    p. cm.
  Includes bibliographical references and index.
  ISBN 0–313–31192–7 (alk. paper)
  1. Developing countries—Literatures—History and criticism—Encyclopedias.
  2. Literature, Modern—20th century—History and criticism—Encyclopedias.
  3. Postcolonialism—Encyclopedias. I. Hawley, John C. (John Charles), 1947–
PN849.U43E53   2001
809'.891724—dc21   2001023317

British Library Cataloguing in Publication Data is available.

Copyright © 2001 by John C. Hawley

Library of Congress Catalog Card Number: 2001023317
ISBN: 0–313–31192–7

First published in 2001

Greenwood Press, 88 Post Road West, Westport, CT 06881
An imprint of Greenwood Publishing Group, Inc.
www.greenwood.com

Printed in the United States of America

The paper used in this book complies with the
Permanent Paper Standard issued by the National
Information Standards Organization (Z39.48–1984).

10 9 8 7 6 5 4 3 2 1

for Trish, Donna, and Chris

Contents

Preface

The increasing globalization of literary studies prompts this reference work, which provides a panoramic snapshot of the ongoing transformation. The term "postcolonial" itself is controversial: which former colonies are to be included in the discussion, and which individuals are to be singled out? How "post" is the current economic situation in destitute newer countries that remain financially linked to, and dependent upon, their former masters? To what extent are European and American scholars recolonizing the cultural world by controlling the publishing houses, choosing the subjects, shaping the future canon? These are among the questions that various entries in this volume address. Whether or not one is satisfied with the analysis that they provide, the issues themselves demonstrate the lively nature of this field, which draws upon history, politics, economics, critical theory, gender studies, and a great many other areas to describe what is going on in literature today. The vibrancy of the exchange suggests that some form of postcolonial studies is likely to become the literary department in universities in the future, collapsing English and modern language departments and inviting further transgression of disciplinary borders. The ramifications of postcoloniality have undeniably enlivened literary and cultural studies in the last decade; the multicultural nature of globalization and the accompanying economic interdependence virtually guarantee that this movement will continue to reshape the literary canon and much else.

Not only students but their teachers as well will continue to play a game of catch-up as the "new literatures" increasingly find a place in the classroom. The need that this volume meets is a single book that introduces, in some reasonable depth, the major concepts undergirding this new field, the origin of its central ideas, and the international nature of the conversation in which they are developing. Such an introduction necessarily focuses heavily on the novelists, poets, and playwrights, generally from the "Third World," who are responding specifically to their status as citizens of "emerging" nations with a colonial history.

Such a book, to be most helpful, must be extensive enough to provide a significant overview of the field but not so lengthy as to render it inaccessible for individual readers. No other such book currently exists. The closest may be Kofi Buenor Hadjor's *Dictionary of Third World Terms* (1992), but Hadjor's book reflects the strengths and weaknesses of a volume written from a single individual's point of view. Two recent books are helpful, but with a limited focus: on the one hand, *Encyclopedia of Post-Colonial Literatures in English* (1994), edited by Eugene Benson and L. W. Conolly, is hugely comprehensive (in two large volumes), but deceptively so. By including so many topics and authors within its covers, the editors leave readers wondering whether sufficient discrimination was guiding the selection that the editors made. More importantly, the motivation for (paradoxically) restricting the coverage to English literatures continues the colonizing bias that postcolonial studies seeks to subvert: these literatures should not be imagined as extensions of any one nation's tenure on communication. A truly representative handbook would necessarily convey the clear impression that the field of postcolonial studies arises in *all* literatures that become available to a large reading audience: anglophone, francophone, lusophone, Chinese, Swahili, Urdu, and so on. It is important that the field be seen as inherently comparative. The other recent book, *Key Concepts in Post-Colonial Studies* (1998), by Bill Ashcroft, Gareth Griffiths, and Helen Tiffin, is closer to the mark. An advantage of the present book over *Key Concepts*, however, is that the broad authorship of our encyclopedia suggests the variety of approaches that are competing for a forum in this contentious field. In his *African Literature and the Crisis of Post-Structuralist Theorising* (1993), Niyi Osundare complains about "the ease and complacency with which Western theories take over the global literary and intellectual arena" and "inscribe themselves as though the other parts of the world were a tabula rasa" (6). A forum for international voices is of paramount importance.

The volume includes alphabetically arranged entries of varying lengths. These entries are devoted to topics and individuals central to the discussion of postcolonial studies, and they are cross-referenced in boldface type to encourage readers to use the book as something similar to a Web site—flipping back and forth and entering increasing levels of complexity. Among the entries on individuals, some are novelists, poets, and playwrights (e.g., Wole Soyinka); others are the major theoreticians of the field (e.g., Gayatri Spivak and Edward Said). Some entries summarize an entire national literature (e.g., Zimbabwean literature); others define key theoretical concepts and offer a history of their development (e.g., Arabism). Individual entries conclude with a (limited) "Further Reading" bibliography relevant to the topic. Since we make an effort to include literatures from nonanglophone countries, and since we also deal with literatures that some would not immediately recognize as "postcolonial," various entries make the case for the expansion of the concept. The focus throughout is upon the writer's (or the idea's) relevance specifically to the field of postcolonial studies. For individual author entries, brief biographical details are included, but the emphasis is upon the postcolonial themes apparent in the writer's major works. For national literature entries, historical background is included, along with attention to any implied conversation ongoing among the national authors. For topical entries, the major theoreticians who have contributed to the development of the idea are discussed. For entries about individual theoreticians an analysis of their idiosyncratic topics is clearly presented with as little jargon as possible.

What (and who) *is* included will be seen to be as controversial as what is *not*. Where possible, individuals are incorporated into larger, national entries in order to present the context that shapes the writer. For some regions, such as the Caribbean, individuals are often discussed separately, lest the entire area be painted with the same brush. Similarly, various national or continental literatures (e.g., Canada, India, Africa) are divided into a limited number of their language groups (with quite separate cultural "arguments" ongoing in the literature). In other instances (e.g., Pacific Island literatures) I have decided to offer a broad survey—not to collapse national cultures into one monolithic whole but to be as inclusive as possible in a book that must remain manageably sized.

As fascinating and vibrant as the field of postcolonial studies seems to many, recent commentators like Kalpana Seshadri-Crooks lament the "melancholia induced paradoxically by its new-found authority and incorporation into institutions of higher learning" (Afzal-Khan and Seshadri-Crooks 2000, 3): the fear is that "institutionalizing the critique of imperialism may render it conciliatory." Such an accommodation to capitalism threatens the enterprise, which "is interested above all in materialist critiques of power and how that power or ideology seeks to interpellate subjects within a discourse as subordinate and without agency" (19). Thus, on the one hand, practitioners of postcolonial studies are among its harshest critics. Their concerns are "addressed" by the enduring amorphousness of the field itself. As Seshadri-Crooks asserts, "it does not have a theory to speak of, concerned as it is with local cultural practices and political issues in the context of transnationalism. Unlike other area studies, postcolonial studies has no identifiable object: it would be impossible to suggest that it pertains to one or the other area of the world or that it is confined to a period, genre, or theme; nor can it name a stable First or Third World subject as its legitimate speaker" (19). Surely, this description is borne out in the present volume, which seeks to avoid (though, inevitably, unsuccessfully) to privilege any voice and, to a somewhat lesser extent, any period. But if some practitioners see this as a cause for melancholy and the wringing of hands, many others welcome it as symptomatic of the breakdown of a hegemonic canonizing and the emergence of new voices and literatures. It is worthwhile to examine a movement once it has become otiose and can be safely poked and dissected, but wrestling with the protean thing itself can be far more bracing.

I am very grateful for the many contributors from around the world who enthusiastically committed themselves to the project because of its perceived importance. Reading their individual entries is an enriching and reliable encounter with the latest thinking in their fields of expertise; reading the book from cover to cover is a stimulating immersion in a torrent of ideas that sparkle in a shared sun. My thanks, as well, to Dr. George Butler, senior editor at Greenwood Press, for his consistent encouragement in the project and to Nicole Cournoyer, production editor for the encyclopedia.

Encyclopedia of Postcolonial Studies

A

Chinua Achebe Chinua Achebe was born Albert Chinualumogo Achebe in November 1930 in Ogidi in eastern Nigeria. Achebe's mother, Janet Iloegbunam Achebe, was the daughter of a blacksmith from Umuike village in Awka. His father, Isaiah Okafo Achebe, was from Ogidi and was baptized into the church by missionaries from the Church Missionary Society in 1904, thereafter being engaged in missionary teaching across eastern Nigeria. Achebe attended schools in Ogidi and Nekede before, in 1944, he earned a place at the prestigious Government College at Umuahia. He was a member of the first class to enroll at the new University College in Ibadan in 1948, recently established as a constituent college of the University of London. He received his B.A. in English literature in 1953.

After a short period teaching, Achebe joined the Nigerian Broadcasting Corporation (NBC) in 1954. He became controller of the Eastern Region of the NBC and in 1961 director of external broadcasting, in effect "the Voice of Nigeria," a position that he took up in Lagos following the award of a Rockefeller travel fellowship in 1960. With the onset of the Nigerian civil war in 1967 Achebe returned to eastern Nigeria and undertook many trips abroad to speak on behalf of the Biafran cause. Following the end of the civil war in 1970, Achebe began a career in university teaching, first at the University of Nigeria at Nsukka and then at a number of institutions in Canada and the United States.

Achebe has written five novels, *Things Fall Apart* (1958), *No Longer at Ease* (1960), *Arrow of God* (1964), *A Man of the People* (1966), and *Anthills of the Savannah* (1987). He has published two short story collections, *The Sacrificial Egg, and Other Stories* (1962) and *Girls at War* (1972), as well as a volume of poetry *Beware Soul Brother* (1971; expanded and revised, 1972, and published as *Christmas in Biafra and Other Poems* in the United States in 1973), which won the Commonwealth Poetry Prize in 1972. An eloquent speaker and essayist, Achebe has published two important collections of essays, *Morning Yet on Cre-*

ation Day: Essays (1975) and *Hopes and Impediments: Selected Essays, 1965–1987* (1988) in addition to his 1984 study *The Trouble with Nigeria*. He has also written four children's books.

Achebe's purpose in writing has always been to provide for African readers images of themselves and to overturn the notion that writing and literature are concepts that come to Africans only from outside. His novels, in particular, portray complex social worlds in Igboland and Nigeria that span the period from the late nineteenth to the late twentieth centuries. *Things Fall Apart* and *Arrow of God* chart the incursion of colonial rule into the world of the Igbo, haltingly in the first novel and more completely in *Arrow of God*. The protagonists of both novels, Okonkwo in *Things Fall Apart* and Ezeulu in *Arrow of God*, are successful and venerated figures, accorded great respect in their communities. Okonkwo is a champion wrestler and the holder of many titles in his village of Umuofia; Ezeulu is the chief priest of the god Ulu, the most powerful deity in Umuaro. Yet Achebe qualifies the achievements of both characters by also making them rigid and inflexible in many of their actions, especially in relation to dealings with the British. In both novels, the ultimate tragedy of the central figure lies in the complexities of power within the local community. Okonkwo and Ezeulu both follow their own sense of purpose and judgment when acting in the best interests of the community, the former reacting to the appearance of the British and the establishment of a Christian Mission, and the latter dealing with the tensions within Umuaro society and the developing nature of the relationship with the British administration. But both find their sense of personal authority at odds with the consensus of the community, with tragic consequences.

Unlike some other African novelists of the 1950s and 1960s, Achebe refused to overcelebrate the nature of precontact society. Both *Things Fall Apart* and *Arrow of God*, by having figures of respect who also possess crucial flaws, present Igbo societies containing contradictions and restrictions. Achebe also stresses that the processes of history took their course and that the British colonial creation of Nigeria was a fact that cannot be disputed. The inevitable nature of historical change is reinforced by his decision to end *Things Fall Apart* with the narrative's moving to the new British district commissioner, who literally takes over the story following Okonkwo's demise. Yet it is precisely by showing Igbo society in such terms that Achebe makes his greatest claims to stress its legitimacy. Such a world is, his fiction proclaims, as full and complex as anywhere else.

In part, the tensions within the local communities of *Things Fall Apart* and *Arrow of God* are Achebe's comment on the dissonances within Nigerian society around the period of independence in 1960. This is made even clearer by his other novels, *No Longer at Ease* being set in Nigeria at the time of independence and *A Man of the People* and *Anthills of the Savannah* dealing with fictional postindependence nations that bear a strong resemblance to Nigeria. All three of these novels explore the tensions inherent in positions of power, especially in a society that is forced to combine the forces of tradition with the modern apparatus of the bureaucratic nation-state. As with the characters in *Things Fall Apart* and *Arrow of God*, Achebe's protagonists in his contemporary novels act in contexts of difficulty and doubt for both individuals and communities.

Achebe can be truly said to be one of the instigators of postcolonial literatures and is a tireless champion of African writing. *Things Fall Apart*, in particular, is undoubtedly one of the most important novels of the twentieth century, a book that in many ways helped formulate the paradigm of "African literature." Achebe has been the recipient of over twenty honorary degrees and the subject of many major conferences and critical studies. His work has been translated into over forty-five languages.

Further Reading: C. Achebe 2000; S. Gikandi 1991; R. Wren 1981.

Stuart Murray

African-Language (Zulu) Literatures   Until the late nineteenth century, Zulu was exclusively an oral language, and the predominant literary forms were *izibongo*, or oral praise poems, and ancestral chronicles. The British empire established itself in the kwaZulu region later than in the Western Cape, and Zulu kings typically met the English with armed resistance until the defeat of the Bambatha rebellion in 1906. Consequently, British missionaries reduced Zulu to a written form later than some other South African languages such as Xhosa and Sotho, and serious literature written in Zulu began to develop only in the 1930s.

John Dube is generally credited with inaugurating this era in 1930 with the publication of the first Zulu novel, *Insila kaShaka* (Shaka's Body-Servant). This novel is set in the 1820s during the reign of Shaka, the great king and soldier who created the modern Zulu kingdom; Shaka's attendant, disaffected by the cruelty of Shaka's warfare, flees the kingdom after the king's death rather than submit to the custom of being buried with his late master's corpse. While Dube frowned on the violence and ruthlessness of Shaka and his successor, Dingane, his novel was the first in a long list of semihistorical novels in Zulu to depict the accomplishments of the great nineteenth-century kings. Many other writers revisited and represented the legacy of Shaka and Dingane in a more positive, or at least more ambivalent, light. R.R.R. Dhlomo, for instance, wrote several novels from the 1930s through the 1950s about the Zulu dynasty; *UShaka* (1937) portrays the king as simultaneously a ruthless tyrant, a respected and paternalistic leader, and a prophet. Kenneth Bengu likewise wrote a series of novels in the 1950s and 1960s using historical settings and recalling the past glory of the Zulu aristocracy. Historical themes have also been taken up in Zulu drama, as in Jessie Gwayi's *Bafa Baphela* (They All Died, 1973), about the female leader Mnanthathisi, and in C. T. Msimang's *Izulu eladuma eSandlwana* (Stormy Weather over Isandlwana, 1976).

The most influential and innovative Zulu writer of the early period is Benedict

Wallet Vilakazi, who published both his first novel and his first book of poetry in 1935. He is best known for his poetry, which was influenced by English Romantic poets as well as Zulu oral tradition and departed significantly from the *izibongo* forms: he broke his verse into stanzas, for example, and experimented with rhyme. He was also among the first serious writers in Zulu to take modern settings and problems as his subjects, as in his depiction of the inhumane treatment of black laborers in the gold mines in his protest poem "Ezinkomponi" (In the Mining Compounds, 1945).

The implementation of apartheid as official policy beginning in 1948 had a profound effect on African-language literature. Because the educational system was forcibly segregated along linguistic as well as racial lines, there was a considerable demand for books in all nine African languages spoken in South Africa, intended for use in the state-controlled schools. Thus, there was an increase in the number of books published in Zulu in the 1950s and 1960s, but most of these prescribed books were intended for pedagogical purposes and of dubious artistic merit. One notable exception and one of the most widely praised Zulu writers is novelist, linguist, scholar, journalist, and publisher C.L.S. Nyembezi. In *Inkinsela yaseMgungundlovu* (The V.I.P. of Pietermaritzburg, 1961), often considered his best novel, a con man defrauds the residents of a small kwaZulu town by posing as a rich businessman from Pietermaritzburg.

Limitations in potential audiences and strict censorship by the white government prohibited most Zulu writers from writing critically against the regime, and they have usually confined themselves to certain themes. In addition to the historically based works, popular genres include the "Jim goes to Jo'burg" plot—James Gumbi's *Baba, Ngixolele* (Father, Forgive Me, 1966), for example, and David Mkhize's *Ngavele Ngasho* (I Said So from the Beginning, 1965)— and the "Prodigal Son" theme, which appears in Bengu's *Baba Ngonile* (Father, I Have Sinned, 1971) and Ntuli's *Ubheka* (The Watcher, 1962), among many others. The lifting of apartheid's strictures, reforms in the educational system, and new developments in the publication of South African literature—most notably, Heinemann's Mamela Afrika Series—may give Zulu literature a new lease on life and open up new possibilities for original, modern storytelling.

Further Reading: A. Gérard 1971; D B. Ntuli and C. F. Swanepoel 1993.

Shane D. Graham

African-Language (Kiswahili; Gikuyu) Literatures   "Titi la Mama ni tamu, ijapokuwa la mbwa" (A mother's breast is sweet, even if it's a dog's). Few critics of African literature are familiar with the works of Shaaban Roberts, a prolific Swahili novelist and poet whose poem "Titi la Mama" captures the essence of linguistic nationalism. Shaaban Roberts' nationalist sentiment is a product of the process of colonization and the subsequent anti- and postcolonial struggles that continue to shape the lives of the entire world population. But Roberts was probably a man ahead of his time because of his ability to anticipate the acrimonious debate during the first meeting of African writers in Makerere, Uganda, in 1962, to which he was ironically not invited. Like his contemporaries Obi Wali and D. O. Fagunwa and a host of other African writers who have followed in their steps, he was cognizant of the efficacy of African languages in "recover[ing] what the colonizing structure has sought to repress" (Simon Gikandi 1991, 9) as well as in articulating the complex postcolonial realities in languages that their audiences could understand. One would argue, as does Nigerian critic Ernest Emenyonu, that "the course of modern African literature as we know it today would have been altered for the good of Africans" (1994, 91) had the writers who assembled in Makerere heeded Obi Wali's suggestion. But what would it have mattered if *its* course were different, given poststructuralist cynicism about the social referentiality of texts that still haunts the academic climate today? One turns with profit to **Edward Said**'s timely observation that various "issues [are] reflected, contested, and even for a time decided in narrative" (1993, xiii).

As the persistence of several African writers illustrates, linguistic nationalism is not just another lofty academic issue. Just as it is almost inconceivable to have a university or college in the United States without a department of English, in Tanzania and Kenya, where Kiswahili is a national language, colleges and universities can boast of sound departments of Kiswahili. But unlike English departments in the United States, Kiswahili departments in these universities are also centers of nationalist consciousness. Questions of nationalism, patriotism, and belonging easily and uncompromisingly blend with academic issues. By the same token, *other* African languages are ubiquitously absent, although in some cases departments append the phrase "and other African languages" to the title. Linguistic **nationalisms**, then, as they pertain to African literature and life, also address simultaneously the possibility of writing literatures that genuinely articulate the historical and cultural experiences and the ways in which, in spite of the postcolonial decay, writing in these languages remains one of the possibilities for an African renaissance and a space for inventing a national community. Furthermore, as the case of both countries illustrates, these concerns are not about to disappear, however elusive the goal might appear. Yet, debates about postcolonial African literatures continue to operate as if Africans write only in European languages. This privileging of European tongues has led to a situation where the current interest in African-languages literatures remains ideologically suspect, if only for the simple reason that few, if any, Africanist scholars seem genuinely interested in those languages and literatures. **Ngũgĩ wa Thiong'o**'s radical decision to write in the Gikuyu language momentarily appeared to animate some interest in such literatures, at least in Europe and North America, for obvious reasons: that Africans write in their own languages remains a matter of curiosity, as many teachers of African literature might attest. Those of us teaching in North America and requiring that our students read Ngũgĩ's *Decolonising the Mind: The Politics of Language in African Literature* are often confronted with the question, "Why don't Africans write in their own languages?" by students and colleagues unaware of the "three traditions in the imaginative verbal production of Africa" (Ngũgĩ 1998, 103).

But as the mixed reception of Ngũgĩ's Gikuyu writings in Kenya, a decidedly multilingual country, illustrates, the dilemmas of linguistic nationalisms are as complex as the legacy of colonialism itself. Contrasted with the case of Tanzania, another multilingual country where writing in European languages hardly exists, Kenya's example challenges us to reexamine the issue of linguistic nationalism vis-à-vis the idea of nationhood, for even if the national boundaries are arbitrary and fictional colonial constructs, there is a sense in which people living within these constructed boundaries have come to perceive themselves as belonging to that nation and simultaneously to resist what they perceive as an emerging *hegemonic* version of linguistic nationalism. Second, Kenya's example also unintentionally foreshadows the conciliatory position that Ngũgĩ himself has taken in his later writing, especially *Penpoints, Gunpoints and Dreams*, where he claims that "nearly *all* African writers have returned to African languages. What they write in whatever language derives its stamina, stature, identity from African languages" (1998, 103). There is no denying that Ngũgĩ's writing in Gikuyu has proved as popular as it is polarizing, *at least in Kenya*. This is a reality that many admirers of Ngũgĩ outside Kenya may not be aware of (see, e.g., Ernest Emenyonu 1994, 91). Ngũgĩ's radical and even visionary decision to take part in the debate raging at the University of Nairobi—over whether European literatures should continue to be taught at the expense of African literatures—by writing in Gikuyu had complicated consequences. At a time when the Kenyan nation was increasingly becoming polarized because of Mzee Jomo Kenyatta's openly tribalist administration, a time when Kiswahili language and literature were inextricably associated with national cultural awareness, Ngũgĩ's act was perceived as a betrayal of the nationalist cause by a cross-section of Kenyan intellectuals and a sizable non-Gikuyu-speaking public. The resentment of what was seen as a bid for Gikuyu hegemony cannot be blamed *entirely* on an opportunistic regime manipulating public opinion. Rather, the cause must be sought in the history of Kenya as a country and Africa as a continent. Tanzania across the border had proven a successful example of what Kiswahili could do for a nation struggling to shake off the legacy of colonialism.

Further Reading: E. Emenyonu 1994; Ngũgĩ 1998.

Katwiwa Mule

Agency   Agency has been an important and prevalent concern within colonial and postcolonial studies since its emergence as a discipline, approximately with the publication of **Edward Said**'s *Orientalism* (1978). Its prevalence is also attributable to the school of criticism known as New Historicism, insofar as it, too, was invested in locating traces of **resistance** to dominant discourses and power structures. Agency presumes a certain autonomy and emancipatory possibilities for the subject, usually identified in terms of either insurgency or complicity. Such an inscription of free will rebuts the narratives of the passive, uninstructed, and duped colonized subject, and it dismantles the attendant binary, which holds that the West wields monolithic power and that the "Third World" is utterly dominated. However, allowing for a narrative of insurgency seems to suggest that colonial power may be easily dissolved through the conscious and revolutionary return of the dominated classes to their rightful state, while, on the other hand, allowing for a narrative of simple compliance seems to suggest that the dominated classes are somehow Rousseauistic—outside the production of knowledge and trapped within civil and social relations that inhibit their natural state of being. The more complicated understanding of agency as operable within moments of both coercion and consent has been shaped by the work of **Antonio Gramsci**, and this insight has served as a means of solving the problem of interpreting the resistance to revolution on the part of the **subaltern** subject. One theoretical pitfall for work on agency and the state of the subject, then, is that it often poses a delimited dialectical model of false versus self-consciousness. Another pitfall is that it relies on Western narratives of agency in its emphasis on autonomy and Enlightenment ideas of the inherently free and reasoning subject, and the problems of mapping this Western model onto a discussion of the subaltern are numerous. Ultimately, agency can be understood as a theoretical abstraction that is based on particular narratives (e.g., "revolution") and particular categories (e.g., "the subject"). In this respect it is paradoxically removed from what it means to represent: the materiality of everyday lives.

Further Reading: D. Haynes and G. Prakash 1992; R. O'Hanlon 1988.

Rita Raley

Aijaz Ahmad   Currently a professorial fellow at the Centre for Contemporary Studies, Nehru Memorial Museum and Library in New Delhi, Aijaz Ahmad is a specialist in postcolonial literature and theory. He is widely recognized for his polemical *In Theory: Classes, Nations, and Literatures* (1992), which is an exacting critique of literary developments in the field popularly known as **colonial discourse** analysis. An expert on Urdu poetry, Ahmad has also edited *Ghazals of Ghalib* (1971).

In Theory gathers together almost all of Ahmad's postcolonial theorizing. In this work, the rigorously Marxist Ahmad openly denounces poststructural theory's clear complicity with the dogma of the bourgeoisie. Ahmad views the project of poststructuralism, particularly its debunking of all "origins, collectivities and determinate historical projects" (2), as inherently opposed to any coherent analysis of colonialism and holds Western Marxism responsible for contributing to the rise of poststructuralism and thereby paving the way for its consequent near banishment from the American academy.

Commenting on the paucity of Marxist thought in American literary theory following 1975, Ahmad insists that the history of materialities is important in interrogating and understanding literary questions of empire and oppression. In addition, Ahmad, who is always resistant to the empire–nationalism binary formulated by many important postcolonial critics, argues that only **Marxism** brings to the fore and hybridizes social formations in areas designated by the West as a singular, homogeneous "Third World." The "fundamental dialectic" of *In Theory*, then, is between imperialism, **decolonization**, and the struggle for socialism (9); the problematic issues for Ahmad are not so much concepts of class, nation, and state as much as ways of talking about class, nation, and state.

Foregrounding Marxism as the primary mode of analysis, *In Theory* concentrates on reviewing some seminal positions in the field of colonial discourse analysis. In taking on the "canons" of postcolonial literature and theory, Ahmad sets himself against the growing tendencies toward homogenizing the so-called Third World, a movement that he understands as emanating from the auspices of the metropolitan academy. Ahmad complains that the Western academy has codified the Third World into a unitary archive that includes only the writers whom the hegemonic literary critics of the metropolitan university think suitable. This archive, with the stamp of Western sanction attached to it, is then redistributed to the "Third World" as a monolithic "Third World literature." In his detailed analysis of how Third World literature is constituted, Ahmad takes up the case of English in India as a study and examines its impact on class formation. The irony, Ahmad notes, is that although this literature allows a conversation between writers from different constituencies of the Third World, it is consumed in English or in other languages of the metropole.

Ahmad also implicates the metropolitan immigrant in the construction of a monolithic Third World. He argues that a combination of privileged class position, their location in the metropolitan academy, and the lack of adequate grounding in a socialist praxis predisposes many of these immigrants toward an "opportunistic Third World-ism" (86). Gradually, differences between the writings that are produced in the actual geophysical spaces of the Third World and writings by the immigrants in the metropole are erased, leading to a simultaneous approval of the latter as the authentic voices of Third World resistance. This is problematic not only because it homogenizes the literatures of the Third World but also because literary migrancy usually subsumes the class question.

Ahmad contests the generally accepted category of "Indian literature" as well. Since the largest record of translations from the vernacular languages exists only in English, it becomes the language in which the knowledge of Indian literature is produced. That English is the most removed, in terms of its cultural and linguistic structure, from the regional languages is an irony that Ahmad is quick to note. Pinning the blame on English departments in India, Ahmad argues that they have not theorized Indian literature adequately primarily because Indian literature always remains a secondary area of specialization well below Shakespeare, Wordsworth, Milton, and so on. This problem is further aggravated by the fact that the only literature that is taught all over India is English literature, ensuring that the educated elite is well versed in the English canon, the standards of which are then used to assess Indian literature.

To construct a category such as "Indian literature," argues Ahmad, English literature needs to be de-privileged and studied in tandem with other literatures of India. Moreover, scholars of "Indian literature" should continuously engage with the lived history of the many literatures of India, always keeping the current *Indian* context in mind. While Ahmad concedes the permanence of the English language—and therefore its literature—in India, unlike many other nativist critics, he also calls for an understanding of the history of English in India and the need to study English not as a Pan-Indian language but as one of India's many languages. Continuing with his critique of the concept of a homogeneous Third World, Ahmad also provides a sustained assessment of the three worlds theory and insists on its need to be constantly historicized. Ahmad demonstrates how this theory changed in terms of who developed its own particular version. For example, there were at least three versions of this theory in circulation: the Soviet version, the Chinese version (which had the most widespread currency), and the Nehruvian version. Ahmad examines the contradictions and slippages in the various constructions of this theory, thus pointing out the difficulty in employing "Third World" as a theoretical category.

While *In Theory* sets out to elaborate many of Ahmad's theoretical positions on terms bandied about in postcolonial discourse, this work is perhaps most controversial for his taking to task writers and theorists such as **Salman Rushdie**, **Edward Said**, and Fredric Jameson. This, however, is linked to the central thesis propounded by his book, namely, the role of Marxism in colonial discourse analysis and the heterogeneity of categories usually designated as a homogeneous whole. Ahmad claims that the metropolitan academy insists on the marginalization of texts that do not ask a "**national** question." Class is also given short shrift; for example, in Salman Rushdie's *Shame* (1983), the experience of a certain (upper) class is pitched as being representative of the national experience.

Ahmad also takes apart Jameson's statement that "all third world texts are necessarily national allegories" and argues that seeing the Third World as constituted only by imperialism and colonialism is erroneous. Claiming that he could not think of a single novel in Urdu written between 1935 and 1947 (the important years immediately preceding decolonization) that is solely about the experience of colonialism and imperialism (118), Ahmad exposes Jameson's privileging of the singularity of the "Third World" experience. In fact, he reverses Jameson's statement and reads it as saying that "only those texts that give us national allegories can be read as third world texts" (107). As a solution, Ahmad calls to replace the idea of a nation with the more pluralistic idea of "collectivity" (110).

Ahmad's review of Edward Said's groundbreaking *Orientalism* (1978) is perhaps his best-known, yet most controversial, contribution to postcolonial theory. Claiming that Said is often guilty of what he sets out to critique, Ahmad exposes the faultiness of Said's assumption of a single, linear Western history that has been complicit in subjugating the "Orient" since time immemorial. According to Ahmad, Said subscribes to the structure of Western metaphysics even while seeming to explicitly censure its contents. Ahmad also criticizes Said and colonial discourse analysis, which is so closely associated with Said, for privileging only the moment of imperialism in cultural and social formation in the former colonies. Ahmad thus condemns both Said and Jameson for their unidimensional understanding of the impact of colonialism. Another notable feature of *Orientalism* that Ahmad takes issue with is Said's tendency to deny any **agency** to the colonized. This is evident in Said's glossing over how and which aspects of colonialism may have been acknowledged, altered, and resisted by the indigenous populace. Ahmad claims that *Orientalism* is unable to articulate a voice of the colonized other than that of Said. Instead, the only voices that emerge in this account of Western hegemony are those of the Western canon that Said claims has silenced the Orient.

Ahmad also defends Marx against Said's criticism of Marx's comments on India. Ahmad claims that Marx's diatribe on India, flawed though it may be, needs to be contextualized and demonstrates that Marx's assorted writings on India are far more diverse than Said admits. However trenchant a critic of the caste and class structure of India, Marx was equally vitriolic in his condemnation of the feudal aspects of European society. Marx's attitude toward colonialism and the colonized space was always complicated. Hence, Ahmad rebukes critics such as Said and French poststructuralists who pull Marx's writings out of their historical, textual, and material contexts. Indeed, in *In Theory* we can see Ahmad's committed effort to read these very contexts into the often hermeneutic world of literary criticism.

Further Reading: M. Levinson 1993; M. Sprinker 1993.

Pallavi Rastogi

Ama Ata Aidoo (23 March 1942–   )   Born in Ghana (then called by its colonial name, Gold Coast), Christina Ama Ata Aidoo was the daughter of a chief in the town of Abeadzi Kyiakor. She grew up in the royal household and attended the Wesley Girls High School in Cape Coast, an old colonial-instated school. From 1961 to 1964, she attended the University of Ghana at Legon, where participated actively in the school of drama and in the writer's workshop. In 1964, *The Dilemma of a Ghost*, her first play, was produced. Between 1964 and 1966, Aidoo was a junior research fellow at the Institute of African Studies at the university, which considerably strengthened her commitment to the use of African oral traditions in her writing. The **Pan-Africanist** and socialist ideas that were prevalent in the 1950s and 1960s in the period leading up to and immediately after the independence of Ghana in 1957 also influenced her greatly. The disillusionment that followed independence, as it became apparent that the national liberation struggle led by Nkrumah had failed to live up to its expectations, greatly affected Aidoo. This can be seen in her collection of short stories *No Sweetness Here* (1970). The roles of women in African society as well as the "been-to" (Africans educated in Europe) are also prevailing concerns in Aidoo's work.

Since the publication of her first play in 1965, Aidoo has published another play, *Anowa* (1970); two novels, *Our Sister Killjoy: Or, Reflections from a Black-Eyed Squint* (1977) and *Change: A Love Story* (1992); two collections of poetry, *Someone Talking to Someone* (1985) and *An Angry Letter in January* (1992); two collections of short stories, *The Eagle and the Chickens* (1989) and *The Girl Who Can* (1997); and numerous essays on African literature and the status of women in African society. Apart from her roles as a productive writer and critic, Aidoo also pursues a career in education, teaching and lecturing in various parts of Africa and the United States. In the early 1980s, she was involved with Ghanaian politics and became minister of education under the Jerry Rawlings government.

Further Reading: A. Azodo and G. Wilentz 1999; V. Odamtten 1994.

Nikolas Huot

Syed Hussein Alatas (1928–   )   Syed Hussein Alatas was born into a family of intellectuals in Bogor, Indonesia, in 1928 and educated at the University of Amsterdam. He has had a distinguished career as a sociologist, culminating in vice-chancellorship of the University of Malaya (1989–1991). He has written over a dozen books in English and Malay, the most influential of which is *The Myth of the Lazy Native* (1977).

The argument in *Myth* is that British colonial administrators (see Alatas' *Thomas Stamford Raffles [1781–1826]: Schemer or Reformer?* [1971] about the "founder" of Singapore) systematically and insultingly created "the lazy native," portraying Malays, Indonesians, and Filipinos as indolent in order to buttress the ideology of "colonial capitalism." This ideology (in Mannheim's sense), which sought a justification of Western rule by denigrating natives, their history, and their society, ranged from vulgar fantasy to refined scholarship. Alatas convincingly shows that "the accusation of indolence was merely a veiled resentment against Malay unwillingness to become a tool for enriching colonial planters" (1977, 80–81).

In spite of careful documentation, Alatas' detractors have accused him of eliding the role of the Malay peasantry itself in supposedly helping construct this myth. Fortunately, Alatas can enlist the support of Donald Nonini, among other sometimes unwitting allies. Work on the **resistance** of the Malay peasantry to the racism of colonial ideology has also been taken up by A. B. Shamsul and K. S. Jomo.

Significant in Alatas' work is his demonstration of how contemporary postcolonial Malay intellectuals simply replicate the colonialist ideology that first cast Malays and other Southeast Asians as "lazy." He places responsibility for this squarely with the elites, as well as responsibility for its dismantling. *Intellectuals in Developing Societies* (1977) is a plea to this class; indeed, Alatas' audience has always been, for him, intellectuals and elites of the postcolonial world first and Western intellectuals and elites second.

Even quintessential **nation** builders, such as Mahathir Mohamed (now Malaysian prime minister), are not spared in Alatas' searching analysis. Mahathir's *The Malay Dilemma* (1970) and the collectively authored *Revolusi Mental* (1971) are shown by Alatas to unquestioningly take over colonial images, thereby confining them to categories of "colonialist capitalist thought."

Alatas would doubtless agree with C. W. Watson (1996) that postcolonialism has brought Malaysia where colonialism always wanted it to be by relying on a rhetoric and political discourse of Malayness but would disagree with Watson that discussion and debate on the future of Malaysia "are likely to be more about post-modernist consumers and less about post-colonial subjects" (Watson 1996, 322). In any event, Alatas' work remains important to any rearticulation of the postcolonial.

His first book was an exposition of democracy in Islam with comparative reference to Western political thought (1956), and his second a series of reflections on the theories of religions (1963). Alatas' demystification of the colonial subject and of Islam thus evidently intersects with **Edward Said**'s own work. In *Culture and Imperialism* (1993) Said describes *The Myth of the Lazy Native* as a great work, likening it to the studies of Peter Gran, Judith Tucker, and Hanna Batatu. Bart Moore-Gilbert (1997) appears, however, to misread Said's reliance on Alatas and Guha, whom Said pairs in opposition to **C.L.R. James** and George Antonius. Seeing the work of the former pair as rejectionist, darkly ironic, and expressive of a hermeneutics of suspicion is high, if belated, praise, not dismissal. It is ironic that Alatas' indictments of the influence of colonial ideology on scholarship and selection of themes are later echoed by **Aijaz Ahmad** (and other detractors) who accuse Said of not acknowledging the importance, and influence on him, of Alatas.

Alatas' project to establish a foundation for a postcolonial methodology of (Southeast) Asian history and society—see his 1998 (coauthored) occasional paper "Malays/Muslims and the History of Singapore" (1998), for instance—has contributed to the literature now emerging from and about Southeast Asia, from Panivong Norindr's *Phantasmatic Indochina: French Colonial Ideology in Architecture, Film, and Literature* (1996) to Lily Rose Roxas-Tope's *(Un)Framing Southeast Asia: Nationalism and the Postcolonial Text in English in Singapore, Malaysia and the Philippines* (1998). Not all (need) acknowledge a debt to Alatas, but all operate within a space opened by his work.

The legacy also continues in the work of his son Syed Farid Alatas' *Democracy and Authoritarianism in Indonesia and Malaysia: The Rise of the Post-Colonial State* (1997), in particular its emphasis on postcolonial corruption. Alatas (senior)'s several books on the topic include the influential *Corruption: Its Nature, Causes and Functions* (1990).

Alatas may have spawned no "school" and may be a recognizable name in Western postcolonial circles only thanks to Said's recent evocations, but he is without doubt a pioneer in postcolonial studies, an early example of a scholar interrogating the ways in which the structures, dominations, and legacies of the colonial world have shaped and are still shaping the postcolonial world.

Further Reading: S. H. Alatas 1977; C. W. Watson 1996.

Shawkat M. Toorawa

Meena Alexander   The eldest of three sisters, Meena Alexander was born on 17 February 1951 in the northern city of Allahabad in the newly independent India. When, in 1956, Alexander's father was requested by the government of India to work abroad in the newly independent Republic of Sudan, she and her mother went with him. In *Faultlines: A Memoir* (1993), Alexander claims that from that moment "my childhood crisscrossed the continents" (6). She successfully pursued studies at Sudan's Khartoum University, earning a first-class B.A. in English and French literature with a minor in philosophy.

Alexander went to Britain and completed her doctorate in English studies at Nottingham University in 1973. Her dissertation was entitled "The Vital Centrality: An Essay in Phenomenological Aesthetics on the Human Self-Image with Special Reference to Romantic, Symbolist and Modern Poetry." Before marrying and emigrating to the United States in 1979, Alexander returned to India and spent some time in Delhi and Hyderabad. She has lived in New York City ever since with her husband, son, and daughter. Alexander is currently Distinguished Professor of English at Hunter College and the Graduate Center of the City University of New York. In addition to English and French, she is fluent in Hindi and her mother tongue of Malayalam and can speak Arabic.

Meena Alexander has received awards from the Arts Council of England, National Endowment for the Humanities, American Council of Learned Societies, the Lila Wallace Foundation, the Altrusa International Foundation, National Council for Research on Women, the New York State Council on the Arts, and the New York Foundation for the Arts. She has been a visiting fellow at the Sorbonne (Paris IV); Frances Wayland Collegium Lecturer at Brown University; writer in residence at the Center for American Culture Studies at Columbia University; University Grants Commission fellow, Kerala University; writer in residence, National University of Singapore; and fellow at the MacDowell Colony. In 1998 she was a member of the jury for the Neustadt International Award in Literature.

Alexander's books of poetry include *River and Bridge* (1995), *House of a Thousand Doors* (1988), and *Stone Roots* (1980). Her prose writings include *The Shock of Arrival: Reflections on Postcolonial Experience* (1996) and *Faultlines: A Memoir*. In addition, she is the author of the novels *Manhattan Music* (1997) and *Nampally Road* (1991). Her poems and prose have been widely published internationally in magazines and widely anthologized. "Notebook" is a cycle of poems that has appeared in English/Swedish from the Bildmuseet and will be included in a work in progress that will appear as a volume of poems called *Illiterate Heart*.

Any discussion of the postcolonial experience is incomplete without the delicate, poetic insights offered by Alexander. Powerfully and politically, she honestly narrates her personal experiences in her memoirs, invokes visionary images in her poems, and constructs characters in her novels who grapple with existence in the margins. Alexander is constantly exploring the boundaries of an identity riddled with dualities. In *Faultlines* she describes her knowledge of the English language as "a pale skin that has covered up my flesh, the broken parts of my world" (73). She fulfills this metaphor by claiming that she must use her teeth and nails, also biological parts of herself, to break free from the ways in which linguistic discourse has subjectified her by masking her "discrepant otherness" (73). Following the metaphor, we are led to see how the act of speech forces Alexander to wallow in an ambivalence since she must utilize different parts of her own body, nails and vocal cords, against one another to escape the internalization of colonial ideology that accompanies knowledge of the colonizer's language. This ambivalence is enforced in the very next paragraph when Alexander writes, "Sometimes I think I have to write myself into being. Write in order not to be erased" (73). In this passage we see how the English language works as a hegemonic discourse that has consumed Alexander's identity to a certain extent but is nonetheless the medium that allows her to write, which, in turn, permits her to disclose her colonial experiences. Readers can thus feel the author's frustrations with those dualities that characterize the life of an immigrant woman of Third World origin. As such, the powerful testimonials offered by Meena Alexander in the contexts of colonialism, womanhood, immigration, and displacement allow readers of her works to step in and assume one of her many selves that have experienced life in the margins.

Further Reading: D. Bahri and M. Vasudeva 1996; E. Duncan 1999.

Rahul Krishna Gairola

Alterity   The term "alterity" stems from the French *altérité* and the medieval Latin *alteritatem* to connote the state of being different and has consequently found an important space in contemporary postcolonial theory. Alterity marks the threshhold of otherness, the site where difference in skin color, geography, sex, sexual orientation, and other historical and biological markers of difference are sociopolitically discoursed. In postcolonial theory, the term has been used interchangeably along with difference and "otherness." The concept of alterity is essential to grasp when we consider the construction of **subaltern** subjects, for the landscape of alterity guides colonial subjects and other minorities toward acceptable notions of their own subjectivity while simultaneously demonstrating the Western perceptions of subjectivity that interpellate peoples of formerly colonized countries. In other words, alterity at once renders subjectivity of minority experience to both the other and the subject who is doing the "othering," and the concept can thus be located in both postcolonial and minority discourse.

A prevalent use of the term stems from Tzvetan Todorov's (1984) reading of Mikhail Bakhtin's *The Dialogical Principle*. Todorov cites Bakhtin for his theory that identification with a narrative subject is an ambivalent act in which the author must relate to the subject and detach from the subject. While the character of a novel is a fictive formulation from the creative essence of the author, Bakhtin asserts that alterity permits the author to feel distance from his or her own creation. As Todorov puts it, "the author is the externality that makes it possible for the character to be seen whole" (100). In accordance to Bakhtin's theories on dialogism, alterity is important, for it is at once the site of difference and the occasion for dialogue since there can exist no dialogue without difference. In other words, the state of being different can be read as an inner conflict within the self that inherently manifests outside the self and creates the conflict that drives narrative.

For example, we see how alterity becomes a dual ambivalence for Pecola in Toni Morrison's *The Bluest Eye* (1970). Racism in the United States manifests through a number of symbolic registers for Pecola, most conspicuously in the blond-haired and blue-eyed dolls that adults encourage her to cuddle with. Though we generally know how whites in the novel view themselves, Morrison powerfully illustrates the deep inscription of racist ideology in Pecola's desire for blue eyes. In this narrative binary of white/black, Pecola views her alterity, her "otherness," as ugliness. Though Peccola's self-perception of her difference is rather traumatic, perhaps equally disheartening is the view of adults in the African American communities around the girl. They, too, view their alterity as a deficiency in comparison to whiteness and hence show how difference can cause profound distress in shaping the subjectivities of a race whose subjectivity has been dictated to them by white, **Eurocentric** standards. In *The Bluest Eye* we see that racism need not be enforced, for blackness as a stigmatized form of "otherness" has been internalized by the black subjects themselves.

Similarly in **colonial discourse**, the concept of alterity has been used to explore the many ways in which "otherness" shaped the discursive trends of Western hegemony in the imperial project of subject construction in Third Worlds. In "Representation and the Colonial Text: A Critical Exploration of Some Forms of Mimeticism" (1984), **Homi Bhabha** speaks of the concept of alterity, which he calls "difference." In the essay, Bhabha argues that the very act of representing the colonial subject impels one to map out the experiences and essence of the colonial through difference—a process that necessarily views native elements of the colonial experience as "an-other history and an-other culture" (98). Bhabha leads us to see that colonialism is rooted in the ontological and epistemological foundations of difference as it continues to support them. Though the attitude of the colonizer can range from a sexualized fetishization of the colonial subject, to a violent racism, it is difference that sets up such relationships between the colonizer and colonized subject.

Some critics have recently pointed out that the term can be problematic, a buzzword that has lost its meaning. For example, critic Philip Tagg holds not only that "alterity" can be difficult to define since its usage in English differs geographically but that we can read difference in the context of mass media and **postmodern** culture. With these many transpositions of the concept, Tagg offers what he calls the "eight dualisms" of alterity, or the eight primary uses of the concept: (1) the popular "other"; (2) the lower-class "other"; (3) the black "other"; (4) the "Third World other"; (5) the female "other"; (6) the national or ethnic "other"; (7) oppressed parts of subjectivity as the "other"; and (8) somewhere else as the "other" place. Tagg's contemporary observations are important in noting the many kinds of alterity that exist and how, in the context of postcolonial studies, one form of otherness may highlight another. In this way, Tagg leads us to see that the colonial other is never without layered differences that further place him or her in the margins, especially during representation.

Further Reading: H. Bhabha 1984; P. Tagg 1996; M. Taussig 1993; T. Todorov 1984.

Rahul Krishna Gairola

Mulk Raj Anand (1905–) Mulk Raj Anand, also known as Narad Muni, graduated from the University of Punjab in 1921 and continued his education in Cambridge and London University. In the 1930s and 1940s he divided his time between Bloomsbury and the Indian independence movement. After the war, Anand made his home in Bombay. In his early novels, his social and political analysis of oppression was influenced by his involvement with the Left in England. *Untouchable* (1935), *Coolie* (1936), *Two Leaves in a Bud* (1937), and the trilogy *The Village* (1939), *Across Black Waters* (1940), and *The Sword and the Sickle* (1942) are strongly socialist. In his later, more autobiographical novels like *The Private Life of an Indian Prince* (1953), *Seven Summers* (1951), *Morning Face* (1968), *Confessions of a Lover* (1976), and *The Bubble* (1984), Anand focuses more on the human psyche and personal struggles. In addition to writing novels, his eclectic interests range from art and literary criticism to **Marx**, Engels, Kama Sutra, and erotic sculpture.

Colonization brings with it a cultural encounter, and the colonized subject is predictably hyphenated. The self-defeating desire of the slave to own the colonizer's world results in a schizophrenic "imitativeness" (see **Frantz Fanon**'s *Black Skin, White Masks*, 1967). Krishan's father in *Seven Summers* and *Morning Face* is the head clerk of the Thirty-eighth Dogra Regiment and a faithful employee of the Angrezi Sarkar. He perceives the nationalists as troublemakers and is content to be a colonized subject. The young Krishnan strives for "imitation Sahibhood." He tries to speak like the British, dress like an Etonian, and play cricket. Bakha in *The Untouchable* is in awe of the British because they wear trousers and sit on commodes.

Anand deconstructs the myth of imperial hegemony and problematizes **Eurocentric** representation of colonization that reinforces rigid oppositions like civilization/barbarism, progressive/primitive. His narratives explore the question of **ethnic** identity in a prejudiced, empowered, hostile dominant culture that pretends superiority. The plantation, where the main objective is economic exploitation and where order is based on terror, hypocrisy, and suppression, is in many ways a microcosm of colonized India in *Two Leaves*. The colonizer's arrogant justification of the ethical benefits of colonialism to enlighten and ennoble a barbaric race is exposed for what it is—a myth. On an almost farcical level, Reggie Hunt's bearer, Afzal, is allowed to play polo because of the shortage of players, but he is not allowed to score a goal.

But Anand does not typically present the colonizers as villains, nor does he completely reject a positive colonial residue. What he does reject are the myth of the progressive role of colonialism and stereotypes about the positional inferiority of the empire's "Others." He himself had a warm affection for many individual Britishers, and his characters display the same realistic ambivalence. For example, Bakha feels that the Tommies treat him more humanely than do the Hindus. The "ethical obligation" of the colonial civilizing mission, however, is satirized in Bakha's encounter with missionary Christianity. Bakha is not convinced by the doctrine of original sin, nor is he desirous of a heavenly abode. Colonel Hutchinson, despite his gospel of equality, can neither articulate Christian belief with any clarity nor persuade Bakha about the need for conversion.

In Anand's narratives the **subaltern** subproletarian takes center stage and speaks and is spoken for. In colonized and decolonized India, casteism and disparity of wealth perpetuate colonialisms. Munoo, the fifteen-year-old orphan, warmhearted and filled with a zest for life, dies of tuberculosis brought on by poverty and malnutrition (*Coolie*). Bakha in *The Untouchable* (1935) resigns himself to his low-caste status. But in *The Road* (1987), despite allegations of "pollution," Bikhu the untouchable helps build the road from the village to the highway. At the close of the narrative, Bikhu defiantly faces the Rajput landowner's son Sajnu and turns purposefully toward the city of Delhi, where anonymity eradicates caste differences. In "Lajwanti" and "The Parrot in the Cage" (*The Lost Child*, 1934), Anand gives voice to the "gendered subaltern." Lajwanti, a young married girl, is tyrannized by her in-laws and attempts suicide. Rukhami loses everything in the Hindu–Muslim partition riots. Anand explores a young widow's terror of Suttee in "Savitri" (*Between Tears*). In the patriarchal rural society of *The Road*, women do not possess the freedom to love. So Rukhmani's attraction for Bikhu the untouchable remains suppressed. In the refreshingly feminist *Old Woman and the Crow* (republished as *Gauri*, 1987), Gauri is sold to an old moneylender. When she returns to her husband, Panchi, he rejects her because of social pressures. Rather than reenact the actions of her prototype the goddess Sita, who chooses death to rejection, Gauri determines to build a new life for herself.

Deeply involved in the freedom struggle, Anand includes the history of colonized India toward self-determination. *Confessions of a Lover*, a deeply autobiographical work, records the influence of Gandhi's Satyagraha. Historical events like the Jallianwallah Bagh massacre in 1919, a tragic result of Western totalitarian "humanism" to control its "anarchic populace," are closely integrated into the fictional narrative of *Seven Summers* and *Morning Face*. *Little Plays of Mahatma Gandhi*, though linguistically sloppy, is Anand's attempt to write back to the empire.

Anand, one of the first Indian writers to write in English, explored alternative forms of English, which in itself is an assertion of power in linguistically colonized India. His characters often speak in sentences that are structurally incorrect by British English standards and that phonetically mock European English. Swearwords and idiomatic expressions are literally translated, and words like "wah," "acha," and "huzoor" are included without translation. The Indianisms in both narration and dialogue symbolically enact the adoption of the "bastard child" (see **Salman Rushdie**'s *Midnight's Children*, 1981) of the colonial legacy.

Anand and other writers like **R. K. Narayan** and Raja Rao helped create a unified imaginative topos and a common national register for a colonized and newly independent India. His counternarratives reveal how literary representation of the empire's "Others" in dominant culture narratives is constructed out of multiple and conflicting discourses. In the process, they deconstruct representations of India and Indians in postcolonial discourse.

Further Reading: S. Cowasjee 1977; R. K. Dhawan 1992; C. D. Narasimhaiah 1987.

Ranjini Philip

Benedict Anderson   Born 1936 in Kunming, China, of English and Anglo-Irish parents, Anderson received a B.A. in classics at Cambridge University in 1957 and a Ph.D. in political science at Cornell University in 1967. His doctoral dissertation, written under the direction of George M. T. Kahin and published as *Java in a Time of Revolution* (1972) dealt particularly with the effect of youths in the Indonesian revolution. Founder and director of Cornell's Modern Indonesia Project, Anderson holds the Aaron L. Binenkorb Professorship of International Studies. Anderson's research has focused broadly on the political culture and historical roots of **nationalism** and militarism in postcolonial societies, specializing on Indonesia and Thailand and, more recently, on twentieth-century Philippines.

His *Imagined Communities* (1983; revised 1991) provides a comprehensive framework for understanding the process by which states, whether kingdoms or colonies, become nations. Anderson finds the origins of nationalism in the shift from the vertical structures of absolutist states and the church in Europe, a process that he sees beginning around 1500, to horizontal relationships among individuals. He diverges from most students of nationalism, however, in locating its first wave in the republics of North and South America that threw off the yoke of colonialism. The rise of the European republics, beginning in the 1820s, constitutes Anderson's second wave, with the last wave coming after World War II in the postcolonial societies of Asia and Africa.

While Anderson's multifaceted theory incorporates a number of factors, its relevance to postcolonialism is particularly salient. He shows that the first wave occurred in the **Creole** communities of the Americas, where newspapers and other forms of print capitalism resulted in a shared sense of resentment against the colonial powers. One of the more controversial aspects of Anderson's theory is his contention that once nationalism developed in the colonial societies of the Americas, it became modular, such that it could be replicated in, and adapted to, conditions in other societies. His encyclopedic grasp of Indonesian cultures, particularly literature and the arts, as well as his impressive knowledge of Thai and Philippine cultures allow him to draw many of his illustrative examples from colonialist, anticolonialist, and postcolonialist circumstances.

Written out of a sense of bewilderment occasioned by the 1978–1979 armed conflict involving Vietnam and Cambodia and then Vietnam and China, *Imagined Communities* breaks with orthodox **Marxism** on at least three important points. One is that nationalism ought not to be seen as an ideology, in the sense that liberalism and fascism are, but as a cultural artifact more like kinship or religion. The second follows from the first: that nationalism ought not to be seen as the bane of an internationalist worldview. Indeed, he points out that every modern revolution not only defines itself in national terms but derives its territory and peculiar identity from its prerevolutionary or colonialist state. Third, in answer to such theorists as Tom Nairn (see, e.g., his *The Break-up of Britain*, 1977) who view nationalism as Marxism's greatest failure, Anderson prefers to see it as an anomaly. Citing Marx's 1848 formulation that in each country the proletariat must settle things with "its own bourgeoisie," he marvels that no serious consideration has yet been given to why a segment of the bourgeoisie should be considered national.

Ultimately, Anderson compels himself to address the vexing question of what makes a nation significant enough that large numbers are motivated to fight and die for it. Inevitably, this question must be placed alongside Nairn's contention that racism and anti-Semitism derive from nationalism. Instead, Anderson locates racism in class consciousness, specifically, in fear of contamination on the part of aristocratic classes and their bourgeois imitators. He adduces examples from the colonial services, which enabled petty bourgeois to act like aristocrats, lording it over the natives and maintaining an aura of white solidarity. As a result, the last wave of nationalism has occurred in the former colonial territories of Asia and Africa, largely in response to extractive economies designed to feed the industrial capitalism of the metropoles. Because large numbers were required to fill the lower administrative echelons of these colonial states, native intelligentsia received a Westernized education and so became privy to models of nationalism celebrated in Europe and the Americas. In support of his view that popular nationalist enthusiasm derives from the colonial state that preceded it, Anderson shows that the census, the map, and the museum were transformed from totalizing instruments of control to modalities by which a people could imagine themselves as a political entity.

Language issues are never very far from Anderson's consciousness. Two essays reprinted in his *Language and Power* (1990), "The Languages of Indonesian Politics" (1966) and "*Sembah-Sumpah*: The Politics of Language and Javanese Culture" (1984), delve into the problem of how Indonesian, rather than Javanese, came to be the national language. Taking issue with those who view the language of Indonesian politics as a pathology (notably, the American anthropologist **Clifford Geertz** and Swiss linguist Herbert Leuthy), Anderson contends that national consciousness in postcolonial Indonesia is shaped as a synthesis of politics and culture. That Javanese, the mother tongue of the majority of Indonesians and especially of those who have wielded the most political clout, was not a suitable national language had little to do with supposed sensitivities of the minority populations. Instead, Anderson shows the impossibility of thinking modern thoughts in a language fraught with centuries of domination by a princely caste in precolonial times. An added complication adduced by Anderson is that Javanese has a high and a low form used according to caste. Considering that literary Javanese always used the high form, the rigid hierarchical social structure thus enforced made that language unsuitable to a nation imagining itself into existence.

Anderson shows that with the advent of print capitalism in the Netherlands East Indies writing in Javanese became obsolete. In co-opting the traditional elite, the Dutch made the traditional literature obsolete because its chief topics, the mystery of traditional Javanese religion and the battlefield exploits of native heroes, seemed ineffectual in the face of decisive Dutch victories in the colonial wars. Consequently, writers attempting to ingratiate themselves with the colonial power and perhaps be heard in the metropole wrote in **Dutch**. Those who wished to address the natives of the Indies wrote in a form of trade Malay that eventually became known as Indonesian. This language became a fertile ground for writers taking a cultural stand against the Javanese language and a political one against the Dutch and their local **subalterns**. When General Suharto came to power in a countercoup in 1965, Anderson and two colleagues at Cornell University circulated their preliminary analysis. Because their informants might be sanctioned, Anderson and his colleagues asked that those receiving the draft treat it confidentially. Nonetheless, the "Cornell Paper," as it came to be called, was leaked, and in 1972 Anderson was forbidden to enter Indonesia, an order that stood until early 1999 in the post-Suharto era. Anderson turned his attention to Thailand and, later, the Philippines. The immediate product of his studies on Thailand, which Anderson calls Siam in deference to notable Thai scholars, at odds with the pretensions of ethnic inclusiveness of successive governments, was *In the Mirror* (1988), an anthology of short stories critical of the effects of the American military on Thai society in the era of the Vietnam War. His extensive historical and critical introduction, which takes up nearly one-third of the book, makes clear that the Thai claim to never having been a colony is a hollow one, given the compromises that had to be made with the British to the west, in Burma, and the French to the east and north in Cambodia and Laos, as well as U.S. **neocolonialism** in the immense military buildup of the 1960s.

Another attempt to rescue an anticolonialist writer from near oblivion is the recent edition of a novella attributed to Carlos Bulosan titled *All the Conspirators* (1998), with a lengthy historical and critical introduction written by Anderson and his coeditor, Caroline S. Hau. Two aspects of that introduction are important from a postcolonialist point of view. One is the theme of these writings, a bitter denunciation of U.S. racism with respect to Filipinos. The other is the paradoxical use of the colonial languages by Filipino writers.

Anderson has many intellectual forebears. Among those whom he acknowledges are Wittgenstein, Auerbach, Benjamin, and, of course, Marx. The notion that print capitalism—later, radio, television, and electronic communication—was everywhere a precursor to nationalism adumbrates Benjamin's theories concerning mechanical reproduction. Less obvious is the influence of his brother, Perry Anderson, the widely quoted theorist of British Marxism and longtime editor of the *New Left Review*, whose essays have dealt with such influential twentieth-century thinkers as Braudel, Sartre, **Gramsci**, Althusser, and E. P. Thompson. In the introduction to *Language and Power* he writes of his joy in discourses with his brother and credits him with providing "a broadly Marxist optic" (10) that enabled him to bring his early studies of Indonesia into comparative perspective.

Further Reading: B. Anderson 1983, 1990, 1998.

Roger J. Jiang Bresnahan

Anglophone Literatures   This is a disciplinary field that links together all writing produced in English, inclusive of British and occasionally of so-termed minority or multicultural American texts as well, although the usual category for the latter is "literature of the Americas." All of the texts once understood as Commonwealth are now more widely understood as anglophone, with the semantic change signaling a de-emphasis of static imperial relations between the metropolitan homeland and its protectorates. Canonical value is no longer imagined to be held exclusively by the **center**, as it was with the discipline of **Commonwealth literature**. In fact, critics such as **C.L.R. James** have argued that the "best" writing in English in the twentieth century was produced by writers who are not themselves English, from James Joyce and Joseph Conrad, to **Derek Walcott**, J. M. Coetzee, and **Kamau Brathwaite**. The international popularity, critical acclaim, and prizewinning status of novels written in English by non-English writers confirm this. Understanding most of twentieth-century writing in English as anglophone acknowledges the difficulties, if not impossibilities, of establishing national identifications for the vast number of transnational or migrant writers who are born in one country and then choose (or are forced to choose) to live in another. In this respect, English studies has swerved away from a nation-based paradigm and toward one that is language-based. "Anglophone literature" also acknowledges the increased production and availability of literary texts from all over the world, although one important pitfall of this expansion of the canon is advocacy criticism, whereby the value of "marginal" writers is determined in relation to the literary value of the center. Such a global literary web also suggests the possibilities of interconnectedness among texts produced in different parts of the world, whether it be through thematic, problematic, style, or narrative structure. A significant and much commented-upon group of anglophone texts are those that fall into the category of "rewriting empire" because they annotate, parody, and otherwise rework the major canonical tropes and figures that have contributed to an understanding of the "Third World" and its subjects. For example, such texts as *The Tempest*, *Robinson Crusoe*, *Jane Eyre*, *Kim*, and *Heart of Darkness* and the figures of Prospero, Caliban, Bertha Mason, and Friday have been reframed and represented by such authors as Brathwaite, Walcott, Coetzee, **Michelle Cliff**, **Chinua Achebe**, Jean Rhys, and Michael Ondaatje. Insofar as the disparate anglophone texts may be said to share disparate concerns, they also may be said to allow for the identification of connections, particularly in their concern with the materiality of violence, Western commodities, migrancy, **nativism**, **identity** and alienation, and the imperial force of English.

The field of anglophone literatures is made up of diverse texts, all of which are written in English. An important question to ask, then, is what ultimately links, for example, **Jamaica Kincaid** to **Wole Soyinka** or to **Salman Rushdie**. One answer to this question has to be that there is a certain connection between the English language and colonialism. The authors understood as anglophone belong to different historical and cultural moments (e.g., South Africa, Pakistan, Antigua), and they belong to distinct moments and distinct spaces, yet they are all still readable if one knows English. This raises an interesting paradox: a sense of the different moments and practices of readings, on the one hand, and an apparent commonality and ease of translation, on the other. Yet, this act of **translation** is erroneous insofar as one cannot comprehend all of the texts equally; certain cultural references or rhetorical styles might always be "foreign" or ungraspable. Thus, the discussion of writing in English presumes a kind of unity and singularity, a unified literature in English, but multiplicity and differences are ineluctable: the field must instead be understood as literature in English*es*. Such a designation is necessary in order to account for the varieties of English that are circumscribed as anglophone, and naming individual dialects such as Jamaican English, Scots, and Nigerian English is not sufficient to account for the innumerable differences in languages among all of the "new" Englishes. These differences, which result from the use of pidgins, **Creoles**, nation languages, neologisms, Standard English, and a hybridity of languages, have been significant enough to prompt the critical suggestion that anglophone literatures would benefit from the methodological approaches of comparative literature and linguistics.

The imperial force of language has become a central thematic in twentieth-century literature and criticism, and the institutionalization of imperial languages (English, French, Spanish) within the colonies has been registered within anglophone literary texts as both a destructive imposition and as a productive, enabling, or even necessary force. **Ngũgĩ wa Thiong'o** and Chinua Achebe have most prominently taken these respective positions within the context of what can be framed as a debate on the use of English by African writers. (It is important to note that this debate on the politics of writing in English is not alone in its basic premise, which is that there is no material difference in the facility with which non-native speakers work within the language.) Achebe articulates both the necessity and the advantages of writing in English in terms of the international audience and currency of the language and in terms of its cultural and literary inheritance. He does, however, allow for English as performing a colonization of the mind, a position most famously taken by Ngũgĩ, who reads language as colonialism's weapon of choice. Ngũgĩ argues that English functions as the language of capital, industry, technology, and war and that the phenomenon of Africans writing in English suggests that the situation for "Third World" writers is neocolonial, rather than postcolonial. Contemporary arguments that have followed in Ngũgĩ's wake have held that the imagined diaspora of English is not just a matter of anglophone unity but also a matter of an anglophone identity intimately allied with a civil and thinly disguised cultural identity. In such a context, to command someone to write in English is not just to command the use of a grammar or vocabulary or to command the demonstration of a technical literacy but is also to command the performance of a particular cultural identity. Such a power/knowledge critique of a one-way flow of information, from the center to the margins, has been modified by an understanding of the use of English as an appropriation, counterinhabitation, and dismantling of a dominant language. It follows that the ultimate argument, made by Chinua Achebe and others, for the use of English depends upon the refashioning and making "new" of English. Such a refashioning finds its perfect metaphor in the title of Louise Bennett's (Jamaica) poem, "Colonisation in Reverse" (1949), which is about the phenomenon of **black Britain** and is itself written in a dialect of English.

One reaction to the "new" Englishes from the metropole has been that the uses of English by anglophone writers have been read as part of the unintelligible background noise of the colony and of the metropole—as imperfect, impure corruptions of a Grand (literary and linguistic) Tradition. But they also have to be read as highly innovative and even emancipatory, whereby a postcolonial writer might appropriate English in order to subvert the tyranny of an imposed colonial language by making a home within it. Amos Tutuola's *The Palm-Wine Drinkard* (1952) is an early and important example, as is Ken Saro-Wiwa's *Sozaboy: A Novel in Rotten English* (1985). What Tutuola, Saro-Wiwa, Michelle Cliff, and **Sam Selvon** achieve in their novels is precisely that: the inhabitation, making indigenous, and subterranean reworking of English. These writers are not in the position of assimilation or **mimicry** or simply producing literature in the canonical or generic mode of the West, but they are instead producing a hybrid cultural form. They are at once severing language from some of its cultural associations (severing English from its ties to Western power and rewriting its racist and colonial ideology) *and* realigning language and culture (providing oppositional representations of "Nigeria" or "Jamaica" in a new language). Their work promises to reconfigure the association of English with power, empire, nation, and culture, and it suggests the extent to which there are fundamental differences between "English literature" and "literature in English." Other Nigerian writers commenting upon the relations between English and power and contributing to a "new" English include Achebe, Gabriel Okara, Ben Okri, **Buchi Emecheta**, Femi Osofisan, and Wole Soyinka.

The "literatures" component of anglophone literatures is equally important, encompassing as it does the classical generic modes of poetry, novels, stories, memoirs, essays, and plays but including as well a number of oral modes such as dub poetry, folk poetry and folk songs, praise songs, calypso, dread talk, curses, and word-songs. These oral modes have directly contributed to the emergence of anglophone Caribbean literature (also named West Indian) as an academic field, insofar as their translation into print form has secured an international audience and insofar as they have helped to inaugurate a literary tradition with which contemporary writers remain in conversation. An important early moment in this field was the BBC-sponsored radio program *Caribbean Voices* (begun 1946), a weekly program broadcast to the West Indies that helped to launch the careers of Selvon, **V. S. Naipaul**, Michael Anthony, **George Lamming**, and Andrew Salkey. A diasporic Caribbean literary community with profound ties to Britain was the result, and the fifty or so books produced by British Caribbean novelists between 1948 and 1958 constitute one of the most significant cultural phenomena at the ends of the British empire. Selvon's *The Lonely Londoners* (1956) was the first Caribbean novel written entirely in the literary demotic and among the first to present Caribbean speech as dignified, natural, and something other than a curiosity. Calypso has had a profound influence on Selvon and Caribbean literature as a whole, as has jazz, and Jamaican writing in particular has evolved in relation to reggae, of which dub poetry, which involves reading against the rhythm of the bass line, is the quintessential form. Black British dub poets such as Linton Kwesi Johnson, Benjamin Zephaniah, and Michael Smith have found a significant audience in London and New York, and they have turned their attention to the problem of race relations in contemporary Britain, much as migrant Caribbean writers living in the United States have turned their attention to race relations here (Paule Marshall, Jamaica Kincaid, Cliff).

Anglophone Caribbean writing is composed of African, East Indian, Carib, and other indigenous cultural influences, but an important divide is epitomized by Derek Walcott and Kamau Brathwaite, insofar as Walcott generally writes in standard English and has achieved a place within mainstream world literature, and Brathwaite generally writes in what he terms "nation language." Another way of tracing the contours of the field is generational (not by age but by moment of publication), with the following writers grouped in the first wave: Louise Bennett (Jamaica), Erna Brodber (Jamaica), **Wilson Harris** (Guyana), Merle Hodge (Trinidad), C.L.R. James (Trinidad), George Lamming (Barbados), Paule Marshall (Barbados), V. S. Naipaul (Trinidad), Jean Rhys (Dominica), Andrew Salkey (Jamaica), and Sam Selvon (Trinidad). The second wave of Caribbean writers would include Kamau Brathwaite (Barbados), Jean Binta Breeze (Jamaica), David Dabydeen (Guyana), Jamaica Kincaid (Antigua), **Earl Lovelace** (Trinidad), Grace Nichols (Guyana), **Caryl Phillips** (St. Kitts), Olive Senior (Jamaica), Derek Walcott (St. Lucia).

Black British writing links together not just Caribbean migrants but African and South Asian as well. Among the more prominent literary figures tied in some way both to Britain and to a South Asian diaspora are Salman Rushdie and Hanif Kureishi. Kureishi is a novelist and short story writer, but some of his most important work has been screenplays (*My Beautiful Launderette* [1986] and *Sammy and Rosie* [1988]), which indicate the extent to which anglophone literatures include all media forms. Other writers who have produced notable works for visual media include Ken Saro-Wiwa, who wrote and directed the popular and critically acclaimed Nigerian sitcom *Basi and Company* (1987), and Michael Ondaatje, whose novel *The English Patient* (1992) was translated into a popular film. The South Asian diaspora has produced some of the most prominent "postcolonial" writers, critics, and critical studies essayists, and after the publication of Rushdie's *Midnight's Children* (1981), a retroactive genealogy of what has also been variously termed as subcontinental, Indo-Anglian, and South Asian literature has been drawn back to Rabindranath Tagore. Such a genealogy includes colonial-era texts by Rudyard Kipling and E. M. Forster and Sri Lankan, Pakistani, Bangladeshi, Indian, and Burmese writers such as Ondaatje (novels), Rushdie (novels, stories), **Bapsi Sidhwa** (novels), **Anita Desai** (novels), Kamala Das (poetry), Rohinton Mistry (novels), **R. K. Narayan** (novels), **Nayantara Sahgal** (novels), Vikram Seth (novels, poetry), Arundhati Roy (novels), Sujata Bhatt (poetry), Sara Suleri (memoirs), and Wendy Law-Yone (novels).

British literature itself is a problematic category, given the most recent revival of Scots, led by award-winning and popular writers James Kelman (novels, stories), Irvine Welsh (novels, stories), Duncan McLean (stories), Janice Galloway (novels), Alex Hamilton (stories), A. L. Kennedy (novels), and Andrew Crumey (novels). Traces of linguistic and cultural autonomy, if not **nationalism**, are present in the latest generation of Scottish writers, as is anticolonial sentiment. So, too, English–Irish colonial relations figure prominently in Irish writing of this century, from James Joyce and W. B. Yeats, to Flan O'Brien (novels), Seamus Heaney (poetry), Eavan Bolland (poetry), Brian Friel (plays), and Roddy Doyle (novels). Anglophone literatures also encompass other national literatures annotated in this volume: Australian, Canadian (English), Filipino, Irish, Native American, New Zealand/Maori, South African, Sri Lankan, and Zimbabwean.

Further Reading: A. Donnell and S. Welsh 1996; D. Walder 1998.

Rita Raley

Gloria Anzaldúa (1946–   )   Gloria Anzaldúa is a Chicana tejana lesbian-feminist who works in multiple genres—mixed poetry and prose (*Borderlands* [1987]), children's stories (*Friends from the Other Side* [1993] and *Prietita and the Ghost Woman* [1995]), interviews (*Interviews/Entrevistas* [2000]), anthologies (*This Bridge Called My Back* [1983] and *Making Face, Making Soul* [1990]), and fiction (*La Prieta* [1995]). Throughout her writings, she draws on her personal experience as a seventh-generation Chicana born in an occupied territory (the Texas–Mexico border) to explore issues highly relevant to postcolonial theory, including U.S. imperialism, bilingualism, and indigenous Mexican history and myth. Her concepts of the borderlands, mestiza consciousness, and the new mestiza inform contemporary debates concerning postcoloniality, subjectivity, lesbian identity, and literary conventions.

A political activist, Anzaldúa uses her writing to encourage social transformation. Editing anthologies contributes to social awareness, builds community, and provides a crucial space of dialogue. *Making Face, Making Soul (Haciendo Caras): Creative and Critical Perspectives by Women of Color* (Spinsters) includes essays, poetry, artwork, and fiction by sixty-two women. Here, Anzaldúa provokes "others" to "decolonize" themselves. She deconstructs categories of fixed identities to encourage bridges across difference. She defines creative acts as forms of political activism and identifies the advantages of taking part in the culture by helping to build it, making space for the self and for others in an ongoing process. Along with Cherríe Moraga, Anzaldúa edited *This Bridge Called My Back: Writings by Radical Women of Color*, a groundbreaking, multigenre volume that expanded previous mainstream definitions of feminism and challenged "white" feminists to examine issues of privilege and responsibility.

Anzaldúa's germinal work, *Borderlands/La Frontera*, defies prescriptive, imperialist defining discourses. Her articulation of the "borderlands" (psychological, sexual, geographic, spiritual, linguistic, and theoretical) posits a border-crossing trope useful for theories of subjectivity. She deploys the term "mestiza consciousness" to identify the plurality of subjectivities that each individual embodies. Occupying a space of "perpetual transition" and "cultural collision" involves a struggle to resist limiting and confining borders. Demonstrating the interpenetration of the many borders, such as ethnic, gender, sexual, linguistic, and religious, Anzaldúa exposes the political forces that construct borders to divide and conquer those least empowered. The fact that the borders are in a state of constant transition gives impetus to movements for social change. Identifying the continual process of plural subjectivities in one individual, Anzaldúa contests the Western philosophical notion of the stable, unified subject (which assumes a white male subject with an authoritative speaking voice).

Drawing on her own experiences, she argues that the work of the "mestiza consciousness" is to transcend dualities by breaking down subject/object binary thinking. Those who are "othered" by dominant culture must resist labels such as transgressors, aliens, inhuman, subhuman, through embodied cultural and political acts aimed at social transformation. Her inclusionary ideology, which refuses to deny any part of herself, provides a model that is now becoming adopted in the academy and reflects the realities of a postcolonial world.

Seeing identity as an ongoing process, Anzaldúa embodies a postcolonial strategic resistance to cultural oppression at the interstices of difference embodied by ethnic minorities, women, lesbians, the poor, and other "othered" groups. Anzaldúa reveals the inextricability of self and actively *producing* self in a social context; she claims that by changing ourselves, we change the world. She describes a simultaneous movement of going deep into the self and also expanding into the world, thus reconstructing society at the same time as re-creating the self in a two-way movement. Connecting the self and society, imbricating the "I" and the "we," reverberates in postcolonial theory.

Discussing the writing process, Anzaldúa rejects postmodernist notions that deny the writer's authority over the text and imperial critics who proceed to deconstruct the text and subsume authority. She identifies such postmodern strategies as part of the old practice of appropriating the text of the "other," of interpreting the text as a product of a cultural matrix, a product that the critic can master and gain power over its meaning. However, she acknowledges the difficulty in preventing oneself from using and being used by the dominant discursive practices.

In an interview with Andrea Lunsford, Anzaldúa directly addresses postcolonialism in terms of issues of identity (*Interviews*). She identifies the powerful white, Euro-American frame of reference within which individuals in most disciplines must operate. Anzaldúa engages the need to be aware of the Euro-American frame of reference in order to participate in, and encourage, sociocultural and economic change and to offer alternative models.

Engaging her own writing, Anzaldúa uses the image of being pulled counterclockwise in order to include the indigenous and Mexican parts of her self. The educational system trained her to look at the world in one way, and to do otherwise necessitates a powerful resistance to the pull to conform and to belong. Postcolonial people must live within this tension between the clockwise of the colonizing cultures and the counterclockwise of the colonized cultures. In terms of style and rhetoric, she wonders how far she can bend traditional, academic theoretical discourse with "code-switching," "Spanglish," and associative writing and still be accepted and recognized by diverse groups of peers—the academics, artists, writers. Such accommodation is a juggling act.

Anzaldúa believes that postcolonial studies are one way to invite students to recognize and appreciate difference and to reflect upon their own ways of being in the world. Postcolonial studies is an emancipatory project that encourages the students to ask questions about who has power, who has voice—whether it is engaging government, anthropology, or composition, for instance. Interrogating the neo-colonialization of people's minds exposes the erasure of certain history, of ideas, languages, and books. She offers the example of the historical events during which Mayan and Aztec codices were burned and evidence of a whole system of knowledge was thereby destroyed.

Anzaldúa delineates the mutual complicity that negates simple binary splits of white and colored, straight and queer, Christian and Jew, self and other, oppressor and oppressed, since the "insider"/"outsider" positions are frequently interchangeable. Speaking of a "geography of hybridity," Anzaldúa echoes and informs many postcolonial theorists and critics. She predicts a world, inside and outside the academy, where a "hybrid consciousness" may be forged.

Further engaging pedagogical issues, Anzaldúa plays with the word "*cono-cimiento*," which is Spanish for "knowledge." For Anzaldúa, *conocimiento* represents counterknowledge. Counterknowledge encourages self-reflection and awareness, enabling students to be open and welcoming to new ideas. There must be an opening, a gate, a "rajadura—a crack between worlds," where interfaces occur, she theorizes.

Here, her thought process obviously crosses linguistic borders, and the border-crossing dynamic creates new ways of knowing and new ways of explaining. *Nepantla* means the space in between, the middle ground, and Anzaldúa uses it to refer to the liminal states of being, the borderlands, the interface between established grounds. With particular significance for postcolonial theory, *nepantla* states create spaces of understanding for experiences and realities that layer and overlap across different cultures and social and geographic spaces. Refusing the reductive limits of traditional Western logical thinking, Anzaldúa produces a cultural matrix that spirals through history and contemporary time and valorizes the unconscious as well as conscious, rational thought.

She rejects traditional systems that reinscribe dominant discourse and force formerly colonized peoples to adopt writing and thinking strategies that are foreign to their own. While she acknowledges that it is impossible for an internal postcolonial author to rewrite ideology from within, she hopes that a community of writers may be able to create new *conocimientos* or different versions of reality.

Crossing linguistic borders in her thinking, Anzaldúa feels that she creates a mixture, a hybridity that valorizes both the indigenous and the Western and acknowledges the reality of her experiences and her life—a liminal state between cultures, between knowledges, between symbolic systems. Including Spanish phrases in her works, which are rich in oral tradition, a tradition in which women have always participated, Anzaldúa refuses to turn away from her own heritage.

Language's powerful role in shaping reality and ordering experience gives it primary significance for promoting social transformation. Acknowledging the significant impact that language has in creating reality and in forming each individual's sense of identity, as well as the potential to displace reality, Anzaldúa laments the hegemony of the English language in the world. She identifies the Internet, the age of globalized industrialization, and the age of electronics as increasingly advancing the English-only environment. Using her own experience, she documents the damage that individuals suffer when forced to adopt a new language and restrict the use of their first language. Enforced use of English evokes memories of her painful childhood experiences in the school situation, adding to her desire to leave those linguistic binds and borders behind through creatively deploying a combination of languages. Anzaldúa refers to the postcolonial setting in which the colonizers' language is a constant reminder of otherness. She provides witness to diverse experiences of "linguistic terrorism." She states that "if you really want to hurt me, talk badly about my language. Ethnic identity is twin skin to linguistic identity—I am my language" (*Borderlands*, 59). In *Borderlands*, her "code-switching" from English to Castillian Spanish to the North Mexican dialect to Tex-Mex to Nahuatl to a mixture of them all creates a "cross-pollination" at the juncture of culture that revitalizes language.

Further Reading: Fowlkes 1997; Keating 1996; Steele 2000; Yarbro-Bejarano 1994.

Lynda Hall

Arjun Appadurai   Arjun Appadurai, currently Samuel N. Harper Professor of Anthropology and South Asian Languages and Civilizations and director of the Globalization Project at the University of Chicago, has made several significant contributions to the field of postcolonial studies. A specialist in the anthropology of **modernity** and the historical anthropology of South Asia, Appadurai's important critical interventions into studies of postcoloniality can be traced to two main sources: *Modernity at Large: Cultural Dimensions of Globalization* (1996) and his contributions as associate editor of the journal *Public Culture*.

Appadurai has written extensively about modernity, particularly in the South Asian context. *Worship and Conflict under Colonial Rule: A South Indian Case* (1981) is Appadurai's first full-length text. Appadurai's most influential text, *Modernity at Large*, collects several articles on modernity and **globalization**, including "Disjuncture and Difference in the Global Cultural Economy" and other influential essays such as "Playing with Modernity: The Decolonization of Indian Cricket" and "Patriotism and Its Futures." Altering the way postcolonialists theorize the role that global capital plays in constructing and producing multiple types of communities, Appadurai's theoretical oeuvre consistently dismantles the reductivist position that a simple **center/periphery** model can explain relations in a postcolonial moment. Instead, the focus on migration, diaspora, and movements of people and capital in a global framework offers a rubric to think about how new types of relations are forged in a transnational world.

In his introduction to *Modernity at Large*, Appadurai emphasizes the role of the *cultural* over *culture*. Thinking of culture as a fixed, static unity, Appadurai argues, is problematic because it implies that culture is an object that can be discretely studied and quantified (12). Emphasizing the *cultural* allows for an articulation of what Appadurai names "situated difference"—the idea that cultures are in flux and never wholly predetermined or fixed. The idea of the *cultural* as process and as dimension of difference denaturalizes the links between group identity and "culture," foregrounding, instead, the fact that national or transnational politics, for example, can mobilize certain ideas of culture to serve the needs of ethnic **nationalist** and transnational movements.

In thinking about emergent global communities in a postcolonial moment, Appadurai argues that mass migration movements have altered the makeup of the world. The groundwork for thinking through the construction of new types of communities is laid in the frequently anthologized "Disjuncture and Difference in the Global Cultural Economy"—also the first chapter in *Modernity at Large*. Extrapolating from **Benedict Anderson**'s work on the role of print capitalism and imagination in creating imagined national communities, Appadurai examines how new, imagined worlds have become a vital part of the global economy. To address the numerous ways that flows of global capital and people construct different types of communities, Appadurai describes five different types of imagined world landscapes: ethnoscapes (people who move between nations, such as tourists, immigrants, exiles, guest workers, and refugees), technoscapes (technology, usually linked to multinational corporations), financescapes (global capital, currency markets, stock exchanges), mediascapes (electronic media), and ideoscapes (official state ideologies and counterideologies). In suggesting that these five landscapes are different types of imagined worlds, Appadurai is not subscribing to a facile and naive celebration of border crossings and traversals in a transnational postcolonial moment. By describing these imagined worlds that traverse the borders of the nation-state, Appadurai makes a timely intervention into postcolonial studies and also provides a critical vocabulary to discuss the different types of economic and social domination that affect postcolonial nation-states. These imagined worlds, Appadurai argues, are increasingly present in the contemporary world, and by emphasizing their presence and growing importance (instead of the imagined community of the nation-state), it becomes possible, perhaps even necessary, to think how communities are forged transnationally, across nation-states through networks of **diaspora**, migration, technology, electronic media, ideologies, and global capital. Appadurai's scholarship in *Modernity at Large* involves a rethinking of the role of the imagination in providing alternatives different from the nation-state. In an era of globalization and mass migration and in a world that is increasingly mediated by electronic media, Appadurai argues that it is exceedingly difficult to separate the world into discrete nation-state entities. Cognizant of the fact that not everyone travels, migrates, or crosses borders, he posits, nonetheless, that few people anywhere in the world do not know of someone who has traveled to different locations in the world. Through what he names "diasporic public spheres" (4), Appadurai contends that modern subjectivities are rendered increasingly unstable. He cites the example of Pakistani taxi drivers in the United States listening to taped sermons from a Pakistani mosque to emphasize how electronic media enable migrants outside the nation-state to imagine themselves as part of an imagined world. Through multiple forms of electronic mediation and imagination, persons and communities are able to traverse boundaries without physically traveling.

Extending this logic, Appadurai's essay "Playing with Modernity: The Decolonization of Indian Cricket" examines how transmission of spectator sports such as cricket via radio, cable, and satellite television as well as print media engenders new, imagined worlds that intersect and pollinate across transnational lines. Appadurai explores how these "mass-mediated forms" enabled cricket— once the repository of Englishness and a tool for colonization—to become a spectacular national passion that is central not only to the Indian imagination in the postcolonial Indian nation-state but also within certain imagined worlds of diasporic communities. Throughout the essay, he examines the role played by corporate sponsors, the entertainment industry, technocrats, and journalists in creating new, imagined communities of cricket spectators in diverse global settings.

His collaborative work with Carol Breckenridge in the collection *Consuming Modernity: Public Culture in a South Asian World* (1995) has also paved the way for serious and nuanced analyses of modernity in South Asia. In "Public Modernity in India," Appadurai and Breckenridge describe modernity as a global experience but qualify this by noting that experience(s) of modernity is varied and heterogeneous. Cognizant of the fact that the term "modernity" is itself a Western historical category, they argue against thinking of modernity as a teleological process with a fixed end point. They suggest that most societies locally produce their own modernities, noting at the same time that movement of people and capital renders it difficult to construct neatly demarcated zones of experience.

Appadurai and Breckenridge also problematize the use of the term "popular culture." Instead, they use the term "public culture" to navigate through and around zones of cultural debate that are an integral part of globalization processes (Appadurai and Breckenridge 5). Distinct from mass, commercial, or popular culture, public culture comes to speak of spaces such as cinema, sports, museums, and restaurants (Conlon 90) where national, mass, and folk culture intersect and challenge each other to produce an effect that is called "modern" within and across nation-states (Appadurai and Breckenridge 5).

Appadurai has also played a vital role in rethinking the role of area studies in the U.S. academy in a post–Cold War era. Linking the rise of area studies departments between 1945 and 1989 to foreign policy needs of the United States, Appadurai argues that the "old way" of doing area studies is no longer tenable. In critiquing the tendency of area studies departments to create rigid maps of the world that fixate on certain geopolitical spaces, he is also cognizant of the importance of creating a space within the academy and society at large to give serious consideration to the world outside "America." He thus asks the important question, How can area studies departments change the way that images and ideas of the world are created from within the United States? For this reason Appadurai emphasizes studying the local production of modernity in discussing issues of globalization, migration, and nationalism.

A final, but crucial, site of intervention into postcolonial studies can be found in Appadurai's involvement with *Public Culture*, a journal that has created a forum to critically study global cultural flows in a postcolonial world and has made several major contributions to the field of transnational **cultural studies**. The analyses of cultural, social, and political differences in public spheres are often concerned with public culture in specific local conditions. As part of a special tenth-anniversary commemorative, *Public Culture* released a series of four special issues—the Millennial Quartet—that addresses the theme of globalization processes. The second volume in the series (vol. 12, no. 2, 2000) is edited by Arjun Appadurai and is titled "Globalization."

In a world that is marked by uneven flows of global capital, peoples, and communities, it is increasingly problematic to use a term such as "postcolonial" to describe the diverse experiences and cultural processes of communities in or from formerly colonized spaces. Without naively seeing the world as an interconnected whole, Appadurai's scholarship has been tremendously useful in thinking about how transnational flows of people and capital create alternative imagined worlds and "scapes" of modernity. Foregrounding the importance of theorizing public culture and the cultural rather than culture, Appadurai helps to establish a new trajectory in postcolonial studies that grapples with the links between nationalism, diaspora, cultural processes, and globalization in a postcolonial moment.

Further Reading: A. Appadurai 1996; A. Appadurai and C. Breckenridge 1995.

Anita Mannur

Arabism   Arabism refers to Arab nationalism, *al-'Urubah, al-Qawmiyah al-'arabiyah*. The term "Arabism" in English was coined by C. Ernest Dawn in his controversial book *From Ottomanism to Arabism* (1973) and resonates with the Arabic coinage, *al-'urubah*. The consensus is that Arabism is, first and foremost, the belief that all Arabs share a common cultural identity and that, despite local and even religious differences, this identity is defined by a common language and a collective history that predate the appearance of Islam. Arab nationalism can be understood as a political, cultural, historical, and ideological phenomenon that disregards exclusionist theories of blood and race. Likewise, as a secular ideology, it purports that Islam is a central *cultural*, but not religious, component to Arab identity.

However, despite this diversity or perhaps because of it, scholars have failed to understand Arabism as a discursive phenomenon with its intellectual roots in the nineteenth-century Arab Renaissance, or *al-nahdah al-'arabiyah*. During this period, Arab intellectuals, Christian, Jewish, and Muslim alike, started to rethink what it meant to be an Arab, vis-à-vis Islam, its religious minorities, and their increasing and ever disproportionate relationship with the West. During the twentieth century, Arab nationalism traveled several roads, splintered off into many different pedigrees, and came to mean a handful of different things to different people, Arabs and non-Arabs alike.

It is virtually impossible to discuss Arab nationalism without discussing its historiography. Arabism, as an ideological and political phenomenon, has been thoroughly studied almost continually since the time of its inception. Within recent decades, it has been much assailed by Western and, to a lesser extent, Arab scholars, undergoing revisions and defenses, some of which have been productive and others pedantic. The fact that few other topics equal the passion and ferocity that the discussion of Arab **nationalism** has inspired is testament to its importance, even centrality, in understanding the Arab world throughout the twentieth century.

The traditional, now outdated paradigm regarding the genesis of Arab nationalism is that the ideology was created by Western or missionary-educated Christian and, later, Muslim Arab intellectuals—based mostly in Beirut and Cairo—during the nineteenth century in reaction to Turkish Ottoman tyranny. This "Turkocracy," as Greek nationalists named it, allegedly resulted in the stifling of innovative Arab cultural and intellectual production as well as the suppression of Arab identity. The writings of the Syrian activist al-Shaykh 'Abd al-Rahman al-Kawakibi (1855–1902) and Najib Azoury (1870–1916) are most representative of these beliefs, but George Antonius' seminal *The Arab Awakening* (1938) is the most prominent and cited source for the historiographical paradigm.

However, by the 1960s Albert Hourani would write the definitive work on the historical context and intellectual environment that would give rise to Arab nationalism. In *Arab Thought in the Liberal Age* (1962), indeed, still a classic and standard reference, Hourani amends the traditional paradigm, focusing on the several intellectual pedigrees that were under formation at the turn of the twentieth century, including, although perhaps oxymoronically, Islamicism, Islamic secularism, and radical Christian secularism.

At this same time, scholars such as Ernest Dawn, Elie Kedourie, and Sylvia Haim were attacking the commonplace understandings of the origins of Arab nationalism. They highlighted the specious claim regarding Ottoman tyranny and downplayed the effects or existence of the pre–World War I "Turkification" initiative of the Committee for Union and Progress (CUP). Likewise, they faulted the historians of Arab nationalism as well as its contemporaneous proponents for having incorrectly and anachronistically associated nineteenth-century Arab intellectuals with what would later become known as Arab nationalism. That is, these "revisionist" historians, many of whom had their own ideological and political bone to pick with Arab nationalism, maintained that the nineteenth- and early twentieth-century intellectuals were either Ottomanists or local nationalists. Scholars, such as Dawn, have maintained that there is an absence of evidence for any substantial participation in such now well-known Arab nationalist "secret societies" as *al-Fatat* or *al-'Ahd*. Consequently, they assert that there was no Arab nationalism before World War I. Furthermore, scholars such as Kedourie theorized that Arab nationalism was a movement created by local elites to stave off or counteract increased pressure on their own political power base.

These scholarly critiques of Arab nationalism by the "revisionist" school inspired a generation of scholars to "return to" or find new sources pertinent to the rise of Arab nationalism and the appeal that it might have maintained in the Arab world. Scholars such as Rashid Khalidi and Marwan Buheiry refocus attention on the press as a valid scholarly source that expressed the sentiments, aspirations, and activities of nascent Arab nationalist organizations and thinkers. Shukru Hanioglu, Phillip Khoury, Hasan Kayali, and Reeva Simon are just a few others who have reexamined foreign consular correspondences, private papers, and Ottoman archives in hopes of gauging the social, class, and political origins of participants in the Arab nationalist movement and their relationship with the Ottoman state as well as the particularities of the latter's policies.

Another fruitful consequence of the often pedantic assertions of the revisionist school has been that historians have expanded their scope of inquiry. In moving away from Arabist activities exclusively in Lebanon, Syria, Palestine, and Egypt, William Ochsenwald, Mary C. Wilson, Reeva Simon, Dina Rizq Khoury, and Lisa Anderson, among many others, have looked at Arab nationalist sentiment and participation in Iraq, Libya, and the Arabian peninsula. Likewise, historians like Beth Baron and Margot Badran have extended the study to women's participation in nationalist ideology, while scholars such as Abdallah Laroui, Bassam Tibi, M. Abed al-Jabari, and 'Aziz Azmeh have broadened the theoretical and political framework of understanding Arab nationalism.

The struggle within the academy and its peripheries over the historiography of Arab nationalism should not be seen as merely an ivory-tower debate. Rather, the passion and proliferation of studies and critiques are particularly pertinent to postcolonial studies, as they clearly demonstrate the nexus between history, historiography, ideology, the academy, and the political arena as well as demonstrate that academic writing was a central stage in the twentieth century where political battles, particularly over the struggle for Palestine and the validity of Arab nationalism as a liberation movement, were fought. Most indicative of this is the avalanche of right-wing and/or pro-Zionist commentaries in mainstream periodicals and newspapers, most notoriously by Orientalist Bernard Lewis, heralding the "end" or "death of Arab nationalism" following Operation Desert Storm in 1991.

A crucial failure of the historiography of Arab nationalism, irrespective of the ideological position taken toward it, has been the inability to understand its discursive origins apart from the context of "awakening" and its germination outside the notion of "a movement." For example, Dawn, who offers the most respectable critique of the "origins of Arabism," cites the writing of Syrian political activist Muhammad Kurd 'Ali (1876–1953), who testified that Egyptian state institutions, not missionary or Western schools, were the fundamental source in "awakening" an Arab national consciousness. Furthermore, he raises issues of statistical quantity, such as how many readers Arab nationalist newspapers actually had before World War I, as a means of casting a doubt on Arabism's mass appeal.

However, we must understand Arab nationalism principally as a discursive phenomenon and, therefore, examine its "epistemological foundation" as laid down in the mid- and late nineteenth century by thinkers like Butrus al-Bustani (1819–1883), Rifa'ah Rafi' al-Tahtawi (1801–1873), Jamal al- din al-Qasimi (1866–1914), Khayr al-din al-Tunisi (d. 1890), and Jurji Zaydan (1861–1914). Although these intellectuals were not Arab nationalists per se, their writings began to reformulate what it meant to be an Arab in the context of their various religious, local, and/or Ottoman identities. In doing so, they all articulated, despite their religious, educational, professional, and local differences, similar concerns and visions of Arabness, that is, a common sense of history, culture, language, and political tradition. Therefore, we follow Rashid al-Khalidi's understanding that Ottomanism and Arabism were *not* mutually exclusive or contrary ideological forces or camps. In doing so, we recognize the discursive depth and elasticity of Arabism that would equip it for the many turbulent years that were to come.

That is, Arab nationalism did not take off as a solidified political movement, with an organization and an immediately recognizable political infrastructure, until the first decade of the twentieth century. Arab nationalist activists were generally members of the reform movement against the autocratic rule of the Ottoman sultan 'Abd al-Hamid. Many nineteenth-century Arab activists and thinkers were involved in, and supported, the CUP revolt of 1906, which reinstituted the Ottoman Parliament, which had been dissolved some thirty years earlier by the Sublime Porte. In fact, many of the most prominent Arab activists became members of the Ottoman Decentralization Party. Despite the mass support for the CUP coup and the parliamentary establishment and despite the claims of fair representation, by 1909 the Arabs and other non-Turkish ethnicities in the empire were underrepresented in the Parliament, while the ruling council consisted exclusively of Turks. To make matters worse, by 1912 the ruling triumvirate attempted to institute an empirewide program of "Turkification," replacing Arabic with Turkish as the language of administration and education in the Arab provinces. Whether Turkification was a real or only perceived threat, this cultural intrusion along with prominent Western political interference and increased and unchecked Zionist immigration into Palestine compelled Arab nationalism as the most natural and articulate vehicle for the expression of Arab independence.

During World War I, Arab nationalism congealed into a political and military movement, revolting against the Ottoman empire and assisting the Allies in the war effort. In an attempt to crush "sedition," the Ottoman governor of Damascus cracked down on intellectual and political activity, and, in 1916 the Arabists had accrued their first martyrs. While several were hanged or jailed for treason,

Abd al-Hamid al-Zahrawi and Shukri al-'Asali, two former Ottoman parliamentarians, were the most prominent who were executed. The Balfour Declaration's support for a Jewish homeland in Palestine and the Sykes-Picot Agreement, carving up Arab lands among France and Britain, confirmed the West's disregard for Arab independence regardless of its support in the war effort. Therefore, Arab nationalism took on the tenor and form of a full-fledged "independence" movement.

By 1921 the French had crushed King Faisal's government in Damascus, and the English and French had summarily divided up control of all Arab lands. Consequently, Arab nationalism, at least in the Levant, Iraq, and al-Hijaz, had become the formidable ideology of mass and elite appeal. Until the loss of Palestine in 1948 with the concomitant dispossession of hundreds of thousands of Palestinians, Arabism was the official ideology of the political elites throughout the Middle East, as well as appealed to the expanding native urban bourgeoisie in those countries. During this period, Arabism's principal spokesman and ideologue was the articulate and tireless Sati' al-Husri, minister of education in Syria and Iraq.

In other words, Arabism lacked the revolutionary elements that it would acquire in the 1950s and beyond. While Arab nationalism explicitly stated its opposition to foreign exploitation and colonial and mandate rule, its proponents were concerned generally with the cultural components of Arabism. The unity of the "Arab people" effectively offered economic possibilities and benefits to their growing economies in addition to providing a convenient way for the justification of the rule of the indigenous and nonindigenous Arab elites. For example, the English installed nonindigenous rulers from the Hashemite clan of the Arabian Peninsula in Iraq and Jordan. Also, in the 1940s King Farouq of Egypt, an otherwise corrupt and notoriously self-serving monarch, became a late advocate of Arab nationalism in hopes of being named the new caliph or king of the Arab lands.

Radical Arab nationalism, however, was simmering at this time. In Syria, which France had carved into several virtually autonomous ministates, three Paris-educated teachers, some former members of socialist- or communist-oriented parties, formed an intellectual-political circle called *al- B'ath al-'Arabi* (the Arab Renaissance). Michel Aflaq (1910–1989), Salah al-din al-Bitar, and Zaki Arsouzi—each from a different religious affiliation—would eventually merge the B'ath Party with Akram Hurani's Arab Socialist Party in 1952. This new brand of Arab socialism took on particular force after the failure of the native elites to protect and defend Palestine against the Zionists in 1948. The movement not only preached the cultural unity of the Arabs but also attacked the native elite's hold on the lion's portion of the state's resources, calling for redistribution of wealth and power. Gradually, the B'ath Party attracted crucial support in the military, allowing it to become the major power broker in Syria. By 1958, the B'ath Party attempted to "unify" with Egypt, forming the United Arab Republic (UAR). Although this unification would prove a disaster, particularly because of Jamal 'Abd al-Nasir's disregard for Syrian opinion in the running of the UAR, it proved to be the first experiment with Arab nationalist unification.

B'athist principles gained deep support in Iraq, and by the 1950s, the party had become a formidable power broker. In 1958, it joined 'Abd al-Karim al-Qasim's revolt against Nur Sa'id and the monarchy. In 1963, the B'ath Party took control of Iraq, overthrowing Qassim, and conducted a sustained pogrom against the Iraqi Communist Party. Ahmad Hassan al-Bakr led the final military coup in 1968 to ensure the control of the Iraqi B'ath Party, of which Saddam Hussein soon emerged as leader. In the meantime, the military element of the Syrian B'ath Party also launched a coup in 1966, which resulted in the exile of Aflaq, Hurani, and Arsouzi, the ideologues of the party. This coup led to the estrangement between the Syrian and Iraqi B'ath Parties. Hafez al-As'ad, also a military officer, arose out of this socialist-Arabist-military element of the Syrian B'ath Party.

Similar, but more dramatic, developments were under way in 1950s Egypt, where Jamal 'Abd al-Nasir (1918–1970) led the Free Officers Coup in 1952 to topple King Farouq. Gradually, the Egyptian genus of Arab nationalism became known as Nasserism, targeting "autocracy, imperialism, and feudalism" in the name of "the Arab nation." No other figure in the history of Arab nationalism has the presence and importance of 'Abd al-Nasir. Despite his many flaws, his increased totalitarian rule, and the expulsion of "non-Arab" minorities (Greeks, Jews, Armenians, and Syrian Christians) from Egypt, 'Abd al-Nasir implemented land redistribution, nationalized the Suez Canal, and became an architect of the Non-Aligned Movement.

'Abd al-Nasir and his discourse of Arab socialism greatly influenced other developments in the Arab world. For example, similar military coups led by socialist-Arabist officers occurred in Libya and the Sudan in 1969, led by Mu'ammar al-Qaddhafi and Ja'fr al-Numayri, respectively. However, despite 'Abd al-Nasir's charisma and popularity, his leadership proved disastrous in the 1967 Arab–Israeli War. The miserable failure of the Arab forces, supposedly championed by 'Abd al-Nasir's Egypt, invigorated the more radicalized **Marxist** Arab nationalist parties.

The Arab Nationalist Movement (ANM) was founded by students of the socialist professor Constatine Zurayq in Lebanon. Truly an assortment of Arabs from various countries, George Habash, Wadi' Haddad, Hani al-Hindi, and Ahmad al-Khatib assumed collective leadership of the ANM, which was committed to the liberation of Palestine and the class struggle as much as the platitude of unification of all Arab peoples. The ANM proved the origins of the most radical and brilliant left-wing activists of the 1960s and 1970s, including Maoist Nayef Hawatmeh and, of course, Leninist George Habash. Although it gradually disintegrated into a variety of left-wing parties, the most famous of which is the Popular Front for the Liberation of Palestine, the crowning achievement of the ANM was successfully seizing power in South Yemen in 1969.

Further Reading: R. Khalidi et al. 1991.

Stephen P. Sheehi

Arabophone Literature   The colonial period in the Arab world—the region stretching from the Persian Gulf to the Atlantic Ocean, most of which had been part of the Ottoman empire since the seventeenth century—began with the French invasion of Egypt in 1798. The French occupation of Egypt lasted only three years, but in 1830 France annexed Algeria, then occupied Tunisia and Morocco in 1912. Spain occupied parts of Morocco in 1886, and Italy occupied Libya in 1911. In 1882 Britain occupied Egypt, and then the Sudan in 1898. In the aftermath of World War I, the remaining parts of the Arab world—Greater Syria (which the colonists divided into what is now Syria, Lebanon, Jordan, and Palestine), Iraq, and the Persian Gulf—were divided into British and French colonies and protectorates, except for parts of the Arabian Peninsula, which remained relatively independent.

Thus, insofar as it addresses the issues arising from Arab societies' experience under European colonialism, modern Arabic literature may be said to be postcolonial. Yet it must also be noted that during the preceding three centuries, Arabic literature had languished in decadence and stagnation within the stifling cultural milieu of the Ottoman empire. In the mid-nineteenth century, however, the new colonial threat led to a movement of "revival" (*Nahda*), which aimed first at borrowing European science and technology but eventually exposed Arab intellectuals to European culture, thought, and literature. *Nahda* intellectuals saw their task as selectively borrowing from Europe while at the same time striving for authenticity with regard to Arab cultural identity. Together with the rediscovery of classical Arabic literature, which came to be seen as the repository of Arab cultural identity, the exposure to European literary styles, genres, and movements revitalized Arabic literature. Much of modern Arabic literature is, therefore, the product of both anti-Ottoman and anticolonialist liberatory impulses, some of which paradoxically aimed at achieving their goal through the selective adoption of Western **modernity** while at the same time resisting Western cultural imperialism. Thus, in a broad sense, a great deal of modern Arabic literature negotiates this complex response to the West, which encompasses many themes such as the problematic relationship between the Arab Islamic cultural tradition and Western modernity, the need for social, political, and religious reform, the status of women, resistance to colonialism and imperialism, the challenges of nation-statehood and of Pan-Arab **nationalism**, and the Palestinian problem, among others.

Not all of these themes are always explicitly or directly tied to colonialism, but they arise out of a social milieu that has been affected in innumerable ways by the multiple forms of political and cultural domination in the Arab world. In the late nineteenth and early twentieth centuries, for example, the renewed interest in classical Arabic literature was, to a great extent, an attempt to revive a cultural identity associated with Arabic civilization at the height of its power.

Not surprisingly, therefore, poetry, which Arabs have always considered one of their greatest cultural achievements, reclaimed its function as the expression of social values and aspirations, as well as an important organ of social and political mobilization. The classical poets were first and foremost public figures, both in pre-Islamic times when they championed their tribe and satirized its enemies or after Islam when they used the conventional ode for personal and/or political ends, praising or denouncing a prince or governor, but in all cases adopting the stance of a sage who formulated maxims and gave memorable poetic expression to prized moral values. In other words, classical Arabic poetry was a powerful form of public discourse in which the poet consciously assumed the role of spokesperson for the community. It is precisely such a role that Mahmoud Sami al-Barudi, the pioneer of "neo-classical" poetry, assumed in the 1860s, when he began to voice opposition to the policies of Egypt's Khedive Isma'il, which led to the British occupation in 1882, after which the poet was sent into exile by the British until 1901. In the following decades, other neo-classical poets, notably, the Egyptians Ahmad Shawqi (who also suffered exile) and Hafiz Ibrahim, the Iraqis Ma'ruf al-Rusafi and Muhammad Mahdi al-Jawahiri, the Palestinian Ibrahim Tuqan, and many others, likewise wrote "poems of occasion" that responded to political events in ways that often galvanized public opinion against colonial powers.

With a few rare exceptions, political commitment has always infused modern Arabic poetry, from neo-classical, to Romantic (between the two world wars), to modernist (since the early 1950s). Faced with the consolidation of colonial rule after World War I, Arab Romantic poets, who rejected many of the conventions embraced by their neo-classical predecessors and instead drew inspiration from European Romanticism, nevertheless saw themselves as actively engaged in cultural resistance. In addition to writing poems that responded to political events, many poets now took aim at Orientalist discourse in ways that emphasized not only politics but also culture as the arena of contestation. By using the inorganic form and conventional desert imagery of the classical ode, argued the leading Romantic poet and critic 'Abbas Mahmoud al-'Aqqad, Shawqi and other neo-classical poets were simply reinforcing colonial stereotypes about the irrationality, incoherence, and ahistorical essence of the "Oriental mind." Thus, as the critic Terri DeYoung (1998) argues, the shift from the neo-classical to the Romantic mode was itself motivated by the need to construct a cohesive Arab self that defied such stereotypes. Further, the revolutionary zeal of European Romanticism appealed to Arab Romantics who came to see in it a reflection of their own rebelliousness against colonial domination. Likewise, argues DeYoung, despite the devalorization of narration in classical Arabic poetry, the "epic turn" in the pioneer of Arabic modernism Badr Shakir al-Sayyab's poetry of the 1950s is part of this attempt to construct a poetic postcolonial narrative that challenges Orientalist discourse. In this way, Arab Romantic and modernist poets were selectively appropriating from European literary history those paradigms, forms, and styles that served their own anticolonial ends.

Drama also participated in the revival of the classical heritage and the assertion of a cultural identity in the face of colonialism. Drama was a newly imported genre with no roots or stylistic models in classical Arabic literature, but its treatment of subjects drawn from ancient Egyptian and Arab history served to raise awareness of Arab cultural identity. Here, too, Arab writers were appropriating European forms to serve the cause of anticolonial resistance. Since Ottoman censorship impeded the development of drama outside Egypt, a country that was relatively autonomous from 1805 to 1882 under the rule of Muhammad 'Ali and his descendants, it was there that the genre developed after first being introduced in Beirut by Marun al-Naqqash in 1847, then in Cairo by Ya'qub Sannu' in 1870. Significantly, two important plays, Farah Antun's *Sultan Saladin and the Kingdom of Jerusalem* (1914) and Ibrahim Ramzi's *The Heroes of Mansura* (1915), depicted the current tension in the region through the theme of the Crusades. Other dramatists were preoccupied with the Westernization of Egyptian society, which was an inevitable part both of the *Nahda* project and of colonialism: Farah Antun's *Modern Egypt, Old Egypt* (1913), Mahmoud Taymour's *'Abd al-Sattar Effendi* (1918) and *The Precipice* (1921), and several plays by Najib al-Rihani. In a similar vein, the theme of Egyptian and Arab great past informs Ahmad Shawqi's poetic dramas *The Death of Cleopatra* (1929) and *The Princess of Andalusia* (1932). The Qur'an inspires the giant of Arab theater Tawfiq al-Hakim's *The Cave Party* (1933), while *The Thousand and One Nights* provides the subject matter for his *Scheherazade* (1934). In these noteworthy examples as well as in many other plays during the colonial period, dramatists drew heavily upon the cultural resources of Egyptian, Arab, and Islamic civilizations in an effort to resist Western cultural imperialism.

In the postcolonial period, Arab dramatists in Egypt and elsewhere in the Arab world, where drama gradually took root, turned their attention to social and political criticism. In countries where the reading public constitutes a relatively small percentage of the population, the popularity of drama is rivaled only by cinema and television miniseries (in fact, recordings of theatrical productions are routinely televised). During the 1940s and 1950s, several plays by Mahmoud Tymour, Tawfiq al-Hakim, and Nu'man 'Ashur attacked the corruption of the aristocracy. The problem of legitimate political authority is the subject of al-Hakim's *The Sultan's Dilemma* (1960), and his political allegories of the 1960s reveal the disillusionment of many intellectuals with the 1952 Egyptian revolution. The plays of Sa'd al-Din Wahba, Alfred Farag, Mahmoud Diyab, 'Ali Salim, Salah 'Abd al-Sabur, and others also addressed the social upheavals of the period and often contained veiled criticism of Arab governments, especially after the 1967 war with Israel. This last theme inspired the Syrians Mamduh 'Udwan, 'Ali 'Uqla 'Arsan, and Muhammad al-Maghut, who wrote two important plays, *The Hunchback Sparrow* (1967) and *The Jester* (1973), as well as Sa'dallah Wannus, author of the satirical play *Celebrating the Fifth of June* (1968), who advocated the "politicization of the theater" and insisted on drama's educational mission.

Like drama, the novel was imported from Europe, although the abundance of other narrative genres in the Arabic literary tradition informed and facilitated the appropriation of the novel. One important example is the genre of *maqama*, a highly stylized, picaresque narrative that originated in the tenth century at the hands of Badi' al-Zaman al-Hamadhani, and featured the roguish 'Isa Ibn Hisham, who lived by his wit. Intended for entertainment, social commentary, and moral instruction, the *maqama* was revived by Muhammad al-Muwailihi, who published *Hadith 'Isa Ibn Hisham* (1898–1902), the title of which clearly established a link across 900 years. The work satirizes Westernization, corruption, and other social and moral ills. The novel as such, however, began with loose translations and adaptations of European novels, notably, by Jurji Zaidan, who also displayed a strong interest in classical Arabic literature. These early beginnings eventually resulted in the birth of the Arabic novel in 1913, with the publication of the Egyptian Muhammad Husayn Haykal's *Zaynab*. Significantly, the novel's explicit privileging of the Egyptian peasantry was presented, in the words of the author, as part of the rising tide of nationalism that led to the 1919 revolution against the British occupation.

Over the next three decades, the genre of the novel reached maturity at the hands of **Naguib Mahfouz** and eventually achieved great popularity throughout the Arab world, arguably greater than that of serious drama or even poetry. Mahfouz's early novels thematized ancient Egyptian history, before depicting, in a series of novels culminating in the famous Cairo Trilogy, the conditions of life in Egypt during the British occupation and World War II. Other novelists during the same period also tackled the relations between the Arab world and Europe with various degrees of emphasis, but the most important among the novels published in the colonial period were Tawfiq al-Hakim's *A Bird from the East* (1938) and Yahya Haqqi's *The Lamp of Umm Hashim* (1944). Both novels depict Egyptian students who travel to Paris and London, respectively, where they pursue their higher education and fall in love with European women. These romantic affairs provide the opportunity for exploring the complexities of Arab–European relations, as well as for criticism of outworn customs in Arab society. This pattern continues in the postindependence period (the 1950s and after throughout the Arab world) to inform a great many novels, most famous among which is the Sudanese **Tayeb Salih**'s *Season of Migration to the North* (1966). Other noteworthy novels belonging to this category are Suhayl Idris's *The Latin Quarter* (1953), Sabah Muhyiddin's *Unfinished Symphony* (1956), the short stories of 'Abd-al-Salam al-'Ujaili, and Ahdaf Soueif's remarkable *In the Eye of the Sun* (1993), which depicts a female student's journey to England.

Since the 1950s, scores of other novelists from Lebanon (Tawfiq Yusuf Awwad, Layla Ba'albaki, Layla 'Usayran, Emily Nasrallah, Hannan al-Shaykh, Ilyas Khury), Syria (Hanna Mina, Muti' Safadi, Halim Barakat), Iraq (Gha'ib Ti'ma Firman) Kuwait (Isma'il Fahd Isma'il), Saudi Arabia ('Abd al-Rahman Munif), Egypt (Mahfouz, **Nawal el Saadawi**, 'Abd al-Rahman al-Sharqawi, Latifa al-Zayyat, Yusuf Idris, Fathi Ghanim), Tunisia (Mahmoud al-Mas'adi, Bashir al-Khurayyif), and Morocco ('Abd al-Karim Ghallab, 'Abdallah al-'Arawi [Laroui], 'Abd al-Majid Ben Jalloun, Muhammad Barradah, Muhammad Zafzaf) have written—sometimes with local and sometimes with Pan-Arab emphasis (see **Arabism**)—about the struggle for independence, nationalism, and nationhood, the status of women, the failures of postcolonial Arab regimes, the Arab–Israeli conflict, the Lebanese civil war, and the ongoing concern with Arab **identity** vis-à-vis Western culture and imperialism. In Algeria, which did not gain independence until 1963, the brutality of the French during the protracted war of independence and the disappointments of the postcolonial period are depicted in the novels of al-Tahir Wattar. Also noteworthy are Tunisian, Algerian, and Moroccan novelists of French expression such as Albert Memmi, Kateb Yacine, **Assia Djebar**, Muhammad Dib, **Tahar Ben Jalloun, Driss Chraïbi**, whose works may be said to belong to Arabic as well as **francophone literatures**. Fewer Arab novelists have written in English, the most important of whom are the Palestinian Jabra Ibrahim Jabra, who also wrote in Arabic, and the Egyptian Ahdaf Soueif.

The devastating defeat of Arab armies in 1967—called *Naksah*, or Setback—signaled not only the loss of more Arab territories but also the demise of Nasserism, the form of Pan-Arab nationalism that represented the culmination of *Nahda* itself. At stake was the very sense of Arab identity revived in the nineteenth century in response to colonialism and cultural imperialism. This crisis of identity, accompanied by disillusionment and frustration with Arab regimes, resonates in countless literary works throughout the Arab world, most important of which are the Syrian Halim Barakat's *Six Days* (1961) and *Days of Dust* (1969), the Iraqi Layla 'Usayran's *Birds of Dawn* (1968) and *The Snake Line* (1972), the Kuwaiti Isma'il Fahd Isma'il's *The 1967 File* (1974), the Moroccan Khanathah Banunah's *Fire and Choice* (1968), and the Syrian Hani al-Rahib's *One Thousand and Two Nights* (1978).

One of the most persistent themes of Arabic literature since World War II has been the Arab–Israeli conflict following the dispossession of the Palestinians in 1948, then in 1967, by Israeli settler colonialism. The year 1948 is referred to in Arabic historiography as the year of *Nakbah*, or Disaster, a term that hints not only at the scope of the plight of the Palestinians but also the magnitude of the historical dislocation felt throughout the Arab world, which was reflected in the literature produced by Palestinians (see **resistance literature**) and non-Palestinian Arab writers alike. Almost all of Palestinian fiction by Ghassan Kanafani, Tawfiq Fayyad, Rashad Abu Shawir, Emile Habibi, and Sahar Khalifa; much of the poetry of Ibrahim Tuqan, Fadwa Tuqan, Tawfiq Sayigh, Jabra Ibrahim Jabra, Tawfiq Zayyad, Salma Khadra Jayyusi, Samih al-Qasim, and Mahmoud Darwish; and the plays of Mu'in Basisu and Samih al-Qasim depict the conditions of Palestinians both in exile and inside Israel and the Occupied Territories.

Further Reading: M. 'Abd al-Ghani 1994; R. Allen 1998, 1995; M. M. Badawi 1988, 1993; T. DeYoung 1998; B. Harlow 1987; S. K. Jayyusi 1977.

Waïl S. Hassan

José María Arguedas José María Arguedas (1911 Andahuaylas, Peru–1969 Lima, Peru) was one of the most accomplished authors dealing with themes of the indigenous and mestizo culture of Peru. Arguedas learned Quechua as a boy from servants in the household of his stepmother and his father, an itinerant lawyer. He graduated from the University San Marcos of Lima as an anthropologist, although he did not finish his doctoral work until 1958. His first publication in 1935 is a collection of short stories titled *Agua* (Water). In 1937 Arguedas was detained for participating in student protests, an experience that served as a basis for his second novel, *El Sexto* (1961), whose title bears the name of the prison where he was imprisoned. In 1939 Arguedas married Celia Bustamante and moved back to the highland region, where he worked as a schoolteacher. He published his first novel, *Yawar Fiesta*, in 1941, which suggests the existence of the spirit of independence and opposition that was to fuel the peasant movements of the 1950s and the breakup of the landlords' rule. Of all his works, *Deep Rivers* (1961; in English 1978) has had the greatest impact on Latin American literature. The novel is a poetic portrayal of unequal power relationships in a country struggling to overcome the feudalistic conditions in the middle of the twentieth century.

In 1962 Arguedas started working at the Universidad de La Molina and in 1964 was named director of the National Museum of History. That same year he published *Todas las sangres* (*All Bloods*) about Peru's aim toward becoming a capitalist society and the impact of this change on the lives of Indians. In 1965 he divorced his wife and traveled to Chile, where he married Sybila Arredondo in 1967. Arguedas' last and unfinished novel, *El zorro de arriba y el zorro de abajo* (The Fox from Above and the Fox from Below), was published posthumously in 1971.

Until his suicide in 1969, this novelist and anthropologist was perhaps more responsible than any other Peruvian for the impassioned defense of the Quechua language (the Indian tongue spoken by more than 10 million people in the Andean area) and cultural autonomy for millions of Quechua speakers, challenging the powerful ideologies of "**modernization**" and "national integration" predicated on the erasure of Peru's indigenous past. Although there was a strong utopian strain in Arguedas, he was interested not just in indigenous traditions. He also wrote about the challenges of migration and modernity, and in a famous speech upon the acceptance of the prestigious Garcilaso de la Vega, El Inca Award, he proclaimed himself not to be an *aculturado* but a modern Peruvian, reflecting his desire for a cultural pluralism for Peru that would go beyond a retreat into a narrow traditionalism.

Further Reading: W. Mignolo 1999; C. Sandoval and S. Boschetta 1998.

Silvia Nagy-Zekmi

Ayi Kwei Armah   Born in 1939 in Ghana and currently living in Senegal, Ayi Kwei Armah has also lived in various other parts of Africa. The themes in his works reflect this familiarity with the continent and its people, myths, and poetics. He is a believer in the necessity of art as a tool for social emancipation, especially of a colonized people. Consequently, he firmly believes that the process of critical response to a work of art is a process of interpretation of that work to one's audience.

The Beautyful Ones Are Not Yet Born is Armah's first novel. Published in 1968, it immediately established Armah as a remarkable novelist articulating the African ethos. Writing so soon after most of Africa was transformed from a colonial society into a hodgepodge of neocolonial dependencies, Armah was one of the first African thinkers to point out that the panacea of independence was only a camouflage for the institution of a more efficient, more avaricious form of colonization at the hands of the indigenous elite.

The next two works, *Fragments* (1970) and *Why Are We So Blest?* (1972), were published almost simultaneously, and they continue the criticism of the African elite and their destructive behavior within the newly independent societies. In *Fragments* we see how this behavior impacts the individual who is naive enough to think that an individual can make a difference. This destructive behavior is linked to the affinity for Western material goods.

In *Two Thousand Seasons* (1973), Armah decides to reassess black history by trying to go to the beginnings of racial self-hatred. The easy assumptions are all cast aside, and he foregrounds the distortion of the black people's history through the growth of negative indigenous rulers who prepare the nation for the exploitation of the strangers. In this work, Armah is careful to use language that shows respect for the black people, closely trying to approximate black/African speech and idiom.

In *The Healers* (1978) Armah attempts to answer the question, When did things begin to go wrong for the black people? But his novel is more than an assessment of Africa's political problems, for Armah also illuminates a strain of healing that runs through black history. He identifies the "healers" as those people who not only are involved in the dispensation of medicines for the healing of the body but also engage actively in an attempt to create a humane society by participating in politics.

As such, Armah recaptures not only Africa's artistic past with *Osiris Rising* (1995) but also its future in the arts with his publishing company. *Osiris Rising* continues to explore the meaning of African art by boldly reclaiming ancient Egyptian history and myths as part of the black people's cultural heritage. While it is true that Armah clearly is aware of the metropoles, he at the same time refuses to acknowledge their definitive role in the cultural struggle of the African.

Further Reading: R. Fraser 1980; D. Wright 1992.

Ramenga Mtaali Osotsi

Art of the Twentieth Century and the (Post)Colonial The history of twentieth-century art in the West is fundamentally shaped by colonialism and **decolonization**. Typically, scholars who chart this history focus on developments in French and American culture, for it is within these arenas that a great many contributions to the avant-garde occurred. Avant-garde refers to creations made by highly individualistic artists who break with artistic and often social conventions. The beginning of avant-garde production dates to the early mid-nineteenth century in the period of Romanticism, when artists, in lieu of working for heads of states, functioned increasingly as entrepreneurs who determined their own briefs in isolation or with support from forward-thinking patrons. Later, nineteenth-century and early to mid-twentieth-century avant-garde art is often referred to as modern art, not only to designate its time frame but to denote an emphasis on simplified form and color, both of which are frequently non-naturalistic and the former of which can be abstract. Modern artists' focus on imaginative versus realistic representation was spurred by a variety of factors, including exposure to non-Western art.

Modern artists in Europe came into contact with non-Western art because of colonialism. By the later nineteenth century and early twentieth century, much of Africa, Asia, and the Pacific was colonized by the British, Europeans, and Americans. Collections of artifacts acquired (often plundered) from colonies were displayed in major cities' ethnographic museums and pavilions set up in large, temporary expositions that promoted national industry and culture. Avant-garde painters and sculptors eager to abandon artistic traditions in favor of new visual forms gravitated toward non-Western material culture for inspiration. Artists such as Paul Gauguin, Vincent van Gogh, and the members of the group *die Brücke* (the Bridge), were impressed not only with the formal properties of these works but with the positive and negative Western fantasies projected onto the artifacts and their makers. For the most part, Westerners imagined that non-Westerners were simpler peoples: either pure souls closer to nature or savage beasts without human decency (these fantasies provided Westerners with justification for "civilizing" those whom they colonized). Avant-garde artists determined to abandon or remake their experience of Western civilization—which they often thought was compromised by loss of faith, social injustice, and destruction of natural resources—and they drew on non-Western artifacts to produce work that critiqued European culture or that envisioned **utopian** alternatives to it.

This exposure to non-Western art and its impact on the avant-garde is called **primitivism**, for Westerners referred and continue to refer to much non-Western material culture—chiefly African, Native American, and Oceanic—as "primitive" (a paternalistic term that communicates Westerners' conceit of having more fully developed civilizations). The French painter André Derain was among the first of the twentieth-century European avant-garde to collect non-Western artifacts and acquired African masks and statues, for which a vogue among his bohemian set soon developed. The brilliant color, aggressive brush marks, and blunt forms characteristic of the painting done in Derain's circle—led by Henri Matisse—were inspired, in large part, by the group's primitivism, which earned them the name *Fauves* (Wild Beasts). From the time of the Fauves' debut on the Paris art scene in 1905 until the beginning of World War II, much of the European avant-garde imagined itself vitalized by its engagement with what it deemed to be primitive art. In most cases, these modern artists knew little or nothing of non-Western artifacts' specific contexts and histories. This is true even in the case of the surrealists, poets and artists who first gathered around the French writer André Breton in 1924 and who at various points in their long history as a group decried colonialism. Breton and his colleagues agitated against artistic, social, and political formations that they found oppressive and in their publications spoke out against Westerners' denigration of non-Western peoples. In 1931, the surrealists demonstrated against the Colonial Exposition in Paris, mounting their own exhibition of non-Western art, which they viewed as a tribute to the creative powers of those colonized. This tribute, however, along with subsequent surrealist celebrations of the non-Western, did not engage artifacts within the conditions of their own making. Instead, surrealists positioned "primitive" artifacts as supposedly irrational objects that incarnate freedom rather than the entrapment that surrealists imputed to Western rationalization. Several non-European modern artists were hailed by surrealists as particularly potent, not only in recognition of their important projects but also because of surrealist infatuation with their otherness. This was certainly the case with the mestizo Mexican painter Frida Kahlo and the Afro-Chinese Cuban painter Wifredo Lam. Both artists' work reflects, among other things, their understanding of their countries' native and mestizo traditions: Kahlo depicted elements of pre-Columbian myth and material culture, and Lam embraced Afro-Cuban subjects and forms.

The success of Kahlo and Lam in Paris and subsequently in New York (which usurped the French capital as the center for avant-garde art during and after the havoc that World War II wreaked in Europe) was an exception to the long-standing rule that Caucasian male creators dominated the art world in the West. The marginal status of women and people of color in the arts continued well into the 1960s, when worldwide struggles for social justice—including battles for decolonization—destabilized hegemonic Western beliefs, practices, and their institutionalization. The wars for independence that the colonized fought against their oppressors from the end of World War II well into the 1960s and beyond dramatically altered power relations in all sectors of Western society. For example, the Algerian and Vietnam Wars not only signaled the partial decline of French and American control overseas but also sparked major civil unrest at home, with populations deeply divided over Western domination of foreign lands. The peace movements embraced after World War II and in the face of Cold War fears of renewed conflict encouraged some Europeans and Americans to extend their critiques of tyranny to their own nations' imperialism, and a number of liberal and radical artists produced openly political work in support of Algerian independence and America's withdrawal from Vietnam. For example, in 1960 and 1961, a coalition of avant-garde European and American artists, including Enrico Baj, Raymond Hains, and Robert Rauschenberg, exhibited work in Paris, Venice, and Milan that decried French violence against Algerians. In 1966 American artists such as Judy Chicago, Irving Petlin, and Mark di Suvero created with their art a peace tower in Los Angeles to protest the Vietnam conflict.

Decolonization abroad and civil rights movements at home broadly politicized the art world; by the later 1970s and in the 1980s, women and people of color increasingly protested their continuing roles as those who inspired male Caucasian artists' production and more frequently exhibited their own work in galleries and museums. In the 1980s in particular, "**identity politics**" often framed the making and reception of art in the West. Artists produced work and curators organized exhibitions that explored the experience of individuals and communities marginalized by dominant culture because their gender, race, class, or sexual orientation was devalued. This linkage of art to lived history was often consciously opposed to the critical reception of **modernism** largely formulated by the American critic Clement Greenberg, who in the 1940s–1960s privileged American abstract painting (notably that of abstract expressionists such as Jackson Pollock) as art that concerned itself only with the formal and material conditions of its own making. Championing social protest art of the 1960s–1970s and touting poststructural theoretical models of society and culture largely developed in France, many artists and critics in the 1980s positioned their production as **postmodern**: work that critiques beliefs and institutions that structured much of prior twentieth-century experience. Among the many notions about Western art that were partially dismantled was its supposed ability to uplift all viewers through aesthetic pleasure and appeals to common humanity. Among the many critiques of existing artworks that were launched was the idea that each work conveyed ideological messages about people's places in society. Within this critical climate, the legacy of colonialism as well as its continued operations were increasingly addressed in the art world.

Nineteenth-century French modern art—for decades celebrated as the most brilliant experimental art in the West—was the first examined in light of its political realities and ideological biases. Art historian Linda Nochlin's 1983 essay "The Imaginary Orient" is notable in this regard for its analysis of the colonialist logic at play in nineteenth-century French Orientalist painting. Indebted to **Edward Said**'s critique of Orientalist French and English literature, Nochlin's reading of academic (hyperrealistic and officially sanctioned) and avant-garde French nineteenth-century painting demonstrates the extent to which both position Near Eastern peoples as debased and often highly eroticized others. She further shows that the academic versions of Orientalist works were successful at the time because their almost photographic style conveyed a sense of objective truth that naturalized the often prurient fantasies about the peoples portrayed. Nochlin condemns the 1982 exhibition (in New York state) and catalog *Orientalism: The Near East in French Painting, 1800–1880* for examining Orientalist painting purely in light of aesthetic and art historical terms, thereby failing to engage the politics of the work.

Many more criticisms were launched against another early 1980s exhibition that concerned modern art and the non-Western, this time the supposed kinship between so-called primitive art and the work of twentieth-century avant-garde painters and sculptors. The 1984 show *"Primitivism" in Twentieth-Century Art: Affinity of the Tribal and the Modern* and its two-volume catalog were produced by the venerated Museum of Modern Art in New York City. The exhibition showed African, Native American, and Oceanic artifacts alongside art by modern masters and argued that the latter intuitively grasped the formal power of the former. *"Primitivism"* implied that all exceptional creators share aesthetic acuity but further suggested that modern artists exposed to non-Western material transcended their sources in their transformations of borrowed form. This paternalistic idealization and subordination of the "primitive" dehistoricized the non-Western material in the show; the work was not examined in its original contexts or in the political contexts of its absorption by Western colonizers and artists. The show was resoundingly criticized for its premise and omissions.

A later 1980s exhibition that attempted to locate the work of non-Western artists on an equal footing with that of Western creators was the 1989 Paris Centre Pompidou blockbuster show of contemporary art, *Magiciens de la Terre*. Renowned Western artists such as John Baldessari and Hans Haacke were exhibited alongside figures less recognized in the Euroamerican art world, for example, Sunday Jack Akpan from Nigeria, Nuche Kaji Bajracharya from Nepal, the Inuit artist Paulosee Kuniliusee, and the Australian Northern Territory artist Jimmy Wululu. Although the show gave some sense of the diversity of contemporary art production across the globe, the title of the exhibition conveyed *Magiciens de la Terre*'s romanticized and depoliticized relationship to the non-Western material displayed. Reanimating a long-standing Western fantasy, the exhibition curators implied that contemporary non-Western art possesses "magic." This premise betrays an exoticizing impulse that suggests that less-than-satisfying Western experience can be reenchanted by an encounter with the other.

Increasingly, non-Western artists active at home and abroad have created their own arenas for the framing and reception of their work, and since the 1960s and 1970s—the decades when many such arenas were launched—artists from former or current colonies have slowly, but surely, gained access on their own terms to the international (read Euroamerican) art world. In the United States alone, numerous cultural centers are devoted to the art of indigenous peoples and those rooted to America through the imperialist operations of slavery and territorial expansionism. Notable examples include the Institute of American Indian and Alaskan Native Culture and Arts Development (a Santa Fe fine arts college launched in 1962); the Center for Hawaiian Studies (founded in Honolulu at the University of Hawaii in 1970); the Galeria de la Raza/Studio 24 (begun in San Francisco in 1970); the Studio Museum in Harlem (opened in

1967); and the Asian American Arts Centre (established in New York in 1974). The critical voices of those once or currently colonized who write about art and culture have since 1987 appeared in the influential journal *Third Text*, published in London and edited by the Pakistani-born artist Rasheed Araeen. Araeen's art—which inserts into minimalist modern forms visual and textual references to "First" World injustice in the "Third" World—like his writing, exposes the repression of non-Western peoples at the core of supposedly enlightened Western culture.

Two 1990s exhibitions of contemporary Maori art are crucial examples of how artists and curators from colonized cultures activate their work within an indigenous context. From 1992 to 1993, *Te Waka Toi: Contemporary Art from New Zealand* toured the United States. Maori works on display were not positioned as mere artifacts but were situated within a ritualized context that saw Maori who visited the show speak with, and emote over, the images. Important organizers of the exhibition, Sandy Adsett (a Ngati Kahungunu artist) and Cliff Whiting (the chairman of *Te Waka Toi*), enabled an experience of living culture by arranging ritual openings of the show at each exhibition site and by displaying art in conceptual arrangements that reinforced Maori protocols. The 1996 exhibition *Patua: Maori Arts in Action*, held at the Wellington City Gallery, also activated space conceptually to create a Maori environment and context for the work on view. In front of the gallery and before the exhibition rooms two facades were erected, with the first functioning as a temporary *marae*, or meeting house, to welcome official visitors. Works in the show were arranged to echo visually and conceptually the architectural elements of the meeting house. Furthermore, in the exhibition's upper gallery, art was hung to convey interrelationships between senior and junior artists.

Virtual space as well as gallery space are rapidly becoming another important vehicle for artists committed to decolonization. Arts organizations with Web sites, such as the Institute for International Visual Arts, and art journals with on-line components, like the *Eastern Art Report*, use the Internet to disseminate art by, and information about, formerly and currently colonized peoples and reach people from all over the world with access to computing technology. Although the Internet's celebrated interactivity and information delivery lack a physical dimension, the rich interweaving of text, image, and sound made possible by digital media provides artists and writers who engage the legacy of colonialism with powerful and compelling communication tools. As we begin the twenty-first century of the information age, artists and art writers committed to (post)colonial perspectives will surely continue to have an increasingly large presence in the art world.

Further Reading: C. Rhodes 1994; *Third Text* 1987.

Andrea Feeser

Australian Literature   A conflict that long plagued Australian literature and literary criticism stemmed from a rudimentary question: Should the literature be "national" or "international"? This opposition was first articulated in 1856, when Frederick Sinnett wrote what is considered the initial critical study of Australian literature. In his essay "The Fiction Fields of Australia" (1856), he argued that "most Australian stories are *too* Australian, and, instead of human life, we have only local 'manners and customs' portrayed in them." The discord over what Australian writers should write continued for another century. The literary nationalists, supported by the influential publication *The Bulletin*, contended that a work should be judged by its "Australianness," and *The Bulletin*'s famous literary "red page" remained allegiant to that dictum. This stance led to the primacy of the bush tradition, which celebrated the exploits of protagonists— most often Anglo-Saxon males—who overcame untold hardships as they struggled to claim and to tame the land. The unswerving account of "manners and customs" did not fade away easily. But in the post–World War II era, an emerging group of young writers agreed with Sinnett's observations and asked, as novelist Michael Wilding did: Must we "write Australian"?

Historians generally agree that Australia started to shed its colonial trappings after World War II and to take its place as a nation among nations, no longer content to drift along as a "dominion" of Great Britain. Of course, no revolution took place, no movement to drive out the settlers, no bloodshed, no struggle that climaxed with a dramatic declaration of independence and a vision of a better tomorrow. Australia, like other **settler colonies**, may not in the strictest sense qualify as a postcolonial nation, so perhaps the literature should not bear that label. Yet as the shape of Australian life altered, so did the creative spirit. Therefore, the original argument over a literature that should celebrate the national and ignore the international can be restated in more contemporary terms, that is, substituting "colonial" for "national" and "postcolonial" for "international." "Internationalism" has always been a kind of catchall term. It did not apply solely to writers who set their work outside Australia, even though that practice was frowned on. It more precisely described the use of literary forms from abroad, such as modernism or other much-maligned models described as "avant-garde." As well, the offensive word applied to work that failed to celebrate Australianness even if set in Australia. Yet the postcolonial writers, for the most part, have not given up Australian materials. They have simply used them in untried and unaccustomed ways. They have depicted human life in its spiritual context as well as its "manners and customs," and they have used their art to scold their fellow Australians for all manner of wrongdoing: hypocrisy, provincialism, masculinist behavior, rejection of the artist, the eager acceptance of American culture, the mistreatment of native Australians, the subjugation of women, the cultural cringe. Above all, they have sought to identify their nation, an objective central to the postcolonial project.

Now that the terminology has been reinvented, it is permissible to call Patrick White Australia's first postcolonial novelist. In his 1958 essay "The Prodigal Son," published in *Australian Letters*, he issued a singular call for a fiction that was "not necessarily the dreary dun-coloured offspring of journalistic realism."

This too-often-quoted statement—more colorful than Sinnett's but similar in meaning—should not be read as a blanket condemnation of all that came before White's novels, even if that is what White intended. Although earlier Australian writers did, for the most part, adhere to the tenets of social realism in their rendition of an insular world, it would be unjust to cast aside a number of those novels that celebrate Australianness. It cannot be disputed, though, that White revolutionized Australian fiction by subverting its most cherished traditions. For example, his first major work, *The Tree of Man* (1955), follows the conventions of the bush novel but blends them into the metaphysical realm, just as *Voss* (1957) turns the heroic deeds of Australian explorers into an abstract quest. As well, the plight of the artist in a postcolonial society figures in *The Vivisector* (1970), and the journey toward self-realization dominates *A Fringe of Leaves* (1976), which painstakingly recounts the colonial era. While White, who received the Nobel Prize in 1973, can be credited with inventing postcolonial fiction in Australia, his monumental work has at times been considered a hindrance in the development of the Australian novel. To some degree, his fiction overshadowed that of his contemporaries, and his legacy continues to aggravate writers. Still, neither did the Australian novel languish during White's productive years, nor did it die in 1979, when he published his last major work, *The Twyborn Affair*. Instead, the novel took on, and continues to do so, diverse shapes in its newfound postcolonial mode.

Thea Astley, a near contemporary of White, has since the publication of her first book, *Girl with a Monkey*, in 1958 recorded the Australian experience but at the same time transformed it into parables of spiritual discontent. In the essay, "Being a Queenslander," she defends the way that she appropriates the state of Queensland in her fiction, calling it a "geographical conceit" and pointing out "that literary truth is derived from the parish, and if it is truth it will be universal." One of her novels, *Beachmasters* (1985), qualifies fully as a postcolonial work; it records a native revolution against leftover French and British colonialists.

Thomas Keneally revisited and revised the convict period in *Bring Larks and Heroes* (1967), and in *The Chant of Jimmie Blacksmith* (1972) he handled the tragic consequences of Aboriginal persecution in a daring manner for that time. Then Keneally literally fell in love with internationalism and shifted away from Australian settings; ironically, he is best known for his factual/fictional account of World War II, *Schindler's List* (1982), which received the Booker Prize.

Like Keneally's work, a number of Australian novels in recent years have been set in Europe, in Asia, and in North America, often with an Australian protagonist and with scenes shifting between home and overseas. Of course, Christina Stead, who rarely wrote about her homeland, could be called Australia's most international novelist. Significantly, she had to wait for the postcolonial era to establish her reputation in Australia, even though her major work had appeared years earlier.

Peter Carey has explored the literary possibilities of postcolonialism fully and originally. In *Illywhacker* (1985) Carey subverts the traditional Australian-celebratory novel by questioning the truth of national mythology. According to Australian slang, an "illywhacker" is a trickster, a confidence man, a liar, which aptly describes the narrator of *Illywhacker* and his preposterous account of Australian history. Carey's richest examination of the postcolonial state comes in his 1994 novel, *The Unusual Life of Tristan Smith*, in which he reimagines Australia into a land called Efica, controlled by a new empire called Voorstand. Like many of his fellow novelists, Carey sees American imperialism—the cultural aspects in particular—replacing the withering influence of Great Britain in Australia. So it is tempting to identify Efica as Australia and Voorstand as the United States. Just as he did in *Oscar and Lucinda* (1988), which received the Booker Prize, Carey returns in his recent novel, *Jack Maggs* (1998), to nineteenth-century Britain and Australia to examine the workings of colonialism, its legacy, and possibly the liberation from it.

David Malouf has utilized conventional Australian materials in most of his fiction, such as his first novel, *Johnno* (1975), which recounts wartime Brisbane, and his 1996 novel, *The Conversations at Curlow Creek*, set in the early colonial period. Yet all of Malouf's Australian-centered work transforms the materials into personal quests that rely on the "parish" but do not depend solely on it for signification. One critic did wonder whether Malouf, who is also noted for his poetry, was indeed an "Australian poet" or an "international poet." This question could apply to his fiction as well, considering that Malouf's best-known work may be *An Imaginary Life* (1978), a mythical account of Ovid's exile.

One important development in Australia's fiction is the emergence of Aboriginal writing. Usually absent from earlier books by white writers, Australia's first inhabitants have revealed their hidden lives through novels, short stories, and personal memoirs. Several anthologies of Aboriginal writing have appeared recently showing the variety and artistry of voices long unheard. Mudrooroo (formerly Colin Johnson) remains the most notable of those who have treated the Aboriginal experience. His neglected 1983 novel, *Doctor Wooreddy's Prescription for Enduring the Ending of the World*, stands as Australia's prime example of a postcolonial novel. It imagines with uncanny precision the first contact between native and settler, and it chronicles dramatically the extinction of the Tasmanian Aboriginals.

Just as it is theoretically possible to identify the first postcolonial Australian novelist, the same can be done with poets. In this case the honors go to Judith Wright and Oodgeroo (formerly Kath Walker). Like White and his successors, Wright made full use of Australianness; but as one critic observed, she freed it from "aggressive regionalism." Her first book, *The Moving Image*—(1946), widened the scope of Australian poetry as it reformed myths and questioned the established ways of viewing the land and its people. As a supporter of Aboriginal rights, she defined the attitudes of white Australians toward Aboriginals in the poem "Bora Ring," and as a nontraditional landscape poet she stressed preservation, not prettiness. Almost twenty years after Wright's first collection appeared, Oodgeroo published *We Are Going* in 1964, a book that has been hailed as the first collection of poetry by an Aboriginal writer. These direct, heartfelt, sometimes angry, sometimes touching poems inaugurated the Aboriginal protest poem, which has been developed further by writers such as Jack Davis, Mudrooroo, Kevin Gilbert, Lionel Fogarty, and Bobbi Sykes.

Australian poetry has taken varied directions since its emergence in the post-war period. It has also been abundant. For some reason poetry has always been a favored genre in Australia. A nineteenth-century *Bulletin* writer once boasted that every sunburned bushman was a poet at heart. While today the poet more likely dwells in the city, there is still no scarcity. In fact, the scandals, upheavals, battling factions, and competing schools that somehow blended together to develop postcolonial Australian poetry make an intriguing story in itself. One school in the 1950s, called the Jindyworobaks, set out to revive literary colonialism by concentrating on the expression of Australianness and eschewing international influences. Although a white writers' movement, the Jindyworobaks insisted on the appreciation of Aboriginal culture, which they apparently wanted to appropriate. In opposition to these isolationists, another group avowed its **modernism** through a literary journal called *Angry Penguins*, published from 1940 to 1946. Advocating international influences, the journal declined in 1944, when it published a group of poems as masterpieces of modernism. In truth they had been written as a ruse by two Australian poets who held that international influences were a deterrent to the progress of Australian poetry. This fiasco, according to many literary historians, thwarted the development of Australian writing for an extended period. A. D. Hope, a poet who found much of his inspiration not in things Australian but in the ancient world, noted that the argument over internationalism (or postcolonialism) had long "bedeviled" Australian writers. Yet in spite of what have been called the "poetry wars," postcolonial poetry in its diverse forms sets out to delineate the new—not to describe the familiar but to enlarge the vision, not to constrain it but to provoke the citizenry, not to bolster national pride but to experiment with new forms.

Although the theater has long been an integral part of Australian life, the development of drama has lagged behind that of the other genres. Here internationalism takes on another dimension, considering that the Australian stage has always welcomed imports from abroad more enthusiastically than home-grown products. During the 1920s a movement got under way to establish a genuine Australian theater that would depict ordinary, rural life. This well-intended effort to create such a drama failed and possibly hindered theatrical progress for many years to come, because audiences continued to prefer plays from overseas. Still, it is possible to name Australia's first postcolonial dramatist: Ray Lawler, whose *Summer of the Seventeenth Doll* opened in Melbourne in 1955 to an unprecedented reception. Significantly, Lawler violated the precepts of the colonial theater movement from the 1920s. Not only did he set the play in Melbourne rather than in the bush, but he challenged the bush legend as well. A well-made drama in the realistic tradition, *Summer of the Seventeenth Doll*

undermined the myths of outback life, such as mateship, masculinity, egalitarianism, and the superiority of the bush over the city. The play, which still holds
up in production, stresses for better or worse the ascendancy of the urban community, where most Australians live. Hailed prematurely as a watershed in Australian theater, Lawler's play and reputation faded.

In the 1970s another development took place when alternative theaters offered
new work by experimental writers such as Alexander Buzo, Jack Hibberd, and
David Williamson. Yet a few decades later the excitement appears to have held
more possibilities than actualities. Although he has been accused of selling out
to the mainstream theater, David Williamson is the only playwright from this
heady era who has continued to enjoy a consistent reception in Australia and
abroad. He has remained true to Australian materials from his earliest success,
The Removalists (1972), which takes a harsh look at masculine dominance, to
plays such as *The Club* (1978), which reveals the distorted role of sport in
Australian society, and *Travelling North* (1980), which records the disillusionment of old age and retirement. Indisputably Australia's major dramatist, Williamson explores personal interaction between urban, most often educated and
professional, Australians, and at the same time places them in the larger postcolonial context.

Plays by Aboriginal writers, previously excluded from mainstream theater,
have become standard pieces and altogether postcolonial in structure and content, such as Kevin Gilbert's *The Cherry Pickers* (1971), Jack Davis' *The
Dreamers* (1982), and Robert J. Merritt's *The Cake Man* (1978). The Aboriginal
writers tend to work in nontraditional forms and use drama as a way to protest
against their precarious place in Australian society. Another recent development
in the theater comes from Australia's large, but long-silent, non-Anglo-Saxon
immigrant community.

It would definitely be mistaken to dispense with Australian theater as a lost
cause, even if it has not gained the reception at home and overseas accorded to
fiction and poetry. From an international standpoint, though, Australian **film** has
received more attention than the stage.

Is Australian literature postcolonial? Certainly, a literature such as Australia's
that has been engrossed—and continues to be—in the search for a national
identity qualifies. In this unfulfilled, perhaps unattainable quest, the literature
has become more international, indeed, postcolonial. The nineteenth-century
critic Frederick Sinnett would surely be pleased not only with the postcolonial
"fiction fields" but with the "fields" of poetry and drama as well.

Further Reading: B. Bennett and J. Strauss 1998; L. Hergenhan 1988.

Robert L. Ross

B

Mongo Beti (also Eza Boto, pseudonyms for Alexandre Biyidi)   A major literary and ideological voice of **francophone literature**, Mongo Beti was born in 1932 in south-central Cameroon, then a French protectorate. Ewondo by birth, Beti attended school at the local mission and completed secondary (lycée) studies in the capital, Yaoundé, in 1951. That year Beti entered the university at Aix-en-Provence, later attending the Sorbonne and eventually passing France's most rigorous examination for the recruitment of teachers (*agregation*). His career included over thirty years of teaching Greek and Latin to French lycée students. During that time Beti was persona non grata in his country and lived in exile for thirty-two years. He returned to Cameroon after retirement, where he launched a bookstore (Peuples Noirs Peuples Africains) in Yaoundé and continues to write.

Spanning half a century, Beti's writing includes fiction and political commentary that can be divided into three periods: (1) anticolonial works written mainly during his student years in France (1953–1958): one short story, "Sans Haine et sans amour," and four novels, *Ville cruelle* (pseud. Eza Boto), *Le Pauvre Christ de Bomba*, *Mission terminée*, *Le Roi miraculé*; (2) postcolonial works written during exile (1972–1991), including the Reuben trilogy, *Remember Ruben*, *Perpétue*, and *La Ruine presque cocasse d'un Polichinelle*, and the two Guillaume novels, *Les Deux Mères de Guillaume Ismaël Dzewatama* and *La Revanche de Guillaume Ismaël Dwewatama*. Nonfiction works include two exposés of the abuses by Cameroonian neocolonial regimes supported by France: *Main Basse sur le Cameroun* and *Lettre Ouverte aux Camerounais*, as well as the *Dictionnaire de la négritude*, where Beti and other contributors provide detailed interpretations of hundreds of subjects related to blacks and their history. In addition to these works, until 1989 Beti edited sixty-eight issues of the journal *Peuples Noirs Peuples Africains*, which he founded with his wife in 1978; (3) since Beti's retirement in Cameroon (1993), he has continued to

write nonfiction: *La France contre l'Afrique: Retour au Cameroun*, a critique
of neocolonial life in Cameroon, particularly as it relates to French interests, as
well as fiction: *Histoire du fou* (1994), *Trop de soleil tue l'amour* (1999), and
Branle-bas en noir et blanc (1999).

Distancing himself in the early 1950s from the romanticized, essentialist view
of precolonial Africa and Africans common to the negritude school, Mongo Beti
was among the first francophone novelists to provide a radical critique of French
colonization. His opposition to the mystification inherent in negritude is evident
from the start in his critique of **Camara Laye** (in 1954 and 1955 issues of
Présence Africaine), becoming more substantial in the *Dictionnaire de la négritude* (1989). His works have continued to jab at the soft underbelly of **neocolonial** collusion that links France to its former colonies. As a result, his writings
have been banned in Cameroon, and the first edition of *Main Basse sur le
Cameroun: Autopsie d'une décolonisation* (1972) was confiscated by the French
government. A common theme running through all of Beti's work is the cor-
rupting influence of illegitimate power, whether imperial, religious, neocolonial,
or that of postcolonial tyrants.

Beti's first four novels counter the official version of France's *mission civi-
lisatrice*, providing an unprecedented view of colonization. Using irony, humor,
and naive narrators to launch his anticolonial attack in the trilogy that made him
famous (*Le Pauvre Christ de Bomba*, *Mission terminée*, and *Le Roi Miraculé*),
Beti throws a radically new light on Christianization and European education.
No longer colonization's twin forces of modernization and progress, Beti clearly
shows how they work to break down the African social fabric. Beti's characters
are caught up in a process that they cannot control but that irrevocably transforms them into misfits who are no longer at home in a traditional African setting
anymore than they are in the European colonizer's world. Beti's early novels
provided readers not only with the first images of colonization's deleterious
effects on the African psyche but also with some of the earliest metaphors for
postcolonized Africa. Bomba's abandoned mission, deserted by its French missionaries, is nothing more than an empty shell robbed of its vitality by the
colonial project. Like the European school, its presence permanently mars the
African landscape.

After a fourteen-year period of silence, roughly corresponding to the end of
French colonial rule and the rise of neocolonial regimes in Africa, Mongo Beti
resumed his critical analysis of the abuses of power. The first of these is a
political pamphlet, *Main Basse sur le Cameroun*, a scathing exposé of collusion
between France and the Ahidjo regime to brutally repress Cameroon's independence movement (l'Union des Populations Camerounaises). In his fiction, Beti
abandons the irony and humor of his earlier works and develops characters that
contrast with the marginalized neophytes in the earlier group of novels. In *Remember Ruben* and *La Ruine Presque cocasse d'un polichinelle*, revolutionary
heroes end their quest for liberty by returning home to rid their villages of
missionaries and tyrannical chiefs. Beti's unusual use of third-person narration

emphasizes the collective nature of nation-building where women play a key role. Beti's metaphorical use of gender is further developed in *Perpétue et l'habitude du malheur*, where Perpetua's betrayal by those around her leads to her imprisonment and death. Her lack of **agency** parallels that of all victims of neocolonial regimes.

Retirement has far from dulled Mongo Beti's pen, positioned as he now is to observe Cameroon's neocolonial regime at close range. He continues to be engaged in political commentary (*La France contre l'Afrique*) and fiction writing (*L'Histoire du fou, Trop de soleil tue l'amour* and *Branle-bas en noir et blanc*). In both genres Beti focuses on the reign of anarchy in Cameroon, where all social and political institutions have been corrupted, serving the interests of the dictatorship or those of the former colonizer. Like the protagonists in Beti's first novels, these characters are constantly threatened by powerful forces around them; however, this is a highly complex and far more dangerous world where the absurd reigns and where the saving grace of solidarity has been reduced to infinitely small proportions.

Further Reading: S. Arnold 1998; R. Bjornson 1991; A. Kom 2000.

Eloise A. Brière

Beur **Writing**   Beur writing is a recent occurrence, dating to the early 1980s. The word "beur" entered the *Dictionnaire Larousse* in 1986. Michel Laronde in his influential work *Autour du roman beur* pinpoints the use of the term "beur" to 1981, when it was first pronounced by Nacer Kettane, disc jockey for Radio Beur. The term, designating a specific group of young daughters and sons of immigrants from the three countries of the Maghreb (Algeria, Morocco, and Tunisia), is a word in a unique French slang known as *vers-l'en*. *Vers-l'en* specifies that all two-syllable words in French can be reformulated by flipping the syllables around, "*à l'envers*" (inversely). The word "beur" is, in fact, the French word "arabe," reformulated in *vers-l'en*. Use of *vers-l'en* is popular with young people of immigrant communities, particularly in large urban centers such as Paris, Lyon, and Marseilles. Rebellious and antiauthority, the coded language of the Beurs is used to subvert feelings of marginalization, isolation, and racism. Young Beurs have sought to gain acceptance in France from the *Français-de-souche* ("pure French" native) population, which, they often point out, is rigid and contrite to the embrace of **multiculturalism** in France. Although born in France, the young Beur population claims that they are treated no better than their immigrant parents. Assimilation into French culture has been difficult. Indeed, lack of acceptance is a principal theme found in the novels of Beur authors. Other popular themes are marginalization, nomadism, racism, language barriers, and the difficulty of adapting to French culture.

The Beur identity has offered the young population of the urban ghettos a means to negotiate between two worlds: one French (the country in which they were born) and the other their parents' homeland, of which they often know little. Caught between these two worlds, the young Beur tries to mediate his or her own place in the world. Attesting to the difficulty of negotiating these opposing worlds, works such as Leila Sebbar's trilogy (*Shérazade: 17 ans, brune, frisée, yeux verts* [1982], *Les carnets de Shérazade* [1985], *Le fou de Shérazade* [1991]) trace the polarity of young Beurs' lives. Sebbar's protagonists often claim that they feel "neither French nor Arab," despite attempts to negotiate some median place between the two. Not having a sense of "place" is a theme evidenced in Farida Belghoul's only novel, *Georgette!* (1986). Written when she was twenty-eight, Belghoul calls attention to one young girl's struggle for acceptance in a world where hostility is the norm. Existence "nowhere" is also a concurring theme in Leila Houari's 1985 novel, *Zeïda de nulle part.* Azouz Begag's *Le Gone du Chaâba* (1986) and *Beni ou le Paradis Privé* (1989) offer a window into the lives of young boys growing up in urban settings where they must fight for acceptance in a world where all odds are against them. Themes of displacement, isolation, urban blight, and lack of opportunity for young Beurs in France are found in works such as Mehdi Charef's *Le Thé au harem d'Archi Ahmed* (1983), Ahmed Kalouaz's *Point kilométrique 190* (1986), Nacer Kettane's *Le Sourire de Brahim* (1985), Jean-Luc Yacine's *L'Escargot* (1986), and Hocine Touabti's *L'Amour quand même* (1981).

While often at times humorous, told tongue in cheek, the underlying thematic currents of Beur literature are generally emotionally painful. Marginalization, racism, and urban violence are always found as undercurrents of the Beur author's text.

Further Reading: A. Hargreaves 1989, 1990a, 1990b; M. Laronde 1993.

Valérie Orlando

Homi Bhabha   Born in Bombay in 1949 Homi K. Bhabha now occupies the Chester D. Tripp Chair in the Humanities at the University of Chicago and is visiting professor at the University of London. Although confused sometimes with India's first nuclear head, Homi J. Bhabha, he is better known in the West than his illustrious uncle. Described by the *Times* as one of the "super-dons" in British academe when he was teaching at the University of Sussex, a more homely description would see him as one of Midnight's Children (one of those born around the time India gained independence in 1947), actively allowing the contamination of diverse traditions in his own life while he theorizes the time of "the scattering of the people." He is editor of the acclaimed collection of essays *Nation and Narration* (1990); the publication of *The Location of Culture* (1994) collected most of his seminal essays, representing over a decade of work. Bhabha's work is famously difficult, and any paraphrasing of his arguments runs the danger of being dismissed as reductive.

The postcolonial perspective, in Bhabha's terms, "revises[s] those nationalist or **'nativist'** pedagogies that set up the relation of Third World and First World in a binary structure of opposition" (1994, 173). This is a conscious attempt to move beyond **Edward Said**'s *Orientalism* (1978) and **Frantz Fanon**'s *The Wretched of the Earth* (1968 [c. 1963]). Although Said deplores the neat distinction often made between colonizer and colonized, the contradictions and tensions that he notices in **colonial discourse** are resolved rather hastily in his work. This is due, as critics have noted, both to his positing of the power-knowledge equation as operating only in one direction and to the way in which he ascribes intentionality in colonial relations. Bhabha, instead, celebrates the early Fanon of *Black Skin, White Masks* (1986). In his foreword to that book, he reads Fanon as suggesting that the subjectivities of both parties must be seen in their necessarily nuanced and politically ambiguous engagements. In a Lacanian move, shifting and dynamic notions of identity are put forward, such that the "familiar alignment of colonial subjects— Black/White, Self/Other—is disturbed . . . and the traditional grounds of racial identity are dispersed, whenever they are found to rest in narcissistic myths of **negritude** or White cultural supremacy" (ix).

The legitimating postulate of colonialist discourse, in Bhabha's formulation, is the notion of "time-lag," of extending the project of modernization to areas outside the West. In the discursive arrangement that colonialism constructs, the tutelage and responsibility for this mission are Europe's. The non-West, by this catalytic intervention, is to hurry up its evolutionary refinement, its journey from the state of nature to that of culture, to become a mirror image of its benefactor. This agenda, which colonialism sets up for itself, places it in an embarrassingly paradoxical position. The transformation of the non-West into a clone of the West would, of course, render the whole project nonsensical, dissolving any sustainable distinction between the West and the rest. Only by reducing the specificity of its essential genius or by self-deconstruction can the project of **modernity** for the darker races bear fruit. This split at the enunciatory site of colonialist logic, according to Bhabha, results in a discourse and social formation marked with a kind of perversion described by Fanon as "Manichean delirium." The West, as a fallout of colonialism, is necessarily "tethered to" the non-West, and the once-colonized societies perforce become "dark shadows" of their erstwhile colonizer, shadows that replicate the conduct of that colonizer at a distance.

A discourse that is sutured so viscerally with contradiction has to rely on the absolute ardor of its enunciatory will. The repetitive address of its humanist progress and civility is made to stick by assumed power. To closely scrutinize the language of colonialism is thus to perceive the play of power even as the erosion of colonialism's cognitive ratiocination proceeds. The rhetoric at work in the scene of colonial administration and the exercise of authority uncovers a terrain, a productive space for an oppositional postcolonial stance. In "The Other Question: Difference, Discrimination and the Discourse of Colonialism" Bhabha explains that the object of colonial discourse is marked by what he terms a productive ambivalence: "that 'otherness' which is at once an object of desire and derision, an articulation of difference contained within the fantasy of origin and identity" (1990, 67).

Bhabha develops the notion of **"mimicry"** in the essay "Of Mimicry and Man:

The Ambivalence of Colonial Discourse" (1985) to further his reading of the fissures immanent in colonial articulation. The normalization of the colonized subject as a "mimic man" again brings to the fore the contradictory, built-in mechanism of colonial discourse. The native is to be Anglicized but not turned into an English clone: "not white/not quite." The contradiction arising out of such a "flawed colonial mimesis" also becomes the occasion for a subversive move. The closer the mimic man resembles the colonizer, the greater the potential for a transgression of authority. "The *menace* of mimicry," he explains, "is its double vision which in disclosing the ambivalence of colonial discourse also disrupts its authority" (1994, 88). Apart from pointing out the significance of dissimulated power and ambivalence in the exercise of colonial authority, Bhabha here suggests that the figure of the mimic man constitutes an undermining moment of differential time that extends in its reach to the **neocolonial** formation. Thus, the very presence of colonialism's mimic man is understood as always-already undermining the structure of colonialist supremacy even from within the neocolonial regime. This view of **resistance**, however, has been criticized for proposing a model that weakens the autonomy of the **agent**.

Attacking the assumption that culture can be located within the bounds of nations, social formations, and time spans, Bhabha argues that modernity as an Enlightenment concept is rooted in Western notions of rationality and historical progress set in a unilinear time frame. Favoring the idea of a contramodernity, Bhabha gestures to the challenge posed by the "peripheral" regions of the world where different temporalities and historicities are juxtaposed on a daily basis, where the traditional and the modern are articulated together, thus opening out a space for alternative possibilities. This clearly interrogates facile ways of thinking wherein the passage from an early primitive phase to a creative, progressive, contemporary phase easily normalizes dominant notions of history and tradition.

This is the insight that anchors the whole of his *Location of Culture*. In treating the idea of culture not simply as a spatial metaphor but also as a temporal one, Bhabha launches his critique of the **postmodern**. In the concluding essay, " 'Race,' Time and the Revision of Modernity," he demonstrates how postmodernism's reliance on the spatial is incapable of revealing the relative nature of the figure of Enlightenment man, the universal status of which is attained only by positing the non-Westerner as belatedly entering history upon contact with the West. The limits of postmodern thinking in its attempts to decenter the sovereign subject are clear even in the works of **Michel Foucault**, **Benedict Anderson**, and Fredric Jameson, who fail to pay sufficient attention to the histories and legacies of colonialism.

That he is not parasitic on French theory but anxiously and actively vigilant is evident when he reminds us that Jacques Derrida's invocation of the Nambikwara Indians and Jean-François Lyotard's turn to the Cashinahua pagans form an aspect of a "strategy of containment where the Other text is forever the exegetical horizon of difference, never the active agent of articulation" (1994, 31). Here he indicts contemporary critical theory for its impetus "to reproduce a relation of domination." His relation to current theory is further complicated by the argument that "the encounters and negotiations of differential meanings and values within 'colonial' textuality, its governmental discourses and cultural practices, have anticipated, *avant la lettre*, many of the problematics of signification and judgement that have become current in contemporary theory" (173). Thus, Bhabha finds in the colonial texts themselves the problematization of issues that condition the theories that are usually applied to such texts.

That the nation is ever unitary or homogeneous is a myth. It is, instead, internally marked by the performative transgression of the metanarratives that claim a singular national identity. This nationalist pedagogy, Bhabha argues, is contested by the scraps and patches of everyday life as well as by voices from the margins of the nation. This "double time" engendered by the nationalist narrative splits the people such that they are objects already scripted in history as well as performers in an unfolding national story. In other words, there is a form of living in the postcolonial nation (often he cites the example of India) that is functional and productive precisely because of cultural or ethnic tensions. He does not argue for the elimination of the category of the nation as such when we still witness people willing to live and die for that form of social organization. While acknowledging its historical limitations, it is difficult to jettison the nation both as a concept as well as a political structure.

In our increasingly transnational world, new ways of thinking about **cosmopolitanism** become indispensable as political thinkers continue to derive models of harmonious global living from older **Eurocentric** forms. Bhabha argues for a new, complex vernacular cosmopolitanism that goes beyond liberalism as we know it, one that accounts for the wider transformation of the public sphere and the process of **translation** at work. This he sees to be exemplified in, for instance, the work of Vandana Shiva, which moves "between contemporary, postcolonial Third World **feminism**, the unsustainable commodification of the world, and the old, dying earth itself" (1997, 3). In other words, cosmopolitanism not merely is rooted in Enlightenment concepts of civility and virtue but is also the historical experience of colonial societies, which have always had to deal with **multicultural** living.

Bhabha's work questions the premises of traditional liberalism that underwrite the multiculturalist credo that different cultures can be harmoniously juxtaposed like a mosaic. Opposing the mantra of cultural diversity, which assumes an understanding of relations between cultures in absolute, ontological terms, he proposes the notion of "cultural difference." The cultural difference of the historically marginalized, the migrant, the refugee is to be seen as an argument not for equality with the dominant group but for a dialogic equality in which no single (normalized) term would allow the de-privileging of specific **subaltern** histories and identities. The prerogative of cultural translation is to recognize not only the shifting character of interacting positionalities but also that it is necessary to revise systems of reference, norms, and values and to go beyond the habitus of accepted modes of change. Negotiating with the difference of the other is to acknowledge the inadequacy of our conceptual resources and systems of signification. Traditional, unrevised liberalism falls short in its task of attempting to provide a measure of justice to what is necessarily foreign to it.

In his essay "The Commitment to Theory," he argues for the dismantling of the false opposition between theory and political practice. Liminality, or the interstitial space, between theory and practice mediates their mutual exchange and relative meanings. Thinking them together is to acknowledge the tension that produces their hybridity. For Bhabha, a response to the question What is to be done? requires the acknowledgment of "the force of writing, its metaphoricity and its rhetorical discourse, as a productive matrix which defines the 'social' and makes available as an objective of and for, action" (23). The category of the liminal is the space between competing cultural traditions and critical methodologies. His model for political change, therefore, is that of the hybrid moment, the translation of elements that are *"neither the One nor the Other but something else besides,* which contests the terms and territories of both" (28). Through his readings of Rushdie, Nadine Gordimer, Walcott, and Toni Morrison, inter alia, and less-known narratives like the rumors of the circulation of chapatis across the rural heartlands of the Indian Mutiny and the film *Handsworth Songs,* he demonstrates that the postcolonial condition, as part of a revisionary time, is central to any notion of the contemporary, not just a peripheral concern. The blasphemy of **Salman Rushdie**'s *The Satanic Verses* (1988) is emblematic of the power of hybridity in bringing newness into the world by questioning the purity of tradition not only in its fundamentalist guise but, more importantly, in its liberal manifestations. Newness must be located outside the continuum of progress in a sort of interruptive history. Shaking postimperial identity to its very foundations, the metropolis is seen as already transformed, even though it may not know it. In the stammering words of Rushdie's Whisky Sisodia: "The trouble with the Engenglish is that their hiss hiss history happened overseas, so they dodo don't know what it means" (166–67).

Said has described Bhabha as "a reader of enormous subtlety and wit, a theorist of uncommon power. His work is a landmark in the exchange between ages, genres and cultures; the colonial, post-colonial, modernist and postmodern" (Bhabha 1994, cover). In the words of Terry Eagleton, he has put the "skids under just about every cherished doctrine of Western Enlightenment" (1994, 28). At the same time, Bhabha has also been charged with being elitist and obscurantist, engaging in word games, privileging the discursive over the economic, relying too heavily on Western psychoanalytical and poststructuralist theory, and—perhaps the most damaging criticism of all—being a privileged spokesperson for the Third World position. In his defense, one can make a case for his refusal to endorse easy assumptions and writing that mimics the very transgression of borders that he speaks about. Accolades and criticism apart, his work has transformed the imaginative landscape of contemporary cultural criticism and enjoys a citation index second to few cultural and literary critics. Concepts like "hybridity," "mimicry," "Third Space," and "sly civility" have become central to any understanding of cultural formations as they continue to impact disciplines as diverse as English and **cultural studies**, political theory, **art** and **film** criticism, history, and anthropology.

Further Reading: H. Bhabha 1986, 1990b, 1994, 1997; B. Moore-Gilbert 1997; R. Young 1990.

Prem Poddar

Black Atlantic This is a term coined by cultural theorist Paul Gilroy as a general name for the interconnected black cultures of Africa, Europe, and the Americas. His book *Black Atlantic* (1993) is a critique of **essentializing** Pan-Africanist or black nationalist theories of culture and is, in part, an extension of his earlier work *There Ain't No Black in the Union Jack* (1987). In that book Gilroy critiques the politics of race and nation that treats ethnic/cultural identities as fixed, pure, and rooted in the past, with its store of supposedly unchanging tradition. Using black British culture as his example, he argues that collective identity is as much a creation of the present as a product of the past. Racial and cultural identities are constantly changing, reinventing themselves from within and being reinvented by interaction with other cultures. This is not, as essentializing theories of race would have it, an undesirable process of dilution or infection; it is the basic, healthy life process of all cultures. The black Atlantic, Gilroy argues, is a particularly good example of robust cultural health.

In *Black Atlantic* Gilroy elaborates a conception of black Atlantic cultures as modern and hybrid. Using **Edouard Glissant**'s concept of black diaspora, Gilroy argues that black Atlantic culture is "transnational," a "non-national nation" that is not so much rooted in tradition as routed through a shared, "non-traditional tradition." That is, the important link between black Atlantic cultures is not their shared origin in some unchanging and traditional African past but their shared capacity for change and exchange in the present. This is most evident in the sphere of music, where the repeated cross-fertilization of African, West Indian, African American, and black European music constantly produces new forms such as reggae, afro-beat, and rap.

For Gilroy, the trade routes that these musical exchanges map across the Atlantic are an important echo and reinvention of the trade routes along which Africans were carried into slavery. Slavery made New World blacks the first modern people, separated from their past, surviving in an unstable and alienating social environment, finding identity and self-expression in those areas over-looked by (white) power—especially in music. Today, power in the Atlantic is transnational, traveling the routes of international commerce; and the cultures that are best equipped to survive and subvert it are those that are likewise transnational. The exchange of subversive black music through the medium of international commerce, Gilroy argues, is evidence of both the black Atlantic's transnationality and its vibrancy.

Some cultural commentators wonder to what extent these black Atlantic cultural exchanges are compromised by the mediation of international capital; Jamaican reggae, for example, gets diluted for the purposes of marketing it to an international audience. There is also reason to fear that the transmission of culture around the black Atlantic is not as equitable as Gilroy supposes; for example, some commentators suspect that musical forms like afro-beat are not evidence of healthy cross-fertilization between African American and African cultures but evidence of Western cultural hegemony or, worse, merely part of a neocolonial program of marketing Western products in the Third World. The black Atlantic may, finally, turn out to be the black American Atlantic.

Gilroy, however, is confident that black Atlantic culture fairly consistently eludes the grasp of international capital and that fears about cultural hegemony and cultural dilution are misplaced. Black Atlantic culture is already a hybrid, the product of centuries of **Creolization**; Jamaican reggae, for example, is already a Creole formation that owes as much to black American music as to Jamaican music. Consequently, Gilroy urges the recognition of the openendedness of black Atlantic cultures, their ability to interact creatively not just with other black Atlantic cultures but with other cultures as well, without losing their integrity.

Further Reading: P. Gilroy 1987, 1993; G. Lipsitz 1994.

Hugh Hodges

Black Britain   This term refers to the common cultural identity shared by British people of African, West Indian, and South Asian descent and gained currency in the 1970s and 1980s. It reflects the attempt on the part of these postcolonial subjects who, for different and often contradictory reasons, had begun to arrive in Britain in significant numbers in the 1950s, to contest not so much their complete exclusion but rather their subordinate *inclusion* within dominant British cultural formations. This identity was forged in the crucible of civil uprisings of this period, provoked by the pervasive and systemic racism of British society. It was sustained by the rigorous and committed work of intellectuals such as **Stuart Hall**, Ambalavaner Sivanandan, and Bhikhu Parekh, the journal *Race Today*, and the Institute of Race Relations. Articulated in vigorous opposition not only to a resurgent far Right but also against elements of the Left that often cynically instrumentalized race, "black Britain" embodied dub-poet Linton Kweisi Johnson's call for an "Independent Intavenshun" within state and civil society. Such an "intavenshun" could be said to have culminated in the ultimately unsuccessful struggle for "black sections" in the Labour Party in the mid-1980s. Two developments contributed to its displacement as a viable political identity in favor of more particularistic and exclusionary identities. The first was the "**Rushdie** affair," which, of course, pitted a large proportion of Muslims against Asians of other religious affiliations as well as against Africans and West Indians. The second was the increasing class divisions between that fraction of "black Britain," notably, East African Asians, who benefited economically if not socially and culturally from Thatcherism and were consequently regarded as a "model minority," on the one hand, and those who continued to be criminalized by the state, on the other.

Further Reading: P. Gilroy 1987; A. Sivanandan 1990.

Samir Gandesha

Black Power Movement   The black power movement was founded by Stokely Carmichael in 1966. In their infamous and influential text *Black Power: The Politics of Liberation in America* (1967), Carmichael and Charles V. Hamilton outlined the material and ideological tenets of black power. Largely influenced by the writings of Frederick Douglass and the ethnopsychoanalytic theses of **Frantz Fanon** and Albert Memmi, the black power movement sought to resist and redress structures of white privilege or supremacy in the United States. In contrast to the civil rights movement, advocates of black power identified strongly with colonized nonwhite peoples around the world. Specifically, the black power movement emphasized the need to acknowledge an African heritage (apropos of the notion of "roots") and to recognize the psychological and so-ciomaterial domination of nonwhites by whites in the United States as a situation of imperialism or colonialism. Indeed, Carmichael and Hamilton affirm that "Black Power means that black people see themselves as part of a new force, sometimes called the 'Third World'; . . . we see our struggle as closely related to liberation struggles around the world. We must hook up with these struggles" (1967, 14). In favor of a more proactive approach in their negotiation of the fundamental issues concerned, proponents of black power also reject the passive rhetoric of "love and suffering" associated with the civil rights movement. Car-michael and Hamilton maintain that appealing to (white and nonwhite) middle-class values and codes of conduct not only leads to a situation of victimization for the African American peoples but also operates to sustain the hegemonic structures of white privilege. Espousing a discourse of black ownership and franchise within the political, social, aesthetic, and economic spheres, the black power movement has gone as far as to advance black separatism as a possible solution to the impasse of racial/class disparity.

It is thus not surprising that, particularly at its inception, there existed a great deal of anxiety among the white and nonwhite middle class or mainstream re-garding the putatively militant or fanatic proposals of this (at that time) radical organization. Chiefly affected by the hyperbolical representations by the mass media and other institutional structures that not only marginalized but also de-monized black **identity**, this collective apprehensiveness toward the black power movement is largely unfounded; the organization employs/ed mainly legally sanctioned and peaceable modes of operation. The more moderate, though no less deliberate, projects associated with the black power movement also hold the primary objective of effecting **agency**, pride, and suffrage for the African American community and individual.

One of the most notable achievements of the black power movement consisted of the **decolonization** and reevaluation of the ways in which African Americans were represented. Abrogating or reappropriating hitherto pejorative stereotypes and appellations, the movement sought to redress the internalized racism instilled in African Americans by structures of white supremacy. As bell hooks notes of the black power revolution, it saw "self-love as a radical political agenda" (1995, 119).

Hence, for example, "Afro" hairstyles became fashionable where they were previously deplored as being "nappy." Indeed, it is significant that the rhetoric of black power targeted and was addressed primarily to the black community, not otherwise. Of particular concern was the internalized (self-)hatred that prevented African Americans from achieving self-esteem and a sense of dignity, as well as the associated—and even more troubling—phenomenon of the color caste system operating within the black community (e.g., see Russell and Hall, 1992).

Although only one faction of various organized endeavors to resist racism and empower African Americans, the black power movement's influence was pervasive, with an increasing incidence of eminent and celebrated persons becoming associated with its cause. For example, on 16 October 1968, John Carlos and Tommie Smith, Olympic medalists in the 200-meter run, gave the black power salute while standing upon the winners' platform in Mexico City. The photograph of the two African American men raising their fists to the sky remains famous to this day.

It is important to note, however, that not only were many black and nonblack factions opposed or antagonistic to black power activism but also that various dialectical and ethical concerns arise in the attempt to account for black power in postcolonial terms. Many of these concerns pertain to a homogenization—and, subsequently, trivialization—of the situation and discursive terms of disparate ethnic, cultural, and racial identities and identifications (see C. Macleod 1997). Indeed, it is often observed that even regarding the black **diaspora** throughout the United States alone, there is such a heterogeneity (syncretism) in sociomaterial situation and politicoideological identification that it is problematic to conceive of or posit generalizations regarding African Americans as a unitary culture. Nevertheless, the political positioning of black power activism is either largely based in, or coincident with, postcolonial formulations. Despite sometimes advocating a radical class/race separatism, black power exponents, along with critics such as bell hooks, Cornell West, **Edward Said**, and others, have endorsed a more heterogeneous perspective in negotiating the material and ontological boundaries pertaining to "race" and **ethnicity**. Anticipating Said's remarks regarding the "octopus" of modern American imperialism, Carmichael invites the conflation. He remarks that "while we disrupt internally and aim for the eye of the octopus, we are hoping that our brothers [outside America] are disrupting externally to sever the tentacles of the United States" (1971, 87).

Further Reading: S. Carmichael 1969a, 1971; F. Chideya 1995; F. Fanon 1967, 1968; b. hooks 1995; C. Macleod 1997; K. Russell, Wilson and Hall 1992.

Matthew Cleveland

Edward Kamau Brathwaite   From the period that produced **Derek Walcott**, **Wilson Harris**, **V. S. Naipaul**, **George Lamming**, and **Sam Selvon**, Edward Kamau Brathwaite is arguably the most original and innovative Caribbean writer of his generation. Born in Bridgetown, Barbados, in 1930, Brathwaite is a historian by academic discipline and has lived and taught in the U. K., Africa, the Caribbean, and North America. In his major works Brathwaite considers the issues that have troubled many of his contemporaries: the nature of Caribbean **identity**, the future of the Caribbean and its people, and the role of the **artist** in Caribbean society. In response, Brathwaite has consistently argued that the contemporary Caribbean is the product of a long process of **Creolization** that continues to affect the islands. Accepting that Caribbean identity is made up of a variety of traditions and cultures, Brathwaite traces his roots back to Africa. He asks that the African contribution to Caribbean life not be forgotten. He is a champion of the survival of submerged languages and their forms in the language of contemporary life, and as an individual and communal poet he seeks to remake in his poetry a new language for a Caribbean future.

To date, Brathwaite has produced at least nineteen volumes of poetry, four collections of prose poems (what he terms "proems"), two volumes of plays for children, eight books of literary and cultural criticism, numerous critical essays, and five studies of Caribbean history. He is a prolific talent. Among these many works, *The Arrivants* (1973), his "New World Trilogy," is still considered by many to be his most significant work. Influenced by **Aimé Césaire**'s *Cahier d'un Retour au Pays Natal* (1939) and comprising *Rights of Passage* (1967), *Masks* (1968) and *Islands* (1969), the poem as a whole is concerned with the fate of the New World Negro as the Caribbean region enters an era of social, political, and cultural independence. *Rights of Passage* evokes an experience of rootlessness and dispossession as the Negro leaves the islands in search of life, love, and labor, while the islands themselves drift helplessly, fermenting **mimicry** and revolution in equal parts. The poet looks with anger and sorrow at the desolation of the New World, but at this stage he can do nothing. In *Masks* the homeless and historyless poet goes in search of spiritual roots, as he reverses the journey of the Middle Passage and returns to Africa. However, this is no simple, romanticized vision of the ancestral past. Born in the New World, the poet recognizes that he can never be wholly integrated into the African past. Instead, he surveys African language, history, and religious ritual for points of connection, moments of ancestral survival and spiritual communion. The most powerful of these is the African talking drum (*"atumpan"*), which sets a rhythm and refrain for the poet to follow. Back in the New World in *Islands*, the poet asserts the presence of Africa in the language and life of the community and works toward the possibility of a spiritual and linguistic reawakening. Significant for the epic grandeur of its thematic design, *The Arrivants* also stands as a testament to Brathwaite's poetic technique. The poem is especially notable for its dynamic, rhythmical structure, its subtle incorporation of several different voices and registers, and its prodigious use of linguistic experimentation and wordplay. Driven by the African drum, *The Arrivants* is rich in allusion to African American jazz and blues, Jamaican reggae and ska, and Trinidadian calypso (see "Folkways," "The Journeys," "Wings of a Dove," and "Calypso"). Written with the voice in mind, the poem also exhibits Brathwaite's ability to capture the speech of ordinary Caribbean folk expression (see "The Dust," "Rites," and "Cane"). More generally, a number of poems are self-consciously concerned with the acquisition of language and the poet's wish for the words that will allow him to hallow and heal the islands (see "Ananse," "Negus," and "Vèvè"). At the poem's close, the poet reflects upon the cruelty and creativity of a New World language that is only just discovering its true potential.

Brathwaite's "New World Trilogy" was followed by a second "Ancestors" trilogy, comprising *Mother Poem* (1977), *Sun Poem* (1982), and *X/Self* (1987). Focused more closely on his native island of Barbados, *Mother Poem* and *Sun Poem* see Brathwaite searching for rehabilitation in a world fractured into silence by the events of imperial history. The mother of *Mother Poem* refers to the poet's own mother, the variety of victimized females of the island, and the island itself. In returning to these sources Brathwaite sees the possibility for salvation and survival. In *Sun Poem* Brathwaite offers an examination of the male figure in the Caribbean. Memories of boyhood are contrasted with a panoply of impotent fathers. Yet, the volume ends on a note of hope as the sons of the Caribbean are given life by the force of the Caribbean sun. Published five years later, *X/Self* marks a shift in the poet's perspective as the personal gives way to the political. Here Brathwaite in the guise of X/Self ranges over failed empires and revolutions in Europe and the Caribbean and offers an apocalyptic vision of the postcolonial world. X/Self is the voice of black rebellion, and like the poet of *The Arrivants* he is also the voice of linguistic rebellion. It is here that we can see the beginnings of what Brathwaite has termed his "post-modem Sycorax video style," in which the words on the page evoke verbal performance, challenge Western logic, philosophy, and linguistics and look back to Sycorax, the mother, in establishing a connection with the ancestral past. This highly individual style has been explored further in such works as *Middle Passages* (1992), *DreamStories* (1994), *Shar/Hurricane Poem* (1990), *Trench Town Rock* (1994) and *The Zea Mexican Diary* (1994). The latter three perhaps offer a third trilogy in which Brathwaite movingly responds to a sequence of personal catastrophes.

In addition to his poetic achievements, Brathwaite has made a significant contribution to Caribbean criticism. Essays worth further investigation include "Jazz and the West Indian Novel" (1967/1968), "The African Presence in Caribbean Literature" (1970/1973), and "Timehri" (1974). In his longer studies Brathwaite has principally focused on questions of Caribbean history and language, out of which two key ideas suggest themselves, namely, "Creolization" and "nation-language." Central to his poetic project, the concept of creolization is most fully explored in Brathwaite's doctoral thesis "The Development of Creole Society in Jamaica 1770–1820" (1971) and *Contradictory Omens* (1979). In the former Brathwaite argues that Jamaican society during this period represented a unique moment in the material, psychological, and spiritual intermixture of whites and blacks. For Brathwaite, Creolization is the name for the acknowledged and illicit processes of acculturation and interculturation during the colonial period. Most importantly, though, he suggests that contemporary Caribbean society can be understood only within the framework of such a persistent and incipient process of dialogic encounter. Reflecting his interest in the survival of ancestral and spiritual roots in language, nation-language is Brathwaite's term for the language that Caribbean people actually speak, that is, the language that is the product of a process of Caribbean Creolization. It is first discussed in Brathwaite's *History of the Voice* (1984). In the **anglophone** Caribbean the linguistic spectrum is broadly made up of English, Creole English, nation-language, and the disappearing fragments of Amerindian, Indian, Asian, and African languages. For Brathwaite nation-language is the closest to the Caribbean experience. It is characterized by a close proximity to the **oral** tradition, a close alliance to the African experience, a dialogic communication with a communal native audience, and the production of meaning in a process of total expression. As a lived, dynamic, and changing phenomenon, nation-language challenges the institutionally imposed notion of Standard English. However, more than just a stratum of language, nation-language also challenges the dominant rhythm of English verbal expression: the pentameter. Instead, the rhythm of nation-language is intimately tied to the natural, environmental experience of the Caribbean as it captures the force of the hurricane that blows from the African coasts to the Caribbean islands. Questioning the logocentrism of the West, nation-language therefore affects and calls for a radical shift in the understanding of postcolonial Caribbean language and life. It suggests continuities in the modern Caribbean with the submerged language of the slaves brought over in the Middle Passage, and it proposes that the language used in contemporary Caribbean literature is "English in a new sense" (1984, 5). At the close of *History of the Voice*, Brathwaite calls for a redefinition of the Caribbean literary tradition and a reorientation of Caribbean criticism so that both might take full account of the scribal and oral cultures in the anglophone Caribbean.

In his major works as poet, critic, and historian Brathwaite repeatedly suggests that Caribbean recovery lies in the greater understanding of the cruelty and creativity of language. In a world of postcolonial encounters Brathwaite's voice may not be the loudest, but it is often the most original, challenging, and engaging.

Further Reading: E. K. Brathwaite 1984; S. Brown 1995; G. Rohlehr 1981.

Simon Beecroft

C

Amílcar Cabral   Born in Bafatá, Guinea-Bissau, on 12 September 1924, Amílcar Cabral grew up in Cape Verde, where his family settled in 1931. After completing his elementary education on the islands, he left to undertake further studies in Lisbon. Cabral graduated from the prestigious University of Lisbon in 1950 as a colonial agronomy engineer. Sometime later he returned to Cape Verde, following the death of his father, and was soon working for the colonial Provincial Department of Agricultural and Forestry Services of Portuguese Guinea. In this capacity Cabral traveled extensively across the country. Moving among the people in the far corners of Guinea in the 1950s, Cabral began to think seriously about the condition of Guineans and, indeed, of all Africans living under Portuguese colonial rule. As fellow lusophone intellectual and political activist Mário de Andrade (1928–1990) noted in a biography of Cabral written for the 1979 edition of Cabral's *Unity and Struggle*, the period spent as a student in Lisbon was crucial to Cabral's intellectual and political development. The company of many other Africans from Guinea, Cape Verde, Mozambique, and Angola, such as Angola's future president, Agostinho Neto, together with his association with Portuguese left-wing political groups, awakened in Cabral a nationalist, anticolonial consciousness.

In Cabral we have one of the most successful examples of an African whom the Portuguese believed to have thoroughly indoctrinated only to discover that the degrees that he gained at the University of Lisbon played a crucial role in his development of a profoundly influential critique of Portuguese and European colonial policies. Through a combination of the anticolonialist philosophies that he developed upon his return from Portugal and the organization of the peasantry into cells of popular resistance to the Portuguese colonial authorities, Cabral set in place the seeds for a political movement that was light-years ahead of anything developed elsewhere in Africa. Through his understanding of Portuguese colonial policies in Africa, he was able to begin working on healing the chasm set in place by the splitting of Africans into categories such as the *assimilados* (Africans deemed by the Portuguese colonial system as having successfully emulated "civilized" behavior) and the *indigenas* (Africans who had yet to begin the journey toward assimilation). Further, in the preferred mode of other earlier postcolonial theorists such as **Frantz Fanon**, Cabral perceived his position as a member of the educated native elite as that of an *"interlocuteur valable"* (1969, 66), articulating in this sense the "authentic voice of the people." This view of the intellectual's role in the **nationalist** struggle as one of leadership and guidance, which Cabral again shared with some of the postcolonial theorists in the early 1960s, reflects his belief that the educated *petite bourgeoisie* would in time join in the struggle toward the reconstruction of the newly liberated nation. But for Cabral such a position of leadership could eventuate only once the elites recognized their own imbrication within the colonial system and actively sought to move outside the ideological limitations of their class structures.

In his influential study of Portuguese **decolonization**, *The Decolonization of Portuguese Africa: Metropolitan Revolution and the Dissolution of the Empire* (1997), Norrie MacQueen suggests that one of the reasons that Guinea-Bissau has experienced a much lower level of political instability and violence than the other Portuguese colonies was the degree to which Amílcar Cabral had prepared the country for the departure of Portuguese colonialism. Cabral's belief that a well-educated, well-fed, and healthy local population would be indispensable once the Portuguese departed had seen him develop a framework of schools, clinics, and agricultural cooperatives that left Guinea particularly well placed for the postindependence period. Further, Cabral conceived of the armed struggle as one of the many simultaneous coordinates in the process of colonization. His often cited assertion that culture was an act of national liberation sought to account for what he understood as a complex, protracted system of "self-making," insofar as the creation of a new culture—a new way of being in the world—was intrinsic to the development of a postcolonial revolutionary consciousness. For Cabral, the "liberated zones" established by the PAIGC (Partido Africano para a Independência da Guiné e Cabo Verde), with their own political, economic, and social structures, represented for the Guinean people the task of taking over responsibility for the future. Cabral's use of the term "culture" thus clearly surpassed Fanon's own views on the subject. For Cabral, decolonization acted at a number of levels, and cultural decolonization, in its most literal sense, was simply one of a number of equally crucial sites of **resistance**.

However, Cabral's most original and lasting imprint on African postcolonial thought was his repeatedly voiced view that the anticolonial struggle was always, first and foremost, fought against a colonial system, rather than against a people. Thus, he stressed that Africans in the Portuguese empire recognized a shared bond between themselves and the Portuguese people; the nationalist war was primarily against a colonial regime supported by world capitalism. Through the articulation of such a stance, at the time well ahead of its intellectual and political contexts, Cabral first set out what undoubtedly constitutes one of the most sophisticated analyses of the postcolonial condition. Anticipating the philosophical impetus of later postcolonial critics such as the British historian Paul Gilroy (1993), the Ghanaian philosopher Kwame Anthony Appiah, and the Indian historian Partha Chatterjee (1986), to name but some of the many authors who, in recent years, have revisited the ground that he first explored, Cabral proposed in his political writings a stance of "double recognition" that sought to move beyond the realm of postcolonial recrimination and into a dialectical engagement with the social and psychological conditions of the encounter between Europe and its Others. Although this was to place him at the receiving end of pointed attacks by other African anticolonial nationalist leaders, he remained convinced that the solution for the future comprised a coming together of lusophone Africans and of a Portuguese people freed of the shackles of António Salazar's dictatorship.

Such a view may be seen as the result of Cabral's conviction that a theory of liberation would be incomplete and utterly ineffective without a continuous interaction with the popular masses. His stay in Portugal and his later encounters with Portuguese soldiers in the battlefields in Guinea-Bissau were crucial to Cabral's growing awareness that the vast majority of soldiers in the colonial army were themselves also trapped within a wider class struggle. Thus, rather than viewing them simply as an obstacle in the way to liberation and decolonization, from very early on in the anticolonial war, the PAIGC sought to encourage Portuguese soldiers to put down their weapons and cross into the liberated zones. The historian Basil Davidson (1992) has convincingly linked the military coup of 1974 in Portugal to the grassroots practice first established by Cabral's conciliatory approaches to the Portuguese army fighting in Guinea.

Class, rather than race or color, represented for Cabral the real crux of a politically effective program of anticolonial struggle. Once again proving to be well ahead of his time and of the views of many of his contemporaries, he perceived colonialism to be inextricable from capitalism. The overturn of the one would not be possible without the demise of the structural apparatus provided by the other. MacQueen's examination of the decolonization of the Portuguese empire has clearly demonstrated how foreign and Portuguese capital were instrumental to the empire's survival and to the maintenance of its armies. Rather, Cabral saw "the struggle of progress against misery and suffering, of freedom against oppression" as one shared by both colonizer and colonized. He exhorted Asian, African, and Latin American leaders and activists to address "one's own weaknesses," referring thus to the dangers inherent in racism, tribalism, and national chauvinism. Cabral's recollections of the comments of another African delegate at the 1961 Tunis All-African Peoples' Conference: "[I]t's different for you . . . you're doing all right with the Portuguese" (MacQueen 1997, 13) suggest the extent of his frustration with what he perceived as Africa's inability to unite against a common enemy.

Although a perspicuous critic and a skillful diplomat, Cabral's prolific and eclectic writing output meant that often it veered between thoughtful commentary and less critically refined pronouncements. He has on occasion been attacked for presenting what are seen as flawed and dogmatic viewpoints on many issues. To some he has seemed far too much the product of a European philosophical tradition based on a hypocritical profession of freedom and equality where race remained essentially an unspoken marker of difference and discrimination. But Cabral's detractors are clearly in the minority. Indeed, in recent years his work has begun to attract the attention of a number of non-Portuguese-speaking critics. In a critique of postcolonial theories, *Beyond Postcolonial Theory* (1998), the American-based Filipino intellectual E. San Juan Jr. suggests that Amílcar Cabral's political views owed much to Fanon's work. Indeed, he suggests, Cabral's views are "essentially Fanonian." Equally significant is San Juan's view that Cabral's ideas stand on a par with those of a larger group of postcolonial intellectuals, such as Fanon, the Brazilian **Paulo Freire**, the Martinican **Aimé Césaire**, and other theorists whom he credits with articulating a viable alternative to the theoretical framework that his own study attacks.

In contrast to the other figures to whom San Juan alludes, Cabral's writings have remained, on the whole, poorly discussed. Indeed, it would seem that, in spite of the greater emphasis on inclusivity and interdisciplinarity brought about by the dissemination of postcolonial critical practices, linguistic barriers still prevent us from benefiting from a truly transcolonial process of analysis that a study of Amílcar Cabral's work would make possible. Cabral's belief in "the need to re-Africanise one's mind" (Handyside 76), argued within a larger theory of national liberation as "an *act of culture*" (*Unity and Struggle*, 143), illustrates the extent to which contemporary African political and philosophical thought might be indebted to his work. Indeed, a study of Cabral's influence on postcolonial African fictional writing, particularly that of the "first generation," remains a timely challenge.

But Cabral was more than just a political and cultural theorist. Most of all, he was a leader of his people, and a truly inspiring force in the complex web of internecine squabbles among different ethnic groups that the Portuguese sought to foster. Today, he remains best known for his ability to bring together the disparate peoples of Guinea-Bissau and Cape Verde into a political entity that he would never see accede to power, the PAIGC. Sadly, though no doubt he would be the first to recognize the perverse irony of the situation, the nation that Cabral fought so hard to unite is now riven by bitter and brutal internal division. The loss to fire of almost the entire collection of the new nation's national archives in late 1998 is, in many ways, symbolic of the way in which Cabral's own contribution to the anticolonial struggle has been swallowed by the realization of his greatest fears: that of the reinvention of colonialism in the form of globalization. In his own words, "**neocolonialism** (which we may call rationalized imperialism) is more a defeat for the international working class than for the colonized peoples" (Handyside 73). Ironically, some of the most influential writings by Amílcar Cabral survive today in a museum dedicated to his work and based in Lisbon, the capital of the former colonial power.

In addition to his political writings, Cabral wrote poetry and short fiction. At an early age he began writing often thinly disguised "imaginings" of his later role in life as a leader of the Guinean people. As a poet, in a soulful and melancholy voice, Cabral articulated the islands' isolation, the suffering of the people, their need to emigrate. In one of the many ironies that Cabral so presciently identified, the people of Guinea-Bissau and Cape Verde shared with the Portuguese nation itself one of the greatest mass migrations of the 1950s and 1960s. For Cabral, the similarities were obvious, and the blame for the suffering of Africans colonized by Portugal rested with a large, institutional, political, and economic system of which the Portuguese people were also victims. He is best remembered in lusophone arts as a muse to a younger generation of Guinean and Cape Verdean poets. Further, while his creative output is clearly negligible, it represents an illuminating map of the development of Cabral—the idealistic adolescent, the young man filled with dreams who left for Lisbon in 1945, the committed leader who returned home in the early 1950s, the politician who, with four other men, formed the PAIGC in 1956 in Praia, the myth who remains forever shrouded by the mystery of a death that came too soon and that much too prematurely deprived a nation of a leader of enormous and proven potential. Cabral was possessed of one of the finest minds among the nationalists of his day, indeed, among those who both preceded or followed him in the anticolonialist struggle. Yet, unlike so many other postcolonial nationalist leaders, for him the nation represented but a transitory stage toward complete decolonization, rather than an end in itself. A number of central themes characterize his work: a concern with theories of colonialism and imperialism, the analysis of class struggles in the capitalist world-system to which colonialism was but a minor element, the role, place, and *meaning* of culture in a postcolonial society, **Pan-Africanism** and solidarity with other revolutionary movements. Cabral was assassinated in Guinea-Conakri on 20 January 1973. Although the circumstances of his death were never convincingly explained, it is generally accepted that it was the work of the Portuguese secret police, possibly with the collusion of disaffected PAIGC members.

Further Reading: A. Cabral 1970; R. H. Chilcote 1991.

Tony Simoes da Silva

Canadian Literature, English Language   Canadian literature in English has always exhibited the awkward doubleness with regard to colonialism that characterizes all **settler colonies**: the invading settlers are colonizers, subordinating the native cultures, but then are often treated like colonized people themselves, especially by their mother country—in this case, England. They usually adopt elements from the new cultures, combine them with parts of the Old World, and in this way create something new and different. The ambiguity or plurality of codes that characterizes postcolonial literatures is, therefore, also noticeable in Canada, as is a concern with **identity**, history, power relations, and opposition to, or connivance with, dominant ideologies. But postcolonial literature in Canada is far from being a unified, monolithic category. Writers and critics usually display no shared agenda or collective consciousness but demand recognition of the specificity of place and time, thus realizing the uncertainties even of postcolonial truth claims.

In Canadian literature, the European and especially English norms, values, and genres survived and prevailed for a remarkably long time, far into the twentieth century. They are visible in the first Canadian novel, Frances Brooke's *History of Emily Montague* (1769), written in the tradition of the English eighteenth-century epistolary novel, and in the nineteenth-century autobiographical sketches of Susanna Moodie, *Roughing It in the Bush* (1852), as well as in Wilfred Campbell's selections for the first *Oxford Book of Canadian Verse* (1913). A new international perspective was put forward by the modernists in the 1920s, in particular, the McGill movement, centered on A.J.M. Smith and F. R. Scott, criticizing the conservatism and colonialism of Canadian literature, to be overcome by adopting international modernist standards and by allowing writers complete freedom in the choice and treatment of their subjects. John Sutherland's introduction to his poetry anthology *Other Canadians* (1947) provided another outspoken attack on Canadian writing as colonial, but his suggestion to replace the old British literary models by U.S.–American ones proved to be problematic, as the United States was already experienced as a far more dangerous colonizer in Canada than Britain. The Massey Commission of 1951 officially identified U.S.–American mass culture as the greatest threat to Canadian cultural sovereignty and initiated important measures against this influence, especially the establishment of the Canada Council for the Encouragement of the Arts, Letters, Humanities, and Social Sciences in 1957. Margaret Atwood's novel *Surfacing* (1972) expresses this old fear of the economic and cultural dominance of the United States again, and it addresses the complexity of colonial issues in Canada by referring to the white treatment of native peoples and the English–Canadian domination of **Quebec** as well as the Canadian connivance in the betrayal of their own culture by adopting the U.S.–American way of life. Atwood describes Canada as a collective victim and oppressed minority due to British and U.S.–American colonialism in her influential book *Survival: A Thematic Guide to Canadian Literature* (1972).

England and France as the dominant colonial powers within Canada were politically and culturally often regarded in the twentieth century as the *Two Solitudes*. Hugh MacLennan's 1945 novel still hopes for a union between them, but the expression has come to signify the almost complete absence of communication and exchange between these cultures. Smaller cultures were, until the 1960s, of even less importance. In 1970, though, the Royal Commission on Bilingualism and Biculturalism made politicians aware of "The Cultural Contributions of the Other Ethnic Groups" (Innis 1973), and a year later Prime Minister Trudeau put Canada's multicultural identity on the official political agenda. It was still a **multiculturalism** within a bilingual framework, though.

The Canadian Multiculturalism Act, declaring as its goal the preservation and enhancement of Canada's multicultural heritage, initiated in 1971, was passed in the House of Commons only in July 1988. Multiculturalism has been called the protective shell of Canadian-style tolerance, resulting in acceptance without concern (August 1974), and it has been blamed by Neil Bissoondath, a Canadian with an East Indian and Caribbean background, as *Selling Illusions* (1994) and as being based on stereotyping and ghettoizing tendencies. Instead of the differences highlighted by multiculturalism, Bissoondath calls for a greater concern with similarities in order to create a nation of cultural hybrids, where every individual is unique and distinct but also Canadian, undiluted, undivided, and unhyphenated. He thus expresses the idea of a cohesive, postcolonial society enlivened by cultural variety within a vigorous unity. This is a version of the "third way" between one-sided extremes developed in postcolonialism as well as in **cultural studies**.

Joy Kogawa equally thinks that the mixing of races and ethnicities is part of the Canadian identity and should not be deplored. Her novels *Obasan* (1981) and *Itsuka* (1990) trace the development of Canada and Japanese Canadians from World War II to the present and describe racism, injustice, and people fighting for redress. Her novels are postcolonial in their rewriting of a national history and giving voice to a muted ethnic group and are at the same time **postmodern** in their interweaving of poetry with autobiography, history, and fiction. Tomson Highway is also looking for the new voice, the new identity, the new tradition combining the best of both worlds in which he has lived, his native Cree culture and that of the white people with whom he grew up when he started school.

The difficulties that nonwhite immigrants to Canada encounter are extensively described by the various writers coming from the Caribbean, such as Bissoondath, Dionne Brand, Austin Clarke, Claire Harris, and Marlene Nourbese Philip. Racial and gender problems are presented, and the issue of finding a postcolonial identity in this mixture of cultures is always prominent. Michael Ondaatje, coming from a Sri Lankan background, has presented similar clashes between cultures in *In the Skin of a Lion* (1988) and *The English Patient* (1992). This literature expresses hope mainly with regard to individual people rather than in connection with abstract generalizations, deforming nation-states, or destructive cultures, which are presented in a state of disintegration and terminal disease, like the English patient. The position of immigrant writers always allows for another double perspective or stereoscopic vision on Canada, experiencing the old and the new cultures in an in-between stance that invites comparisons and evaluations as well as new combinations of styles, voices, and literary forms. This crossing of different perspectives often works as an anticolonial strategy or one that opposes totalitarian systems of all descriptions. The South Asian perspectives of Rohinton Mistry, M. G. Vassanji, or Arnold Itwaru again reveal the diversity of these writers, who are not an easily unifiable group.

Although Canada has from the beginning been a clearly hybrid culture often likened to a mosaic, unlike the U.S.–American melting pot, this concept has become really prominent in literature only since the 1960s, when extensive discussions about Canadian identity arose in the contexts of the threat of Quebec separation, civil rights movements, and the calling into question of all authorities, which has also led to postcolonialism. Representative examples of postcolonial writing implying reconstructions of standard genres, revisions of official history and the involvement of the neglected perspectives of natives are provided by Rudy Wiebe, for instance, in *The Temptation of Big Bear* (1973) and *The Scorched Wood People* (1977), where the languages, voices, and worlds of the British with their imperialist ideology and of the Plains Cree people, respectively, of the Métis political activist Louis Riel, are contrasted with each other, and orthodox British readings of history are replaced by different visions.

Postcolonial revisions of European, especially British cultural codes, often involving a rewriting of canonical European narratives, are provided by Margaret Laurence, whose *The Diviners* (1974) reallegorizes Shakespeare's *The Tempest*, Timothy Findley's revision of Conrad's *Heart of Darkness* in *Headhunter* (1993), or Ken Mitchell's use of *Othello* in his play *Cruel Tears* (1976). Thomas King's short story "One Good Story, That One" (1988) and his novel *Green Grass, Running Water* (1993) juxtapose the Bible with native creation myths and make fun of Christian rules and religious dogmas. As King puts it in the introduction to his anthology of contemporary Canadian native fiction, *All My Relations* (1990), the Judeo-Christian concern with good and evil, order and disorder, is replaced with the more native concern for balance and harmony. This concern implies the responsibility of every member of the universal family to live in a harmonious and moral manner with the others, their relations.

Regionalism has been an important aspect in Canadian literature at least since the 1920s novels of Raymond Knister, Martha Ostenso, and Frederick Philip Grove, but it has become particularly relevant since the 1960s, as it offers a sense of identity based on the land, the region. The material aspect of the country and its influence on the imagination as well as the workings of the imagination on the land are all equally important. This produces a new awareness of the constructedness of what is usually taken to be a simple fact of nature. Such awareness is of particular importance in the postcolonial context, as it raises similar questions of dominance, power, and political influence. Regionalism in Canada is inseparable from politics and (post)colonialism, as the identity of the Canadian West, for instance, depends as much on the literature of Ukrainian immigrants (such as Maara Haas and Myrna Kostash) as on that of writers with an Icelandic background (Kristjana Gunnars, Laura Goodman Salverson, William Valgardson) or a Japanese ancestry (Kogawa, Hiromi Goto, Roy Miki). For William H. New, *Articulating West* (1972), therefore, means much more than just a language with a regional bias; it is the articulation of the tension between order and disorder, myth and reality that is also found in postcolonial writing.

Robert Kroetsch has perhaps most consistently demonstrated the decreative energy of texts for a postmodern and postcolonial debunking of myths, ideologies, and traditional genres. For him the task of the Canadian writer is not to name experience but to un-name, to "uninvent" the world so that people can construct a new one. What Kroetsch (1989, 63) calls the "ultimate *contradiction*" is a typical paradox of **modernity**: "[P]eople uncreate themselves into existence." Only thus can they tackle the task of creating **narratives** and myths appropriate to their own experience. This constructive and postcolonial element in Kroetsch's deconstructive work is of particular importance in the literature of women, natives, and **ethnic** groups that acknowledge the need to construct an identity, however temporary, fragile, and fragmented.

Women have had an outstanding position in Canadian literature from the beginning, often presented as twice colonized and victimized, in the nation and also in patriarchal families. But women have not only described their subordination but also insisted on the constructedness and therefore the mutability of gender roles. Excellent examples are provided by Sandra Birdsell's *Agassiz Stories* (1987), Dionne Brand's *No Language Is Neutral* (1990), Marian Engel's *Bear* (1976), Mavis Gallant's *Home Truths* (1981), Aritha van Herk's *No Fixed Address* (1986), Daphne Marlatt's *Ana Historic* (1988), Alice Munro's *The Progress of Love* (1988), Sharon Pollock's *Blood Relations* (1981), Audrey Thomas' *Real Mothers* (1981), and the many other texts by women that interrogate history, power structures, traditional concepts of time, space, identity, and value and are in this respect also postcolonial.

In the **natives**' protests against political injustices, in their endeavors to rewrite Canadian history, to develop a new language and create a new sense of location out of the elements of the past, postcolonialism rings loud and clear, too. The natives' world is always rich with meaning, and life is not a straight line ending in death or an endless struggle for redemption but, as Highway, Drew Hayden Taylor, Emma LaRocque, and others put it, a continuous cycle and a joyous celebration. The idea of the relatedness of all things, animate and inanimate (humans, animals, the land, reality, and imagination), which is an essential part of native mythology, provides the postcolonialism of native literature with an extremely important holistic notion, necessary for the creation of meaningful identities (and also dominant in **constructionism**). One such explicitly postcolonial and revisionist work is Jeannette Armstrong's novel *Slash* (1985), dealing with racism, sexism, and classism as by-products of colonialism affecting natives in Canada. Armstrong identifies decolonization as the solution to systemic oppression but also as a long, painful process involving individuals and local communities as well as nations. The book also speaks of the need to create a vital third way between assimilation and extermination. Maria Campbell's *Halfbreed* (1973), Beatrice Culleton's *In Search of April Raintree* (1983), and Minnie Aodla Freeman's *Life among the Qallunaat* (1978) are also texts advancing a feminism of decolonization. It should be noted, though, that natives often reject the term "postcolonial," because they find it **Eurocentric** and unnecessarily restrictive in describing the cultural ferment that is going on in the Aboriginal community. Their work can be read for a critique of sexism, racism, colonialism, and economic exploitation as well as for its marks of cultural, not **essential** or universal, differences.

Other versions of Canada's past, present, and possible futures are now being written through people's awareness of, and involvement in, the complex discourses of multiculturalism and postcolonialism. Canada is often regarded as a positive example for other nations in the postcolonial context, because problems are not denied but relatively openly discussed and dealt with. It also often appears as a country in which the national aspect is less important than other ways of defining unity. Bissoondath's, Kogawa's, King's, or Highway's notions of "Canadian" are clearly different from 1950s concepts of the term, which, above all, meant "not American"; they also mean much more than simply French- or English-speaking, and they are certainly different from each other. But it is a difference that at the same time tries to establish or at least look for similarities as well, for new *relations*.

Further Reading: D. Brydon 1995; C. Klinck 1976, 1990.

Klaus-Peter Müller

Alejo Carpentier (1904, Havana, Cuba–1980, Paris, France) Without any doubt, Carpentier is one of the most significant writers of the twentieth century. Born in Cuba to a French father and a mother of Russian origin, he opted for writing in Spanish, which was not his first language, and he became one of the great masters of the Baroque writing in Spanish. As he himself said, "The Baroque is the legitimate style of the modern Latin American writer." Carpentier, who was the first Latin American writer to be recognized with the Miguel Cervantes Saavedra Prize of the Royal Academy of Spain, has one of the most substantial and prolific bodies of work in the narrative field: journalism, cultural promotion, essays, musicology, radio, and publicity. In his novels he laid the foundations for Latin America's literary renaissance after his naturalist precursors, thus giving rise to the so-called literary boom in Latin America.

In the prologue of his novel *El reino de este mundo* (The Kingdom of This World, 1949) Carpentier excoriates European surrealism for its empty falsity. He coined the term *lo real maravilloso* (marvelous reality), which was transported into the Latin American literary consciousness as "magical realism." This term appeared as a critical term for the arts, and later it extended to literature. It was first used by the German critic Franz Roh in 1925 to characterize a group of postexpressionist painters, but the term was later replaced by "new objectivity." Despite this change, the term **magic realism** survived to define a narrative tendency in Latin America from 1949 to 1970. The novel itself was inspired from a voyage to Haiti and is focused on the life of Ti Noël, a black slave within the historic background of a rebellion by another slave, Mackandal, whose objective was to establish an African kingdom on an island dominated by the French.

Another one of Carpentier's groundbreaking novels is the *Pasos perdidos*

(The Lost Steps, 1953), where the author looks back at nature and the unattainable possibility of utopia in the New World. In the end the return to nature in search of transcendent truths is but a Romantic notion. Civilization may offer modern humankind many ideas, but, unfortunately, there are no utopias left to escape from the contingencies of time, space, history, and culture. Like *El reino de este mundo*, this novel stems from travel experiences, this time in Venezuela. According to González Echevarría, *Los pasos perdidos* transcends the autobiographical experience and becomes a synthesis for the literary tradition of Latin America. This self-reflexive dimension, together with the heterogeneity evidenced in the multiple literary formats included (journal, autobiography, confession, anthropological field diary), leads to the questioning of the novel as a form of literary expression.

Carpentier's greatest contribution to Latin American literature seems to be his interpretation of history. He published several collections of short stories, among them *Guerra del tiempo* (Time War, 1958). Other novels by Carpentier include *El siglo de las luces* (The Century of Enlightenment, 1962), about the historical impact of the French Revolution on the Caribbean. In a masterly twist, Carpentier tells the story of the French Revolution from the perspective of Guadeloupe based on its only connection to France, the ever-sporadic mail service. News of events in France come by mail long after they had occurred there. The role of history and our interpretation of it is questioned in this novel.

Satire was not foreign to Carpentier. In *El recurso del método* (A Recourse of the Method, 1974) is a significant satire of the horrific Latin American dictatorships that were booming at that moment in South America. His account of the Cuban revolution, *La consagración de la primavera* (The Consecration of the Spring, 1978) has been widely criticized for its melodramatic, triumphalist overtones. However, the (unusual) interpretation of history and historical figures remained one of Carpentier's recurrent themes. In *El arpa y la sombra* (The Harp and the Shadow [1994]) Columbus is represented as a genius impostor.

Further Reading: Henighan 1999; Zamora 1997.

Silvia Nagy-Zekmi

Cartography   As a representation of the physical world, cartography seems innocent in its direct, if crude, representationalism. Etymologically, however, cartography signifies the drawing (from the Greek *gráphein*) of a chart (from the Latin *carta*), the latter of which is also antecedent of "charter," the listing of rights and rules, as in the British Magna C(h)arta. This contractual aspect of cartography is evident in the first known institutionalized mapping: the regulation of gardens in ancient Egypt to exact the pharaoh's taxes. The importance of cartography to the regulation, maintenance, and exploitation of areas shows why cartography has been integral to the political arena. European colonialism, for instance, would have been nigh impossible without cartography, and Britain's Great Survey of India, whose meticulous mapping took from 1802 to 1852, is but one example of the centrality of cartography to the control of foreign lands.

But although there has long been acknowledgment of the political ends to which cartography is frequently employed, what has rarely been acknowledged is the political nature of cartography as such. When Pythagoras, in the sixth century B.C.E., mapped the world at the center of a universe in which the distances to heavenly bodies correspond to musical intervals, he postulates an order and thus a truth to be found "outside" culture and cultural biases that, nevertheless, conforms to Greek epistemology and music theory. The fifth-century B.C.E. historian Herodotus locates Greece at the center of his map of the world, and six centuries later the most influential of Greek cartographers, Ptolemy, author of *Géographiké hyphégésis* (Guide to Geography), articulates both the scope and confident representationalism of his work when he writes that mapmaking "represent[s] in picture . . . the whole known world, together with the phenomena contained therein." Ptolemy provides latitudes and longitudes for some 8,000 places, and this geometric ordering of the earth is central to colonization, whose etymological roots reach to the Latin *colere*, to till, and thus "furrow" a land with lines of order and control. Mechanical advances (e.g., the magnetic compass and precise timepieces necessary for calculating longitude at sea) improved Europe's ability to order and thus colonize spaces and "the phenomena contained therein." But what is most interesting from a postcolonial perspective is understanding how—as evident already in ancient Greece—maps can confirm the "truth" of a culture's knowledges and thus "naturalize" imperial attitudes.

For instance, the T-form maps, called *mappaemundi*, of the Middle Ages divided the world into three parts: Europe, Asia, and Africa. From this "production of space" (to borrow the title of Henri Lefebvre's seminal 1974 book, *Production de l'espace*, trans. 1991) comes the continued practice of categorizing, as a continent, the appendage of Asia known as Europe—a spatial status (large and independent of Asia) integral to Europe's self-definition. Similarly, the placement of Jerusalem at the center of *mappaemundi* not only reflected and reproduced values of medieval Christianity but—under the presumption that it is human nature to protect that at the center of one's world—"naturalized" the Crusades. Postcolonial theory looks at how cartography works to make culturally specific stories into "verities" whose "grounding" in the "natural order" promotes and justifies the subjugation of others.

As **Edward W. Said** shows in both *Orientalism* (1978) and *Culture and Imperialism* (1993), European cartography has constituted an "imaginative geography" in the service of empire. These imaginings, as Derek Gregory discusses in *Geographical Imaginations* (1994), have produced "geographic anxieties" based on binary oppositions that **V. Y. Mudimbe** shows, in *The Idea of Africa*, map the outer region of Europe's medieval world as "objectively a *terra nullius* (noman's-land)." The "feminized" and virgin "blankness" of this outer region was seen by Europeans as in need of "masculine" exploration to open it up to Christianity and, eventually, foreign stewardship. Reinforcing these impetuses came science and the dualism of René Descartes' *res cogitans* and *res extensa*, which solidified an objectivist epistemology that understands itself capable of enframing reality in all its "truth," a truth confirmed by the profitability of European expansions.

Europe's expansions included measuring and naming physical features, flora, fauna, habitations, and peoples as part of a systematization whose supposed objectivity worked to delegitimate other systems of knowledge. In, for instance, Richard F. Burton's travel narrative *First Footsteps in East Africa* (1856), we have not only a title that erases the presence of peoples in East Africa but also a text whose maps and attention to latitudes, longitudes, and altitudes signify its "truth" in contradistinction to the superstitions generated by the "vacant mind[s]" of Africans. The "truth" of cartography confirms, for the colonizer, the "truth" and thus the ultimate beneficence of the colonial project, including that project's redefinition of places and the peoples who understand themselves in relation to those places.

Postcolonial thinking critiques colonial definitions of space as it works to develop alternatives to the divide-and-conquer geography that John Willinsky, in *Learning to Divide the World* (1998), characterizes as a "conceptual instrument that the West used both to divide up and to educate the world." Postcolonial thinking explores how to "map" the world in ways less violent to cultures and groups that have been and continue to be disrupted by political and cultural imperialisms; how, if not to achieve **Derek Walcott**'s "geography without myth," then at least what **Ngũgĩ wa Thiong'o**, in *Moving the Centre* (1993), calls "the right to name the world" as part of "recasting [that] world" (to adapt the title of a collection edited by Jonathan White) in ways that take seriously "non-Western" and "minority" cultures and systems of knowledge.

For instance, how does the division of the world into nations, Michael J. Shapiro asks in *Violent Cartographies* (1997), produce tension, conflict, even war? Should the "geographic imaginary" that we call "**nation**" be replaced by what Paul Gilroy, in *The Black Atlantic* (1993), calls a "transcultural reconceptualisation"? In *In My Father's House* (1992), Kwame Anthony Appiah proposes that a reconceptualization is under way when he notes that "Africa's postcolonial novelists . . . are no longer committed to the nation" as they search for other spatial conceptions for the organization of **identity**.

Understanding not only "nation as **narration**" (to quote **Homi Bhabha**, echoing **Benedict Anderson**'s *Imagined Communities*, 1983) but also ideas of East and West, First World and Third World, and even—as Martin W. Lewis and Karen E. Wigen in *The Myth of Continents* (1997) argue—landmasses as sociocultural constructions opens intellectual spaces for developing what **Edouard Glissant**, in *Caribbean Discourse* (1989), calls "cross-cultural relationship[s] . . . not fixed in one position." Although postcolonial theories of geography acknowledge the current necessity of nation to effect political change, a major goal is to move beyond the violence of the "either/or" logic of colonial and national discourses to develop multiple "hyphenated geographies" that form, shift, rupture, and reconfigure in quest of what Jacques Derrida, in "Violence and Metaphysics" (1978), calls "the lesser violence within an *economy of violence.*"

Postcolonial theory emphasizes that cartography is not Descartes' objectivist science discovering, like Archimedes from his theoretical point, the truth but is instead a "drawing" whose marks both shape and are shaped by not only discourses of science but also such discourses as politics, economics, and anthropology. This is not to propose that cartography is independent of the earth's physical features but merely to realize that lands are interpreted and in that interpretation constitute texts whose "readings" are inseparable from cultural concerns. The postcolonial concern to work toward a more ethical, equitable, and convivial world will necessarily redefine the imaginary lines with which we inscribe and divide our world.

Further Reading: D. Gregory 1994; J. Willinsky 1998.

Kevin Hickey

Center/Periphery (Related terms: metropolitan, metropole/marginality) The binary of center/periphery is a fundamental concept of **colonial discourse**, which **Edward Said** (1978) explains as a system that has organized the colonial and postcolonial world. According to this neat division, the colonizing center is home to science, order, and **modernity**, while the colonized periphery harbors superstition, chaos, and backwardness. Following this logic, the colonizing center must control these negative aspects of the periphery in order to protect both the center and the periphery from itself. This is also the principle according to which one of the purported goals of colonialism was to "raise up" the colonized. Numerous challenges have pointed out the contradictions in this binary logic. Based in spatial and geographical concepts, the dichotomy of center/periphery might seem to carry the supposed impartiality of topography. As numerous writers have noted, however, whatever the objective topography may be, mapping it is an intensely subjective and power-determined experience. Whose center and whose periphery, after all, are in question? Since the early eighteenth century, the West has had the power to arrogate to itself the position of center by marking all else as peripheral. Colonial relations have involved a particularly brutal application of this practice, although, as Said has noted, this division was also constructed by those without colonial possessions or, in some cases, even pretensions. As in most dichotomies, the two sides are involved in an unequal relationship in which the first term is privileged.

The simple installation of a new person or group in the role of power does nothing to weaken the dichotomy that says some cultures and peoples are central and important, and others are not. The end of colonization did not mean the end of this dichotomy. Thus, following many colonial independence struggles, a newly independent **nation** might relegate some part of itself to the margin or suppress it altogether in order to reassert the centrality of its own existence. Algeria, for example, has ignored its Berber populations, while proclaiming itself a unified Arab nation. This kind of nationalism has been critiqued as a **mimicry** of the imperial logic of the colonizing center. **Frantz Fanon** was perhaps one of the first to note that if newly independent nations merely replaced the former colonizer with a new elite imbued with European ideals and education, they were likely to continue imperialist values in the name of **decolonization**.

The distinction between center and margin is, of course, not solely geographic, as can be seen in a colonial context where the colonizer culturally and politically belongs to the center, while physically living in the colonial periphery. In contrast, the colonized subject who travels to the colonizing center for education or work, no matter how much metropolitan culture he or she may acquire and internalize, will remain in terms of power and political status on the periphery. **Benedict Anderson** (1983) discusses this movement of colonized individuals from the colonized margin to the colonizing center and back again. No matter how long the individual may remain in the metropole for education, he (and it was usually men who made this journey) must eventually return to the periphery, even if to another section of the periphery.

Albert Memmi, among many others, notes the intertwined relationship between center and periphery in the person of the colonizer and colonized but asserts that the line between colonizer and colonized or center and periphery may be crossed only by becoming what is on the other side. Should the colonized assimilate so far as to aspire to colonizer status, he endangers the entire colonial enterprise since, without a colonized subject, there can be no colonial system and hence no colonizer. The colonizer must therefore guard against any change in the status quo. Perhaps for this reason, the logic of the colonial binary allows for no differentiation regarding class or gender within either side of the binary. All members of the periphery, just as all members of the center, must conform to certain criteria; any variation simply cannot be accounted for within the dichotomy.

Several other writers, including figures as diverse as Said and **Homi Bhabha**, have described the importance of the binary in creating and maintaining a colonial power structure. They also note, however, the fragility of the structure. In this regard Bhabha, for example, has examined issues surrounding the profound ambivalence of the stereotype. Bhabha's discussions of stereotypes (1994) are particularly relevant to the dichotomy of center/periphery. In his formulation, a stereotype recognizes and denies difference at the same time, thus rendering the colonized subject both Other and completely knowable. This double status, however, means that the supposed **essential** difference is always in danger of being unmasked as a fraud, thus revealing that the difference between center and margin is equally precarious. This is all the more true in that the fixed **identity** of the colonized is one of unpredictability. The stereotype must be constantly repeated in order to allay the colonizer's fear that perhaps the colonized are not so different after all.

The distinction between center and margin has been forcefully challenged in practice by immigrants and the children of immigrants living in the metropolitan center. Immigrants are located geographically in the center while occupying politically and culturally the periphery, a situation that undermines clear distinctions between center and periphery. This situation is reproduced in spatial arrangements in many European cities, where low-income housing developments and their large immigrant communities are relegated to the outskirts of major cities. The children of immigrants, although often born in the metropolitan center, nonetheless find that the center is unwilling to recognize them as full members. These immigrant communities have increasingly put into question the dichotomy that places them culturally and politically on the periphery of European cities even as they establish themselves in the heart of Europe. The most interesting challenges, however, are not asking for inclusion in an already defined center but instead claiming the right to determine what the center will look like. Some fiction by **Beur** writers in France, for example, argues that having been born and educated in France, they are as French as anyone in France, and therefore what they contribute to French culture must be considered French.

A center implies a monolithic nation opposed to outside forces, cultures, and peoples. This conception of the center, however, depends on a narrow conception of what goes into making it and an obsessive concern with borders. Much postcolonial literature seeks to underscore the way the center is and always has been home to the supposed periphery as well and how the boundaries between the two may not be at all clear. Franco-Algerian writer Leila Sebbar, for example, not only portrays the contributions of the periphery to the center but reminds her readers of how the two have always been involved. In her *Shérazade* (1982) trilogy, for instance, she recalls Arthur Rimbaud in order to discuss his and his family's connections to Africa. She does not seek to create a new canon or center but merely points to connections that have always existed. As well as dividing people, the dichotomy center/periphery has been used to divide cultural works. Again, the division between the two sides of this dichotomy are anything but clear. Writers from the so-called periphery (whether that of the colony or of the *banlieue* [suburbs]) both before and after the end of formal colonization have sought to publish in the metropole, usually for a European readership. While this may be due, in part, to the economics of publishing (European presses tend to have bigger budgets and a larger readership), it is also related to the sometimes very real pressures of censorship in the former colony. As Hafid Gafaiti (1997) has observed, after independence newly established national publishing houses expected writers to contribute to national rebuilding with literature that emphasized content over form and demonstrated a commitment to the political direction of the new nation. Since these national publishing houses often monopolized the national publishing market, experimental and oppositional writers have often had little choice but to publish in the former colonial center. As Christopher Miller (1998) notes, the situation was similar under colonialism, as, for example, in France when work by the colonized was published in the metropole even as its distribution was banned in the colony.

In a postcolonial context, when publishing in the metropolitan center, a writer is most often obliged to publish in the language of the center, especially if he or she is aiming for a large European or American readership. That the writer is competent in this language or may even speak it as a first language is often due to cultural policies of the former colonizer, which seek to maintain cultural and linguistic ties where military and political ties may have been severed at independence. Thus, for example, France's Ministry of Culture sees to the establishment of centers of French language and culture in its former colonies and encourages the spread or maintenance of **francophone literature**. Ironically, the promotion of *francophonie* throughout former colonies and other areas of influence excludes France itself, which, while it may produce French literature, does not produce francophone literature. This distinction is re-created on bookstore shelves in France, where literature is divided into French (i.e., from France) and francophone (i.e., everything else written in French but not from France). Even after colonialism the periphery must not be allowed to be confused with the center. Remarkably, this same distinction is sometimes applied to literature produced by immigrants and children of immigrants residing in France who produce works in French—as though to underscore their permanent status as members of the periphery, albeit a periphery located within the geopolitical boundaries of France itself. Work like Sebbar's and that of other postcolonial writers is often productively read through the lens of **transculturation**. For good or ill, cultures interact, and texts travel.

Transculturation as described by Françoise Lionnet is a process wherein texts, traditions, and symbolic systems interact and, through exchange, affect each other. Lionnet's interpretation of transculturation, like Gérard Genette's ideas regarding intertextuality, is concerned with the relation of different cultural texts to each other. Intertextuality refuses a boundary between a textual center and margin and even among different centers, as the texts of different nations mingle. In their most positive incarnations, texts like Sebbar's succeed in showing the chimerical aspect of any distinction between center and margin. The resulting hybridity, or *métissage*, to use Lionnet's term, has been proposed as an alternative to the rigid center/periphery dichotomy. The promotion of *francophonie* and the continuation of French cultural hegemony, however, have been seen by many as one downside of such works. Others have argued that theories of *métissage* and hybridity ignore the unequal power relationship between those whose cultures are blending to form a hybrid newness. Even if the relationship could be equalized, maintaining a concept of center/periphery maintains the center as the location of all power and value (whoever may occupy it), leaving others without power or value. Still others, like Fanon, mentioned earlier, have argued that valorizing hybridity risks moving a new group into the center rather than deconstructing and eliminating the idea of center altogether.

Abdelkebir Khatibi raises many of the same issues in his discussion of marginality. What is particularly disturbing about the binary logic of center/periphery is that it purports to account for everyone and everything. There is no acknowledgment that individuals and their experiences may not always fall neatly into a system of classification. According to Khatibi, the only way to confront such a binary is to subvert it, and for that he advocates what he calls plural thought, which acknowledges that it cannot encompass all. Whereas totalizing thought, according to Khatibi, is the kind of thought that seeks to dominate and control, plural thought allows for people and ideas that might fall right at the bar between center and periphery. Thought that arises from its poverty as Khatibi calls it (and here he is not referring to material poverty but rather to thought that acknowledges its own incomplete character) allows one to imagine a space between the dichotomy of center and margin.

Further Reading: H. Bhabha 1994; A. Khatibi 1983.

Annedith M. Schneider

Aimé Césaire (1913–) Internationally renowned for his poetry, dramas, postcolonial theory, and statesmanship, Aimé Césaire is widely acclaimed for his demand for a valorization of African culture and advocacy of self-determination for blacks throughout the world. An important figure in world history, his life and politics straddled both sides of colonialism, first as a colonized subject of the French empire in Martinique, then as representative of a self-governed Martinique in the French National Assembly. He first came to international attention during the 1940s, when, as a student in Paris, he became a leading proponent of an artistic and political movement called **negritude**. Begun primarily as a reaction against white Western cultural domination, negritude sought to situate a critical racial identity for blacks against colonial oppression. His long poem, *Cahier d'un retour au pays natal* (Return to My Native Land, 1939), is widely considered his masterpiece; the poem typifies both his adoption and adaptation of surrealism as a movement that postulates liberation from Western rationalism and, by extension, advocates political liberation as well. Lesser known is Césaire's *Discours sur le colonialisme* (Discourse on Colonialism, 1972), where Césaire anticipates many of the concerns of later postcolonial theory. Césaire's role as artist, theorist, and statesman has had a profound effect on the role that blacks play in aesthetics and politics.

Born in the French Caribbean colony of Martinique, Césaire grew up experiencing the poverty and oppression of the island's black population. At the age of eighteen he won scholarships to study literature and philosophy in Paris at the École Normale Supérieure. Paris of the 1930s was a political and cultural center for movements such as surrealism and **Marxism**. As a young student, Césaire met Léon Damas and Léopold Sédar Senghor and began to construct an aesthetic that was influenced by the aesthetic revolutionary potential of surrealism and the political revolutionary potential of Marxism. The friends founded a magazine entitled *L'Étudiant Noir* (Black Student), in which Césaire first developed his notion of negritude. By claiming the inherent value of black culture and averting their contemporaries' gaze away from the supposed superiority of French culture, Césaire and negritude set the stage for many political changes that would take place after the war. Césaire fully developed his notion of negritude in his long poem *Return to My Native Land*. First published in 1939 in the magazine *Volontés*, a second version appeared in 1944 with a preface by French surrealist André Breton; finally, a definitive addition was published in 1956. The long poem is broken into three parts and mirrors Césaire's own return to Martinique. The first part is written while still in Paris and is a reflection on the poverty and oppression visited upon Césaire's native land. It is also, more importantly, a diagnosis of the psychological effects that colonization has on the black inhabitants; colonization has perpetuated a self-loathing that continually undermines access to empowerment. In the second part, Césaire returns to Martinique and moves toward claiming his negritude by trying to loosen the hold of French rationality that has instilled the defeatism of his people. In the final section, Césaire adopts a new language of negritude, which he links to the volcanic eruptions that created Martinique. Calling upon and inventing a language of explosive, dynamic, and life-giving energy, Césaire sought to situate his poetics themselves within his native culture and land. The power that Césaire evinced in this important work led surrealist André Breton to claim that this work was "nothing less than the greatest lyrical monument of our time" (1971, 17). While Césaire's poetics of negritude seemed to have some surrealist heritage, it is equally true that Césaire was not recognized as having any surrealist lineage until Breton came to the island while fleeing World War II. This marked, from the very beginning of his writing career, Césaire's ability to traverse worlds. His work was simultaneously empowering for blacks against their French oppressors and warmly adopted by a series of well-respected white French intellectuals from Breton to Jean-Paul Sartre.

Césaire remained in Martinique during the war, and he and his wife, Suzanne Roussi, took posts as teachers in Césaire's former school in the capital of Martinique, Fort-de-France. During this time, he turned to more engaged forms of politics; he officially joined the Communist Party and was elected as the mayor of Fort-de-France and the deputy for Martinique in the French National Assembly. In 1941 Césaire founded the literary journal *Tropiques*, which continued his commitment to blacks' right to self-determination and also, with Breton in Martinique, reinforced Césaire's adaptation of surrealist poetic techniques in the service of negritude. Over the next decade Césaire was a prolific poet, publishing several volumes of negritude poems. He published *Les armes miraculeuses* (Miraculous Weapons, 1946), *Soliel cou-coupé* (Beheaded Sun, 1948), and *Corps perdu* (Lost Body, 1950). The style of the volumes is often reductively referred to as surrealist; rather than being a mere continuation of the project begun by

Breton, Césaire's poetics continued to be animated by the linkage to the African, the land, and the violence of slaves against their masters. Césaire actualized the notion of the slave's using the master's language against him. He enacted a violence against the French language itself in a mode that radically displaced the rationality that constructed the system responsible for the subjugation of blacks.

By 1950 Césaire launched a direct attack against fascism and imperialism in his *Discours sur le colonialisme* (Discourse on Colonialism, 1950). Often ignored as just a theoretical diversion from his more important literary work, *Discourse on Colonialism* had a profound effect on such thinkers as **Frantz Fanon** and helped to establish Césaire as one of the leading figures in what came to be known as postcolonial theory. Coming in the aftermath of World War II, his book is a wide-sweeping critique of the West in light of its fight against fascism. After a war in which the "civilized" countries of Europe fought against any notions of racial superiority, Césaire points out the fact that most European countries are hanging on to their colonies with a similar view of racial superiority that is conflated with a version of **humanism**. He challenges the insidious effects of the West's notion of humanism, which claims a certain universality, all the while at the expense of humans who supposedly don't conform to the categories that are established as universal. In a manner that would greatly influence and adumbrate similar theories from Fanon, **Homi Bhabha**, and **Edward Said**, Césaire also attacked the "discourses of civility" that were promulgated by colonizers. In the name of the betterment of humanity, Césaire argues, colonizers imposed Western culture with a notion of racial superiority and effaced the distinctiveness of local cultures. This theoretical gesture is important for his later aesthetics as he traces out what occurs when blacks inherit and internalize notions of their own inferiority. Ultimately, *Discourse on Colonialism* indicts the West for perpetuating the same totalitarianism that it had declared itself against. This maneuver shored up the deep paradoxes in Western thought that animated the disgraceful maintenance of colonies after World War II.

Césaire's commitment to communism, as for many Western intellectuals, was revoked in 1956, when the Stalinist Soviet Union invaded Hungary. Césaire's many hesitations and rejections of communism are outlined in his *Lettre à Maurice Thorez* (Letter to Maurice Thorez, 1956). This led to the founding of the Martinique Progressive Party in 1957, of which Césaire was elected president. During the 1960s, he continued to produce volumes of poetry, *Ferrements* (Shackles, 1960) and *Cadastre* (1961). *Ferrements* is a pun on both political ferment and the shackles worn by black slaves—a continuation of his project both to call attention to colonial oppression and to invoke blacks to recognize the ways in which they've adopted the shackles. However, the 1960s was dominated by Césaire's turn toward the theater as a site where he felt he could have more direct political effect. Perhaps in response to critics who claimed that his poetry was too erudite and therefore too alienating for the very readers whom he was trying to reach, perhaps as a counter to Stalinist realism, Césaire's plays reestablished his importance for thinking about colonial/postcolonial issues.

Césaire's first play was written in 1956 in the surrealist-inflected language of the poetry from that period. *Et les chiens se taisaient* (And the Dogs Were Quiet, 1956) is primarily an attack on the Caribbean people whose deep apathy left those who attempted to lead in lonely and tragic positions. This was to be a constant theme for most of his important dramas of the 1960s. *La tragedie du roi Christophe* (The Tragedy of King Christophe, 1963) is a biographical dramatization about revolutionary hero Henri Christophe, who led a successful revolution against French colonists in Haiti and became Haiti's king from 1811 to 1820. Eventually, there is a rebellion by the black inhabitants, who oppose what they see as his despotic authority; the result is the suicide of Christophe. The play at once celebrates the rebellion against colonial rule and lauds one of the most important rulers in Caribbean history. At the same time, Césaire makes scathing claims against the Haitians, who believed that revolution means taking the place of the French oppressors to the extent of putting down other blacks just as the French did. Césaire problematizes the role of revolution by questioning who suffers in the name of a concept inherited from the very people against whom they are revolting. Césaire was also making a commentary against the various despots who adopted heroic and revolutionary pretensions in postcolonial Africa. This play also marked his evacuation of his surrealist-inflected writing and a turn toward a cycle of plays that took as their focus the historic struggles of blacks against colonial oppression.

Une saison au Congo (A Season in the Congo, 1967) continued the historical cycle by focusing on Patrice Lumumba, the first president of the Republic of the Congo in 1960. Like *Christophe*, the play follows Lumumba's struggles to liberate his people from Belgian colonial rule, follows him through successful revolution and, independence and, finally, to his assassination by competing political opponents in 1961. Césaire again problematizes the use of power within the revolutionary modes adopted by the Africans against their oppressors. In this play, Lumumba is portrayed as a messianic figure who is martyred by his own people. Césaire intended to complete this historical cycle with a play about the assassinated black Muslim leader Malcolm X in America. Never completed, Césaire's intention was to underscore once again the deep division in black consciousness, which, instead of unifying blacks throughout the world, has incorporated the contention against blacks that has been enacted against them for centuries.

Perhaps Césaire's most popular play is *Une tempête: adaptation pour un théâtre nègre* (1969). As an adaptation of Shakespeare's *The Tempest*, Césaire's play takes on one of the most revered texts of the English language to shore up the deep racism that pervades its structure—especially in the context of the colonial annexing of Caribbean islands. Césaire recasts the characters of *The Tempest* to highlight the imperialist structure and racial conflict of the Shakespearean original. In Césaire's *A Tempest*, Prospero is considered a white colonialist, Ariel is a mulatto slave who capitulates to Prospero's wishes, and Caliban, the hero of Césaire's play, is a black slave who is unwilling to serve Prospero. Ultimately, Caliban refuses to allow Prospero to name him, insists on being referred to as "X," and begins a revolt against Prospero's tyranny. The revolution is unsuccessful but results in X's and Prospero's insistence of a claim to the island and the proclamation that they will resist each other with violence if necessary.

Césaire's *Oeuvres complètes* was compiled in 1976 and does not, therefore, include his work since that time. Continuing to be active in politics and writing, Césaire published *Moi, laminaire* (Me, Laminar) in 1982. He also continued to serve as mayor of Fort-de-France until 1983 and as Martinican deputy of the French National Assembly until 1993. Césaire has been criticized for being too strictly tied to Europe in his conceptions of negritude. In the political sphere, he has always argued for a continued relationship of Martinique to France instead of complete independence; meanwhile, his aesthetics appear to be dominated by the very colonizers against whom he is arguing. His choice to continue to write in French, for example, is seen by some as a capitulation to imperialism. Some, however, argue that this is precisely Césaire's strength: his ability to traverse the French world and the black world. The very fact that he grew up learning a colonizer's language was what animated his attack against the "master's" language. Further, Césaire's relationship to surrealism is often overstated. Both Césaire and Breton have accounts that demonstrate that Césaire had begun to revolt against the French language in advance of his experience with surrealist doctrine. At Breton's urging in 1944 Césaire attempted to use surrealism to heighten negritude's poetics. It is precisely from the position of both a colonized subject and one who is able to participate in the colonizer's world that Césaire was able to have such dramatic and important effects on both how the French perceived their colonies and how the colonized blacks were able to envision themselves within and against the colonial system.

Further Reading: A. J. Arnold 1981; S. Frutkin 1973.

Erich Hertz

Patrick Chamoiseau   The winner of numerous literary prizes, Patrick Chamoiseau studied law in Paris before returning to his native Martinique. He is the author of many novels, including *Solibo Magnificent* (1988/1997), and *Chronicle of the Seven Sorrows* (1986/1999), as well as nonfiction work, including his most controversial, *Eloge de la Créolité* (1989). Cowritten with Jean Bernabé and Raphaël Confiant, it challenges **Aimé Césaire** and his **"negritude"** movement, criticizing its relevance to contemporary Martinican society. In this text, the authors introduce a new approach to conceptualizing Martinique and its relationship with the Caribbean and France through "Créolité": a political and linguistic manifesto that emphasizes the multicultural and hybrid nature of the island and supports the establishment of **Creole** as the true linguistic expression of Martinique.

In 1992, Chamoiseau won France's prestigious Prix Goncourt for *Texaco*. A historical novel that spans the period of slavery and the end of the plantation economy, it is written in an ever-changing voice through Chamoiseau's creative use of Creole and French. Indeed, the search for an authentic linguistic expression is central to Chamoiseau's work. In *School Days* (1994/1997), children are encouraged to favor the French language over the native Creole. It is ironic that Chamoiseau himself has had to resort to using the French language to portray his Creole identity, a common dilemma in postcolonial studies. Following a similar theme, *Strange Words* (1998) emphasizes the importance of oral tradition. In this collection of Creole folktales, Chamoiseau's voice, as the storyteller, is punctuated throughout his writing as the storyteller's voice breaks in the middle of the stories, imparting an interactive quality to the text. The richness of this work lies in its engagement with the reader, and while the customary responses from an audience are missing, the emergent voice of the storyteller is very evident, establishing his ease with the written word.

Further Reading: D. Anderson 1995; C. Bongie 1998; S. Cudjoe 1980; L. Taylor 1998.

Grace Ebron

Chicano/a Studies   Chicano/a studies aims to focus attention on the knowledge systems—including history, culture, and politics—of Mexican-heritage U.S. residents and to authorize the development of a unique sense of self within a white-dominant mainstream that has historically denied the brown subject **agency**. Chicano/a critical theory gravitates around themes such as the politics of authorship, canonicity, exile and diaspora, and home and dislocation.

The field of inquiry grew out of the powerful civil rights wave of Chicano/a activism/intellectualism, making the Chicano/a's layered history as a colonized subject—the victim of both Euro-Spanish conquests of Latin America and Euro-Anglo imperialism in the United States—increasingly visible. During the first wave of postcolonial critique and **resistance**, Chicano/a activist intellectuals sought to intervene primarily at the political and cultural levels. In 1969 a cultural nationalist manifesto, "el plan espiritual de Aztlan," unified Chicanos/as across the Southwest, making visible en masse their unique culture and history of marginalization. While "el plan" spurred many writers to symbolically reclaim the Southwest from the Anglo colonizers (see Rudolfo A. Anaya's *Bless Me, Ultima* [1972], *Heart of Aztlan* [1981], and *Tortuga* [1979]), it wasn't only a cultural model. Coupled with civil rights protests, "el plan" led to the strong celebration of Indian heritage.

As much as this first wave gave shape to, and positively valenced, "Chicanismo," its Us-vs.-Them racialized model reproduced the dominant system's exclusivity, ignoring those who didn't pass racial litmus tests and oppressing women, gays, and lesbians. Soon the publication of *This Bridge Called My Back*

(1981), an anthology edited by Cherrie Moraga and Gloria Anzaldúa, introduced a powerful new wave of Chicana **feminist** critique of these **essentializing** paradigms: in Aztlan one wouldn't heroize men and relegate women to the kitchen. Chicana writers and intellectuals such as Anzaldúa, Moraga, Norma Alarcon, Sonia Saldivar Hull, Rosa Linda Fregosa, and Chela Sandoval have further **decolonized** and denaturalized the hierarchies between brown and white, man and woman, straight and **queer**. They have revised the old-school, patriarchy-based Chicano counterhegemonic narratives. For example, in *Borderlands/La Frontera* (1987), Anzaldua dismantles the hypermacho, heterosexist idea of Aztlan to celebrate a more diasporic-mestiza-feminist- and *atravisado* (border crosser)-inclusive borderland subjectivity. She writes, "As a mestiza I have no country, my homeland cast me out; yet all countries are mine because I am every woman's sister or potential lover. As a lesbian I have no race, my own people disclaim me; but I am all races because there is the queer of me in all races" (88). According to Anzaldúa, at the social and economic outer edges—oppressed because of phenotype, gender, and class—the mestiza becomes the ultimate site for contestation of the status quo. To survive, the mestiza slips and slides through different modes of existence, all while exposing the Euroamerican mainstream's strategies to contain the ethnic subject. Norma Alarcón (1993) celebrates a mestiza subject who, along with her Third World sisters, must construct "provisional identities" to actively inhabit cultural, racial, and gendered hybrid zones within the historical and imaginary shifting national borders of Mexico and the United States Chicana feminist critics have dramatically altered the way that ethnic **identity** is understood today, creating an oppositional "bridge consciousness" for expressions of difference.

Riding along this second wave's crest is an articulation of the Chicano/a as existing within borderlands of racial, sexual, and gendered identity. Such a move to articulate the Chicano/a as a hybrid, borderland subject has redeployed the Western-origin view of reality and its construction of the mestizo/a subject as a distorted "other." In much the same vein as Indo-British postcolonial critics, Chicano/a critics define postcolonial identity not as a reinforcement of, but as a hybrid, simultaneous mocking and **mimicking** of, (neo-)colonial authority. As Tomas Ybarro Frausto writes of Chicano/a art generally, the "rasquache" aesthetic of recycling and invention grows out of having to inhabit in-between racial, cultural, geopolitical spaces. Alfred Arteaga (1997) uses the Nahuatl poetic device known as *"difrasimo"* (a single idea expressed in two words) as the template for articulating a Chicano/a identity that performs with a double voice (Spanish/indigenous, Mexican/American, Castillian/English); in his model, a single self contains many selves, and speech acts with multiple meanings and layers (what he defines as "heterotexts"), slipping and sliding between restrictive racial, cultural, sexual, and national paradigms. José David Saldívar (1997) similarly defines an in-between subjectivity, looking to contemporary literary, visual, and aural aesthetics. Saldívar discusses the ways a punk group such as Los Illegals and a rap artist such as Kid Frost reflect the hybridizing borderland ideal of

Tijuana—a city that resists categorization. In a like mode, performance artist and intellectual Guillermo Gómez-Peña clears space for a more complicated Chicano identity. In his performances, the old-school paradigms—brown versus white, Chicano versus Mexican, pre-Columbian pastoral versus Western super-tech modern—are remapped. Gómez-Peña portrays the "other" 's shape-shifting tactics for evasion and subversion, as the structures that contain and control the racialized subject become increasingly sophisticated—as infrared panoptic surveillance cameras and supercharged Jet Ranger helicopters patrol U.S./Mexican borders, for example. Of course, while such transborder critics and performance artists endeavor to denaturalize hierarchies of difference, they build into their critiques a strong awareness of the violent marks that those real borders leave on **subaltern** bodies and consciousnesses.

Further Reading: G. Anzaldua 1987; G. Padillo 1993; R. Perez-Torres 1995; V. Ruiz 1998; J. Saldívar 1997; R. Saldivar 1990; T. Ybarra-Frausto 1991.

Frederick Luis Aldama

Chinese Literatures   China's reaction to the phenomenon of semicolonialism has yielded profound consequences for modern Chinese literatures. From the mid-nineteenth-century Opium Wars through 1949, China's national identity and its literature were fractured due largely to the various waves of colonial on-slaught. Though not enveloped by European powers the way that some colonized societies were, the partition of China's lifeline, the coastal treaty ports where most intellectuals live, carried with it the powerful hegemonic discourse of **mo-dernity**, a discourse that legitimates the linear trajectory of Western history. This legitimating discourse has depicted traditional China as a refractory society, obsessed with its own particular problems, set against the West, which suppos-edly embodies the universal culture of **humanism**. The struggle between the alleged universal, which is "modern" and "individual," versus the particular, a China that is misogynist in its treatment of women and superstitious in its prac-tice of religion and science, pervades modern Chinese literature. The thematic battleground for this struggle has been subjectivity; the structural one has been language. Filiality constituted the traditional Chinese subject position, a rela-tional subjectivity operating within a web of rituals designed to integrate oneself into an ancestral, patriarchal line. One became a "self" by performing certain memorial rituals that sought to revivify deceased ancestors. This was codified in ancient Confucian texts and reworked countless times in traditional Chinese literature. Though long and complex, modern Chinese literature has moved from an ambivalent attitude toward traditional culture, to radical critique, and back to a modified celebration or at least a fascination with it.

The anachronism of traditional Chinese language and ideology is no more pointedly laid bare than in Liu E's *The Travels of Lao Can* (1907). Though structured along the lines of a traditional Chinese novel, the themes—the utter debasement of Chinese culture, governmental corruption, and the emergence of the West as the great, global challenge—reflect a profound shift in the concerns of Chinese literature. In it, the protagonist Lao Can roams the Chinese landscape, encountering various inequities of feudal China. At points the work is dreamy and allegorical, such as when Lao Can imagines an imperiled ship with crew and passengers at each other's throats. In their distrust of modern (read "foreign") invention, they refuse the use of a compass to guide them to safety. The novel progresses in a desultory fashion, with the only constant thread being Lao Can, the iconoclast with superior insight yet with no one to appreciate and utilize his talents. Just as the eremitic intellectual Lao Can is shown to be insignificant in his attempt to "save" Chinese society, the novel itself similarly identifies social problems but doesn't possess the language to fully articulate them. It would take something far more revolutionary to transform Chinese culture.

Lu Xun and the "May Fourth" generation of writers turned the ambivalence of Liu E into an unremitting critique of Chinese culture itself, ill equipped in its parochial obsessions and superstitious ways. A protest against the forcible ceding of Chinese territory to the Japanese as part of the 1919 Treaty of Versailles, members of the May Fourth movement expressed unprecedented disaffection with traditional Chinese values and social institutions even while they became more nationalistic in their desire to recast China in the mold of Enlightenment nation-building. Lu Xun exemplifies the spirit of May Fourth, a paradoxical notion that suggested that traditional culture must be repudiated in order to save the nation. In works such as "Kong Yiji" (1919), whose name alludes to Confucius, Lu Xun attacks the traditional scholar elite and unveils the callousness with which ordinary people treat each other. Suggesting that traditional Chinese culture is "cannibalistic," Lu Xun appropriates colonial imagery to interrogate Chinese culture in stories such as "Medicine" (1919) and "Diary of a Madman" (1918). "Diary of a Madman," the first genuinely modern work of Chinese fiction, works simultaneously on the levels of language and ideology. Ideologically, it critiques filial rituals and popular "superstitions" regarding herbal medicine. Linguistically, "Diary of a Madman" performs the conflict between the archaic language of classical Chinese and a new, more flexible modern vernacular. Lu Xun's radical critique, revolutionary style, and precision as a writer have guaranteed his place as the first and most important, truly modern Chinese author. The dissolution of the subject and the difficulty in representing the peasantry in elite discourse are the central themes of his short story "New Year's Sacrifice" (1924). The story is told from the point of view of a modern, rather self-satisfied intellectual, stripped of his pretense by an illiterate peasant woman. She asks if "there *really* is a soul after death?" He attempts to placate her by saying there is. But she responds by asking if the soul then could continue to suffer. Realizing the implications of his hasty appeasement, he escapes her queries. She has rendered him silent, reversing the representational apparatus so that the silenced one, the illiterate **subaltern**, quells the voice of the intellectual. The narrator then recalls the peasant woman's plight, which delineates the breakdown of the traditional Chinese subject position.

Ding Ling, the most important modern Chinese female author, extended Lu Xun's exploration of the psyche and experimentation with language in her fictional narrative "Miss Sophia's Diary" (1927). The diary consists of several passages written in a seemingly haphazard style that actually restructures Chinese in the form of European syntax. Sophia, a European name whose root, "sophos," means "to be clever" presents the reader with a stunning narrative of female subjectivity—sexual, tempestuous, hypochondriacal, and helplessly smitten by a half European businessman from Singapore who touts the speeches of Woodrow Wilson and avidly reads the English newspapers. All the rage in Shanghai at the time, "Miss Sophia's Diary" positions the modern female individual in direct opposition to traditional Chinese patriarchy.

After 1949, literature was divided between socialist realism in mainland China, made up primarily of long communist hagiographies of war, land reform, and other topics, and modernist tendencies among writers who mainly published in Taiwan. Reminiscent of Lu Xun, the Taiwan-based Wang Wenxing's *Family Catastrophe* (1971) addresses the conflict between traditional Chinese filiality and the emergence of the individual subject in language that continues to contest premodern literary and linguistic norms. Yet, unlike Lu Xun, whose critique is radical and absolute, Wang Wenxing's is ultimately open-ended, doubly inscribed, and deeply ambivalent. The reader cannot confidently ascertain whether the author is condemning traditional culture or illustrating the negative characteristics of a subject trapped between tradition and modernity. The novel features Fan Ye, searching for his missing father. The search takes place in the narrative present, interspersed with flashbacks recounting the history of the family. From the history, we learn of the uneasy relationship between the son, an individualist enamored of European writings, and father, who bemoans his son's lack of filial respect and scorn for ritual obeisances. As the novel depicts the split in the character's psyche between the traditional "filial" subject and the modern, atomized one, it also expresses this stylistically through the bifurcated narrative, one line of which is antifilial in tone, the other of which is nostalgic. The language of the antifilial narrative is colloquial, modern vernacular, punctuated with neologisms. A newspaper ad beseeching the father to return, written in classical Chinese, begins almost all passages of the nostalgic narrative. The result is arguably the most uniquely constructed literary text in modern Chinese fiction.

Such literary experimentation did not come to the People's Republic of China (PRC) until after the death of Mao and fall of the Gang of Four. Recent Nobel laureate Gao Xingjian was a bold innovator in the late 1970s and early 1980s whose appropriations from French modernism largely echoed those done in Taiwan during the late 1950s. Perhaps the most concerted attempt to reassert the power of an independent, educated elite has come from the "Seeking Roots" writers who have turned once again to a fascination with rural folk and traditional Chinese cultural practice. Wang Anyi's *Baotown* (1985), for example, is at once a limpid, endearing story of village life in rural China and a searing critique of the representational apparatuses of party-sanctioned socialist realism. Returning to the subject of filiality and the problem of language, Wang Anyi presents Dregs, an ordinary boy posthumously canonized as a socialist hero. Dregs befriends Old Fifth Grandfather, the last of his line, who bemoans not having an heir to carry on his ancestral line. Dregs almost instinctively serves as a filial surrogate to the old man and even gives his life trying to rescue him from a flood. Wang Anyi's insertion of an additional level of narration, the literate peasant Bao Renwen, allows her to illustrate how such filial gestures could be reinterpreted as communist hagiography. His depiction foregrounds the issue of language, for Renwen's representation of Dregs' story itself is reworked by party hacks into that of a proletarian hero.

The fractured state of political affairs that epitomized Chinese society for the 150-year-long colonial period virtually has ended. However, with a regime in Beijing still resistant to the autonomy of the educated elite, the stubborn resurgence of premodern cultural practices such as filiality, and the unresolved question of Taiwan, Chinese literatures persist in a fragile state. The recent accolades bestowed on Gao Xingjian, whose monumental works such as *Soul Mountain* and *One Person's Bible* are banned in China and must be published in Taiwan, are a testament to the necessity of characterizing modern Chinese literatures in the plural.

Further Reading: R. Chow 1991; Y.-T. Feuerwerker 1998; C. Lupke 1998a, 1998b.

Christopher Lupke

Driss Chraïbi   Driss Chraïbi was born in Mazagan, Morocco, in 1926. At the age of two his father sent him to the Qur'anic school. Later he was one of only two Moroccan students to attend the French lycée in Casablanca. In 1945, he left for Paris to prepare a degree in chemical engineering and neuropsychiatry. He eventually abandoned his scientific pursuits for journalism and literature. After traveling throughout Europe, he finally married a Frenchwoman in 1962 and settled in France, his present country of residence.

Chraïbi's early work is tainted by an angry and revolutionary tone. As a young Moroccan trapped between two contradictory and irreconcilable cultural codes, he first revolted against his own society and unequivocally rejected his people and his past. His first novel, *Le passé simple* (1954) rewrites the colonial encounter as it is manifested microcosmically in the household of Haj Fatmi or, as he is symbolically nicknamed, *Le seigneur*. *Le passé simple* suggests that underdevelopment, social injustice, and hypocrisy are not only the outcome of colonial incursion but the direct consequence of 1,300 years of Islamic rule. Angry in tone, determined in its condemnation of all aspects of Moroccan society, Chraïbi's first novel offers some of the most scathing self-criticisms. Through the character of *Le seigneur*, the young novelist exposed the ways that Moroccan bourgeoisie made use of the colonial presence and how it commandeered Islam to exploit the masses. *Le passé simple*, therefore, remains an attempt to foreground those aspects of Oriental society that official rhetoric tries to hide. It potently and blatantly debunks Moroccan precolonial history and identity. When it first came out, it was greeted with a spate of criticisms from both sides of the colonial divide. Moroccans attacked it as an unrealistic and highly subjective treatment of society, while French critics used it as an obstreperous testimony from within Morocco to justify their colonial rule.

The wedge between the values of liberty, fraternity, and equality that the French tout and their actual treatment of North African immigrant workers is the subject of Chraïbi's second novel, *Les boucs* (1955). After being disappointed with his own culture and society, Chraïbi now exposes the hypocrisy of French society. As a precautionary step, he chose an Algerian as the protagonist of his new novel instead of a Moroccan. Yalann Waldik, which in Arabic means "may your parents be cursed," is a writer who has come to France to fulfill his dream of freedom and justice only to become the subject of French racial prejudice. *Les boucs* is, thus, one of the very early narratives that address the dilemma of immigrants in France. Through the character of Waldik, it shows the hardship and lack of integration in French society. Waldik and his compatriots will always remain by French standards mere Arabs/Berbers, uncivilized, backward, and undeserving of equal rights.

Succession ouverte (1962) brings the protagonist of *Le passé simple*, Driss Ferdi, back to his native Morocco to attend the funeral of *Le seigneur*. This gives him an opportunity to check on the progress of his society after official independence. Even though *Succession ouverte* lacks the angry and revolutionary tone rampant in the first novels, it still highlights the fact that nothing has changed much even after the French have departed. Driss realizes now that neither his country of birth nor his host country meets his universal aspirations for human love. "I have seen," he laments toward the end of the novel, "the West preach **humanism** and practice cruelties. And seated between two closed doors, I cried out so much for human brotherhood and mutual understanding" (105).

La Civilisation, ma mère! . . . (1972) is the antithetical text of *Le passé simple*. The same mother who is described in the earlier text as meek, subordinate, and a mere pregnancy box takes now the center stage, while the figure of the once-tyrannical father is relegated to background information. Set in colonial Morocco, *La Civilisation, ma mère!* . . . traces the development of a Moroccan bourgeois woman from a traditional housewife to an educated woman and a political activist defending the liberation of women and advocating human rights. Written in a cheerful and humorous tone, Chraïbi's eighth novel is a potent statement on the importance of the mother figure in Moroccan culture and the necessity of her liberation. It is also an allegory for all oppressed nations that aspire to independence and freedom.

Chraïbi's later work, notably, *Une Enquête au pays* (1981), *La Mère du printemps* (1982), *Naissance à l'aube* (1986), and *L'Homme du Livre* (1995), is more interested in his own ethnic group (the Berbers) and Islam. These later novels rewrite the Arabo–Islamic conquest of North Africa and show how the Berbers reacted to the new conquerors. Through the character of Raho Aït Yafelman, who appears in more than one work, Chraïbi evinces the cultural confrontation between Islam as a religion and the Berbers' paganism and attachment to land.

Chraïbi's later work testifies to the fact that the once-young and rebellious author has broadened his interest from the specific problems of Moroccan society to the more universal concerns of all oppressed minorities and peripheral cultures. Instead of the confrontational aspect of the early narratives, Chraïbi's more recent work opens up new cultural spaces where civilizations meet with, rather than oppose, each other. It more and more emphasizes the shifting and hybrid nature of identity and culture. Chraïbi's lifelong quest for self-discovery in the midst of different histories and identities makes him **Homi Bhabha**'s ambivalently positioned colonial subject par excellence. Literary teratology, acculturation, ambiguity, and alienation are frequently encountered vocabulary in scholarship about the **francophone** writers of North Africa. Having opted for the language of the erstwhile colonizer, these writers continue to operate along the borderline of two sociocultural orders—an indigenous Islamic heritage and French colonialism. The founding father of this literature is the Moroccan novelist Driss Chraïbi. For almost half a century his oeuvre has tried to grapple with the dynamics of Moroccan postcolonial identity as it is caught between native mores and the demands of secularizing Western thought.

Further Reading: K. Houaria 1986; D. Marx-Scouras 1992; J. Monego 1984.

Salah M. Moukhlis

Michelle Cliff (1946–) Michelle Cliff was born in Jamaica, the light-skinned daughter of a family comprising both former slaves and former slave owners. After living in New York as a teenager and later in London, where she completed a dissertation on the Italian Renaissance, she now lives in California.

Although she had always wanted to be a writer, Cliff started writing only when she was about thirty, in an attempt to address her own personality conundrum as an almost white, middle-class, lesbian **Creole** in a Caribbean society that, in spite of a formidable social and cultural complexity, is strictly stratified and still characterized by colorism and homophobia. The titles of her first two collections, halfway between poetry and prose, *Claiming an Identity They Taught Me to Despise* (1980) and *The Land of Look Behind* (1985), which contains an essay entitled "If I Could Write This in Fire, I Would Write This in Fire," testify to her determination to resort to speech and subjectivity to decolonize the self and to her will to use the fragmentation inherited from history as a means toward wholeness.

A similar quest for self-identification characterizes her fiction, especially her first two novels, *Abeng* (1984) and *No Telephone to Heaven* (1987). These partly autobiographical works are best read together, as they share the same heroine,

Clare Savage, whose dual name crystallizes the **identity** dilemma at the heart of all Cliff's writing. The direct heir of Bertha Rochester (the madwoman in the attic in *Jane Eyre* but the protagonist of Jean Rhys' *Wide Sargasso Sea* [1966] as well), Clare Savage embodies the divided consciousness of white Creoles and their difficulty in positioning themselves in formerly colonized societies that reject any form of ambivalence. In *Abeng* the young Clare achieves integrity by unearthing the silenced history of Jamaica and identifying with such historical figures as Nanny, the female Maroon leader, but also with Anne Frank. In *No Telephone to Heaven* this sense of self is reached through political commitment and a physical bond with the Jamaican landscape, perceived as essentially female and associated with the women ancestors. *Free Enterprise* (1993), Cliff's third novel, explores the **diasporic** dimension of her identity by delving into the history of other oppressed peoples, mostly African American and Jewish. Unlike the official written record, which she shows to be mendacious or, at best, incomplete, Cliff's imaginative reconstruction of the American past foregrounds the role of female **resisters** in the fight against the slave trade and oppression in general. Like the rest of her writing, *Free Enterprise* combines **narrative** gaps, multivoicedness, and wide-ranging cultural allusions to provide a thought-provoking challenge to the monolithic master tale often viewed as white and male.

Cliff is also the author of two collections of short stories, set in the Caribbean and the United States, *Bodies of Water* (1990) and *The Store of a Million Items* (1998), notable for combining unsentimental lyricism with subversive power.

Further Reading: F. Lionnet 1992; M. Schwartz 1996.

Bénédicte Ledent

Colonial Discourse   Colonial discourse analysis emerged as a scholarly field after the publication of **Edward Said**'s groundbreaking work, *Orientalism*, in 1978. In *Orientalism*, Said draws on **Michel Foucault**'s work on discourse theory and **Antonio Gramsci**'s political writings in order to identify the ways in which the West produced a geographical and cultural entity, the "Orient," for the consumption of a European market. By drawing on the discursive similarities of a range of texts written in the nineteenth century by learned scholars, poets, novelists, travel writers, and state legislators, Said calls into question the "objective reality" that these texts purport to convey. In fact, he demonstrates that putatively objective academic works, particularly those in the social sciences and humanities, were strongly implicated in the project of European colonial expansion by producing forms of knowledge about the Other that led to the cultural, economic, and military control of foreign territories.

According to Said, the Orient does not exist; rather, the Orient is the site of a projection of European fantasies about the East. He describes the discursive features of a range of texts that describe the Orient as a place of irrationality, eroticism, and superstition. The Orient, claims Said, was constructed in negative terms and was represented as the inverse of the West. If the West embodied Enlightenment concepts of rationality, scientific and technological progress, and individual liberty, then the Orient emerged as the site of backwardness, irrationality, superstition, and despotic rule.

Thus, not only did the Orient represent the projection of Western fantasies, but its production as a site of radical difference from the West enabled European nations to establish truth-claims about non-European nations and cultures in order to advance their military and economic control over regions that they sought to control. In other words, the textual production of the Orient through colonial discourse enabled colonial governments, inspired by economic and military gain, to justify their control over territories that were represented as radically different from the West and in need of guidance from more "civilized" Western nations.

Colonial discourse, argues Said, is characterized by sweeping generalizations of the various non-European cultures in the Middle East—the geographical area upon which Said focuses. The construction, in colonial texts, of Middle Eastern peoples as belonging to an indeterminate mass rather than distinct individuals accomplished two important ends. First, the representation of indistinguishable masses of people under despotic rule worked in direct opposition to the representation of the enlightened subject in a democratic European nation. Second, stripping the "Oriental" of individuality enabled the production and the circulation of colonial stereotypes. Stereotypes of the lazy, sly, ignorant indigenous subject worked as further justification of a Western presence as a civilizing influence.

In *Time and the Other: How Anthropology Makes Its Object* (1983), Johannes Fabian emphasizes the idea of temporal difference as an important characteristic of colonial discourse as deployed by the (European) anthropologist. Fabian argues that the anthropologist, in his or her studies of non-European cultures, situates the Other in the past tense, thereby relegating non-Europeans to a past moment in a linear historical narrative. Europeans, by contrast, are situated at a more progressive or advanced stage of human development. By denying "temporal coevalness" to the colonized Other, the colonizing force can justify its civilizing mission of enlightening primitive peoples and their cultures. Fabian's work on temporality and the discursive production of colonized peoples as the inverse of the colonizer complements Said's position regarding the production of the Orient and "Orientals" in negation to the West. This form of negation results in the affirmation of a powerful subject status for the West and places the Orient in the position of the object—to be known, to be desired, and to be controlled.

Although Said's work on colonial discourse theory is acknowledged as groundbreaking and as having established a field of academic scholarship, there have been three important criticisms leveled against it. First, *Orientalism* represents a homogeneous view of colonial discourse and therefore reproduces the same problems that result from Western generalizations about the East. Second,

Said's analysis of the pervasive discourse of Orientalism does not account for the heterogeneity of Oriental **resistances**—evidence of which can be found in colonial texts. Third, Said neglects to offer a gendered analysis of Orientalist and colonial discourse in his work.

These absences in Said's work have been productive, as other critics have built upon his thesis in order to further develop or critique his original premise. In *Colonial Encounters: Europe and the Native Caribbean 1492–1797* (1986), Peter Hulme works against the idea that colonial texts represent the colonized in solely negative terms. Hulme shows the complexities of colonial discourse as it produced both positive and negative representations of indigenous cultures. These conflicting representations of various cultures in the Caribbean, Hulme argues, were informed by their relationship to colonialism; those cultures that resisted colonial invasion and control were described as barbaric cannibals—in need of the civilizing and controlling presence of the colonizing power. Those cultures that accepted colonial rule and facilitated the colonial presence were represented as civilized in relation to their barbaric counterparts.

In *Critical Terrains: French and British Orientalisms* (1991), Lisa Lowe argues that there are radical differences between French and British Orientalisms and that each specific historical, cultural, geographical moment produces varying Orientalist representations. Lowe's argument can be seen as a direct challenge to Said's contentious claim that the Orient allowed itself to be Orientalized, thus divesting the Oriental subject of **agency** in the face of a homogeneous and hegemonic colonial discourse. The diversity of French and British representations of the Oriental other, suggests Lowe, allows for a range of possibilities for postcolonial interventions and resistances.

In *Imperial Eyes: Travel Writing and Transculturation* (1992), Mary Louise Pratt builds on the notion of the heterogeneity of colonial discourses by situating her analysis in what she terms "the contact zone." Pratt's "contact zone" refers to the space and the moment in which the colonizer and the colonized come into contact with each other and define the ways in which subjects come into being in relation to each other. Rather than configuring the colonizer/colonized in positions of radical difference, Pratt uses the "contact zone" to describe their relationship in terms of interaction and co-presence, albeit within an unequal structure of power. Once again, the recognition of the heterogeneity of colonial discourses produces the possiblities of resistance as opposed to the hegemonic model proposed by Said.

Homi Bhabha, who draws upon **psychoanalytic** theory in his approach to colonial discourse, further destabilizes Said's representation of the homogeneity of colonial discourse by describing how it can start to fracture through the process of repetition. In "Signs Taken for Wonders: Questions of Ambivalence and Authority under a Tree outside Delhi, May 1817" (in Bhabha 1994, 102–22), Bhabha offers a reading of a Christian missionary's account of the discovery and circulation of the Bible in an Indian Hindu community in Meerut. In Bhabha's reading of this missionary tract, the discovery of the Bible signifies at one and the same time the authority of the civilizing, enlightening colonial presence and the ambivalence of colonial rule, for the translation and the repetition of the word of God in the wilds of colonial India are filtered through the process of *Entstellung*, which Bhabha defines as "a process of displacement, distortion, dislocation, repetition" (105).

Although the missionary document celebrates the circulation of the Bible in colonial India, Bhabha draws out the ambivalences at the heart of this colonial moment. The Bible as representative of the word of God and of truth circulated among the colonized, but with a difference: vegetarian Hindus refused to accept that the Bible was sent to them by the Europeans, not least because the Europeans ate meat. The Hindus rejected the idea of the Sacrament, as they saw eating the flesh and drinking the blood of Christ as a barbarous act. Thus, while the Bible circulates successfully in colonial India, its presence as signifier of British authority is destabilized as stereotypes of the barbarity of colonized subjects and the civility of European colonizers are reversed. Bhabha points out the ambivalence of colonial discourse by arguing that the colonial presence is always split "between its appearance as original and authoritative and its articulation as repetition and difference" (107).

The notion of the splitting of colonial discourse and the idea of repetition as difference relates to another important concept in Bhabha's work: **mimicry**. Colonial mimicry, argues Bhabha, was a strategic project to create a class of "domesticated Others," representatives of the colonized class who would assist the colonial project by acting as intermediaries between the colonial presence and the colonized peoples. But the discourse of colonial mimicry is structured around an ambivalence that accentuates the difference between the Anglicized mimic man and British colonial authority. Mimicry, in fact, always produces a slippage between that which it is meant to represent and the representation itself. This slippage between the discourse of mimicry and that of mockery produces the threat of menace to the civilizing mission. The figure of mimicry repeats, rather than represents, argues Bhabha, and this process of repetition, through the ambivalent discourse of mimicry, includes the partial presence of the colonial subject. Thus, the presumed totalizing aspect of colonial discourse is always threatened by the partial presence of the colonial subject, and the disciplining gaze of the colonizer is displaced by the mocking return gaze of its colonial double.

The notion of the partial (if occluded) presence of the colonial subject within colonial discourse is an idea to which Ranajit Guha and **Gayatri Chakravorty Spivak**, in their work with the **Subaltern Studies** Group, have devoted much attention. The Subaltern Studies Group borrows the term "subaltern" from Gramsci's writings, in which it refers to an individual's subordination in terms of class, caste, gender, race, language, and culture. The Subaltern Studies Group argues that official documents or historical narratives tend to be written from the perspective of the colonial power. The category of the subaltern, constituted by dominant discourses, thus emerges in the interstices of dominant discourses, through their gaps and silences. In those texts where there is some representation of members of the colonized culture, the voice of the small and privileged class of "native elites" is foregrounded at the expense of the interests of the larger indigenous population. Theorists of subalternity believe that subaltern voices are silenced by the official and dominant discourses of colonialism and indigenous nationalism—and that the figure of the subaltern can be found by reading the gaps, the fissures, and the silences in colonial texts. Spivak is particularly interested in the figure of the subaltern woman, and in a famous essay, "Can the Subaltern Speak?" (1989), Spivak analyzes the figure of the subaltern woman who is the victim of a double colonization—European colonialism and indigenous patriarchal **nationalism**. The figure of the subaltern woman is caught between these two dominant and oppressive discourses, and therefore, Spivak concludes, the subaltern woman cannot be "heard"—her voice cannot register within dominant Western (colonialist) discourses or indigenous (anticolonial) discourses.

Spivak's concern with the silenced voices of subaltern women leads to the third and final critique of Said's *Orientalism* and the field of colonial discourse analysis. The absence of a gendered analysis of colonial discourse has been addressed by a few critics, most notably by Sara Mills in *Discourses of Difference: An Analysis of Women's Travel Writing and Colonialism* (1991) and by Reina Lewis in *Gendering Orientalism: Race, Femininity and Representation* (1996).

Although such critics as Peter Hulme have analyzed the heterogeneity of colonial discourses, the **travel writings** of women who wrote about the Orient have been, Mills argues, for the most part neglected. Mills points out that although women's travel writing was widely read and popular at the time of its publication, these works are generally overlooked or neglected in the male-dominated field of colonial discourse analysis. Any analysis of these texts usually comes from feminist critics who, according to Mills, tend to celebrate these women travelers as heroic and adventurous feminist figures rather than as agents in the mobilization of colonial discourses.

Mills finds that Western women's travel writings about the Orient offer strong examples of the diversities, the ambivalences, and the contradictions within colonial discourse. Western women, caught between the discourse of colonialism and the discourse of **femininity**, have an ambivalent relationship to the colonial project. Mills writes that while the discourse of colonialism demands an active and intrepid narrator interested in exploration, the discourse of femininity demands a passive narrator who focuses on nurturing personal relationships. Although Western women's writings tend to be stereotypically colonial in terms of their content and their style, Mills argues, the Western woman writer was unable to adopt a straightforwardly colonial voice of authority as she faced the contradictions between the discourses of colonialism and femininity. She thus saw herself on the margins of what remained a predominantly male colonial enterprise.

Like Mills, Reina Lewis believes in the important participation of women in the production and dissemination of colonial discourse. In *Gendering Orientalism*, Lewis asserts that women did, indeed, produce images and writings supporting the colonial project. She argues that an analysis of colonialist representations by Western women will help develop an understanding of the interdependence of the ideologies of race and gender in colonial discourse. Lewis goes on to state that the difference between Western men and Western women's colonial discourses is, most importantly, one of degree; Western women's discourses participated less in representing the Oriental Other as radically different and backward in relation to the West.

Meyda Yeğenoğlu, however, would disagree with both Lewis' and Mills' more generous analyses of Western women's writings about the colonial Other. In *Colonial Fantasies: Towards a Feminist Reading of Orientalism* (1998), Yeğenoğlu argues that stereotypical colonial representations of the Orient emerged in the writings of Western women—and that these images remain unabashedly similar to those that emerge in the writings of men. Contrary to Mills and Lewis, Yeğenoğlu believes that although Western women emerged as the Other in relation to Western men, they adopted a masculine subject position in relation to Oriental women. She traces the development of a European feminism that is necessarily and unambiguously tied to the colonial enterprise.

Since the inception of the field after the 1978 publication of *Orientalism*, colonial discourse analysis is necessarily broadening in scope to incorporate not only issues of colonial resistance but a fuller articulation of gender and of feminist complicity in the colonial enterprise.

Further Reading: M. Yeğenoğlu 1998; R. Young 1995.

Nima Naghibi

Colonial Patronage Patronage of many kinds had been central to most European power structures through the earlier colonial periods; colonial governors obtained patronage and thus preferment from aristocratic figures in government and were likewise in a position to extend patronage to their lesser-ranking applicants. Patronage as a principle of social ordering allowed the privileged to exercise power but through its casual and even accidental nature allowed a measure of social and professional mobility. However, this mobility was predicated on the assumption that the client would, in many ways, serve the interests of the patron, in the very least by becoming a "product" of which the patron could be proud and that he could display.

Transferred into the colonial field, this system worked effectively in Macaulayan schemes of generating a privileged minority through which the larger society could be administered. Thomas Macaulay's project, to "form a class who may be interpreters between us and the millions whom we govern, a class of persons Indian in blood and colour, but English in taste, in opinions, in morals and intellect" ("Minute on Indian Education" [1835]), was attempted with varying degrees of success in a number of colonies. A small percentage of the colonized populace was viewed with special favor if they imitated the behavior and dress and, above all, the language of the colonizers. Typically, this attempted Europeanization of indigenes left them alienated from their local culture and not always able to take significant roles in racist colonial administrations.

Missionary societies mirrored the way that colonial administrations patronized one cultural grouping in order to administer the country. In the Ugandan Protectorate, the British had worked through the Baganda in order to dominate the region politically. The Church Missionary Society (CMS) at least initially concurred with this approach and debated as to whether a Bible should be produced in other languages such as Lunyoro at all. Many CMS missionaries argued in the 1890s and the early 1900s that Luganda was a superior language, that the spread of a common language would extinguish tribal divisions, and that producing the Bible in multiple languages would make excessive demands on the meager printing capacities of the CMS.

In the missionary field the system of patronage became clear, as missionaries would typically choose a few of those whom they took to be their brighter charges and send them to training institutes in the colony or the colonial center. In this way the Church Missionary Society's Henry Venn arranged for three West African students to be sent to Edinburgh for medical training; one of these, Dr. James Africanus Horton, born in Sierra Leone of Ibo parents, became the author of *West African Countries and Peoples* (1868). This personal patronage often developed into close friendships with apparently mutual respect but is usually narratively represented in missionary reminiscences as a rescue of a potentially valuable human being from what would otherwise be a worthless and savage life. Insofar as this kind of personal patronage celebrates the elevation of the individual, it represents the working out of ethnocentric ideologies of individualism, which contrasted sharply with many indigenous beliefs in the community.

Forms of cultural production other than writing were discouraged. Art, dance, and oral literatures were seen as distinctly inferior forms of culture compared to writing. T. O. Beidelman's *Colonial Evangelism* (1982) notes that the Kaguru of East Africa were forbidden by CMS missionaries to dance and engage in many rituals. He also points out that many Kaguru managed to live in both Christian and pagan worlds, balancing the demands of each (135–38). Yet there is no doubt that missionary patronage, with its promises of salvation and, more pragmatically, better jobs and social status, played a central role in skewing indigenous cultural production toward those forms approved by Europeans. At best, these kinds of patronage may have effected the transformation of indigenous languages into a written form; very occasionally, an indigenous authority, such as Samuel Crowther in Nigeria, was active in this. At worst, however, this kind of education was directed at discouraging the use of local languages in preference for the colonizer's language. Indeed, the very idea of an indigenous literature of any value was usually dismissed outright by missionary and colonial authorities such as Macaulay. However, both these systems of linguistic patronage proved less than stable. While the missionaries successfully encouraged the publication of the Bible in indigenous languages, these tools of publication were utilized for indigenous expression and, ultimately, anticolonial aims.

The history of publishing in many colonized lands is linked to missionary presses. To consider Africa once again, this connection is apparent in the history of Yoruba literature, where missionaries, including Crowther, converted the Yoruba language into Roman orthography and encouraged publishing efforts. These included the bilingual newspaper *Iwe-Irohin*, produced by the Church Missionary Society's Henry Townsend, who trained Nigerians in printing. These trainees, J.F.A. Ajayi notes, went on to develop a tradition of newspapers and small printeries in Lagos and Nigeria more generally (1965, 159). Much that was produced in early phases of publication in Nigeria were works of history, readers, hymn books, or educational materials. However, E. M. Lijadu, associated with the CMS, published a collection of songs under the title *Kekere Iwe Orin Aribiloso* (A Small Book of Ariboloso's Songs, 1886) and later published a book of Yoruba sayings.

Many writers from colonized countries reflect on the role of missionary and colonial patronage on African life and writing. **Ngũgĩ Wa Thiong'o** notes in *Decolonizing the Mind* (1986) that literacy was confined to those inducted into pragmatic minor functionary roles such as "clerks, soldiers, policemen, and the petty civil servants" (67). However, literacy and literary production were encouraged by colonial Literature Bureaus, but, as Ngũgĩ observes, the writings were "censored either directly through licensing laws or indirectly through editorial practice" (67).

Critics have noted that the problems of patronage have not disappeared in the postcolonial world (Kotei 1995). International presses centered in London or New York still determine what is to be published and, in concert with the literary academy, assist in determining the African canon and the canons of other formerly colonized countries. There are few resources in many formerly colonized nations for publishing in languages other than English, so that, to some extent, systems of patronage remain determinative of cultural content.

Further Reading: J.F.A. Ajayi 1965; T.O. Beidelman 1982; S.I.A. Kotei 1981; Ngũgĩ 1986.

Simon Ryan

Commitment Literature. *See* Resistance Literature

Commonwealth Literature   This is a term formulated both to describe and to define the study of literatures in English originating from member countries of the British Commonwealth. The Commonwealth itself was formed in 1931 to formalize the economic relationship between Britain and its independent "white dominions"—Canada, Australia, South Africa, New Zealand, and so on. However, with the sharp acceleration of decolonization following World War II in response to powerful independence movements demanding self-determination, the character of the association changed substantially from being a "white nations' club" into a body encompassing most of the nations to emerge from the collapse of the British empire (notable exceptions being Eire, which refused to join on attaining formal independence, and South Africa, which was later to be excluded during the apartheid era).

The earliest university courses to take as their subject "Commonwealth" literature emerged during the 1940s in the United States but focused exclusively on the already established literature of the white **settler colonies**. The 1958 Modern Language Association annual meeting saw the inaugural meeting of what would become the Conference on British Commonwealth Literature, and the first general introduction to the new field, *The Commonwealth Pen*, was written by A. L. McLeod of the State University of New York in 1961 and extended the field beyond the former white dominions. This was a recognition of the cultural stimulus of the independence movements of the 1950s and 1960s, from which had emerged a new wave of writers who would gain international recognition, including **Chinua Achebe** in Nigeria, **Wilson Harris** in Guiana, **Ngũgĩ wa Thiong'o** in Kenya, and Raja Rao in India. Publishers had also begun to respond to the demands of both new authors and readers with the launch of Heinemann's highly successful African Writers series in 1962, to be followed in the succeeding decade by Caribbean and Asian series as well as Longman's Drumbeats series. This, in turn, finally brought major institutional recognition in England and elsewhere.

The 1964 Conference on Commonwealth Literature at the University of Leeds proved a seminal event for both writers and academics. Its aim was not only to review current work in the new field through the delivery of conference papers but to ensure its establishment as a recognized subfield of English literature in universities in Britain and throughout the Commonwealth. However, in tacit recognition of the greater level of organization that had already been made in the United States, no delegates were invited from the United States for fear that they would overrun the new subject. This conference also saw the establishment of *The Journal of Commonwealth Literature* (still in print today) and the founding of the Association of Commonwealth Language and Literature Studies, which encouraged academic exchange programs and organized a triennial conference. Courses in Commonwealth literature were soon established in a number of universities in Britain and other Commonwealth countries as well as in Europe.

Not only academics were drawn to this conference. Chinua Achebe delivered his famous paper "The Novelist as Teacher," and it was stated that an aim embodied in later conferences would be to encourage the interaction of both writers and critics, which was, in part at least, realized. However, the published proceedings of the conference under the editorship of John Press (who had been seconded to the conference by the British Council), *Commonwealth Literature:*

Unity and Diversity in a Common Culture, demonstrates that in these early years the field was dominated by academics and writers from Britain and the white settler colonies. Moreover, as this title suggests, a number of assumptions underlay this inaugural conference that remained influential until the 1970s. Both "unity" and "common culture" presumed that British culture, particularly, the "great tradition" of English literature, provided the comparative frame against which Commonwealth literature was to be judged and understood. This effectively discouraged the consideration of literature from former colonies as contributing to the formation of a distinct national literature—an aspiration dismissed as being of no more than local interest in comparison to the "universal" themes of the English literary tradition. The next conference in Brisbane in 1968 reinforced this subtle priority of the "**center**" over the "margins."

However, even in 1964 dissent from this Anglocentric conception of the subdisciplne was evident. Indeed, S. Nagarajan in his conference paper "The Study of English Literature in India" complained that while the diversity was evident enough, the unity was not so obvious. Further, Achebe's contribution to the conference, the last essay in Press' collection, highlights the divergence between African writers like himself and the normative critical values operating in the metropolitan universities. In the years that followed, further fault lines became evident, with critics even from the white settler colonies questioning the appropriateness of literary models from Britain to understand the representation of unique experiences and spaces of their homelands and whether the comparative model would even be appropriate between other settler colonies. The notion of Commonwealth literature increasingly came to be seen as too restrictive by precluding other **anglophone literatures** like that of the Philippines that might provide a more relevant candidate for comparison with the anglophone literature of Singapore than that of the Caribbean. Even the centrality of the English language came to be seen as increasingly anachronistic, with debates that suggested that francophone African literature would have more in common with anglophone African literature than the English tradition. What of American literature? As the first British colony to gain independence, arguments were advanced to claim this as a more appropriate comparative frame, as well as growing interest in the African American literary tradition. Many writers from the Commonwealth had also explicitly rejected the "Commonwealth" label, including **V. S. Naipaul**, Lloyd Fernando, and Clark Blaise. **Salman Rushdie's** 1983 essay "Commonwealth Literature Does Not Exist" recapitulates this position.

As arguments over the exclusion of "English" literature gained ground, so the influence of British-based academics like Norman Jeffares, the convener of the 1964 Leeds conference, waned. By the mid-1970s Commonwealth literature as a unified subdiscipline was in crisis, and a fundamental paradigm shift was in process, with the debate assuming an increasingly political character that would ultimately see the emergence of a "postcolonial" criticism. Subsequent postcolonial theorists have been harsh in their judgment of Commonwealth literature.

Homi Bhabha makes a number of dismissive gestures in his early essays "Representation and the Colonial Text" (1984) and "Signs Taken for Wonders" (1985), and **Gayatri Chakrovorty Spivak** scarcely refers to this earlier tradition at all. Indeed, many readers and textbooks in postcolonial studies simply make no mention of their immediate predecessor, implying a fundamental break that, in fact, does not exist. Somewhat ironically, one of the most vociferous opponents of postcolonial theory, **Aijaz Ahmad**, has also decried Commonwealth literature as being little more than a vehicle to further the aims of the British Council. However, much of his critique of postcolonial theory is shared by contemporary practitioners of Commonwealth literary studies, now incorporated within a broad-based postcolonial criticism or the study of new literatures in English. Postcolonial theory has, in turn, been criticized by a Commonwealth literature studies reconstituted within postcolonial criticism both for its obsessive engagement with **colonial discourse**, to the extent that the cultural production of the postcolonial world is at risk of being overlooked, and for an unnecessarily mystificatory vocabulary that is too reliant on French high theory. The coordinates of this criticism reflect two of the strengths of Commonwealth literary studies. While influential figures within the subdiscipline emerged, it was never dominated by any single theoretical critical approach. The most influential means of its expression was the volume of collected essays rather than the single totalizing reading by celebrated theorists. With the waning of British influence, the close associations with authors and cultural movements in formerly colonized nations gained in importance, as did intellectual and cultural exchange. Rather than the one-way academic migration to metropolitan universities for which Ahmad has attacked postcolonial studies, there was a genuine circulation of both authors and academics throughout the Commonwealth and beyond.

Despite the flaws of its conception and the initial limitations of its scope, Commonwealth literary studies fostered an international consciousness of the literature of colonialism, independence movements, and the emergence of long-suppressed nations that enabled postcolonial studies to emerge—a tradition that persists to this day in the healthy tensions within postcolonial criticism.

Further Reading: H. Maes-Jelinek, Petersen, and Rutherford 1989; J. Press 1965.

Lawrence Phillips

Comprador   In **Marxist** theories of imperialism, "comprador" refers to a native mercantile class in a colonial or **neocolonial** society whose members act as intermediaries and agents for foreign capitalists. Members of this class buy and sell goods on behalf of foreign investors and multinational corporations, thus helping transfer the country's wealth and resources to the European metropole and contributing to the nation's continuing dependence on foreign capital. In the essay "The Pitfalls of National Consciousness" (1965), **Frantz Fanon** explains that after political liberation from the European powers, the leaders of **nationalist** movements in Africa and elsewhere become the ruling class but find themselves with little economic power or expertise in government and so turn to capitalists from the former colonial power for help. Similarly, Michael Barratt Brown notes the tendency of nationalist movements to move toward accommodation with the former ruling nation after formal **decolonization**. He identifies the comprador class, a holdover from the colonial era, as one of three key elements in the new ruling class, along with native capitalists and feudal landlords. Paul Baran applies the term "comprador regime" to the governments of nominally independent nations that sell off natural resources to multinational corporations, citing certain Latin American countries and the oil-producing nations of the Middle East as examples. The politicians and businessmen in these comprador regimes, rather than working toward true industrialization and economic development, typically keep the profits for themselves and maintain ostentatious lifestyles, while most of the residents of the country remain mired in poverty.

Further Reading: P. Baran 1957; M. Barratt Brown 1974.

Shane D. Graham

Maryse Condé　　Born in Point-à-Pitre on the island of Guadeloupe in 1937 to a family that valued intellectual pursuits, Maryse Condé (née Boucolon) went to Paris to study at age sixteen. Despite colonial and racial prejudice encountered in France, Condé completed study in English and classics at the Sorbonne, rematriculating in 1970 to pursue a doctorate in comparative literature after traveling and teaching in the Ivory Coast, Ghana, Guinea, and Senegal. Condé worked for the groundbreaking journal *Présence Africaine* and joined the Sorbonne faculty, completing her first novel, *Heremakhonon*, in 1976. Condé returned to Guadeloupe in 1986; she has since held positions at many major U.S. universities.

The author of stories, plays, children's books, and critical essays, Condé is most renowned for novels that explore the complexities of Afro-Caribbean history and **identity** in a postcolonial political, economic, and cultural order. Recipients of numerous awards for **francophone literature**, most of her novels have been translated into English in the past decade. Condé's work expands imaginatively on extant historical documents, fleshing out references to black African and Caribbean individuals and events and providing both voices **resistant** to a monologized European history and an Afro-Caribbean context for that history. Her work is sometimes described as "marvelous realism" for its use of ancestral spirits who represent connections with a past too often denigrated.

Critics often divide Condé's work into stages that mirror her intercontinental travels. Her first novels, the so-called African novels, have been described as explorations of **negritude** and **Pan-Africanism**, although Condé herself resists such categorizations because of their reliance on a monolithic notion of the black African (generally male) that emphasizes racial continuity over cultural, class, and gender difference. Although these novels explore the common heritage of

West Indians and Africans, the search for "authentic" identity is often frustrated by the political turmoil that embroils the characters and the nation, particularly in *Heremakhonon* (published in French in 1976; English translation, 1982) and *A Season in Rihata* (1981, 1988). *Segu* (1984, 1987) and *The Children of Segu* (1985, 1990) trace the generational decline of a West African Kingdom (Mali) under the pressures of colonialism, the slave trade, and the coming of Islam. *I, Tituba, Black Witch of Salem* (1986, 1992) represents a departure from Condé's African settings, implicating the colonial United States as a corner in the triangular slave trade through the voice of a Barbadian woman. *Tree of Life* (1987, 1992) links familial life in Guadeloupe with U.S. economic interests and construction of the Panama Canal, recontextualizing the **multicultural** world of the Caribbean in relationship to its "New World" circumstance rather than to France and Africa. *Crossing the Mangrove Swamp* (1989, 1995) and *The Last of the African Kings* (1992, 1997) continue her exploration of Caribbean and American relationships. *Windward Heights* (1995, 1999) reimagines Brontë's *Wuthering Heights* from a Guadeloupean perspective.

Condé's writing reflects her suspicion of monolithic ideologies and is often overtly critical of créolité, antillanité, africanité, and Western **feminism**, preferring instead the values of pluralism that these movements sometimes elide.

Further Reading: D. Perret and M.-D. Shelton 1995; *World Literature Today* 67.4 (1993).

Joseph Slaughter

Constructionism   Constructionism is an approach employed in understanding reality in such diverse fields as biology, neurophysiology, sociology, psychology, anthropology, history, **cultural studies**, and literary criticism. It is particularly attractive because it might bring the arts and sciences closer together again. Bluntly stated, it means that reality is not simply "out there" waiting for human beings to inspect and thus understand it correctly. Constructionism rejects such simple forms of realism, empiricism, and positivism. Instead, it underlines the importance of the human mind (and body) for any understanding of reality and claims that reality not only is obviously there but is also constructed by human beings, in particular, by their giving value and meaning to it, so that reality is "the embodied mind." This construction of reality must not be seen as an act of solipsism or idealism, though. Constructionism avoids the one-sidedness of idealism as well as that of materialism. Reality is there, but the way in which human beings look at it and the meaning that they attribute to it depend on many complicated individual, biological, and cultural factors. Even such seemingly factual properties as color and smell are actually actively constructed by human beings through neuronal activities. The difference between a colonial and a postcolonial world makes the constructedness of reality more immediately evident and reveals the fundamental changes in the value systems that occur when a colonial reality becomes postcolonial. For constructionism, an adequate description of reality always consists of an analysis of both the facts (including practices) and the values or meanings given them (as in cultural studies). In postcolonial theory, constructionism has shed light on the intricate relationship between colonizer and colonized and the possibility of **resistance** and change in human societies; in postcolonial practice, it helps people to create their **identities** through an awareness of the numerous influences that they are under and of the possibilities that they have. Constructionism emphasizes efficiency and practicability in everyday activities; it illuminates the cognitive processes of human life and is a complex, pragmatic, and holistic approach.

Further Reading: J. Holstein and G. Miller 1993; H. Maturana and F. Varela 1984; K.-P. Müller 1999; F. Varela, E. Thompson, and E. Rosch 1991.

Klaus-Peter Müller

Cosmopolitanism   A true cosmopolitanism, from a postcolonial perspective, is an attempt to reconcile the local and the universal (à la **Salman Rushdie, Derek Walcott, Wole Soyinka,** et al.) while going beyond the built-in **Eurocentrism** of earlier efforts to forge a notion of humankind living harmoniously together. The provincial **universalism** in the Stoic and Cynic idea of a "cosmopolis," Cicero's commonwealth of all creatures endowed with reason and speech, and, later, Kant's proposal for "perpetual peace" are repeated in our times in Martha Nussbaum's influential position, which sees the task of the citizen of the world as consisting in making human beings more like our "fellow city dwellers," grounding our deliberations on "that interlocking commonality." **Homi Bhabha** questions the givenness of such a commonality based on the liberal, benevolent idea of the "empathetic self," which is conceptually inadequate for recognizing the predicament of refugees and migrants. His challenge to such forms of liberalism is put forward in his notion of a marginal or vernacular cosmopolitanism that is informed by the performativity of everyday life, the particularity of human experiences. In moving toward a certain "affective and ethical identification" with globality that is not divorced from "transhistorical memory," he warns against an intellectual ethic that may be blind to, say, the manifestations of Americanness abroad. In critiquing communitarian assertions that the lives of all individuals as well as families are centered around a common national culture, Anthony Appiah's notion of a "rooted cosmopolitanism" suggests instead that what enables the centering of myriad heterogeneous cultures and lives is a shared commitment to constitutional institutions. **Ashis Nandy** echoes Bhabha's concerns about allowing European Enlightenment values to be assumed as definitionally universal and argues for alternative formats of dialogue that are nonhierarchical, nonoppressive and equal and take cognizance of non-Western multicivilizational entities. It is only then that a truly pluricultural universe with a nonsynchronous future can be assured.

Further Reading: T. Brennan 1997.

Prem Poddar

Creolization   The term refers to the word "Creole," which is a derivative of the Spanish/Portuguese word *"criar"*—to bring up, to raise. In early texts, Creole designates parts of the population made up of Caribbean descendants of colonists, born and brought up in the New World. Depending on the region in Latin America or the Caribbean, it can refer to indio-mestizo, to white, or, especially on the former plantation-islands, to American-born and thus acculturated black people. Above all, however, the term "Creole" denotes the languages that have developed during the process of colonization. The term "creolization" has a very brief history in scientific terminology and was initially used to describe the formation and changeability of these languages. Creole languages were already studied in the nineteenth century (Hugo Schuchhardt, 1882–1891) but were conceived merely as a deficient zero-grade of European national languages such as English, French, Spanish, Portuguese, and Dutch. Not until the 1960s (1959 Mona Conference in Jamaica) did Creole languages come to be seen as an autonomous language system and the linguistic term received a certain importance, which, in turn, led to the founding of the scientific field of Creole studies.

In the context of postcolonial studies, the term "creolization" is conceived as "the process of intermixing and cultural change that produces a Creole society," especially in the Caribbean (Ashcrofts, Griffiths, and Tiffin 1998, 58). Similar to the precise outlines of creolization in linguistic terms, this definition restricts the application of the term to a well-defined geographical region. For a general hypothesis of cultural intercourse, a biological term like hybridization seems to be much more adequate. However, in linguistic research, a growing number of Creoles have emerged all over the world. Some linguists have even started to claim that every language has been creolized to some extent during its history. In this way, the meaning of the term "creolization" is becoming as global and general as that of hybridization. However, unlike the biological term, creolization can describe situations dominated by the facts of lingual, social, and cultural fusion without referring to an initial purity or **essentiality**.

The population of the Indian Ocean, West Africa, the Caribbean, and the Pacific, which are the main areas where Creole languages spread, had to manage situations of trade and to maintain hegemonic relations. The example of the Caribbean plantation societies demonstrates how heterogeneous the lingual and cultural basis has been and how important it was to find a common medium of communication. The European colonizers and settlers (with their different European idioms—including a great variety of dialects and slangs), the autochthonous population (although nearly destroyed by murder, diseases, and corporeal overtaxing), and the slaves arriving from Africa created a melting pot where a great variety of voices left its marks. In the nineteenth century a large number of Asian laborers migrated to add to the ethnic, cultural, and linguistic mix of the archipelago.

To further reinforce the image of a multilingual setting, the creolist Robert Chaudenson claims, for example, that the complexity of French-based Creoles is even greater than was thought in earlier research. In fact, the French language involved in Creole language construction was not a single, standard language but different popular and regional language varieties of seventeenth-century France. All these voices, present in one way or another within the plantation community, constituted a new language: Creole. The most outstanding characteristic of Creole languages is their variability and their competence for rapid change, adapting quickly to new situations. Both their heterogeneity and transformability can lead to overall changes that may even touch the whole structure of the language. The highly elaborated production system of the plantation economy and the specific historical and social conditions created a complex semiotic system, equally constituted by all members of this act of communication in the emerging community of culture and language. The aspect of purity does not mean anything for Creole languages, which are fundamentally the product of language and culture contact and different communicative strategies.

The linguistic accounts of Creolization are subsequently extended by scholars and writers from different disciplines to cultural exchange and variety and its various phenomena in the Caribbean area. When in **cultural studies** the structure of culture is declared a semiotic system, it can be easily compared to the semiotic system per se, the structure of language. Hence, at the very moment that the studies of Creole languages came to consider Creoles as original languages, the term "creolization" could be translated to cultural phenomena. Creole languages are no longer seen as a product of the decline of European languages but as an independent product in which different systems overlap and interfere and by these means are able to produce something new. Since the nineteenth century, Creole languages have been looked at in a holistic way. The formation of Creole studies as an independent discipline stands for a paradigmatic shift in the research of these non-nationalized language forms. It incited numerous surveys, at least in all those parts of the world that had undergone a colonization period and had thus created a pidgin or Creole language. It was now that creolists established that these languages were an outstanding object for studies in the biogenetical functioning of language in general (Bickerton 1981). At the same time, it was in the interest of the United States to describe the postcolonial situation after World War II and the decline of the European colonial empires.

Nevertheless, European cultural studies shows a trend toward questioning the old-fashioned terminology in which the constant flux of cultures has been described. Cultural history, which was formerly written with a **nationalist** orientation, is giving way to an internationalization or **globalization** of cultural values. The work of the British historian Peter Burke is paradigmatic in this respect. After important contributions to the study of the Italian Renaissance, Burke has tried since 1997 to deal with the adoption and transformation of

European cultural practices in the New World. Rather than turning away from the European cultural history of the early modern period, this exemplary study of cultural appropriation in the American context is aimed at a more general methodological reflection. Burke asks whether a fixed terminology is able to describe the consequences of cultural contact and undertakes a preliminary account of cultural history in which he outlines new perspectives, considering a "new conception of culture as bricolage, in which the process of appropriation and assimilation is not marginal but central" (1997, 208).

Moreover, Western cultural historiography continues to limit its field of investigation to an elitist high culture that represents the spirit of a nation, while today's conditions of globalization are forcing it to turn away from identity problems toward possibilities of **transculturation**. For this reason, Burke proposes to borrow the terminological apparatus of American social scientists who were the first to deal systematically with phemomena of mixing and interrelations, irrespective of the hierarchies of the concepts of modernity.

The terminological arsenal that we owe to these studies includes four central terms: hybridity, syncretism, metissage (or mestizaje), and creolization. These four terms are used by scientists of New World civilizations to explain different forms of intercultural transfer. But these terms describe, at the same time, a terminological topography within the American-Caribbean area. The term "hybridity" recently incited, apart from **Homi K. Bhabha**, extensive debates on Mexican culture when Néstor García Canclini propagated "hybrid cultures" (1989) such as the Tex-Mex culture on the North American–Mexican border. The second term, "syncretism," is mainly applied in the Spanish Caribbean. The objects of investigation here are religion and music, for example, the Afro-Cuban Santería and the Afro-Cuban Son, that is, exactly those phenomena of Afro-European syncretism that the Cuban cultural scientist Fernando Ortiz analyzed in the first part of the last century. The ideal object was the Afro-Cuban religion, where Yoruban deities were projected onto Roman Catholic saints. In the same way as hybridity, the term "metissage" is charged with a long tradition of biologically, genetically, and racially motivated distinctions of the pure and the unpure. The multiple terminological transfers from one object of scientific research to another made it inevitable to look at the individual elements of meaning that such terms are taking with them when they are dislocated. The cross-breeding of two plants or animals of different biological species is called hybridization; that is, it refers to a fertilization against natural tendencies that steer in the opposite direction of their separation. This element of meaning has been the conceptual basis for the term "metissage," which describes the hybridization of human beings implicating a distinction into different races. The concept came into being after the radical changes brought about by the history of colonization. Hence, the terms "metissage" and "hybridity" always include the racist susceptibility of procreation and breeding. These distinctions are forcing contemporary scholars to use them repeatedly as a counterdiscourse to these traditions.

As the history of the Smaller and Greater Antilles has been marked from the beginning by different migration flows, Creole identity seems to be especially heterogeneous and discontinuous. Apart from their historical implications, a variety of religions—Catholic, Protestant, Hindu, or African and, for some years now, revivalist churches—as well as pan-nationalistic movements such as black consciousness, **negritude** (**Aimé Césaire**), Antillanité (**Edouard Glissant**) and créolité (Jean Bernabé, **Patrick Chamoiseau**, **Maryse Condé**, Raphael Confiant) and, last but not least, the tourism industry have formed a very high grade of pluralism. On the other hand, Caribbean identity is not founded on a common, autochthonous country of origin that already existed before colonization. The founding stage of Caribbean history is, rather, the heart of the slave plantation as meeting ground and battleground of the colonial act and the relationships between master and slave. Finally, Caribbean people have always been susceptible to a form of nomadism that today is called **cosmopolitanism**. In the beginning of the 1950s, the famous Martinican psychiatrist **Frantz Fanon** insisted in his foundational work *Black Skin, White Masks* (1952) on the alienation of the colonized subject. In adopting the values of white colonial power, the **subaltern** black people deny their own identity and are thus led into a psychotic condition that can be cured only by a complete physical and psychological **decolonization**.

In contrast, writers, theorists, and linguists, especially from the French Antilles, are looking for a possible identity based on this premise. They underline the uniqueness of the historical and geographical situation fueled by the understanding that Caribbean culture and identity are the positive products of a complex and multiple set of local historical circumstances and try to conceptualize it in terms of creolité intended to lead Caribbean people to a new identity, assuming the fact of their history without linearity. But the endless circulation of people from the islands to the European metropoles reinforces even more the vision of a nomadic population without a fixed or fixable identity. These are some of the reasons that the possibility of a homogeneous Caribbean identity derived from a common history is constantly being questioned. The fragmentation into separate islands, whose national unity is defined by the colonial hegemony without the advantages of participation in their history, is reflected in their textual production, which designs a **cartography** of gaps and differences.

The poet and historian **Edward Kamau Brathwaite** was the first to link the term "creolization" to his own definition of slave societies embracing all the groups resident in the Caribbean during the period of slavery. His theoretical concern was to show an original Creole culture emerging from plantation economies. His point of departure is not the linguistic paradigm of creolization but the clearly defined topographic and historical setting of the Jamaican Creole culture from 1770 to 1820 (1971). With this particularization of the Creole society, he is drawing a consistent image of the origin and evolution of a specific cultural formation, the different sections and groups of the population of that period, and how these managed to construct a new community. His intention to recognize a Caribbean cultural entity is maintained in his theoretical work by the diachronical reconstruction of a Creole being with a great implication of the African descendants and is featured by the picture of racial and spiritual dispossession in his poetical writings.

The Swedish professor of social anthropology Ulf Hannerz uses the term to describe the multidimensionality of "transnational connections" (1996) in the postcolonial era. He tries once again to do away with the unilateral vision of **center and periphery** and to deal with culture as a "network of perspectives," which, in an ongoing debate, reorganizes its own values and perspectives over and over again. The main question for a global investigation is whether the linguistic term "creolization" is more appropriate than the notion of hybridization to describe the different processes of "cultural complexity" (1992) and the various manifestations of culture to which they give way. "It suggests that the flow of culture between countries and continents may result in another diversity of culture, based more on interconnections than on autonomy" (1992, 266). His endeavor to juxtapose Caribbeans in terms of an ethnic group to his definition of cultural complexity is not aimed at getting deeper inside Creole cultures. One of the most important claims of his analysis is that from the research results of the investigation of Creole language and culture an adequate model can be extracted to describe globalizing flows in general.

Many Caribbean writers have theorized their practice through the medium of genres other than philosophical discourse. Their fiction, poetry, or dramas bear the traces of a theoretical reflection that questions by that means, academic discourse and represents the polyphony of the oral tradition. The effort of the poet, novelist, and philosopher **Edouard Glissant** is to make use of the poetical discourse in order to realize an interdiscursive integration where all the different voices of Caribbean history can take part. His book *Traité du Tout-Monde* (1997) is a collection of varying textual forms aligned next to each other to unfold the notion of creolization within the shape of what he calls a "poetics of relation." The narrative text is based on fragments that he sees as recitations, alluding to oral figures of speech with their constitutive character of repetition. He elucidates a network of related issues connecting and disconnecting them in a continuous flow of varying discourses. Not repetition word by word but the impetus of the storyteller presents his stories always in a different variant, thus forming a new one. With this procedure Glissant is aiming at the reappropriation of history and the problematizing of identity. In subverting his poetic writing in French by mixing Creole words into the text or transforming standard French in order to achieve a subtle dislocation of the norm, Edouard Glissant is developing what he describes as creolizing language. For the French-Antillean writer the question is not whether to write in French or Creole to fulfill a strategic use of language. The poet endeavors to write with all the existing languages in mind and to find a mode of cultural resistance to those homogenizing tendencies that try to stop the ongoing process of Creolization in a movement of reterritorialization.

Glissant's work echoes French poststructuralist philosophy, mainly the theory of rhizomatic networks of Deleuze and Guattari. But their critique of the logocentric European history is translated into his own postcolonial perspective to explain the becoming of a culture based on orality and diversity. His writing began to focus on the idea of antillanité in his *Poetics of Relation* (1990), which laid the groundwork for the Creolité movement. In his early essays he focuses on the term "metissage," which he abandoned finally in *Traite* to replace with the term "creolization," which in his eyes is more appropriate to describe the productive effects of the cultural amalgamation process in the Caribbean. He is juxtaposing the terms "globalization" and "creolization" and emphasizes the particular situation at the end of the twentieth century marked by new qualities such as the worldwide contact of cultures, which at this point of their expansion cannot be held back. Yet the energetic vision of the Caribbean as a world in transformation should be able to produce an emerging global consensus. Nevertheless, it is not the way in which the worldwide imperial culture industry is spreading out that the author is drawing on but an unforeseeable and intentionless process of dissemination that cannot be used for strategic purposes.

The focus of the Cuban writer and theorist Antonio Benítez-Rojo is on the description of the Caribbean in terms of chaos theory. For him the "plantation-machine" (1996), as he puts it, is not only the purely exploitative economic adventure of European colonizers who built up the barbarian system of slavery, subjugating millions of peoples and destroying their families and cultures, but also the basis for the globality of today's Caribbean culture. "It is the bifurcated center that exists inside and outside at the same time, near to and distant from all things that I can understand as my own: race, nationality, language, and religion" (1998, 54). Similar to Glissant, he points out that there is no organization such as history or family trees to find in this space and that creolization is the main and never-ending movement in the Caribbean. In opposition to Glissant, he does not use the term "creolization" as one of process, because this would imply a forward movement. Rather, he speaks of a state that is marked by a "discontinuous series of recurrences," also called "happenings" because of their performative character. He detects a prolonged explosion that has projected everything outward, splitting it into an uncountable mass of fragments that are disseminated all over the world in food, language, sound, rhythm, or dance to "re-form and pull apart once more, and so on" (1998, 55). The best infrastructure for this globalizing of Caribbean culture is, of course, the media. In his country, Cuba, for instance, the recording industry and the cinema have since the 1920s been widely transmitting rumba, son, and conga. Cuban poetry of Nicolas Guillén was followed by the **magic realism** of **Alejo Carpentier** and the paintings of Wifredo Lam and are all now forming part of the industry of global culture. The plantation represents, at the same time, order and disorder and in terms of chaos theory the "strange attractor" of all of the possible states of Creolization.

For both authors, the unpredictability of Creolization prevents its exploitation as a weapon for essentialist **identity politics**. When Glissant describes the polyphony of Caribbean languages and literatures, it is the complex polyrhythmic system for Benítez-Rojo that came from "the African diaspora, the memory of sacred drums and the words of the griot," which derived from the plantation system. But there are also "the rhythms of the sugar mill's machines, the machete stroke that cuts the cane, the overseer's lash, and the planter's language, music, and dance. Later there came other rhythms, from India, from China, and from Java" (1998, 58). The example of musical symbiosis of separate elements best portrays the movement of reflection, refraction, and fragmentation. This network of rhythmic flow was incited by the "big-bang" of the plantation and is now inscribed in the memory of the Caribbean population. Due to these creolizing movements, the rich artistic potential of the region has been a function of its diverse cultural outcome and the evidence of the capability of amalgamation and adaption of Caribbean people, language, and culture to their environment, which is constantly in motion. The "supersyncretic artefact" is not a synthesis of two or more different objects but rather is made up of differences that cannot be reduced to an entity while they keep creolizing themselves. Ulf Hannerz and Edward Kamau Brathwaite make use of the term "Creolization" in their respective disciplines, applying it to conditions of intermixing and diversity. The former starts from a specific topography that he wants to describe; the latter puts it as an abstract model of cultural complexity. They are more or less using it for scientific purposes. In contrast, Glissant and Benítez-Rojo are trying to mingle their conception of the term "creolization" with a poetic praxis. The basis for their creativity is the recombination of fragments. For Benítez-Rojo, "The performer, through his or her performance, can resolve the paradox of his or her identity. But only poetically" (1998, 61). Both authors are trying to find out what role fictional representation can play in this process.

The main assumption here is that a movement from the local to the global level can be traced, from the microcosm of the Caribbean archipelago to the macrocosm of the whole world. This shift is based on the argumentation that the present state of the world, a global space with cultural interconnections, has been created by colonial expansion. The infrastructure of colonialism may serve as a surface on which the process of creolization can globalize itself. These are, therefore, the complementary tendencies of the postcolonial era, and the claim is that no politics of national identity will be able to offer resistance to them in the long term. As a second result it seems obvious that plantation societies have been experiencing and anticipating for some time what the contemporary world condition is reflecting today. As far as the chaotically moving exchange of cultural values is concerned, the presumably underdeveloped Caribbean seems to be on a par with the most advanced regions. Moreover, the term "creolization" applied to postmodern societies always addresses Creole societies. Nevertheless, compared to the biological and racial metaphors, it does not have a negative implication of unpurity but refers to a positive representation of diversity as origin.

Further Readings: B. Ashcroft, G. Griffiths, and H. Tiffin 1998; K. Balutansky and M.-A. Sourieau 1998; A. Benítez-Rojo 1996, 1998; D. Bickerton 1981; E. Brathwaite 1971, 1974; P. Burke 1997; N. García Canclini 1989; E. Glissant 1997, 1999; U. Hannerz 1996; H. Schuchhardt 1882–1891.

Andrea Schwieger Hiepko

Cultural Studies   Cultural studies is a fairly recent cross-disciplinary field concerned with all aspects of the investigation of cultures. A culture is always a specific form of sense-making, though neither uniform nor monolithic. Consequently, one very generally accepted definition of culture in cultural studies sees it as a contested and conflictual set of practices of representation bound up with the processes of formation and re-formation of social groups. A culture in this sense is a productive network of power relations, the embodiment and site of antagonistic relations of domination and subordination. This applies equally to colonial and postcolonial cultures, and cultural studies helps to analyze these different forms. Cultural studies is not a tightly coherent, unified movement with a fixed agenda, though, but embodies the results of the crises and contradictions in the humanities and social science disciplines and makes use of, but also influences, many other fields concerned with understanding and changing human life, such as **feminism**, postcolonialism, deconstruction, **psychoanalysis**, and ethnology.

Cultural studies developed out of the political climate of the 1960s and 1970s neatly expressed in a slogan at the walls of the Sorbonne University in Paris in 1968: "Art is dead. Let us create everyday life." The artful and sometimes artificial world of high culture was to be replaced by everyday life in its totality as the subject of investigation. Raymond Williams, one of the main founders of cultural studies, had already claimed in 1958 that culture is ordinary and voiced his concern about the exclusions practiced by selective traditions of culture. His understanding of culture as "meanings in negotiation" also emphasized the point that a culture is always complex, full of oppositional layers of meaning. In this context, some people stressed the importance and influence of dominant political, social, and economic structures as determinants in people's lives, while others pointed out that life was constructed by human beings and could therefore be changed by determined human action. **Stuart Hall** described these different attitudes as two basic paradigms in cultural studies, the first representing various forms of determinism (as in one-sided versions of **Marxism** but also in structuralism), and the second emphasizing social practices as the constitutive activity in a culture, thus underlining human **agency** (as in the works of Williams, E. P. Thompson, or Richard Hoggart). This dichotomy, however, needs to be overcome in cultural studies, and Williams already supplies the basis for combining the two opposites in his extremely useful definition of culture as being always *both* the lived traditions, practices, and material conditions of life *and* the meanings and values connected with them. Hall also speaks of the necessary dialectic between conditions and consciousness, reductionism and idealism, which have represented the poles of cultural studies from its beginning. Cultural studies is always a dynamic, dialectic, multifaceted enterprise trying to find a third way between the one-sided and therefore unacceptable extremes of materialism and idealism.

Concern with everyday life lay behind the decisive interest of early cultural studies in working-class and popular culture, the mass media, and all those aspects of normal life that had usually been taken for granted. These were new objects of study and perspectives and accompanied the establishment of, for instance, media studies at universities in the 1960s but also the new interest in history "from below," history influenced by the common people (such as in Angus Calder's influential *The People's War* [1969]), rather than by outstanding personalities. One's own culture became an object of study like any other. The investigation of everyday life is connected with the new awareness that when people are at their most natural, their most everyday, they are also at their most cultural. The roles that seem most obvious and given are recognized as constructed, learned, and far from inevitable. Cultural studies has always wanted to make people aware of this constructedness of lives and cultures, and it has therefore been involved in enlightening people, in pointing out the ideologies behind power structures, and in this way also in empowering people. The strong link between cultural studies and politics is based on the fundamental tenet that it is not enough to describe the material facts and human activities in a culture but that the values and meanings connected with them need to be elicited as well. The critique of ideology and of myths thus is an essential element of cultural studies and includes the question as to why certain behavior is regarded as normal, natural, or inevitable. All endeavors to interpret the cultural as the natural and the historical and political as the universal tend to establish ideologies and myths; they are part of the bourgeois (described in Roland Barthes' *Mythologies* [1957/1978], for instance) as well as of the patriarchal or the colonial ideologies. The criticism and exposure of ideologies and myths in cultural studies are, therefore, also an essential element in feminism and postcolonialism. As no culture is without myths as providers of meaning, cultural studies needs to distinguish productive myths from destructive ones. This is particularly relevant in politics, in analyses of power structures, and in all discussions of authenticity and **identity**. Early work in cultural studies, for instance, reveals that newsreels on television do not simply reflect reality but construct it and are highly charged with ideologies and myths. Reality, even in the news but also in the sciences, is always mediated, never encountered directly, but always through signs, especially language.

The development of new perspectives, new subject areas, disciplines, and corresponding institutions went along with the breaking up of subject boundaries and a revived interest in interdisciplinary work. At the same time, personal judgments, evaluations, and even feelings were now acknowledged in research, and the traditional assumption that science should be and can be objective was abolished. **Michel Foucault** and Jürgen Habermas were among those who showed that no research is really objective, that there is always an inseparable connection between "knowledge and human interests," that there are always feelings and aspirations to power involved in the production and distribution of knowledge. Cultural studies explicitly acknowledges the involvement of the researcher in the world that is investigated, even if this world is a foreign culture.

Culture is obviously a category that transcends and transgresses disciplinary, theoretical, and methodological boundaries. That is why cultural studies has challenged the restrictions implicit in the divisions of academic organization and knowledge production; it even constitutes a fundamental challenge to the whole (Western) quest for (scientific) certainty, in fact, a challenge to all one-sided forms of epistemology. Basically, two different types of approach can be distinguished: the empirical, quantitative approach of the sciences and the interpretive, qualitative approach of the humanities. Ideally, cultural studies employs both kinds constructively and at the same time, but actually cultural studies methodology often is a kind of *bricolage*: one is pragmatic and strategic in choosing and applying different methods and practices, and in selecting a method, one does not necessarily want to adopt the whole scientific paradigm to which it belongs.

A very pragmatic consequence of the vastness of the field and the diversity of approaches and theoretical backgrounds is cultural studies' concern with a number of individual studies rather than with a single monolithic description— analyses of the many different aspects of a culture, rather than of culture as a comprehensive whole. As it is impossible for a single person to grasp all aspects of today's culture(s), and as every researcher necessarily lives in only a small section of the world and even of his or her culture(s), a very useful approach has been to limit the scope of a study to what sociologists have called a "life world." The term has been transferred to other disciplines, and it is extremely appropriate for cultural studies, where the concept is also referred to as "the practical world," "everyday life," "the local community," or (as Angela Mc-Robbie put it in *Postmodernism and Popular Culture* [1994]), the "nearest appropriate constituency" (41). A life world provides people with very specific functions and identities, a sense of coherence and belonging that enables them to find or create meaning in their lives. The family, school, university, work, and leisure-time activities can all provide such life worlds. The starting point for a cultural studies investigation of life worlds is not an abstract theory (for instance, about the working class in Britain) but the concrete living conditions, activities, discourses, and values of people in a specific area. For such descriptions, cultural studies uses the tools of anthropology (e.g., ethnography and ethnomethodology), employs the language and stories of the people investigated, and applies sociological strategies to the depiction of milieus. The integration of such facts into meaningful contexts involves interpretation from the beginning, though, and the life world approach again combines quantitative and qualitative methods. A life world can also be regarded as a module in a network, a microculture within a macroculture that can perhaps not really be completely

investigated or at least requires research in its subsections to help in the understanding of the whole. For this problem of quantity in cultural studies, the network concept of culture and the concentration on specific life worlds offer a
pragmatic solution.

The emphasis on everyday life implies a concern with the importance of
individuals, and cultural studies is currently most interestingly engaged in sup-
plying a theory of the individual and of subjectivity as a decisive element in
cultures (cf. Cohen 1994). Such a theory has significantly been neglected in
Marxism, structuralism, and poststructuralism, where the individual is always
seen as a rather passive element subjected to overpowering determining influences. Such influences as the society as a whole, the media, dominant discourses,
and so on are certainly not neglected in cultural studies, but they are seen against
the possibilities with which individuals have to come to terms and creatively
change. There is an evidently growing concern in cultural studies with the social
construction of subjectivities (cf. Johnson 1986–1987; Certeau 1998).

Cultural distinctions and meaning systems are studied from the point of view
of both actors and structures. Meaning and subjectivity are the productions neither of absolutely free and authentic individuals nor of some transcendent absolute. Cultural studies again looks for a middle way between these extremes,
and this middle way has many similarities with the third way described in postcolonial literature and theory, the development of novelty out of the often conflicting influences of, say, colonial and postcolonial powers. Cultural studies is,
in this way, both deconstructive and reconstructive. Again, like feminism and
postcolonialism but unlike **postmodernism**, cultural studies cannot do away
with ethics, politics, history, truth, identity, and meaning. Rather, it is, through
its analyses of cultures, inevitably concerned with them. This implies a concern
with the signs used to express history, truth, and so on. As Quine had already
made clear in his "Two Dogmas of Empiricism" (1953), distinctions between
truth and nontruth enter our conception only as cultural posits. Such distinctions,
like all valuations, depend on the entire existing set of beliefs, truth claims, or
attitudinal dispositions that happens to prevail within some given community of
knowledge. In other words, they depend on the culture in which they are made;
thus, culture is what determines people's real lives, their identities, their values.
Culture inevitably defines and "constructs" reality. This construction is not only
material but also conceptual, if not idealistic. It is certainly inseparable from
signs.

Culture, it seems today, is most successfully investigated when regarded as a
sign system. This again allows for the combination of scientific methods with
hermeneutic approaches and emphasizes a perspective succinctly expressed by
Clifford Geertz, who says that an analysis of culture is not an experimental
science in search of law but an interpretive one in search of meaning. The
combination of the description of facts with values and meanings provides a
cultural analysis in which the material and the symbolic are seen in relation to

each other, as Raymond Williams already demanded. This has many intriguing consequences, as, for instance, the use of symbolic interactionism (rooted in American pragmatism) in sociology and cultural studies (see Denzin 1992); but, above all, this results in a semiotic approach to culture on the assumption that everything in a cultural analysis can be regarded as a sign system or text. A text in cultural studies goes far beyond the discrete boundaries of the page or the book into the institutional practices and social structures of a culture. A bus ticket, for instance, taken as an item of a particular culture, is then incorporated into texts (including all relevant contexts) that tell the stories of a specific transport system in a particular community, of the people who use it, work in it, and organize it, of the money that is needed for it, of the advantages and disadvantages that it has in comparison to other means of transport, and so on.

In this way, cultural studies is always connected with narratives and with human activities. Narration, in particular, is regarded as a basic activity giving meaning to human life (cf. Nash 1990). The social production and circulation of meaning in a specific culture are the subject matter of cultural studies as it tries to read the signs of the times where material artifacts are always symbolic, and all practices also signify. A text, then, is a network of connections in which each element is conceived as being relational rather than substantial. Everything in a culture receives its value and meaning through its position in that structure conveniently called text, because this is a suitable metaphor for the marking or tracing of pure relationality. In addition to this metaphorical use of the term, textual analysis is also an already well advanced approach that can be usefully employed in cultural studies until better tools for an understanding of culture have been created.

The development of a "poetics of culture" in New Historicism reflects the importance of narration, the inseparable link between culture and signs, and the investigation of culture as text. As poetics is concerned with the general laws of creating, distributing, and perceiving texts and with the interpretive competence of people dealing with specific genres that serve particular purposes and invite some forms of discourse rather than others, and so on, the term "poetics" is quite appropriate for the definition of the work done in cultural studies. A cultural poetics today is necessarily descriptive rather than prescriptive. The poetics of an everyday world investigates the forms (the styles of clothing, housing, work, and so on but also of language, the discourses, ideologies, and so on) that constitute a specific life world and create a meaningful story for the people living in this world. Empirical tools, which help define the social milieu, the institutions involved, the economic and political situation, and so on, but also the language used, are again employed in connection with hermeneutical tools, which serve to understand human actions and place them in a specific system of meanings and values. Texts are developed in the life world as well as in cultural studies that produce meaning and reveal the need of human beings for meaning (as investigated by Wolfgang Iser, e.g., in the context of literary anthropology). These texts need not be nonfictional, as fictional ones can equally reveal a certain concept of a life world. In New Historicism, the difference between literary and other texts has practically been abolished.

Cultural materialism, an approach developed in the 1970s and 1980s in British literary and critical studies, provides good examples of the importance of literary texts in an analysis of cultures (even though this importance has also been recognized by many historians, such as G. M. Trevelyan). Cultural materialists claim, for example, that Shakespeare's history plays provide a better understanding of the culture described in them than contemporary history books, because the latter often make sense of the past in a very partial and ideological way, whereas the literary texts provide space for subversive voices and dissenting opinions. This unique ability of literature to represent complexity, plurality, contradictoriness, and inconsistency is a substantial reason for the inclusion of literary texts in cultural studies. Cultural materialism also claims that meaning is created not by individuals or by abstract entities, such as class, gender, nation, or race, but only in specific contexts that constitute a culture. The cultural materialist Alan Sinfield has expressed this with regard to the notion of political awareness, which is an essential element in cultural materialism and which, he says, arises from involvement in a milieu, a subculture. This life world furnishes political awareness as well as emotional security, specific practices, and a sense of identity. It provides people, as Sinfield puts it, with stories that work, and it is these stories, in the vast complexity of the poetics of culture or of cultural materialism, that cultural studies needs to investigate and describe. The life story of every person is meaningful only in the context of a specific life world. No text is autonomous, and every text is a site of cultural contest. That is why, for Sinfield, culture as a whole is constituted by the perpetual contest of stories striving for dominance and recognition. But for cultural materialism it is not enough to acknowledge the great variety of texts and their readings. In contrast to most postmodernist approaches but in accordance with postcolonialism, cultural materialism does not want to produce just different readings; it also wants to shift the criteria of plausibility of the texts. These criteria necessarily derive from the living conditions of people, their material, political, social, and economic situation in connection with their feeling and experience of life as expressed in their life stories. Cultural materialism does not deny the agency of human beings and their possibility of actively changing cultures, of creating better life stories not only on a blank page but in reality. Such agency is not always acknowledged in cultural studies; it is almost nonexistent in New Historicism, but it is of essential importance in feminism and postcolonialism.

Discourse analysis is another useful approach in cultural studies, again combining very different methods: a text is described linguistically, and the speakers and topics are analyzed, as are the social positions of the speakers and the power structures in the communicative situation; and, eventually, the world that is created in the text is compared with the worlds established in other texts. The point here is that a text does not reflect a world that exists outside of a text but that reality is always connected with texts and actually constructed in texts. Reality is a text. Or, to make this more palatable for people still believing in realism or even positivism, reality can be best described and understood as text, and all of reality that human beings can understand is therefore a text. Derrida's statement that there nothing outside the text makes much sense in that everything is relational and has meaning only in connection with other things, that is, in a culture, a system, a network, a text. In **discourse** analyses, these networks (or at least the most important modules in them) are investigated, and the use of language in specific contexts is analyzed. That is why one now thinks that every theory and practice of discourse always imply a theory of the society or culture investigated. For Stephen Greenblatt, for instance, culture is therefore an ensemble of discourse formations, a network of multiple texts whose analysis discloses the behavioral codes, logics, and motive forces controlling a whole society. Discourse analysis reveals the constructedness of culture again and the tenuousness of the claims of any single power structure or fixed worldview. Both feminist and postcolonial discourse analyses have made this very evident and have also shown that it is absolutely essential for people to become linguistically and semiotically visible, in order to be acknowledged as really existing. There is, indeed, nothing outside a text; nothing exists unless human beings speak about it, and the way they speak about it determines its place in society. In this sense, discourse is power, and those who can represent themselves and others through discourse are powerful; those who cannot almost don't even seem to exist at all.

As cultures are characterized by specific discourses (including particular metaphors and ways of describing and defining reality), different cultures develop different styles (in speaking as well as in behavior, dress, and so on) and also create different histories. The rewriting of colonial stories and histories in postcolonialism is a striking example of these new styles, stories, and histories that cultural studies needs to investigate comparatively as well as historically, for its concern with everyday life implies a concern for the past, the present, and even the future, no less than for the workings of class, racism, colonialism, sex, and gender. It also necessarily includes cultural politics, dealing with all questions of the political influence, power, and relationships of the various cultures in a certain area.

As cultural studies is concerned not only with facts but also with meanings and values, all of which depend on contexts that determine meanings, and as these contexts change, cultural studies is endless and never reaches final conclusions. In addition to this, every symbolic representation necessarily includes ambiguity and doubleness, that is, always the possibility of oppositional and critical representation, as it is quite clear that the chosen form is just one of many possible ways in which reality can be represented. A representation requires the consent of people in order to establish itself as a culture. The complexity of this situation is further increased through the fact that cultures as texts are not only read and interpreted but also written by those who investigate them.

Through the criteria, perspectives, and the language employed by the researcher, the observed culture is already partly predefined. This fairly recent focus on text-making highlights the constructed nature of cultural accounts and the inseparable connection between cultures and signs once again (cf. Clifford and Marcus 1986). Something else is made evident in this way, too, namely, the close relationship between the foreign culture and the culture of its observer. The result is that the other is always a construct and a part of oneself. Any description of others as foreigners and as different mirrors the expectations, criteria, hopes, and fears of the observer. That is why cultural studies introduces people not only to other cultures but always also to their own and to themselves. Cultural studies is, in this sense, always intercultural and self-reflexive: it helps people to learn about other ways of life as well as to develop a better understanding of their own lives. Self-reflexivity implies a critical account of one's own motivating questions and thus of the frameworks and rules by which the cultural studies research imperatives are formed. It also helps to accept the partiality, the incompleteness, and the open-endedness of all research.

The development of cultural studies has coincided with postcolonialism and so shares with it many interests and perspectives, such as the concern with everyday life and the power structures that influence human activities; the importance of signs as markers of identity or dependence; the emphasis on values and meanings; the questions of human agency and involvement in the construction of cultures; the thoroughly ambivalent character of social control exercised through culture. Postcolonialism is an excellent example of the constructive power of members of a culture to bring about radical change. The theory of subjectivity that is still missing in cultural studies would have to take into account this impressive achievement, and it would shift the focus of attention much more to production, after a long period of interest in consumption. But the most interesting studies in media consumption, such as Ien Ang's investigation of soap opera, have shown that even consumption is a locus of active cultural production, of selective appropriations and innovations of cultural forms in people's daily lives. Such constructive appropriations are of importance in cultural studies and in postcolonialism, but they also reflect the creative potential of human life generally. Cultural studies is involved in investigating this constructive human capacity, and it currently finds much support in **constructionism** for its understanding of this creative quality of human cultures. It is only at the beginning of its work, still creating and defining its place in the world and in the institutions of human knowledge, but it is evidently concerned with some of the most vital problems of today.

Further Reading: Y. Lotman 1990; G. Turner 1996.

Klaus-Peter Müller

D

Decolonization   It appears that a German scholar, Moritz Julius Bonn, coined the term "decolonization" in 1932 in his contribution on "Imperialism" for the *Encyclopedia of the Social Sciences* (edited by Edwin Seligman). However, the term attained general currency only after World War II, when, during the period from the late 1940s to the mid-1970s, the great modern European empires were dismantled one after the other. As late as November 1942, British prime minister Winston Churchill was declaring, "I have not become the King's First Minister in order to preside over the liquidation of the British Empire" (quoted in Sarkar 1983, 376–77). But less than five years later, at midnight on 15 August 1947, Jawaharlal Nehru took Britain's most valued colony, the jewel in the crown, out of the empire, became the first prime minister of independent India, and spoke of his country's "tryst with destiny." During the thirty-year period that followed, "decolonization" became the omnibus term for a similar retreat of different varieties of European political and economic power from other colonies around the world. The term has by now come to refer mostly to the historical transformation of the Dutch, Portuguese, French, and British empires in Asia, Africa, and the Caribbean.

In this sense, "decolonization" is linked terminologically to "Third World," another term—coined apparently by the French demographer Alfred Sauvy in 1952—that came into popular usage during the same period (see Harlow 1987, 5). The latter term refers to a third grouping of nations, independent of the Western bloc (led by the capitalist United States of America) or the Eastern bloc (led by the communist Soviet Union). When considered in conjunction with "Third World," decolonization becomes apprehensible as the process of the emergence of this third grouping onto the world political stage. In 1955, at a meeting in Bandung in Indonesia, this linkage between the disappearance of colonies and the appearance of a new coordinated consciousness in world politics was made most dramatically visible. The Bandung conference brought together the leaders of twenty-nine Asian and African countries representing over 50 percent of the world's population. In his address to the meeting, President Sukarno of Indonesia declared that "we are united by a common detestation of colonialism, in whatever form it appears" (quoted in Betts 1998, 42). Held only ten years after the end of World War II, the Bandung conference indicated the extent to which the colonial world had changed.

But where had this change come from? In one sense, the period before World War II was the high point of imperialism. The modern European colonies reached their greatest physical extent when the Treaty of Versailles, concluded among various European powers at the end of World War I, brought fresh territories within the colonial system. What explains, then, the rapidity with which the apparently impregnable fortress of European imperialism was first breached and then overrun in the years following World War II?

In recent years, as the hope of decolonization has passed into historical fact, a lively debate has taken up this question. One side of the debate has emphasized developments within metropolitan societies (i.e., within colonizing nations), while the other side has emphasized developments among the colonized. The former finds the roots of decolonization mainly within the changed consciousness and material circumstances of metropolitan societies; the latter, within the renewed vigor of the colonized.

It is not really contestable that World War II did, indeed, severely shake all the main combatants, including those who eventually emerged victorious. While France was actually occupied by Germany during the war, Britain's resources were stretched to the limit. All the European powers emerged from the war in a weakened condition, affecting their ability to maintain their control over their colonies. In addition to these material constraints, the psychological advantage enjoyed by the European colonial powers had been compromised by the defeats that the Japanese had imposed on them in Asia. The war made palpable to the colonizers (as well as to the colonized) the severe limitations of European power. Many colonies—such as the Dutch colony of the East Indies—fell into Japanese hands for a number of years, during which period political institutions independent of the former colonial masters were allowed to grow. Thus, the conclusion of World War II found the European powers in a far different situation than previously.

As a related point, it should be observed that the years following World War II also witnessed the usurpation of global power from Western Europe, first by the United States and then by the Soviet Union. The United States, the new superpower, regarded decolonization with ambivalence. On the one hand, the notion found some resonance within American anti-British republicanism, even as it fit in with expanding American ambitions by providing an opportunity to replace a global Pax Britannica with a Pax Americana. On the other hand, decolonization also provided an opening to the Soviet Union, the United States' archrival in the race to global hegemony. As Western Europe was consolidated into a position of subordination to American power, then, the United States came to see countries like Britain, Belgium, France, and Portugal as proxy states whose colonial relationships could be used to contest what was seen as Soviet expansionism. Accordingly, American enthusiasm for decolonization progressively cooled during the period of the Cold War between the United States and the Soviet Union.

A similar admixture of moral and material support and strategic maneuvering can be seen to characterize Soviet attitudes to decolonization. The strong valence of **Marxism** and socialism within most decolonization movements, found in an uneasy alliance with **nationalist** ideology, tended to bring Soviet support, even as American support was alienated. These kinds of strategic considerations, typical of the Cold War, were behind the complications, for example, that attended the drives to decolonization in Indochina as well as central and southern Africa, leading to civil wars in Vietnam, the Belgian Congo, Angola, and Mozambique. At the same time, the Cold War provided some decolonized countries, too, with unique opportunities to maneuver. Both decolonization movements and decolonized nations found themselves able to pit one superpower against the other and garner support for themselves. Finally, in the context of our review of changes in metropolitan societies relating to decolonization, some historians have also suggested that decolonization is of a piece with the growth of liberal politics within these societies. Thus, decolonization may be seen to be complementary to such other developments as the welfare society and the civil rights movement. With the spread of liberal values through Western European societies, it is argued, colonialism lost popular support.

Many historians regard the causes for decolonization laid out thus far—focusing on changes within metropolitan societies—as the most important. For example, in *European Decolonization 1918–1981: An Introductory Survey* (1985), R. F. Holland makes the following rather polemical observation: "It is one of the central themes of this study that European decolonizations after 1945, particularly in their African dimension after 1956, arose more directly from changing conditions *within* the metropoles than they did from any metamorphosis at the periphery" (191). From a different perspective, this assessment of decolonization might be regarded as undervaluing the contributions of the colonized themselves to their emancipation.

What were these contributions? Here, again, only a brief and illustrative survey is possible. To explain decolonization with reference to changes within colonial societies requires a retreat to the period immediately preceding decolonization—though it must be noted that periodization is always a perilous matter when discussing a global phenomenon. In the case of some colonies, the dates are earlier, and in others later, and what is offered here is only a general outline. In this spirit it might be noted that if the interwar period saw the territorial apotheosis of modern European colonialism, it was also the period of growing opposition within the colonies. A variety of social and political processes led to the rapid development of anticolonial and nationalist—the two are linked but not necessarily the same—sentiments within different colonies. The appellation "nationalist" is more properly given to those mass movements (mostly led by the bourgeoisie and the petty bourgeoisie) that tended to articulate self-conscious ideologies of nationhood as a way of contesting colonialism. In the Indian context, an example of such an articulation is to be found in Jawaharlal Nehru's historical work *The Discovery of India* (1946), written during a period of imprisonment by the British colonial masters.

Broadly speaking, at least two dimensions to changes within the colonies during the interwar period deserve special mention in the context of our discussion. In 1916, V. I. Lenin in *Imperialism, the Highest Stage of Capitalism* had pointed to the specifically economic nature of colonial exploitation. During the interwar period, the exigencies of this exploitation combined with the spreading effects of the Great Depression to increase restiveness and resistance in the lower reaches of colonial societies. Widespread and anticolonial agrarian unrest characterized many colonies, including, for example, the French colonies of Indochina. Since the colonies were, in the main, still agrarian societies, the significance of this unrest cannot be overstated. Simultaneously, the interwar period saw the successful emergence of an autonomous, though small, indigenous bourgeoisie—composed of professional and business classes—in many colonies. The classic example of this phenomenon is India. The burgeoning ambitions of these classes drove the rapid transformation of the Indian National Congress into a mass movement under the charismatic leadership of M. K. (Mahatma) Gandhi. Since the bourgeoisie possessed the resources to develop institutions and social mechanisms capable of contesting colonialism on its own terms, the significance of this restless reaching after power on the part of this group also cannot be overstated.

Agrarian unrest and bourgeois ambition, then, may be regarded as two important intracolonial causes contributing to the vigor of the decolonizing process after World War II. In a successful decolonizing movement, one was linked to the other through the development of organizations with the ability to mobilize large sectors of society. In his little-known work entitled *Nkrumah and the Ghana Revolution* (1977), **C.L.R. James**, radical West Indian student of decolonization, set out to demonstrate precisely this thesis with regard to the Gold Coast (later, Ghana). More conventional historiography has tended to emphasize that the initial resistance to colonialism came from an organization of the African elite called the United Gold Coast Convention (UGCC). In contrast, James locates the impetus for decolonization in the workers, the market women, and the primary school-educated youth. The UGCC, founded by J. B. Danquah in 1947, was a moderate party aiming at a smooth transfer of power within the colony to elite African hands. The successful drive to decolonization under Kwame Nkrumah, however, hijacked this limited agenda in a more radical direction. In 1949 Nkrumah, who had been invited back from London to become the secretary of the UGCC and popularize it, broke with the party to set up his own, called the Convention People's Party (CPP). The CPP successfully linked bourgeois ambition to mass aspirations, and, consequently, in 1957, Ghana became the first British colony in sub-Saharan Africa to become independent.

The example of Kwame Nkrumah and the Gold Coast also points to another important factor in decolonization: the growth of what may be called intercolonial associations and collaborations. These associations and collaborations were especially important in the African context, because of the "toing and froing" across what Paul Gilroy has felicitously called "the **black Atlantic**" in his book of the same title. Nkrumah himself was educated in the United States, came into contact with West Indian proponents of African decolonization such as George Padmore in London, and participated in the important 1945 Pan-African Conference, also attended by Kenyan nationalist Jomo Kenyatta. Indeed, this particular Pan-African Conference, which played an important role in giving a radical impetus to African decolonization, was only one of a series. The first such meeting had been organized by the African American W.E.B. Du Bois and the Senegalese Blaise Diagne, collaborating in the traditions of the black Atlantic in Paris in 1919. Thus, we can conclude that in the African context, notions of continental or even racial solidarity vied with a more conventional nationalism for the status of chief ideological opponent of colonialism.

Such, then, were a few of the causes of decolonization relevant to a consideration of the contributions of the colonized. The debate over how best to understand decolonization—whether as driven primarily by metropolitan concerns or by changes within the colonial world—may probably be satisfactorily resolved by noting that both contributed to the process. Furthermore, this is a good point on which to resist generalization and aver that, in the case of a particular colony, the former set of causes may be more relevant, while, in the case of another, the latter may. However, such neat resolution, persuasive though it may be at many levels, should not lead to an underestimation of the need *to decolonize the story of decolonization*. After all, the story of decolonization can be, and has been, told in many different ways. Which way comports best with a decolonized perspective?

However we may understand decolonization, the dates and the facts are by now well known. If the independence of India in 1947 may be regarded as a key event heralding the age of decolonization, then 1975, the year of independence of the last substantial Portuguese colonies in Africa (Angola and Mozambique) and of the United States' exit from Vietnam may perhaps be regarded as closing the age. Colonies remained after 1975, but they were few and anomalous. By 1975, for the most part, decolonization, understood as the achievement of political independence as a national entity, had passed from the subjective realm of hope to the objective condition of fact. Within this thirty-year sweep, smaller patterns are discernible. Most Asian colonies had achieved independence by 1960. The great period of African decolonization was from the late 1950s to the middle of the 1970s. Other important dates here are 1948, when the communists vanquished their opponents in China and achieved control over what had been a quasi-colonial territory; 1949, when Indonesia achieved independence from the Dutch; 1956, when the British and the French attempted to overthrow President Nasser of Egypt through an old-fashioned use of imperial power and were rebuffed; 1957, when Ghana became the first sub-Saharan African country to achieve independence; and 1962, when Algeria achieved independence from France after a protracted and violent struggle.

Such a condensation of dates and facts cannot but be superficial; and perhaps precisely because of this, it is useful in indicating some of the inadequacies in the most prevalent conceptions of decolonization. A geographical focus on colonialism as a European phenomenon discounts the role of the United States, which, while ambivalent with regard to colonialism in the ways previously discussed, was nevertheless also an imperial country similar to a European power like Britain. Indeed, Philippines, an American colony, was the first Asian country to decolonize (in 1946), even if it did not prove to be the important model that India was.

A temporal focus on decolonization as a phenomenon of the post–World War II era shows up even more vexing anomalies. Ireland, arguably the country to be colonized the longest by Britain, was decolonized (for the most part) in the interwar period. In focusing on decolonization after 1945, it is easy to overlook the importance of the Irish struggles for independence for anticolonialism in general. Moving even further back, we see that such a temporal focus glosses over the movements that swept through Latin America during the nineteenth century, as what is often referred to as the first imperial age came to an end. These movements loosened the grip of Spain and Portugal, the earliest colonial powers, on this vast terrain and left **Creole** nations in their wake. Then, of course, it is possible to make the argument that the first experience with decolonization occurred in Haiti in the late eighteenth century. Haiti achieved independence from France in 1801. While the case of the United States, which, too, achieved independence in roughly the same period, shows many radical differences from the decolonizing movements after World War II—not the least of which is the articulation of a colonialist ideology of Manifest Destiny—Haiti, as the already mentioned C.L.R. James argued in the concluding pages of his monumental study of the Haiti revolution entitled *The Black Jacobins* (1938), can be easily seen to have particular relevance for European colonies in Africa.

The import of this discussion of the inadequacies in our account of decolonization thus far is to draw attention to the temporal and geographical boundaries appropriate to the term "decolonization." Such attention does not necessarily invalidate a focus on the African, Asian, and Caribbean colonies of European powers after 1945, but it does caution us against glib generalizations and make us attentive to the historical complexity of decolonization. Perhaps the point may be made by recourse to Fredric Jameson's useful distinction in *The Political Unconscious* (1981) between history and historicism (18). To be historical is to be attentive to the vital links between different times; to be historicist is to be attentive to the past but without regard for such links. History, rather than historicism, is the imperative in any account of decolonization.

Thus far, our narrative has taken for granted the self-evident nature of the fact of political independence and proceeded to account for decolonization on its basis. Beginning from a notion of cultural independence, however, provides us with a different narrative. **Frantz Fanon**, in *The Wretched of the Earth* (c. 1963), especially in the chapter "On National Culture," was among the first to draw attention to what may be called the cultural and psychological dimensions of decolonization. As various commentators since then have suggested, a sensitivity to cultural issues provides us with a different temporality for decolonization. Reduced or raised, depending on your attitude, to anticolonial sentiment, "decolonization" as a term escapes the temporal straitjacket imposed by the political event of independence. In this sense, decolonization is to be found even at the original moment of colonization, in the **resistance** encountered by the British colonizers, for example, from the Ashanti in the Gold Coast. Decolonization becomes comprehensible in this context as total dissent from the seductions and repressions of colonialist ideology. Fanon opens *The Wretched of the Earth* by foregrounding this notion of decolonization, suggesting that it "is quite simply the replacing of a certain 'species' of men [*sic*] by another 'species' of men [*sic*]" (35). Going on to note that "we could equally well stress the rise of a new nation," he declares that he chooses to regard decolonization rather as "the minimum demands of the colonized" (35).

At first glance, this culturalist and psychological conception of decolonization would seem to retrieve an expanded notion of the **agency** of the colonized—that is, it would seem to recover a richer understanding of their capacity to act in ways independent of the power of the colonizer. This conception of decolonization would underline for us the ways in which the colonized, even at the moment of their defeat (i.e., colonization) emerge victorious (i.e., dissent from colonization). However, a corollary to this culturalist or psychological interpretation of decolonization would, in fact, encourage a less sanguine attitude to the question of the agency of the colonized. The flip side of pushing notions of "decolonization" back so that they include resistance to colonialism is to query whether decolonization is, in fact, achieved at the moment of political independence, whether in a cultural and psychological sense ("deep" sense as opposed to the superficial fact of political independence) colonial societies have, in fact, been liberated from colonialism. The result, then, is to pose the following choice: postcolonialism or **neocolonialism**? Which follows decolonization? The former term would imply an optimistic assessment of the achievement of decolonization, that decolonization had certainly enabled a radical departure from the disabling effects of colonialism. In contrast, the latter would imply a pessimism regarding decolonization. It would suggest that decolonization has meant really the transformation of colonial mechanisms to fit a different age. The real effects of colonialism—economic subordination, cultural imperialism, and psychological anxiety—it would suggest, survive the trivial detail of independence.

Undoubtedly, independence and its aftermath were hardly ever unaccompanied by disillusionment. The tragedy of the partition of colonial territory into two separate nations and the displacement and death of millions in sectarian strife heralded India's journey into independence. Within a few years after its independence, Ghana plunged into chaos, and Kwame Nkrumah, erstwhile hero of African decolonization, was forcibly ejected from power. Poverty, illiteracy, civil war, unemployment, malnourishment—the litany of postcolonial failure tells a story of hopes deferred and opportunities squandered. In the African context, generations of novelists like the Kenyan **Ngũgĩ wa Thiong'o** and the Ghanaian **Ayi Kwei Armah** have explored this desperate territory. In Asia, the Pakistani Faiz Ahmad Faiz and Indonesian **Pramoedya Ananta Toer** have made similar contributions. As the raw passion that accompanied political independence grows ever fainter with the passage of time, it seems pertinent to raise questions about postindependence achievement.

Postcolonialism or neocolonialism? It is undeniable that the postcolonial condition, to use a favored current locution, deserves urgent remedy. The question is whether blame for this state of affairs is to be assigned to former colonial, now neocolonial powers. Nowhere did colonial powers retreat without determined efforts to leave institutions in place that would permit them to control the future of decolonized countries. The experience of francophone Africa is, in this sense, exemplary. As part of its decolonizing effort, France set up an organization that would bind its former colonies to it in a close economic and political relationship. Refusal to join this organization would mean the complete withdrawal of the French. When Guinea decided not to join the association, the French interpreted complete withdrawal in a rather startling way. "When Guinea opted for independence," writes historian Raymond Betts, "the French expressed the exactness of their intentions by taking as much equipment as they could when they departed, including telephones off the walls" (1998, 31). Surely, part of postcolonial disillusionment has to do with the realization that the achievement of nominal independence is one thing, and the transformation of economic relationships of subordination and dependence is another. In this context "neocolonialism" seems an appropriate term.

Yet, it would be wrong to conclude, therefore, that decolonization has been in vain. The achievements of independence struggles have been significant, even if they have not remained uncontested later. Perhaps the best way to describe the contemporary condition of the formerly colonized world is as both postcolonial and neocolonial, successfully decolonized in some respects and still subject to updated colonial mechanisms in others. Decolonization was always a difficult and complicated undertaking. That it has not delivered colonial societies into the fresh air and pure light of paradise, that it has not yet, in the words of Fanon, "set afoot a new man [sic]" does not detract from what it has made possible, if not real (1968, 316).

Finally, as the words of Fanon illustrate only too vividly, if unintentionally, the story of decolonization, understood as a contest for state and other such forms of power in colonial territories, has largely been a masculine affair. Part of the task of decolonizing the story of decolonization must be to explore why this has been the case and in what ways decolonization has faltered—as it surely has—because it has been so.

Further Reading: R. Betts 1998; F. Fanon 1968.

S. Shankar

Dependency Thesis   Contemporary literature usually includes several themes, sometime competing but each having some relevance, that "explain" Third World underdevelopment. They are (1) Rostownian stages of growth, (2) Keynesian capital accumulation, (3) Lewis' "surplus-labor" framework, (4) the dependency thesis, and, more recently, (5) the neo-classical free-market counterrevolution model. The first three, much in vogue till the early 1970s, mainly focused on internal factors (insufficient saving/investment, lack of education/ skills, changes in economic structure, etc.), with assistance from abroad; and the fifth is the global extension of the 1980s neo-classical free-market paradigm, which used to be advocated during early post–World War II, postcolonial years. However, the dependency thesis gained momentum in the 1970s, especially among Third World intellectuals (though not exclusively), as a result of disenchantment with existing explanations and widening global disparities. Indeed, this thesis inspired the now-dormant 1974 United Nations (UN) New International Economic Order Declaration.

Numerous names are identifiable in the literature: Samir Amin, Paul Baran, Benjamin Cohen, Keith Griffin, John Gurley, Colin Leys, Patrick O'Brien, Theotonio Dos Santos, Immanuel Wallerstein, and others. However, about the most durable and forceful proponent of this thesis has to be Andre Gunder Frank, for whom the state of "underdevelopment" of the poor countries was itself created or "developed" by the actions of the rich countries. Thus, the "automatic" functioning of the international economy, dominated by Europe, created underdevelopment and then hampered efforts to escape from it; thus, underdevelopment is seen as a product of the historical processes.

The dependency thesis views developing countries as beset with institutional, political, and economic rigidities, both national and international, and trapped in a dependence/dominance relationship with developed countries. The developing countries, though politically independent, are viewed as still part of the neocolonial **center–periphery** linkages. Whether the rich countries are intentionally exploitative by design or benignly neglectful, the coexistence of rich and poor nations in an international capitalistic system, dominated by unequal power relationships between the center and the periphery, renders attempts by the developing countries to be self-reliant and independent rather difficult, if not impossible.

In addition, it is argued, some groups within the developing countries (landlords, military, entrepreneurs, public officials, etc.) hold superior socioeconomic status and political power. They serve and are rewarded by the international special-interest power groups, including entities such as the multinationals, aid agencies, World Bank, and the International Monetary Fund. Such organizations are argued to be tied, by their structure or funding, to the developed nations. Consciously or not, the controlling elites often engage in activities that run counter to the well-being of the wider population and, in some cases, may even lower levels of living and perpetuate underdevelopment. Thus, the dependency thesis claims, a large part of the Third World impoverishment is the result of policies of the developed countries and their cohorts in the developing countries, plus compatible international organizations. Underdevelopment is seen as externally induced; essentially, poor countries are poor *because* rich countries are rich. The interdependence relation between two or more economies, through trade and other links, leads to a set of relationships whereby the dominant countries can pursue self-sustained expansion, while others can do so only in the shadow of that expansion, with either positive or negative effects on their immediate development.

Dependence takes many forms, some of them visibly economic. The international transmission of technology through capital imports and of tastes ("McDonaldization") through increased circulation of the mass media and international tourism reveals the great penetration of the values of affluent countries. Control of the rich countries over technology and finance makes the other countries "dependent." Increased international specialization—the division of labor on an international, rather than a local, basis—furthers dependence. Such **globalization**, it is argued, induces further dependence.

It may be noted that a large part of the appeal of the dependency thesis stems from its normative character, evidenced by advocacy of massive reform or even revolutions and its manifest concern for the poorest, both domestically and internationally. Thus, these reflexive incursions into normative issues lead some critics to dismiss the argument ("devil's theories") as a branch of ethics rather than analytical economics. To be fair, however, the dependency theorists advocate a scientific approach, both holistic and more modest than the aims of the purists: holistic in the sense that they would go beyond economics and incorporate political, social, and cultural variables in the discussions and more modest in that some proponents explicitly avoid claiming that they seek general theories. Rooted in the details and circumstances of history, in national and international situations seen as unique and therefore nonrecurring, in places where personality and power arise in complex combinations that can never be duplicated—these analyses may defy easy application to other poor countries and other eras.

Interestingly, the benign roots of this neo-Marxist thesis go back to the famous work by the Nobel laureate Gunnar Myrdal, *Asian Drama* (1968), in which he talked in terms of "circular and cumulative causation," though with the main focus on internal less developed country (LDC) dynamics. Further, a similar, again obviously non-Marxist and less provocative perspective is proposed by the Vatican. The 1988 Encyclical Declaration, *Solicitude rei socialis* (The Social

Concerns of the Church), denounced the various economic-financial-social mechanisms maneuvered by the developed countries, because they "favor the interests of the people manipulating them. But in the end they suffocate or condition the economies of the less developed countries."

Dependence theorists alert us to the significance of the structure and operations of the global economy and the ways in which decisions made in the developed countries can affect millions in the developing world. Whether or not those activities are deliberate or benign is often irrelevant. The fact is that the vulnerability of the underdeveloped countries to decisions made in Europe and North America (or Japan), in addition to those made by the World Bank and the International Monetary Fund (IMF), persuades one to recognize the validity of the propositions suggested by the dependency school.

Further Reading: D. Buck 1999; S. Chew and R. Denemark 1996; K. Griffin 1973.

S. M. Ghazanfar

Anita Desai Born in 1937 of mixed Bengali and German parentage, Desai has been ideally placed to interpret India to the West and to investigate the cultural crises of the Anglicized Indian bourgeoisie in the postcolonial world. In her early novels, *Cry, the Peacock* (1963), *Where Shall We Go This Summer?* (1975), and *Fire on the Mountain* (1977), India is presented through the eyes of this class' discontented, psychologically disturbed wives as an unromantic, dull actuality from which refuge is sought in fantasy and neurotic delusion. In *Clear Light of Day* (1980), Desai turns from private, solitary obsessions to public, sociohistorical themes and familial and communal responsibilities. This novel charts the disintegration of the postcolonial **nation**-state, its political violence, and the relocation of its populations through the fragmentation of an aristocratic Delhi family that is meant to represent an older, more accommodating and tolerantly interethnic India. After partition a brother defects to the Muslim north, and a sister to Europe, while the protagonist, taking on the symbolic matriarchal role of Mother India, remains to nurse her retarded younger brother whose arrested development is an image of petrified national progress.

In subsequent novels India's material squalor, from which the wives of the early books are protectively cocooned, is graphically evoked, and the style acquires a new, hard-grained social realism. *In Custody* (1984), the tale of a professor's disastrous bid for fame by interviewing a famous Urdu poet, is set in the dusty, disease-ridden city of Mirpore, where even the most exalted art cannot be distilled from degradation. The Calcutta and Bombay of *Baumgartner's Bombay* (1988) are places of filth and stench, and the novel's eponymous German Jew is a putrescent presence who ends his days in a seedy, alcoholic expatriate community, cut off from comprehension of the Indian world and the colonial and religious wars in which he finds himself interned and dispossessed. Even in *Journey to Ithaca* (1995), which charts the quest for the enigmatic Franco–Egyptian Holy Mother of a Himalayan ashram, the pilgrim's hospices and shrines are given their full quota of horrors, and slums are more powerfully evoked than scenic delights. Though it is focused with a softer lens than Desai's 1980s fiction, the novel's worldview is a rationalist one that remains skeptical of ascetic mysticism in the face of material want and commercial greed and uncomprehending of the spell cast by India over the Holy Mother and her hippie disciples. In *Fasting, Feasting* (1999), Desai returns to the theme of siblings and the family as cultural microcosm and to the parallel perspectives of East and West, domestic servitude and expatriate emancipation.

Desai has scant recourse to indigenous storytelling traditions or mythology and the unapologetically Europeanized perspective of her later novels has fueled charges by Indian critics that they are essentially expressions of an outsider's sensibility. Limited in range and formal innovation though her fiction is, it does, however, achieve an unrivaled lyrical and psychological intensity in its presentation of Indian women in a variety of family roles.

Further Reading: U. Bande 1988; R. K. Dhawan 1989.

Derek Wright

Mahasweta Devi   Mahasweta Devi (1926–   ), a graduate in English literature from Calcutta University, worked as a teacher and journalist. Her first book, *Jhansi Rani* (1956), marks the beginning of a prolific literary career: Devi has published more than twenty collections of short stories and close to 100 novels, primarily in her native Bengali. She has been the recipient of several literary awards—the Jnanpith (1996), the Padamasree (1980), and the Magsaysay (1997).

Postcolonial discourse that focuses on texts written in English veer toward "academic **neocolonialism**." The focus on the **subaltern** frequently has excluded work *by* the subaltern; vernacular and popular cultural texts that embody a literature of self-awareness continue to remain ghettoized. Fortunately, writers like **Gayatri Chakravorty Spivak** who translate Devi's work into English help reinscribe a more authentic postcolonial discourse.

Devi writes and works for the subaltern—the Denotified and Nomadi tribes—for whom independence has not yet come. In 1871 the British classified these tribes as criminal, and independent India ratified that decision by a 1952 act. While expatriate writers like Bharathi Mukherjee and Chitra Divakaruni reiterate the discourse of freedom from the oppression and limitations of postcolonial India to freedom in the First World, Devi's life and work offer no script of escape.

Her narratives demonstrate how decolonized India repeatedly reinscribes the violence of colonization. In the story of Mato the young Buno boy and his goat Arjun, the oppressive power of superstition concludes with the boy's death (*The Armenian Champa Tree*, 1998). In "Bayen" Chandi is declared a witch and made to live in utter seclusion, estranged from her husband and her son. When she dies and prevents a major train disaster, the embarrassed villagers find their "bayen" elevated to a martyr. "Rudali" (1980) revolves around the life of San-ichari, a poor, low-caste woman who adroitly survives in a restrictive rural socioreligious system that reiterates a larger discourse of exploitation and power. Focalized through a subaltern perspective, the text deconstructs the myth of the pastoral.

For Devi, independence is a "failure," and India remains "diseased" (*Rediff* Interview, 24 December 1997). The failure of **decolonization** is symbolized by Jashoda the "Breast-Giver," who nurses high-caste children and dies of breast cancer (*Breast Stories*, 1997). *Mother of 1084* (1997) reflects the Calcutta of the 1970s, when a city disillusioned with independence is filled with revolu-tionary fever. Devi poignantly narrates the grief of an upper-middle-class woman whose son is killed for his Naxalite beliefs. All that is left of him is an identity tag that identifies him as No. 1084.

Independence has certainly not brought economic liberation for the subal-tern—for bonded laborers like Douloti, whose name ironically means wealth ("Douloti the Beautiful," *Imaginary Maps*, 1995). The daughter of a tribal bonded worker, she is abducted and sold by upper-caste Indians into bonded prostitution. In postcolonial India bonded laborers occupy a space of non-subjectivity that does not even allow ownership of their own children. Dying of venereal disease, Douloti lies literally and metaphorically "spread-eagled" over the floor-map of India.

In postcolonial India there exist extravagant and useless attempts to celebrate India's martyrs. In "Statue" (*Old Women*, 1999) the Calcutta Secretariat decides to raise a bronze statue for freedom fighter Dindayal Thakur in his home village of Chhatim. This decision of postcolonial India is triggered by a Ph.D. disser-tation that none of the some thirty literate people of Chhatim would read. The 74,851 rupees spent on the statue that will soon be covered with crow shit and dirt could have been used for a road, health center, and hospital.

Colonial authority continues to work via postcolonial India's cultural depen-dency on a colonial educational system and via English, which remains the language of privilege and elitism. This linguistic colonialism shapes the way that postcolonial India sees itself/others and its/their being in the world. Writers like Devi suggest that the devaluing of local and regional culture in favor of a "neocolonial" one is an assault on an integrated "cultural self." This conflict between **nativism** and a growing cosmopolitanism that embraces colonial resi-due is explored in Devi's short story "The Son." Ramapathi and Niraja's desire that their son succeed in life explicitly includes a rejection of Indian "culture" and ratification of a First World "other." Shubhro's English medium education makes him equal to 100 of the vernacular schoolgoing children. But an adult Shubhro, who embodies the hybrid syncretic of postcolonial India, is distanced from his parents. His aging father asserts that his son belongs to a different generation—one that he does not know or trust. Is Shubhro, then, a "hyphen-ated" Indian? By Devi's standards, which veer toward cultural **essentialism**, he is. But in the world of "The Son" this integration of the values of the ex-colonizer and the decolonized is more smooth.

In Devi's texts, climactic events that display the rupture of colonial power by an unempowered colonized subject border on fantasy. On the day of the spring festival in "The Hunt" (*Imaginary Maps*), Mary Oraon, the illegitimate daughter of a tribal woman by an Australian plantation worker, ritualistically slaughters the contractor who sexually victimized her. The aboriginal Dopdi Mehjen ("Draupadi," *Breast Stories*), after a night of repeatedly being raped, walks into the daylight unclothed, her thighs and pubic hair matted with blood, her breasts and nipples bloody and torn. Laughing, her arms on her hips, her lips bleeding, she spits at the frightened police chief Senanayak and defies them to rape (*koun-ter*) her again. In Devi's works, ethics and aesthetics combine. Her texts veer toward didacticism; density of details and regionalisms cloud her narrative. But the concreteness of her language, the vividness of her characters (like Dulali and Andi in *Old Women*), and the poignancy of the "story" keep one enthralled. Devi's works cannot leave one unmoved. She directs our attention to those who live in the margins of society—oppressed and colonized in a postcolonial nation. The oppositional nationalism that her texts articulate is an attempt to fuel the decolonizing process of the subaltern in independent India. Her narratives re-count discourses of colonization and freedom in the Third World rather than an enthusiastic affirmation by neocolonial subjects of emancipation as immigrants in the First World.

Further Reading: Rediff 1997; S. Bandypadhyay 1986; G. C. Spivak 1995.

Ranjini Philip

Diasporic (exilic; migrant) Writings   The traditional notion of exile/diaspora indicates a certain dislocation from the normal or "natural" place of living or way of life. It is predicated on a level of involuntariness or helplessness. The dislocating force may be direct and coercive or diffused and subtle, such as lack of opportunities for social or economic advancement. It can be caused by mo-mentous events such as mass expulsions or "cleansing" or a creeping sense of desperation that overcomes a group or an individual. The varied motivations that underpinned movements of individuals/groups in different parts of the world and in different periods make it difficult to define the phenomenon with accuracy and validity across space and time. While the notion of exile has largely retained the element of compulsion or conditions of unfreedom as a causal factor in the dislocation or uprooting, the term "diaspora" has acquired varied **postmodern** connotations and is currently used loosely to cover different types of migration.

Exile/diaspora is an important area of postcolonial studies, as colonialism resulted in a voluntary or a forced movement of the colonizer and the colonized alike. However, in the case of the colonized, the movement has been more traumatic and conforms more to the Jewish model, the forced movement of Jewish people described in the Bible. Colonial reformulation of the global economy to suit the interests of the "mother" countries led to a large-scale reordering of the space and ways of living of a vast number of peoples throughout history. The pace and geographical spread of such dislocation as a result of European colonization over the last 500 years or so have been more extensive and damaging than any similar exercise of imperial power. Slave trade in Africans and indentured labor export from the Indian subcontinent ("a new form of slavery") are often seen as more recent examples of exile/diaspora in the Jewish model that emphasize the element of force and/or unfreedom in the movement of people.

Colonial and postcolonial developments affected different movements of people, and their influence can be seen in all the categories of diaspora that Cohen identifies in his book *Global Diasporas: An Introduction* (1997): Victim diasporas (Africans and Armenians), labor and imperial diasporas (indentured Indian and British), trade diasporas (Chinese and Lebanese), homeland diasporas (Sikhs and Zionists), cultural diasporas (Caribbeans), and **globalization** diasporas (international migration). Traditional/modernist approaches to migrations, by and large, produced neat binaries between the origin and destination, a colony and its "mother" country, guest and host communities in the "mother" countries, and colonizer and the colonized in the colonies. Postmodern approaches, on the other hand, decenter unitary identities that characterize traditional/modernist notions of exile, diaspora, periphery, **center** and the **nation**-state. The growth of communication technologies, especially the Internet, has facilitated postmodern trends not only through minimizing power differentials in communication but also by creating a new public space for "virtual" existence where exile/migrant/diasporic identities can be made and lived more easily than in the "real" world.

While the terms "exile" and "diaspora" both indicate the involuntary nature of the movement/migration, the former has been used, more coherently and consistently, to imply unfreedom as a/the factor that starts and sustains a life away from one's normal place of residence. Also, the term "exile" is associated with ideological disagreements much more than the term "diaspora" and has been used to refer to movements caused by extreme/distorted applications of ideologies, both on the right and the left. Thus, a large section of Russian/Soviet, South African, Chilean, and Cuban migrants during the twentieth century was considered to be in exile. However, the term "diaspora" has had a varied use over the years. The original use of the term by the Greeks connotes a triumphalist migration/colonization (*speiro* = to sow; and *dia* = over) from the point of view of the colonizer/occupier. Notions of civilizational/masculine superiority underpinned such a use of the term. The biblical use was one of "scattering," what the Lord would do as a punishment for not observing the divine laws (Deuteronomy 28: 58–68). The Hebrew equivalent was *galut*, which meant exile. The Hebrew usage and Jewish experience of expulsion and exile from Jerusalem provided the basis for the use of the term well into modern times, especially in the case of African diaspora created by the transatlantic slave trade.

The postwar use of the term "diaspora" is more inclusive than the preceding usage and foregrounds particular periods of colonial history or movements directly defined by the interests of the colonial power(s). The migratory patterns are more diffused now and involve a variety of remigrations from places of first migration. However, diaspora as a concept involving a forced migration or something that can be located in a place or a people sharing a particular language, faith, historical experience continues. Thus, in the contemporary media one hears not only of Irish, Armenian, and Palestinian diasporas but also of Sikh, Kurdish, and Tamil (Sri Lankan) diasporas.

Debates on the theorization of the term "diaspora" are influenced by colonial and postcolonial developments. The nation-state model of political organization that characterized colonial states led to the evolution of postcolonial states along similar lines. Such a model was not suitable for many situations and did not satisfy the political aspirations of several groups. But the model created, in many cases, alienation, strife, and displacement within and without the borders of the nation-states. This resulted in a steady stream of displaced people/exiles. The link between oppression and migration was evident as Cold War polities created more ideological polarizations within and between states. Commentators sought to distinguish between exile, expatriation, and economic migration. The dominant notion of diaspora was still one of victim-migrant and close to that of exile.

With the ending of the Cold War and the gathering pace of globalization in the 1990s, the term acquired new connotations. The theoretical strength/weakness of the term "diaspora," in its current usage, is that it can refer to a wide range of situations. It could cover the migration that was/is essentially "exile," that of people fleeing situations of conflict and insecurity, but it could also account for people living away from one's country/place of normal residence for economic/cultural reasons. With the weakening of the role of the individual nation-state in a globalized and globalizing world, "diaspora" as a descriptive term to cover the whole of a migrant community also helps in bypassing the divisions made in earlier literature between the first and subsequent generations of migrants, that is, between expatriation and exile. The emphasis on migration or movement along several axes—often from the "periphery" to the "center"— has also given rise to the term "axial" to describe the condition of migrant societies.

However, the marginalization of the nation-state in the process of globalization/homogenization of economic institutions and political ideologies has led to the foregrounding of alternative identities, subnational as well as supranational. **Ethnic**/cultural identities that predate the evolution/imposition of the nation-state under colonial conditions find resurgence, and the term "diaspora" captures, in part, the assertion of identities. Thus, "diaspora" becomes a useful term to recognize and study migration without too specific a reference to its initial circumstances. The term provides a working definition of the postmodern condition, especially in global cities with a heterogeneity of nationalities and races interacting with each other in an ever-increasing multiplicity of identities. While the traditional definition of the term in the biblical-Roman-Jewish tradition emphasized the circumstances of the origin of the migration, the recent usage emphasizes the end result of the migration—the presence of diasporic communities. The term now captures the sense of the self for various communities in the decentered, postmodern, and globalized world.

One of the most discussed and theorized, but also controversial, applications of the exile/diaspora can be seen in attempts to define historical as well as contemporary experience in the African communities of the United States, the Caribbean, and the United Kingdom. African diaspora has features of a typical victim-diaspora: awareness of the historical and continuing injustice, a positive self-image that negates past and present negative value systems, idea of returning to the homeland (real and metaphorical), creating a positive image of the homeland, and articulating overarching homogenizing ideologies that cement intragroup discontinuities of history and differentials of power in terms of social groupings, especially that of gender and class. While there are attempts to highlight the human and aesthetic aspects of diaspora in essentialized racial categories, one also comes across powerful voices in favor of recognizing the impossibility of re-creating/returning to the past and the futility of the excessive obsession with origins.

New fomulations of diaspora focus on negating or bypassing the limitations created by the nation-state. It is argued that the concept as well as the actual working of the nation-state are rigid, hierarchical, and modernist, less suitable to the realities of the present-day postmodern society. Alternative conceptions based on sub- or supranational networks and identities are seen as opening up more creative and fulfilling opportunities not only to diasporic communities but also to the "community of communities" (the *Parekh Report on the Future of Multi-Ethnic Britain*, The Runnymede Trust, October 2000) in which they live. Notions of hybridity and in-betweenness are seen as potentially positive. Postmodern/pluralist definitions of diaspora are in direct opposition to the monochrome and limited identities on which nation-states are built. Political, cultural, and social dimensions of the centrifugal tendencies embedded in diasporic existence and articulation of difference challenge the centripetal and centralizing attitudes and structures of the nation-state. One of the sensitive areas in this dialectics of change and progress is the weight of the past and the willingness in the present. The finer points of *The Parekh Report* on the condition of multiethnic Britain were drowned in the media criticism of its suggestions to rethink the national story and the British identity.

(Re)defining diasporic identities in frameworks outside of, or in partial or total opposition to, that of the nation-state is based on recent developments in the world economy and politics. The globalization of capital flows, production processes, and consumer markets has undermined the authority of the state and, with it, the arguments about the exclusive distinctiveness of its social and political formation. Globalizing forces of colonialism organized along national/nation-state lines in the past have given way to new forms of regional political organization putting former competitors in roles of friends, in the European

Union, for example. This is by no means universally welcome in the countries affected by it. Traditional political parties are split over what aspects of public/ private life should be "surrendered" to the new "superstate."

Which symbols of national sovereignty are worth swapping for the actual/ anticipated economic prosperity? Which democratic institutions earned through years/centuries of political struggle for wider social participation in public life can be handed over to technocrats and bureaucrats?

(Re)defining diasporic identities at a time of rapid economic and political transition and change is probably inevitable and necessary, but not necessarily easy to accommodate even within a liberal view of the nation-state. Rooted in the self-assurance of Orientalist binaries and a moral certitude of a liberal de- mocracy, the dominant discourse is one of a gradual assimilation and dissolution into the underlying ethos of a tolerant society or that of a melting pot with the American Dream at the end of the road. Multiethnic identity is seen as divisive, and identity markers such as language, religion, dress, and food represent some of the faultiness in the discourse. However, changes are never unidirectional, and the communities face flux and change in the weakening of nation-states and rise in the clout of diasporic communities. With ancestral, commercial links to some of the fast-growing areas in the global economy, particular diasporic com- munities (e.g., Irish, Chinese, and Indian) have been able to gain more visibility and international mobility.

Defining exilic/migrant/diasporic writing is a difficult task. Apart from the preceding international migrations, there has been a range of internal migrations that took place during and after the colonial period in what have now become successor states. For example, the tea plantations in Assam in the northeast of India were built on the labor recruited from central India. Should this type of emigration be recognized as being on a par with the indentured labor migration overseas? Further, categories and definitions of exile/diaspora are externally as well as internally defined. Thus, we are left with the undefined status of writers who would like to use self-definitions that reject the ascribed status that the preceding adjectives project on the writing/writers.

The confusion and overlapping nature of the subject area are seen within the varied terms used in mapping and framing of exilic/migrant/diasporic writings in the academy. For example, a recent advertisement by a university in the United States for a teaching position in global literature (a term that largely covers this area by being selective about the term "global") includes the follow- ing possible specializations: colonial/postcolonial studies (any historical period from the Middle Ages onward), contemporary "mongrel" British literature, post- colonial theory, **subaltern studies**, exile and diaspora, transatlantic and trans- pacific cultures, **Creole** studies, nationalism and postnationalism, international gender studies, border crossing, contact zones, and the globalization of culture. Similarly, in the academic curriculum of a British university Bessie Head and **Salman Rushdie** were moved from modules in African and contemporary lit- eratures in English, respectively, to a module on the literature of the margins.

Leaving aside the confusion over the inclusion/exclusion criteria, one can notice some of the broad themes that this body of writing covers. While nostalgia for the lost place or way of life is always present in some form or other, the literature would also project a certain determination to find relevance in the new environment. Symbolic links with the "imagined community" of the diaspora in other parts of the world or with the past through sagas/plots across generations would be established. Such a combination of history and literature would stress the symbolic, subversive nature of literary **narrratives**. Themes and techniques in exile/diasporic writings revolve around adoption/absorption/retention/(re)invention of several cultural domains, especially those of religion, race, dress, food, and music.

Experimentation with the form that one comes across in exilic/migrant/diasporic writing is both a valid literary activity as much as a refusal to conform to the narrative patterns of the given, dominant tradition of the colonial and/or patriarchal systems. This involves conscious attempts to use oral narrative styles that emphasize distance from the European models of written narratives, especially in the genre of the novel. But there are also attempts to evolve new styles through selective borrowing and mixing of different inheritances that exile/diaspora juxtapose. At the other end of the spectrum, exile/diaspora fuses into the dominant tradition, and the writing is distinguishable mostly in the location and concerns rather than in the techniques of the narrative, as in the case of **V. S. Naipaul**. The duration of the exile/diaspora often affects the narrative style, replacing naturalistic/direct accounts of the pre-exile period by symbolic/metaphoric ones, as in the case of Alex La Guma.

The language/dialect of exilic/diasporic literature raises issues of language maintenance, language death, and language revival. Given the association between the nation-state and its dominant language(s)/language variety, exilic/diasporic literatures swim against the current to maintain the language through bi/multilingual creativity and validation of pidgin/Creole writing as "national language" writing or defend the use of diasporic language varieties. Writers belonging to colonizing/imperial diasporas display a classic dilemma common to writers operating outside the linguistic parameters of the standard language/variety of the imperial nation-state: how to assert a local/social/gender identity in the text of the narrative by going beyond the caricaturing of the linguistic Other? How to bring the use of the authentic language from the margins (set-piece dialogues for "flat" characters) to the very center of narration? On the one hand, language is a part of the process of defining and expressing self and collective identities, and, on the other, there is a need to reach a wider audience who are likely to favor high-prestige languages. The choices made by writers in exile/diaspora range from making minor or no variations to the status quo, to inventing styles and idioms that match the anticipated audiences' image of the characters' language (as in the case of **Sam Selvon**'s *The Lonely Londoners*). Exilic/diasporic writing is also a fertile site of language contact, facilitating the production of literature in **translation** and intertextuality in narratives inscribing cultural interactions.

The emergence of new technological modes of communication, especially the

Internet, has facilitated the survival and development of exilic/diasporic writing. A range of "virtual" associations has come into being, some building on the old diasporas and some developing new diasporas based on newfound or hitherto underexpressed identities, such as the Hindu (religious) diaspora and the Telugu (language) diaspora. Most of these "virtual" diasporic communities use Web sites, discussion lists, E-mails, bulletin boards, and phone calls made affordable by advances in communication. The ease of using different scripts has also helped in the use of languages with non-Roman alphabets. While the use of digital texts of exilic/diasporic writings is largely limited to pedagogic institutions, active exchange of views on these writings is not uncommon in the previously mentioned range of communications in the public space created by new technologies. Literary magazines, critical discussions of authors/texts/contexts in discussion lists, and publicity for writings and e-commerce in books have increased the accessibility of exilic/diasporic texts. More importantly, they nurture a critical tradition, which, for any writing, is indispensable. While these advantages are available to all writings, the role of new technologies in the case of exilic/diasporic writing is crucial, as these writings often operate against a current of assimilation and powerful structures of the monolingual nation-state.

Further Reading: M. Busby 1993; R. Cohen 1997; Writing Diasporas 2000.

Balasubramanyam Chandramohan

Assia Djebar   Assia Djebar was born in 1936. By 1962 she had completed four critically acclaimed novels in French and had successfully established herself as a major Maghrebian author by age thirty. Shortly thereafter, she renounced fiction writing in order to take a position as a professor of history at the University of Algiers. For the next twelve years, Djebar refused to write fiction, preferring to concentrate on bridging the gap between French and Arabic through **film**. Her film *La Nouba des femmes du Mont Chenoua* was awarded the Venice Biennale prize in 1979. In her film, Djebar interviews women in Arabic about the roles that they played during the 1954–1962 war of liberation from the French. Her novels often take up the role of women's voice in the making of Algerian history. Establishing voice for women in a history that has been written down by males is a theme of particular importance in all of her novels. Her most recent works include *Oran, langue morte* (1997) and *Le blanc de l'Algérie* (1995). In the 1980s Djebar concentrated her efforts on her Algerian Quartet, novels that elaborate on the importance of Algerian women throughout the history of her country. *L'amour, la fantasia* (1985) is the first novel of the quartet. This book was followed by *Ombre Sultan* in 1987. The third novel in the quartet is *Vaste est la prison*, published in 1995. These novels are a cumulation of autobiographic experience and records of the tumultuous history of Algeria.

L'Amour, la fantasia constructs a hybrid narrative of culture, language, and historicity. In this novel Djebar reconsiders and renarrates the legacy of French colonialism, which has altered the identity of Algeria. As a social commentary, *L'Amour, la fantasia* confronts difference and marginalization and champions the important roles of voice, ethnicity, and diversity in forming a historical narrative. Djebar employs a multivalent perspective to reinscribe the multiple stories of Algeria's past and present. She seeks not to wipe the historic slate clean of the former colonial presence in her own country but to refocus the reader's perspective on overlooked events in France's archives on Algeria.

Vaste est la prison is a study of exile and duality. It is equally an evaluation of the current political situation and issues affecting women in Algeria. The freedom that Djebar finds in exile allows her to critique social, cultural, and historical events that have influenced women's lives in Algeria. Within her space of exile, the author negotiates new **feminist** parameters for all women of the Maghreb. However, such parameters are not formed easily. Djebar must first define an intellectual space of **agency** where she sets herself and her female protagonists beyond established stereotypes concerning Algerian women. The new parameters that Djebar forges begin with her autobiography and move to other narrative modalities that encompass colonial/postcolonial revision and even cinematographic journalism (drawing on her career as a filmmaker). It may be said that the author's works are polyphonic. Such polyphony requires constant metamorphosis; therefore, no single site of fixed ideology or subjectivity is favored. The author writes in a transitory space for all her feminine characters. By writing in the transitional, Djebar is setting a new tone for feminine writing and social ethics for the Maghreb.

For Djebar, writing is the only means of protesting the current political unrest and violence in Algeria. It is only from her polyphonic place of exile that she finds the means to break free of the violence that characterizes Algeria today. The author must live outside her home country as a dissident in order to continue to contest the injustice that is imposed there. She insists that a dissident voice is the only manner in which an author, placed in an unstable and unjust world, will succeed in developing his or her own discursive strategy and agency. Assia Djebar's ultimate objective is to forge a new space for future Algerian intellectual discourse, a space that will displace the violence of a country that has been in turmoil for over two centuries, while fostering the remembrance (and subsequent rewriting) of a forgotten history. Writing in exile as a "fugitive who doesn't know it," as she puts it, Djebar nurtures the voice within her Self and within the women of her country.

Further Reading: F. Lionnet 1992; R. Merini 1999.

Valérie Orlando

Drama. *See* Performance

Dutch Caribbean Writing This is the literature of the Netherlands Antilles (Aruba, Bonaire, Curaçao, Saba, Sint Maarten, Sint Eustatius) and Suriname.

Among its better-known authors are Curaçaoan Frank Martinus Arion and Surinamese Astrid Roemer. Whereas Martinus Arion's long poem "Stemmen uit Afrika" (Voices from Africa, 1957) subscribes to the **negritude** ideology, Roemer's collection *Noordzeeblues* (North Sea Blues, 1985) revolves around the alienation of a Surinamese immigrant. The relationship between former Dutch Guiana and the kingdom is in the foreground of Roemer's *Suriname Trilogy* (1996–1998). Martinus Arion's *Dubbelspel* (Double Play, 1973) is the first Dutch Caribbean novel available in English translation. Both Martinus Arion and Roemer have also contributed to postcolonial discourse in their essays. Other Surinamese writers include Bea Vianen, whose "Punishment Coop" (1972) portrays the horrors of a Catholic boarding school, Hugo Pos, whose "Juditha Triumphans" (1993) reacts to the "December Massacre," and Ellen Ombre, who depicts the ambiguous benefit of "First World" values in "Maelstrom" (1992).

Further Reading: A. J. Arnold 2000; H. V. Yoder-Neck 1998.

Doris Hambuch

E

Eastern European/Post-Soviet Literatures Eastern European literatures include, for the purpose of this entry, the former European communist countries that were not part of the Soviet Union. Eastern European literatures and the post-Soviet literatures belong to peoples of various linguistic stock (Slavs, Romance, Baltic, etc.) but sharing a troubled history of aggressions from various empires. The succession of empires (Byzantine, Ottoman, Austrian, Russian, and, after World War II, Soviet Union) was sometimes met with hope but finally proved disastrous for the aspirations of the peoples in the area. In the nineteenth century and the beginning of the twentieh century **nationalisms** seemed to be the answer to the problems of the areas. Literatures nationalistic in spirit and realistic or romantic in most of their manifestations dominate this period.

Geopolitical arrangements, political treaties, and spheres of influence carved new frontiers, scarring the ethnic body of the peoples in the area. Literatures belonging to the same **ethnic** tradition were separated forcibly through the game of frontiers and came to be a minority literature in one area while maintaining its status of mainstream literature in another area (for instance, Hungarian literature in Romania and Hungary; Romanian literature in Romania and the Soviet Republic of Moldova).

Thus, Eastern European literatures and post-Soviet literatures belong, in various degrees and with different tension, to two paradigms: the **center/periphery** paradigm and the metropolis/colony paradigm. While sharing with the areas having belonged politically to some colonial empire the military defeat, the subordination to a center of power (Vienna, Istanbul, Moscow, London or Paris), the hybridity and cultural polyvalence, and the marginality as a source of both energy and inferiority complexes, Eastern Europe also has its own specific features.

Eastern Europe is doubly alienated as compared to the colonies. It is alienated from the centers of power because it has always been a sphere of influence. It is also alienated from the colonies because it has always tried to **mimic** the centers of power on the grounds of a common belonging to a dominant Europe. Rivalries between different centers of power also resulted in fierce rivalries between these countries. In spite of great moments of communication, the Eastern European literatures have been rather separated and looking at the faraway center, forgetting about their neighbors, though they all shared different repatternings of the great "–isms" of the nineteenth and twentieth centuries and a rash and superficial, incomplete **modernization**. Eastern European cultures are defined by conflicting attractions toward European integration and simultaneity and the craving for the protectiveness characteristic of "minor" cultures. There has always been in these cultures and literatures a desperate effort to recover lost time, an obsession about "keeping up the pace." Sometimes quick and incomplete modernization gave birth to "forms without matter," institutions, mores, and literary patterns abruptly supplanted in order to accelerate Westernization seen as an absolute synonym of progress.

Post-Soviet literatures come much closer to colonial literatures, the oral Siberian literatures, for example, closely reiterating similar experiences in Africa or North America. At the same time, a longed-for mimicry of the latest literary novelties from the West must be put into contrast with the imposed mimicry of the realist socialist models during the Stalinist period. In such a context, hybridity is a kind of nationalist appropriation, even a "domestication" of exterior and often contradictory models. By this token, laws of protection of the national languages (in Armenia, Estonia, Ukraine) and the rejection of the Cyrillic alphabet (in Moldavia and Tadzhikistan) constitute a kind of nationalist framework for post-Soviet literatures. Bilingualism, by this logic, is rejected in order to protect ethnicity.

Further Reading: A. Babeti and C. Ungureanu 1997; M. Muthu 1995.

Mihaela Mudure

Buchi Emecheta   Buchi Emecheta is a preeminent Nigerian writer who has produced novels, children's books, plays, and nonfiction. She is best known for her novels, among which are *In the Ditch* (1972), *Second Class Citizen* (1974), *The Bride Price* (1976), *The Slave Girl* (1977), *The Joys of Motherhood* (1979), and *Destination Biafra* (1982). She was born Florence Onyebuchi Emecheta in Lagos, Nigeria, in 1944, and her parents came from Ibuza in Igbo country. She had excellent primary and secondary schooling in Nigeria, married Nduka Sylvester Onwordi, and migrated to England in 1962. She had five children before the marriage ended because of Onwordi's infidelity and abusive behavior. Emecheta raised her five children as a single parent, attained a bachelor's degree in sociology (with honors) and a master's degree in philosophy, and also began her career as a writer. Her autobiography, *Head above Water* (1986), candidly discusses her life as a single mother, immigrant, and writer.

Emecheta's novels articulate a postcolonial **feminism** through a primary focus on the lives of Igbo women and their struggles under multiple forms of social, cultural, and political oppression. Her writing is "postcolonial" because it emerges after Nigeria's political **decolonization** and also because it (to borrow Leela Gandhi's definition in *Postcolonial Theory*, 1998) interrogates the colonial past and its aftermath. Emecheta documents resistance to colonialism as well as complicity with it during and after political decolonization, particularly from a woman's perspective. She writes of women's exploitation by precolonial, colonial, and **neocolonial** cultures. Still, there is much critical debate about Emecheta's feminism. Emecheta herself refuses to embrace the Western version wholeheartedly, although some African critics see her feminist strategies as privileging the agenda of Western feminists. Florence Stratton argues that some of Emecheta's critics have appropriated her work to "foreground a particular type of feminism" (1994, 109). Other critics like Tuzyline Jita Allen classify her as womanist because she critiques white women's insensitivity to race and class issues that black women face both in the Third World and when they are immigrants in the First World.

Her novels address different postcolonial feminist themes. For instance, she documents Igbo women's struggles with traditional Igbo male-centered social practices such as polygamy, bride-price, and wife inheritance in *The Bride Price*, *The Slave Girl*, and *Kehinde*. *Kehinde* and *The Bride Price* also speak of the challenges that women experience when they transgress traditional values. Whereas the protagonist of *Kehinde* is an educated "been-to" (i.e., been to Europe, usually for education) woman, and Aku-nna in *The Bride Price* spends much of her life in an Igbo village, both pay a heavy price for their rebellion. Emecheta does not see such rebellion as the outcome of Westernized education but as a product of a woman's inner spirit. In her own life Emecheta names this inner spirit "the Presence," and in her novels it is the protagonist's *chi*.

Emecheta's first two novels, *In the Ditch* and *Second-Class Citizen*, and her more recent novel, *The Family/Gwendolen*, focus on black women's experiences with immigration and racism in Britain. The first two novels draw upon Emecheta's own life to critique racism in England of the 1960s and 1970s, where Africans could not rent homes because they were black and where the welfare system allowed a single mother some opportunity to raise her children but condemned her to poverty for her entire life. Both her early novels (published eventually as *Adah's Story*) stress the camaraderie among the working classes and the poor, where individuals transcend race boundaries in a limited way to forge communal bonds.

Emecheta also addresses black women's lack of political power in *The Rape of Shavi* and *Destination Biafra*. In both these novels, she argues for women's participation in national politics and suggests that women bring an alternative, compassionate social vision that both traditional and neocolonial societies lack. Both these novels stress female heroism and dismantle the idea that myths of male heroism are central to national history. Other themes in Emecheta's fiction include black women's education, black women's experiences with domestic violence and incest, and the destruction of traditional family structures and values because of colonialism.

A major critique often leveled at Emecheta is that, in her female-centered fiction, her male characters are often violent, abusive, and morally weak. Many of the husband figures like Albert in *Kehinde*, Francis in *Second Class Citizen*, Ete Kamba in *Double Yoke* seem to be modeled after Sylvester Onwordi. Occasionally, she portrays men as victims of colonialism (especially father figures like Aku-nna's father) whose cultural values were eroded by the English presence and who were emasculated in the employ of the English. Her most positive male figure is Bill, a Canadian librarian friend of Adah's who encourages her writing career, and he is white. There are no positive African or black male portrayals in her fiction or in her autobiography with the exception of an occasional male child.

From a postcolonial perspective, her writing could be critiqued for its lack of a finely nuanced national historical vision. She is more interested in individual women's lives, even in her most political novels like *Destination Biafra* and *The Rape of Shavi*, and historical events often form the backdrop to their individual trials and tribulations.

Emecheta's major contribution to postcolonial literature is that she places African women's lives at the center of the African novel. In this respect, she challenges the point of view of her compatriot, **Chinua Achebe**, in whose novels African history and traditions are celebrated, but women's roles are marginalized, and their experiences with polygamy, bride-price, and domestic violence are ignored. She popularized African women's issues in the West and has carved out a space for black women within feminist fiction. Her vision earlier in her career was very Igbo-centered but has since evolved to include others of African descent in the diaspora, as seen in *The Family/Gwendolen*, where the emphasis is on the Afro-Caribbean world.

Further Reading: F. Stratton 1994; M. Umeh 1996.

Nalini Iyer

Essentialism   Essentialism is a viewpoint that attempts to explain the properties of a complex whole by reference to a supposed inner truth or essence. Such an approach reduces the complexity of the world to the simplicities of its constituent parts and seeks to explain individuals as automatic products of inner propulsions. Essentialism also operates on the premise that groups, categories, or classes of objects have one or several defining features exclusive to all members of that category. With regard to race and gender, the essential characteristics distinguishing one race from another or the feminist from the masculine are then emphasized over other qualities.

Colonial discourse drew attention to essentialist categories through the norms and theories employed to create notions of inferiority regarding the colonial subject. Such categories functioned to reinforce hegemonic control over the colonized by manipulating dominant modes of public and private representation. The colonial system also relied on an interpretation of ethnicity as fossilized and immutable for administrative and exploitative purposes. Power used as a force of social oppression cements itself with dual structures and totalizing logic on social subjects, while repressing differences. Oppressive structures, however, are never total, and differences are always in some way expressed, such as through **mimicry**, ambivalence, hybridization, and fractured **identities**. The rejection of essentialism is hinged on a negation of the binary provisions on which the colonialist worldview is predicated. Thus, antiessentialism holds that the world is not inherently divided into segmented and opposing camps (**center** versus periphery, First World versus Third World) but rather is and always has been defined by innumerable partial, mobile differences.

Postwar national liberation movements were based on essentialist modes of thought in terms of recovering or developing a people's sense of local identity and distinction, which had been damaged by imperial and colonizing discourses and policies. Essentialism also infiltrates indigenous construction of ethnic identities. The powerful revival of identity politics has been of a hybrid or symbolic variety but also embodies an exclusive or "essentialist" quality. The postcolonial project, then, is to affirm the multiplicity of differences so as to subvert the power of the ruling class over peripheral actors.

Critiques of language by poststructuralist theorists such as Jacques Derrida, Jaques Lacan, and **Michael Foucault** have been used to argue that essentialist categories of culture were flawed. Various writers have used this concept to critique the institutions through which individual subjectivity achieved a sense of identity, for example, ideas of race or nation. **Homi Bhabha** points toward a **utopian** ideal where the binary and totalizing structures of power are fractured and displaced, leaving room for an existence-based community (which Bhabha describes as a community of the "unhomely"), a new internationalism, and a gathering of people in the **diaspora**—the opposite of societies created by systems that rely on isolation and fragmentation. The affirmation of difference and hybridity is itself, according to Bhabha, an affirmation of community. Bhabha argues that the seeds of the alternative community arise out of close attention to the locality of culture, its hybridity, and resistance to the polarizing nature of social hierarchies, all of which have been constructed by the oppressor. Alternatively, **Gayatri Spivak** stresses the need for the **subaltern**/oppressed to go beyond their essential subjectivity in which their beings are formed within discourses and institutional practices that give them a voice. In an attempt to clarify the political force resonant in her theory, Spivak speaks of the need to embrace a *strategic* essentialism to counter the effects of colonial and **neocolonial** oppression. Writing on the black diaspora, Kobena Mercer also highlights how white racism and racial stereotypes have contributed to reflectionist and social engineering arguments for essential black representation and recognition. Other writers discuss the notion of an essential womanhood common to all women, whereby the female figure is inherently suppressed by "the patriarchy." Impulses to homogenize or rely on essentialism can, in the preceding cases, be seen as a product of racial and gender discrimination.

Postcolonial studies expose essentialist tendencies with regard to identity formation when categories like gender, race, class, and sexuality intersect. For a better understanding of essentialism as a theory, Teresa de Lauretis calls for further elaboration of the relationship between experience, social power, and resistance within feminist theory. Others, such as Andrew Ross, question the notion of an essentialist and reductionist view of sexual difference on issues such as consumption of pornography. In addition, he explores how medical, legal, literary, and psychological terms like "heterosexual" and "homosexual" map peoples' worlds in a polarizing fashion that is full of implications for personal existence. He cites Foucault's thesis that modern Western culture has placed what it defines as sexuality in an increasingly distinctive, privileged relation to the constructs of individual identity, truth, and knowledge. Foucault argues that sexuality was a "historical apparatus" that had developed as part of a complex web of social regulation that organized and shaped ("policed") individual bodies and behavior. Sexuality could not act as resistance to power because it was explicitly linked to the ways in which power operated in modern society.

Postcolonial theory holds that essentialist categories view the world in terms of binary divisions. This condition is seen as being hinged on notions of totality, identity, homogeneity, and the wholeness of social subjects. Such conceptions of the world imply the essentiality and homogeneity of each opposing identity. By focusing on the relationship that develops across a separated, central boundary, all experiences became subsumed within a coherent social totality. In this Hegelian dialectic of a coherent totality, essentialized social identities automatically face each other in opposition.

Further Reading: T. de Lauretis 1993; S. Hall 1997; A. Ross 1993; G. Spivak 1987, 1991; J. Weeks 1997.

Saheed Adeyinka Adejumobi

Ethnicity   This is the sense of identification of oneself or of others as belonging to a group of people who share (real or putative) common ancestry, language, blood ties, religion, customs, memories, and/or phenotypal features. Even though ethnicity is a concept that refers to both the self and the other, in postcolonial studies its emphasis is on marginalization and the discourse of Otherness. This may be rooted in its etymology: the Greek word *ethnos* was used for large groups of people without distinctive characteristics, thus referring to the other, rather than the self. Its biblical use as heathen or pagan persisted in the English "ethnic" up to the mid-nineteenth century, after which it was used as a synonym for "racial." The noun itself came into use in the mid-twentieth century to replace the biological and genetic focus of the term "race," thus rejecting Third Reich ideology. In the 1960s ethnicity became a buzzword in the social sciences but for a while remained undefined and vague, especially in its relation and disputed synonymity to the term "race," a position that is largely determined by a preference for a biological/genetic or a social behavioral perspective. Among proliferating theories of ethnicity in the late twentieth century, two major positions developed: a view of ethnicity as a primordial, stable given, on the one hand, and one of ethnicity as a situationally **constructed** resource, on the other. The latter position enabled the acknowledgment of a common black experience, not based on **essentialisms** but constructed historically, culturally, and politically. As a political instrument of self-assertion, ethnicity has been crucial for **identity formation** of the formerly colonized and works on a more local level against the tendency of **globalization** toward a uniformity of cultures. On the other hand, a focus on ethnic identity in postcolonial studies has been criticized for blurring class and power relations, and more recently the term has been negatively connoted with **nationalism** and ethnic cleansing in former Yugoslavia.

Further Reading: N. Glazer and D. Moynihan 1975; W. Sollors 1996.

Susanne Reichl

Eurocentrism Understanding oneself and one's culture in ways that both emphasize and empathize with what is near and familiar is a common, if not universal, human tendency. What is most noteworthy about the European-centered thinking known as "Eurocentrism" is, thus, not so much the privileging of a certain area's dominant beliefs but the global scope and impact of what is frequently referred to as "Western thought." Especially over the last five centuries, this thought has developed with an increasing material exploitation that has strengthened Western domination vis-à-vis other regions and, for many, worked to confirm not just the material "superiority" but the "truth"—and thus inherent justice—of Western knowledge. As potential antidotes to the biases—and thus injustices—of Western knowledge, postcolonial studies works both to reveal the conceptual limits (e.g., contradictions, blindnesses, violences) of Western thought and to sustain, develop, and disseminate other ways of knowing.

In such works as **V. Y. Mudimbe**'s *The Idea of Africa* (1994), Martin Bernal's *Black Athena* (1987, especially volume 1), Emmanuel Eze's *Racist Enlightenment* (1997) and *Postcolonial African Philosophy* (1997), Susan E. Babbitt and Sue Campbell's *Racism and Philosophy* (1999), J. M. Blaut's *The Colonizer's Model of the World* (1993), John McCumber's *Metaphysics and Oppression* (1999), Jacques Derrida's *Writing and Difference* (1978), Robert Young's *White Mythologies* (1990), and, most famously, **Edward W. Said**'s *Orientalism* (1978), critical theory helps reveal how the discourses with which Europeans have understood themselves "produced" a world that—as G.W.F. Hegel puts it in *Philosophy of History* (Vorlesungen ueber die Philosophie der Geschichte, 1975)—already "looks" or is destined to look "Europe-wards" (zu Europa hingewendet).

This is the Eurocentrism that Samir Amin in *Eurocentrism* (trans. of L'eurocentrisme, 1989), describes as a worldview that "present[s] itself as **universalist**, for it claims that imitation of the Western model by all peoples is the only solution to the challenges of our time" (vii). Amin, an economist born in Egypt, stresses the role of capitalism in the postmedieval "mythological reconstruction of the history of Europe and the world" (ix), which, for Amin, characterizes Eurocentrism.

Redressing the continuing economic injustices of a global capitalism whose modus operandi is the exploitation of "non-Western" regions and minority groups constitutes much of the ethical impetus of postcolonial studies. But although postcolonial studies can partly be understood as a critique of capitalism to facilitate what Amin describes as the "more humane future" of a "truly polycentric world . . . that has resolved the legacy of the unequal development inherent to capitalism" (151–152), postcolonial studies remains wary of teleologies whether based on the historical materialism of Amin or the declaration in Francis Fukuyama's *The End of History and the Last Man* that "the ideal of liberal democracy [can] not be improved on" (1992, xi).

Like **Marx**, Hegel, and before them, Immanuel Kant, both Amin and Fukuyama promote ideals of European political thought as "end points" of human evolution and thus political conceptions that are universal and proclaim what Michael J. Shapiro, in *Violent Cartographies* (1997), describes as "an end to ethics and politics." Amin works against the Eurocentric roots of his political thought by defining his end point of "socialist universalism" as both "based on the contributions of everyone" and beyond prediction. Fukuyama is more certain in his vision of the future as a "wagon train" in which everyone "will discover that to get through the final mountain range [all] must use the same pass" (1992, 338–339). But despite political differences, both Amin and Fukuyama cling to the certainty of foundationalism.

The three main sources and continuing engines of Eurocentric thinking (Judeo-Christianity, Platonisms, and science) all cling to foundationalisms that, as David Scott writes in *Refashioning Futures* (1999, 49), inscribe "the non-West into [their] privileged telos." This continues the legacy of one ultimate truth articulated in the binary (hierarchical) logic of René Descartes, "father of science" and "architect of foundationalism," whose *res cogitans* and *res extensa* propose a pure objectivity to the thinking mind. This binary logic is also expressed in the foundationalism of Kant's *Critique of Judgment* (Kritik der Urteilskraft, trans. Wemer Pluhar, 1987, 318–319), which proposes that the "ultimate purpose of nature" is that nature transcends itself in a "culture of discipline" that will free humankind from "the despotism of desires." This emphasis on an objective and disciplined rationalism (long Eurocentrism's defining mark of "Europeanness" in contradistinction to the rest of the world) is also what subtends Marx's reference to the "Oriental despotism" of India, which, Marx tells us, needs to be destroyed so as to allow Asia to move into the future by adopting "the material foundations of Western society."

Europe's dominant religious, scientific (e.g., cartography, geography, anthropology, evolution), economic, and metaphysical discourses worked to place Europe at the center of geographical spaces and at the forefront of time—leading the world into the future. Increased distance from Europe was frequently equated with increased primitiveness. Nearly everything that diverged from the supposed European norm—warmer climate, darker skin, less clothing, less materialistic, less environmentally destructive—signified "less developed" and worked to naturalize Europe's "masculine" penetration and control of supposedly feminine (or childlike) peoples in need of stewardship.

Although current Western social-political thinking increasingly insists on non-Western input and the unpredictability of where best to "end up" (even Fukuyama states that the world's people may reach the end of their Manifest Destiny to the land of liberal democracy yet "set their eyes on a new and more distant journey"), Eurocentric thinking remains in presumptions that there are no viable destinations other than those espied from the promontory that is Europe. The division of the West from the rest of the world, writes Tsenay Serequeberhan, continues to mark the division of "the real in contrast to the unreality of human existence in the non-European world" (1997, 143).

As knowledges continue to circulate, the already blurry distinction between "Western" and "non-Western" will still further fade. Postcolonial studies, however, insists upon a future open to more than hybrid Eurocentric possibilities, to more than merely joining a way of knowing whose heritage includes what Edward Said, in *Orientalism*, describes as the production of "racism, cultural stereotypes, political imperialism, [and] dehumanizing ideology" (27) paraded under the banner of "universal enlightenment"—a heritage that continues to produce and justify the **neocolonial** economic, social, and political relations that still dominate the world at the start of the twenty-first century.

Further Reading: S. Amin 1989; D. Chakrabarty 2000.

Kevin Hickey

F

Frantz Fanon (1925–1961)   Frantz Fanon was a **francophone** psychiatrist of Caribbean descent whose writings and participation in the Algerian struggle against French colonialism have been a major source of inspiration and ideas for contemporary theorizing about racism, anticolonialism, Third World **nationalism**, and postcoloniality. The power and popularity of his work derive from the clarity and vigor with which specific types of colonized minds are analyzed, while suggesting general applications relevant to all the historically and geographically divergent manifestations of colonized minds and communities. Fanon wrote at a time when Algeria was still fighting for freedom. In later, postcolonial times, his views have proved amenable to a variety of approaches and appropriations, both practical and theoretical.

Fanon was born in Martinique in 1925 and grew up in a colonial culture that was used to looking up to France as its mother country. During World War II, at the age of eighteen, he volunteered for service with the Free French Army, served at the front for two years, was wounded, and received the *Croix de Guerre*. After the war, he returned to Martinique and then came back to France to study medicine and psychiatry at the University of Lyons. There he married and began writing. His experience of racism during the war and as a student was to displace his initial colonial identification with the French and lead to the writing of his first book, *Black Skin, White Masks* (1952).

Intent on working in Africa, in 1953 Fanon accepted the position of head of psychiatry in a French hospital in Algeria. Shortly afterward, the Algerian war of independence began. Fanon's experience of treating patients from both sides, during a period that saw much violence from both sides, crystallized, in the form of a politically committed anticolonialism, the antiracist convictions with which he had come to North Africa. In 1956, after having participated covertly in the activities of the Algerian National Liberation Front (FLN), Fanon resigned from French service and was expelled from Algeria by the French government.

He moved to Tunisia, where he combined the practice of psychiatry with political activism on behalf of the Algerian struggle for independence, writing for a number of periodicals, including Jean-Paul Sartre's *Les Temps Modernes, Présence Africaine*, and the FLN newspaper, *el Moudjahid*. By 1956, the Front had mobilized support across the entire region, and in 1958 a government-in-exile was set up in Tunis, with Ahmed Ben Bella as the political leader and Houari Boumedienne in charge of the military wing. Fanon worked actively for the Front in a variety of ways, surviving several assassination attempts and sustaining injuries in one of them. While working as ambassador to Ghana in 1960, he contracted leukemia, for which he received treatment briefly in Moscow, but resumed work during a period of remission. This soon led to a rapid deterioration of his health. Finally, with Central Intelligence Agency (CIA) assistance, he was flown for treatment to Washington, D.C. It has been claimed that he was left alone there in a hotel room for eight days before being admitted to hospital, perhaps because the CIA was more interested in information on guerrilla activities in North Africa than in his health. At any rate, by that time, his illness had advanced to a terminal stage, and he died in the National Institutes of Health in Bethesda, Maryland, on 6 December 1961, at the age of thirty-six. His body was taken back to Algeria, as he had requested. The Algerian government-in-exile buried him with full military honors.

A recent feature film called *Frantz Fanon: Black Skin, White Mask* (1995), directed by Isaac Julien, offers an interesting collage of interviews with friends, relatives, and contemporary academics, as well as documentary footage, readings from his work, and dramatizations of key moments in his life. As for the subsequent history of the country on whose behalf Fanon devoted his energy and his life, Algeria achieved freedom from France in 1962, with Ben Bella as president. He was deposed in 1965 by Boumedienne, who ruled until his death in 1978. During his tenure, the country adopted **Marxist** socialism in the National Charter of 1976, while Islam was made the state religion.

Fanon's first book, *Peau noire, masques blancs* (1952; trans. as *Black Skins, White Masks*, 1967), is one of the most direct and powerful books on the causes, effects, and mechanisms of racism written in the twentieth century. Fanon's understanding of racial consciousness in the Caribbean and his experience of racial prejudice during World War II and later as a student in France are refracted through the rationality of his psychoanalytic training and his critical engagement with the views of a wide variety of writers, including Jean-Paul Sartre, **Aimé Césaire**, and Jacques Lacan. Fanon's characteristic mode is to focus sharply on specific examples but as exemplifying general tendencies characteristic of all contemporary colonialist cultures. He treats the black Antillean as a type with analogues all over the world: colonized by whiteness and European culture, as these are mediated through the colonizer's language, institutions, practices, and values. The sexuality of the colonized person is shown as fraught with racial tensions concerning dominance and submissiveness. It is argued that male sexuality is shaped by the ambivalent desire for conquest over, or violation of, the white woman, and female sexuality is characterized by the black woman's desire for acceptance by, or submission to, the white man. The sexuality of the colonized person is thus rendered as depraved in itself and threatening to whiteness. The effect is to alienate men and women from their own bodies and their skin color. Colonialist ideology teaches the colonized to believe and accept that they are ugly. It also implies or asserts that the technological and military dominance of Europe over its colonies is a "natural" consequence of their own inferiority. They internalize the "guilt" of not being white and end up hating themselves. As the only recourse in this asymmetry, they acquire—or get taught—the desire to transcend the limitations of their status by aspiring to the culture of the colonizer. However successful they may become at this imitative assimilation, the aspiration keeps them trapped in the role of a symbolic scapegoat for European myths of progress, civilization, liberalism, education, enlightenment, and refinement. Fanon urges **resistance** to the Manichean characterization of blackness as evil and to all the other binaries that are generated by the colonial opposition between white colonizer and black colonized. The solution that he proposes in this book, which was completed before his move to Algeria, is that both blacks and whites must learn to free themselves from their "Manichean delirium," so that human beings can interact as equals without the mediation of the false dualities associated with skin colors.

His second book, *L'An V de la révolution algérienne* (1959; trans. as *A Dying Colonialism or Studies in a Dying Colonialism*, 1965) sprang directly from his passionate adoption of the cause of Algerian independence. The book was banned in France. It is propagandist in tone and intent on arguing for a sympathetic account of how the militant struggle for political freedom has mobilized Algerian society toward a wider social emancipation from its traditional mindset. Fanon is keen to emphasize how militancy against the French colonialists has created greater unity among the colonized and a more progressive attitude toward women, whose enthusiastic support of the nationalist cause is treated as a catalyst for wider changes in their social position in a very traditional and conservative society. Colonialist claims that Western forms of **modernity** when applied to social issues, such as teaching Algerian women to abandon the traditional veil, are dismissed as blind to the ethos of a culture that they try to change from the outside. The revolutionary struggle is given credit for a more organic activation of the force of modernization in the new attitude among Algerians, not only to the role that women played in the revolution but also toward modern technology, as exemplified by the radio. Fanon points out that the war of liberation made the North African aware of the radio as a means of disseminating information and affecting opinion, thus helping a traditional community move toward a new openness to change. Fanon's own experience as a doctor provides him with data and hypotheses to show how even Western medicine gets practiced in a colonial context with results that leave doctors and patients ambivalent about the kind of efficacy taken for granted in a Western context. Fanon's awareness of his own relation to, and difference from, the

African, the Arab, and the Jewish peoples is discussed in the context of a political opposition to racism as an instrument of colonial domination. Fanon's second book thus finds its focus in a sustained opposition to racism as assimilated into colonialism, which renders racial difference and prejudice into a systematic form of oppression and exploitation. It treats both as contingently empowered by technological superiority but inherently unstable because of internal contradictions.

The essays and articles that represent Fanon's regular and occasional contributions to the Algerian liberation movement (from before the time of his leaving French service as the medical director at the Psychiatric Hospital of Blida-Joinville in 1956, to his death in 1961) were collected in the posthumously published *Pour la révolution africaine: Écrits pólitiques* (1969, trans. as *Toward the African Revolution*, 1988). The essays are generally short, and their intent is vigorously polemical. Their tone is animated by a fervent conviction that the era of French colonialism is about to end when an entire colonized nation has finally become aware of itself in terms of the right to justice and freedom. French colonialist practices are criticized on a number of grounds. The principle of colonialism is vilified as involving the systematic deculturation of peoples, which foists upon them a false identity as "natives." Fanon acknowledges that for the typical West Indian who habitually thought of himself as superior to Africans (and not as a Negro, except when facing the white man), the downfall of France in World War II was like the death of the father. This view suggests, in contrast, why he looked for a cause in colonial Africa—rather than the Caribbean—to which he might dedicate his life. In Africa, the damage done to the colonized was at its most obvious and objectionable. Fanon blames French intellectuals for an abdication of moral responsibility in the face of the many kinds of violence, from torture, to rape, to massacre, that the colonialists are accused of perpetrating in their belated efforts to stem the tide of the inevitable. Fanon has no objections to the use of violence by the liberationist cause, since he sees it as a necessary and justified form of counterforce. He places the struggle for independence in a global perspective, as the augury of a new **humanism** that will address human issues in a more wide-ranging perspective than the **Eurocentrism** that gets dissembled as Western humanism. In the Cold War status quo that had already established itself between the United States and the USSR, he recognizes that the Western world fears to give up its territorial conquests, as that would weaken its economies, raising what Fanon dismisses as the bogey of an ever-strengthening communism. The struggle in Algeria is aligned with, and follows upon, the liberation already achieved by nations under leaders such as Nehru, Nasser, and Sukarno. Fanon hopes that the struggle for **decolonization** will unite Africa. He would like to see anticolonialism and resistance to "metropolitan" capitalism combine as forces that will replace the idea of race (as a category on which identity can be built) with the notion of a **Pan-African** unity. The two dangers that he foresees as threatening this ideal are regional tensions between neighboring communities and borders and the likelihood that the middle class will achieve power once nationalism had won the day, and in the ensuing era of "**neocolonialism**," this middle class will adopt an "annexationist" policy picked up as a vice from their erstwhile colonial masters. He predicts that Africa's real enemy will not have been colonialism, but "the absence of ideology." For him, liberation means the right to self-determination. He argues that the freedom to this right is not part of some inevitable necessity built into history seen as a dialectical process. It is a goal to be achieved by focused revolutionary action. Subsequent developments have shown how justified were Fanon's fears and how difficult of achievement his ideal.

Fanon's final book, *Les Damnées de la Terre* (1961, trans. as *The Wretched of the Earth*, 1963), has proved to be a very influential work. In an exhortatory preface, Sartre applauds Fanon and admonishes the Western world for not having had the sense to appreciate the implications of his achievement for European culture and humanism. The essays in the book are analytic in tone and diagnostic in mode. Fanon reiterates the absolute need for an organized and educated counterviolence if the struggle for self-determination is to succeed against the Manichean violence that created "native" consciousness and frustrated its collective energies. His focus here has shifted from the struggle between colonialism and anticolonialism to the pitfalls facing decolonized peoples, whose entry into their new histories as nations is accompanied by an inevitable and desperate need for a stake in the global redistribution of wealth. Fanon places the problems of these emergent nations in the broader context of the global contestation for power between capitalism and socialism. He again identifies the principal danger for underdeveloped nations as the rise to power of a native bourgeoisie. He warns that the native middle class lacks the technical and economic strengths to build up a stable and prosperous nation. Instead, it is liable to turn its back on the masses and concentrate, in narrow greed, on substituting itself in the positions of advantage once occupied by the former colonial masters. Once the masses discover that the new nation does little to improve their condition, in their disappointment and apathy they are likely to revert from the idea of nation to older and regressive affiliations of tribe and race. Fanon urges native intellectuals to take an active interest in shaping national consciousness in order to forestall corrupt leadership, antidemocratic regimes, and economic regression. The decades of African history since Fanon's death have more than confirmed the accuracy of his apprehensions, though what he had hoped for did not materialize. By and large, neither did the masses get adequately educated and mobilized to sustain into the building of nations the cohesiveness and participation that had gained independence, nor did native intellectuals succeed in providing the critical mass or energy to affect the turn of events in the new nations of Africa.

Writing in 1960, Fanon argues that in the postcolonial struggle to achieve the legitimacy of the claims of a nation, a national culture has to be fostered. In this attempt, the native intellectual, who is generally fearful of being reabsorbed into the culture of the former colonizer, can end up either making or finding a real or imagined value in the native culture that preceded colonization. He warns that while this can serve to give the past a value that got obscured by colonialism, such evocations are no guarantee of an adequate culture for the present or future needs of emergent nations. Fanon acknowledges the role of Islamic consciousness and of the **negritude** movement in fostering a new African consciousness but warns that the goal of a racial, as against a national, identity would be a mistake. According to him, the movement of the native intellectual and writer toward a more integrated role in the creation of a national culture involves three phases. In the first, he is still a creature shaped by colonial values; in the second, he moves away from this assimilated existence but cannot embrace native themes and materials except awkwardly; and in the third, he finally identifies himself with the native masses, whose consciousness he begins to shape. History has shown that Fanon's picture may have been too optimistic, but it continues to offer a schematic path that writers and intellectuals from the underdeveloped world have found unavoidable. Critics point out that Pan-Africanism may have seemed a tempting panacea to Fanon in his time but has had little practical power to unify the vastly differentiated affiliations that constitute the postcolonial history of the diverse nations and cultures of Africa.

Fanon wrote at a time when the challenges that he named, the goals that he set, and the dangers that he warned of were part of a sweeping reconfiguration of the geopolitical map of the earth. After his death, his first and last books, in particular, have had a great impact on intellectuals, radicals, and writers all over the Third World, where issues of race, decolonization, and national consciousness have become the primary concerns of underdeveloped nations and oppressed minorities. Fanon's works have found a large and sympathetic readership in the intellectual Left in Britain and Europe. In the United States, his ideas on racial consciousness and sexual identity have influenced black figures such as Malcolm X, Eldridge Cleaver, and Amiri Baraka. More recently, Fanon has been enlisted by the academic **Homi Bhabha** into a poststructuralist argument that goes against the grain of Fanon's overt political idealism to develop a theory of the subversions and slippages to which identity and authority are prone in a **subaltern** context. Dominance and subjugation have been studied by other academics like Abdul JanMohamed, using Fanon's metaphor of the Manichean aspect of racial difference. Meanwhile, an academic who is also a committed political writer, **Edward Said**, has commented that while Fanon made a vital contribution to the ideologies of resistance, decolonization, and liberation, he neither did, nor could, provide strategies for how postcolonial nations might avoid the dangers that he foresaw all too accurately. Nevertheless, for the nations of Africa, Fanon continues to serve as a voice of exhortation and warning.

Further Reading: A. C. Alessandrini 1999; L. R. Gordon, T. D. Sharpley-White, and R. T. White 1996.

Rajeev S. Patke

Nuruddin Farah   The Somali novelist Nuruddin Farah is one of the most multiliterate and multilingual of African writers (English is his fourth language). Born in 1945, he comes from a nomadic tradition and has been a global nomad, living in a score of countries over four continents. His fiction is richly diverse in origin, drawing upon Western, Arabic, Islamic, and oral sources, and is a living testament to the process of cultural hybridization that has become a hall-mark of the postcolonial world. Farah's writing is a forum of debate for com-peting voices and ideas, opposing a tolerant multiplicity of viewpoints and fluid, open-ended narratives to the tyrannies of closure, monologue, and omniscience, which he associates with dictatorship.

Though Farah has revisited Somalia only once in his twenty-five-year exile, the bulk of his writing depicts his country's oppression by the clan-based post-colonial dictatorship of Siyad Barre, which held power from 1969 until 1991. Only his first novel, *From a Crooked Rib* (1970), which charts the flight of an independent-minded nomadic woman from bartered marriages and pastoral slav-ery to urban prostitution, is set in the colonial period. Farah has said in interview that, although the former imperial powers, Britain and Italy, were responsible for sabotaging the structures of African society, and the neoimperial ones, Russia and America, helped to keep the dictator in power, the key betrayals of the ideals of independence came not from colonialism but from within the Somali nation, clan, and family. In the trilogy *Variations on the Theme of an African Dictatorship* (1979–1983), tribalism and Islam are no less complicit than **Marx-ism** with the new political totalitarianism into which Barre's post-1969 revolu-tion, simultaneously celebrated and censured in the earlier *A Naked Needle* (1976), has drifted. Moreover, military despotism is revealed to be but a pro-jection of authoritarian family structures that condition people to institutional tyranny. The twin repressive institutions of family and state, household and political patriarchy work in negative collaboration and mutual reinforcement, invoking each other's authority and sanctioning each other's violence. In *Sweet and Sour Milk* (1979), patriarchal bigotry and state terrorism work hand in hand in the form of the father Keynaan, who combines the roles of police torturer-cum-informer and terrorizer of his wives and children, stamping out subversion at both political and domestic levels by his connivance at the death and defa-mation of his highly placed dissident son. In *Sardines* (1981), a government minister brings the wrath of the regime down on his head when he dares to evict his tyrannical mother, and in *Close Sesame* (1983), a father who is of the same clan lineage as the dictator is forced at the latter's personal behest to bludgeon to death his own son for subversive underground activities.

A striking feature of the *Dictatorship* trilogy is Farah's ingenious combination of the techniques of the detective novel, political thriller and dystopian forms, and oral narrative to create a deranged world of rearranged history and disap-pearing "unpersons" in which the protagonist's hold on reality is never secure. This uncertainty is compounded by the regime's privileging of the **oral** culture, from which its security corps of illiterate spies and informers is drawn, and its unofficial endorsement of the oral code's unstable, inconclusive order of meaning as the political status quo. In the menacing atmosphere of fear and distrust fostered by an obscurantist dictator, no one can trust anyone else's testimony, truth dissolves in a welter of conflicting oral rumor and hearsay, and reality becomes an unravelable hermetic text, an unwritable plot in which rival orders of meaning cancel one another out. Thus, when the veteran anticolonial hero Deeriye dies in a futile attempt to assassinate the tyrant at the conclusion of *Close Sesame*, so many rival interpretive options are present—revenge, religious or political martyrdom, suicide—that the event hovers between a polyvalency of meaning and an impenetrable aporia.

Postmodernist and postcolonial elements continue to converge, in more intensified form, in Farah's sixth novel. Set during the 1977 Somali-Ethiopian War in the Ogaden, *Maps* (1986) unfolds an intricate fable of individual, **ethnic**, and national identity through the relationship of the orphaned Ogadenese-Somali child Askar and his adoptive Oromo-Ethiopian mother Misra, with whom he develops a close physical intimacy that overrides national enmities. As the mythic offspring of two patriotic martyrs, Askar personifies Ogadenese nationalism, his childhood history analogous with that of his parentless nation, but he is also a straddler of boundaries. To the problematic borders of nation and tribe that generate awkward questions about Somali identity are added those of gender, status, and age. Askar claims to be simultaneously male and female, half-man and half-child, a real and a mythological miracle-child, thus figuring dually in the narrative as a creature of history and of his own intellectual fantasy. His principal obsession is with the redrawing of the questionable colonial maps of his homeland, but the new cartographic hegemonies that he promotes are, like the old ones, unstable figmentary constructs that seem to bear little relation to human geography. Like the real Misra (whose name means "the foundation of the earth"), the neutral, disputed strip of land over which the war is fought does not discriminate between its diverse occupying nationalities and the rival ethnocentric maps that overlay it like a palimpsest.

After a brief return to conventional realism in *Gifts* (1992), a love story that explores the psychology of donorship in the context of international aid, Farah in his eighth novel extends *Maps'* skeptical line of inquiry from national to clan identity and assesses the damage that clan fanaticism, even more than nationalism, has done to his country. In the last days of the Barre regime and under the shadow of impending interethnic warfare that will make clan identity a matter of life and death, the protagonist of *Secrets* (1998) seeks to determine his ancestral lineage, only to find that origins, whether of individuals or nations, are obscure, imponderable, and finally irrelevant. The progeny of a gang rape, he discovers only a host of untraceable fathers from nameless and unnumbered clans, and he learns of people what Askar learns of countries in *Maps*: that they have many parents; that the kinship groups into which they are formed have no primordial authenticity but are man-made, opportunistic political inventions camouflaging powermania and greed; and that (as Askar learns too late) the

emotional bonds of parents and children who choose each other are more liberating than identities constructed along bloodlines. Truth in this novel, as in
Farah's others, exists at "the crossroads where several worlds meet."

Further Reading: P. Alden and L. Tremaine 1999; D. Wright 1994.

Derek Wright

Feminisms As political interventions with considerable epistemological impact on struggles over race, gender, **ethnicity**, national identities, and imperialisms, both postcolonial praxes and feminisms have had a long and fruitful
relationship, each correcting and redefining the field of the other. Articulated
together under overlapping rubrics, these interventionist projects have restruc-
tured the cartographies of political struggle across divergent geopolitical contexts and disciplines. Chandra Mohanty (1991) shapes "Third World feminist
politics" as an analytic category that allows for coalitional alliances between
progressive theorists and activists across the world. She insists on postcolonial
feminisms (in the plural) as praxes of reorientation and reinvention: the acts of
reading both politically progressive (e.g., white feminist, postcolonial, or Third
World **nationalist**) and regressive (e.g., racist, imperialist, or sexist) discourses
against the grain and constructing new understandings, histories, agendas. In
such tasks feminisms understood in the context of postcoloniality—an experience carrying its own formidable refigured epistemologies—have challenged,
extended, and refined the vectors of both feminist and postcolonial studies.

Postcolonial feminisms draw on the internal critiques of white, middle-class
feminism by second-wave feminists. Since the start of the 1980s we have witnessed enormous challenges to the notion "woman" as a unitary category, for
analysis or for political mobilizations (Denise Riley 1988). Women in different
contexts seem variously inclined and engaged in disparate issues, debates, and
agendas pertinent to the modalities of power in *their* lives; moreover, they inhabit multiple sites of struggle, not necessarily limited to gender as the primary
determinant of action. Hence, scholars, critics, and activists from different quarters insist on gender as a *historical* category, understood within a particular
historical juncture and in the intersections of multiple "relations of ruling" (Dorothy Smith 1987).

Black feminists heralded this critique in their interrogations of the racism and
of the white, middle-class privileges of speaking for *all* women (for instance,
see bell hooks 1984; Cherrie Moraga and Gloria Anzaldúa 1983; Pearlie McNeill
and Pratibha Parmar 1986; Hazel Carby 1995). They argued that the shunting
of all women into one class, which assumed common histories, experiences, and
interests, often served to jeopardize other possible and contingent collective
links—such as, in the Anglo-American case, alliances between black women
and men in antiracist struggles in the United States and Britain. Along with
these realizations came the call for attention to relationships between classes of
women from feminists like Aída Hurtado (1996); on another front, lesbian fem-

inists attacked the implicit heterosexism of white feminism (Adrienne Rich 1977). In turn, this gave rise to an acknowledgment of differences between women, differences along multiple vectors of power, including differentials along the lines of sex and gender (Joan Scott 1988).

The feminist emphasis on situated identity formation and site-specific **resistance**, as well as the renewed attention to the power of discourse in constructing the rubrics for identification and struggle, ran parallel to the poststructuralist and postmodern critiques of all grand *récits*. These latter gestures questioned other *progressive* visions, such as the leftist horizon of class struggle. **Marxist** feminists like Michele Barrett (1992), for example, theorized gaps in Marxist conceptions of domestic labor (specifically, Marx's dependence on *wage-labor* as a unit for measuring exploitation), reproduction, and patriarchy, elisions responsible for the inattention to gender inequities in Marxist analyses of power. By adding gender and sexuality as analytic categories for political critiques of *regressive* visions, such as imperial dreams or state policies, theorists further refined and realigned feminist understandings of the modalities and the multiple locations of power and resistance. For example, Ann McClintock's (1995) tracing of "race" and its impact on forms of desiring, for both men and women, revised the colonial record of the daily reinscription and the superstructural exercise of power. These interventions served to locate **identity** as irrevocably plural and political interests and practices as therefore contingent on the specific moments of articulation. The recognition that neither the study of gender nor political organizing around gender categories could have transcendent historical or geographical horizons, led to revisions of scope followed by a movement toward location-specific analyses.

The epistemic break described earlier has everything to do with the category "postcolonial feminisms," for the term derives its value, at least initially, as a critical interrogation of white, middle-class feminism located in the First World. As an *epistemological* category, it was unequivocally a part of this general challenge, yet with a cartographic twist: the historical perception that a substantially large part of the world, heuristically understood as the "Third World," *did* share experiences of postcoloniality, and, hence, the interests and agendas of men and women in this *geopolitical* arena necessarily would be different from their counterparts based in the "First World." I do not belabor the argument that Mohanty (1991) makes so well about the geopolitical congruence of the "postcolonial" with the "Third World," a rubric that she uses because of its considerable historical (epistemological) force and endurance in contemporary discursive cartographies of power. But Mohanty's concretization of the "postcolonial" as a collection of *geopolitical* sites rather than *subjective locations* (understood as sites of identity and struggle) proved to be an important moment for theorizing postcolonial feminisms, for while the assertions of subjective sites of multiple identity formations were significant to understanding the difference of *postcolonial feminisms* from *white, middle-class feminisms*, the physical limits of geopolitical location were an undeniable corollary to the postcolonial condition; postcoloniality has always been about the aftermath of territorial conquest and about links, transgressions, and border-crossings. This is not to suggest that territorial locations are somehow more "real" or relevant to postcolonial politics than imaginative acts of self-location. Yet, it is increasingly evident in the recent discourse on migration, exile, and nomadism that, in a century that has seen more human migration than at any other period in history, most postcolonial peoples substantially experience the physical limits and constrictions of geo-political boundaries—especially women, whose bodies constitute some of the most visible of transnational flows—hence, the relevance of the *cartographic* carving out of "First" and "Third" Worlds, as differential materially experienced spheres, and the subsequent acknowledgment of the "Third World" within the geopolitical boundaries of the "First" (this zone on the "inside" becoming the site for alliances between, say, women of color in London with their sisters in New York, Kano, or Delhi).

The feminist perception of postcoloniality as a shared historical experience, rooted in colonial **modernity**, drew from epistemological revolutions in another quarter—the wing of poststructuralist discourse that engaged with unpacking the colonial recits of progressive modernity and found them lacking. With inaugural moments in **Frantz Fanon, Edward Said**, and **Gayatri Spivak**, there came a wave of deconstructing, criticizing, and evaluating the colonial archive, culmi-nating in the field of postcolonial studies, initially an oppositional epistemology in the "First World" (a boundary that is sometimes, but not entirely, commen-surate with "the West" or "the North," in this discursive field), then gradually gaining momentum from massive anticolonial nationalist and internationalist re-sistances from the postcolonies. The postcolonial critiques of the project of mo-dernity and the Enlightenment, as exampled in the work of the **Subaltern Studies** collective, looked inward self-reflexively at the process of knowledge production *both* by postcolonial metropolitan elites and by the colonizers, cou-pled with concerted attempts to situate heterogeneous modernities in different postcolonial contexts.

If one of the results of these investigations was to reconstitute the subject of power and the object of discourse, women were historically primed to be ex-emplary figures of subalternity. Feminists working in postcolonial studies now turned to the implications of these critiques for women, as the historical subjects of *both* colonial and indigenous patriarchies. Gayatri Spivak's (1987) articula-tion of the gendered subaltern (like the Rani of Sirmur), produced in masculinist British colonial *and* Hindu Brahmanical discourses, is perhaps the best marker for this moment in postcolonial theoretical conjectures. Joining the general poststructural attack on grand universal frameworks, Spivak raises key questions about *representation*, both political (who speaks for whom?) and aesthetic (how is she spoken of?). Who, asks Spivak in the case of the Rani of Sirmur, speaks for this woman? Do we ever have access to her as a subject? Do we ever hear her "speak"? Or is she the figural product of discursive genuflections on the gender issue by two patriarchal narratives, the one on a civilizing mission and the other honed to reformist zeal?

What has emerged in postcolonial studies, then, is a significant archive on different histories, agendas, and issues for women and men as postcolonial subjects. To pick a contemporary example: in analyzing the rape, mutilation, kidnapping, and repatriation of women during the partition of India and Pakistan, Urvashi Butalia and Ritu Menon (1998) offer revised histories of partition violence etched on the bodies of women, narratives lost in the nationalist accounts of the period. They remind us, for instance, of a fact seldom mentioned in all the postcolonial discussion on the exchange of population and properties in 1947: that the Inter Dominion Treaty did not allow *women* to choose their national affiliations but rather ascribed them citizenship based on the chosen national loyalties of their fathers, brothers, husbands, and other patriarchal guardians—hence, the "problem" of "recovered women" on both sides of the border after partition. The state-sponsored ownership of women as individuals, of course, had everything to do with the ways in which Hindu, Muslim, and Sikh men worked out trauma of *their* border-crossings by violating the mobile property of the "other"—wives, sisters, mothers.

These revisionist explorations inevitably become implicit critiques of political structures (here, the "liberated" postcolonial state) and movements, as well as of existent historical accounts (including progressive anticolonial history-writing) seeking to document all forms of oppression, violence, and exploitation. The nation, the nation-state, and nationalist historiography have emerged as central objects of critical investigation for many postcolonial feminists, questioning the formulations of gender roles and citizenships in these new polities. Deniz Kandiyoti's (1991) work on women's participation in the Algerian anticolonial struggle and their further role in nationalist politics offers a rereading of liberatory anti-imperial rhetorics and policies. Anticolonial Third Worldist nationalist projects, suggests Kandiyoti, in identifying women as the bearers of cultural identity often seek to control women's sexuality and economic and political power, thereby preventing their emergence as full-fledged citizens. From Gandhi to Kenyatta to Nkrumah, nation-makers seem at odds with their women citizenry, even as there is the wide recognition that the organized political struggles of women in the postcolonies cannot be understood outside of the colonial/postcolonial script.

What these investigations imply are *differences* in the political *feminist* impetus of women and men in the postcolonies, differences that substantially revise First World understandings of women's liberation, particularly the liberal discourses on rights and choices. Haleh Afshar (1996) draws our attention to anti-imperial struggles that fruitfully utilize socially prescribed or traditional gender roles that are not seen as liberatory within mainstream First World feminisms, for instance, the acceptance of the veil by elite Iranian women as a non-negotiable emblem of the Islamicization of the country or the placing of motherhood at the center of feminist struggle by women in Latin American countries. The staging and performance of motherhood as political praxis and the even more confounding fact that often these women do not see themselves as *gendered* actors in their daily resistances (Caldeira 1990) necessitate revised notions of feminist praxis, the feminist political actor, and the object of feminist analyses.

I return to these revisions and expansions shortly, but to continue with the double-pronged postcolonial feminist challenge to First World feminisms and postcolonial studies that I have been developing so far, I perceive the changes in the vectors of scrutiny to be deeply linked to the question of political **agency**, an issue that goes hand in hand with the discomfort over the politics and aesthetics of representation. Here, too, the postcolonial feminist criticism of the First Worldist production of a non-Western other who must be rescued—explicit in Spivak's work but even more urgent in development theory critics (for instance, see Marian Lazreg 1994; Chandra Mohanty 1991; Aihwa Ong 1988)— has been categorical and substantial. Feminists now routinely explore hitherto uncharted arenas of struggle, such as mobilization around motherhood, family, or femininity, or nongovernmental organization (NGO) organizing outside of structures of power delineated in political theory.

This is not to say that there are no lasting reservations about embracing these unconventional forms of struggle *as* feminist resistances, especially since they might entail redefining prior feminist equations such as the one between women and pacifism. This equation has been a particularly beleaguered one in the contemporary conversations on women icons in India's Hindu militant right wing, for example, women leaders who have exhorted Hindu men to kill Muslims and rip Muslim children from their mother's wombs (Amrita Basu 1998). While fully ratifying masculinist ideologies of chastity and vigilance, these women present spectacular examples of female empowerment, while the unprecedented political mobilization of women by the Hindu Right outnumbers the previous wave of women's participation in nationalist struggles (during the anticolonial era). These curious facts have sparked a furious debate on empowerment, resistance, women's activism, and violence (Tanika Sarkar 1995; Amrita Basu 1998), leading to the consolidation of an archive on the women's organizations in the Hindu right coalition (see, for instance, Paola Bacchetta 1999).

Of course, there is another great pitfall in postcolonial feminist studies—one of becoming so specific as to occlude any common alliances and patterns between feminists that might work toward progressive futures. In the interface of the "postcolonial" with the "Third World," there are implicit geopolitical traversings, multiple and crisscrossing lines of resistance to "scattered hegemonies" (Grewal and Kaplan 1994). New cartographies are in order in our current moment of **globalization**, perhaps more than ever before, as the transnational flows of similar objects and the commensurability of global economic restructurings *do* beg for comparative analyses and alliances across local sites of struggle. Consider, for example, the political relevance of Jacqui Alexander's exegesis on sexual legislation against **queer** bodies in the Bahamas (read as the government's response to the perceived permeability of national borders, in Bahamas' state-sponsored exploding tourist economy) to discussions of the visual panics in the current Indian cultural context of Hindu militant border-drawings, the deliberate marking of queerness as a signifier of contaminating global presences within the nation-state (most recently witnessed in the controversy over Deepa Mehta's 1997 film, *Fire*). Such new mappings of resistance and power can serve as bases to build political alliances between feminists, queer activists, and progressives across nation-state boundaries at a moment when the fragmented, displaced, yet overwhelming, specter of late capital seems unassailable in its enchroachments. Several collections on Third World women's movements and political praxes offer a space for such geopolitical border-crossings, with feminists engaged in reading the intersectionality of women's resistance with superstructural modes of power (authoritarian regimes, fundamentalisms, ethnic nationalisms, etc.). Significantly, these border-crossings remain cautious, wary of postcolonial feminist deconstructions of **dependency theories**; we can see this quite clearly in the guarded discussions of human and woman's rights in recent years (Nancy Fraser and Linda Gordon 1994). Saskia Sassen's (1998) reenvisioning of global terrains of power and resistance, when one uses gender as the analytic category, provides an excellent example of exciting possible reformulations. Sassen reminds us that globalization theories, too, often map transnational financial terrains as *the* definitive mode of global restructurations; yet, in the global cities that are her sites of analyses, she records other links of power *between* migrant women, networks whose existence may remain undocumented by the nation-state or by global macropolitical structures such as the United Nations. Through these examples, I have been suggesting the *double valence* of the term "postcolonial feminisms" in challenging both feminist and postcolonial work—a radical linkage of epistemological and geopolitical significance.

For the balance of this exploration, I provide some examples of how the category has reshaped both the subjects and the objects of feminist discourse. In doing so, I hope to offer a sense of the term's value and its limitations. One of the significant changes engendered by postcolonial feminist discussions has been to contest the fixity of the political actor, for neither the national citizen nor the transnational cosmopolitan seems a category adequate to the understanding of complex feminist resistances in the postcolonies. One's particular place on the map, stratified as it is by ethnicity, class, sexuality, and migration (Chandra Mohanty 1991), produces the mobile, contingent, and plural individual subject who may become a political actor at many levels—daily lived practices; local, national, or international organized struggles; or sustained participation in a feminist movement. The critique from black and Third World feminists of feminist practice, analyses, and the color and location of feminist agents has thus changed older perceptions of both *what* consitututes praxis and *who* might be engaged in these acts of resistance. These revisions in the subject and object of *feminist* work affect disciplines as diverse as political theory, history writing, cultural criticism, and ethnography; I pause only on one example of disciplinary restructurations to make my general point.

In the field of political theory, Nira Yuval-Davis and Ruth Lister (1997) have contributed to the feminist reconstructions of the idea of citizenship by taking into account exclusions based on gender, ethnicity, and national borders. Keeping in mind the multiple possibilities of feminist praxes and placing the recognition of difference at the heart of citizenship, they reconfigure a citizen as a "multilevel" relation to sources of governance above and below the state. Hence, a key concept of political theory—citizenship, as the relation of the individual subject to the nation and the state—is rearticulated in the wake of postcolonial feminist discourse. Other critics have challenged First World recommendations for democratic woman's rights, based on evidence that in new democratic regimes (like those overseen by the International Monetary Fund [IMF]) women have, in fact, become increasingly marginal as political actors and often subject to revived local patriarchalisms (Catherine Eschle 2000). The discussions of states, nations, and citizens have increasingly engaged postcolonial feminists as sites of struggle over meaning and identity, with the intent toward feminist organizing around transnational effects of racism and imperialism (Cheryl Johnson-Odim 1992; Charlotte Bunch 1987). While these efforts revitalize *existing* sites of political analyses, others place unobstrusive objects in full critical view. An example of this may be found in Aihwa Ong's (1987) work on transnational political economies, where she places the Malay female body in the center of discourses on late capital and its effects. In doing so, she emphasizes the need for "specific ethnographies" and the "politics of embodiment" (Tani Barlow 1997, 4).

Although, in recent years, history writing and political economies have been the major subject of postcolonial feminist discussions, in delineating the historical scope of the category, one must recognize the earlier sites of inquiry, postcolonial feminist cultural criticism (for instance, see Rey Chow 1991 or Norma Alarcon, 1993) and ethnography (Trinh T. Minh-ha 1989, on the racial and sexual basis of the anthropological object). After all, these critiques substantially deconstructed (and still continue to do so) the colonial gaze and the making of the non-Western "other," not to mention revitalizing the links between subjectivity, consciousness, and writing (which had fallen into disrepute after the "disappearance of the subject" in high poststructuralist discourse).

In fact, it is in these last two fields of inquiry, cultural criticism and ethnography, that postcolonial feminists have most rigorously questioned *their* own projects, their cosmopolitan gaze and text-making functions. Indeed, as Spivak (1987) and Arif Dirlik (1997) have noted in discussions on the postcolonial value, a category such as "postcolonial feminisms" inevitably produces "surplus value" in First World cultural economies, laboring to fill that desire for samples of other worlds. This, I think, will always be generally true of knowledge production in the field of postcolonial studies—hence, the call on the part of postcolonial feminists "to make sense of the unequal relations of feminist writing projects" (Tani Barlow 1997). Yet the unevenness of epistemological and political terrains does not diminish the **utopian** value of postcolonial feminisms, for most of the field's practitioners remain committed to making contingent alliances in transnational, national, and local spheres: what Chandra Mohanty and Jacqui Alexander (1995) have eloquently envisioned as "democratic futures" forged by progressive forces across geopolitical boundaries.

Further Reading: T. Trinh 1989; C. Mohanty 1991.

Bishnupriya Ghosh

Filipino Literature The unique postcolonial situation of the Philippines—three centuries of Spanish colonial administration (1565–1898) and fourty-eight years of American administration (1898–1946), interrupted by the four-year Japanese occupation during World War II—has led to a complex network of social and cultural practices in the country, generally characterized by its palimpsestic nature, the process of history, and the creation of culture having been inscribed and reinscribed by successive generations and colonizations. The country contains a racial blend of Malay and Chinese, with a cultural heritage that is a fusion of Asian, Spanish, and American; Roman Catholicism is the dominant religion. Filipino and English are the official languages, with interventions from over eighty languages of the diverse provinces.

Before any colonial encounter with the West, literature was performed and written in many languages by the groups of people who eventually formed the Filipino "**nation**." Literature in these languages continued, and still continues, to be produced along with writing in the languages of the colonizers. During the Spanish occupation, Francisco Balagtas wrote *Florante at Laura* (1861), a metrical romance in Tagalog (now called Filipino), a classic of Philippine literature. The first works of Filipino literature of international renown were written in Spanish. José Rizal's *Noli Me Tangere* (1887)—written two years after the first Filipino novel, Pedro Paterno's *Ninay* (1907)—and *El Filibusterismo* (1891) exposed Spanish colonial atrocities and led to his execution. A decade after the American government established the public school system in 1901, the use of Spanish had declined, and writers began experimenting with the new language and the forms and imagery offered by English and American literature. Early Filipino writers in English sought to articulate Philippine experience in the recently acquired language and by the 1920s exhibited genuine development in literature. A parallel development in Tagalog fiction, poetry, and drama by Lope K. Santos, Inigo Ed. Regalado, and Jose Corazon de Jesus, among others, developed through publication in hundreds of periodicals and magazines. Zoilo Galang's *The Child of Sorrow* (1921) is considered the first Filipino novel in English. Other early writers of fiction in English were Paz Marquez-Benitez ("Dead Stars" (1925), "A Night in the Hills," 1926), Vicente Hilario, Paz Latorena, Loreto Paras-Sulit, Fernando Maramag, and Mauro Mendez. Much of this early writing was characterized by melodrama, unreal language, and unsubtle emphasis on local color. Jorge C. Bocobo and Carlos P. Romulo developed nonfiction prose in English. The *zarzuela*, in Tagalog as well as in other Philippine languages, the dramatic form of the 1920s and 1930s, was gradually replaced on the city stage by dramas by American and English writers and later by Filipino playwrights Wilfrido Maria Guerrero, Severino Montano, and Alberto Florentino.

After this initial development, the central concern of Filipino writers in English was to create a national literature that would reveal authenticity of experience and artistic originality. Emphasis on craftsmanship made José García Villa, novelist and poet, the leading literary figure of the period of American colonization. His first collection of stories, *Footnote to Youth: Tales of the Philippines and Others*, was published by Scribner's in 1933. This period produced writers of fiction in English who continued to write after independence from the United States, incorporating contemporary themes and issues, such as massive Filipino immigration to North America and the Marcos dictatorship, as well as experiments with literary styles and forms. In recent decades, Filipino writers have become increasingly conscious of the gap between critical expectations and definitions inherited from culturally dominant societies and the literature that must help develop national and cultural **identities**. The sense of discontinuous history and cultural hybridization, produced by a long history of both cultural assimilation and conflict, leads writers to work within a heterogeneous overlapping of cultures with their attendant myths, religious and ethical philosophies, aesthetic ideologies, political systems, and economic modes. Noteworthy writers of fiction include Manuel E. Arguilla, who explores the authenticity and poetic quality of rural life ("Morning in Nagrebcan" [1940], "A Son Is Born" [1940], "How My Brother Leon Brought Home a Wife" [1936]); Bienvenido Santos, chronicler of the dramas of Filipino exiles (*What the Hell for You Left Your Heart in San Francisco* [1987], "Scent of Apples" [1948], "The Day the Dancers Came" [1955]); Arturo B. Rotor, whose stories expose the inner life of the city ("At Last This Fragrance" [1937], "Deny the Mockery" [1937]); Carlos Bulosan, who lived the injustice suffered by migrant Filipino laborers in the United States (*America Is in the Heart* [1946], "As Long as the Grass Shall Grow" [1943]); and N.V.M. Gonzalez, whose Filipino stories emphasize the culture's intrinsic doubleness (*The Woman Who Had Two Navels* [1961], *Bread of Salt and Other Stories* [1993], *The Bamboo Dancers* [1959]). Nick Joaquin's novel, *Portrait of the Artist as Filipino* (1961), deals with a Filipino's growing historical awareness of himself as a blend of Western culture imposed on an Asian setting, inaugurating a new form of Filipino originality through the creation of a symbolic vocabulary from indigenous objects and imagery. In short stories like "May Day Eve" (1947) and "Summer Solstice" (1947), he produces conflict by blending the palimpsestic strands of belief and ritual at the root of Filipino culture. Stevan Javellana's *Without Seeing the Dawn* (1947) is emblematic of Philippine historical fiction.

Contemporary writing displays more confidence in the use of Filipino English, tinged with Spanish or Filipino words or expressions that at best, articulate the writer's awareness of the consequences of the between-world position on literary discourse. This maturity is evidenced in the works of contemporary poets such as Emmanuel Torres, Rolando Tinio, Alfredo Navarro Salanga, Alfred Yuson, Ramon Sunico, Bienvenido Lumbera, Marjorie Evasco, Gemino Abad, Luisa Aguilar-Cariño, Ricardo de Ungria, Rofel Brion, and Benilda Santos; in fiction by Francisco Arcellana, Nick Joaquin, Bienvenido Santos, N.V.M. Gonzalez, Edilberto Tiempo, F. Sionil José, Ninotchka Rosca, Kerima Polotan, Linda Ty-Casper, and Jose Y. Dalisay, the most significant fictionist in English of this generation.

Further Reading: L. Casper 1991; C. Hidalgo 1998.

Rocío G. Davis

Film and Other Media   It is possible to argue that the Hollywood film industry and U.S. media in general are postcolonial industries, that is, that they are a historical part of the establishment of self-**identity** and **settler** indigenousness in a country previously mostly under British rule, a case, therefore, of New World differentiating from Old, the repudiation of imported European models and the following of an independent path.

It is equally possible to argue that the hegemonic position of anglophone Hollywood and U.S.-controlled media conglomerates in the contemporary world media is a supreme act of imperialism that creates "colonized" situations elsewhere by suppressing, for example, not only non-Western media development but national identity in the non-anglophone countries of Europe and places limits on the degree of regional independence worldwide by favoring U.S.-focused news, information, and entertainment. Time Warner, after all, has used this most famous of catchphrases: "The world is our audience." New media industries, such as those concerned with computer software and the Internet, both largely controlled by U.S. interests, help only to heighten this situation.

Though both of these positions are viable, neither is usually what is meant by the terms "postcolonial film" and "postcolonial media." Mostly, these terms tend to refer to the development and discussion of film and media by **First Nation** peoples, to indigenous settler film and media, and to non-Western media industries, both within non-European countries "physically" colonized by Europeans and in opposition to the broadcast or screening of nonindigenous media products in those countries. This, development of the "postcolonial" film industry is often included in a discussion of "Third Cinema," while in media terms it is included in the empirical and theoretical consideration of the growth of "indigenous" media industries. Such discussions can include the development of non-anglophone media industries in predominantly anglophone countries, such as Welsh-language broadcasting in Great Britain on Welsh television stations such as S4C and the Irish-language television broadcasting on Teilifís na Gaeilge (TnaG) in Ireland, as well as the development of film and broadcasting controlled by First Nation peoples, such as Aboriginal and Torres Strait Islander filmmaking in Australia, Inuit filmmaking in Canada, and Maori broadcasting in New Zealand.

Michael Meadows, writing in Albert Moran's *Film Policy: International, National and Regional Perspectives* (1996), talks in this regard of "a new spirit of cooperation between indigenous and non-indigenous filmmakers" heralding a "new era of representation" (270). While Wimal Dissanayake, writing in *The Oxford Guide to Film Studies* (1998), points out that while the concept of Third Cinema is widely used to differentiate it from First Cinema (mainstream Hollywood) and Second Cinema (European arthouse), critics such as Paul Willeman note rightly that the term should not be seen as a homogenized one nor damp down discussions about the relationship between cinema and **nation** or cinema and race.

In important ways, many of these issues are engendered in the internal situation of the United States as well as in a discussion of its external influence. While this undoubtedly strays into a discussion of the nature of media **globalization**, the two discussions are intimately connected.

Included here is the willingness to reflect on the relationship between non-anglophone and nonsettler industries and the dominant white settler, English-speaking media. There are likewise the questions of region versus nation and the internal hegemonies that favor, for example, urban over rural perspectives. As Rob Nixon points out in his chapter in Kate Darian-Smith's *Text, Theory, Space: Land, Literature and History in South Africa and Australia* (1996), the rural is seen as a place of exile, spatially, economically, and culturally, but also as a place of indigenous tradition. That the majority of the world's media industries have an urban base only helps to reiterate that the physical location of media production often engenders a residual imperial factor.

The following analogous situation is also notable. A great deal of film is produced in the United States outside Hollywood. We only need think of the strong state-based industries of Texas or New York. Likewise, a lot of U.S. film is made by independent production companies. Yet, as Steve Neale and Murray Smith point out in *Contemporary Hollywood Cinema* (1998), it is only through such government legislation as the Paramount Decrees of 1948 that the small number of companies that controlled the film industry was obliged to divorce their interests in exhibition from those in production and distribution. Even now, American film and Hollywood studio film are often viewed as synonymous, and independent, non-Hollywood filmmaking is seen as "other." Thus, Native American filmmaking, nonanglophone filmmaking, and geographically "regional" filmmaking are marginalized. It would not be unfair to view this as continued evidence of a colonial privileging of the "**center**."

An analogous, but even more complex, situation exists in postcolonial India. The Indian film industry has grown to become the most prolific in the world, producing over one-third more films per annum than the United States and second only to China in the total size of its annual cinema attendances. It is true to say, however, that the Western world commonly sees Indian cinema as equaling Hindi cinema, tends to include all Indian cinema under the pejorative banner "Bollywood," and mostly knows the work of one or two key names, of which Satyajit Ray is dominant. The differences between such language cinemas as Assamese, Bengali, Bhojpuri, Gujarati, Hindi, Kannada, Malayalam, Marathi, Oriya, Punjabi, Rajasthani, Tamil, and Telugu are rarely recognized. If media globalization promotes a centralizing cultural hegemony, then this is one obvious form of a powerful Western imperialism.

The reality of post–World War II Indian cinema is vastly different from this. Indian cinema is intimately connected with the foundation of Indian **nationhood**, and government policy toward it has been firmly grounded in prioritizing film projects devoted to the promotion of cultural identity, often in a state version of realism, and connected with a perceived need to integrate the region's cultures into one nation. Undoubtedly, Ray's work itself played a primary role in promoting such integration, albeit with one set of aesthetic tools. In addition to this, Indian cinema has strongly debated such aesthetic and political points as the difference between realism and **modernism**, the cultural position of high and low art, and the specifics of precolonial aesthetics.

Indeed, direct state intervention is a feature of India's postindependence film history. The formation of the Film Finance Corporation (FFC) and reports on state intervention (the Film Enquiry Committee Report of 1951) and on film censorship (the Khosla Report on Film Censorship of 1969) reflect the importance that many postcolonial countries have placed on managing the growth of their indigenous media industries. Similar state interventions, for example, can be seen in the media industries of both Australia and Canada.

The intervention of the Australian government in the growth and focus of its national filmmaking culture took place largely in the 1970s. Only fifteen feature films were made in Australia in the 1960s, and the majority of these were financed and controlled by non-Australian interests. Likewise, as Tom O'Regan notes in *Australian National Cinema* (1996), even in the 1980s only between 5 percent and 21 percent of the local cinema box office was made up of local product. What filmmaking did occur within Australia prior to the 1970s owed a great deal to the use of Australian settings, Australian literature, or Australian myths for what were essentially British films.

This worked in two ways: first, to engender stereotypes about the Australian character and lifestyle and, second, to give access for local settler filmmakers to modes and techniques of filmmaking not well developed in their own country. We need only look at Harry Watt's *The Overlanders* (1946), Jack Lee's *A Town like Alice* (1956), or Michael Powell's *They're a Weird Mob* (1966) and the less naive, less romanticized pictures of the Australian environment presented in Nicolas Roeg's *Walkabout* (1970), with its often horrific images of decay and voracious animal life, and Ted Kotcheff's *Wake in Fright* (1971), with its interest in barbarism and the harshness of male society.

These stereotypes involve now internationally familiar pictures of "bush life," tales of "pioneering," and images of sun-bronzed "ockers" (someone overtly displaying characteristics of the white Australian associated with "the outback," rugby, and beer drinking), despite the fact that the majority of the Australian settler population has always lived in the lower southeast corner of the country in urban areas based around Sydney and Melbourne.

Though the stereotypes were not largely displaced in the 1970s and continued well beyond the international success of *Crocodile Dundee* (1986), the notion of a national media culture was supported by the establishment of a number of funding and development agencies and reflects a new feeling of independence brought about largely through Australia's turning away from an economic association with Britain and toward one with the United States and, later, Asia. These included the Australian Film Development Corporation (AFDC), the Experimental Film and Television Fund (EFTF), and the dedicated training facility, the Australian Film, Television and Radio School (AFTRS).

Despite this intervention, Australian filmmakers were still faced with the problem of convincing distributors to screen their films, and Australian screens remained dominated by Hollywood products. Tariff control was recommended, though never implemented; but the realization that the Australian government was prepared to legislate to protect and promote its media industries was enough to spur the local industry. Yet, the first commercial successes of the Australian film "revival" were not always seen as culturally significant or even as aesthetically attractive. This was the era of such films as *The Adventures of Barry McKenzie* (1971), *Stork* (1971), and *Alvin Purple* (1973), films that owed no small debt of influence to the British school of *Carry On* comedy.

The formation of the Australian Film Commission (AFC) in 1975 and the international success of more culturally and aesthetically pleasing films such as Ken Hannan's *Sunday Too Far Away* in the same year are seen by critics such as Stephen Crofts in *Australian Cinema as National Cinema* (1995) as a watershed in the history of Australian postcolonial filmmaking. Neither cured the penchant for stereotyping or immediately brought international commercial recognition. However, it is from this, and the subsequent establishment of tax concession schemes that offered generous breaks for film investors and the later Film Finance Corporation (1988), that the contemporary Australian film industry emerged. This is represented, not least, by such internationally recognized Australian film directors as Peter Weir, Dr. George Miller, Phil Noyce, Bruce Beresford, and Gillian Armstrong and, in perhaps a more localized way, by Australian-based directors such as Rolf de Heer and Tracey Moffatt.

Moffatt, however, stands out from this list in being an Aboriginal filmmaker. The support for First Peoples film and media making in Australia has been substantially slower in coming than that for the settler community. That the majority of representations of Australian Aboriginal peoples has been from non-Aboriginal perspectives has struck a particularly strident chord. Walter Saunders, a member of the AFC's **Indigenous** Branch, has gone so far as to suggest that one solution might be to "stop non-indigenous film-makers from using government money to make films about indigenous people, or to allow only collaborative projects which ensure that Indigenous people have the right to creative and artistic control" (1994, 7). The postcolonial history of First Peoples media in other contemporary postcolonial countries such as Canada, Algeria, Senegal, Cameroon, India, and New Zealand, and, most poignantly in recent times, South Africa reveals similar concerns. The recognition of the distinct styles and subjects of First Peoples media is, recently, a further declaration of the move from a colonial to postcolonial ethos in many countries. However, this recognition is still far from being universal. The work of filmmakers such as Tracey Moffat and Kevin Lucas in Australia and of program makers such as Tainui Stephens in New Zealand is helping to address this situation.

Film and television, as naturally generative visual and aural media, acknowledge what is perceived as much as what is the case in actuality. With this in mind, the perception of many postcolonial film and television cultures as peripheral to world media culture continues, regardless of their actual indigenous success. This is more than an economic position; it reflects the strength of U.S. focused media in promoting their own cultural, aesthetic, and interpersonal perspectives. Though media tend to transgress national boundaries far more easily than, say, literature, it is still the case that the closer a country is to U.S. influence, the more engulfing it must be. The colonial history of Canadian film and media is a case in point.

Always faced with overshadowing by its Hollywood neighbor, in 1939 Canada created the National Film Board (NFB) for the purposes of developing films whose purpose it was to interpret "Canada for Canadians and the rest of the world." These are identical terms to those used in the 1969 Australian Council of the Arts report, which stated that cinema was seen as important in kindling "Australia's efforts to interpret itself to the rest of the world." This is not at all far removed from Indian government efforts to promote nationalist, realist, and integrationist agendas.

The NFB allowed for the creation of a "parallel" film industry to maintain Canadian interests regardless of the increasing power of the U.S. machine nearby and was led by the distinguished British documentarist John Grierson (1898–1972). Grierson's influences on the forms and styles seen in the early years of the board are well recognized and can be seen directly even as late as the 1960s in such films as Donald Brittain's *Memorandum* (1965) and Allan King's *Warrendale* (1967). However, a further ideological complication had already arisen.

The problem of discrimination against **Quebecois** film and media was, by the 1950s, being significantly highlighted. When the NFB moved from largely English-speaking Ottawa to largely French-speaking Montreal in 1956, this further illuminated the problem. In 1957 Guy Roberge, the French Canadian appointed commissioner of the NFB, was seen as one of the key forces in addressing this problem. Later developments included the establishment of the Canadian Film Development Corporation (CFDC) in 1968 to stimulate private sector film production and the launch in 1982 of Telefilm Canada, which took

over from it. Telefilm Canada also administered the Broadcast Fund, whose
protectionist policies allowed Canadian television producers to access production
funding and thus work competitively in light of more cheaply available imported
American programs. Similarly, the NFB was the model for the development of
regional film funding organizations such as those in Nova Scotia and British
Columbia, organizations not dissimilar to the state-based funding organizations
in Australia.

The Quebecois question reminds us that the majority of the discussion so far
has centered around anglophone postcolonialism. Dina Sherzer's excellent collection *Cinema, Colonialism, Postcolonialism* (1996) addresses the question of
francophone postcolonialism. Indeed, the francophone history parallels the anglophone. In cinema, it follows the change from colonial films (such as Jacques
Feyder's *L'Atlantide* [1921] and Edmund Greville's *Princesse Tam Tam* [1935],
which romanticize and exoticize the non-Western), through those films that show
early criticism of European imperialism (such as Chris Marker's *Les Statues
meurent aussi* [1952] and Jean Luc Godard's *Let Petit Soldat* [1960]), to filmic
discussions about the past by colonizers in Aleandre Arcady's *La Coup de Si-
rocco* (1978) and those that deal with colonialism as a topic, such as Regis
Wargnier's *Indochine* (1992).

Francophone postcolonial cinema has also seen First Peoples and indigenous
exiles approaching questions of their own cultural identity and history: "**Beur**"
cinema, or cinema by people of Maghrebian origin, such as Cedric Kahn's *Trop
de bonheur* (1995), and "black" cinema such as Coline Serreau's *Pomauld et
Juliet* (1988). Finally, there are the filmmaking and media making of the former
French colonies: films like *Camp de Thiaroye* (1988) by Ousmane Sembene
from Senegal, *Quartier Mozart* (1992) by Jean-Pierre Beloko from Cameroon,
and *Chroniques des annees de braise* by Lakhdar-Hamina from Algeria.

The biannual Pan African Festival of Film and Television of Ouaguadougou
(FESPACO), organized in Burkina Faso, is, in fact, the largest film festival in
the world, with the purpose of promoting African films in a variety of languages.
However, in general within sub-Saharan Africa imported cinema from Hollywood, Hong Kong, and India substantially marginalizes local products.

Even if allegory gave to character and event only a deeper moral meaning,
South American cinema would stand as an exemplar of the politically charged
visual heritage of colonial and postcolonial environments. Brazil's Cinema
Novo, notably, with its historical interests, experimental explorations of film
language, and slick shifts between comedy and tragedy, is so thoroughly infused
with the movement between realism and mysticism, remembered past and observed reality, individual life and holistic society that it captures perfectly many
postcolonial societies' poignant struggles with identity, place, and reason. This
is seen, not least, in the work of Glauber Rocha, who died young in 1981, but
not before he could produce such superbly metaphorical films as *Deus e o diablo
na terra do sol* (1964) and the brilliantly stylized *Antonio das Mortes* (1969), a
mix of fact and fiction, epic and cinematic poetry. Rocha joined Cinema Novo

in the early 1960s, a group fathered, he noted humbly, by Nelson Pereira dos Santos. In 1965 he produced his now well-known manifesto, *The Aesthetics of Hunger*, critiquing the group. Most importantly, this manifesto set out his idea that the moment when the colonizer becomes aware of the existence of the colonized is the moment of violence. Rocha proved, on that basis, that allegory in cinematic colonial terms is more than simply imbuing character and event with deeper moral meaning. Rather, it is the invention of a new visual and aural language, layered with spiritual as well as political intent.

Like Indian and Canadian film and media, the "postcolonial" history of Hong Kong media focuses on the story of competition between languages. In the case of Hong Kong cinema, the competition has been between Mandarin (the official Chinese language) and Cantonese (the local dialect). Filmmakers emigrating from China to Hong Kong in the post–World War II period, working in Mandarin, formed the basis for the eventual supremacy of Mandarin cinema over Cantonese in the early 1970s. Cantonese cinema, however, certainly didn't die at that point; and the contemporary history of Hong Kong cinema is tied up with the influence of the traditions of one language cinema on the other, theatrical traditions drawn from indigenous and imported cultures, and the cross-fertilization of genre, not least in highly successful martial arts films and in comedy. Of course, the idea of "postcolonial" media in Hong Kong might well be premature, given Hong Kong's only very recent change of colonial status.

If a paradox seems clear in the discussion of postcolonial film and media, it is that the birth of mass media in the post-1950s period has occurred alongside what should have been increased independence for former European-colonized countries. There have been new modes of media production and distribution whose global intentions and Western perspectives have created a new mode of imperialism. The conditions of postcolonial filmmaking, therefore, work as a useful case study and are not far removed from those of broadcasting or, more recently, of multimedia. If, in literature and in history, we saw evidence of a move from the colonial to the *post*colonial in the latter half of the twentieth century, in film and media the situation is not so straightforward. The current state of play in the world's digital media industries suggests that this paradoxical situation will continue in the immediate future.

Further Reading: A. Moran 1996; D. Sherzer 1996.

Graeme Harper

First Nations   First Nations is a contemporary term of political and legal significance that has been appropriated by Canadian aboriginal communities to designate a group of people with a shared language, history, and culture who identify with each other as belonging to a common political entity. The term reconceptualizes the historically racist misnomer "Indian" used by Europeans to identify the aboriginal peoples of the Americas but does not replace individual, culturally specific tribal names (e.g., Dene, Gitxsan). In its current usage, First

Nations signifies the historic rights of aboriginal peoples to a distinct sociopolitical legal status within Canada as "Nations or Tribes" designated in the Royal
Proclamation of 1763, as signatories of treaties between the British Crown and
band members, and as "bands" under the Indian Act. Contemporary First
Nations issues in Canada include land claims settlements, self-government, sovereignty, recognition of treaty rights, recognition of cultural diversity and renewal, and enhancement of educational and economic opportunities.

Further Reading: P. Dickason 1992; J. Woodward 1989.

Cheryl Suzack

Michel Foucault   Michel Foucault was a poststructuralist historian and philosopher whose work has had an enormous influence on postcolonial studies.
Born in 1926 in Poitiers, France, Foucault went on to study philosophy and
psychology, earning the Diplôme de psycho-pathologie from the Institut de Psychologie of Paris in 1952. After holding numerous academic posts in France,
Sweden, and Germany, in 1970 he was awarded a chair at the Collège de France,
which he held until his death in 1984.

Foucault's work is largely concerned with providing a "history of the present," or in other words, performing an archaeology of "truth" in order to understand how social norms and discourses (any body of knowledge) have shaped
its construction throughout history. The anti-Enlightenment and antihumanist
stance that informs this undertaking is evident in Foucault's critique of rationality and the universal subject that have characterized epistemology since the
beginning of the modern era. His early works, *Madness and Civilization* (*Folie
et déraison*, 1961) and *Birth of the Clinic* (*Naissance de la clinique*, 1963), for
instance, focus on the origins of clinical medicine and the emergence of madness
as a clinical disease. In these works, Foucault endeavors to explain how attitudes
toward madness and disease were produced by shifts in belief concerning the
individual and deviant behavior. Ideas about madness are seen by Foucault not
as representative of any objective or scientific knowledge of mental illness but
rather as categories used to marginalize individuals and groups that do not conform to the dominant political interests of the time.

Foucault's antihumanism is more explicit in his books *The Order of Things*
(*Les mots et les choses*, 1966) and *The Archaeology of Knowledge* (*L'Ar-
chéologie du savoir*, 1972), where he sets out to map the various discourses that
inflected the formation of the human sciences and the rise of the "author function" in literary criticism during the seventeenth century. In these works he is
concerned with determining the "conditions of possibility" that specify what can
be "known" about any given subject and the limitations and constraints of
knowledge practices expressed through discourse at any point in history. He
refers to these organizing assumptions as the "episteme." In this context, the
individuality of the author of knowledge becomes less significant than it has
been constructed in the history of ideas. Here, what it means to "discover" the

world through scientific practice, exploration, observation, and imaginative or philosophical contemplation is seen as embedded in the discursive conditions of the age. Foucault thus locates the concept of "human nature" and the belief in a pregiven self as a product of the modern episteme and undermines the notion that individual intention plays a substantial part in the meaning of any text. It is on this basis that Foucault declares the "death of Man."

In *Discipline and Punish* (*Surveiller et punir: Naissance de la prison*, 1975) Foucault investigates how disciplinary practices inflect the simplest activities of the subject at a microphysical level so that his or her identity is produced by, and is subject to, various discourses in an everyday context. Power in the modern era is thus viewed as relational and productive and exercised through discourses that impinge on the most intimate of activities such as thought and speech. Foucault's discussion of Bentham's panopticon is suggestive of a society that he associates with the modern era where the subject surveils his or her self, internalizing norms and attitudes that come to be accepted as common sense. This research points the way to his later interest in governmentality or "the art of government"; in this understanding, the modern state is conceptualized as "employing tactics rather than laws, and even of using laws themselves as tactics—to arrange things in such a way that, through a certain number of means, such and such ends may be achieved" (1991, 95). Though not specifically addressed by Foucault, his definition of the modern regime of power casts light on the ways in which colonizers sustained their domination by enrolling the support of their colonized subjects.

In subsequent works such as the three-volume set of *The History of Sexuality* (*L'histoire de la sexualité*, 1976, 1984, 1984), Foucault becomes increasingly interested in the ways in which subjects and discourses are shaped by the limits and constraints placed on knowledge by institutions and society. Knowledge is seen as interested and informed by power relations rather than as innocent and objective. Foucault's famous formulation, power/knowledge, seeks to emphasize the political and strategic character of knowledge production in all disciplines. Postcolonial studies has used this insight to help make visible the Eurocentric assumptions that pervade the academic disciplines such as anthropology, biology, history, psychology, literature, and philosophy—disciplines that helped legitimate the colonial project.

The influence of Foucault's work on the field of postcolonial studies is first evident in what has come to be known as **colonial discourse** analysis. This is an area that grew out of **Edward Said**'s investigation of what he termed Orientalist discourse in his seminal work on the subject, *Orientalism* (1978). Following Foucault, Said rejects the repressive hypothesis and the Marxist notion of ideology as a false consciousness as the basis for the formation of colonial views on the Orient. Instead, he offers a definition of Orientalism as a discourse that produces (rather than merely reflects) the idea that there is essential distinction between the Orient and the Occident that serves as an alibi for colonialism. This represented a shift in understanding about colonialism's modus operandi—from something that was primarily conceived of as economic and political, to something that relied on cultural, textual, and epistemological factors to justify its activities.

In keeping with Foucault's understanding of "the will to know," Said argues that discourses about the East have sought to define "the truth" about the Orient and served the interests of Europeans who endeavored to subject it to management and control. Like Foucault, Said sees literature as disciplined by Orientalist discourse. However, a key distinction that Said makes between Foucault's and his own methodology is the **agency** that he attributes to individual authors whose work he sees in a dialectic with the episteme as a whole. It could be argued, however, that Foucault's later work on *askesis*, or self-fashioning, accommodates the role of the author in this sense.

Aijaz Ahmad's critique of *Orientalism* in his book *In Theory: Classes, Nations, Literatures* (1992) cites Said's invocation of Foucault as central to signaling an all-too-convenient shift to post-Marxism in the study of imperialism at the onset of the Reagan/Thatcher era. Not only does Ahmad have trouble reconciling Foucault's notion of power with his own Marxist outlook, but he contends that Said's work in *Orientalism* is caught in a methodological contradiction. On the one hand, the invocation of Foucault implies a critique of **humanist** assumptions; on the other hand, Ahmad sees Said as reproducing humanist assumptions in his presentation of the Western literary tradition as continuous.

Foucault's work has also facilitated the critique of nationalist discourse in postcolonial studies, resulting in a more self-reflexive engagement with conflicts within and between colonized subjects. Central to this rethinking of **nationalism** has been the work of the **Subaltern Studies** Group and, in particular, Partha Chattterjee's *Nationalist Thought and the Colonial World* (1986). With reference to the contradictory political rhetoric that informed struggles for independence in India, Chatterjee draws on Foucauldian insights to argue that anticolonial nationalism is a discourse that legitimates its claims for nationhood on the basis of a unique cultural identity even while it embraces the universalizing rhetoric of **modernity** that underpins the formation of the modern state. Despite the natural and shared conception of identity that this implies, Chatterjee's analysis illustrates how this discourse unwittingly privileges an elite, masculine, and autonomous citizen-subject with **essentialized** notions of cultural distinctiveness. Chatterjee's analysis explores how even while modern nationalist discourse attempts to distinguish itself from the attitude of the colonizer, it "accepted the very intellectual premises of 'modernity' on which colonial domination was based" (30).

The influence of Foucault's work on the subject can be seen in **feminist** postcolonial research in the way that it works against the romanticization of women's voices in texts written by or about women. The notion of a free or entirely original expression of "the self" is untenable if one accepts that the disciplinary apparatus cannot be transcended. Instead of attempting to recover the voices of women in some sort of imaginary prediscursive form, outside the influence of patriarchal, colonial, class, or nationalist discourses, the feminist postcolonial critic is focused on how the utterances of the gendered subject are inflected by the power/knowledge of the prevailing discursive conditions. She is interested in both subverting and displacing rather than escaping those conditions. Susie Tharu and K. Lalita's two-volume *Women Writing in India* (1991) is an example of a feminist postcolonial project where the notion of women's authorship is investigated in this context.

Gayatri Chakravorty Spivak takes up Foucault's work at numerous junctures in her oeuvre but nowhere more contentiously than in her essay "Can the Subaltern Speak?" In this essay she addresses the problem of how the gendered subaltern is represented in Western discourse, both critiquing and extending Foucault's notion of the subject. She argues that the subject requires a "still more radical decentring" (1989, 271) than it is given in Foucault's work, which she argues still works from a Eurocentric gaze. Spivak argues that Foucault's critique of the sovereign subject is undermined by his failure to recognize the dialogue between ideology and discourse in the formation of the subject so that institutions like capitalism and colonialism are reified in discussions of the agency of the subaltern. Following Derrida and Marx, Spivak contends that a deconstructive and fully textual analysis of institutions, practices, and agency discloses the necessarily interested character of representation, thus requiring the intellectual's constant vigilance against rendering his or her interests transparent. Elsewhere, Spivak characterizes the failure to account for this undecidability of representation as a form of "new orientalism."

Homi Bhabha's readings of colonial stereotypes about the other in terms of fetishism rely on Foucauldian insights in their articulation. Foucault's notion of the all-encompassing network of power relations that inform relationships between rulers and those whom they rule accounts for the instability of hierarchies between the colonizer and colonized that is crucial to the ambivalence that Bhabha locates in colonial stereotypes about the other. Bhabha's focus on this ambivalence in colonial discourse is indebted to Foucault's view of power's both inciting and prohibiting identification with the other. The *simultaneous* "recognition and disavowal of racial/cultural and historical differences" (1990b, 75) in colonial discourse that this underscores are key to Bhabha's effort to track the process of subjectification of the colonial other and, in turn, understand how colonial otherness is both produced and sustained.

Anthropologist Ann Laura Stoler's work on the sexual politics of race in *Race and the Education of Desire* (1995), extends Foucault's discussion of the intersection of sexuality and power in *The History of Sexuality* and in the French recordings of Foucault's 1976 lectures at the Collège de France to the imperial context. In her analysis of how the discourse of race and sexuality intersect in the colonial body, Stoler contends that Foucault's late work was increasingly preoccupied with sketching out a genealogy of race as it relates to his concept of biopower. Stoler uses the insights from this work to explore how the colonial order of things was concerned with "the discursive management of the sexual practices of colonizer and colonized" (4). Stoler thus considers Foucault's views on the birth of the European bourgeois subject in terms of the discourse of race as it emerged within the apparatus of colonialism. She argues that practices inflecting "racialized bodies" are bound up in, and serve as a contrast for, Foucault's "healthy vigorous body" (7) and that the colonized served as a "racially erotic counterpoint" (6) in the discourse of colonial sexuality. The "education of desire" that is the focus of Stoler's book refers to the elaborate rules of conduct governing the interaction of children and native servants, colonizers and colonial subjects whose necessarily intimate interaction required constant surveillance in order to both promote and sustain the hegemony of the colonizer.

The criticism made most often of Foucault's conceptions of power/knowledge and the disciplinary society is that they fail to propose a way out of the agonistic struggle against domination—a concern quite important to discussions of **decolonization**. In fact, in *The History of Sexuality*, Volume 1, *An Introduction* (*L'histoire de la sexualité, I: La Volonté de savoir*, 1976), Foucault suggests that "where there is power, there is **resistance**," and, as a consequence, points of resistance proliferate throughout the power network (96). Resistance is thus redefined by Foucault's work as the "odd term in relations of power" that produces "cleavages in a society that shift about, fracturing unities and effecting regrouping, furrowing across individuals themselves, cutting them up and remolding them, marking off irreducible regions in their bodies and minds" (96). From Foucault's perspective, "the strategic codification of these points of resistance" (96) produce the kind of revolution in thinking, acting, and being that the process of decolonization requires. On the whole, postcolonial studies has built upon, and interrogated, the limits of Foucault's work and helped to make visible the coimplication of European and postcolonial critical concerns.

Further Reading: G. Deleuze 1988; P. Rabinow 1984.

Jill Didur

Francophone Literatures   Francophone literature is literature written in French by people who read, write, and speak French outside France. This literary genre also encompasses *Beur* literature (novels written by second-generation sons and daughters of Maghrebian immigrants residing in France) as well as authors who are not French but who live in exile in France. The term "francophone" was first coined by the geographer Onésime Reclus at the end of the nineteenth century. For Reclus the term was both sociolinguistic and geopolitical, encompassing French-speaking peoples of the world. In the 1960s the term was used more widely in literary journals to discuss the phenomenon of writing in French outside France (see B. Jack 1996a, 17).

Francophone literature as a genre is largely a twentieth-century concept, dating to the postcolonial period (after 1950). An exact date when francophone literature was considered a genre (and not an appendage to the French canon) is still debated due to the unevenness of its development throughout the French-speaking world. The culturally pluralistic nature of francophone literature is due to the multitude of countries and histories that are represented within its scope. When the term "francophone" is used, it globally refers to literatures written in French from Africa, Madagascar, South America, North America, Europe, parts of Asia, the Antilles Islands, Haiti, Mauritius, and La Réunion. Each region has been influenced by France in a unique manner. For some countries such as Algeria, Tunisia, Morocco, Cameroon, and Senegal and islands such as Haiti and Madagascar, the francophone novel has evolved out of revolutionary movements, developing a certain political power in postcolonial arenas. In French-speaking Canada, *littérature québécoise*, also considered under the francophone rubric, has developed differently, emphasizing antagonisms with Anglo influences that have constantly threatened the production of literature written in French in Canada. French literature from Switzerland and Belgium also has an incongruous history compared to that of other Francophone writing.

Taking the preceding into consideration, France's influence on the literature of a particular country or region must be considered within varying terms and boundaries: (1) the history of brutal colonialism, which gave way to anticolonial revolutions (as in the case of the majority of former French colonies in Africa, Madagascar, and Haiti, as well as anticolonial struggles in Guadeloupe and Martinique [islands that continue to function as French protectorates]), (2) the history of regional influence, as in Belgium and Switzerland, where writing in French is due to proximity to France, and (3) imperialist influences (Asia and Canada) wherein France abandoned its efforts to colonize, but the French language remained in use (today this is less evident in Asia, as French is being replaced more widely by English).

Africa and the Caribbean

In the last twenty-five years, francophone literature of Africa and the Caribbean written by both men and women has shaped new areas in postindependence thought. Replacing revolutionary schemata are issues of postcolonial concern. Poverty, corrupt governments, the rise of religious fundamentalism, and questions of language (i.e., should one continue to write in the language of the former colonizer?) are taken to task by contemporary francophone authors.

When considering francophone literature, colonialism comes to mind. The majority of contemporary texts written in French come from the former colonies in Africa and Haiti. Novels from the Caribbean, notably Guadeloupe and Martinique, although still under French rule, are often engendered from themes stemming from anticolonial struggles and/or colonial history. With the exception of a few texts written in French in the nineteenth century by Africans and Haitians such as Anténor Firmin, who wrote the pivotal *De l'égalité des races humaines* (1885), francophone literature of Africa, the Caribbean, and French Guiana may be thought of as a twentieth-century phenomenon. Martinican René Maran's 1921 novel *Batouala* was the first major work of Africa and the Caribbean to be recognized in France. Maran, who lived a number of years in Africa and was schooled in France, won the renowned French literary prize the Prix Goncourt for the novel, which exposes the life of the colonized African *through his own eyes*. Maran's work is essential because it formed the basis for a new anticolonial African consciousness (see K. Walker 1999, 27). The voice of the African man was heard in Maran's work, constructing the foundation of later anticolonial, black, revolutionary intellectual movements. Other earlier remarkable works, such as Gilbert Gratiant's *Cris d'un jeune* (1926), exposed the beauty of writing in Martinican Creole.

The issues raised in these earlier works culminated in the **negritude** movement begun by three students in Paris in the 1930s: **Aimé Césaire**, Léon-Gontran Damas, and Léopold Senghor. The *Revue du monde noir* (established in the 1930s primarily by Paulette Nardal and Andrée Nardal) and the political literary manifesto *Légitime Défense* (1932), which includes contributions by three Martinican intellectuals (Jules Monnnerot, Etienne Léro, and René Ménil), launched a political platform for African writing while denouncing the bondage of colonialism. However, Damas' *Pigments* (1937), Césaire's *Cahier d'un retour au pays natal* (1939), and Senghor's *Chants d'ombre* (1945) founded a new vision for antirevolutionary movements across the French colonies. The poetic and literary context of the negritude movement later influenced more intense anticolonial manifestos such as Martinican **Frantz Fanon**'s *Peau noire, masques blancs* (1952), *L'an V de la révolution algérienne* (1959), and *Les Damnés de la terre* (1961).

Since the 1950s, francophone texts from sub-Saharan African countries such as Cameroon, Senegal, Mali, Benin, Ivory Coast, and Zaire have proliferated. Authors such as **Mongo Béti** (*Le Pauvre Christ de Bomba*, 1956), Bernard Dadié (*Climbié*, 1956), **Ousmane Sembène** (*Xala*, 1976), Birago Diop (*Leurres et lueurs*, 1960), **Ferdinand Oyono** (*Une vie de boy*, 1956), **Ahmadou Kourouma** (*Les soleils des indépendances*, 1968), Yambo Ouologuem (*Le Devoir de violence*, 1968), **V. Y. Mudimbé** (*Entre les eaux*, 1973), and Tchicaya U tam'si (*Les Cancrelats*, 1980) have contributed significantly to the postcolonial canon. Notable women authors and playwrights include Nafissatou Diallo (*Le Fort maudit*, 1980), Calixthe Beyala (*C'est le soleil qui m'a brûlée*, 1987), Véronique Tadjo (*A Vol d'oiseau*, 1986), Werewere Liking (*Elle sera de jaspe et de corail*, 1984), Mariama Bâ (*Une si longue lettre*, 1979), and Marie Ndiaye (*Comédie classique*, 1986). It was particularly difficult for francophone women to establish a literary voice in Africa prior to the postcolonial era due to their minimal access to education. Traditional mores also impeded women's success in untraditional careers such as those of authors and journalists. However, since the 1970s women have become more educated and have begun to speak out, touching upon issues from the beauty of the traditional African family, to women's sexual emancipation. Throughout Africa, women are establishing themselves as major players in the francophone literary arena. Women authors who have spoken out the most forcefully are Mariama Bâ (*Un Chant écarlante*, 1981), Calixthe Beyala (*Tu t'appelleras Tanga*, 1988), Aminata Sow Fall (*L'Ex-père de la nation*, 1987), Angèle Rawiri (*Fureurs et cris de femmes*, 1989), and Véronique Tadjo (*A Vol d'oiseau*, 1986).

In Guadeloupe and Martinqiue, authors such as **Patrick Chamoiseau** (*Texaco*, 1992), **Edouard Glissant** (*Le discours antillais*, 1981), Léonard Sainville (*Dominque*, 1951), Vincent Playcoly (*La Vie et la mort de Marcel Gonstran*, 1971), Xavier Orville (*Délice et le fromager*, 1977), and the pivotal theoretical work *Eloge de la créolité* (1989), written by Patrick Chamoiseau, Jean Bernarbé, and Raphaël Confiant, are forging new inroads to innovative postcolonial perspectives favoring the individuality of French Creole writing in the Antilles. Women writing from the islands have also contributed to the singularity and unique style of francophone literature of the Antilles. Mayotte Capécia's early work, *Je suis martiniquaise* (1947), although condemned by Frantz Fanon for what he thought was a manifesto for the degradation of the black man, marked, nonetheless, a beginning point for women's strong contribution to the literature of the Antilles. Myriam Warner-Vieyra (*Juletane*, 1982) presents an interesting perspective on Guadeloupe as an exiled author living in Dakar. **Maryse Condé**, who is perhaps the best-known contemporary francophone woman author, has contributed to the literary production of the French Antilles with novels such as *Hérémakhonon* (1976), *Ségou* (1984), *Moi, Tituba, Sorcière . . . Noire de Salem* (1986), and *Traversée de la mangrove* (1989). Simone Schwarz-Bart (*Un Plat de porc aux bananes vertes*, 1967; *Pluie et vent sur Telumée Miracle*, 1972; and play, *Ton beau capitaine*, 1987) has also contributed extensively to shaping a feminine literary voice for the region.

Haiti, although liberated from French colonialism in 1804, has incorporated a rich French literary history into its unique canon. In the 1830s Coriolan Ardouin and the Nau brothers formed a group of young literary intellectuals to compose the idea of "a distinctively Haitian literature in French" (Jack 1996b, 134). This literature rallied around the idea of creating a lasting bond between French and the *créolité* inherently found in the voice of native authors. The influence of the Parisian symbolists at the turn of the century created a certain aesthetic that appealed to indigenous poets of the island who sought to mix traditional literary paradigms with inherited French culture (in which they had been imbued throughout the nineteenth century). The idea of *Haïtianisme*, a Haitian literature built around the tenants of the negritude movement while also espousing the unique **multiculturalism** of the Haitian culture, was supported by authors and poets such as Price-Mars (*Ainsi parla l'oncle*, 1928), René Depestre (*Enticelles*, 1945), and J.-F. Brierre (*Le Drapeau de demain*, 1931). In the later part of the twentieth century, francophone novels of Haiti were more critical of the corruption and poverty inflicted on the people of the island. Jacques-Stéphen Alexis (*Compère général Soleil*, 1955) and Pierre Roumel (*Les Arbres musiciens*, 1957) attest to this political criticism, while blending a literary voice that is multicultural and representative of the diversity of Haiti's people: African, Indian, French, and American. In Haiti realism has dominated francophone literature since the 1960s, particularly with regard to political realism. Authors such as Emile Ollivier (*Mère-Solitude*, 1983), living for years in exile in Montreal, have continued to criticize their homeland in overtly political novels, hoping eventually to bring positive change (Jack 1996b, 142).

The Maghreb

In the Maghreb (Morocco, Algeria, Tunisia), contemporary francophone literature has primarily developed out of bloody revolutionary movements. Tunisian Albert Memmi, known for his pivotal work *Portrait du colonisé* (1957), with a preface by Jean-Paul Sartre, and the works of Martinican Frantz Fanon, who denounced France's occupation of Algeria, forged the theoretical skeleton of late twentieth-century francophone writing in the Maghreb. Algeria has by far produced the most francophone authors of this region. In general, francophone literature of the Maghreb may be classified into three stages of development since the first novella written by an Algerian appeared at the end of the nineteenth century. The first stage, beginning in 1891 and lasting until the end of the 1930s, reflects some nationalistic writing but is more profoundly characterized by Algerian writers who attempted to assimilate and mimic the literary style of the colonizer. This mimeticism stems partly from the French process of *assimilation* (indoctrination) of the French language and culture. Assimilation was carried out most effectively by the French school system, set definitely into place by the 1880s.

The second stage of writing in the francophone Maghreb reflects a militant nationalist influence. The massacres at Sétif, Algeria, on 8 May, 1945 (during which many Algerians were killed for demanding independence from the French) set off a wave of anticolonial literature, thus commencing the resistance era, during which novels such as Algerian Kateb Yacine's *Nedjma* (1956) and Mohammed Dib's *L'Incendie* (1954) made their first impact. New, young, politically charged authors Mohammed Dib, Malek Haddad, Kateb Yacine, and Mouloud Mammeri published their works in numerous "revues culturelles" such as *Simoun, Forge, Terrasses, Soleil, Progrès*, and *Consciences maghrébines*. As their articles attest, these authors did not seek to hide their political and anticolonial agendas and thus openly fueled the rhetoric of the revolutionary process. *Nedjma*, Kateb Yacine's 1956 novel, foregrounds a definite thematic rupture with former Maghrebian novels written in French. Yacine's novel is filled with allusions to the social struggle going on in Algeria at the time of the novel. The word "Nedjma" connotes not only the name of the elusive female figure who is a constant object of desire for the four male protagonists in the work but also the word for "star," principal emblem for the "étoile nordafricaine" and the secular symbol for Algerian independence. *Nedjma* is a novel that raises crucial questions concerning the identity of the Algerian people as well as hope for their independence.

The third stage encompasses texts written after independence in the Maghreb. Themes include concerns associated with feminine identity, immigration, and exile. Such themes in Maghrebian francophone texts began to proliferate after 1962, immediately following the end of the Franco–Algerian War. Authors writing during this time seek to define the parameters of a much more socioculturally based literature that incorporates thematical areas other than those of **nationalism** and revolution, prevalent in the 1950s. During this third stage, postrevolutionary narratives are centered less on the duality and divisions between the worlds of colonizer/colonized and more around questions of individualism and how to cope with living between two histories, two cultures, and two identities. Nabile Farès' *Yahia pas de chance* (1970), Driss Chraïbi's *Les boucs* (1955, reedited in 1984), and Albert Memmi's *Le Scorpion* (1969) seek not only to explore the historical legacy of colonialism and militancy but also to cope with issues (such as **identity**) inherently important to recently independent nations. These issues also grapple with the complications associated with the use and place of the French language and the heritage of French culture in postrevolutionary societies. More and more, francophone novels from authors of the Maghreb attest to the question of identity and place in the modern world. Authors such as Rachid Boudjedra (*La Répudiation*, 1969), **Tahar Ben Jelloun** (*L'enfant de sable*, 1985, and *Hospitalité française*, 1984), Tahar Djaout (*Chercheurs d'os*, 1984), Mohammed Haddadi (*La malédiction*, 1988), Mourad Bourboune (*Le mont de genêts*, 1989), Hedi Bouraoui (*Tunisie Plurielle*, 1997), Abdelkebir Khatibi (*Amour bilingue*, 1983), and Rachid Mimouni (*La Fleuve détourné*, 1982) seek to define the identity of the postcolonial Maghreb by asking questions such as, What is my identity as an immigrant in France? and "How do I live in two worlds, juggle two conflicting political spheres—one secular and one Muslim? These questions become even more complex when considering the Beur authors (second-generation sons and daughters of Maghrebian immigrant parents residing in France). The Beurs' unstable situation is often evoked in the French press or by the government as being one of those "precarious and fragile groups" whose destiny within the social order of France is still unknown. In recent years, more and more Beur writing by authors such as Leïla Sebbar (*Shérazade: 17 ans, brune, frisée, les yeux verts*, 1982) and Azouz Begag (*Béni ou le Paradis Privé*, 1989) has drawn the French-reading public's attention to the deplorable plight of a lost generation that has found it impossible to fit into French society.

Novels by Maghrebian francophone women writing in the postcolonial era take on new contours, exploring questions of feminine identity and sexuality. Works such as **Assia Djebar**'s *Les Enfants du nouveau monde* (1962) and *Les Alouettes naïves* (1967) posit a new **feminine** voice for Maghrebian women who seek to redefine their place in history as well as contemporary society. Traditional Muslim culture juxtaposed to encroaching European **modernization** and the ensuing debates and concerns with respect to women are constant areas of sociocultural discourse within Djebar's later novels, *L'amour, la fantasia* (1985), *Le blanc de l'Algérie* (1995), and *Oran, langue morte* (1997). Feminine sexuality and identity of the new modern Algerian woman are central forces not only in Djebar's postcolonial narratives but also for others such as Djamila Debèche (*Aziza*, 1955), Yamina Mechakra (*La Grotte éclatée*, 1979), Aïcha Lemsine (*La Chrysalide*, 1976), Malika Mokeddem (*L'interdite*, 1993), Hajer Djilani (*Et pourtant le ciel était bleu*, 1995), Khalida Messaoudi (*Une Algérienne debout*, 1995), and **Fatima Mernissi** (*Les sultanes oubliées*, 1990). These women are changing the contours of the francophone text in the Maghrebian postcolonial era (V. Orlando 1999).

French Canada

Canada's **Quebec** region was first settled in 1604. The largest wave of French immigrants came in 1663–1673, when many Jews and Huguenots fled Cardinal Richelieu's religious oppression in France. Since this time, the region of Quebec has struggled to hold onto its "Frenchness" while fighting against Anglo encroachment. In the twentieth century, Quebec also battled economic hardships and poverty due to the primary rural and poor urban proletariat of the larger cities and economic domination by the richer Anglo regions of the country. Anglo cultural oppression, certainly of the French language, was for centuries a constant threat to the well-being of Canada's Quebecois population. However, with the education act of 1964, which safeguarded the teaching of French in Canada, the "Frenchness" of French-speaking regions has been maintained. Contrastingly, modern authors writing in French still argue that they are forced to write within colonized boundaries. Laurent Girouard noted in 1963 that "the alienation from which we have suffered is multi-leveled, stemming from the fact that we are colonized and exploited . . . on the political, economic and cultural levels" (Jack 1996a, 62). Years later, francophone authors continue to write against the de facto Anglo-*culturalization* of French Canada by championing a brand of difference known as *québécité*. Beginning with the first half of the twentieth century, Louis Hémon's *Maria Chapdelaine: récit du Canada français* (1914) set the tone for the individuality of *la littérature québécoise*. Works of the 1940s by authors such as Gabrielle Roy (*Bonheur d'occasion*, 1945) became internationally recognized. Roy was the first Canadian author to win the prestigious French Prix Fémina for her work, which concentrated on exposing the poverty and hardship of a poor working-class Quebecois family during World War II. Roy launched what has been considered the first wave of protest literature, shaping a voice for francophone Canadian literature devoid of Anglo-American influences. Roger Viau's *Au milieu, la montagne* (1951) solidified the genre of the Quebec urban novel (Jack 1996a, 77). Novels by authors such as Réjean Ducharme (*L'Avalée des avalés*, 1966; *L'hiver de force*, 1973; *Les enfantômes*, 1976) explore questions of language, multiethnicity, and Canada's overbearing traditional sociocultural systems. Other novels that examine traditionalism and its impact on the lives of the Quebecois population are Jean Basile's *La Jument des mongols* (1964), Marie-Claire Blais' *Une Saison dans la vie d'Emmanuel* (1965), and Roch Carrier's *La Guerre, Yes Sir!* (1968). Quebecois poetry also has made significant contributions to the Canadian francophone canon. Notable poets are Paul Camberland (*L'Afficheur hurle*, 1964), Michèl Lalonde (*Song de la fiancée détruite*, 1958) and Gatien Lapointe (*L'Ode au Saint-Laurent, précédée de j'appartiens à la terre*, 1963). Perhaps the best-known female author in Canada of recent years is Anne Hébert, known for her passionate and often violent novels. Her acclaimed *Kamouraska* (1970), *Les Enfants du sabbat* (1975), *Héloïs* (1980), and *Les Fous de Bassan* (1982) are haunting and dramatic tales of witchcraft and murder. Her stories often tackle questions of place and of identity in a world surrounded by Anglo-American influences that impede the traditional values of her protagonists. In *Les Fous de Bassan*, for example, the murderer has spent time in the United States, where, it is implied, he was corrupted and enabled to return to his homeland to commit a heinous crime.

Vietnam

In the early nineteenth century, France set its sights on Indochina for new imperial conquests. In 1836 Commandant Laplace navigated his vessel, *L'Artémise*, toward "Indochine." Cochin-China (southern Vietnam) was over-taken in 1859. Succinctly, Vietnam and Cambodia were both named as French protectorates, with Laos added in 1893. Although De Gaulle refused to acknowl-edge Ho Chi Minh's declaration of independence in 1945, he later was forced to grant it when the French were defeated at Dien Bien Phu in 1954. Although French influence was relatively superficial in the region, late nineteenth- and early twentieth-century Vietnamese authors writing in French did make some literary contributions. Today, few contemporary authors write in French. In an effort to encourage use of French, France has renewed its literary ties with Vietnamese authors, translating numerous novels into French in recent years. On the screen in the 1990s, France's rekindled love affair with Vietnam is noted in neocolonial films such as Alain Wargnier's *Indochine* (1992) and Jean Jacques Annuad's *The Lover* (1994).

From 1862 to 1954, nourished by centuries of patriotic protest against Chinese rule and French imperialism, Vietnamese authors writing in French and Viet-namese have sought to create a new platform of literary **agency** addressing contemporary concerns. Historically, Chinese and French writing influenced the movement known as the Dông-kinh (School of Just Cause). Founded in 1906, it blossomed and created an intellectual group of authors who remain today very politically engaged. Vietnamese writing in French sought to mediate a dialogic space *in-between* the exoticized image "L'Indochine," represented for the former imperial power, and the modern sociopolitical changes and upheavals that have plagued the region since the installation of communist rule in 1975. Narratives in French of the 1960s include Pham Van Ky, *Perdre la demeure* (1961), and Nguyen Cong Hoan, *Impasse* (1963). In later works, Vietnamese authors treat France's contemporary political, cultural, and literary roles in Indochina in such works as Duyen Anh, *Un russe à Saigon* (1986) and *La Colline Fanta* (1989) and Duong Thu-Huong, *Les paradis aveugles* (1991). In recent years, Vietnamese literature written in French has become something of a rarity (authors today write in either Vietnamese or English). Critical texts on francophone authors of Vietnam such as M. Durand and Nguyen Tran Huan's *Introduction à la littérature vietnamienne* (1969), Jean Hougron's *Les Asiates* (1954), and Raphaël Barquissau's *L'Asie française et ses écrivains* (1949) offer comprehensive overviews of the history of France's influence on literature in Vietnam.

Further Reading: I. Almeida 1994; B. Jack 1996a, 1996b; J. Meyer 1991; L. Kesteloot 1991; V. Orlando 1999; K. Walker 1999.

Valérie Orlando

Paulo Freire   Paulo Freire was a Brazilian educator, politician, writer, and social theorist whose work has influenced teachers, cultural workers, and communities throughout the world. It is all too rare that he is discussed in a specifically postcolonial context. Particularly in North America and Europe, he is often engaged only as a resource for thinking about issues of pedagogy and as the founder of "The Paulo Freire method." Moreover, he is often depoliticized in his Western incarnations, despite his insistence that to be an educator is always to be a politician. Freire consistently resisted being classified as a member or founder of a pedagogical school. He would contest any effort to describe his pedagogical theory that might restrict its continued development—crucial for Freire was the fact that he never finished learning and that each experience would help to refine and critique his past work. Such resistance to restrictive categories should not, however, deny the constants in his thinking and writing. His work is always historically and contextually grounded and consistently challenges societies that function by means of oppressive social control and domination. Domination, Freire claimed, is the defining "theme" of our "epoch," and through his teaching and writings—through his *praxis* (a key term for Freire)— he attempted to assist in the struggle of dominated and oppressed peoples to gain liberation and to reform society.

Freire was born in Recife in the northeast of Brazil in 1921, into a middle-class family. When the family suffered severe economic hardships during the depression of the 1930s, Freire saw firsthand, for the first time, how hunger affects one's ability to learn. In 1941 he began teaching Portuguese in Brazilian schools and in 1947 began working for the welfare-oriented SESI (Social Service of Industry). He spent the years until 1961 continuing his work with SESI (as a director and superintendent of various SESI educational and cultural divisions), working in teacher training, and adult education and as an education consultant in many areas of Brazil. After completing a doctoral thesis in 1959 on the subject of contemporary Brazilian education, Freire took a professorial position at the University of Recife and worked throughout Brazil to improve literacy, particularly among the rural peasantry. In 1964, by which time he was engaged in literacy programs with millions of Brazilians, Freire was imprisoned by the military after a coup-d'etat, before going into what would be a sixteen-year exile, during which time he worked in other South American countries, North America, Europe, Africa, and Asia and with the United Nations Educational, Scientific, and Cultural Organization (UNESCO), the World Council of Churches, the Institute for Cultural Action (of which Freire was a founding member), and various political regimes, including many ex-colonized nations. During his exile, Freire continued to develop his pedagogical principles and his critique of the oppressive nature of capitalist society and published most of his major works, including *Education as the Practice of Freedom* (1967—this date and others refer to the original Portuguese publication, which may precede the English-language version by as much as six years), *Pedagogy of the Oppressed* (1968), *Cultural Action for Freedom* (1968), *Education for Critical Consciousness* (1973), and *Pedagogy in Process: The Letters to Guinea-Bissau* (1977). Returning to Brazil in 1980, Freire once again took up a university position, and in 1989 he was appointed minister of education for São Paulo, in which capacity he continued his radical programs for education and literacy. Many of Freire's later writings took the shape of what he called "talking books," in which he would engage in a dialogue with, for example, Ira Shor, Donaldo Macedo, or Antonio Faundez to discuss matters pedagogical and political. Freire died of heart failure in May 1997, at the age of seventy-five.

Freire's diagnosis of the modern capitalist world, which is expressed clearly in his most famous work, *Pedagogy of the Oppressed*, has particular valence to postcoloniality since, as a diagnosis of oppressive regimes, it bears direct relevance to the situations of colonized peoples. Oppressed peoples, Freire suggests, have been stripped of their subjectivity and are prevented, by various acts of oppressive regimes and dominating groups (such as colonizers), from being fully cognizant individuals. Specifically, he argues that traditional educational methods and institutions play an important role in maintaining social structures of oppression by denying the oppressed the chance to be active participants in the creation of knowledge. In an argument that chimes with Althusser's notion of the school as an ideological state apparatus, Freire sees education as serving the dominant (oppressive) ideology by figuring students as the objects into which knowledge is deposited by teachers, who are the only active subjects in this kind of educative process, which Freire calls "banking education." Knowledge itself becomes dead matter in this formulation, and what is defined as knowledge is strictly controlled by the dominant social group. Oppressed peoples are thus disfranchised from the act of knowing and become dependent on others for sanctioned knowledge, while what they themselves know, what they have learned from their historical, political, and social realities, is deemed useless.

The solutions for such oppressive situations differ according to the particular historical and social conditions in each case. However, constant is the need for a "problem-posing," humanizing pedagogy in which the oppressed people and educators engage in a dialogic relationship with one another. Such an education does not simply offer nuggets of preformed wisdom to students but instead sees knowledge as created by teacher and student, both of whom have something to learn. In addition, knowledge is not sanitized and dehistoricized in a problem-posing education. Rather, Freire's goal is that the oppressed will come to a "critical consciousness" of their own oppression and the world in which they live. The process of coming to such a consciousness is called *conscientização* and enables oppressed peoples to engage in "praxis." For Freire, praxis is the highest form of social action, in which the subject proceeds by means of both action and critical reflection, two processes that are in an ongoing dialectical relationship with one another.

Similar theoretical issues had engaged Freire in his first book, *Education as the Practice of Freedom*. Here he discusses in detail the ways in which a society can become *mystified*. In terms of postcolonial theory, this notion of a mystified society adds something to a more familiar concept of hegemonic, **colonial discourse**. A mystified society is one wherein the (oppressed) people have become separated from their historical reality and are dehumanized. Mystification occurs when the dominant, oppressive classes spread myths throughout the culture—using mass media, for instance—that impede the people's potential to understand and critically relate to their contextual situations and, further, suggest bogus solutions to the problems faced by the people. What makes this concept different from many ideas of colonial discourse is that it is grounded in a **Marxist** sensibility. Freire suggests that dehumanizing myths work in tandem with a capitalist means of production, which serves to alienate the masses from the products of their labor. Mystification is thus a two-pronged attack on the people, who are held back from achieving subjectivity or **agency** in the larger social processes by cultural *and* economic forces.

As a way of working with such an alienated population, Freire discusses the use of "culture circles"—a concept that appears in his practical and written work throughout his career. Culture circles are often the place where *conscientização* occurs and are of particular interest since they offer a site wherein the oppressive structures of power that have been built up by the dominant group are challenged. A group of educators and students (though these terms are misleading, since the educators and students alike educate and learn in a culture circle) engages in dialogue that focuses on the existential realities of the particular local situation. Such discussions allow the participants to realize their potential to exert agency in the world; to begin to dissect and critically confront and examine their culture, their hopes for that culture, and their own futures within it; and to make significant strides toward literacy by discussing key "generative words."

While neither *Pedagogy of the Oppressed* nor *Education as the Practice of Freedom* could be labeled a purely theoretical work, concerned as they are with the practice of education in oppressive societies, neither of them gives the insight into the workings of one of Paulo Freire's educative ventures that is found in *Pedagogy in Process: The Letters to Guinea-Bissau*, which details one of many educative initiatives in which Freire participated in ex-colonized nations. This later work takes the form of a series of letters that Freire wrote to the (then) newly formed education authorities in Guinea-Bissau when he and a team of educators from the Department of Education of the World Council of Churches and the Institute for Cultural Action worked with the new Guinean government to implement a literacy program; also included are an extensive introduction and postscript, which give further information about Freire's involvement with the African Party for the Independence of Guinea and the Cape Verde islands (PAIGC) and commentary on the letters. This text is crucial for an understanding of Freire in terms of his relation to postcolonial studies, since Guinea-Bissau had only recently gained its independence from Portugal when Freire and his team arrived. Moreover, through the course of this book and other reflections that Freire was to make on the situation in Guinea-Bissau, he goes some way to writing a history of the transition of a young, ex-colonized nation, detailing the kinds of difficulties and joys that a newly independent nation faces.

Freire's analysis of the colonial past of Guinea-Bissau fits well with his idea of mystified societies. He charges the colonial rulers with de-Africanizing the Guineans and suggests that their education system—imported prefabricated from Europe—served to alienate the people from their local contextual situations and prevented them from participating in the processes of social decision making. While his mandate was to help institute a program of literacy reform, the letters and introduction detail that Freire recognized his work as crucial to the political and social regeneration of the newly independent nation. Unlike the Portuguese colonizers, Freire respected the precolonial history of the Africans and wanted the educational reforms that he and the Guineans would institute through a dialogic process to help undo the repression of the local culture that the colonizers had instituted. Necessary, he argued, is that any postcolonial system of education focus on local geography and history—including the history of resistance to colonial oppression—and that texts that had been ideological mainstays of colonial syllabus be discontinued. As well as integrating the nation's indigenous history into the discourse of education, Freire hoped to be able to help integrate the nation itself, asking that urban students move their schooling and teaching to rural areas so that they might interact with the agricultural and rural peasant classes of the nation. This was especially important, since 90 percent of Guinea-Bissau's economy was then focused on agriculture. A second key goal of this interaction would also, then, be to bring the site of education closer to the site of production, making for a more complete and critically stimulating education.

A major issue for Freire and the people of Guinea-Bissau was that of language, which has long been crucial to the postcolonial debates. In what language would the literacy education be conducted? What language would the people learn to read and write? **Ngũgĩ wa Thiong'o** has discussed similar linguistic issues in East Africa, suggesting that for an ex-colonized nation to escape the ideology of the colonizers, indigenous languages must be embraced. Like Ngũgĩ's, Freire's argument is that the promotion of local languages and Creoles will help locals in their journey to personal and communal subjectivity. Despite this argument, the literacy campaign in Guinea-Bissau was conducted in Portuguese, which fact has long been contentious and for which Freire has been much criticized. However, Freire would later claim that he had vigorously campaigned to resist teaching Portuguese, fearing that it would only serve to continue the colonial process of mystification but that the new national government wanted to keep the colonial language. After much discussion, Freire had to abide by its wishes, hoping that the practical process of literacy education itself could be part of the revolutionary transformation that the nation was experiencing, no matter what language it was conducted in.

Letters and indeed many of Freire's other works that have not been discussed here offer a way to think about diagnosing, critiquing, and eventually over-throwing situations that thrive on oppression and domination. Whether one is an educator or not, his work is a call to those in positions of power to consider their relations to those who are not, and it stands as a strong critique of the ways in which colonial discourse has embedded itself in global political and social practices. Moreover, Freire calls upon his readers to critique his work as they negotiate their own contextual situations. Such critiques have suggested that Freire lacks a consideration of the workings of patriarchy in dominative systems and that he did not consider enough the ramifications of gender in both oppressive and educative situations; likewise, he has been questioned in terms of his seeming ability to unquestioningly delineate terms such as "oppressed" or "the people." These and other critiques have led him and his commentators to make many adjustments to his thinking, and continuing dialogues with his work and legacy mean that his theories should remain a work in progress.

Further Reading: P. Freire 1997a, 1997b.

Daniel L. Silverstone

G

Clifford Geertz (1926–)   A cultural anthropologist whose ethnographic studies focus on Bali, Java, and Morocco, Clifford Geertz has written on a variety of Third World topics, ranging from the bazaar economy, to kinship, to cockfighting, but he is most widely recognized for his redefinition of the term "culture" and a distinct methodology for analyzing it. Geertz attended Antioch College and Harvard University, earning his Ph.D. in 1956. During the 1950s and 1960s he did field research in Indonesia and Morocco, where he developed his definition for culture and reflected on the act of interpretation in anthropological study. He continued to work on these ideas at the University of Chicago from 1960 to 1970, pioneering a "symbolic anthropology" movement focusing on cultural signs and their meanings. A fellow of the National Academy of Science, the American Academy of Arts and Sciences, and the American Philosophical Society, Geertz has been a professor in the Department of Social Science of the Institute for Advanced Study in Princeton, New Jersey, since 1970.

In *The Interpretation of Cultures* (1973), Geertz conceptualizes culture as a system of symbols used to impose meaning upon experience (45). He identifies a symbol or sign as "any object, act, event, quality, or relation which serves as a vehicle for conception" (91). After defining culture and its components, his methodology calls for the grouping of systems of symbols under general categories of aesthetics, sports, religion, entertainment, law, and so on. These various signs and the corresponding systems exist in continual interplay, creating an intricate mosaic of meaning that Geertz studies as culture proper. With his emphasis on all things semantic, Geertz transforms ethnography from "an experimental science in search of law," to "an interpretive one in search of meaning" (5). After the observing and recording of signs in the field, Geertz employs the practice of "thick description." Thick description usually begins with a specific, yet cursory, presentation of a distinct cultural sign, like a ritual, a myth, an anecdote, a piece of art, an institution, a historical episode, a local custom. Geertz "thickens" the description by reading out any number of semantic possibilities inherent to the sign. In the course of the analysis, he establishes the sign as a text to be read, insisting that the ethnographer can read culture as the literary critic reads a novel. From this perspective, Geertz elaborates in scrupulous detail the text before him, and here is where the true "thickening" takes place. He produces a very complex reading of the sign by examining the systems of perception that inform it—working through the web or tissues of conceptual structures, social institutions, local conventions, and individual motives that make the isolated sign meaningful.

With reference to postcolonial theory, Geertz's redefinition of culture and the notion that signs and meanings are the keys to interpretation demonstrate that the ideas of a fixed concept or law regarding what to look for in an ethnographic study are bunk. In exchange for rigidity, Geertz uses a fluid concept of relative meanings. He moves away from the **essentializing** Western tendencies to construct a "native" from a privileged point of view, to finding meanings in the particular actions, expressions, or relations of the native. He makes a general step toward a more self-conscious practice of ethnography to avoid portraying static, ahistorical others. While he can never escape the colonialist roots of ethnography or the privilege of being the one who inscribes the representation of a studied group, Geertz begins a process of conciliation between the empowered and the powerless.

More recently, Geertz has concentrated on the more overt postcolonial implications immanent to anthropology. In his book *Works and Lives: The Anthropologist as Author* (1988), Geertz suggests that the anthropologist's practice, specifically, the textual record, needs to be examined. This provocative comment redirects the possibilities for interpreting anthropological studies. The idea that questions of method or perspective in ethnography are at the center of critical inquiry significantly changes how we look at anthropological reports. Postcolonial critics—or any critical reader, for that matter—are no longer required to ask what the ethnographer extrapolates but how he or she extrapolates. Within this glacial shift of critical priorities, Geertz asks critics of anthropology to think through the actual relationships between what the anthropologists wrote and the historical conditions under which they wrote. He points out that because modern anthropology grew up and took form during a period in which Western imperialism was strong in Africa and the Pacific and various other places, its methods and claims need to be examined for their complicity with the imperial project. However, Geertz is quick to admit that just as anthropology is compromised by its relationship with colonialism, we are all compromised by whatever relationships that we have to power: nobody works in a political vacuum, including the "objective" ethnographer (*Works and Lives*).

As an early proponent of the concept of "reflexivity," the recognition that the observer is inevitably part of the observation, Geertz is also especially relevant to postcolonial scholarship in his reflections upon the subjective role of the anthropologist in the practices of ethnography. For Geertz, the extent to which the anthropologist is conscious of his or her own subject position (gender, race, political affiliation, national background) allows for a closer analysis of those who represent and those who are represented. The acknowledgment of a subjective ethnographer opens up the possibilities for study by inviting a critique of the writer by his or her informants. A concern with describing cultures in ways that acknowledge personal perspectives and the ambivalent role of the ethnographer as mediator between cultures incorporates the other as a participant in the dialogue of representation. Geertz does not specifically give the writing over to his informants, but he does create a space for their voices, enabling a more self-ascriptive method of ethnography where the voice of the anthropologist coexists with the voices of the informants.

Further Reading: C. Geertz 1973, 1988.

Jason A. Clark

Edouard Glissant Born in Sainte-Marie, Martinique, on 21 September 1928, the political activist, theorist, novelist, playwright, and poet Edouard Glissant grew up in that town, where his father worked as a plantation manager. Studying at the Lycée Scholcher in Fort-de-France, Glissant played a significant role in the election campaign of the acclaimed **Aimé Césaire**. Between 1946 and 1953, Glissant studied philosophy at the Sorbonne and ethnology at the Musée de l'Homme in Paris. Between 1953 and 1959, he played an active role in the political arena. Maintaining an active involvement with the Société Africaine de Culture, he cofounded the Front Antillo-Guyanais pour l'Independance with Paul Niger and was subsequently forbidden to travel outside France. In the years that he spent in France, Glissant began his career in writing. His first collection of poetry, *Un Champ de l'îles*, was published in 1953. In 1956, the first volume of his essay collection, *Soleil de la conscience*, was published. His first novel, *La lézarde* (recipient of the Prix Renaudot), was published in 1958, followed in 1961 by his first play, *Monsieur Toussaint*. When the travel ban was lifted in 1965, Glissant returned to Martinique, where he assumed a position as professor of philosophy at the Lycée des Jeunes Filles in Fort-de-France. In 1974, Glissant played an instrumental role in establishing the Institut Martiniquais d'Etudes (IME). Because it offered courses on Antillean history and emphasized cultural activities, the IME was praised for providing an alternative to the French government's public school system. In 1980 Glissant returned to France, assuming an editorial position at the United Nations Educational, Scientific, and Cultural Organization (UNESCO). During his stay in Paris, he completed the poetry collection *Pays rêve, pays réel* (1985), the critically acclaimed volume of essays *Le discours Antillais* (*Caribbean Discourse: Selected Essays*, 1989, trans. J. Michael Dash), and the novels *La case du commandeur* (1981) and *Mahagony* (1987). From 1988 to 1994, Glissant served as distinguished professor and director of the Center for French and Francophone Studies at Louisiana State

University. Since 1995 he has served as distinguished professor at the City University of New York.

As J. Michael Dash explains in *Edouard Glissant* (1995), an exhaustive analysis of the author's work, Glissant is one of the most important writers and thinkers from the French West Indies (3). In addition to the texts already mentioned, he is the author of several critically acclaimed novels, plays, and collections of essays and poems, including *La terre inquiète* (1954), *Les Indes: poème de l'une et l'autre terre* (1954), *Le sel noir* (1959), *Le sang rivé* (1960), *Malemort* (1975), and *Faulkner, Mississippi* (1995). Although his writings have had a profound impact on Afro-Caribbean, African American, and **francophone** postcolonial literary and cultural studies (e.g., a special issue of the journal *World Literature Today* on the work and critical studies of Edouard Glissant, J. Michael Dash's text, and Debra Anderson's 1995 work *Decolonizing the Text: Glissantian Readings in Caribbean and African-American Literatures*), his writings have been less influential on scholarship in **anglophone** postcolonial studies, partly due to the fact that much of Glissant's oeuvre has not been translated into English.

This imbalance, however, may be shifting in a positive direction. Situating Glissant's work in relation to the work of established postcolonial theorists such as **Edward Said, Homi Bhabha, Gayatri Spivak**, the authors of *The Empire Writes Back* (Bill Ashcroft, Helen Tiffin and Gareth Griffiths, 1989) and **Frantz Fanon**, Celia M. Briton's recent monograph *Edouard Glissant and Postcolonial Theory: Strategies of Language and Resistance* (1999) makes a valuable intervention into the Anglo-dominated field of postcolonial studies and is one of the few texts that attempt to bridge the gap between anglophone postcolonial studies and francophone postcolonial studies.

Like many postcolonial writers, Glissant destabilizes the colonizer's language by *writing* in that language. In *L'intention poétique*, he clearly states that he has no intention of rejecting French. Rather, he uses the language creatively so as to destabilize its status as the authoritative master language. Not only does he coin theoretical words that do not translate easily (e.g., *détours, retours, errance, Creolité, Antillanité, relation, opacité, totalité-monde*), but he also infuses the oral and aural qualities of Creole in his writing. Moreover, as critics, including J. Michael Dash and Betsy Wing, have noted, Glissant evokes a wide range of thinkers, including continental philosophers such as Hegel, Kant, and Nietzsche, U.S. authors like William Faulkner, activists like Nelson Mandela, and scientific thinkers such as Albert Einstein (in Glissant's formulation of chaos theory). He also makes use of the Icelandic sagas, Homeric verse, and Greek and Roman tragedy. Numerous Caribbean authors and thinkers, including St. John Perse, **Derek Walcott**, Frantz Fanon, and Aimé Césaire, also feature prominently in Glissant's theoretical work. The language of these thinkers is thus fused with his thinking and his writing.

Although the body of Glissant's writing consists primarily of novels, drama, and poetry, his theoretical writings have been tremendously influential in terms of offering a radically different way to conceptualize the relationship between language, history, culture, and tradition in the postcolonial French West Indies. Although it is a false distinction to separate Glissant's literary works from his theoretical work, postcolonial critics and scholars will find of particular interest *Le discours Antillais* (Caribbean Discourse) and *La poétique de la relation*. In *Le discours Antillais*, a 490-page text that J. Michael Dash (1995) describes as an elaboration of discourse in the Caribbean rather than a prescriptive mediation on Caribbean culture and history (152), Glissant offers numerous ways to think through the multiple connections and intersectionalities between race, class, gender, language, space, and place in the Caribbean so as to posit a theorization of *Antillanité*, or Caribbeanness. The text also provides thoughtful inquiries into numerous aspects of Antillean literature and history and attempts to see the Caribbean—indeed, the Americas as a whole—as interconnected.

In the introduction to *Writing in Limbo: Modernism and Caribbean Literature* (1992), the postcolonial literary critic Simon Gikandi explores how Glissant's work offers a different historical narrative of the Caribbean. Where French colonial history writes the history of Martinique to create a continuous French history, emphasizing the centrality of events such as the temporary abolition of slavery in 1794 or emancipation in 1848 and departmentalization in 1946, Glissant foregrounds the discontinuity that underlies the apparent seamlessness of the history of the Caribbean in relation to French colonial history (Gikandi 8). Part of Glissant's "postcolonial" sensibility can be detected in the way that the historical circumstances of colonization are reimagined in his literary works. While he is not interested in accessing some primordial moment of origin, emphasis in Glissant's theoretical and literary works is, nonetheless, placed on history, as Gikandi has observed. Similar to many other postcolonial authors, Glissant offers creative reenactments of defining colonial moments, such as Christopher Columbus' "discovery" of America. Like the novel *The Harp and the Shadow* (1990) by the Cuban author **Alejo Carpentier**, for instance, which rewrites the story of Columbus' discovery of America, Glissant's poems "Les Indes" (1955) and "La terre" (1955) offer interpretive rereadings of this event, which has shaped the course and nature of political, social, and cultural history in the Caribbean.

In anglophone postcolonial studies, this style has been described by Bill Ashcroft, Helen Tiffin, and Gareth Griffiths as "writing back." Glissant, however, theorizes this process in a different way. In contradistinction to the binary logic embedded in the notion of "writing back," Glissant's essay "Le retours et le détours" in *Le discours Antillais* introduces an alternative model to conceptualize how postcolonial authors rewrite the historical legacy of colonialism: the concept of *détours* and *retours* (diversion and reversion). Through this model Glissant offers a way to rethink reductive and linear definitions of community and identity. Transplanted diasporic populations are initially compelled to maintain the order of values from the homeland in the "transplanted locale." For persons transplanted to the Caribbean via the **black Atlantic** slave trade, the desire to return to a primordial state of being in the motherland (*retours*) becomes an obsession. Discussing the contingency of historical-cultural memory, Glissant argues that reversion, or *retours*, is untenable in the Caribbean precisely because populations in the Caribbean—transplanted by the slave trade—are temporally and spatially distant from Africa and thus cannot generate sustained, vibrant memories of the mythic "motherland."

In the section following "Retours," Glissant describes "Détours," or diversion, as a strategy deployed by populations who seek to better understand issues of **identity**—not by returning directly to the source/origin but by navigating an alternative route: the use of Creole, the importance of Joual in **Quebec**, syncretic religious fusions in various Brazilian rites and "Vaudou" practices (34)—all are described as "diversionary" strategies. Acts of syncretic fusion become vitally regenerative strategies for establishing new types of communal bonds. *Détours* cannot, and must not, simply function as a tactic that celebrates syncretic fusion; it must *lead* "somewhere." *Détours* does not pretend to be able to access some primordial originary **essence**, but its "success" is contingent upon its ability to provide alternative paradigmatic formulas to understand one's (or a culture's) roots and origins. Thus, as Gikandi notes, the twin concepts of *retours* and *détours* perform the "double gesture" of affirming the presence of Africa in the Caribbean imagination and also recognizing the spatiotemporal differences that make it problematic for postcolonial nations in the Caribbean to connect with Africa (1991, 12).

In *Poétique de la Relation* (1997), Glissant elaborates on arguments first presented in *Le discours Antillais* to problematize the notion that the postcolonial Caribbean has a direct etymological link with African ancestral "roots." In describing the diverse culture of the Caribbean—music, literature, folk—Glissant alludes in greater detail to the figure of the rhizome, a plant with roots that spread horizontally rather than vertically, to describe the connection between diverse cultural histories in the Caribbean. Introduced by Gilles Deleuze and Félix Guattari in *Mille plateaux*, the rhizome is, as Keith Allan Sprouse (2000, 80) notes, "an assemblage of connected multiplicities, without center or origin." Glissant connects the idea of errance or errantry with the metaphor of the rhizome. Citing Frantz Fanon's trajectory from Martinique to Algeria and Saint John Perse's work as examples, Glissant establishes that errantry is not an apolitical category that naively celebrates totality. Rather, the errant—not a traveler, conqueror, or discoverer—strives to understand the totality of the world but is cognizant of the problematic nature of this quest.

In *La poétique la relation* and, to a lesser extent, in *Le discours Antillais*, Glissant emphasizes the theme of relation. With a marked emphasis on parallel histories that become intertwined, Glissant's elaboration on relation is a radically different way of conceptualizing links between communities, peoples, and languages that have been affected by colonialism. In his theorizations of *antillanité*, errance, *retours* and *détours*, or **Creolization**, Glissant evokes the idea of relation. Knowing the specifics of one's culture or history is important, but equally important is a knowledge of that of others. For persons, nations, and communities in the postcolonial nations of the Caribbean, this process emphasizes rhizomatic links of affiliation between different groups rather than searching for a myth or origin.

To list all of Glissant's contributions to the field of postcolonial studies is simply not possible here. Although a significant number of Glissant's works remain untranslated, the fact that there is growing awareness and interest in his ideas in anglophone postcolonial studies and that both *Le discours Antillais* and *La poétique de la relation* are available in English translations that also critically introduce Glissant's work is an encouraging sign that this important thinker from the Caribbean will help to shape the terrain of postcolonial studies in the new millennium.

Further Reading: C. Briton 1999; J. M. Dash 1995.

Anita Mannur

Globalization is the name that has been given to the social, economic, and political processes that have, taken together, produced the characteristic conditions of contemporary existence. In particular, globalization refers to the ways in which previously distant parts of the world have become connected in a historically unprecedented manner, such that developments in one part of the world are now able to rapidly produce effects on geographically separated localities. This, in turn, has made it possible to begin to imagine the world as a single, global space linked by a wide array of technological, economic, social, and cultural forces. This conception of globalization is echoed by all of its major theorists. Globalization has been characterized variously as "the intensification of world-wide social relations which link distant localities in such a way that local happenings are shaped by events occurring many miles away" (Giddens 1990, 64); as "time-space compression" (Harvey 1989, 147); as "the stretching out of the geography of social relations" (Massey 1997); as "the receding constraints of geography on social and cultural arrangements" (Waters 1995); and as "the compression of the world and the intensification of the consciousness of the world as a whole" (Robertson, 1992, 8).

Over the past decade, globalization has become a ubiquitous term in a wide range of different discourses. It is a concept that has now been used to describe almost any and every aspect of contemporary life, from the complicated machinations of contemporary capitalism, to the erosion of the nation-state system and the rise of transnational organizations and corporations, to the threat posed by global culture to local cultures and traditions, and to the communications revolution introduced by new technologies like the Internet. For this very reason, globalization is a concept that is already in danger of becoming simply a short-lived buzzword of the age. While the term seems to capture a genuine sense of the dizzying changes that have transformed the world, especially during the second half of the twentieth century, the real explanatory value of globalization has been placed increasingly in doubt over the past several years.

The relationship between globalization and the characteristic concerns of postcolonial studies, is of necessity, extremely complicated. Though it might seem natural to expect a theoretical confrontation between these concepts in a manner akin to the engagement between the postcolonial and the **postmodern** (as in the work of Kwame Anthony Appiah and Linda Hutcheon), there has, in fact, been very little written that explicitly takes up the position of postcolonial studies in relation to globalization. This can be explained, in part, by differences in emphasis and by the disciplinary origins of these two concepts. Globalization remains a term employed primarily in the social sciences and is used to describe contemporary Western experience (whether it realizes this or not), while postcolonial studies are rooted in the humanities and focus on the experiences and practices of non-Western countries, especially as they relate to Western cultural, economic, and political domination. There is, nevertheless, a sense in which these concepts occupy roughly the same conceptual ground. Part of the hesitation of postcolonial theorists to address the issues and themes raised by globalization seems to stem from the implicit challenge that it poses to the broad theoretical framework of postcolonial studies. The characteristic concerns of postcolonial studies have been defined in relation to the complicated legacies of nineteenth- and twentieth-century imperialism and colonialism. While globalization also has its roots in the European projects of imperialism and colonialism, it also names a set of contemporary transformations that have directly undermined some of the animating concepts of postcolonial studies, such as place, identity, the **nation**, and the modes of **resistance**.

Though globalization refers to the present, it is important to point out that the phenomena that it describes are hardly new. For example, there have long been discussions about the possibility of a global economic system, a world culture, or a world literature. In the *Wealth of Nations*, Adam Smith identifies the global character of Western capitalism from the outset, foreseeing the "mutual communication of knowledge" and "an extensive commerce from all countries to all countries" (1961, vol. 2, 141) that would be of benefit to all parts of the globe. Famously, in a phrase that at least partially echoes Goethe's discussion of *Weltliteratur*, in the *Communist Manifesto* Marx and Engels link the global spread of capitalism to the production of a global culture. For them, the constant revolutionizing of bourgeois production and the search for new markets that fueled imperialism meant that "national one-sideness and narrowmindedness become more and more impossible, and from the numerous national and local literatures there arises a world literature" (1976, vol. 6, 488). For all their other differences, both Smith and Marx and Engels viewed the process of economic and cultural globalization as leading toward a genuine universalism on the other side of the false particularities produced in the era of nations and nationalisms. There remains a strong undercurrent of universalism in some variants of the concept of globalization, especially insofar as it seems to inexorably suggest the production of a single, homogeneous planetary space.

In the twentieth century, the current uses of the term "globalization" were anticipated both in Marshall McLuhan's vision of a "global village" produced by the worldwide diffusion of communication technologies and in Immanuel Wallerstein's "world-systems theory." At the core of Wallerstein's theory, as first developed in *The Modern World System* (1974), is the claim that the world economic system has been a capitalist one since its first emergence in the sixteenth century. Developed as an alternative to modernization theory, world-systems theory explains the economic "underdevelopment" characteristic of colonial and many postcolonial countries as a function of their position within an overall capitalist world-system. These "peripheral" areas, which are exploited for their raw materials and/or their cheap labor, are structural requirements for the development and growth of capitalism. However, even given its various points of nascent emergence, and even though the high point of Western imperialism and colonialism at the end of the nineteenth century represented a degree of economic and political integration that has remained unmatched even to the present day (Linda Weiss 1998), the term "globalization" first came into common use only in the mid-1980s. Before this time, the increasing connection between disparate people and places on the globe continued to be described in the older vocabulary of the relations between nations, that is, as "internationalism" or "transnationalism." As much as it seems to refer to an entirely new set of phenomena—or at least the unmatched intensification of older ones—it is therefore worth remembering that globalization is a theoretical construct whose emergence at this time needs to be carefully considered.

While there are many reasons for this emergence, one of the reasons that it became necessary to talk about the world as a whole is related to the end of the Soviet empire in 1989. The decline of the Eastern bloc as an opposing force to the West necessitated a rethinking of the entire system of international politics and the development of new discourses to explain the characteristics and nature of the "new world order" propitiously announced at the end of the Cold War. Part of the ambiguity and confusion surrounding the concept of globalization derives from this point of origin. As Paul Hirst and Grahame Thompson, two of the leading critics of the concept, suggest, "globalization has become a fashionable concept in the social sciences, a core dictum in the prescriptions of management gurus, and a catch phrase for journalists and politicians of every stripe" (1996, 1). In the discourse of business and politics, globalization has served as a justification and as an ideological screen for the rapid, global spread of a pernicious neoliberal capitalism intent on reversing the social gains of the past five decades and in introducing an economic rationality into the public sphere. What has given globalization much of its rhetorical power in this respect is its function as a periodizing term, that is, as the name for the "natural" economic and political order existing at the "end of history." For this reason the academic fascination with globalization has been treated by many critics (such as Arif Dirlik and Masao Miyoshi) with a great deal of suspicion. Critical or not, the academic study of globalization has tended to reinforce both the idea of globalization's empirical reality (as in claims that the decline of the nation-state means that it no longer has the power to intervene in economic decisions) and its historical inevitability, in ways that have legitimated the use of the concept in international business, global politics, and the popular press.

Given these complexities, it is hardly surprising that theorists of globalization have differed widely on its historical specificity, its geographic reach (is the global equivalent to the planetary?), and its primary causes and effects. As a temporal marker, globalization is taken most commonly to refer to the immediate present. However, it has also been suggested that it is a long-term, ongoing process that originates in the very earliest moments of human cross-cultural contact, accelerating with Columbus' discovery of the Americas over 500 years ago. In the popular press, globalization is also commonly discussed as if it were an inexorable phenomenon that now occurs everywhere on the globe. However, many critics have been careful to point out that the world has been globalized unequally, with both the benefits and pitfalls of globalization being realized to different degrees in different parts of the world. For instance, while the Internet has become an important new medium of commerce, entertainment, and communication in the West, making nearly instantaneous global communication possible for many people, there, nevertheless, remain numerous places in the world where there is limited or no access to even very basic phone service.

For a variety of reasons, globalization has been seen as primarily an economic phenomenon that has, in turn, had a determinate influence on social, political, and cultural life. The emergence of globalization has been linked both by cultural critics, such as Fredric Jameson, **Arjun Appadurai**, and Lawrence Grossberg, and by social scientists, such as David Harvey, Giovanni Arrighi, Manuel Castells, and others, to a late twentieth-century shift in capitalism from Fordism to post-Fordism, regimes of flexible production and accumulation, and finance capitalism. Economically, globalization is associated with the transnationalization and deterritorialization of capital and industry, which have allowed companies to transcend national boundaries and to move across the globe to take advantage of cheap labor and to develop new markets for goods and services. The mobility of contemporary capital has challenged the ability of both governments and nongovernmental agents, such as labor movements and environmentalists, to control some of the more rapacious aspects of contemporary global capital. This has included the creation of deindustrialized regions (such as the American Rust Belt), the renewed global use of child labor, the creation of exploitative zones of economic production (such as the Mexican *maquilladoros*), and the largely unchecked, worldwide degradation of the environment. Economic globalization has also been associated with the emergence of international free trade agreements, such at the General Agreement on Tariffs and Trades (GATT) and the establishment of an around-the-clock global financial market.

With the generalized spread of capitalism into every space on the globe, Ann Cvetkovich and Douglas Kellner have suggested that a global system of mass production and mass consumption now exists that "disseminates throughout the planet fantasies of happiness through consumption and the products that allow entry into the phantasmagoria of consumer capitalism" (1997, 6).

A great deal of discussion has also centered on the political implications of globalization. In particular, much attention has been focused on the threats that globalization poses to the power and sovereignty of nation-states (examined in different ways by David Held, Manuel Castells, and James Rosneau) and, correspondingly, on the emergence of new sites of transnational politics centered in global cities (as described by Saskia Sassen), international organizations (including nongovernmental organizations [NGOs] and the United Nations), and transnational corporations. Examinations of the politics of globalization include assessments of the increasing militarization of global relations, the emergence of new nationalisms and ethnic conflicts, and massive migrations of peoples across regions or even across the globe, a process that has put significant strains on definitions of citizenship and cultural belonging in almost all Western countries.

Globalization has also been discussed in reference to the development of new communication technologies that have played an essential role in collapsing the globe spatially. As **Benedict Anderson** has argued with respect to the relationship between the novel and the nation, these global communication technologies have made it possible to conceive of the globe as a single space shared by all of humanity. It is not just that computer and communication technologies have made it possible to instantaneously transmit information across the world but that the circulation of information, ideas, and images has meant that, increasingly, people (especially global elites) around the world have come to share a common range of cultural referents. The emergence of a "global culture" has, thus, been largely made possible due to the availability of new technologies. The same news events and entertainment programs can now be seen by people in very different locales. Brazilian youth can enjoy American pop songs, while their counterparts can listen to Tom Ze and Caetano Veloso, and U.S. film production is increasingly geared toward a world cultural market rather than to the domestic U.S. market.

For all of the interesting hybrid cultural forms that have emerged out of global culture—from Bhangra (Punjabi music filtered through London to the West), to Latin pop, to fusion cuisines—it is, nevertheless, clear that the global dissemination of cultural forms and ideas is hardly equal. Much of the interest of cultural critics in globalization has focused on the impact of the global spread of a capitalist culture anchored in the United States and on its explicit threat to the continued existence of local cultures and traditions. It is perhaps here that the study of globalization and that of postcolonial studies most clearly overlap. One of the major imperatives of postcolonial studies has been its insistence on the cultural dimensions of imperialism and colonialism. Far from being secondary to the politics and economics of imperialism and colonialism, postcolonial critics have convincingly argued that culture must be seen as essential to the creation, production, and maintenance of colonial relations. From this perspective, especially in the context of the spread of a global mass culture, globalization may be seen as the continuation and strengthening of Western imperialist relations in the period after decolonization and postcolonial nationalisms. Yet even if the processes associated with globalization have meant that the structure of world power relations has remained largely the same since the beginning of the twentieth century, it is, nevertheless, important to see the current period of global neoimperialism as different in kind from earlier forms of imperialist power, especially insofar as it has become, at one and the same time, centered in the United States and supra- or transnational, dispersed into fully deterritorialized logics and circuits of power. This is particularly true for examinations of forms of contemporary cultural imperialism, as this is a concept that has become considerably more complicated than its seminal expression in Ariel Dorfman and Armand Mattelart's *How to Read Donald Duck: Imperialist Ideology in the Disney Comic* (1975).

Worries about cultural imperialism, especially understood as the global diffusion of American cultural products and values, constitute, in fact, perhaps the earliest development of the idea of globalization. The threat associated most commonly with the idea of global culture is that it will eventually result in a homogeneous world culture, erasing existing differences between local cultures and leaving in its wake an impoverished, soulless, Americanized culture of commodity consumption. As in postcolonial studies, the study of globalization thus involves questions about the nature and survival of social and cultural identity. From its outset, one of the singular contributions of postcolonial studies to contemporary thought has been its understanding of the dialectic relationship between colonizer and colonized. The colonizers not only shape the culture and identities of the colonized but are, in turn, shaped by their encounter with the colonized, in ways that have been perceptively explored by theorists from **Edward Said**, to Gauri Viswanathan, to **Homi Bhabha**. In a similar fashion, the work of theorists like John Tomlinson and Néstor García Canclini has been important in drawing attention to some of the problems and limitations of the cultural imperialist thesis, especially in its most pessimistic articulations, for while it is true that much of modern cultural life around the globe has become defined by commodity culture, it is also a mistake to equate the global penetration of Western culture with the automatic and total evisceration of local particularities. The persistence of cultural difference can be seen in the variety of ways in which cultures have entered global modernity. Modern Islam is one example of a distinctive relationship to globalization that is characterized neither by a rejection of modernity (as some commentators such as Benjamin Barber have suggested) nor by its claim to some unassailable "local" authenticity (an always already suspect concept) that prevents Islamic culture from engaging in global markets or with global culture.

While it is worth remembering that the spread of global commodity culture is motivated by political and economic concerns, it is thus essential to see the "local" and the "global" as in a dialectical relationship that predates current discussions of globalization. By the time the local is developed as a discursive concept, it has already been thoroughly globalized such that claims to the authenticity of the cultures that exist there are questionable at best. In other words, even though the rhetoric of an unfettered cultural imperialism is still frequently employed by governments and the popular press and in academic circles, the reality of cultural globalization is better captured by Roland Robertson's term "glocalization." Just as the global modifies the local, so, too, local practices have had a determinate impact on the global. Transnational corporations intent on spreading their products across the globe have understood the need to modify their products and sales pitches in terms of local cultural practices. Anthropologists have shown the very different role that, for example, the fast-food chain McDonald's plays in different countries. Lastly, Ien Ang's pioneering study (1985) of the audience reception of the American soap opera *Dallas* suggests that non-Western cultures engage in a very active cultural process of understanding and decoding Western media images. This may not constitute local or cultural "resistance" in the strongest sense of this term, but it does show that the global cannot simply usurp the local in any uncomplicated manner.

Finally, as much as one might worry about global culture's impact on individual identity formation, this, too, needs to be seen as an ambiguous, dialectical process. On the one hand, images of Western iconic celebrities, from Madonna, to Schwarzenegger, to Bart Simpson, as well as visions of the capitalist good life, provide seductive raw materials for the formation of new identities that, one imagines, can be fully assimilated into the phantasmagoria of global capitalism. However, this pessimistic view of a relationship between global culture and local identities fails to account for the hybrid character of these new identities, which are neither fully global nor local. It also unduly and uncritically romanticizes the local over and against the global as a "natural" site of difference. It should be remembered that the local is also the site of sometimes constrictive social and gender roles, traditions, and practices; in many cases, the intersection of the global with the local provides the imaginative resources for the creation of new identities that are able to challenge these constrictions on identity formation. For this reason Arjun Appadurai has claimed that "the imagination is now central to all forms of **agency**, is itself a social fact, and is the key component of the new global order" (1996, 31). The relations between global and local are complicated and ambiguous and require precise, case-by-case analysis. Though it should once again be emphasized that contemporary identities and cultural spaces are heavily overdetermined by global capitalism and its attendant social and political relations, the idea of resistance to imperial power that has been an important element of postcolonial studies is immeasurably complicated by the operations of culture within globalization.

For all that has been said, it is readily apparent that there are deep homologies between postcolonial studies and the critical study of globalization. Both of these concepts exist at the intersection of imperialism, capitalism, and **modernity**, and both deal with the effects and consequences of the unequal relations of power between different sites on the globe, as they are articulated economically, politically, and, especially, culturally. Culture forms a central locus for understanding the character of contemporary reality for a number of reasons. If globalization is characterized by a kind of "complex connectivity" (John Tomlinson), it is precisely through culture that this is symbolized and understood and also through culture that this connectivity becomes reflexive in the manner outlined earlier in the confrontation of the local and the global. Even if the economic continues to be imagined as the central axis of globalization, as it so often is, it is necessary to remember that the present is defined by "the becoming cultural of the economic, and the becoming economic of the cultural" (Jameson and Miyoshi 1998, 60).

Although globalization and postcolonial studies are thus related, it would, nevertheless, be a mistake to simply subsume globalization into postcolonial studies or, on the contrary, to simply see globalization as an alternate term for postcolonialism—the name for postcolonial studies in the twenty-first century. There remain a number of important conceptual relations that would need to be worked out more thoroughly before this becomes possible. For instance, globalization has also been seen as a substitute term for postmodernism, or, at the very least, the postmodern can be seen as the Western cultural response to those underlying shifts in the capitalist economy that we now refer to as globalization. Indeed, it would not be difficult to reimagine Frederic Jameson's characterization of postmodernity as the "cultural logic" of late capitalism in the newer vocabulary of globalization. Given the vexed relationships between the postmodern and the postcolonial, there is no reason to assume that globalization and postcolonialism can occupy the same space without difficulty. Furthermore, social theorists such as Anthony Giddens, Ulf Hannerz, Ulrick Beck, Mike Featherstone, Scott Lash, and John Urry have examined, and continue to examine, globalization with respect to a modernity whose assumptions are often antithetical to those articulated within and by postcolonial studies. Certainly, the universalistic impulse at the core of many conceptions of modernity stands in stark contrast to the postcolonial emphasis on the value and necessity of difference. It is perhaps most fruitful to see the concept of globalization as offering a productive challenge to some of the underlying concepts of postcolonial studies, and vice versa. The postcolonial offers a necessary reminder of the imperialist origins of globalization and of the Western location of contemporary power, no matter how deterritorialized culture and politics may have become. On the other hand, the discourses surrounding globalization may be able to push postcolonial studies to consider more fully the impact of contemporary global economics and mass communications technologies on contemporary reality, as well as the radically disembedded character of contemporary identities and cultures, which necessitates the elaboration of new models of power and resistance.

Further Reading: A. Appadurai 1996; M. Hardt and A. Negri 2000; J. Tomlinson 1999.

Imre Szeman

Lorna Goodison   Poet, painter, and **short story** writer Lorna Goodison was born in 1947 in Kingston, Jamaica. She has lived and taught in Jamaica, Canada, and the United States. Her poetry is frequently concerned with reclaiming that history of Jamaicans not found in colonial textbooks and with celebrating the people, especially the mothers and grandmothers, who lived that untold history. The Jamaican identities that emerge are joyously hybrid. Reflecting that hybridity, the poems often use a range of Englishes, shifting between Standard Jamaican English, Jamaican Creole, and **Rastafarian** Dreadtalk, extracting unexpected significance from apparently simple phrases. This attention to the way that subtle changes in sound and verbal emphasis can affect meaning reflects Goodison's deep awareness of West Indian **oral** traditions. Trickster stories, revival hymns, and folk songs are an integral part of her art. Much of her poetry is also deeply religious, and here, too, it is hybrid, employing imagery from all of Jamaica's richly various religious traditions. Her collections of poetry include *Tamarind Season* (1980), *To Us All Flowers Are Roses* (1995), and *Turn Thanks* (1999).

Further Reading: L. Goodison 1999; D. Kuwabong 1999.

Hugh Hodges

Antonio Gramsci (1891–1937)   A founding member of the Communist Party of Italy, Antonio Gramsci's writings have made a significant posthumous contribution to **Marxism**, political theory, and **cultural studies**. The intellectual Left across the world, including the Indian **Subaltern Studies** group of historians, draws upon his writings for an understanding of the concept of hegemony, the role of intellectuals in civil society, and the theme of subaltern **resistance** to reactionary and fascist modes of thought and power.

Gramsci was born on 22 January 1891 into a middle-class family in Sardinia. The poverty and backwardness of the south of Italy, when compared to the industrial north, gave him his first understanding of the regional aspect of economic inequality. He grew up learning to cope with the physical, social, and psychological consequences of suffering from a curvature of the spine and abnormally short stature. His father was a minor public official whose brief imprisonment on charges of mismanagement was to reduce the family circumstances and interrupt his early education. He had his first contact with politics through the Italian Socialist Party (PSI) at eighteen. In 1911 he went on a scholarship to the University of Turin, where he studied linguistics and became involved in PSI activity. He broke off studies in 1915 to take up a career in political journalism, closely linked to factory councils and the labor movement. In 1919 he founded the weekly *L'Ordine Nuovo*. Strikes in Turin during 1920 first raised, then dashed hopes of a revolution led by workers. Gramsci advocated reform of the PSI, but his ideas did not get party support. In January 1921 the Left faction of the PSI which included Gramsci, seceded from the PSI to form the Communist Party of Italy. Its objective was to bring about a workers' revolution in society. Its opponent was Mussolini's increasingly powerful Fascist Party, which united northern industrialists, southern landowners, and the bourgeoisie in a conservative alliance. In 1922 he was sent to Moscow by his party. Illness was to keep him there for two years, a period in which he could watch political events in Moscow from close quarters while, at home, the Communist Party lost power to the fascists. In Moscow he met his future wife, Julia Schucht. In 1923 he was transferred to Vienna. In 1924 he returned to Italy under parliamentary immunity as an elected deputy and became leader of the Communist Party. Meanwhile, in Moscow Julia gave birth to their first child. In 1925 mother and son came to live briefly in Rome, returning the next year to Moscow, where a second son was born. Gramsci never saw them again. In November 1926 Gramsci and other leaders of the Communist Party were arrested. He was to spend the remainder of his life in a succession of jails. His sister-in-law Tatiana kept in constant touch over these eleven years. In May 1928 he was sentenced to twenty years' imprisonment. In February 1929 he started work on his *Prison Notebooks*. The project lasted until June 1935, with three periods of intense writing interrupted and finally halted by worsening health. Meanwhile, his wife suffered a breakdown in Moscow. In November 1932, as part of a general amnesty, his sentence was reduced. He died in April 1937, three days after being granted freedom. It had been a life of heroic stoicism in the face of constant adversity, sustained by a resolute commitment to the political and the intellectual elements in life.

Gramsci's *Prison Notebooks* consists of thirty-three handwritten school exercise books, totaling 2,848 pages. Twenty-nine of these contain his thoughts on a range of political, economic, historical, and cultural topics. Selected letters were first published in Italian (1947), followed by the notebooks (1948–1951), which had been smuggled to Moscow after his death by Tatiana. The first English selection came out in 1957. The most thoroughly annotated translations of the notebooks are by Joseph A. Buttigieg (2 vols., 1992, 1996), supplemented by the *Pre-Prison Writings* (1994, ed. Richard Bellamy) and the *Letters* (1994, 2 vols., ed. Frank Rosengarten). Giuseppe Fiori's biography (1970) has been translated into English by Tom Nairn.

Gramsci's journalism from the period before his imprisonment is the work of a political activist, not a closet intellectual. It is occasional in nature, immersed in the details of day-to-day politics but informed with the same larger concerns that are evident in the prison writings. Over the years, some of his views changed, but there is an overall consistency between the work written before imprisonment and that during imprisonment. The *Prison Notebooks* was composed under difficult circumstances and remains fragmentary. The notes vary in length and scope. Issues are taken up in apparently random order, sometimes revisited, sometimes revised in subsequent notebooks. They place a special interpretive responsibility on the reader.

Gramsci was preoccupied by the failure of the hope of a proletarian revolution in Italy. He also wanted to stand back from topical issues in order to reflect in a more permanent way on the implications of his political experience. The focus in a large proportion of the notes is on Italian themes. These are discussed in the context of conditions in Europe and elsewhere. They include the factors in Italian history that led to a crisis of political leadership before and after World War I, the role of the Catholic Church in modern Italian history, and the contemporary significance of Italian thinkers such as Machiavelli and Benedetto Croce. A more contemporary theme concerns the set of industrial practices associated with the scientific management of production under American Fordism. Gramsci was apprehensive and anticipatory about its implications. He predicted that similar practices would have to be adopted by the rest of the world, transforming the entire culture of work, consumer practices, and lifestyles.

His contribution to Marxist theory includes the notion of "historic bloc," which is a more complex model than that associated with Marx, who had believed that the economic bases of production determined the social and political institutions in society. Gramsci rejected such economism. He reinforced the Leninist belief that revolution would not follow spontaneously upon the worsening of workers' conditions under capitalism. He also recognized that revolutionary politics would have to become "national-popular": capable of assimilating a broad range of popular interests transcending narrow class values. He transformed the study of the exercise of power in society by arguing that the direct domination available to the political state through the coercive force of its legislative and juridical functions related complexly to the workings of what Russian Marxists in the 1880s had called "hegemony." They used the term to signify the power of leadership to shape a revolutionary political consciousness. Gramsci extended the notion to signify the power exercised by a dominant group in society through the creation of consent for its own values and ideas among subordinated classes. He showed that the coercive power of the political state interacted with the consent created by hegemony in civil society, using the Hegelian term "civil society" to include all the institutions in "private" society other than the state (i.e., the family, the church, schools, trade and cultural organizations, etc.). He described the history of Italy's nineteenth-century reunification as the result of changes brought about by the hegemonic dominance of a specific class. He used the notion of "passive revolution" to characterize such historical phenomena, in which large-scale social changes came about without the participation of the subordinated classes affected by those changes. Gramsci argued that economic crises would not lead to revolution by the working classes in the countries of Western Europe without long preparation through "a war of position." He argued that in Russia's "war of movement," workers had successfully seized power because Russian society lacked the institutional structures of civil society evolved by the advanced capitalist countries. He argued that such institutions acted as buffers against a direct causal connection between economic crises and revolution.

Marx had treated ideology as distorted consciousness. Gramsci moved away from this negative connotation to the sense of an organic ideology that signified the ideas and values that organized the consciousness and social practices of a class, growing out of popular culture and interactive with the "common sense" of the masses. He emphasized the role of education in the transformation of the subordinated and attached great importance to the role of intellectuals in promoting the interests of the group to which they were "organic." He argued that in modern society, technological progress had generated new classes that had evolved their own "organic" intellectuals. Meanwhile, types such as the clergy, who had seen uninterrupted historical continuity, treated themselves as autonomous and assumed the more conservative role of "traditional" intellectuals. Gramsci treated the continual struggle for dominance in society as the outcome of changing balances between the interests of traditional classes and the new classes created by **modernization**, with "traditional" and "organic" intellectuals struggling for hegemonic control over the institutions of civil society. Developments subsequent to Gramsci's death have confirmed the continuing relevance of many of his ideas.

Further Reading: D. Forgacs 1988; A. Gramsci 1999; http://www.italnet.nd.edu/gramsci; http://www.soc.qc.edu/gramsci/

Rajeev S. Patke

H

Stuart Hall   Stuart Hall is internationally renowned as one of the principal founders of the interdisciplinary field of **cultural studies**. While its continuing reception of new models of theoretical discourse has led to considerable shifts of emphasis since its inception in the early 1970s, cultural studies represents the attempt to rigorously think through the complex relationship between the "social" and the "symbolic." Having emerged as a distinct political intervention within the British public sphere, its translation to a North American context and beyond has left the politics of cultural studies rather less defined and more ambivalent. The influence and abiding impact of Hall's pathbreaking work within cultural studies lie in its insistence on the inherently fluid and therefore continually contestable nature of culture; because of this inherent dynamism, signifying practices are open to conflicting inflections that themselves operate within fields of power/knowledge. The influence of Hall's work can be discerned across the range of disciplines and fields that it has touched: from the social sciences, particularly political science, the sociology of communications, and media studies, to literature, fine arts, and **film studies**, to race and ethnic studies. Hall's work has also had a palpable impact upon the art world, in particular, the films of Issac Julien and John Akomfrah and the Black Audio and Film Collective.

That Hall's work has had such a remarkable impact comes as little surprise when one considers that his own biography converges at crucial points with some of the most important events of the last half of the twentieth century. Born into an ethnically diverse, "extremely respectable" middle-class family in 1932, Hall became involved in the nascent anticolonial politics in the country of his birth, Jamaica. In 1951 he made what was to become a familiar journey for **diasporic** intellectuals: he traveled from the **periphery** to the very seat of imperial power/knowledge, Oxford University, on a scholarship ironically named after Cecil Rhodes. Like **Frantz Fanon, Amílcar Cabral, Aimé Césaire,**

Kwame Nkrhumah, and countless other intellectuals who made similar journeys, Hall deconstructed colonial cultural formations in such a way as to open them up and use their contradictory elements to disrupt colonial power itself; Hall's own biography is an extraordinary instance of the very politics of culture that he would later theorize.

While at Oxford, Hall met a number of independent leftists (i.e., those who were not formally members of the British Communist Party), including Perry Anderson and Canadian philosopher Charles Taylor. In collaboration with Taylor, Hall engaged in a rigorous study of Marx's important "Economic and Philosophical Manuscripts." In the wake of the invasion by the Soviet Union of Hungary in 1956 and the mass exodus of many radicals from the Communist Party, intellectuals and activists on the Left felt the need to develop philosophical and political positions outside the stifling atmosphere of orthodoxy. This drive to problematize both the theory and practice of **Marxism** led to the formation of the New Left, and Hall immediately became one of its foremost intellectuals. Along with Taylor, Raphael Samuel, and Gabriel Pierson, Hall became an editor of *Universities and Left Review*, which was later to become *New Left Review*.

In 1964 Hall moved to the University of Birmingham, where he and a number of colleagues at the Center for Contemporary Cultural Studies began developing the incipient field of cultural studies. In this they were building on the ground that had already been prepared by Richard Hoggarth and Raymond Williams. During this period Hall did some of his most interesting collaborative work, reinterpreting **Antonio Gramsci** through the prism of structuralism and poststructuralism in such a way as to illuminate a diversity of phenomena that had hitherto been either marginalized on the Left or overlooked altogether: youth subcultures, leisure, and communication, among others. Upon leaving Birmingham, Hall moved to the Open University, which provided him with an opportunity to engage cultural studies with a broader, nontraditional, academic audience.

It is possible to understand Hall's work as comprising roughly three "moments." The first was constituted by the need, after the disaster of 1956, to rethink the categories of Marxism so as to avoid economism, on the one hand, and the political dogmatism to which it gave rise, on the other, while remaining firmly within the tradition of historical materialism. Such an imperative led Hall and many other members of the New Left in Britain to a long and extremely productive dialogue with the theoretical and political legacies of Gramsci. The second moment, largely made possible by the first, consisted of a rethinking of a wide range of what Gramcsi called "repertories of resistance"—forms of culture that had been, at best, marginalized or, at worst, dismissed as irrelevant or reactionary by orthodox Marxism. The third and perhaps most fruitful and enduring moment was the rethinking of politics and ideology, or what Hall would later simply call "discourse," as not the fully formed, coherent worldviews of particular social classes but, rather, as forms that comprised a wide range of signifying practices. This led to the notion that the ideological sign is multivalent or constantly "in play." Ideology does not consist, in a straightforward way, of the ruling ideas of a particular epoch but, rather, is that structure that intervenes to arrest the flow of signification in such a way as to attempt to "fix" its meaning; power is this capacity to enact closure or a fixity of meaning. Discourse, in this sense, comprises the manner in which social phenomena are mapped, classified, and divided or situated within what **Michel Foucault** called the "order of things."

Hall's distinctive contribution to postcolonial studies can be discerned at all three levels. First, by critiquing the economistic or reductionist forms of Marxism, Hall, like theorists such as Fanon and Cabral, challenged its **Eurocentrism**. This meant that the specific Marxist narrative of the succession of modes of production, contradiction between relations and forces of production, the presupposition of a homogeneous time of a single mode of production within a given social formation, the revolutionary role of the industrial proletariat, and so on had to be seriously rethought. This also opened up a theoretical space in which the specificity and "relative autonomy" of race, ethnicity, and **identity** from the economic instance could be thought without, at the same time, **essentializing** these categories.

In an important paper presented to a conference sponsored by the United Nations Educational, Scientific, and Cultural Organization (UNESCO) in Paris in 1985, for example, Hall sketches out the new possibilities for theorizing race opened up by Gramsci. There he suggests several ways in which the latter's work can illuminate the specificity of race and ethnicity. First is its emphasis on historical specificity; for instance, in the British case, **colonial discourses** around race are different from those that emerge in a postcolonial society in a period of economic decline. Second is its focus on the often considerable regional differences and contradictions within a particular **nation**-state. Third, it insists upon the irreducibility of racial and ethnic identities to class. Fourth, it suggests a contingent or non-necessary relationship between relations of exploitation at the level of the economy and the more differentiated nature of racial and ethnic differentiation that can cut across it. Fifth, it raises the political or strategic implications of the noncorrespondence of economic structure and political and ideological superstructure. Sixth, it suggests that the state has to be understood in terms of both its coercive as well as its "educative" role, which enables us to better grasp the dynamics of racism within the liberal state as well as the specificity of the postcolonial state. Seventh, it opens up a consideration of the role of racism and ethnic identity as bearers for certain nationalist forms of "common sense" or localized knowledges of the everyday.

In his "conjunctural" analyses of Thatcherism, the political discourse that has probably had the biggest and farthest-reaching impact on the Western world since the end of World War II, Hall showed how irreducible its deployment of racial, ethnic, and national elements was in generating a hegemonic project. Given that Thatcherism was a principal harbinger of **globalization**, Hall's work could be said to have anticipated well in advance the deeply contradictory resurgence of new forms of ethnic particularity vis-à-vis the increasing global penetration of capital. Hall argued that problems of identity played a pivotal role in Thatcherism's ability to stage a hegemonic project in the midst of the most "organic" crisis of British society. Thatcherism was much more than a code word for neo-liberal economics; rather, it was what Hall called "authoritarian populism"—a discourse that fused together or articulated free-market economics and a conservative privileging of social institutions such as "community" and the family within an overarching framework of a redoubled emphasis on "law and order." Because it was more fluid and unstable than most discourses, it required particularly affective forms of signification to hold its extremely contradictory elements in place. This work was done by way of a deployment of the explosively charged figures of race and ethnicity. Thatcherism, in other words, conjured the specter of the "old," particularistic identity of Englishness. It was precisely such a form of identity that worked to stabilize the new "historical bloc" that Thatcherism represented by sharply delimiting "friend" and "foe," those who belonged and who did not belong to the nation.

The flip side of the analysis of Thatcherism's strategic deployment of race and ethnicity is that these identities are nothing essential. Rather, they are what Hall calls "floating signifiers"; that is, the meaning of each term has no necessary meaning but is constantly struggled over by contending social forces. Such a politics is therefore utterly without guarantees or certainties but rather depends upon the conjunctural or historically determinate relations between such forces; the "fact" of racial or ethnic difference could not guarantee in advance the success of a given politics. Identity politics, therefore, labored under much the same illusions as reductionistic forms of Marxist theory. Here Hall's historicist or antiessentialist understanding of identity echoes the critique of **negritude** in *The Wretched of the Earth* (1965), where Fanon argues that such categories have only a provisional meaning dependent upon the shifting vicissitudes of the liberation struggle itself. Rather than doing away with the concept of ethnicity altogether, as the orthodox Left seeks to do, on the one hand, and rather than essentializing it, on the other, Hall argues that ethnicity is, indeed, a vital way for postcolonial subjects to situate themselves historically and culturally. However, rather than simply retreating to past forms of ethnicity—as in the return of a repressed "Englishness" in Thatcherism—he argues for the construction of "new" forms of ethnicity, new possibilities that do not simply lead to the repetition of an allegedly "authentic" past but take on the difficult work of negotiating a novel relation between past and future.

While Hall has contributed immeasurably to the development of postcolonial studies, he also differs from the predominant approaches to it. While much postcolonial theorizing, as in **Edward Said**'s seminal text *Orientalism* (1978), aims at problematizing Occidental constructions of the periphery as "other," that is as the abjected antithesis of the West, which as a consequence legitimates in advance the West's imperial project, Hall's "conjunctural" or historical analyses unearth the location of the "other" not outside, but at the very heart of, the West's dominant cultural formations.

Moreover, grounded as it is in a materialist cultural studies, Hall's work, while clearly attentive to the complex and multiform inner workings of the "text," is nothing if not sociologically and historically grounded in the "world." In contrast, then, to the privileging of the literary moment within postcolonial studies, Hall's work aims at unraveling the mutual implication of the "social" and the "symbolic." Unlike the somewhat easy institutionalization of cultural studies and postcolonial studies in particular, especially within the North American academy, Hall's work always manages to wrestle free from a complete incorporation in what **Gayatri Spivak** calls the "teaching machine."

Hall's unwillingness to be "disciplined" by the academy can be attributed to his stubbornly ethical adherence to the Gramscian ideal of the "organic intellectual," which entails two distinct kinds of responsibilities. First, it necessitates the nondogmatic, open-ended drive to locate new avenues of theoretical and empirical research rather than simply recognize what was supposedly always already known. Second, it involves the impulse to disseminate such knowledge dialogically with those who are not professional intellectuals. Only through the difficult labor of bringing both of these moments into a critical tension would it be possible to construe intellectual work as part of a larger political project. Unlike many postcolonial writers whose work is directed primarily at an academic audience, Hall has disseminated his rigorous analyses in a wide range of forums such as the now-defunct *Marxism Today*, public lectures, and public policy debates at the national and international levels.

Because he attempts to relate the workings of power and signification, Hall is deftly able to avoid the tendency toward either a kind of a **postmodern** emphasis on the endless play, or jouissance, of the text, on the one hand, or a structural determinism, on the other. Because he understands power as the always contingent or provisional will to arrest the flow of signification, to enact closure within the text, there is always the possibility of undoing or deconstructing such forms of naturalized or fixed meanings that are a function not just of texts themselves but of the larger institutional structures and knowledge practices of particular societies. Because of this, never is it the case that the **subaltern** subject is unable to speak.

Further Reading: S. Hall 1990; D. Morley and K-H. Chen 1996.

Samir Gandesha

Wilson Harris (1921–   ) Wilson Harris, poet, novelist, and critic of mixed European, Amerindian, and African descent, was born in Guyana, where he worked as a government surveyor until he emigrated to England in 1959. The many expeditions that he led into the Guyanese interior considerably influenced his perception of landscape as a living, never passive environment, permeated with the silent, ghostly presence of vanished Amerindian peoples—hence, his obsessive attempt in both fiction and criticism to retrieve a subterranean native tradition as a counterpoint to Western culture, in a possible harmony free of binary opposition between conqueror and conquered, Christian and pagan. He thus detects strange affinities between Renaissance Europe and the pre-Columbian Americas, representations or cultures that are *partial* masks of a "universal unconscious." This is the source of his postcolonial philosophy and cross-culturalism, which he sharply distinguishes from multiculturalism, in his view an umbrella term covering a surface mosaic of cultures tolerant of each other but still distinct and self-sufficient. In *Explorations* (1981), *The Womb of Space. The Cross-Cultural Imagination* (1983), *The Radical Imagination* (1992), and *Selected Essays*. In *The Unfinished Genesis of the Imagination* (1999), Harris has commented extensively on cross-culturalism as a multilayered concept implying a mutuality between different cultures but also between dominating peoples or individuals and "still or silent eclipsed voices" outside and within the self. This explains his view of the human personality as a cluster of inner selves, "the crew every man mans and lives in his inmost ship and theatre and mind" (*Palace of the Peacock*, 1960, 1998, 44).

All of Harris' novels are expeditions into outer and inner landscape, the "womb of space," physical territory, boundless metaphor, and psychical ground of exploration where the brutal legacy of past and recent history (as in *Jonestown*, 1996) is confronted and transformed into a possible source of rebirth. Indeed, the very fragmentation of self and community, central to the Caribbean experience, its catastrophic events and traumas mutate in his fiction into gateways toward the reconstruction of the self, though never finally achieved: "[A] balance exists between wreckage and unfinished genesis, between loss and gain, between dismemberment and re-memberment" (*Resurrection at Sorrow Hill*, 1993, 134). Harris' first book of essays (*Tradition, the Writer and Society*, 1967), in which he anticipates by some twenty-five years **Edward Said**'s correlation between the rise of the novel in Europe and the growth of imperialism, initiates his lifelong exploration of the nature of fiction, of creativity, above all, of imagination as the major agent of transformation and renewal in a world beset by conflicts of power and moral crises. Already in *Palace of the Peacock*, an allegorical reconstruction of the New World conquest and original search for El Dorado, the conqueror's reconciliation with the Amerindian people, symbolized by an Arawak virgin and Christ, is essentially a figment of the imagination as the conqueror's vision shatters before being refashioned. As a dream emerging from the narrator's unconscious, it dismantles the Western, self-assured sense of being in favor of a fluid ontology, simultaneously breaking down all aspects of realism, which, in the author's view, reproduces a recognizable picture of society but neglects buried layers of partial existences within the self, what he calls "the cross-cultural psyche." Harris' conviction that all structures and images are partial and that wholeness (different from totality) is inaccessible to people also accounts for his anticolonialism and repudiation of any absolute, his objection to any consolidation whether of identity or power.

Harris began by writing poetry (*Fetish*, 1951; *Eternity to Season*, 1954) until he found his appropriate form with *The Guyana Quartet* (*Palace of the Peacock* 1960; *The Far Journey of Oudin*, 1961; *The Whole Armour*, 1962; *The Secret Ladder*, 1963). It offers a composite picture of Guyana and indirectly evokes the historical legacy that generated its heterogeneous population: slavery, East Indian indentureship, the flight of Amerindians into the jungle, then of runaway slaves and the impact of their descendants' retrieval from oblivion on the modern Guyanese consciousness. In *Heartland* (1964), the protagonist's lonely journey and disappearance into the interior epitomize the unfinished quest and "drama of consciousness" that erode the individual's certainties and rigid sense of self prior to his acceptance of responsibility for personal and community relations. In the next cycle of novels (*The Eye of the Scarecrow*, 1965; *The Waiting Room*, 1967; *Tumatumari*, 1968; *Ascent to Omai*, 1970), each protagonist experiences a state of loss and psychological void from which she or he emerges through the dual (re)creation of a self freed from former prejudices and of a fiction (for Harris, "living text" and reality) that "consumes its own biases."

Myth also plays a major part in bringing to light the regenerative capacity of catastrophe and is a way of coming to terms with the irrational forces that people tend to ignore at their cost. In his collections of stories, *The Sleepers of Roraima* (1970) and *The Age of the Rainmakers* (1971), Harris reinterprets Amerindian myths and legends. "Yurokon," in particular, is a further exploration of cross-culturalism through the bone-flute metaphor (also used in *Jonestown*), the instruments carved by the Caribs from their cannibalized Spanish enemies to penetrate their mind and intuit their intentions. The Caribs saw in the bone-flute the very origins of music. Since destruction (cannibalism) and creation (music) come together in the instrument, Harris expresses through this metaphor his conviction that "adversarial contexts" (the encounter of inimical cultures) can generate creativity. Subsequent novels further modulate his approach to creativeness and, for the first time, take place mainly in the United Kingdom, though they also bridge continents, like *The Angel at the Gate* (1982), located both in London and in India. *Black Marsden* (1972) is set in Edinburgh, where Clive Goodrich comes upon Black Marsden and brings him to his house together with his agents, characters in their own right but also part of Goodrich's tabula rasa inner theater, who threaten to impinge on his freedom of judgment and show that the deprived "other" can become possessive in turn. Goodrich and Marsden reappear in *Companions of the Day and Night* (1975), set in Mexico, which initiates what Harris called "the novel as painting" developed from "convertible images" (protean metaphors), particularly substantialized in *Da Silva da Silva's Cultivated Wilderness* (1977) and *The Tree of the Sun* (1978). In these two novels DaSilva, reborn from death in *Palace of the Peacock* and *Heartland*, is a painter engaged in a profound "re-vision" of the experiences evoked on his canvases. In these and his later fictions Harris elicits correspondences between various forms of art, writing, music, painting, and sculpture as well as between art and science, particularly quantum physics with its assumption of "simultaneous possibilities," parallel universes, and relativization of categories of being. In *Genesis of the Clowns* (1977), published in the same volume as *Da Silva da Silva*, a government surveyor remembers the expeditions he led thirty years before in Guyana and realizes that the sun of empire under which he exploited his crew is being decentered, setting in motion a "Copernican revolution of sentiment" in a globe immobilized in the days of empire and stimulating the rebirth (genesis) of the crew, whose deeper feelings are at last acknowledged.

From the *Da Silva* novels onward Harris' metaphorical writing increasingly blends with metaphysical, abstract reflection on the nature of creativity without relinquishing the sensuousness characteristic of all his fiction. *The Carnival Trilogy* (*Carnival*, 1985; *The Infinite Rehearsal*, 1987; *The Four Banks of the River of Space*, 1990) is an ambitious project that rewrites canonical European grand narratives and myths, *The Divine Comedy, The Odyssey*, and *Faust*, suggesting that, however admirable, the absoluteness of the ideal worldview that they present has become obsolete and may endanger the future of humanity. They also offer revised conceptions of comedy, allegory, and epic as well as an impressive sample of the Old World–New World symbiosis that informs Harris's cross-culturalism. Throughout his fiction, the carnival metaphor stands, among other things, for endless creativity, the emergence into being under different, partial masks of the formerly eclipsed, whose residues and legacies of experience have accumulated into an "unattainable wholeness" and are transformed into the sacred. In *Carnival* the protagonist, guided by Everyman Masters, explores the colonial inferno of New Forest (a barely disguised Guyana) but also, like Dante, the possibilities of rebirth. However, he does not move toward the eternal but discovers that the Inferno, Purgatorio, and Paradiso are fluid, overlapping states in the endlessly changing, self-renewing existential process. This endless evolution, involving backward and forward movements, as in *Heartland*, is further elaborated in *The Infinite Rehearsal*, a phrase that sums up the creative process, "the unfinished genesis of the imagination," the instrument of renewal itself in need of regeneration. It also describes the protagonist's ceaseless "re-vision" of the past from different angles and with a growing consciousness in his quest for value or, as he puts it, for the "original nature of value and spirit" (vii). The shifts between past, present, and future announce a similar approach to time, inspired by the Maya, in *The Four Banks of the River of Space* and, above all, *Jonestown*, both novels weaving a cross-cultural bridge between a pre-Columbian and a modern scientific perception of the universe. Metamorphosed Homeric figures have peopled Harris' writing from his earliest works, and *The Odyssey* is a palimpsest to many of his novels as a frequent source of revisionary myths and metaphors. *Four Banks* "re-writes" *The Odyssey* with English and Guyanese characters, but Ulysses is "fragmented" into a number of actors who share the burden of his strong personality and become partial selves susceptible of compassion and forgiveness, in contradistinction to the original hero's terrible nemesis, a motivation redeemed here, as in *Jonestown*, by imaginative insight.

The Resurrection runs as a major theme through Harris' work and takes on many forms: it can be the paradoxical presence of life in death, the emergence in the characters' consciousness of a previously ignored individual or historical past, and the reappearance of characters who died in earlier narratives. In *Resurrection at Sorrow Hill*, it takes the form of a schizophrenic, but regenerating, impersonation of figures like Montezuma, DaVinci, and Socrates by the inmates of an asylum. Harris adheres to Michael Gilke's concept of "creative schizophrenia" in the Caribbean, postulating that self-dividedness can offer an opportunity to break up a static condition (here blocked psyche) before a therapeutic reconstitution. Through their split personality, the "clowns of Sorrow Hill" (the novel is partly a sequence to *Genesis of the Clowns*) illustrate the doubling in characterization frequent in Harris' fiction and show the need to conciliate the variegated parts of their cultural inheritance both in themselves and in a place dense with the psychological vestiges of conquest. Like Sorrow Hill, Jonestown, the location of Harris' latest novel, is an actual marginal place evoking a victimized humanity, here the massacre ordered by a charismatic cult leader, Jim Jones, of about 1,000 followers, an extermination paralleled with the unexplained disappearance of Amerindian peoples and with contemporary holocausts and genocides. Like earlier Harrisian protagonists, its sole survivor, Francisco Bone, writes a "dream book" "edited" by W. H., whose narrative shifts between past, present, and future in the course of the redemptive journey that he undertakes to bring to light motivations and responsibilities and validate his conviction that "the heart of the wild is susceptible to change" (215). With the possible exception of Donne in *Palace of the Peacock*, Bone, who wishes to "open up a human-centred cosmos," travels farthest of all Harris' characters into mythopoeic and archetypal dimensions. One of Harris' most original contributions to the novel form is to have relativized humans' place in the universe, extending their personality to the extrahuman (including the animal and the divine) and traveling into inner/outer space that reaches from the deepest recesses of the psyche to cosmic heights, blending many cultures past and present. His narratives evince an extraordinary intertextuality. They have also freed language from conventional structures and patterns through the blending of various categories of being, startling orchestrations of images, composite and paradoxical metaphors.

Further Reading: H. Maes-Jelinek 1991, 2000.

Hena Maes-Jelinek

Hispanophone Literatures Hispanophone literatures and their critics have long engaged with the complex issues now subsumed under the postcolonial rubric. Yet, as hispanophone literary studies increasingly incorporate postcolonial approaches, three questions arise. Is postcolonialism another neocolonizing discourse? Do **anglophone** postcolonial paradigms silence the contributions made by Latin American writers who have developed their own modes of cultural production and analysis for dealing with the region's complex colonial legacies? What do the terms "colonial" and "postcolonial" signify in relation to literature in the Spanish-speaking Americas?

Responses to these polemical questions have been varied. Many modern writers locate the origins of Latin American literatures in the narratives of the conquest and colonial era. However, some critics insist that up to the late eighteenth century, texts merely conveyed a Castilian, rather than "American," worldview. According to this position, Spanish American postcolonial literatures emerged in tandem only with the decolonizations from Spain in the early nineteenth century. Other critics argue that an autochthonous and continentally viable postcolonial gaze is first identifiable in the 1880s and 1890s, either in the Nicaraguan Rubén Darío's *modernista* poetry or in the Pan-American vision of the Cuban revolutionary **José Martí**. Some observers suggest that a hispanophone colonial discourse analysis—the identification and critique of the "New World" as a European discursive and mythical construction—emerged with the publication of works like the Cuban Fernando Ortiz's *Contrapunteo cubano del tabaco y azúcar* (Cuban Counterpoint, Tobacco and Sugar, 1940), which inaugurated **transcultural** discourse, and the Mexican Edmundo O'Gorman's *La idea del descubrimiento de América* (The Idea of the Discovery of America) in 1952 and *La invención de América* (The Invention of America) in 1959. Finally, it has been claimed that postcolonial hispanophone criticism is a late twentieth-century phenomenon, part of a broad theoretical and international trend—influenced by **feminism**, poststructuralism, and the work of "Third World" intellectuals—concerned with displacing **Eurocentric** grand narratives and the epistemological primacy of the humanistic male center. Underpinning many of these approaches, however, is agreement that anglophone and hispanophone conceptions of postcolonialism and postcolonial literature must be distinguished; "Latin America" signifies a continent in which colonization generated geopolitical, cultural, and racial heterogeneities not replicated in other parts of the world.

The year 1492 provides an inaugural date for the Spanish conquest and for specific "New World" tropes such as that derived from the "cannibal" first described in Columbus' *Diario* (Diary) and letters. The epistemological impacts of these discursive inventions on "America" prefigure but remain distinct from colonial discourses generated in later centuries, places, and stages of capitalist development (e.g., Orientalism, the "dark continent" of Africa). While colonialism has not ended for the continent's indigenous peoples, the Spanish colonial period lasted until 1826, by which time most of Spain's American colonies attained independence. Nation formation in Latin America thus preceded the appearances of many European states and long predated the **decolonizations** in Africa and Asia after World War II. The newly independent United States itself emerged as the continent's key imperial player, its desire to displace European imperial hegemony announced by the Monroe Doctrine of 1823. The United States' territorial expansions were decisive. Mexico lost its northern half (the region from California to Texas) to the United States by 1848. Spain was forced to relinquish its two remaining American colonies in 1898, with the result that

while Cuba gained independence as a U.S. client state, Puerto Rico was transferred to U.S. colonial control. U.S. military interventions continued in the twentieth century, often with the support of some local sectors. A number of Latin
American revolutionary movements emerged after World War II, but unlike
anticolonial struggles in Africa and Asia with which they were contemporaneous, such movements targeted white **Creole** control of national projects and
resources, U.S. cultural and capitalist domination, and the region's many U.S.-
backed military dictatorships. Disparities in experiences of modernization, access to institutional power, and wealth continue under the so-called neoliberal
democracies that emerged in the 1980s. In an era of global capitalism, transnational trading structures requiring massive labor and capital flows, in and
between nations, are also transforming the demographic and cultural contours
of the hispanophone Americas.

If hispanophone "postcolonial" literatures emerge out of this historical complexity, they are also affected by profound intranational urban and rural tensions and equally profound regional variations, here roughly schematized: the
European-dominated southern cone (Uruguay, Argentina, and Chile); the mestizo (mixed Indian and European race) and indigenous Andean and Amazonian
areas (Peru, Ecuador, Bolivia, Paraguay, the hinterlands of Venezuela and Colombia); the African-European Antilles (Cuba, Puerto Rico, the Dominican Republic, the coastal zones of Venezuela and Colombia); the indigenous and
mestizo Central America; and Mexico, a mestizo nation with large indigenous
populations, which, more than any other Latin American state, is confronted by
proximity to the United States. Indeed, the illusoriness of "a" Latin America is
confirmed in the United States itself. As a result of both its imperial expansions
and mass migrations to it, the United States is now the fifth largest Spanish-
speaking country and home to 30 million people with Latin American ancestry
or affiliations. While Spanish is the predominant Latin American language
alongside Brazilian Portuguese, many indigenous languages and literatures have
survived 500 years of European cultural impact. At the same time, English and
English–Spanish fusions, Spanglish or *caló*, have joined Spanish as quotidian
and literary languages for U.S.-based Latinos.

Hispanophone postcolonial literary studies are inevitably concerned with making sense of the continent's heterogeneities as outlined here. Recent critical
interest in the narratives of the conquest and colonial era have desimplified the
conception of literatures in Latin America. Critics now tend to recognize a labyrinthine textual history spanning 500 years and to examine why Spanish American definitions of literature in the nineteenth and twentieth centuries were
stretched to encompass the colonial era as a site of nonliterary forerunners and
intertextual resources. Colonial-era texts do not represent a homogeneous body
of works that invariably replicated a monolithic Spanish imperial imaginary.
Such texts confirm that many purportedly "postcolonial" struggles over cultural
and political representation and cultural exchange and transformation were identified and discussed in sixteenth-century narratives. These narratives included

generically hybrid chronicles, *relaciones* (accounts or reports), and romances by explorers and *conquistadores*. They include natural histories modeled on classical prototypes (Pliny, Herodotus) but impelled into new generic shapes by the epistemological demands of "knowing" and literally narrating a New World. This is especially evident in the hybrid ethnographic, natural scientific, and theological texts written by priests who were impelled to "know" Indians in order to convert them. Many clerics learned Amerindian languages, mediated Indian testimonies of Spanish conquest, and potentially provided bilingual and bicultural accounts of Indian **resistances** to, and opinions on, conquest and colonization. Alongside works by clerically trained mixed-race and Indian writers, such histories of "America" make evident "colonized" challenges to monological "official" versions of imperial history. Signs that "Europe" was under signifying pressure by American conditions are exemplified by Alvar Nuñez de Vaca's *Naufragios* (Shipwrecks, 1542), the account of a Spanish soldier shipwrecked in what is now the southern United States and whose survival depended on his accession to Indian modes of cultural organization. At times, Spanish women escaped from metropolitan gender prescriptions by finding a space in the American colonies, as attested by the memoirs of Catalina de Erauso (1626–1630), a nun who abandoned a Spanish convent in order to pass as a man in Peru and, later, Mexico. In the imperium itself, the Spanish literary gaze was also adjusting to the New World. For instance, at the end of Quevedo's *La vida del Buscón llamado Don Pablos* (The Swindler, 1626), Don Pablos articulates a desire to improve his fortunes in "the Indies."

Debate among critics continues with regard to the autochthonous contours of literary productions from the seventeenth and eighteenth centuries, the colonial period whose dominant culture has often been designated Spanish American baroque. A case in point is the colonial era's most important Creole writer, Sor Juana Inés de la Cruz (1651–95), a Mexican nun, protofeminist, and author of chronicles and poems, among many other genres, whose fame eventually attracted disciplinarian attention by the Inquisition. Two twentieth-century responses suggest Sor Juana's postcolonial relevance as a pivotal literary forerunner. First, the study by the Mexican poet Octavio Paz, *Sor Juana de la Cruz, o, las trampas de la fe* (1982) (*Sor Juana: Her Life and Her World*, 1988), constructs an American literary lineage that includes Sor Juana's definitive contributions to a locally generated colonial Baroque. Second, the Chicana Alicia Gaspar de Alba's novel, *Sor Juana's Second Dream* (1999), writes back to Paz in order to reclaim the nun's erased erotic life, to emphasize the patriarchal constraints under which she labored, and to imply her exemplary relevance to current Chicana struggles against dominant cultural representations of women that emanate from both the former Spanish imperium and the postcolonial nation, in this case represented by Mexico and the United States.

Sor Juana's experiences with the Inquisition serve as a salutary reminder of Spanish power over the colonial publishing apparatus—most evident in prohibitions on American publishing of certain literary genres and the cultural hegemony exercised by the empire's main administrative centers, Mexico City and Lima. Not until the late colonial period was the Spanish center's control of New World representations challenged. Indeed, it is difficult to speak of hispanophone American literatures before the 1800s, not only because "literature" itself was an early nineteenth-century concept but because local literatures as would be recognized today are closely associated with national construction. Thus, while genres such as epic poetry were written throughout the colonial period in Mexico City and Lima, the first Latin American novel, *El periqullo sarniento* (The Itching Parrot) by the Mexican José Joaquín Fernández de Lizardi, was published only in 1816. Locally published literary texts concerned with post-Spanish identifications and imaginations in an American context are a nineteenth-century phenomenon.

In that century, the novel emerges as a primary, but embattled, cultural resource for national projects as conceived by Creole intellectuals and elites, often in contexts of dictatorship and civil war and violent intra- and international tensions. A number of factors characterize postcolonial literary productions in the new nations. First, drives for independence neither signified the collapse of European colonial epistemes nor precluded **neocolonial** dependencies. For the white Creole ruling classes, blood purity continued to be traced back to Spain, and France was esteemed as the source of "high" European cultural capital even as the socioeconomic structures established by Spain were transformed by the impact of British and, later, U.S. capital. Second, colonial legacies of mass illiteracy and of acute divisions between rural and urban sectors meant that literature was a cosmopolitan or elite cultural medium in contradistinction to the largely oral and popular cultural forms practiced by most Latin Americans. Third, writers regarded themselves as the local mediators of civilizing ideals. Ambivalences and contradictions thus characterized literary productions as writers looked to Europe as the source of literary modes and ideals by which "Latin America" could be narrated into modernity. The Argentinian Domingo Sarmiento encapsulated these postcolonial ambivalences in his *Facundo: civilización y barbarie* (Facundo: Civilization and Barbarism, 1845), in which he posed the cultured, urban "man" against the barbarous, populist forces of dictatorship, while also romanticizing the telluric, pioneering "American" qualities of the gaucho. However, another significant Argentinian foundational text, José Hernández's epic poem of gaucho life, *Martín Fierro* (1872), championed Argentinian popular rural culture in opposition to educated, urban elite accounts of nation. Elsewhere, writers engaged with colonial legacies and transformed "received" cultural capital in ways that prefigured literary production after 1900: the Colombian Jorge Isaacs provided the exemplary American romanticist melodrama with *María* (1867); the Dominican Manuel Jesús de Galván's historical novel *Enriquillo* (1882) detailed the conquest of Santo Domingo's Indian population; the Peruvian Clorinda Matto de Turner's *Aves sin nido* (Birds without a Nest, 1889) was one of the first *indigenista* novels to tackle the plight of contemporary Indian peoples; and the Cuban Cirilo Villaverde's *Cecilia Valdés*

234 Hispanophone Literatures

(1882) was one of the first novels to provide a mulatto (mixed African-European race) perspective.

Key postcolonial literary breakthroughs occurred at the century's end. *Modernismo*—a specific literary movement not synonymous with anglophone notions of modernism—is widely regarded as a successful attempt from the Latin American periphery to challenge Europe's representational power to construct the New World, even as the elite movement drew on French symbolism as its foundation. Rubén Darío's 1888 poetry collection *Azul* (Blue), in particular, is claimed to have circumvented the European gaze by drawing on American symbols and history from pre-Columbian times and sending back to European readers a New World, written in distinctly Latin American Spanish, not countenanced in the metropolis. Martí's poetry had a similar impact, but essays like "Nuestra América" (Our America) went further. His *creolización* (**Creolization**) provided a politicized vision of a Latin American culture that targeted both European cultural and U.S. imperial designs on the continent. A parallel continental imaginary underwrites the Uruguayan Enrique Rodó's *Ariel* (1900), one of the first hispanophone writings, back to *The Tempest*. Here, however, a "cultured" Latin American Ariel is confronted by the materialistic barbarity of the Calibanic United States. Rodó's book also inaugurated a hispanophone critical tradition that echoes **francophone** and anglophone revisions of *The Tempest*, a notable example being the reworking of Caliban into a symbol of American revolutionary possibility in the Cuban Roberto Fernández Retamar's *Calibán: Apuntes sobre la cultura en nuestra América* (Caliban: Notes on Culture in Our America) from 1972.

The literary productions and cultural concerns of the nineteenth century thus provide a postcolonial basis for the literatures of the twentieth century, in which, by the 1960s and 1970s, Latin American authors—most notably, the so-called Boom writers, Gabriel García Márquez, Mario Vargas Llosa, Carlos Fuentes, and Julio Cortázar—were attracting readers outside the continent. The literary text continued to function as a privileged cultural site in which metropolitan–periphery relations were cast as a problem of multiple hegemonic "centers": the Spanish imperium; the cultural **center** such as Paris; the United States as continental power; and the Latin American nation-state's capital city or urban centers. Writers were preoccupied with literary **mimicry** and appropriation—in particular, with regard to the "imposition," "borrowing," and potential local transformation and valency—of literary models and philosophical or political currents from elsewhere. Many writers and critics responded to the problem of how to imagine the continent and of how to develop appropriate literary and linguistic forms by which to represent local realities and incorporate indigenous, mestizo, and African cultural contributions and aspirations. Two events in particular—the Mexican revolution (1910) and the Cuban revolution (1959)—resonated for continental writers, the first foregrounding Indian sectors' survival against the grain of national revisionism on mestizo lines and the second providing the locus for overt antagonisms between Anglo and Latin American imaginations. Literary productions also generated a range of debates about the political and creative role of the intellectual and/or literary writer who regarded himself or herself as the ideal local mediator or transforming vector for national, avant-garde artistic or modernizing projects or as the conduit through which **subaltern** indigenous, mixed-race, or working-class subjects could be represented and spoken for.

The first half of the twentieth century saw regionalist literary trends characterized by distinct, but homologous, racialized and cultural emphases and varying degrees of counterdiscursive ambition. The recuperation and celebration of African popular-cultural forms and contributions to Antillean cultural identity were announced by the Afro-Antillean or *negrista* movement and realized in the poetry of the Puerto Rican Luis Palés Matos (1920s) and the Cuban Nicolás Guillen (*Motivos de son* [*Son* Themes], from 1930, and *Sóngoro Cosongo*, from 1931). The exploration of African popular-cultural signs and of the Afro-Antillean cultural base characterized later work by the Cubans **Alejo Carpentier** and Severo Sarduy and novels by the Puerto Ricans Luis Rafael Sánchez and Rosario Ferré, the latter authors also concerned with the not yet "post"-colonial problem of Puerto Rican identity. In Argentina, the gaucho narrative (*gauchismo*) continued with such texts as *Don Segundo Sombra* (1926), by Ricardo Güiraldes, the romanticized gaucho symbolizing a national sensibility in a perceived context of rural and urban, traditional and modern rivalries. Other regionalist novels that explored these rivalries included *La voragine* (The Vortex, 1924) by the Colombian José Eustasio Rivera and *Doña Barbara* by the Venezuelan Rómulo Gallegos (1929), both also part of a Creole-centered tradition (*Criollismo*) that equated national or continental identities with the land.

One pivotal trend is the *indigenista*, or Indian-centered narrative. This was a literary form of political protest concerned with questions of indigenous socio-economic, cultural, and racial marginalization. Many responses to "the Indian problem" were conceived from urban elite perspectives but, nonetheless, diverged from romanticizations of the Indians as noble victims of European civilization or as foundational symbols to be appropriated by white Creole writers when asserting their distance from Spain or from other Latin Americans. After the Mexican revolution, the official recuperation of an indigenous past as the basis for a posited national mestizo identity—articulated in such works as José Vasconcelos' *La raza cósmica* (The Cosmic Race) from 1925—appeared to replicate or refigure colonial discourses and racialized hierarchies. In Mexico, as in other mestizo nations, the official celebration of *mestizaje*, or racial and cultural hybridity, deflected attention away from institutionalized racism and white Creole control of the means of production. In Octavio Paz's influential *El laberinto de la soledad* (The Labyrinth of Solitude, 1950), the racial question is posed as a psychic conundrum attributed to the national anxieties stemming from the literal production of mestizos in the rape of indigenous women by male European colonizers. Nonetheless, writers in Mexico, Central America, and the Andean nations attempted to acknowledge the role of Indian cultures in national, regional, and continental terms and to desimplify conceptions of the sociopolitical, economic, racial, and cultural relations between Indian, mestizo, and European sectors. Essayists like the Peruvian Manuel González Prada and the Marxist **José Carlos Mariátegui** (*Siete ensayos de interpretación de la realidad peruana* [Seven Interpretative Essays on Peruvian Reality] from 1928) attempted to critique and pose solutions to the gap between Indian and European-dominated sectors. Key texts of *indigenismo* include the Bolivian Alcides Arguedas' *Raza de bronce* (The Bronze Race, 1919); the Peruvian Ciro Alegría's *El mundo es ancho y ajeno* (Broad and Alien Is the World, 1941); the Mexican Rosario Castellanos's *Balún canán* (Nine Guardians, 1957); the Guatemalan Miguel Ángel Asturias' *Hombres de maíz* (Men of Maize, 1949); and the Peruvian Manuel Scorza's five-volume work *La guerra silenciosa* (The Silent War). The five volumes are *Redoble Por Rancas* (Drums for Rancas, 1970), *Historia de Garabombo el Invisible* (Garabombo, the Invisible, 1972), *El Jinete Insomne* (The Sleepless Rider, 1977), *Cantar de Agapito Robles* (The Ballad of Agapito Robles, 1977), and *La Tumba del Relámpago* (Requiem for a Lightning Bolt, 1979). The Peruvian **José María Arguedas**'s writings were also significant, the author's bicultural and bilingual background informing his ethnographically modulated novels and his decision to write poetry in Quechua rather than Spanish. Critics of *indigenismo* have questioned the intellectual mediation of indigenous culture and knowledge underpinning such texts, particularly when "**translating**" Indian culture for nonindigenous audiences or claiming literary resolutions of racialized and socioeconomic inequities.

Alongside *indigenista* narratives and often sharing some of that tradition's concerns while expressly engaging with European artistic movements is a web of *vanguardista* (avant-garde) tendencies that includes such poets as Vicente Huidobro (Chile), Pablo Neruda (Chile), César Vallejo (Peru), and the poet, short story writer, and essayist Jorge Luis Borges (Argentina). Vanguardist literatures were irrevocably transformed by the key political event of the post–World War II era, the Cuban revolution, which coincided with profound shifts in the ways that many writers conceived their literary productions and social function. Writers associated with the 1960s "Boom," for example, asserted their creative independence and break from literary precursors and traditions. Some of these writers—most famously, García Márquez and his *Cien años de la soledad* (One Hundred Years of Solitude, 1967)—are associated with a particular Latin American literary phenomenon, **magical realism**, an attempt to move beyond realism in order to account for Latin American realities characterized by the pluralization of worlds and intersections between rational and prerational epistemes and modern and traditional cultural practices. This genre has a champion and exemplary writer in the Cuban Alejo Carpentier. Outside Latin America, magical realism has often been regarded as paradigmatic of modern hispanophone literature and, indeed, of postcolonial Third World literatures (e.g., Fredric Jameson). However, not only have many of the writers associated with the genre worked with other literary forms, but postcolonial literary productions in the Americas are far more heterogeneous and contested than such readings suggest. For example, the Chilean Isabel Allende mixed magical realist and realist modes in *La casa de los espíritus* (House of the Spirits) from 1982 in reaction against the androcentrism of much magical realist narrative. Moreover, the rise of **testimonio** (testimonial narratives) in the wake of the Cuban revolution as a political medium for recording, presenting, and circulating subaltern voices both coincided with the Boom and persisted beyond it. The Guatemalan Rigoberta Menchú's *Me llamo Rigoberto Menchú y así me nació la conciencia* (I, Rigoberta Menchú, 1983) is the best known *testimonio* and continues to center debates about the textual mediation of subaltern voices, the textual viability of subaltern resistances, and the supposed victory of truth over fiction attributed to the genre. *Testimonios* have been written by Indian, working-class, and peasant subjects and, in the era of military dictatorships, prison and torture victims. These works may reflect the impact of **liberation theology**, while also suggesting links with the exile literatures that arose in response to the military regimes of the 1970s and 1980s.

The writers of the Boom, as well as the *indigenista* María Arguedas, inspired what has been regarded as the most important hispanophone postcolonial mode, **transculturation**. The main critic was the Uruguayan Ángel Rama, whose yet to be translated *Transculturación narrativa* (1981) adapted the Cuban Fernando Ortiz's original conceptualization (1940) in order to account for Latin American regionalist narratives. Rama sought to show that local or regional vernacular literatures could be produced and analyzed on local terms without replicating philosophical discourses, literary genres, or language uses derived from, or sanctioned by, the Creole national elite or the European imperium. Nonetheless, Rama's successors have been forced to accommodate two critiques: he neglected literary texts by women, and he privileged the "high" cultural literary text and the mediating role of the writer-intellectual in generating and defining autochthonous culture. In the late 1980s the Latin American Subaltern Studies group emerged with the aim to counter the perceived elite literary contours of Latin American postcolonial studies. This group highlighted how postcolonial debates are modulated and challenged by feminists and by postmodernist writers (e.g., the Mexican Néstor García Canclini) who focus not on colonial legacies but on the continent's responses to global capitalism and the transnationalization of culture, peoples, and nations. Finally, U.S.-based Chicano and Latino literatures and criticism have also impacted on hispanophone postcolonial debates. Regarded in the 1960s as a sector subject to internal colonization, Chicanos in particular have developed alternative cultural studies modes in response to their position inside the U.S. borders. A key example is Gloria Anzaldúa's "Borderlands" concept as a place of danger and state apparatus attention that is also a metaphor for new cultural identities forged in the interstices of Anglo and Latin Americas.

Hispanophone literary texts appear as cultural forms in which the colonial legacies of multiple signifying systems, cultural typologies, and languages are at work. These legacies have impelled Latin American writers to define or secure an autochthonous Latin American literature in terms of national, regional, continental, and global aspirations and exchanges. Critical attentions to the specific historical preconditions for hispanophone postcolonial literary and critical traditions are the prerequisites for future productive dialogues between anglophone and hispanophone postcolonial theory. Such dialogues already exist. They are evident in the new cultural studies practices enabled by the importation of Indian subaltern studies to Latin American terrains, the various appearances of the Caliban trope in three languages, and the slow spread of transcultural discourse to anglophone postcolonial studies. Finally, postcolonial lessons can be learned from Latin American and U.S.-based Latinos, interrogations of the United States' imperial history and current geopolitical power, and its dissemination of anglophone cultural paradigms.

Further Reading: W. Mignolo 1995; S. Spitta 1995.

Paul Allatson

Humanism In the context of postcolonial discourse, humanism does not refer primarily to the European Renaissance ideal of making human beings the proper objects of human study, in imitation of the achievements of classical Rome and Greece. It foregrounds a specific historical implication of the traditional sense and refers to the post-Enlightenment tendency to treat European norms about humanity as if they were universals transcending ethnic and cultural diversity across history and geography. This connotation is the result of the decolonizing argument fostered by intellectuals such as **Frantz Fanon**, that when traditional humanism is practiced in a colonial context, it becomes part of what **Antonio Gramsci** called hegemonic dominance. Fanon argued that intellectuals from the colonized world are susceptible to assimilating European ideals, just as European intellectuals are prone to disseminating them, whether consciously or unconsciously, as universals of human experience. This has the effect of consolidating a European monopoly on defining the human, while alienating the colonized from their selves and cultures. Humanism is thus complicit with the force of European colonialism and capable of dehumanizing colonized subjects, who, once they fall into the habit of equating the human with the European, tend to associate any departure from this (European) norm of the human as confirmation of their own natural inferiority. It is argued that colonial cultures and nations must resist this effect of European humanism if they are to foster an independence of mind that can lead to the revival of old, or the creation of new, local cultures.

Concurrent with, and in part as a sympathetic reaction to, the many struggles for independence from European colonialism that followed the defeat of fascism and Nazism in World War II, the intellectual Left in Europe (especially France) developed its own reaction to the modern implications of traditional humanism. It led communists like Georg Lukács and Jean-Paul Sartre to formulate varieties of new humanism, which would replace the Enlightenment concept of an unchanging (**essentialist**) human nature with a sense of the human as a changing product of the human actions that constitute the ongoing process of history; in the case of structuralists like Roland Barthes, Claude Lévi-Strauss and Louis Althusser, it led to a critique of traditional and Marxist humanism.

More recently and provocatively, **Edward Said** has argued in *Culture and Imperialism* (1993) for a new humanism that will respect, yet transcend, boundaries of race, culture, and history, including the histories of colonialism and postcoloniality.

Further Reading: F. Fanon 1963; R. Young 1990.

Rajeev S. Patke

Hybridity.   *See* Creolization; Miscegenation

I

Identity Politics The possibility of a postcolonial identity generates much debate in postcolonial studies. Debate occurs because two apparently incompatible models of identity are assumed, dividing postcolonialist critics into **essentialists** and **constructionists**. Essentialism is typically associated with nationalist movements. **Nationalism** argues for a precolonial identity, positively re-presenting a distinct racial essence that is assumed invulnerable to individual, cultural, and historical differences. Constructionism disturbs the assumption of invulnerability by arguing that social, psychical, and linguistic structures determine identity. Determination by other forces generates a split identity, which is also a point of focus for constructionism. Splitting is sometimes assumed to do away with the concept of identity altogether, endlessly pluralizing/relativizing it in the extreme. Between essentialism and constructionism, two models of identity that are vulnerable to deconstruction, is strategic essentialism. The latter utilizes Western conceptual categories for political purposes, with an insight into their linguistic/ideological underpinnings. Essentialism, constructionism, and strategic essentialism represent the main points of focus for a discussion of identity politics.

A politics based on the essentialist model of identity extends the liberal **humanist** understanding of the individual as sovereign regarding meaning and action, to identities previously denied this privilege on the basis of race, **ethnicity**, and nationality. Given that identity is considered to be a white (Western, middle-class, heterosexual, Christian, male) prerogative, its extension to nonwhites constitutes a radical gesture. **Resistance** to what **Aimé Cesairé** refers to as "thingification" necessitates the claiming of sovereignty on the part of other, typically colonized identities. Equally capable of achieving self-knowledge and self-mastery, the latter generally focus their energies on a negative critique of imperialism and/or a positive representation of national identity. Postcolonial critics, particularly those associated with the **negritude** and the **Pan-African** movements, unmask the barbarism of Western civilization, along with contesting the harmful stereotypes perpetrated by the West in its endeavor to maintain global authority. For example, Cesairé references imperialism, "Hitlerism," and American racism in order to challenge the assumption that the West is civilized. Negative critique is also accompanied by the discovery of an essential black identity that exists apart from racist ideologies, along with transcending the divisions brought about by African diaspora. So-called pure and original black traits such as sensuality and community, for instance, are positively re-presented, challenging the content, if not the form, of Western imperialism. In other words, colonial categories make possible a postcolonial criticism that mobilizes itself on the basis of a precolonial identity. Although undeniably effective in helping to bring formal colonialism to an end, a nationalist politics of identity is problematic to the extent that it essentializes, homogenizes, and universalizes postcolonial identities irrespective of individual, cultural, and historical differences. For example, black **feminism** highlights the way in which "blackness" is typically defined according to patriarchal ideology, with nationalists privileging black masculinity as essential to identity politics.

A politics based on the constructionist model of identity negotiates critically with essentialism, rejecting the possibility of racial, ethnic, and national essences, together with repudiating the liberal humanist assumption of sovereign identity. Following **Marx**, Freud, and Saussure, constructionists argue that both essence and identity are socially, psychically, and linguistically affected. Constructionism empowers an oppositional politics to the extent that it insists on the illusoriness of the hierarchical relationship between colonizer and colonized, for example. With the colonizer's superiority in question, postcolonial criticism is rendered possible. Constructionism also emphasizes a split identity, along with the heterogeneity of postcolonial identities. Divided on the issue of **agency**, constructionists envisage political identity as either dialectically negotiated or absolutely determined. For instance, early postcolonial critics, **C.L.R. James**, Cesairé, and **Frantz Fanon** among them, "stretch" Marxism to include an analysis of the relationship between class and race, representing the colonized as willing revolutionary change via dialectical negotiation with Western capitalism. Liberation is possible because neither ideology is absolutely determining, ensuring that identity is relatively autonomous. To argue otherwise is not only to prohibit change but also to take responsibility for oppression away from dominant groups. Constructionism as involving endless deferral allows the business of oppression to continue as usual, inadvertently recentering dominant groups via decentralization. Moreover, decentering problematizes organized resistance, with infighting sometimes occurring between different marginalized groups. Constructionism also functions in much the same way as essentialism, with social, psychical, and linguistic structures seemingly incapacitating identity as "nature" once did. As it turns out, both models of identity politics uncritically reinforce the conceptual categories that postcolonial criticism should be calling into question. For example, essentialism and constructionism sanction binary logic regarding sovereign identity. Whether affirmed (sovereign) or abandoned (nonsovereign), this Western conceptual category is central to both politics of identity. Further, *pre*colonial and *post*colonial identities assume the possibility of exteriority with respect to colonialism. In so doing, essentialists and constructionists leave unacknowledged the fact that exteriority, together with the related concepts of sovereignty and autonomy, ultimately accords with **colonial discourse**.

Essentialist and constructionist identity politics leave postcolonial studies in something of a theoreticopolitical impasse. However, an identity politics based on strategic essentialism offers the potential for a radical critique. Postcolonial theorists who advocate strategy in relation to essentialism include, most notably, **Gayatri Spivak** and **Stuart Hall**. Strategic essentialism departs from the other two models of identity politics because it recognizes the impossibility of exteriority. Rather than searching for a true precolonial/postcolonial identity that is uncontaminated by Western conceptual categories, strategic essentialism critically engages with essentialized notions of race, ethnicity, and nationality. Critical engagement involves the recognition that black identity, for example, is a linguistic effect that is strategically used in order to empower antiracist politics. Further, strategic essentialism acknowledges that it is enabled by rhetoric— metalepsis and catachresis. However, rhetoric is also disabling because it holds no guarantees regarding meaning and reference, a risky situation for identity politics to concede; particularly, as "[t]he old ethnicities still have dominance, they still govern" (Hall 1997, 20). Strategic essentialism's turn toward language, particularly the rhetorical dimension of language, apparently prevents it from formulating a response powerful enough to end the harm generated by the old ethnicities. However, this overlooks the point that the latter acquire sovereignty through the marginalization of other ethnicities. An insight such as this compels recognition regarding the centrality of others, which, in turn, destabilizes the binary logic of, say, black and white. It also allows "black" to enter the theoreticopolitical scene, problematizing the privilege typically accorded to "white." Further, strategic essentialism's linguistic turn is criticized because it apparently signifies indifference to human suffering. However, this leaves unacknowledged the fact that stereotyping has its basis in language, with "hate speech" explicitly emphasizing the relationship between violence and discourse. What is also important about strategic essentialism is that it does not represent itself as having the final word on the politics of identity. Rather, its emphasis is on ensuring a future for debate via the preservation of difference. A rhetorically enabled/disabled politics, although provisionally securing identity in order to critique the old ethnicities, is also vulnerable to undoing, which allows other ethnicities to participate in theoreticopolitical debate.

Further Reading: S. Hall 1997; G. Spivak 1987.

Bella Adams

Indian-Language Literatures In current postcolonial discourse as influentially formulated by works such as *The Empire Writes Back* (Ashcroft, Griffiths, and Tiffin 1989) and the *Encyclopedia of Post-colonial Literatures in English* (Benson and Conolly, 1994), Indian-language literatures are literatures from the former colonies written in English and dating from the very moment of colonial intervention, which is to be called postcolonial. While such a definition may be apt for the literatures produced in the white **settler** colonies such as Australia, New Zealand, and Canada (areas from which both the books just named originated and that have, in any case, hardly any other writing to show for themselves), and while it may also fit, by and large, some nonwhite areas such as the West Indies and Africa (notwithstanding their older **"orature"** and a recent gesture of defiance through writing in Gikuyu by **Ngũgĩ wa Thiong'o**, e.g.), it rules out of consideration an overwhelmingly large and significant proportion of Indian literature. For one thing, extant writing in India dates from much before the moment of Western colonial intervention (c. 1750), going back as it does in Sanskrit to c.1500 B.C.; for another, with no more than 5 percent of the population knowing any English even now, the rest of the vast and traditionally multilingual country still speaks, reads, and writes in one or more of the eighteen modern Indian languages officially recognized by the Constitution and/or in hundreds of smaller regional languages. Thus, Indian writing in English, at present the best-known fraction of Indian literature outside India mainly because of the reach and clout of its global medium, still remains rather like the creamy layer on top of a large jug of milk or even the thin crust of ice over a long and deep lake.

Given the intertextual persistence of classical influences in a literary culture that has remained continuous for over 3,000 years, it may not be safe entirely to exclude even Sanskrit from the domain of the English-only postcolonial, for the "dead" language continues to feed into not only writing in the Indian languages but even contemporary Indian writing in English. Raja Rao's *The Serpent and the Rope* (1960) has a Brahmin hero equally at home in Sanskrit and French, while the title of the novel evokes the Upanishadic philosophical ambiguity between the world as reality or as illusion (*maya*). **Salman Rushdie**, among the most Westernized of Indian writers in English, has his hero Saleem in *Midnight's Children* (1980) say that the god Ganesha served as an amanuensis to the poet Valmiki as he dictated the epic *Ramayana*—in a gross error (or an instance of "unreliable narration," as Rushdie himself claimed post facto), for Ganesha did so for the poet Vyasa as he dictated the other foundational Sanskrit epic, the *Mahabharata*. Shashi Tharoor's *The Great Indian Novel* (1989) puns on the very title of the *Mahabharata* and then proceeds to echo the names of nearly all its major characters and to borrow its structure, in a debt rather more obviously (and superficially) signaled than Joyce's to *The Odyssey*. In **R. K. Narayan**'s *The World of Nagaraj* (1991), the would-be novelist hero thinks constantly of the mythological divine sage Narada, the original teller (and carrier) of tales among the Hindu gods, as a predecessor and possible role model.

Of all the Indian languages, it was, indeed, Sanskrit to which the British in India were first attracted, and the subsequent "discovery" of Indian literature and philosophy through translations from it caused such enthusiasm and excitement in Europe that Raymond Schwab has described the impact as an "Oriental Renaissance." In the context of **Edward Said**'s postcolonial formulation that by acquiring knowledge of the East, the West equipped itself to rule the East better, it may be salutary to recall that the first effect of Orientalism on the West was to leave it full of wonder and admiration. That knowledge can be power for the ruled no less than for the rulers was demonstrated strongly in the latter half of the nineteenth century, when Indian writers put Western Orientalist discourse to their own cultural-nationalist use. As Sanskrit literature was acknowledged to contain both religious and literary works that were quite as sophisticated as anything produced in English (e.g., with the Sanskrit playwright Kalidasa, fourth century A.D., being called "the Shakespeare of India" by his first English translator, Sir William Jones, in 1789), while it was also clearly older, a patriotic resurgence was generated among English-educated Indians enabled by a feeling of cultural seniority as well as superiority. An early subversive translator of Shakespeare's *Comedy of Errors* into Hindi, Ratna Chand, found opportunities in his version (1882) both to glorify India and bawdily to mock England, and Sanskritic themes were often worked up into novels and plays extolling the glory of ancient India while exhorting the readers, at least by implicit contrast, to do something about the lamentable present state of the country. A work of seminal influence that similarly glorified medieval India, the *Annals and Antiquities of Rajasthan* (2 vols., 1829, 1835), compiled with naive credulity from oral bardic sources by an English army officer, Col. James Tod, served writers from many Indian languages as a sourcebook for numerous instances of glorious Hindu resistance against the earlier Muslim invaders, which were now allegorically reinscribed to signal similar opposition to the new invaders, the British.

In the reconstitution and renewal of Indian writing under Western impact throughout the nineteenth century, Michael Madhusudan Datta (1824–1873) stands out as a case exemplifying both the lure and the countereffects of hybridity. He converted to Christianity, married an Englishwoman, went off to live in England and France, and wrote in English, but then he returned home, now to write in Bengali both a magnificent Miltonic epic radically reinterpreting the oldest Indian story, that of the *Ramayana*, and more personal and patriotic verses in a form new to the language, the sonnet. The novel and the periodical essay were also genres new to the Indian languages, and the first major Indian novelist, Bankimchandra Chatterjee (1838–1894), is also regarded as the first cultural-nationalist writer of modern India. Outside Bengal, which (as the area around the British capital Calcutta) bore the brunt of early colonization and at the same time proved the most vulnerable to Western cultural penetration, Vishnu Krishna Chiplunkar (1850–1882), a Marathi writer, feared that our freedom had been "crushed by English poetry," while Bharatendu Harishchandra

(1850–1885) in Hindi thoroughly Indianized *The Merchant of Venice* in his adaptation (1880), wrote a play of his own that satirizes the absurdly arbitrary procedure for dispensing justice adopted by the king in his *Andher Nagari* (City of Misrule, 1881), while even in his encomia to British royal personages and to Pax Britannica generally, he found occasion to complain that under British rule the wealth of India was drained abroad.

A new phase in the colonial history of India and in its (post)colonial literature was inaugurated in 1905, when the viceroy Lord Curzon's highly unpopular decision to partition the province of Bengal provided a rallying point for anti-British feeling in the whole country. In 1907 an allegorical Marathi play by Krishnaji Khadilkar that portrayed Curzon under the name of Kichaka, a villain from the *Mahabharata*, was promptly banned by the government. (In fact, the substantial archive of literary and discursive writing in the Indian languages that the British found it necessary to proscribe, especially under the dreaded Vernacular Press Act, constitutes a rich resource of a radical aspect of Indian postcolonialism.) Bal Mukund Gupt (1865–1907), as editor of a Hindi journal, addressed several open letters to successive viceroys, including Curzon, in the persona of a merry bhang-swilling Brahmin who had traditionally enjoyed the privilege of untrammeled freedom of speech. Even Rabindranath Tagore, who had in 1913 won the Nobel Prize for *Gitanjali*, a slim volume of late-Orientalist mystical poems such as several readers in the West still identified India with, wrote two political novels depicting various shades of contemporary nationalism, *Gora* (name of the hero, 1910), and *Ghare Baire* (Home and Abroad, 1916).

The arrival of Mahatma Gandhi on the Indian political scene beginning effectively with his first nationwide movement of 1920–1922 and his profound influence on all aspects of national life has been acknowledged by Sisir Kumar Das, eminent literary historian, as "one of the most memorable phenomena in the history of Indian literature." The literary response to Gandhi was surprisingly instantaneous and wholehearted. Poets such as Vallathol (Malayalam), Namakkal Ramalingam (Tamil), Akbar Allahabadi (Urdu), and Nazrul Islam and Satyendranath Datta (both Bengali) hailed and glorified him, often as a new prophet. In fiction he tended to be represented by major novelists such as Premchand (1880–1936, Hindi) and Unnava Lakshminarayana (1873–1958, Telugu) and, after the coming of independence in 1947 and Gandhi's assassination in 1948, by Satinath Bhaduri (1906–1965, Bengali) and Phanishwar Nath Renu (1921–77, Hindi), not directly but through the depiction of a Gandhian hero, some unsung local follower of Gandhi who similarly held up the virtues of nonviolent opposition to exploitation and injustice, fierce personal integrity verging on the ascetic, devotion to the truth as revealed through the voice of conscience, and a thoroughgoing civilizational critique of the West.

Gandhi also inspired writing on some new themes, most notably, the destitution of the villagers, as in Sumitranandan Pant's volume of poems *Gramya* (Hindi of the village 1940), or the cruelly circumscribed and exploited life of the untouchables, as in Shivaram Karanth's *Choman Dudi* (Kannada Choma's

Drum 1933). Beginning in the mid-1930s, many writers began to show an unlikely, but potent enough, blending in their works of the influence of Karl **Marx** and the Russian Revolution with the abiding influence of Gandhi and his homespun and rather different model of peaceful revolution. Gandhi also gave rise, among the illiterate or semiliterate masses whom he was able to mobilize politically for the first time, to many folksongs and new legends. This was truly the voice of the **subaltern** beginning to be heard, notwithstanding a strand of postcolonial theory according to which she or he cannot speak.

The coming of independence was accompanied by the partition of the country into India and Pakistan, and if much of the literature relating to the period dwells more on the tragic latter event than on the triumphant former, it is perhaps due to a universal literary bias by which the saddest thoughts make for the sweetest songs. Khwaja Ahmad Abbas (1914–1987) in a **short story** written in 1947 told of a victim of partition whom neither the Hindu nor the Muslim refugee camp would feed until he could tell which of the two religions he belonged to, a fact that he has traumatically forgotten but then refuses to declare even when he can remember it. Another Urdu short story by Saadat Hasan Manto (1912–1953) describes the official exchange between the two countries on the basis of religion even of the residents of lunatic asylums, a bizarre transaction which comes to a climax with the refusal of one of the madmen to budge until he eventually falls dead athwart the new international border.

The high hopes aroused by independence soon began to be interrogated by the literature of what in Hindi, the national or official language of free India in name if not de facto, was called *mohabhanga*, or disenchantment. Dharmavir Bharati's *Andha Yug* (Hindi, The Era of the Blind, 1955) offered an allegorical commentary on contemporary affairs by reviving a story from the *Mahabharata* in which the king is blind and the queen in sympathy blindfolded, and Girish Karnad's *Tughlaq* (Kannada, name of the hero, 1964) similarly reworked a theme from medieval Indian history in which the king is (rather like the first prime minister of India, Jawaharlal Nehru) so rational and idealistic as to be an absurd failure in practical terms. The satirical novel *Rag Darbari* (Hindi, The Sycophants' Song, 1969) by Shrilal Shukla has for its main target the newly empowered rural elite, while Alka Saraogi's *Kali-katha: Via Bypass* (Hindi, 1998, with the first word punning on the name Calcutta, where the novel is set) not only recounts a 150-year-long diaspora of a desert community from west India to the new imperial capital over a thousand miles to the east but also contrasts through narrating a family saga the selfless idealism of the period of the nationalist struggle with the affluent, but corrupt, self-centeredness of the postcolonial and postliberalization India. As if to acknowledge the new and dominant status of Indian writing in English even within India, this novel also takes a couple of parodic bows in the direction of Salman Rushdie.

Of the authors and works mentioned, only a tiny fraction is available in English translation outside India. Even an India-based postcolonial critic, **Aijaz Ahmad**, has stated that not enough Indian literature is yet available in English translation for him to be able to adequately theorize it. It is as if the proof of the pudding of postcolonial Indian literature were not in the eating but in the aftertaste, in that "afterlife" of a text through translation, as Walter Benjamin put it.

Further Reading: S. K. Das 1991, 1995; H. Trivedi and M. Mukherjee 1996.

Harish Trivedi

Indigenismo. *See* Mariátegui

Indigenous Peoples Aboriginal or indigenous peoples are those populations that were already resident when Europeans or other colonizers invaded, occupied, and/or settled their traditional territories. However, such a general definition of indigeneity—"original inhabitants"—is of limited use when applied to examples of colonial, postcolonial, or neo-colonial encounters in specific locations. Distinctions can be drawn, for instance, among indigenous peoples who have remained majority populations in their homelands (e.g., in parts of Africa, Asia, Oceania, and South America); indigenous peoples who were dislocated to foreign territories, where they may have displaced other indigenous peoples (becoming, in effect, "settlers" themselves) and where they may have become either majority or minority populations (e.g., African peoples in the Caribbean and other parts of the Americas); and indigenous peoples who have become minorities in lands that they once controlled (e.g., in the so-called breakaway **settler colonies**, American Indians, Alaska Natives, and Native Hawaiians in the United States; **First Nations** peoples in Canada; Aboriginal peoples in **Australia**; and Maori in Aotearoa/New Zealand; as well as, less obviously, Numerically small Indigenous Peoples in the Russian Federation; Saami in the Scandinavian countries; and Ainu in Japan).

Defining indigenous minority identities in First World settler nations like the United States, Canada, Australia, and Aotearoa/New Zealand has proven especially difficult and politically volatile. Government officials, social scientists, and indigenous peoples themselves have disagreed over whether biological kinship, language, culture, group consciousness, community endorsement, personal declaration, or some combination of these "objective" and "subjective" criteria should be used to recognize "authentic" indigenous status. Some scholars and activists question the usefulness of so-called objective criteria altogether, especially in situations where there are long histories of racial mixing, migration, forced relocation, genocide, and/or high levels of linguistic and cultural assimilation. Mixed-blood individuals and communities have been perhaps most vulnerable to state-imposed criteria for recognizing indigenous status, such as systems of blood quantum in the United States (which divide the "degree" of an individual's indigenous blood into descending fractions of one-half, one-quarter, one-eighth, and so on) or requirements of patrilineal descent in Canada (which nullify the indigenous identity of individuals born to an indigenous mother and a nonindigenous father). Ongoing conflicts over definitional control indicate just how much is at stake for settler-invaders and their descendants: both the right to claim and to control tangible economic resources like land, minerals, timber, and fisheries and the right to claim and to control intangible, but nonetheless highly valuable, political, social, and symbolic resources like authenticity and legitimacy. For indigenous peoples, also at stake are fundamental rights to self-definition, both as individuals and communities. These rights have drawn considerable media attention when self-proclaimed indigenous writers or spokespersons have been suspected or exposed as impostors.

There has been increasing debate over whether the circumstances under which contemporary indigenous minorities live in First World settler nations are best described as "colonialism," "postcolonialism," "internal colonialism," "domestic imperialism," or something else. Additional generalizing labels have been affixed to indigenous minorities along these different lines, some generated by indigenous peoples themselves, including the relatively politically neutral terms "original nations," "domestic nations," or "nations within" and the more overtly politically radical terms "internal colonies" and "captive" or "occupied" nations. Some Maori activists, for example, designate New Zealand as "Occupied Aotearoa." In Canada, both indigenous peoples and settlers currently use the term First Nations to refer collectively to American Indian, Inuit, and Metis peoples as a group; some U.S. American Indians employ it as well. This term is notable for its implications of historic memory coupled with its relative political neutrality: First Nations suggests both prior occupancy of territory and prior political organization (and thus self-determinacy) without overtly carrying accusations of violence or theft against Canada's or the United States' majority populations of European-descended settlers. In Australia "Aboriginal" is still used as an umbrella term for various indigenous peoples, although regional terms are increasingly common, including Koori in Southeastern Australia, Murri in Queensland, and Nyoongah in Western Australia. In the international arena, two generalizing labels for indigenous peoples have come into common currency. First Peoples is a United Nations term that is applied to indigenous peoples in all parts of the world, whether they are majority or minority populations, while Fourth World is a more politically radical term that is often, though not always, limited to indigenous minorities. Both terms acknowledge indigenous status—claims of deep historic, cultural, and spiritual ties to specific lands—as a legitimate rationale for collective political identity at local, national, and potentially international levels.

Resistance by indigenous peoples to colonial and settler domination has been well documented at the local level since the beginnings of European conquest and, in some cases, at the national level as early as the late nineteenth and early twentieth centuries. In settler nations like the United States and New Zealand, however, a highly visible indigenous activism emerged at national and then international levels only in the second half of the twentieth century, as was the case for large-scale **decolonization** movements in Africa, Asia, and the Caribbean. In the United States, for example, the explosive indigenous activism of the 1960s and 1970s can been seen as a direct response to American Indian involvement in World War II and to the federal government's initiation of termination and relocation policies in the mid-1950s, as well as to the examples set by the African American civil rights and **black power movements**. Organized as Indians of All Tribes, the American Indian Movement (AIM), Women of All Red Nations (WARN), red power, and other local, regional, and national protest groups and indigenous activists and their allies deployed a "politics of embarrassment" through direct confrontation and media exposure. They staged marches and sit-ins, occupied confiscated lands and sacred sites, took over Bureau of Indian Affairs (BIA) buildings, and, most famously, held federal forces at bay in an armed struggle at Wounded Knee, South Dakota, in 1973. Indigenous activists in other settler nations formed similar organizations, often led by charismatic leaders, and staged similar, highly visible confrontations with dominant power, including the Aboriginal Tent Embassy erected on Australia Day in 1972 and the 1975 national Maori Land March. In the courts, indigenous individuals and groups also deployed a "politics of rights" by litigating against settler governments over historic and ongoing grievances.

Although a number of international organizations had lobbied for indigenous rights, some beginning as early as the 1920s, including the International Labor Organization (ILO), the International Work Group on Indigenous Affairs (IWGIA), Survival International, and the World Council of Churches, it was not until 1975 that the first international coalition organization formed and run by indigenous peoples themselves, the World Council of Indigenous Peoples (WCIP), held its first meetings. Led by George Manuel, a Shuswap leader from British Columbia who was also president of Canada's National Indian Brotherhood (NIB), the WCIP composed a "Solemn Declaration" of indigenous identity that foregrounds self-selective criteria such as indigenous memory and consciousness. More recently, the United Nations (UN), which recognizes the WCIP and a number of other indigenous organizations as nongovernmental entities with "consultative status," has been preparing a Declaration of Indigenous Peoples Rights. In 1993, designated as the International Year of the World's Indigenous People, the UN completed a Draft Declaration that mixes "subjective" and "objective" criteria for indigeneity such as priority in time, voluntary perpetuation of cultural distinctiveness, self-identification, and experience of subjugation, dispossession, and marginalization by a dominant society.

In the First World settler nations, indigenous activism has shared many of the same goals as other minority initiatives, including voting and political rights, access to better health care, relief from poverty, and protection from police or military violence. But it is distinguished by ethnopolitical struggles for corporate land rights and some degree of corporate sovereignty, as well as for the right to maintain (or revive) cultural and linguistic distinctiveness from the dominant society. Sometimes these struggles are conceived explicitly in terms of **nationalism**. In this way, indigenous minority activism often has as much or more in common with anticolonial struggles in so-called developing nations (e.g., the efforts of indigenous peoples in the Pacific Islands to reclaim lands that were confiscated for military use by the United States and France) than it does with other minority struggles. In fact, indigenous minority activists often resist efforts to redefine their communities as simply one of many similarly distinct cultural or **ethnic** groups in the contemporary "**multicultural**" settler nation. They argue that such redefinition enables dominant power to continue colonial practices of reframing indigenous corporate political *identities*, which are often affirmed in treaties and other binding agreements, as individual political *interests*. In addition, indigenous minority activism has addressed issues such as ongoing paternalism in the state administration of indigenous resources; persistent negative stereotyping of indigenous peoples within dominant popular culture, media, and systems of education; attempts to commodify treaty and aboriginal rights; the appropriation of indigenous intellectual and cultural knowledge; and the repatriation of sacred objects and human remains from museums and universities.

Indigenous minority writing also has a long history, although, like indigenous minority activism, it saw a dramatic increase in the 1960s and 1970s with the emergence of writers such as N. Scott Momaday and Leslie Marmon Silko in the United States, Witi Ihimaera and Patricia Grace in Aotearoa/New Zealand, Oodgeroo Noonuccal and Jack Davis in Australia, and Maria Campbell in Canada. This trend has continued in all genres into the twenty-first century. Two issues have been central for indigenous minority writers, namely, how to define a contemporary indigenous identity and how to narrate the experience of being indigenous in a context of deep settler colonization. Works of both fiction and nonfiction foreground themes of indigenous identity, including pride in ancestors, strong community values, the social significance and aesthetic excellence of oral traditions, a persistent spiritual affinity with specific lands, and a history of resistance. Further, these works critique colonial practices such as the political and social marginalization of indigenous peoples, racial violence, the breaking of treaties and other formal agreements, the disruption of indigenous families, attempts to wipe out indigenous languages and cultures, and ongoing assaults on indigenous lands through flooding for hydroelectric projects, mining, weapons testing, and hazardous waste disposal. Indigenous writers also have documented the devastating legacies of acculturation, such as high rates of alcoholism, suicide, and family disintegration, and revealed the political and economic corruption of some indigenous elites. In these texts, traditionalism tends to be equated with strengthening the indigenous community rather than with the maintenance of particular precolonial technologies or lifeways. Where indigenous languages remain extant, writers have had to choose whether to compose in their own or in the colonizer's language. However, in many parts of the world the potential reading population for specific indigenous languages is tiny or nonexistent. Like other postcolonial writers, indigenous writers often deploy individual untranslated words or phrases as markers of difference and remake colonial languages like English into distinctive or hybrid forms.

As greater numbers of indigenous individuals have entered academe since the 1960s, they have begun to deconstruct the Western academy's dominant assumptions about the production, dissemination, and preservation of knowledge. Sometimes referred to as "indigenous theory," this emerging body of critical work is marked not only by an analysis of **colonial discourses** but also by a focus on indigenous survival, endurance, and transformation. Indigenous historians like Vine Deloria in the United States and Ranginui Walker in Aotearoa/ New Zealand are rewriting their peoples' histories in ways that valorize indigenous memories and forecast indigenous futures. Indigenous scholars of literature and culture like Gerald Vizenor, Elizabeth Cook-Lynn, and Craig Womack in the United States, Hirini Melbourne and Ngahuia Te Awekotuku in Aotearoa/ New Zealand, and Mudrooroo Narogin in Australia are developing sophisticated analyses of indigenous representation, as well as specific and pan-indigenous traditions of aesthetic criticism.

Further Reading: L. Smith 1999; *Voice of Indigenous* 1994.

Chadwick Allen

Indonesia. *See* Benedict Anderson

Irish Literature By the mid-1200s the Anglo-Normans held about 75 percent of Ireland. The Statutes of Kilkenny (1366) were an attempt by the British Crown to prohibit the descendants of the Normans from integrating themselves into Irish life, speaking Gaelic, dressing like the Gaelic-Irish, or marrying them. The British Crown took greater and greater interest in Ireland in the ensuing years, and the Battle of Kinsale along with the "Flight of the Earls" marked the end of the old Gaelic order and established England as the conqueror of Ireland. The seventeenth-century "plantations" by the British were the most important development in Irish history since the arrival of the Celts. The plantations divided Ireland apartheid-like into two hostile camps. Oliver Cromwell, appointed lord protector of Ireland by the English Parliament, arrived in 1649 with thirty-five ships and the determination to terrify Ireland into submission. His troops massacred residents, including unarmed women and children. The Cromwellian Plantation, which followed, reduced Catholic ownership of land from 59 percent to 22 percent. After the Battle of the Boyne the Williamite Plantation reduced ownership to 14 percent.

The eighteenth century was a time when Catholic ownership of land further declined from 14 percent to 5 percent. Catholics were prohibited from purchasing realty or from educating their children in the Catholic tradition. The last of the Penal Laws in 1727 denied Catholics the right to vote. A series of uprisings broke out; in reaction to the Rising of 1798, the Irish Parliament voted for its own dissolution, and in 1800 the Act of Union was passed by the British Parliament. Effective on 1 January 1801, Ireland became an official part of the

United Kingdom. The statesman Daniel O'Connell launched a grassroots campaign to repeal the Act of Union in 1837, but it was unsuccessful.

The Great Hunger, the potato famine that struck when a fungus ravaged the potato crop in 1845, 1846, and 1848, devastated the Irish Catholics and had profound effects on the entire island. Before the Great Hunger, the population of Ireland was 8.5 million. After the famine the population had dropped to 6.5 million. The drop resulted from both starvation deaths and emigration. By 1881 the Irish population had declined to 5 million. The other profound effect that the famine had on Ireland was that the Gaelic language was irretrievably lost. Because the famine hit hardest in the areas where Gaelic was spoken, in the span of just one decade, the language of Ireland shifted almost completely from Gaelic to English.

England's unsympathetic response to the plight of the starvation caused by the famine galvanized Irish ire, and in the late nineteenth century new leaders emerged to challenge British hegemony. Societies such as the Irish Republican Brotherhood and the Fenian Brotherhood championed an aggressively nationalist agenda. The wildly idealistic, but poorly planned, Easter Rising of 1916 began with Padraic Pearse's orating from the steps of the General Post Office in Dublin and declaring "the right of the people of Ireland to the ownership of Ireland." The rebels lasted for five days before being forced to surrender to the British. Within days fifteen of the rebels were executed. While the Easter Rising did not initially have popular support, support was rallied when the execution of the rebels had the effect of creating martyrs.

The Dáil Eireann was subsequently created. Both a Declaration of Independence and a resolution declaring that this government body had the exclusive power to make laws binding on the Irish people and that the British Parliament no longer had any jurisdiction over Ireland were written. Guerrilla warfare immediately erupted after this session. The British prime minister David Lloyd George invited the Irish to negotiations for a treaty. The result of the negotiations was the partition of Ireland into two entities: (1) a twenty-six-county, self-governing dominion called the Irish Free State and (2) the six northern counties formally named Northern Ireland, which remained part of Great Britain.

The treaty passed the Dáil by a vote of 64–57, and the Irish Free State was born on 7 January 1922. The Irish civil war, which lasted for over a year, began almost immediately as pro- and antitreaty factions fought each other. The Republic of Ireland came into being in 1948, when Ireland became a full republic outside the Commonwealth. By midcentury focus had tended to center on Northern Ireland, where the Catholic minority continued to be persecuted. On 30 January 1972, a day commonly referred to as Bloody Sunday, British troops opened fire into a crowd of unarmed civil rights demonstrators. The impact of Bloody Sunday forced the British Parliament to accede to Irish Republican Army (IRA) demands, and a number of reforms were enacted. For the IRA, however, civil rights legislation was not enough; nothing short of a united Ireland was acceptable.

After reading this survey of Irish history we may legitimately ask the question, Where does Irishness, if there is something that we can call Irishness, lie? Following critics like **Aijaz Ahmad** and Anne McClintock, it is very difficult in this sense to pinpoint exactly where postcoloniality starts. As Declan Kiberd notes, "[P]ostcolonial writing does not begin only when the occupier withdraws: rather it is initiated at the very moment when the native writer formulates a text committed to cultural resistance" (1995, 6). Kiberd locates this first authentic decolonizing moment in the seventeenth-century writings of Seathrún Céitinn when he, in his *Foras Feasa ar Éirinn* (A Basis for the Knowledge of Ireland, 1857), establishes himself as a counterimperial historian. Kiberd likewise identifies decolonizing impulses in the works of subsequent Anglo-Irish writers like George Farquar, Richard Brinsley Sheridan, Oliver Goldsmith, Jonathan Swift, and Edmund Burke.

The Irish Literary Revival is the movement very often associated with Irish postcoloniality. Starting in or about 1890 and ending in about 1922 with the end of the Anglo–Irish War and Irish independence, the movement is generally associated with William Butler Yeats and his colleagues. In the early 1890s Yeats decided to shift the emphasis from land reform and home rule back to Irish cultural production, the ultimate goal being to create an Irish literature that would be a rebirth of true Irish forms, themes, and genres and not merely a replication of English literature. He and Lady Augusta Gregory founded the Abbey Theatre, whose goal was to create a venue for the production of new Irish plays for an Irish audience. The emphasis at the Abbey Theatre and in the Irish Literary Revival as a whole was the creation of uniquely Irish forms. Yeats was a proponent of a re-creation of ancient themes, motifs, and stories. His particular favorite was Cú Chulainn, the hero of the *Táin bó Cuailnge* who became for Yeats the embodiment of heroic nationalism. Yeats wrote an entire Cú Chulainn cycle of plays for the Abbey stage and a number of poems about the ancient Irish hero. The Irish hero embodied Yeats' hope for a unified Irish culture based on ancient nobility. This search on Yeats' part was for an authentic Irish past, which was for him and his colleagues more attractive than that offered by colonial histories.

Yeats' well-known fascination with metaphysics and the occult has, according to many theorists, a strong link to issues of the Irish postcolonial. **Edward Said** and Seamus Deane both observe Yeats' fascination with the occult. Said sees Yeats' use of metaphysics as a way of leaving the historical world and contributing to his own particular creation of Irishness. Seamus Deane has been a bit less sympathetic; his observation that Yeats distorted history in the service of his myth is often quoted as a critique of the Irish Literary Revival and its methods.

The Irish Literary Revival was not endorsed by every Irish writer of the time, nor is it universally appreciated now. The Gaelic League (Connradh na Gaeilge) was established in 1893 with the express purpose of buttressing the use of the Irish language in the face of a meteoric decline in its usage due to emigration and abandonment in favor of English. The Gaelic Leaguers, most predominantly Douglas Hyde, the president and one of the founding members, believed that the Irish language was the prime indigenous cultural characteristic that defined Irishness and that the use of the English language, as favored by the writers of the Irish Literary Revival, was not a way to assert an Irish identity against the English; the league contested the validity of the term "Anglo-Irish," maintaining that the language itself defined Irishness. Thus, the league aggressively promoted Irish cultural events of many different kinds. While the Gaelic League held a great deal of sway in Irish politics and policy formation of the time, ultimately it was not successful in doing more than reintroducing the Irish language into the school curriculum; in the end, the Irish Literary Revival's belief that a valid and exciting Irish literature written in English could be an Irish literature prevailed.

James Joyce, for the most part, disassociated himself from the methods and beliefs of the Irish Literary Revival. He criticized the central tenets of the movement as well as many of the central figures. Joyce himself lived the greatest part of his life in self-imposed exile on the continent. He was not, however, disinterested in the question of Irishness and **nation**. The hero of *A Portrait of the Artist as a Young Man*'s (1916) famous dictum that his soul was the site of the creation of the conscience of the Irish race demonstrates Joyce's intense preoccupation with issues of Irish nationalism. Despite his self-imposed exile, all of Joyce's major texts are set in the "centre of paralysis" that was Dublin in 1904. Declan Kiberd offers a postcolonial reading of Joyce when he observes that each of the short stories in *Dubliners* documents a thwarted attempt at freedom on the part of each individual protagonist, an attempt that is predetermined to fail for the very reason that it couches itself in the forms and languages of the erstwhile colonizer. In Kiberd's reading, this designates failure for a nationalism that confines its definitions of itself to the categories designed by the colonizer. For Joyce, as for many Irish writers of this time, Irish was not a viable literary medium. Joyce mocked the aspirations of a Gaelic language revival; instead he invented another form of English completely. Read in an Irish postcolonial context, Joyce's linguistic pyrotechnics can be seen as the invention of a uniquely Irish form of English.

In 1980, the Field Day Theatre Company was founded in Derry, Northern Ireland. The founding of Field Day, about a dozen years after the beginning of the present political crisis in Northern Ireland, was in response to the perceived need of a contemporary cultural and artistic response to political crises on the entire island. The Field Day enterprise is threefold. It consists of theater, the Field Day pamphlets, and *The Field Day Anthology of Irish Writing* (1991).

The theme of "**translation**," whether it be linguistic or cultural, undergirds the main theatrical events of the early Field Day enterprise. Brian Friel's play *Translations* (1981) was the first play written and performed for Field Day. It was followed by plays like Thomas Kilroy's *Double Cross* (1987) and Tom Paulin's *The Riot Act* (1985), an adaptation of *Antigone*. These plays all have in common a preoccupation with the effects of traumatic change, change of the sort brought about by colonialism. In Friel's play *Translations*, the citizens of a small village in Donegal in 1833 witness the effects of the British ordnance survey that sets out to map and transliterate the Gaelic place-names in their region. The play sets up a dialogue between the proponents of the English language and **modernization** and those who are committed to the Irish tradition. Friel includes in his text the components of an emerging national dialogue.

Friel was not a proponent of dreamy nostalgia. His was not the backward gaze of the revivalist who posited Irishness over all. Instead, Friel combines intense realism with the nostalgic backward gaze. The play, written in English, is to be imagined by the audience as enacted in Irish. The great irony that results contributes to the overriding sense of the play as a whole. While examining the results and mourning the loss of the Irish language, the English language is being enriched by the addition of the play into the canon of Anglo-Irish theater.

Intimately related to the theme of the plays are those of the pamphlets, the second part of the Field Day enterprise. The pamphlets analyze rhetorical strategies in Irish literature and the criticism that mediates the literature. Most of the pamphlets are written by Irish critics, but a well-known pamphlet compiled of essays by Terry Eagleton, Fredric Jameson, and Edward Said brought great attention from outside Ireland to the Field Day enterprise.

Finally, the third Field Day project was *The Field Day Anthology of Irish Writing*. The anthology covers a span of 1,500 years of Irish literary, political, economic, and philosophical writings. The intention was to present Irish writing in an entirely Irish context, to bring writers like Swift, Berkeley, Goldsmith, Burke, Shaw, Yeats, Joyce, and Beckett outside the British canonical context and to create an opportunity to read them in an entirely Irish context. Very contemporary novelists like Seamus Deane, Roddy Doyle, Edna O'Brien, and Patrick McCabe are writing texts that continue to interrogate the issue of contemporary Irish identity in a postindependence context. Edna O'Brien's early texts like *The Country Girls Trilogy* (1986) and *A Pagan Place* (1970), while often read as indictments of the repression of female sexuality in Irish rural society, also participate in the broader project of revisionist historiography whose chief aim was to demolish the nationalist mythology that had been in place from roughly 1916 to 1966. O'Brien's texts challenge the myth promulgated by Eamonn de Valera in his Constitution of 1937, which positions the Irishwoman as the center of the home and the home as the center of the fledgling nation-state. O'Brien's very contemporary "Ireland Trilogy," *House of Splendid Isolation* (1994), *Down by the River* (1997), and *Wild Decembers* (1999), is heavily under the influence of **postmodern** trends that adhere to the tenet that identity is pluralistic and always in the process of becoming.

Patrick McCabe, like Joyce before him, uses the form of the bildungsroman to great effect as a metaphor for nation in both *The Butcher Boy* (1992) and *The Dead School* (1995). In both of these narratives, instead of mastery as the ultimate outcome of the bildungsroman narrative, the heroes devolve into incoherence and ultimately into insanity. *Breakfast on Pluto* (1998) has in Patrick "Pussy" Braden what is perhaps the most Irish of all contemporary Irish characters in this postmodern context. *Breakfast on Pluto* is primarily a novel about shifting identities. What the text says about shifting gender identities it seems to say about Irish identity as a whole. *Breakfast on Pluto* asks the implied question, Is there such a thing as Irish identity? McCabe seems to condemn the primordial vision of identity and seems rather to opt for the performative view as we see Pussy unable to piece together a stable and unshifting coherent identity. These themes are also apparent in the work of the filmmaker Neil Jordan. His *The Crying Game* (1993) demonstrates a similar interest in the fluidity of contemporary Irish identity.

A contemporary move back to writing in the Irish language is being performed by writers like Nuala Ní Dhomhnaill and Michael Davitt. Nuala Ní Dhomhnaill sees the Irish language to both assert Irishness and to recover the female voice in Irish poetry that the English male tradition has eclipsed. Ní Dhomhnaill takes her material, as did the Revivalists before her, from Irish literature and legend. Ní Dhomhnaill infuses her poetry with images of strong women, goddesses and queens from the ancient Celtic tradition where women wielded authority equal to, or greater than, that of their male counterparts.

A wealth of fresh and exciting literature with postcolonial themes has been produced in Ireland in the last several decades. Besides the writers already discussed there is the prose of writers such as Jennifer Johnston, Mary Lavin, Molly Keane, Anne Enright, William Trevor, and John Banville. Derek Mahon and Medbh McGuckian write poetry, and Brian Friel and Tom Murphy continue to write provocative plays for production both inside and outside Ireland.

Further Reading: T. Eagleton et al. 1990; D. Kiberd 1995.

Kathryn L. Kleypas

Islamism.   *See* Arabism

J

C.L.R. James   Cyril Lionel Robert James was born into a black middle-class family in the small village of Tunapuna, Trinidad, in 1901. Although struggling financially, the family participated in bourgeois culture. Shakespeare and Thackeray, along with a colonial English education, were available to James. "Englishness" was not adopted uncritically insofar as he rebelled against his Oxbridge masters and pursued an interest in Caribbean popular culture. After leaving school in 1918, James worked short-term at a sugar estate and was later employed as a teacher. Increasingly involved with the Trinidadian artistic/intellectual scene, he produced fiction about the Caribbean that privileged the life of the ordinary people. His interest in rhetoricity/ordinariness dovetailed on encountering Captain Cipriani, a local political leader, who promoted, in James' words, "self-government, federation . . . [and] the barefooted man" (Farred 1996, 18).

James left for the metropolis in 1932, pursuing his writing career as a cricket reporter for the *Manchester Guardian*. Political issues were more obviously on the agenda for James in this working-class region of England. During this period, James became a Trotskyist and a **Pan-Africanist**, political ideologies that demanded critical engagement with capitalist/imperialist discourses. He brought them together, albeit uneasily, in The *Black Jacobins* (1938). James' links with American Trotskyism and the Harlem Renaissance effected his move to the United States in 1938. An important period in his life, 1938–1953, saw his break with the Trotskyist movement because of its limited engagement with both the Russian question and "the Negro question" (1938). In addition to a critique of Trotskyism in *State Capitalism and World Revolution* (1950), James examined American culture in *Mariners, Renegades and Castaways* (1953), identifying Herman Melville as essentially American. Using his Melville book to protest against McCarthyism, which affected him personally insofar as he was imprisoned and expelled for un-American activities, James politicized scholarship in a way that is praised by postcolonial theorists, particularly **Edward Said** and Henry Louis Gates.

From 1954 onward, James resided mainly in the Caribbean, invited back by Eric Williams, the leader of an independent nationalist Trinidadian movement. Controversy surrounded their alliance, as James remarked in *Party Politics in the West Indies* (1962). He also wrote *Beyond a Boundary* (1963), an analysis of cricket in the context of the anti-imperialist struggle. Retiring from active political life in 1962, James moved to London, where he spent his time tackling the relationship between art and life, discussing Shakespeare, Michelangelo, Picasso, Pollock, and "Three Black Women Writers" (1981). As well as offering black feminists an alternative to white Euroamerican **feminism**, James' work inspired black American activists/intellectuals during the 1960s and 1970s. James the novelist, journalist, **Marxist**, Pan-Africanist, Americanist, and populist guided many black political/intellectual figures, including those who visited him at his home in London until his death in 1989. Engagement with the Jamesian oeuvre involves both celebration and critique, with many of his critics honoring him as one of the twentieth century's most outstanding figures.

The Jamesian oeuvre is often divided into four parts, according to geography, history, and intellectual production: Trinidad and literature; England and *The Black Jacobins*; American civilization and *Mariners, Renegades and Castaways;* the Caribbean and *Beyond a Boundary*. Certain postcolonial themes recur in James' works: the language/experiences of ordinary black people and their capacity for self-emancipation; the relationship between race and class; the possibility of destabilizing oppressive regimes from within; a critical negotiation with powerful ideologies (imperialism, Marxism, and black nationalism); a complex, if not universalizing, vision of the dialectical interrelatedness of past/present, global/local, and metropolis/periphery.

Following a "bookish" childhood, James involved himself with Trinidadian artists/intellectuals. He embarked on a literary career, writing short stories like "La Davina Pastora" (1927) and "Triumph" (1929). These stories, together with his novel *Minty Alley* (1936), voiced new possibilities for **anglophone** literature. The voices that James represents reflect the diversity of Caribbean life. For instance, "Triumph" opens with an educated narrator commenting on the barrack yard with an insight into its imperialist history. This narrator also has knowledge of metropolitan culture, and his reference to Kipling and Shaw accords them significance in a way that also seeks to promote Caribbean popular culture. Offering a realistic representation of unadorned human life, "Triumph" describes the changing fortunes of Mamitz, a woman who resists destitution via the commodification of her sexuality. Similarly, the Nurse in *Minty Alley* succeeds by appealing to her "whiteness" and to her professional status. Both texts problematize orthodox Marxism by representing the ways in which it is complicated by **ethnicity** and by gender. Moreover, barrack-yard women are revealed to self-empower through compliance with dominant ideologies—patriarchy, capitalism, and imperialism. This complex negotiation; which highlights both the benefits and the limitations of Western discourses, is also evidenced in relation to language. The **subaltern** voices in James' fiction are in the vernacular, contrasting with the Standard English of his narrators. A radical response to this mode of writing understands it as establishing, if not celebrating, Caribbean cultural distinctiveness via the vernacular. Further, rigid aesthetic categories are problematized by literature that voices the ordinary people. The use of Standard English resists the colonialist assumption as regards the unenlightened colonized, along with potentially signifying the latter's equality with the colonizer. The possibility of surpassing the colonizer is also promoted, which is a key point in James' *The Black Jacobins*.

James' change in emphasis from literature to politics was enabled by his move to England, where he published *The Life of Captain Cipriani* (1932) and *The Case for West Indian Self-Government* (1933). Developing his political interests through theory (Marxist books) and practice (working-class Lancashire), James also raised the issue of the black struggle, particularly in relation to Pan-Africanism. He responded to the emphasis in both Marxism and Pan-Africanism of remembering the past, typically in opposition to the capitalist/imperialist misrepresentation of history. Critical of the victim stereotype in relation to blacks, *The Black Jacobins* discusses the French and the San Domingo (i.e., prerevolutionary Haiti) revolutions, ultimately centering revolutionary consciousness in nonmetropolitan cultures. Europe as bringing about enlightenment (liberty/equality) is called into question, and its revolutionary ideals are revealed to mean more to the black masses, both past and present. *The Black Jacobins* undermines the authority accorded to a white European intelligentsia by imperialism, along with challenging those Marxists, Trotsky among them, who regard race (and popular culture) as marginal to the revolution. As James sees it, the black struggle requires a more critical negotiation by Marxism, although this is not to privilege race over class. Rather than adhering to binary logic, *The Black Jacobins* negotiates a dialectical relationship between race and class; it also proceeds dialectically regarding France/San Domingo, proletariat/slave, colonizer/colonized, and past/present. Noting similarities and differences between the two revolutions, together with the differences among the revolutionaries in San Domingo, James is also vigilant as regards the dilemma that confronts powerful figures, particularly those in the political domain. For example, the French model of revolutionary leadership adopted by Toussaint L'Ouverture in San Domingo brought him both success and failure, empowering him to mobilize the black masses as well as to forget them and what they represented— a postcolonial nation. James' complex perspective is discussed by Said, who praises his critical understanding of both Western imperialism and black nationalism.

The problem with power, whether in the hands of Toussaint, Kwame Nkrumah, or Captain Ahab, is that it often stifles the creative spontaneity of the populace. James identifies bureaucracy as generating dictatorships in San Domingo and Ghana and on the *Pequod*. His return to literature through a study of Melville is not at the expense of politics because *Mariners, Renegades and Castaways* understands *Moby Dick* as allegorically representing power relations in both Russia and America. What is also significant about this book is that James appeals to it in order to avoid deportation, arguing that his celebration of Melville demonstrates an unwavering commitment to American civilization. James has been criticized for his "frothy" espousal of liberalist rhetoric and for his silence regarding "the topic of genocide, territorial theft, and cultural degradation of the native populations" (Ross in Farred 1996, 76, 80). While it is important not to bypass these criticisms, James' commitment to the American populace is also worth considering. He claims that black nationalism within America, a contradictory situation that has been criticized for not conceding black autonomy, represents a revolutionary force in both metropolitan and colonial cultures. Radicalism is accorded to black Americans because they are doubly oppressed by racist/capitalist ideologies. Moreover, their theaters, dances, churches, and writings evidence black radicalism. This understanding of popular activities as a site of **resistance** is also discussed by James in relation to the American culture industry. In his opinion, the popular arts reveal the consumer's independence, albeit by refusing blatant propaganda from the producer. Locked into a modern version of the master–slave dialectic, the consumer and the producer participate in an agreement that accords a degree of power to both.

The radical potential of popular activities, meaning cricket, is discussed in more detail in James' *Beyond a Boundary*. Resonating with cultural significance, cricket generates a number of postcolonial interpretive possibilities. Along with acknowledging the part played by sports in establishing colonial authority, *Beyond a Boundary* discusses Caribbean politics, with major Trinidadian cricket clubs representing race, caste, and class divisions. For example, James affiliated himself with Maple, a brown-skinned, middle-class club. This affiliation brought him up against Shannon, a black, lower-middle-class club, which outplayed Maple in both cricket and politics. Shannon also "showed" metropolitan cricket teams, representing the interests of all black Trinidadians. This movement from national to international politics renders *Beyond a Boundary* postcolonial in the sense that it understands cricket as analogically representing colonizer/colonized relations. Cricket is organized according to a code that grants ultimate authority to the umpire/empire, determining the experiences of those inside/outside the field of play. The rigid hierarchies involved apparently render "cricket" useless in the anti-imperialist struggle. However, James draws attention to its misrepresentation by the colonizer, a misrepresentation that has its basis in brutal discrimination. Committed to white supremacy, the English evidence their suspect ideological commitments by excluding the best men from captaincy because they are black, replacing them with incompetent whites. In so doing, the colonizer fails to live up to its own standard of fair play, a standard that, in part, justifies its colonization of an "unenlightened" Caribbean. Moreover, this failure enables critique on the part of the colonized, who are also revealed to be properly committed to equality in both cricket and politics. In a Caliban-type gesture that perhaps most adequately represents his approach, James appropriates "cricket" in order to bring about postcolonialism. It is possible to understand appropriation as indicating compliance with Western discourses, perhaps representing an early, if not a naive, stage in postcolonial studies. However, the recognition of inescapable imperialist structures and their contradictory capacity to enable/disable also resonates with a more recent analysis, namely, deconstruction, which is one of the many directions open to those currently debating the Jamesian oeuvre.

Further Reading: G. Farred 1996; A. Grimshaw 1992; P. Henry and P. Buhle 1992.

Bella Adams

Tahar Ben Jelloun   Moroccan-born Tahar Ben Jelloun (1944–   ) is a poet, novelist, essayist, and journalist. He has written for the French newspaper *Le Monde*. In 1977 he completed a doctoral dissertation in social psychiatry, from which he wrote his first novel, *La plus haute des solitudes*. Subsequently, he published numerous novels, among which the best known are *La réclusion solitaire* (1976), *Moha le fou, Moha le sage* (1978), *La prière de l'absent* (1981), *L'Écrivain public* (1983), *L'Enfant de sable* (1985), and *La nuit sacrée*, which won the prestigious French literary prize, Le Prix Goncourt, in 1987. His study *Hospitalité française* (1984) scrutinizes the difficulties that the North African community faces in France. This work particularly accentuates the social responsibilities of the host country toward the immigrant community as well as those of the immigrant who comes to reside and work there.

Ben Jelloun is noted for his exploration of the margins of two worlds: one French, the other Moroccan. In order to develop his unique perspectives on these two historically and culturally conflicting worlds, the author creates a third space—a space of mediation—from which to write. His stories often weave narratives of marginal figures who, like himself, do not fit in, but are repudiated, handicapped, or different from the rest of society. Often these individuals are women who seek to tell their life stories. Ben Jelloun's most famous novels, *L'enfant de sable* and its sequel, *La nuit sacrée*, are told through a woman's voice. Because the leading figure is female, she falls prey to the worst atrocities of Moroccan (Maghrebian) society. The author's ultimate goal, however, is to find a space of empowerment for himself and his feminine character. For Ben Jelloun, crossing the gender line also aids in metaphorically mediating the fine line between reality and the imaginary or between the modern Western world and the Moroccan world of legend and myth. Both these worlds constantly push at the author's pen, forcing him to negotiate between these two very different spaces. Ahmed/Zahra is his mediating character. She is left in the in-between of exile to search for her identity. Both novels depict the painful struggle of one woman to gain access to her identity, sexuality, and femininity. Born as the eighth girl child to a wealthy Moroccan merchant in the first novel, *L'enfant de sable*, Ahmed is forced by her father to "become" a boy in order to provide an heir to the family's fortune. Her masculine role condemns her to an existence pulled between both the masculine and the feminine. Under her mask, she is never quite man, nor can she ever be totally woman. The desire to discover her true **femininity** and to shed her masculine mask eventually forces her to embark on a quest. This quest is followed up in *La nuit sacrée*, which further explores the theme of the heroine's duality. In the final scenes of this second novel, Zahra finally transcends the material world when she enters an illuminated paradise of true feminine identity, accepted by her peers for who she really is.

Metaphorically, these two novels offer the reader a study of body politics while alluding to the hermetically sealed roles of gender within the parameters of Muslim society. As the author indicates in his novels, gender politics define and shape every aspect of feminine and masculine space within Moroccan culture. Therefore, how one defines oneself individually as a woman or as a man depends very much on one's predefined space within the larger social whole. These spaces are concretely indicated and usually leave no room for transgression. Yet the author's characters do find ways to transgress. This is perhaps why Ben Jelloun has repeatedly been shunned by his fellow countrymen and women as too reactionary, "Westernized," and even corrupt. These issues have pushed Ben Jelloun to the margins of his own society.

The narrative freedom that the author establishes in *L'enfant de sable* also generates a significant amount of intellectual questioning. Stylistically, blending the narrative mythic time of Maghrebian folktales with the French language leads the author to create an a-centered narrative. This genre of **narrative** is found on the borders of all preestablished norms. Through this freedom, the author is able to tackle fundamental problems such as how to reconcile **identity** and status with regard to his culture, society, and history.

Ben Jelloun's *L'enfant de sable* and *La nuit sacrée* demonstrate more than just the author's fascination with the feminine side of his self. They are studies of a marginalized position in society, or a critique of the politics of exclusion. They are personal reflections of a **francophone** author who scrutinizes the intricacies of being an intellectual, author, and critic in exile. In Ben Jelloun's literary space exists his own politics of mediation through which culture, identity, race, and language are transcended to seek out a truer reality wherein ideologies centered around femininity, masculinity, Islam, the East, and the West may be negotiated.

Further Reading: J. Erickson 1993; L. Ouzgane 1997.

Valérie Orlando

K

Cheikh Hamidou Kane (1928–) Senegalese governmental administrator and novelist—author, most notably, of the 1961 book *Ambiguous Adventure*— Cheikh Hamidou Kane was born 3 April 1928, in Matam, in northeastern Senegal along the Senegal River. Kane was born into an aristocratic Islamic Tukuleur family—one of the groups of West African Fulani (or Peul or Pulaar) peoples along the southern Sahara. Until age ten, Kane attended Qur'anic school and spoke only his maternal Peul. He then attended the local French school and traveled to the capital, Dakar, where he earned his *baccalauréat* at the French lycée (high school) in 1948. In 1952 Kane traveled to Paris, earning a *licènse* (master's degree) in law and philosophy in 1956, followed by a two-year course in administration from the École Nationale de France d'Outre Mer (French National School for Overseas Territories). Kane's immersion in the French educational system, beginning in his Matam youth, gave him a deep sense of the gap between the traditional and Islamic values of his upbringing and what he saw as the West's more technocratic, economic, materialist, nonspiritual values. Feeling this divide sharply in Paris, Kane wrote his great philosophical novel *L'Aventure ambiguë* (Ambiguous Adventure) soon after arriving, though it was not published until 1961.

In 1960 Kane returned to newly independent Senegal and began a thirty-year career in public administration. From 1960 to 1962 he was governor of the Thiès region just east of Dakar, and in 1962–1963 served as director in Senegal's Ministry of Development and Planning. Subsequently, Kane worked from 1963 to 1972 as a senior administrator with the United Nations Emergency Fund and United Nations International Children's Emergency Fund (UNICEF) in Lagos, Nigeria; Abidjan, Ivory Coast; and Dakar. Since then, he has had senior positions in Senegal: director in the offices of Youth and Development (1972–1973), chairman of the Development Authority for Shipyard and Port Facilities of Dakar (1977–1978), minister of industrial development (1978–1983), deputy minister for African economic integration (1983–1988), minister of commerce and crafts (beginning in 1993), and in 1999 minister of defense.

Kane's highly practical career as a postcolonial administrator seems to have little connection with (or perhaps has resolved) his masterful *Ambiguous Adventure*. The novel is set in the land of the Diallobé—the region in which Kane grew up—at a time of growing French colonial influence. The plot centers on young Samba Diallo, the honored son of the aristocratic leader of the Diallobé (who is known in the novel simply as *le chevalier*, or the Knight). Deeply religious, young Samba, an introspective, philosophical, often sad boy, is subjected to the extreme physical and spiritual rigors of his Islamic instructor, Thierno. Early in the text, his community, after a wrenching discussion, decides that Samba will shift to the local French school for a practical education ("to learn to join wood to wood"), in order that their community might best survive the colonial regime. Samba and his father engage in deep conversation with Jean and Paul Lacroix—a classmate of Samba's and his colonial administrator father.

The story then shifts to Paris, where Samba Diallo continues his studies, conversations, and reflections. Among his Paris contacts are the hospitable white French family of pastor Paul Martial and their daughter Lucienne, a classmate of Samba's; and an older West Indian lawyer, Pierre-Louis and his family— especially their daughter, Adèle. Toward the end of the story, Samba's father writes and tells Samba to return home. Samba does, but his former Qur'anic teacher has died, and Samba himself seems to have lost his faith. In an impressionistically rendered scene at the end of the book, Samba is killed at his teacher's grave site by a man known as the Fool, who long ago lost his mind in French military service.

Ambiguous Adventure was a success from the start, winning the Grand Prix Littéraire d'Afrique Noire in 1962. It has been translated into nearly twenty languages, has been continuously in print (and in print in English since 1963), and is one of the most studied and taught works in all modern African literature. The text has succeeded in spite of, or perhaps because of, its demanding, lyrical, philosophical style. In French it is technically a récit (story) rather than a novel (*roman*). Most of the book consists either of deep conversation or of reflections on the state of Samba's mind, rather than action or social commentary. The novel's principal contribution has been its rendering of the colonized *mind*: the ways in which colonialism operates not only on the body but also on the spirit. In Kane's words, "behind the gunboats, the clear gaze of the Most Royal Lady had seen the new school"—the colonial school that "bewitches the soul" and "makes conquest permanent."

Since its publication, critics have discussed *Ambiguous Adventure*'s Sufi Islamic themes, its strong portrayal of women, its portrayal of the dilemmas of the European-educated (sometimes called "been-to") African, its account of deep colonial power and its aftermath, its universal appeal as a story of vexed youth, and its classical style. Less positive comments have noted its false binarism between Africa and the West, or the spiritual versus the material, and its lack of overt political or protest content. As an enduring classic in the postcolonial era, it reminds one that mere "flag independence" does not result in total liberation.

In 1995 Kane published his second novel, *Les Gardiens du Temple*, written from 1963 to 1967 but withheld based on his own political judgment. The book, less successful than his first, begins before independence, describing the conflict between tradition and modernity in a village's burial of its *griots* (oral historians) upright in baobab trees. The narrative moves to the postindependence capital (the country is unnamed but resembles Senegal), where a highly Westernized son of the village becomes president, loses touch, provokes a popular revolt, and is deposed by an honorable army. This text has not yet fully been assessed by critics.

Further Reading: K. Ansell-Pearson, B. Parry, and J. Squires 1997; A. Coulson 1997.

David Chioni Moore

Jamaica Kincaid   Born Elaine Potter Richardson in Antigua in 1949 to parents whom she describes as "poor ordinary people" (Selwyn Cudjoe interview 1989), the Caribbean writer Jamaica Kincaid experienced firsthand the daily inequalities of colonial domination, which she continues to explore in her autobiographically based fiction. Kincaid's early novel *Annie John* (1985), for instance, narrates events similar to those in Kincaid's youth, which was marked by a tumultuous relationship with her dominating mother and dissatisfaction with Antigua's intellectually stifling colonial culture.

Like many colonized people, Kincaid saw self-exile as an escape. In 1965, as later fictionalized in *Lucy* (1990), Kincaid moved to the United States, briefly working as an au pair while continuing her education. In 1974 she began to write for *The New Yorker*, where she first published many of the stories collected into her first book, *At the Bottom of the River* (1983) and where she continued as a staff writer until 1995. After her twenty-year absence from Antigua, Kincaid first revisited her island home in 1986, an experience reproduced in her 1997 novel, *My Brother*. That trip also inspired *A Small Place* (1988), an essay condemning British colonization, tourism, and Antiguan postcolonial self-rule with such vehemence that Kincaid was briefly prohibited from visiting the island. Much of Kincaid's work concerns interactions of the family, particularly the mother–daughter bond, which critics and Kincaid herself interpret as allegorical of imperial relations. As Kincaid explains, "[T]he mother I was writing about was really Mother Country" (Ferguson 1994). Kincaid further explores this imperial legacy in her fiction by meditating on the postcolonial themes of race, language, education, and landscape.

Though race factors into all of Kincaid's works, *The Autobiography of My Mother* (1996), which juxtaposes Afro-Caribbean, Carib Indian, and Anglo-Caribbean racial combinations, provides her most provocative comments on the complex racial stratification and amalgamation of the Caribbean. The narrative links characters' racial identification with their colonial and social status. Xuela, the novel's protagonist, like Kincaid's own mother, is the daughter of a Carib Indian mother and a half-Scot, half-African father. Kincaid's repeated remarks on the red hair and pink skin of Xuela's father, for instance, tie his mixed race to his economic success, dishonesty, and complicity within the colonial system. Similarly, Xuela's Carib-Indian mother's death symbolically repeats the fate of the marginalized and extinct Carib race.

Kincaid also examines the linguistic mix of the postcolonial Caribbean by comparing the Antiguan Afro-Caribbean patois with Anglo-American English. In *My Brother* (1997) particularly, Kincaid juxtaposes her own Anglo-American speech with the dialect of her dying brother. She admits that their linguistic dissimilarity also marked social barriers, for Kincaid's difficulty understanding her brother's patois is matched by his mocking dismissal of her Anglo-American English. As well, Kincaid's writing style, her use of repetition, listing, and dialect, reproduces the rhythms of the Caribbean voice for her Western readers.

Through her fictionalized accounts of her youth, Kincaid scrutinizes colonial education, as well. In *Lucy,* for instance, she relates her anger at British-imposed norms through the bitter memory of being forced to memorize Wordsworth's "Daffodils," though as a child of the tropics she had never seen a daffodil. In *Annie John,* Kincaid describes how she resisted that colonial education by defacing a textbook illustration of Columbus. Though education often equals inculturation in Kincaid's work, reading often symbolizes freedom, just as the dilapidated library in *A Small Place* becomes a symbol of potential, squandered by the corrupt postcolonial Antiguan government.

Also important in Kincaid's work is landscape, for she often contrasts spaces (feminine domestic interiors and masculine public spaces, her Antiguan and American homes, the tropical island landscape with the New England metropolis and idealized English countryside) to highlight postimperial social and economic inequalities. She returns to the garden as a symbol of empire in her recent collection *My Garden* (1999). "The garden," Kincaid explains in an earlier interview, "has a peculiar side to it, a qualifying side. For instance, most of the nations that have serious gardening cultures also have, or had, empires" (*Snell* 1997, 30). Kincaid continues to live in the United States, in Vermont, with her husband and children, currently teaching at Harvard University.

Further Reading: H. Bloom 1998; L. Paravisin-Gebert 1999.

Rebecca Weaver

Ahmadou Kourouma Born in 1927 in Boundiali in the Ivory Coast, Kourouma received his early education in Guinea and Mali. After serving in the French army, he trained as an actuary in Lyon, graduating in 1959, and has since held important positions as a banking and insurance executive in Paris and Abidjan. He has published two novels, separated by a gap of twenty-two years.

In *Les Soleils des indépendances* (1968; *The Suns of Independence*, 1982), both the precolonial past and the postcolonial present are the targets of bleak political satire. For the two one-party states straddling the ancient Malinke kingdom of Horodugu, independence means only taxes and dues, forced labor camps, famine, and loss of trade. In the capitals the French live on in neon-lit neocolonial luxury, while street-sellers are attacked by hordes of ferocious beggars. The last of Horodugu's legitimate Dumbuya rulers is the protagonist Fama, an aging ex-trader and pariah who lives by scrounging alms at funerals. Demoted by French colonialism and ignored by one-party socialism, Fama's ancestral kingdom has now shrunk to a few decrepit huts and starving villagers. Nevertheless, he nurses grandiose aspirations to party office and, with an odd mixture of degraded hauteur and comic hubris, continues to affect the status of a proud Dumbuya descendant, scorning all "sons of slaves," whether they be colonial or party officials.

Fama's vision of independence, though an unreliable one warped by wounded vanity and delusions of grandeur, focuses Kourouma's political satire on one-party regimes, one of which forces farmers to abandon harvests for "self-help" bridge-building projects, while another vindictively backdates opponents' party dues for the period spent in opposition. Problematically, Kourouma's sardonic, bantering modern narrator alternately indulges and derides Fama's dynastic beliefs, thus coloring large stretches of the narrative with an obsolescent and increasingly irrelevant worldview, according to which approaching calamities are always heralded by omens and can be averted by seeking out the correct propitiation rites. Thus, a plotting minister could have survived an antigovernment conspiracy by the timely sacrifice of an ox, and Fama himself would not have embarked from his village upon a journey to imprisonment and death if he had heeded the priest's inauspicious omens and the ancient prophecies of the Dumbuyas' demise. The signal for the politicians whose dull officialdom has "unmagicked" Africa is that they need communal early warning systems, modern equivalents of the fetish, to divine their people's unrest and prescribe remedial action. Kourouma's portrait of traditional life is far from nostalgic. But Fama's death (devoured by the sacred crocodile) and his undying faith in the vitality of his royal ancestors are invested with a tragic dignity; and Horodugu, with its ritual hunting lore and oracular oral wisdom, remains a resilient kernel of African identity that pre- and postdates Islam, colonialism, and the **nation**-state. Something of it will still be there when the suns of independence have passed away.

In his long-awaited second novel, *Monnè, outrage et défis* (1990; *Monnew*, 1993), Kourouma switches the focus from postcolonial to colonial history and to the world that Fama has lost. The novel traces the changes wrought by French colonialism in the fictional Malinke kingdom of Soba and the different aspects of *monnew*—shame, dishonor, humiliation—that its people are forced to endure. Its absolute ruler, Djigui Keita, is a proud, dignified, and devoutly Muslim monarch who, in the course of his long reign, is transformed into a numinous, almost supernatural figure. His spiritual elevation is, however, accompanied by demotion and decline at the political level, with the result that his death at the extreme age of 125 marks the end of the order that he embodies. Djigui is, in fact, blindly complicit with colonialism, allowing himself to be co-opted into French supremacist regimes and his people to be siphoned off to European wars, while failing to repair the inner dissensions that prevent united Soban opposition to imperial conquest. Paradoxically, his royal griots who keep the Keitan dynasty alive in legend hasten its historical demise because, in their roles as intermediaries, they misinterpret negotiations between Djigui and the French administrators. Subsequently, the novel develops a self-conscious preoccupation with the use of language and the diglossic dilemmas of the translator who interprets a conquered culture to a conquering one. *Monnew* is an altogether more speculative, disengaged work than Kourouma's first book, lacking its satiric energy and written at a greater historical distance from its subject, but it remains a complex and strikingly original novel.

Further Reading: K. Ogungbesan 1979; H. Zell, C. Bundy, and V. Coulon 1983.

Derek Wright

L

Jacques Lacan. *See* Psychoanalysis

George Lamming George Lamming was born in Barbados in 1927. He attended school on the island, partly on a scholarship that allowed him access to a traditional British-modeled education. Leaving Barbados in 1950, Lamming settled in London, where he worked for the BBC radio and began to write professionally. He has since moved back to the Caribbean and spends his time between North America and Barbados. He has written a total of six novels, as well as a collection of nonfictional essays, *The Pleasures of Exile* (1960). In addition, he has written poetry and short stories.

Although renowned primarily for his fictional work, and in particular, for his rewriting of canonical texts of colonial literature such as *The Tempest*, Lamming's influence reaches well beyond the realm of literary studies. The inclusion of complete or edited sections of his work in a number of recent readers of postcolonial theory shows how Lamming's reputation has settled equally successfully within postcolonial academic critiques of colonialism. Significantly, his novels were at the forefront of a theorizing of the ideological structures of a Western imperial paradigm only much later taken up by postcolonial academics.

Lamming is now recognized as one of the preeminent symbols of a contemporary search for a Caribbean sense of **national** belonging. Indeed, few Caribbean writers are as overtly identified with their region's struggle for freedom and independence from colonialism as Lamming. At once angry and articulate, lyrical and political, his work reflects the Caribbean subject's schizophrenic notion of selfhood in its most visible complexity. Central to the concerns of his novels is the psychological conflict between selves that simultaneously attract and repel each other, illustrating the predicament that **Derek Walcott** expresses so poignantly in his verse.

Thus, in his first novel, *In the Castle of My Skin* (1953), Lamming offers one of the most insightful critiques of the effect of colonial ideologies on the colonized. Set in Creighton Village, the novel is considered a classic of postcolonial writing in English. Lamming uses the boy "G." to offer a candid, but sophisticated, depiction of the "marking and splitting" (**Homi Bhabha** 1984) experienced by the colonized. Indeed, his treatment of issues as deeply imbricated in the European colonial project as race, class, gender, education, and history writing makes him a more radical critic than postcolonial theorists such as **Cabral**, **Fanon**, or Memmi. Faced with this element of his work, critics often settle for noting that it is difficult and complex.

But while *In the Castle of My Skin* accounts for much of his reputation as a postcolonial intellectual, it was primarily with *The Pleasures of Exile*, a semi-theoretical work that reflected a preoccupation with the role of the intellectual in a changing society and as a Caribbean (colonized) subject, that Lamming established himself as a "household" name within postcolonial studies, for here Lamming undertakes what is possibly one of the earliest attempts to theorize the writing emanating from the formerly colonized territories. The essays anticipate some of the fundamental tenets of postcolonial critical theories and reveal Lamming's engagement with the anticolonial struggle in a way that the novels are unable to do. In their dialectical complexity, the essays strive, if not always successfully, to go beyond the irretrievably polarized stances of a Hegelian master–slave dichotomy intrinsic to the colonial enterprise. Conscious of the bitterness of tone that permeates some of the essays, reflected primarily in the subversive irreverence of a reading of *The Tempest* that places the ability to act with the figure of Caliban, Lamming has noted that the figure of Caliban is in his narratives symbolic of the Caribbean subject.

Recent criticism of Lamming's novels has focused on some of the gaps and silences at the heart of his treatment of the colonial presence in the Caribbean (Pouchet-Paquet 1992; Jonas 1996; Nair 1996; Simoes da Silva 2000), for in Lamming's postcolonial society the female character, for one, is almost always synonymous with a danger to, or the potential for violence against, the Caribbean nation. She acts as the site of an ambiguous relationship with society that places her *outside of*, or *beyond*, the discourse of **nation(alism)** that impels the works. While such a stance needs to be placed within the wider context of all writing of the first generation of nation-building, it highlights the paradoxical nature of a narrative in which a genuinely original and powerful critique of colonialism exists side by side with a bleakness of vision through which the portrait of the Caribbean is often one of despair and disillusion.

Concerned as he is with the ongoing influence of colonialism on the colonized's psyche, Lamming refuses to foretell the death of colonialism. Rather, in his fiction and his nonfictional writings, Lamming stresses that for the Caribbean subject the colonial encounter was/is a *lived*, ongoing experience. Ironically, it is precisely through this focus on a stance not unlike **Antonio Gramsci**'s own "interregnum" that Lamming ultimately falls back into a somewhat restricted and potentially despairing view of the Caribbean. In novels such as *The Emigrants* (1954), *Of Age and Innocence* (1958), and *Season of Adventure* (1960), he revisits time and again themes of nationalist oppression and chauvinism. After an interregnum of his own, in *Water with Berries* (1971) Lamming openly addresses the one issue central to the whole of his work, the dyad Prospero/Caliban. Significantly, in addition to a recognition that the conflict between colonizer and colonized would be resolved only through dialogue, the novel was also the last one of his works to be set in San Cristobal, the fictional island in which four of his six novels are set.

As in earlier works, in his last novel to date, *Natives of My Person* (1972), Lamming once again undertakes a deeply nuanced examination of the mechanics of colonialism. To the extent that the novel now seeks to reinvent the conditions for a possible encounter between the Old and the New Worlds and through its thoughtful treatment of gender relations, *Natives of My Person* comes closest to presenting Lamming's newfound sense of hopefulness for the future. Perhaps typically, however, the narrative goes on to betray the same sense of ambiguity and ambivalence that characterized his four "middle" novels. While Lamming is often quoted as saying that he is now engaged in the writing of a novel dealing with the events of the 1930s in Barbados, the one gap that he suggests his work contains, it would seem unlikely that he should once again find the rationalized anger that so inspired his first work of fiction and his nonfictional work. Lamming's continued struggle with the novel as a genre, especially with its ability to transcend the cultural and political baggage of colonialism, demonstrates one of the most poignant assertions he has made: "The colonial experience . . . is a continuing psychic experience that has to be dealt with long after the actual situation formally 'ends' " (Kent 1993, 92).

Further Reading: F. Birbalsingh 1996; S. Nair 1996.

Tony Simoes da Silva

Language. *See* Center; Nation; Ngũgĩ wa Thiong'o

Law, International International law developed from medieval European practices of treaty agreement and customary relations that focused mostly on territorial disputes and treatment of nationals abroad. In the twentieth century the League of Nations, United Nations, and International Court of Justice (ICJ) became the primary organs for the implementation of international law, an institutionalization that corresponds with movement away from mercantile and militaristic forms of colonialism. Increasingly, international law, whose principles are described in the ICJ Statute as those recognized by "civilized nations," has taken interest in a self-determination that is more broadly defined than the purely imperial notion of national sovereignty.

By the end of the nineteenth century, Europe had divided much of Asia and most of Africa. The West African Conference of Berlin (1884–1885) enlisted the "rationality" of international law into the service of colonialism. Under the pretense of curtailing the slave trade and "opening up" Africa to "free trade," the fourteen nations convened in Berlin authorized Belgium's claim to the Congo and developed guidelines for the "scramble" for Africa. The "General Act of the Conference of Berlin" supplemented older forms of military conquest and mercantile colonization with legal mechanisms establishing the use of consensual international law among the "conquerors" to divide up colonial territories.

Disavowing territorial gain as an objective in World War I, the victors developed the League of Nations' mandate system for distributing the holdings of the Ottoman and German empires. Mandates represented an Allied compromise that balanced increasing anticolonial sentiment with the "need" to dispossess the vanquished of their colonies. Under Covenant Article 22, the league developed a three-tiered system of mandates, grouping territories according to their perceived capacity for self-rule: Class A mandates (former Turkish colonies, including Iraq, Lebanon, Palestine, and Syria distributed between France and England, were determined to be nearly self-sufficient and slated for "early independence"); Mandate B territories (Germany's African colonies, divided among France, Belgium, and England, consisted of Ruanda-Urundi, Tanganiyka, and parts of Togoland and the Cameroons); Class C mandates (from the ex-German empire, were incorporated as territory of the new colonial power and included Southwest Africa [given to South Africa], New Guinea [Australia], Western Somoa [New Zealand], western Pacific Islands [Japan], and Nauru [Australia, England, and New Zealand]). The mandate oversight committee had minimal power; instead, the system instituted a new form of colonial administration answerable, in theory, to the rule of international law.

Like the mandate system, the 1946 United Nations' (UN) trusteeship system emerged from the experience of war. Again disclaiming the goal of territorial gain, the World War II Allies' trusteeship system enabled the redistribution of the holdings of Germany, Italy, and Japan, including Togo, the British and French Cameroons, Somaliland, Tanganiyka, Western Somoa, Ruanda-Urundi, New Guinea, Nauru, and Pacific Islands. Article 73 of the charter also provided for an oversight committee, most of whose duties were assumed by a Special Committee on **Decolonization**, formed in the wake of 1960s independence pressures. Operation of the Trusteeship Council was suspended in 1994 with formal independence of the remaining Trust Territory, Palau.

Responding to the rise of independence struggles in many of their holdings, members of the UN passed resolution 1514, "On the Granting of Independence to Colonial and Dependent Peoples," in 1960. Although resolved in the climate of superpower competition, the resolution implicitly recognized the discrepancy between "sovereignty" vaunted in the UN Charter and the practice of the trusteeship system and other forms of continued colonial subjugation. The resolution provided an international legal basis for independence claims.

With the addition of many recently independent countries and the growing influence of nongovernmental organizations, the UN has begun to address post-colonial independence and self-determination (described in the charter as the right of a people to associate itself as a state and of a state to choose its social, political, economic, and cultural systems) in a number of instruments. The "Right to Development," which recognizes national and individual sovereignty over resources, culture, and economic development, and the "Draft Declaration on **Indigenous Peoples**" reflect movement away from militaristic and mercantile forms of colonialism toward more ubiquitous cultural, legal, and economic **globalized** influence.

Further Reading: J. Fox 1992; M. Hardt and A. Negri 2000; T. Pakenham 1991.

Joseph Slaughter

Camara Laye (1928–1980)   Guinean novelist Camara Laye was born in Kouroussa, Upper Guinea, French West Africa, on 1 January 1928. (Laye's first or given name is Laye, and his family name is Camara, but he always referred to himself as "Camara Laye.") Laye was born into a lineage of Malinké (or Mande) blacksmiths and goldsmiths. During his childhood in Kouroussa and his mother's village Tindican, Laye absorbed the traditional, not heavily French-inflected culture. Laye attended Qur'anic and French schools in Kouroussa, and at age fourteen traveled to Conakry, Guinea's distant coastal capital, to continue his education. There he succeeded in his studies in auto mechanics. In 1947 he traveled to a cold, lonely Paris to continue his studies. There he also worked at the Simca automobile factory and in Les Halles food market and did further studies in engineering and toward the *baccalauréat*.

In 1953 he published his first novel, *L'Enfant noir* (*The Dark Child*, 1954—later titled *The African Child*), a gentle, touching, seemingly nonradical, highly autobiographical first-person story of a Guinean boy's life from his Kouroussa childhood, through development in Conakry, until his departure for France. The book won the Prix Charles Veillon in 1954. Laye quickly followed *L'Enfant noir* with the very different *Le Regard du roi* in 1954 (*The Radiance of the King*, 1956). This book reverses the classic colonial or postcolonial "been-to" theme of the African who travels to Europe, since it concerns a white man, Clarence, who goes to Africa to seek his fortune but fails and then embarks upon an increasingly strange and alienating quest toward the southern jungles in search of recognition by the African king. With these two novels, among the earliest major **francophone** African texts, Laye became famous worldwide as a chronicler of the colonial relation. He returned in 1956 first to Dahomey (now Benin), then to Ghana, and then to newly independent Guinea, where he held several government posts. In 1965, due to political troubles, he permanently left Guinea for Senegal. In 1966 his third novel, *Dramouss* (*A Dream of Africa*, 1968), appeared. *Dramouss* continues the autobiographical account of *L'Enfant noir* but is much more bitter, emphasizing a political critique of Guinea's corrupt leadership. It can be classified with the immediate postcolonial late-1960s wave of African "novels of disillusionment" (of which the best is **Ayi Kwei Armah**'s *The Beautyful Ones Are Not Yet Born*, 1968), which tell of the failed promises of the independences.

In 1970 Laye's wife, Marie, returned to visit Guinea and was imprisoned for seven years; in that time Laye took a second wife, for which Marie divorced him. He fell ill with a kidney infection in 1975 and received treatment in Paris. In 1978 his fourth and last work appeared: *Le Maître de la Parole—Kouma Lafôlô Kouma* (*The Guardian of the Word*, 1980). Its subtitle translates the main title into Malinké. This work renders the monthlong 1963 narration by the Malinké griot (traditional storyteller or oral historian) Babou Condé, of the famous Soundiata (or Sundiata or Sunjata) story: that of the legendary, powerful, crippled thirteenth-century founder of the empire of Old Mali. Laye terms himself "merely the modest transcriber and translator." Camara Laye died on 4 February 1980 in Dakar of his kidney infection, at age fifty-two.

Laye's postcolonial legacy is mixed. *L'Enfant noir* is recognized as one of the early international African literary landmarks, though it has been seen more as a "soft" account of colonial education than as a political critique of the French system. It remains widely taught, read, translated, and critiqued worldwide. *Le Regard du roi* has attracted almost as much critical attention by postcolonial scholars for its complex plot, nearly unique "white reversal," resonance with Kafka and other Euro-modernist writers, and more. *Dramouss*, perhaps due to its bitter account of the immediate postindependence era, is infrequently taught or read. *Le Maître de la parole*, finally, has received some postcolonial critique, particularly in the relation of literature to **orature** and history and the ways in which postcolonial authors renarrativize the precolonial African past. Unfortunately, a smaller number of specialists are qualified to work with such texts. Overall, Laye's four books make him one of the most interesting colonial/postcolonial bridge writers.

Further Reading: A. King 1980; S. Lee 1984.

David Chioni Moore

Liberation Theology Liberation theology constituted a paradigmatic shift from the mainstream Western tradition of theology, stressing a historicist, contextual, and existentially relevant approach to theological formulations. In moving away from an anthropological dimension and emphasizing a historical approach, it introduced a strong social justice component to theorizing and praxis in theology.

Liberation theology questioned the long-accepted dualisms between the spiritual and material, the sacred and the secular, religion and politics. It challenged the emphasis on transcendence in Christian teaching and in the life of the church and called for an incarnational theology rooted in the mundane and familiar.

Liberation theology introduced a new and radical biblical hermeneutic. Taking the central themes of liberation and salvation in the Christian gospel, it called for a reinterpretation of them. By locating theological reflection in the context of the "real situation of the poor" and by rereading the Bible in the light of the hermeneutical privileging of the poor, it developed a stringent critique of oppression and discrimination on the basis of class, race, and caste. Liberation theology aimed at transformation from economic and political oppression to political empowerment and economic development. It encouraged a moving away from an individualistic approach in matters of faith and urged societal freedom and communal solidarity. In the face of often instransigently oppressive regimes, it advocated revolutionary means in the quest for a just peace.

In questioning and rejecting the dominant theologies of the West, liberation theology also focused on religiocultural liberation. It called for reintegration of the core symbols of Christianity and encouraged the development of indigenous expressions of spirituality, culture, and identity.

While liberation theology was spearheaded in the 1970s by Latin American theologians who were strongly influenced by **Marxist** critique and drew attention to the enslavement to Western capital that many developing countries experienced, it evolved different dynamics and emphases. Some of the clusters of liberation theology are Third World liberation theology, black theology, African theology, Dalit theology, Minyung theology, and Asian theology, each with its own particular historical and discursive trajectories. Among its well-known proponents have been Gustavo Gutierrez in Latin America and Archbishop Desmond Tutu and Allan Boesak in South Africa.

Further influences of liberation theology are noteworthy here. In developing a relevant Christian ethic, it aimed at the liberation of nature/creation. In addition, it has influenced **feminist** liberation theology, which, drawing from feminist thinking as well, has highlighted the struggle against oppression resulting from patriarchy, sexism, and androcentrism. Liberation theology also made a significant impact on the development of critical pedagogy (and postcolonial **pedagogies** in general) through the work of **Paulo Freire**.

Further Reading: G. Gutierrez 1974; U. King 1994; B. Tlhagale and I. Mosala 1986.
Devarakshanam Betty Govinden

Shirley Geok-lin Lim Born in Malacca (then known as British Malaya) in 1944, Lim received a B.A. in English from the University of Malaya in Kuala Lumpur, Malaysia, in 1967 and a Ph.D. from Brandeis University in 1973. Since 1990 she has taught women's studies and English at the University of California, Santa Barbara. Both a celebrated creative writer and a critical theorist, she has focused her writing and research on the experiences of Asian and Asian American women.

Lim's first collection of poetry, *Crossing the Peninsula and Other Poems* (1980), was awarded the Commonwealth Poetry Prize. In that volume, as in subsequently published collections of poetry and short fiction, the theme of the *"peranakan"* woman predominates. Also known as Straits-born Chinese, Baba, or Nyonya, this ethnic group originated with Chinese men who were brought into Malaya by the British in the nineteenth century to work the tin mines and married Malay women, thus forming a distinctly syncretic culture. Like other segments of the ethnic Chinese population, the *peranakan* occupy a precarious niche in the economic structure and social fabric of postcolonial Malaysia.

Among the White Moon Faces (1996) contains Lim's reflections on coming-of-age as a semi-outsider in a **decolonizing** society and her subsequent experiences as an outsider in American society. Recounting her early years in the Roman Catholic convent school in Malacca, Lim reveals her first inklings of the racialized colonial society and the evident damage that a British colonial education did to her sense of herself as a Malaysian. She wonders, for instance, what role the Celt ballads, which formed a staple of the music curriculum, were expected to play in the students' futures. She asks, in retrospect, whether those melancholy airs were not intended to reproduce an imperial narrative of "the tragedy of failed Scottish and Irish **nationalism**" (68) as an admonition to independence-seeking youth.

Shortly before Lim departed for graduate school in the United States in 1969, Malaysia experienced several days of race riots directed against the ethnic Chinese. Lim's regret is palpable when she observes that these events dashed her hopes for "a multicultural egalitarian future" (1996, 136) and initiated a race-based scheme favoring Malays. Yet she acknowledges a continuing ambivalence concerning whether she ought to have remained to help define the Malaysian polity.

Further Reading: S. Lim 1995, 1996

Roger J. Jiang Bresnahan

Linguistic Nationalism.   *See* African-Language Literatures; Indian-Language Literatures

David Lloyd   David Lloyd's scholarship draws attention to Irish, Welsh, and U.S. multiethnic cultural forms of "self-estrangement" that speak to and against oppressive colonial and neocolonial nation-states. For Lloyd, aesthetic culture is not a discrete sphere of domination but an area for contestation by an outsider who can transform the material structures of exploitation. Denied access to traditional venues of power, "minoritarian-informed" aesthetics become a powerful vehicle for political intervention. Not surprisingly, Lloyd's studies often explore what it means to be the artist and/or intellectual who simultaneously stands within and outside a marginalized people. He asks questions such as, Can a postcolonial aesthetic critique and resist dominant structures of oppression when minoritarian intellectuals must stylize the voice of their people in order to be heard?

Lloyd throws his critical net far and wide. In his mapping of the contours of postcolonial culture, identity, and **nationalism**, he refers to nineteenth- and twentieth-century poets, writers, and intellectuals: For example, theories by John Stuart Mill, Immanuel Kant, Mikhail Bakhtin, and **Frantz Fanon** frame a discussion of Seamus Heaney's Irish nationalist poetics and/or Jean Genet's counterhegemonic, nonheteronormative thematics. To Lloyd, Samuel Beckett is less an angst-ridden modernist than a postcolonialist making a cultural intervention through a pared-down storytelling form that unsettles political subjectivity and promotes an antinationalist stance. Lloyd catalogs ways that such postcolonial intellectuals and/or writers deterritorialize "developmental narratives which perpetuate hegemonic culture."

Building on Frantz Fanon's work, David Lloyd continually questions whether it is possible for postcolonial subjectivity and **agency** to be truly representative and counterhegemonic. He is critical, for example, of Heaney for serving as an easily swallowed pill of Irish folk nationalism (even tribalism) that strips down an otherwise complex Irish-Anglo conflict. Yet, in the book *Anomalous States* (1993), Lloyd does describe an aesthetic culture that can work "outside the terms of representation." The postcolonial intellectual/writer can occupy a contestatory position by inhabiting "anomalous states" of multiple location (insider and outsider, colonial and postcolonial subject). Intellectuals inhabit these states by keeping their fingers on the popular pulse, using, yet not internalizing, the dominant institutions of the colonizing power. The popular street ballads and folk songs ("tonally inassimilable to nationalist culture") remain sites of aesthetic contestation because, as Lloyd writes, they "constantly exceed the monologic desire of cultural nationalism."

Lloyd's work on the complex relationship between the postcolonial intellectual and the formation of representative aesthetic counternarratives crosses the Atlantic in *The Nature and Context of Minority Discourse* (an anthology co-edited with Abdul JanMohamed, 1993). Here Lloyd is less concerned with tracing the postcolonial aesthetic spaces of Britain than with delineating a program for multiculturalist intervention in the United States. He seeks to make visible multicultural voices traditionally suppressed within a mainstream U.S. education system that relies on "monologic humanism" (his term) to naturalize hierarchies of difference. His essays focus on Asian American, Chicano/a, African American, and American Indian aesthetic cultures that share a self-avowed "antagonistic relationship to the dominant culture."

Lloyd's postcolonial-informed analysis seeks to complicate—and not dissolve—local and cultural difference and to construct bridges between different, multiple-layered, and constantly evolving "minoritarian" aesthetics as they come to exist within "univocal" (his term) nation-states. While he is centrally concerned with the role of the intellectual in the formation of **resistant** postcolonial cultural nationalisms, his work, taken as a whole, destabilizes Western intellectual traditions that favor the colonizer and deconstructs nation-state narratives that naturalize hierarchies of racial, sexual, and gendered difference.

Further Reading: F. Fanon 1980; A. JanMohamed 1983; A. JanMohamed and D. Lloyd 1990; D. Lloyd 1987, 1997; L. Lowe and D. Lloyd 1997.

Frederick Luis Aldama

Audre Lorde (1934–1992)   Audre Lorde, a self-described "Black Lesbian, Mother, Warrior, Poet," was born in New York City on 18 February 1934 to immigrant parents from Grenada and Barbados. She received her B.A. from Hunter College and her M.L.S. from Columbia University, after which she married Edward Ashley Rollins and had two children, Elizabeth and Jonathan. Lorde and Rollins divorced in 1970. In 1968, with help from a National Endowment for the Arts (NEA) grant, Lorde published her first collection of poetry, *The First Cities*. It took two more volumes of poetry for Lorde to be picked up by a major publisher, but in 1976 W. W. Norton published *Coal*, which brought Lorde a wider audience. Two years later, she published *The Black Unicorn*, a book of poetry exploring the relationship between the black diaspora and African mythology, generally regarded as her poetic masterpiece. Lorde published two prose works about her battle with breast cancer—*The Cancer Journals* (1981) and *A Burst of Light* (1986)—in an effort to break the silence surrounding this disease. Additional prose works include Lorde's "biomythography," titled *Zami: A New Spelling of My Name* (1982), and a collection of essays, *Sister Outsider* (1984), which has proven an important contribution to **feminist theory**. In addition to writing and teaching, Lorde cofounded Kitchen Table: Women of Color Press, which publishes and distributes works by women of color from various communities. Shortly before her death in St. Croix in 1992, she took the name Gamba Adisa (Warrior: She Who Makes Her Meaning Clear).

Prominent in many of Audre Lorde's works is the figure of the trickster, called, alternatively, Eshu and Afrekete. In *The Black Unicorn*, the poet glosses Eshu as MawuLisa's "youngest and most clever son"; in *Zami*, she writes that Afrekete is MawuLisa's "youngest daughter, the mischievous linguist, trickster, best-beloved, whom we all must become" (255). A figure of ambiguous sexuality, Eshu/Afrekete becomes, in Lorde's works, a means for the outsider—by virtue of gender, race, and sexual difference—to refuse to be silenced and rigidly categorized into fragments of identity. Kara Provost explains that just as Eshu acts as a translator between the gods and between gods and humans, Lorde attempts to communicate between groups that either cannot or do not interact, including blacks, whites, women, men, homosexuals, heterosexuals, working-class people, and academics (Provost 1995).

In *Zami*, the figure of Afrekete appears as the lover of the character Audre, allowing for a mythical doubling of the poet herself. Lorde calls *Zami* a biomythography, emphasizing both her use of a fictionalized identity and the importance of subjective interpretation in constituting reality (Dhairyam 1992). The title of the book is explained in its epilogue: *"Zami. A Carriacou name for women who work together as friends and lovers"* (255). It is an exploration of the poet's connections to women, all of the various sorts of connections that exist between women, beginning with the link between mother and daughter and coming together in the poet's sense of self.

Sister Outsider, whose title emphasizes Lorde's liminal position with regard to each of the groups with which she identifies, is a collection of essays that deal with sexism, racism, homophobia, and U.S. imperialism while examining the importance of poetry, the power of the erotic, and the utility of anger. In "Poetry Is Not a Luxury," Lorde describes the power of poetry to overcome the white European rationalist model, which emphasizes the rational and the outward at the expense of the emotional and the inward. "Poetry," she writes, "is the way we help give name to the nameless so it can be thought" (37); instead of, "I think therefore I am," Lorde posits, "I feel, therefore I can be free" (38). Throughout *Sister Outsider*, she emphasizes the need for new means of "relating across difference" (123). Without new modes of relating, she insists, people who are not white, heterosexual males will never be free of oppression in the form of racism, sexism, and homophobia, because "the master's tools will never dismantle the master's house" (123).

Further Reading: C. Birkle 1996; A. Keating 1996.

Jennifer C. Rodgers

Earl Lovelace   Earl Lovelace was born in Toco, Trinidad, on 13 July 1935. He studied at the Eastern Caribbean Institute of Agriculture and Forestry and Howard University. He has been editorial writer, reviewer, and columnist for the *Trinidad and Tobago Express* and has served as visiting writer and teacher at institutions in America and the West Indies. Unlike West Indian writers of an earlier generation, Lovelace remained at home to explore the physical and metaphysical contours of his complex society.

Lovelace's fiction is preoccupied with the problematic nature of West Indian **identity** in a postcolonial society crippled by chronic poverty, metropolitan neglect, and the psychic scars of slavery. The individual's sense of personhood is the hub around which his stories turn. Walter Castle, the embittered hero of *While Gods Are Falling* (1965), is the precursor of Lovelace's questing men, for example, the self-effacing Assivero of *The Schoolmaster* (1968), for whom manhood and self-esteem are crucial, and Aldrick, the hobbled dragon of *The Dragon Can't Dance* (1979). Walter Castle, whose impotence is suggested in his bandy legs, is a small man lost in a marginal society apparently deserted by God. His desire to be a person in a world that seems determined to deny him that elementary need is a strong theme in Lovelace's fiction. The residents of Calvary Hill, the slum setting of *The Dragon Can't Dance*, also feel abandoned, and they are obsessed with their identities in a community where a pervasive nihilism can be alleviated only by the escapist rite of carnival and furtive sex. But Aldrick's restlessness cannot be quelled by the annual carnival, which brings neither salvation nor self-affirmation. When, however, he discards his dragon persona, symbol of a sham personhood, he exposes his deeply buried self and achieves a new faith in the efficacy of his own inner strength.

Lovelace's women have a strong sense of purpose and are equally obsessed with wholeness and identity in a society infected with the virus of materialism and scorn for the African past. The hardy women of *The Schoolmaster* are prototypes of Eva, the stalwart wife and mother of *The Wine of Astonishment* (1982). Although her life is circumscribed by poverty and religious persecution, she is sustained by a resolute faith in her value as a person. Lovelace subtly parallels Eva's and her husband's determination to maintain their religious integrity, which is of a piece with their dignity and self- respect, with the persistence of nature's elemental forces.

In *Salt* (1996), which won the 1997 Commonwealth Writers Prize, Lovelace, using more than one narrative voice, explores the complexity of postcolonial contemporary West Indian society as it has been shaped and reshaped by Africa, Europe, and India. Out of these often antagonistic relationships, the novel suggests, a wholesome West Indianness can emerge.

If Lovelace's work has a central theme, it may well be the struggle of individuals to overcome the physical, moral, and psychic restrictions imposed upon them by colonialism and other systems that suppress self-affirmation.

Further Reading: H. Barratt 1984; E. O'Callaghan 1989.

Harold Barratt

Lusophone Literatures   The term describes a body of writing produced in Portuguese by writers working in Brazil or in African nations formerly colonized by Portugal. Largely used to refer to African and Brazilian literature, it alludes inevitably also to a common Portuguese cultural and linguistic heritage, a set of "pre-texts" (Slemon 1995) on which it is modeled, and to which often it addresses itself. Indeed, while it is arguable that lusophone African writing is less dependent on the revisionist impetus of its **anglophone** counterpart, there is, in verse especially, a focus on a soulful, quasi-melodramatic tone that betrays its emotional attachment to the language and "voice" of the sixteenth-century Portuguese poet, Luiz Vaz de Camões.

Of these two geographical locations highlighted, the Brazilian strand is by far the older and may be said to have begun with the very first piece of communication between the newly discovered colony and Portugal, the *Carta* sent by Pedro Alvares Cabral's scribe, Pero Vaz de Caminha, to the king in 1500. As Nunes notes, however, the first exemplar of *Brazilian* lusophone literature dates from much later, after the declaration of independence of 1822. Since then, Brazilian writing in Portuguese has grown dramatically: writers like Jorge Amado (b. 1912) and Clarice Lispector (1920–1977) are both widely appreciated in translation and are the focus of nuanced critical studies. Indeed, prior to the Nobel Prize being awarded to Portuguese novelist José Saramago in 1999, Amado was himself touted as equally deserving of that recognition. Similarly, in *Memórias Póstumas de Brás Cubas* (1881), Joaquim Maria Machado de Assis (1839–1908) wrote what is possibly one of the earliest "postmodern novels," as **Salman Rushdie** comments on the cover of its English translation.

Further, while male authors clearly outnumber female writers, in recent years Lispector and Nélida Pinón, in particular, have done much to shift the coordinates of that situation. Following in the footsteps of Júlia Lopes de Almeida (1862–1934), Raquel de Queiróz (b. 1910), and Lygia Fagundes Telles (b. 1923), they have made inroads into an area of Brazilian arts that has always been largely a male domain. However, in the theater, one of the most innovative areas of Brazilian literature, men continue to dominate. In addition to the best known of Brazilian playwrights, Abdias do Nasciment (b. 1914), founder in 1944 of a group designed to foster and produce black theater, the Teatro Experimental do Negro (TEN), figures such as Ariano Suassuna (b. 1927) and Joao Cabral de Mello Neto (b. 1920) have in recent years come to be seen as contributing to postcolonial drama in very productive ways.

It is a sign of the strength of Brazilian lusophone writing that literature is now not only actively engaged in the process of "writing back to the center" (Ashcroft, Griffiths, and Tiffin 1989), albeit taking second place alongside the extraordinarily more influential soap operas, but, in fact, dictating the way that non-lusophone works appear in Portuguese. For reasons to do with demographics and economics, multinationals are more likely to publish in Brazilian Portuguese than in the "original" linguistic model. To this extent, the dialogue between the Portuguese **"center"** and its Brazilian margin is now being conducted along a postcolonial paradigm in which the language of colonization constitutes a crucial site of a **decolonization** of the mind defended by **Ngũgĩ wa Thiong'o** (1986).

The situation differs greatly in lusophone Africa. Although in recent years a number of writers have attracted international attention, as is the case of the Mozambicans Mia Couto, Lina Magaia, and Paulina Chiziane, the Angolan Pepetela, the Cape Verdean Vera Duarte, and others, it remains poorly appreciated outside the lusophone world. Among the most influential earlier voices within lusophone African literatures, the Angolans Agostinho Neto (poetry) and Luandino Vieira (fiction), the Mozambicans José Craveirinha (poet) and Bernardo Honwana (fiction), and the Cape Verdeans Jorge Barbosa (poet) and Vasco Cabral (poet) stand out. Not surprisingly, with rare exceptions such as Noémia de Sousa (b. 1926), the Mozambican poet, here, too, the vast majority of writers have been male.

Contemporary lusophone African writing is marked by a recognition of the insignificant place accorded the arts during the colonial period. Indeed, Craveirinha (1993) has since lamented the continued marginalization of literature in postcolonial lusophone Africa, a view that is shared by a group of younger poets to whom the highly politicized dimension of the first generation no longer holds much attraction (Hamilton, 1995). As with some of the most original voices in anglophone writing, Couto's highly original "Africanization" of the language, in particular, demonstrates the sort of subversive talent found in the use of Portuguese by Brazilian writers. Indeed, although Couto is by far the most consciously "African" in his abrogation of the Portuguese language, writers such as Boaventura Cardoso, Pepetela, Chiziane, Duarte, Suleiman Cassamo, and Maria Alexandre Dáskalos reveal in their work a similar commitment to ensuring that African Portuguese reflects the reality of the people for whom it constitutes a link between the various ethnic groups.

Perhaps the greater obstacle to African lusophone literature, however, remains the absence of a local readership capable of providing the support that these writers need. Similarly, the fact that the majority of literary works by lusophone authors continue to appear first, and often only, in Portugal and elsewhere, rather than in the territories, combined with the raft of natural and man-made disasters that have assailed most of the former Portuguese colonies in the last two decades, has meant that the conditions for the growth and development of a genuinely lusophone African literature remain woefully inadequate.

Further Reading: R. Hamilton 1993; P. Chabal et al. 1996; A. Gomes and F. Cavacas 1997.

Tony Simoes da Silva

M

Magical Realism   Although the term "magical realism" was originally used to describe painting and opera in Europe during the 1920s and 1930s, Arturo Uslar Pietri appropriated it during the 1940s as an apt description of a literary form that he saw developing in Venezuela. Until the international success of Gabriel García Márquez's 1967 novel, *Cien años de soledad* (One Hundred Years of Solitude), however, the term languished in relative obscurity, after which it began to be widely used to describe literary and filmic texts that combine realistic and fantastic elements. While there is still some debate about the nature of magical realism, the basic characteristic of magical realist texts is that they combine factual (realistic) settings, characters, and situations with counterfactual (supernatural/counterrealistic) elements and present those counterfactual elements *as factual*, thereby changing the order of the fictive world. Examples of this are *Midnight's Children* (1980), by **Salman Rushdie**; *Chronique des sept misères* (1986), by **Patrick Chamoiseau**; *Beloved* (1987), by Toni Morrison; and *The Famished Road* (1991), by Ben Okri. In Rushdie's work, 1,001 children born in the hour surrounding the birth of the independent nation of India (midnight of 15 August 1947) are blessed or cursed with both extraordinary abilities and a profound link to their new nation. Chamoiseau, using magical realism within the *Créolité* (Creoleness) movement, writes about the characters who once frequented the old market in Fort-de-France. In the United States, Morrison tackles the bloody heritage of slavery with the help of a persistent ghost. Okri weaves tales about a boy-hero, Azaro, who can move easily between the worlds of the living and the dead.

The subversive power of magical realism comes from this juxtaposition of objective and subjective realities in ways that call the objective into question, allowing authors to challenge official readings of social, political, and historical events. Because the setting is realistic (the fictive world parallels the real world), when the category of the real is upset within the fiction, the world outside the fiction is made less certain as well. This distortion of the existing world is precisely what distinguishes magical realism both from the fantastic and from other, related literary forms, such as **Alejo Carpentier**'s *real maravilloso*, in which subjective beliefs and superstitions are described but not posited as real. While fantastic literature allows authors to address social issues through the defamiliarizing lens of fantasy, and marvelous realism describes unique physical and psychological landscapes from an objective perspective, magical realism brings reality as we know it into sharp focus, in order to cause a paradigm shift. Thus, while some authors and critics have contended that the phrase "magical realism" is an unfortunate, empty paradox that sensationalizes a serious literary form, in more than one sense, "magic" is the precise description of what magical realist texts achieve. Like stage magicians, magical realist authors create an illusion in one hand while revealing reality in the other, making it difficult to tell the two apart. To create an illusion, the magician has to manufacture just enough distraction that the audience misses the trick without realizing that there was anything to miss. For the magical realists, this means introducing just enough magic that reality shifts, noticed only as a fait accompli. Sometimes, this is done to undermine the all-too-human tendency to deny what is terrible or terrifying. It can help a sane reader to understand madness, make a foreign reader feel less alien (or a native reader feel foreign), or add just enough of the strange that an accepted fact is defamiliarized or a long-held belief stops making sense. It is a trick, cleverly done, that reveals the magician's skill even after it has been unraveled and laid out for critical analysis.

This is not to say, however, that magical realism is all play. While its narratives share with other **postmodern** texts a tendency toward self-reflexivity, fragmented narrative structures, and nonlinear chronologies, they tend to be very firmly grounded in a social critique that is anything but playful. On the level of the theoretical, the multiple voices and meanings of magical realist texts are inherently political, challenging the univocality of official histories and scientific rationalism. Additionally, these texts are steeped in the everyday violence of race, class, and gender-based oppression (compounded by problems of nationalism and imperialism) that exists in the world today. Magical realist texts work on both the symbolic and representational levels to reveal and challenge the social problems facing their authors' societies.

This potential of magical realism to serve as a vehicle for social protest has drawn the interest of many postcolonial authors and critics. The "impurity" (**Edward Said**) and "hybridity" (**Homi Bhabha**) of the mode have been addressed in such influential texts as Ashcroft, Griffiths, and Tiffin's *The Empire Writes Back* (1989); Said's *Culture and Imperialism* (1993); and Bhabha's *The Location of Culture* (1994).

Nonetheless, it is important to note that some authors and scholars have raised serious objections to the classification of texts as "magical realist." They view the literary form as a commodification of Third World difference by and for First World publishers, readers, and academics (L. Connell 1998). When using the term, therefore, one should be aware that "magical realism" is a contested site and may provoke controversy. It is also important to note that serious work has been and is being done to focus the category of magical realism and make it a precise literary term that describes without ghettoizing (A. Chanady 1985).

Further Reading: J.-P. Durix 1998; L. Zamora and W. Faris 1995.

Jennifer C. Rodgers

Naguib Mahfouz One of the more prolific writers of the Arab world, Naguib Mahfouz has published over thirty novels as well as numerous short stories. An avid reader of nineteenth-century European novelists, Mahfouz started writing novels at a time when the genre itself was discredited in the Arab world on two counts: its foreign origin and the belief that it was a lesser art form than poetry, for centuries the dominant literary form in Arabic. However, along with such contemporaries as Emile Habiby, Hanan Shaykh, **Tayeb Salih**, Emily Nasrallah, and Edward Khayyat, Mahfouz has transformed the Arabic novel into a prestigious and widely accepted art form with a large readership in various parts of the Arab world. Today, Mahfouz's novels have millions of readers in the Arab world, and his Western audience has been growing steadily, especially since he was awarded the Nobel Prize in 1988.

Mahfouz was born in Cairo on 11 December 1911, the youngest of seven children in the middle-class family of a civil servant. Egypt was then officially under Turkish rule, and the young Mahfouz grew up amid politically turbulent times that peaked in a violent uprising against the British protectorate in 1919, followed by the negotiation of a constitutional monarchy in 1923 and the overthrow of that monarchy in 1952 in an officers' coup headed by Pan-Arab nationalist Gamal Abdel-Nasser. Mahfouz's own writing reflects this volatile history, as changes in his narrative style are directly related to political events.

Mahfouz entered the University of Cairo in 1930, graduating with a degree in philosophy in 1934. While at the university, he befriended the socialist thinker and publisher Salama Mousa and began to write articles for the latter's journal, *Al-Majalla al-Jadida* (The Modern Magazine). While he is now recognized primarily as a novelist, Mahfouz never stopped writing newspaper articles and was still publishing a weekly column in the country's major newspaper, *Al-Ahram*, when he was awarded the Nobel Prize. In fact, because of lax or nonexistent copyright laws in the Middle East, Mahfouz could not support himself with royalties from his books and worked as a civil servant from 1934 to 1971, supplementing his salary with profits from the adaptation of sixteen of his novels for film and television series. His own experience provides the model for the frustrated middle-class clerks who people many of his novels.

Mahfouz's earliest novels, published between 1939 and 1944 under King Farouk's rule, are set in ancient Egypt yet are at times thinly disguised allegories of the turmoil in Egypt in the first decades of the twentieth century. Undeterred by criticism from the king, who resented Mahfouz's portrayal of the spiritual dilemmas of the modern Egyptian people, in 1945 Mahfouz made a decisive shift from short stories, articles, and historical novels toward the realist novel and a portrayal of the contemporary Cairene middle and working classes. The Cairo Trilogy (1956–1957), which consists of *Bayn al-Qasrayn* (Palace Walk), *Qasr al-Shawk* (Palace of Desire), and *Sukkariuya* (Sugar Street), follows three generations of a Cairene family between 1918 and 1944 and is often considered his masterpiece. It earned him the State Prize for Literature in 1956, as well as the beginning of international renown and critical praise. The trilogy features nineteenth-century novelistic strategies such as chronological plot, unified characters, and a panoramic view of society expressing social commentary steeped in a strong moral and humanistic perspective.

Three years after the Cairo Trilogy, Mahfouz published one of his more controversial novels, *The Children of Gebelawi* (1981), a religious allegory depicting prophets as socially conscious civilian reformers, rather than religious figures. The book, which had appeared in serialized form in Cairene newspapers between 1967 and 1969, greatly angered orthodox Muslims, was banned in all Arab countries except Lebanon (where it was published in book form), and remains unpublished in Mahfouz's own country to this day.

Mahfouz's sociopolitical approach took another turn in 1959, as he became openly critical of the Nasser regime, which he had initially supported but which had failed to bring about significant change in the Egyptian people's circumstances. After 1967 and Egypt's defeat in the Six-Day War with Israel, his style became extremely bleak, reflecting the Egyptian people's sense of helplessness, frustration, and shattered illusions. In 1979, following his support of Egypt's peace treaty with Israel, his books were again censored or banned in all Arab countries, except Lebanon. In the meantime, Mahfouz's style continued to evolve, to combine traditional Arabic narrative forms with European-style stream of consciousness. Mahfouz's more recent novels, however, while still openly critical of various political parties and rulers, have moved away from the realist style to emphasize subjective awareness in a more fragmented, even absurdist manner. Despite international recognition and praise for his work since the mid-1950s, Mahfouz himself has rarely traveled outside Egypt, which is the locale of all of his novels and short stories, and his novels chronicle the social and political life of twentieth-century Egypt. Time, Mahfouz claims, is the real protagonist of his novels, as his characters negotiate their identity as heirs to the great civilization of the ancient Egyptians 7,000 years ago, while making the adjustments necessary in a modern industrial society that has cast off foreign and undemocratic rule.

Mahfouz was awarded the Nobel Prize in literature in 1988 at the age of seventy-seven, and at the Nobel reception, as he addressed a Western audience for the first time, he chided Western leaders for having benefited from the exploitation of the Third World only to abandon it to its poverty and underdevelopment. In 1994 he was the target of an assassination attempt by a suspected Islamic fundamentalist who was later executed, and in 1997, at the age of eighty-six, Mahfouz published *Echoes of an Autobiography*.

Further Reading: R. El-Enany 1993; E. Said 1990.

Nada Elia

Malaysia. *See* Shirley Geok-lin Lim

Marginalization. *See* Center

José Carlos Mariátegui Through his acute understanding of capitalism and its impact on land and labor and through his biting, direct critiques of politics and culture, José Carlos Mariátegui (1894–1930) stands as one of Peru's most famous political theorists and one of the most influential Latin American writers of the twentieth century. Known primarily for his **Marxist**-inspired analysis of colonialism and independence in *Seven Interpretative Essays of Peruvian Reality* (1928/1971), Mariátegui was an intellectual, journalist, editor, and party member of APRA (Alianza Popular Revolucionaria Americana). His activities in APRA created an important schism between revolutionary groups of the 1920s, while recent scholars such as Michael Pearlman, Marc Becker, Jorge Chavarria, and Harry Vanden still debate whether Mariátegui is the founder of communism or of socialism in Peru. Postcolonial critics most often associate him with indigenismo (study and promotion of the indigenous), but it is important to recognize that this term represents an entire political and literary agenda that was shaped by both autochthonous and European forms and values.

Mariátegui's contemporaries, among them Cesar Vallejo (Peru), José Vasconcelos (Mexico) and Jorge Luis Borges (Argentina), represented the literary vanguard of Latin America, while he found diverse inspirations in Inca civilization, Enlightenment thought, and the Russian voices of revolt. Modern-day inheritors of his ideas include controversial groups such as the Shining Path, el Sendero Luminoso (the Shining Path of José Carlos Mariátegui), and the United Mariáteguista Party (PUM), as well as Cuban and Nicaraguan revolutionaries of the 1950s and 1970s.

As an author of two major books, *Siete Ensayos de la Realidad Peruana* (1928) and *La escena Contemporánea* (1925); a novel, *La novela y la vida* (1929, 1955) and dozens of essays and speeches and as an editor of *Nuestra Epoca*, *Labor*, and *Amauta*, Mariátegui's polemics span from 1914 to 1930 (Pearlman 1996, xxxiii). Two significant works are available in English: Marjory Irquidi's *Seven Interpretative Essays on Peruvian Reality* (1971, 1990) and Michael Pearlman's collection of his shorter articles, *The Heroic and Creative Meaning of Socialism: Selected Essays of José Carlos Mariátegui* (1996). These two texts are especially useful to postcolonial studies because they contextualize the struggles between the landholding class and the masses, between the Coast and the Sierra, between the caudillo (the military leader) and the campesino, between tradition and **modernity**, between Europe and its former colonies, and, most importantly within an international context, between the capitalist and worker.

Born in Moquegua, Peru, in 1894 to lower-middle-class parents, Mariátegui had only a primary education, one interrupted and ultimately ended by childhood illness (Pearlman 1996, xv). Mariátegui's father abandoned him and his two surviving siblings; therefore, his mother, Amalia La Chira Vallejos, supported and raised the family. Though of peasant origins, La Chira was, nevertheless, "cultivated" and "very well informed" and worked as a seamstress in bourgeois homes (Mariátegui Chiappe as qtd. in Stein 1997, 63). Despite being deprived of formal schooling, Mariátegui became a precocious and voracious reader, learning the rudiments of French and perusing books in the wealthy residences that he visited while under his mother's care.

Establishing himself as a journalist from 1914 to 1919, Mariátegui observed and responded to political corruption in Lima; his insights led to sharp *La Razón* editorials that exposed and disturbed the Augusto Leguía presidency (Basadre 1971, xii–xiii). From 1919 to 1923, Leguía forced Mariátegui into exile in Europe, where he learned to speak French fluently and kept company with radical Parisian workers. By 1920 he had moved to Italy, where he mastered Italian and married Ana Chiappe, who, along with their four children, would eventually collect his writings into twenty volumes (Basadre, xiii; Becker 1993, xviii). Europe played an important role in his philosophy because it helped him to place the history of Peru in a broader context, and, indeed, through his study of Marx and through his support of Lenin's Bolshevik Revolution in 1917, Mariátegui was able to import revolutionary ideas into Latin America.

His contributions to postcolonial studies can be measured in his arguments on land tenure, education, religion, and regionalism and his placement of Peruvian literature on trial. Discussion of these topics comes filtered through a labor-oriented perspective, but not through hackneyed complaints about capitalism. Rather, Mariátegui's journalism, and especially those essays gathered in *Seven Interpretative Essays*, condemns Lima's ineffectual bourgeoisie for refusing to embrace its own capitalist future, instead, leaving foreign entrepreneurs to manage Peruvian affairs.

The first chapter of *Seven Interpretative Essays* outlines Peru's economic evolution. Mariátegui begins by illustrating how the Spanish broke Peruvian continuity, for before the Conquest, the Inca were "industrious, disciplined, pantheist and simple," able to provide for their population of 10 million (3). By contrast, the conquistador ushered in a self-indulgent "military and ecclesiastic rather than a political and economic power" that reduced the Inca to 1 million people (4). When recounting such disasters, Mariátegui favors the steady voice of the social theorist, laying claim to the simple, but illuminative, principle that people's deeds are revealed better on an economic, rather than a political, level. This principle he adheres to throughout his work, exposing the misleading oratory of his colonial ancestors as well as that of his optimistic counterparts. He contends, for example, that Liberal rhetoric hides the fact that *latifundistas* (large-land owners) benefit from the government's sluggish enforcement of laws. In fact, Mariátegui views the landholding class as impervious to legal adjudication. After exposing the hypocrisy and ineptitude of Criollo society, "An Outline" uncovers three primary problems in Peru's economic evolution: first, the republican ignorance of the spirit of capitalism; second, the replacement of food crops with those demanded by foreign companies; third, labor. Since these views are at the heart of a postcolonial condition, they merit fuller examination.

In the nineteenth century, Peruvian caudillos seized governmental control after independence, adopting, but not enacting, the discourses of development. Military leaders were satisfied to grow wealthy as individuals rather than to establish a national economy. As Peru lacked a strong liberal bourgeoisie, Mariátegui argues, it lacked the ability to temper corruption or plan its own economic agenda (11). Oblivious to the spirit of capitalism, the Criollo landowner, instead, relied on his class and education—these blinded him to the fact that capitalism fragmented and did not protect his feudal holdings. Meanwhile, the hacienda of sugar and cotton closed its doors to local life, deepening the isolation of the wealthy class in Peru (21).

Further delaying development was the fact that Peru relinquished its nineteenth- and twentieth-century enterprises to foreign management. Like many Latin American countries, Peru sought the "machinery, techniques, and ideas of the Europeans, the Westerners"; more specifically, the British empire stood as a model of "capitalist civilization" with its "industry and machinery" and "clear sense of destiny" (9). Indeed, Mariátegui credits England for funding Spanish American independence through its banking. Yet all of this progress came with a cost. In signing the Grace Contract, for example, Peru lost administration of its railroads to England, which had financed them (13). Further, Peru grew sugar and cotton on the Coast for export, rather than producing crops for local consumption. The country's newer productions—copper and petroleum—served North American companies without establishing sustainable local economies, and manufacture, and mining employed relatively small numbers compared to agriculture. Thus, communities throughout the country had been displaced by capitalist enterprise; subsequent chapters discuss this displacement and the historical degradation of the Indian.

In "The Problem of the Indian," Mariátegui insists that neither education nor law nor faith in man's conscience can amend the condition of the peasant, whose fate resides in the reform of land tenure. Although such measures as the Homestead Act of 1918 promised change, Peru continued to be dominated by the feudal lord, the *latifundista* or *gamonal*, who has little to fear from the law because his work is practical, real, while the law is theory, merely administrative. Further, Mariátegui contends that the colonial and, later, the republican government depended on abuses of land and workers for its power.

In the essay "The Problem of Land," Mariátegui explains that by the nineteenth century, a time of industrialization elsewhere, Peru should have moved away from feudalism after independence. Instead, he observes that "great agricultural property actually has grown stronger and expanded, despite the theoretical liberalism of our constitution and the practical necessities of the development of our capitalist economy" (32). Peru's Civil Code removed obstacles to democratize rural property, but it lacked bite, giving no protection to Andean peoples. Following the examples of Central and Eastern Europe, with which Mariátegui grew familiar in exile, he believed that Peru should break up the land into small property and limit ownership. Indeed, Mariátegui points out that the Indian community, the *ayllu*, survives because of its agrarian and social nature. Moreover, through comparative analysis, "The Problem of Land" then hypothesizes that the capitalist system does not necessarily work better than Indian cooperatives in yields. Mariátegui concedes that under capitalism, there might emerge a free market of wage earners, rather than serfs. But as the average Peruvian is not an individualist and has not been educated in Enlightenment thought, he would be unlikely to be incorporated in such a system. Further, Spanish American culture has actively worked against the education of the Indian—the thesis in "Public Education."

Mariátegui admits three influences in Peru's public education—the Spanish, the French, and the North American—however, only the Peninsular legacy still dominates primary, secondary, and university schooling. The problem of Spain's legacy lay in its "aristocratic attitude and [in its] ecclesiastical and literary concept of education, which closed the university to mestizos and made culture a class privilege" (79). He believed that Peru should follow North America's lead on practical training in the arts and sciences—through trade and vocational schools. But such institutions are repugnant to Criollo "humanists" who abhor any affiliation to manual labor. Regardless of its associations, Mariátegui emphasized that such skills-based education is essential to industrial growth and economic incorporation of indigenous people. While he documents and supports Pan-American student protests about exclusive practices in the university, overall he exposes the rather short-term energy of such clamorous movements, which promise much but only perpetrate the status quo.

This status quo exists, in part, because of the palimpsest of religions in Peru, and the superimposition of Catholicism onto sites and values of Inca worship is the subject of "The Religious Factor." Here he explains that common to both the Indian and Spaniard are the ideas of obedience, respect for social hierarchies, and communal organization; absent from both, however, is the individualist spirit. He then compares the medieval and stagnating culture of Peru's aristocracy to the industrious settler culture of North America—what Max Weber identified as the origins of capitalist spirit. But while North America managed its territories according to the Protestant work ethic, only an obscure sense of purpose pervades Peru's three regions: the Coast, the Sierra, and the hazily defined Montaña (jungle).

Nor does Mariátegui believe in the regional and centralist split, as revealed in "Regionalism and Centralism." Here he associates centralism with governmental control in the capital, where *civilistas* promote the benefits of their class. Similarly, regionalism is associated with Liberal politics, which in theory means self-government and laissez-faire and in practice only sustains the abuses of the oligarchy at the expense of the masses. Regionalism also suggests distinct areas for development, yet the divisions between the Coast, Sierra, and Montaña are arbitrary and reflect poor colonial and republican planning, and the country is disconnected in its transportation, communication, and commerce systems. For Mariátegui, the crux is not only technology or a "pluralism of local or regional traditions"(164). Instead, "what has to be solved is a dualism of race, language, and sentiment, born of the invasion and conquest of Peru by a foreign race that has not managed to merge with the Indian race, or eliminate it, or absorb it" (164). In this case, Mariátegui does not see mixing as the answer. His romanticization of the Inca rather than the mestizo, in this case, departs from such postcolonial thinkers as José Vasconcelos ("The Cosmic Race") and **José Martí** ("Our America"), who celebrate Spanish American hybridity.

If the Indians have not been eliminated, Mariátegui seeks to reclaim and better them through land, labor, and education reform but also through cultural production. "Literature on Trial" validates authors who represent the autochthonous, what he calls "Peruvianness," which is distinctly Andean. Toward that end, Mariátegui traces three stages of literature: the first connects colonialism with the metropolis; the second, cosmopolitanism with foreign influences; and the third and most important, **nationalism**, with Peru's own literary and personal sentiments. He notes in the first and second stages the continued ponderous influence of Spanish colonial writers, such as Góngora. The third stage welcomes the popular, Indian poetry of Mariano Melgar, Abelardo Gamarra, and José Santos Chocano, as well as honest criticism of the Spanish legacy; here Mariátegui joins Valdelomar's literary "insurrection against academicism and its oligarchies, its emphasis on rhetoric, its conservative taste" through *Colónida*. A short-lived journal of 1916, *Colónida* published avant-garde literature and railed against national writers, whom they "denounced as a vulgar imitation of second-rate Spanish literature" (227). He also published *Nuestra Epoca*, also short-lived, which published for the masses (229).

While *Seven Interpretative Essays* offers lengthy arguments on Peru, Pearlman's *The Heroic and Creative Meaning of Socialism* offers shorter journalistic pieces on Europe and North America, the anti-imperialist struggle, Peruvian reality, Latin America, Marxism and philosophy, and literature, art, and culture. Of particular note in this collection is "Feminist Demands" (1924), which dismisses machismo rhetoric in order to sponsor women's participation in the workforce and in politics. In addition, "The Indigenist Question," penned in 1929, argues that race misleads social reformers because the problem is not one of race, but rather of class and land tenure; only through the dissemination of socialism will Peru progress. Here he advocates the worker's right to organize, to work an eight-hour day, and to receive compensation for injuries in the line of labor. Soon after these demands were published in *Amauta*, as part of the

Constituent Congress of the Latin American Trade Union Confederation, José Carlos Mariátegui succumbed to a devastating illness at the age of thirty-five. Thus, though his career was a relatively short one, Mariátegui spent his life writing, organizing, and working on socioeconomic theories to break ground for a new generation of postcolonial thinkers.

Further Reading: M. Becker 1993; J. Mariátegui 1971, 1996; W. Stein 1997.

Luz Elena Ramirez

José Martí   José Martí, modernist poet and Cuban liberator, professor, and social critic, represents the revolutionary spirit of fin-de-siècle Latin America. Born in Havana to Spanish parents, Martí witnessed the Ten Years' War with Spain (1868–1878) and formulated radical political views at the early age of sixteen. In 1869 these views landed him in the National Prison and later in a forced-labor quarry. There he penned "Political Prison in Cuba" (1870), which uses his characteristic style—striking imagery and stirring rhetoric—to shame colonial powers. Even so, rather than serving the full sentence for his rebelliousness, Martí accepted exile in Spain, where, by 1874, he obtained a university education in Madrid and Zaragoza, earning a doctoral degree in philosophy and the humanities.

Exile broadened the perspective of this writer-statesman, as it had for fellow Latin American thinkers such as **José Carlos Mariátegui**. In his continental and American peregrinations, Martí observed the growing animosity between classes. Indeed, "The Truth about the United States" (1894) argues that since its heroic revolutionary inception, blind self-interest and divisiveness have weakened the country. This idea, in varying degrees, infuses his journalism, which records momentous events of the time—from the "Memorial Meeting for Karl Marx" (1883), to the "Dedication of the Statue of Liberty" (1887), to the "Funeral of the Haymarket Martyrs" (1888). Yet Martí did not merely rail against the status quo; he changed it by helping to educate and organize Cuban and Puerto Rican laborers in New York and Florida.

His contributions to postcolonial studies include this activism and the manipulation of European literary forms to suit Antillean sentiment and imagery—this is especially true of his books of poetry, *Ismaelillo* (1882), *Versos sencillos* (1891), and the posthumously published *Versos libres* (1913). Postcolonial critics will also find controversial his insistence that there are no races, neither black nor white; we have only traits that, true to Enlightenment thought, one must improve upon. In line with this thinking, "Our America" (1891) praises the "natural man" unsullied by **modernity**. Martí scorns book learning if it creates social barriers, and he advocates a return to nature, coupled with practical instruction to improve people's labor and to give them faith in their government. "Our America" warns, however, that a nation's government must be recognized by its neighbors, particularly the "giant" of the North, and it should be shaped according to internal elements, not as an amalgam of foreign ideas. The key for Martí and his successors, among them Fidel Castro, is to create, not to imitate.

At the same time, Martí used the past strategically, as when he honors Simón Bolívar and José San Martín for their liberation of Peru, Venezuela, Ecuador, Bolivia, Colombia, Argentina, and Chile. Set within this context, he authored speeches and essays demanding organized action in Cuba, as in "With All, for the Good of All" (1891), "Our Ideas" (1892), "The Cuban Revolutionary Party" (1892), and "Manifesto of Montecristi" (1895). While encouraging the strong and dutiful Cuban character, these works also expose the tension between the noble soldier or peasant and the greedy politician or landowner, a tension leading to endless bloodshed. Thus, while reflecting on the premature Ten Years' War, Martí cautions his countrymen not to wantonly kill Spaniards but rather to understand their uneasy situation. Only those who interfere with human rights are appropriate subjects of warfare, only those who benefit from a predatory sugar economy. For Martí, the War of Independence (1895–1898) was the only way to establish a new republic, to create order from Cuba's confused historical origins. To this end, he helped assemble the Cuban Revolutionary Party, enlisting support from others living abroad. In 1895 he, General Máximo Gómez, and their revolutionary forces invaded Cuba from Santo Domingo; Martí died in battle in May, only one month after reaching his homeland. Though under U.S. military rule, Cuba was free from Spain by 1899.

Further Reading: J. Kirk 1983; D. Shnookal and M. Muñiz 1999.

Luz Elena Ramirez

Marxism   Marxism has been absolutely essential to the struggles of anticolonial independence movements around the world. From China to Guinea to Cuba, the fight against imperialism frequently took inspiration both from Marxist political and social theory and from the success of the Russian Revolution in 1917. Following the post–World War II consolidation of the United States as *the* hegemonic power of the postcolonial period, Marxism provided almost the only legitimate counternarrative against the unfettered expansion of capitalist **modernity**. At the same time, the repressive character of many of the self-identified postcolonial Marxist states ultimately tempered enthusiasm for Marxism as a political and conceptual system that could solve the problems of the colonies. Even given its undoubted influence on postcolonial political movements, within the field of postcolonial studies, Marxism has at times been met with a great deal of suspicion, if not outright hostility. Nevertheless, Marxist analyses remain essential to any complete account of the development of colonialism, imperialism, and its subsequent mutations in the postcolonial period.

While Marx wrote little about imperialism beyond his now controversial accounts of British rule in India, his elaboration of the fundamental logic of capitalist development shows the absolutely integral relationship between capitalism and imperialism. As Marx noted in the *Grundrisse* (1973), "the tendency to create the world market is directly given in the concept of capital itself. Every limit appears as a barrier to be overcome" (108). Structurally, capitalism needs to look outside its own established spaces in order for it to avoid crisis. In capitalist economies, profit is generated by the difference between the wages paid to laborers and the total value that they produce. At an economic level, the establishment of colonies allowed capitalism to avoid a crisis by opening up new markets so that surplus value could be realized as profit. At the same time, the colonies provided new sources of capital, in terms of both new sources of labor power and raw materials, that allowed European industry to further expand its power, influence, and wealth. More explicit Marxist analyses of the logic and function of imperialism can be found in V. I. Lenin's *Imperialism: The Highest Stage of Capitalism* (1933), Rosa Luxembourg's *The Accumulation of Capital* (1951), and in Nikolai Bukharin's critique of Luxembourg, *Imperialism and the Accumulation of Capital* (1972), as well as in the writings of numerous other classic and contemporary Marxist theorists.

Beyond offering an understanding of the general economic and historical logic of capitalism, Marxism has also introduced concepts such as alienation and labor exploitation into postcolonial studies. As indicated earlier, it has also been the basis of a revolutionary, anti-imperialist political discourse that was essential to the international movement against imperialism. Furthermore, two of the key concepts in postcolonial studies can be seen to have roots in Marxism. The concept of the **subaltern** or subalternity emerged out of the work of **Antonio Gramsci**, specifically, his "Notes on Italian History" (1971). Second, while the concept of the "Other" is most commonly attributed to Jacques Lacan, its use in postcolonial studies also owes a debt to Alexandre Kojève's Marxist re-reading of Hegel's *Phenomenology of Spirit, Introduction à lectures de Hegel* (1947), particularly the section on the master–slave dialectic, which added a historical, revolutionary dimension to Hegel's idealism. Finally and perhaps most importantly, Marxism has continually emphasized the material basis of colonial exploitation, without denying the existence and importance of the sociocultural formations that both produced and reproduced the colonial relationship.

Postcolonial critics have identified a number of problems with the use of Marxism in the elaboration of the postcolonial situation. While few critics would argue that Marxist theory provides important insights into colonialism and imperialism, a great deal of caution has been expressed about the uncritical acceptance of Marxist thought as a whole. There is, first, what might be termed a **nativist** reaction to Marxism that has seen it as yet another foreign conceptual import with little organic relationship to the reality of the colonial situation. To a degree, this criticism is valid even within terms of Marxist theory, since all Marxist revolutions of the twentieth century have occurred in very different circumstances than Marx might have imagined—not in the heavily industrialized North and West but in the agrarian, colonial South and East. In this respect,

Maoism and Che Guevara's *focismo*, among others, represent indigenous adaptations of Marxism to local needs and circumstances.

Second, worries have been expressed about the implicit (and explicit) teleology of Marxism. As in both the philosophy of Hegel and the very worst forms of modernization theory, Marxism seems to view societal development as attached to a strict temporal framework that obliges each society to move through a necessary sequence of economic stages (as in the infamous "Asiatic mode of production"). Inevitably, this means that the colonies are seen as temporally "behind" the West in their development. In order to overcome their problems, their goal must therefore be to "catch up" with their Western counterparts. While this view of history is clearly **Eurocentric**, Samir Amin, Gyan Prakash, and others have been careful to point out that the general framework of Marxist analysis can be utilized even without adopting its problematic teleology. A third, related criticism (most clearly articulated by Robert Young), which originates at the intersection of postcolonialism and **postmodernism**, rejects Marxism because it offers an insupportable "metanarrative" of historical development. Finally, concerns have been raised about Marxism's traditional focus on the dimension of class to the exclusion of race, gender, and **ethnicity**, conceptual categories that have been of particular importance in postcolonial studies. While early Marxist thought might not have even seen class as a category applicable to colonial societies (which were taken to be "feudal" or "Asiatic"), contemporary Marxism has exhibited a much more nuanced approach to the ways in which class cuts across other social categories in complex and contradictory ways.

While it is thus not without problems, the Marxist analysis of the capitalist system and its attendant social and political ills has nevertheless contributed immeasurably to an understanding of imperialism and neoimperialism. Even in the wake of the end of state socialism in 1989, Marxism has retained a strong presence in contemporary postcolonial studies. A number of prominent figures in the field of postcolonial studies have claimed Marxism as at least part of their intellectual heritage, such as **Aijaz Ahmad**, Chidi Amuta, Selwyn Cudjoe, Geeta Kapur, E. San Juan Jr., and **Gayatri Spivak**. The generation of thinkers who helped to define postcolonial criticism, such as **Frantz Fanon**, **Amílcar Cabral**, and **C.L.R. James**, were directly influenced by Marxism, and a number of early studies of postcolonial literature (especially in the area of African literature) approach it from a Marxist or materialist perspective. In addition, some of the most important critics of development and modernization theory, such as Samir Amin, Immanuel Wallerstein, and Andre Gunder Frank, draw their critical models and concepts from Marxist thought. What is still the most widely known Marxist "intervention" into postcolonial studies—Fredric Jameson's (1986) article on Third World literature and Ahmad's (1987) critical response to it—provides a poor understanding of the ways in which the characteristic concerns of Marxism and postcolonialism overlap. This is due less to the validity of

Jameson's claims about the function of postcolonial "national allegories" than to the fact that his hypothesis about Third World literature has been taken reductively as representative of Marxist thinking about the postcolonial as a whole. As Aamir Mufti and Ella Shohat (1997) have suggested, given Marxism's longstanding interest in colonial and postcolonial relations, it is more productive to see its relationship to the postcolonial as the latter's "defining tension," a conceptual framework that it must always come up against in its attempt to map out the present.

Further Reading: A. Brewer 1980; M. Hardt and A. Negri 2000; K. Marx 1973; A. McClintock, A. Mufti, and E. Shohat 1997.

Imre Szeman

Fatima Mernissi   Fatima Mernissi is one of the foremost feminist scholars in the Muslim world, a sociologist whose work examines the dynamics of contemporary Muslim women as they maneuver between the conflicting sociopolitical forces of rapid urbanization and fundamentalist conservatism. Mernissi, who describes herself as "incorrigibly optimistic," argues that the postcolonial turn toward fundamentalist conservatism in various Muslim countries is a distortion of the true spirit of Islam, which affirms the potential equality between men and women. Her writings reveal a thorough knowledge of ancient Islamic texts from poetry, to philosophy and religious documents, and she argues that **feminism** is compatible with the spirit of Islam as practiced during the Prophet Mohammad's time and that Islamic faith has historically been compromised by despotic leaders seeking to maintain their authority despite the people's desire for democracy. Women's oppression is then seen as the result of male-dominated social institutions and customs, ungrounded in Islam, that seek to control women by denying them access to the political and social power that is rightfully theirs.

   Many of Mernissi's books are written in response to immediate circumstances that seek to strip women of their historical legacy of power. Her books include *Beyond the Veil: Male–Female Dynamics in Modern Muslim Society* (1975; rev. 1987); *Doing Daily Battle: Interviews with Moroccan Women* (in French 1984; in English 1988); *Women in Muslim Paradise* (1986); *The Veil and the Male Elite: A Feminist Interpretation of Women's Rights in Islam* (in French 1987; in English 1991); *Islam and Democracy: Fear of the Modern World* (1992; inspired by the Persian Gulf War); *The Forgotten Queens of Islam* (1993; providing the biographies of eighteen Muslim queens and debunking the claim made by the Pakistani Islamic Democratic Alliance, upon the occasion of Benazir Bhutto's winning of the 1988 presidential elections, that no Muslim state has ever been governed by a woman); the autobiographical *Dreams of Trespass: Tales of a Harem Girlhood* (1994); and *Women's Rebellion and Islamic Memory* (1996). Mernissi has also written the text for a multimedia exhibition, *The Harem within: Fear of the Difference*.

   Mernissi was born in 1941 in Fez, Morocco, one of the centers of the **na-**

tionalist movements against French colonization, and has benefited from her country's decision to admit girls to the nationalist schools in an effort to hasten independence. She has studied at the Mohammad V University in Rabat and the Sorbonne in Paris and graduated with a Ph.D. in sociology from Brandeis University in Massachusetts. She has taught at the Mohammad V University in Rabat, Morocco, the University of California, Berkeley, and Harvard University. She currently holds a research appointment at Morocco's Institut Universitaire de Recherche Scientifique.

Further Reading: L. Ahmed 1992; D. Kandiyoti 1996.

Nada Elia

Mestizo. *See* Miscegenation

Metropolitan. *See* Center

Mimicry Mimicry is a strategy that results from misreadings of **colonial discourse** and power by the colonized subjects. As the colonized performs according to the protocol of the colonizer, he or she inevitability is both the same and different. This gap between the two positions unsettles the power of the colonizer; for at the same time that the colonized subject appears to participate in the imperialistic regime, he or she also misappropriates and misrepresents the dictates of colonial discourse. This tension creates a site of **resistance**.

The debate on mimicry began in the nineteenth century among Western scholars regarding the critique of subservience of local literary styles to Western literary tradition. **Frantz Fanon** and **V. S. Naipaul** in the twentieth century further critiqued this phenomenon. For Fanon, mimicry results from the exertion of colonial power on the colonized in such a way that he or she loses the possibility of an autonomous cultural identity; legitimacy is gained through the taking on of Western ideals—or what he has called "white masks." Fanon wants writers to escape mimicry.

V. S. Naipaul, on the other hand, takes the position that there is no alternative to becoming "mimic men." According to Naipaul, a central tendency of a colonial society is to mimic the colonial power. This analysis informs his view on cultural politics as well as writing, and he takes for granted the underlying insecurity of colonial cultures that unsettle the colonial power's attempt to assert a stable position over the colonized. In considering how mimicry challenges and undermines even as it copies, Naipaul's approach shifts the focus away from a consideration of domination and coercion as a battle between essentialized social and political groups.

Naipaul's approach to mimicry bears some parallels to the work of **Homi Bhabha**, a postcolonial literary theorist who draws from **psychoanalysis**. Bhabha has further revised our understanding of the term, and he notes that the performance of mimicry is marked by ambivalence. As mimicry stages an ambivalent response to the Other, it also challenges its authority, and in this case mimicry *repeats* rather than *represents*.

At the same time that one is adopting the style of the colonial other, he or she is also critiquing the positionality of the colonial power. In other words, the adaptation is always, already partial. According to Bhabha, a classic text of such partiality is Charles Grant's "Observations on the State of Society among the Asiatic Subjects of Great Britain" (1792). Though Grant wanted to achieve missionary education in English, he aimed for a partial influence as Christianity colluded with caste practices. Macaulay's "Minute" (1835) picks up on Grant's thinking and asserts that to be Anglicized is emphatically not to be English. According to Bhabha, these mimic men connote a partial presence, and their presence of difference counteracts narcissism of colonial authority. Bhabha develops his notion of mimicry by drawing on the work of Jacques Lacan, who regards mimicry as a form of camouflage. This notion of mimicry offers a third solution to Fanon's critique that one must give in to the exigencies of whiteness or simply disappear.

Literary mimic men who mix Western genres with local content provide examples of mimicry. Raja Rao's *Kanthapura* (1971[1938]) focuses on the impact of Gandhi's words on a small Indian village. In the novel, Rao refuses to give up the use of English; he prefers to create a hybrid form of the novel in which the story is told through English using Indian cadences and rhythms. Rao's interest reflects the interest in not simply replacing a Western cultural paradigm with its non-Western counterpart, and he also avoids making an appeal to an "authentic" or "**essential**" Indianness.

Further Reading: H. Bhabha 1994; F. Fanon 1967.

Kanta Kochhar-Lindgren

Miscegenation (Related terms: **amalgamation, Creolization, mestizo,** hybridity)   The term was coined by journalist David Croly in his 1864 pamphlet *Miscegenation: The Theory of the Blending of the Races, Applied to the American White Man and Negro.* In order to incite controversy and reinforce antiblack sentiment in the United States, he asserted disingenuously that "[i]f any fact is well established in history, it is that the miscegenetic or mixed races are much superior, mentally, physically, and morally, to those pure or unmixed" (15). According to Croly, miscegenation, derived from "the Latin *miscere,* to mix, and *genus,* race, is used to denote the abstract idea of the mixture of two or more races" (vii). This term is related to amalgamation, which describes the process of blending two metals (Oxford English Dictionary) and symbolizes more general forms of blending or mixing. In contrast, miscegenation never functioned as a "neutral" scientific term. It was used rhetorically to invoke negative sentiment about racial mixing and the contamination of supposedly "pure" racial ancestry.

Croly's introduction of miscegenation into popular discourse was a calculated response to growing anxiety about recently freed slaves. The disruptive potential of miscegenation was so threatening that it became a legitimating powerful concept almost immediately. Racists and prohibitionists alike deployed the term as they debated the fate of the black population at the end of the Civil War.

Although cross-racial sex was not a new phenomenon, the renewed focus on miscegenation was part of the dominant class' attempt to coalesce its fragmented position after the Civil War. In doing so, whites in power reproduced the racial hierarchy of their former colonizer (England) by defining themselves in opposition to "others" (nonwhite/disempowered inhabitants). As early as 1661, when the states were still governed by British colonial law, interracial marriage, although criminalized, existed. Laws designed to maintain class distinctions in England were translated into antimiscegenation statutes that reproduced the racialized power structure that deemed whites as citizens and blacks as property (Saks 1988, 43).

Croly conflated multiple concerns about power, property, race, gender, and sex into one term. Antimiscegenation discourse was so successful that it forced anyone who advocated civil rights for blacks and other nonwhites to explicitly deny that she or he was promoting interracial sex. In an attempt to police interracial relations and racially mixed people spectacularized by Croly, the majority of white Anglos defined themselves in opposition to blacks, to anyone with black ancestry, and to those who were unable to legitimate their white status. This insistence on the black–white binary overshadowed the complex subject positions of individuals and communities not easily contained by reductive racial categories. Given the long-established histories of identity formation in multiple geographic sites (such as North America, the Caribbean, Latin America, Africa, and Asia) characterized as diasporic, mestizo, **Creole**, and "hybrid," it became evident that cross-racial mixing was/is certainly not limited to black–white unions in the United States. This rhetoric, though initially aimed at black–white liaisons, extended across multiple racial/ethnic boundaries and impacted people in most "other" non-Anglo (white) categories, including, but not limited to, Asian, Native American, and Latin American.

The ways in which the historically embedded discourse of miscegenation has been employed, rearticulated, exported, and challenged, despite its intransigence as a black versus white issue in the popular imagination, are instructive. By insisting on cross-racial relations as solely the corruption of "pure" white and black lineage, miscegenation rhetoric often produces contradictions and fails to contain the racially diverse "subjects" of its discourse. Although those who transgress racial/ethnic lines are policed by antimiscegenation discourse, the act of crossing regulated borders still disrupts the narratives that seek to prohibit it. Those who have been "colonized" by antimiscegenation discourse often resist by reclaiming and transforming the strict formulations that confine them. In addition to identifying the ways in which the conventional language and patterns of miscegenation are played out, it is possible to read against these conventions and disturb their repetitive impulse.

In Spike Lee's film *Jungle Fever*, despite the dominant narrative that tracks a failed black–white relationship, two minor characters, African American Orin Goode and Italian American Paulie Carbone, are able to sustain one. They transcend the overpowering racism of both working-class Italian and middle-class African American communities because of their common educational aspirations, as well as their recognition of an interrelated history of oppression as racial/ethnic minorities in the United States. Similarly, Julie Dash's *Daughters of the Dust*, a contemporary film about the diasporic identities of African Americans on Sea Island, Georgia, indicates that all descendants of Africans are ethnically/racially mixed and contests the rhetoric of "pure" racial lines. Dash's narrative allows for a romantic union between African descendant Iona Peazant and Cherokee St. Julian Last Child (Reid 1997, 113), which generates a new multiracial alliance that challenges the colonization and genocide of **indigenous** (Native) and black diasporic communities in the South. These representations of successful cross-racial liaisons not only present alternatives to antimiscegenation narratives but also reclaim agency for those whose bodies/lives have been controlled. They envision the crossing of racial, ethnic, and national borders in ways that oppose hegemonic discourse, power, and policies that deem those who transgress racial lines uncivilized, aberrant, and unnatural.

Earlier responses to antimiscegenation emphasize its function as a colonizing discourse. These representations range from Frantz Fanon's *Black Skin, White Masks* (1967), a psychoanalytic reading of interracial liaisons born of the legacy of colonization, to James Baldwin's *Giovanni's Room* (1956), which can be read as a miscegenous liaison in interethnic, transnational, same-sex terms. Works like Nella Larsen's *Quicksand* (1992 [1928]) and James Weldon Johnson's *Autobiography of an Ex-Colored Man* (1912 [1992]) relocate "postcolonial" characters to sites distant from their "homes" where racist antimiscegenation discourse runs rampant. These figures reformulate identity transnationally, in opposition to the imperializing "normative" categories that formerly confined them. Successful or not, their actions reveal the power of the discourse to reproduce a system of oppression that must be escaped, challenged, or redefined. Suzan-Lori Parks presents a postmodern representation of postcolonial cross-racial relations in *Venus* (1990), a dramatic portrayal of Saartje Baartman, the "Hottentot Venus." This play addresses the transnational, cross-racial spectacularization of miscegenation and its relationship to imperial power as Saartje is displayed onstage as the object of the objectifying imperial gaze. Parks foregrounds the political, gender, and racial politics that "trouble" the original "exhibit"; her contemporary piece "strikes back" at the colonizing miscegenation discourse that pathologized Baartman's body.

Further Reading: D. Croly 1864; J. Dash 1992; H. Elam and A. Rayner 1998; F. Fanon 1967; J. W. Johnson 1965 (1912); N. Larsen 1928; S. Lee 1990; S. L. Parks 1990; M. Reid 1997; E. Saks 1988; W. Sollors, 1997.

Diana Rebekkah Paulin

Missionaries. *See* Colonial Patronage; Liberation Theology

Timothy Mo   Timothy Mo was born in Hong Kong in 1950 of mixed Chinese and British parentage. He has published six novels to date, the last two under his own imprint. His first, *The Monkey King* (1978), was set in Hong Kong and deals with patriarchy. With the second, *Sour Sweet* (1982), which deals with immigrants in London, Mo moved into the world of ambiguities, which he has since stressed. *Sour Sweet* was nominated for the Booker Prize, but his third novel, *An Insular Possession* (1986), really established Mo. It presents the beginnings of Hong Kong from the point of view of two American youngsters whose criticism of the opium trade sets the moral tone of the work. As an account of what might be termed adolescent development, the parallels in the novel (the American youngsters, America as a nation, the new colonial establishment) are extremely illuminating. Mo's next novel is perhaps his finest. *The Redundancy of Courage* (1991) deals with what is clearly East Timor and subtly explores questions of national identity. The pessimistic conclusion seemed natural when it was written, though recent events allow for a more promising view of **identity**.

Mo then published *Brownout on Breadfruit Boulevard* (1995) on his own, and the opening coprophiliac scene may explain why. The novel is not pleasant, perhaps reflecting Mo's perception of the Philippines, or rather of some aspects of its ruling class. The latest novel, *Redemption* or *Halo-Halo* (2001), again about the Philippines, dwells again on violence and social corruption in a depressing manner. The writing continues to be powerful, but the current concentration on esoteric elements will inevitably restrict Mo's market.

Further Reading: E. Ho 2000; R. Wijesinha 1993.

Rajiva Wijesinha

Modernity   The term denotes the state or quality of being modern, that is, contemporary, topical, new, not oriented toward the past. Since Charles Perrault's *Paralèles des Anciens et des Modernes* (1687), also marking the beginning of the Enlightenment, the moderns have been placed above the ancients, and modernity has implied progress in all areas of human life. Life in modernity no longer depends on the past and the eternal truths expressed by ancient authorities (Plato, Aristotle, or the Bible) but on the ingenuity and creativity of human beings. Truths need to be found, described, and established and are no longer regarded as already clearly defined. The inductive, experimental approach of the new sciences became dominant in modernity and brought about a new understanding of nature as well as many advances in technology. Modernity is, therefore, also connected with industrialization and the consequences of the social, political, and economic developments in the modern nations since the eighteenth century, in particular, with individualization, differentiation or specialization, abstraction, and democracy. This means that the premodern, holistic world, in which individuals had a secure, well-defined position and identity in a relatively stable "chain of being" ultimately ordained by God, was gradually replaced by a world where individuals can theoretically become everything (from dishwasher to millionaire, from movie star to president). Modernity thus accords great freedom and importance to individuals but at the same time removes the security provided by close, stable communities and the roles and identities of premodern societies. The freedom allowed by modernity is, therefore, inseparable from *angst*, the feeling first described by Kierkegaard in *The Concept of Dread* (1844) and later by Sartre, Camus, and others of existential emptiness that can be overcome only by decisive human choice and resolute action— though such action never provides a perfect sense of identity, authenticity, and completeness. Modernity is characterized by this constant merging of very different elements that cannot be separated without destroying the whole. Hegel's and Marx's dialectics perfectly exemplify this complex modern unity, assuming the principle that an idea or event (*thesis*) generates its opposite (*antithesis*) and leads to a reconciliation of opposites (*synthesis*), which then becomes a new thesis, the process being endless. Freud's division of the human psyche into the ego, the id, and the superego is another example of the differentiation, fragmentation, contradictoriness, and intricacy of modernity. All of these elements, though, need to be integrated for a comprehensive understanding of the whole. Modernity thus is never one-sided; it is characterized by at least a duality or bipolarity, usually even by a polymorphic plurality in its components.

The order, structure, or hierarchy of these components is not preestablished and eternally valid but depends on human choices. Thus, another key term in modernity is *anomie* (literally, "lawlessness"), which describes the sense of absurdity encountered in a world without God-given meanings, as discussed in Camus' *Myth of Sisyphus* (1942). Anomie is also connected with human despair at such an orderless and senseless world, so that Durkheim holds anomie mainly responsible for the high number of suicides in modern society. As norms for conduct are either absent, weak, or conflicting in modernity, people experience rootlessness, social disconnectedness, and alienation, and suicide seems the only very personal solution in a world that incites infinite aspirations but provides inadequate means for their realization. The result is an increase in suicide, crime, and mental disorder, so that for C. G. Jung schizophrenia is a typically modern disease.

Modernity is also, as Max Weber put it, connected with a sense of utter disenchantment. All the superhuman and supernatural forces, the gods and spirits with which premodern cultures populate the universe and to which they attribute responsibility for the phenomena of the natural and social worlds, are eliminated and replaced by the modern scientific interpretations of nature, which are regarded as uniquely valid. The social institutions of modernity also act according to the methods and findings of science and work on the rational and impersonal precepts formulated by experts. These alienating tendencies in modernity have been countered by a growing emphasis on the missing opposite components (e.g., feelings in the context of modern bureaucracy) and on seeing human beings not in isolated situations (e.g., only in terms of new technologies) but always in more complex and holistic contexts. This complexity as an essential element of modernity is found not only in whole cultures or nations but also in smaller life worlds, the everyday lives of individual people. The concrete experience of life is fundamental in modernity as the modern world is always constructed by human beings. History is, therefore, inseparable from modernity (for Schelling and Hegel, modernity was, above all, the experience of history), and so is self-reflexivity, because people in modernity necessarily think about themselves, the reasons that things are what they are and how human life could be improved. Modernity has also produced a new kind of irony, described by Kierkegaard, that provides people with a sense of freedom from the world and is, above all, a means for survival, then a way of expressing the ambiguities of life, and only eventually a form of criticism.

Modernity is inseparable from the postcolonial context, because all of its characteristics apply to both the colonial and the postcolonial situations. This is most evident with industrialization, where the Western experience has been the model for the world. To become modern was to become something like Western industrial society, and the new technologies reveal that this process is being repeated. What has happened at the same time on another level, though, is no less typically modern: people have reconstructed the world in their own way, and this has always implied giving meaning to themselves and to others. In this sense, modernity will persist in its concern with individual lives and the endless battle of conflicting powers over people, their histories, and meanings. As long as these conflicts continue, modernity has not yet ended. **Postmodernity** has not put an end to human worries about the meaning of life; it has only shown again that such meanings are never absolute but always temporary and culture-specific. Anthony Giddens' suggestion that postmodernity is just one of *The Consequences of Modernity* (1990) makes much sense when one sees that postcolonial literature has adopted postmodern elements but has not really stopped asking the questions of modernity about meaningful lives, especially in the usually very contradictory contexts of colonial and postcolonial powers, modern and premodern influences, native and foreign traditions. The postcolonial countercultures of modernity, discussed by Paul Gilroy (1993) and others, are then most usefully investigated not as postmodern but as part of a second modernity (Ulrich Beck 1992), opening up a new historicity as well as a new future. The paradoxical dialectics of modernity contain the rise of colonialism as well as its dismantling in postcolonial contexts.

Further Reading: U. Beck 1992; P. Gilroy 1993; B. Turner 1990.

Klaus-Peter Müller

Prafulla Mohanti (1936–) is an author and painter who in many ways epitomizes the postcolonial, diasporic character. Born in the village of Nanpur,

Orissa, India, Mohanti showed exceptional promise as a youth and eventually made his way to Bombay, then to England, where he has lived since 1964. Mohanti began in Leeds as an architect/town planner, then moved to London, where he has since remained—although he has returned for several months annually to his native village. Nearly forty years of shuttling between remote village and global metropolis has defined Mohanti's life and is also central to his work. His paintings, held in many public and private collections internationally, are informed by the bright colors and religious symbolism fundamental to Nanpur life. Mohanti has always been intrigued by what the abstract forms tied to Hindu spiritualism in some of his paintings "mean" to his native villagers, as opposed to audiences in England and Europe. His efforts to articulate the development of his own cultural hybridity and his experience of painful acculturation to the West are detailed in his autobiographical work *Through Brown Eyes* (1985). His other works are efforts to "allow the village to speak" to Western readers: *My Village, My Life* (1973; also produced as a BBC documentary), *Changing Village, Changing Life* (1990), and *Indian Village Tales* (1975). While he has spent most of his life in London, Mohanti regards himself as a villager, asserting that he has never felt accepted in Britain, although he also does not consider it feasible to return to the village to reside permanently.

Further Reading: G. Kain 1999; G. Mishra 1985.

Geoffrey Kain

V. Y. Mudimbe (1941–)   Congolese scholar, novelist and poet, V. Y. Mudimbe was born December 8, 1941, in Likasi (then Jadotville) in the southern Shaba (formerly Katanga) province of the Belgian Congo (Zaire from 1970 to 1997, now Democratic Republic of Congo). Born Valentin Yves but using the African name Vumbi Yoka under Mobutu's 1970s "authenticity" policy, Mudimbe has always gone by "V. Y."

His brilliance recognized from a very early age, Mudimbe spent eight years of his boyhood in an African Benedictine monastery, where he studied Greek and Latin and prepared for a religious life. Turning from this, he received his *Licence* in Romance languages from Lovanium University in Kinshasa, Congo, in 1966, did graduate work at the University of Paris, and received his Ph.D., with a dissertation on the concept of "air" in ancient Greek and Latin from Louvain University in Belgium in 1970. After holding junior academic posts in Belgium and France, Mudimbe held several academic appointments in Zaire from 1970 to 1980. He then left Zaire under political pressure and has since held endowed professorships in sociology, Romance languages, comparative literature, cultural anthropology, African studies, and modern thought at Haverford College and Duke and Stanford Universities. He has been married to the scholar Elisabeth Mudimbe-Boyi since 1966 and has two children.

Mudimbe's work includes over twenty books, many edited volumes, and scores of essays, in numerous domains. His early scholarship focused on Romance linguistics and philosophy. His three books of poetry—*Déchirures* (1971), *Entretailles* (1973), and *Les Fuseaux Parfois* (1974)—have attracted critical attention. His four novels are considered masterpieces. *Entre les eaux* (Between Tides, 1973) concerns an African Catholic priest struggling with the attractions of a militant, revolutionary, postcolonial **Marxism**. *Le Bel immonde* (Before the Birth of the Moon, 1976) chronicles the vexed relations between a senior African politician and his rebel mistress. *L'Écart* (The Rift, 1979) is the anguished diary of the last days of a European-trained African historian of Africa who cannot begin to write. *Shaba Deux* (untrans., 1989) is the narrative of an African nun in crisis at a time of revolution. All four texts meditate intensively on the psychological, philosophical, political, and religious dimensions of the postcolonial situation.

Equally importantly, Mudimbe's more recent scholarship has been extremely influential across African studies and in allied fields. In books such as *L'Autre face du royaume* (1974), *L'Odeur du père* (1982), *The Idea of Africa* (1994), and especially *The Invention of Africa* (1988), Mudimbe argues that it is impossible to consider Africa "simply as it is." Rather, one must pass through European, American, and Afro-diasporic writing on Africa—what Mudimbe calls "the colonial library"—to come to a common, dialogic understanding of Africa and the West. Here Mudimbe's work is marked by **Michel Foucault**, is allied with scholars such as Paul Gilroy, Paulin Hountondji, and **Edward Said**, and is opposed to African "authenticity," "African personality," and Afrocentrism. In all his works, Mudimbe embodies a remarkable postcolonial synthesis of high European and African influence, continually negotiating and disturbing the boundaries between Africa and the West.

Further Reading: M. Diawara 1991; K. Stadtler-Djedji 1995; W. Slaymaker 1996.

David Chioni Moore

Multiculturalism In its wider sense, multiculturalism denotes diversity of race, class, gender, language, culture, sexual orientation, or disability within one society. In its narrower sense—the one that is more pertinent for postcolonial studies—it refers to ethnic diversity within one society. The underlying premise of both senses is a recognition of diversity, as opposed to a monoculturalistic attitude that is based on a belief in the supremacy of one social/cultural group and demands a monocentric assimilation to the dominant culture. In its ideal form, multiculturalism respects boundaries between cultures in the private domain but requires the acceptance of a single culture and a single set of individual rights in the public domain. Originally a concept in social anthropology— J. Furnivall's field studies of 1939 were the first to focus on plurality within a society—multiculturalism has turned into a household word as well as a technical term used in such diverse fields as politics, sociology, education, economics, literature, urban planning, law, and psychology. As a result there is now no common agreement as to the nature of multiculturalism beyond the rather broad definition given earlier. This is partly due to the open-endedness of multiculturalism itself. The fundamental question is whether multiculturalism is to be seen as a set of identifiable features of a particular community, as a political attitude, a philosophy, a movement, or even measurements to encourage diversity within a community and promote equal opportunities for minority groups. A further dimension applicable to both the wider and the narrower views is the question of which of the two constituents in the basic ideal of diversity in equality is to be given preference and how they can be reconciled, an issue made even more complex by changing definitions of the concept of culture itself. Whereas in earlier approaches to multiculturalism culture was largely seen as an **essentialism** that was a property of a particular social group, under the influence of poststructuralist ideology and increasing migration, **globalization**, and delocation of culture, the more contemporary branch of multiculturalism tends to see culture as a dynamic, unstable, open construct. This clearly allows for a more flexible notion of multiculturalism as a process rather than a state, one that involves the continuous reforming and reconstituting of social groups with open boundaries. Of course, the practice of multiculturalism in various nations is as varied as its underlying ideologies: although multiculturalism commonly arises as an effect of colonization, its particular realizations in postcolonial societies are varied: Canadian multiculturalism, for instance, originating in two colonizing nations, has been established by law since 1988 and is often compared in its kaleidoscopic nature to a mosaic, especially in opposition to U.S. multiculturalism, the famous melting pot, which is based on the expectation that ethnic minorities should blend into the majority culture and which has been criticized for being an ill-concealed monoculturalistic position. British multiculturalism, after post–World War II migration from the New Commonwealth, is essentially an inner-city phenomenon. Recently, in the wake of the fiftieth anniversary of the arrival of Caribbean migrants to the U.K. on the *Empire Windrush* in 1948, the creative side of multicultural Britain has been stressed, while racism and discrimination are seen as problems belonging to the past, that is, the 1970s and 1980s. A concept that finds so many diverse realizations is bound to be criticized. The main argument against multiculturalism held by monoculturalists is the position that diversity disrupts the fabric of social life rather than maintaining the unity of a social group. Another criticism, held by multiculturalists themselves, is that a liberal focus on diversity upholds the status quo of power relations by keeping ethnic minorities from effectively gaining equality, while only theoretically acknowledging equal rights.

Further Reading: A. Gordon and C. Newfield 1996; C. Willett 1998.

Susanne Reichl

N

V. S. Naipaul   Born in Chaguanas, Trinidad, in 1932, Vidiadhar Surajprasad Naipaul is a descendant of the indentured laborers who arrived in the Caribbean from India in the nineteenth century. A bright student, he was awarded one of the scholarships conferred annually by the colonial authorities to study in the metropolis and obtained a literature degree from Oxford.

Naipaul's first two novels published, *The Mystic Masseur* (1957) and *The Suffrage of Elvira* (1958), together with the short story collection *Miguel Street* (1959), echo street life in the colonial Caribbean, with a wide array of multi-cultural, often picaresque characters. *A House for Mr. Biswas* (1961) is widely believed to be his masterpiece; the protagonist is based on the figure of Naipaul's father, Seepersad, a local journalist and short story writer. Biswas' ambition to have a house of his own has been read as a metaphor of the quest for **identity** of the colonial individual.

Naipaul's subsequent fiction is more overtly political. Although some pieces are still set in the Caribbean, other world scenarios are prominent. *The Mimic Men* (1967) is narrated by a cultured and sensitive expatriate who lives in a state of almost complete withdrawal and is engaged through writing in a quest for self-knowledge. He bears an obvious resemblance to the author's own life, as happens with similar Hindu first-person narrators in later works. This new stage in Naipaul's career is also marked by recurrent depictions of turmoil in postcolonial territories where Westerners try to live exotic adventures that are frustrated because of their failure to understand those societies. *Guerrillas* (1975), about the activities of marginal West Indian revolutionaries, is based on real events already reported by Naipaul for the English media; this provides the reader with an exceptional opportunity to appreciate and contrast the writer's technical handling of both genres, fiction and journalism. *In a Free State* (1971), Booker Prize winner, and *A Bend in the River* (1979) offer somber accounts of chaos at the time of the African transition to postcolonialism, foregrounding the lack of a coherent ideology or leadership that might fill the vacuum left by the old political order.

Naipaul's ceaseless traveling activity has also resulted in a number of articles and travelogues, mainly concerned with sociopolitical affairs. Well before this became staple economic theory, he advocated deregulation and market economy for the collapsed societies of formerly affluent countries such as Uruguay and Argentina; in the same volume (*The Return of Eva Perón*, 1980) he condemns the brutality and the intellectual platitude of self-styled revolutionary African regimes. In *Among the Believers* (1981) and its sequel, *Beyond Belief* (1998), Naipaul exposes the double moral standards of radicals from Iran, Pakistan, Malaysia, and Indonesia who despise Western civilization and, at the same time, profit from its technological progress; he also criticizes the obliteration of rich pre-Islamic traditions in the countries visited, as well as the fanaticism associated with Muslim fundamentalism. *A Turn in the South* (1989) explores the complexity of racial issues in the United States. India, the land of his ancestors, is portrayed in three works. The writer shifts in this series from the fierce criticism of *An Area of Darkness* (1964), softened in *India: A Wounded Civilization* (1977), to a more sympathetic attitude of understanding and appreciation of this country's rich cultural and spiritual heritage and of the social transformation and economic achievements evinced in *India: A Million Mutinies* (1990).

V. S. Naipaul considers that his connection with his Indian traits, including religious belief, has been affected by the passing of time and the obvious geographical gap imposed by the migration of his ancestors, although critics believe that his Brahminical background stands out prominently in his career and accounts for his peculiar behavior and attitude of superiority. He has similarly expressed his disaffection toward his native Caribbean, a region that he sees hampered by poverty, political instability, and the minor significance of the islands on a worldwide scale. Naipaul also resents the situation of East Indians there, where rivalry with the black population has resulted in violence and discrimination against them. As a consequence, Naipaul feels that he is a man without roots. He has been living in Britain since his time at the university, but he still makes a point of considering this residence as temporary. Not committed to any particular civilization or location, his restless traveling activity complies with his determination to consider himself a citizen of the world.

Naipaul has progressively earned a reputation as a supercilious, sulky person who has even alienated many of his closest friends. His gratuitous comments on certain countries and ethnic and social groups have not helped to improve his public image. However, he tends to be sympathetic with oppressed individuals in hostile environments, and in his extensive writing we find appreciative portraits of the man in the street, the small entrepreneur or farmer. Above all, he is always ready to condemn the neglect or abuse of human rights.

Naipaul has referred extensively to his belief in the death of the novel as a classical form since he no longer thinks it useful to reflect the circumstances of the contemporary world. Thus, two of his latest works, *The Enigma of Arrival* (1987) and *A Way in the World* (1997), although labeled as novels in some editions, can be better classified as documentary or autobiographical accounts of his life experience; they even echo many of the views expressed by the writer in articles and interviews.

Vidia Naipaul has been awarded most of the major literary prizes in the English language and has been knighted. His readership has expanded greatly, and he is now accepted in academic circles as a master of English prose. When he refers to his ambition to become a full-time writer, trying to find an appropriate and original subject matter, we recognize the archetypal anxiety of postcolonial intellectuals facing the confrontation between a non-European background and the metropolitan artistic and linguistic models. He is especially relevant when dealing with topics such as exile, **mimicry**, and **universalism**.

Further Reading: B. King 1993; T. Weiss 1992.

Jesús Varela-Zapata

Ashis Nandy   Political psychologist, sociologist of science, and social activist, Ashis Nandy is actively involved with the study of Indian public life and the culture of politics. The versatile Nandy, who is also a prolific writer, has authored a number of important works, including *The Savage Freud and Other Essays on Possible and Retrievable Selves* (1995); *The Illegitimacy of Nationalism: Rabindranath Tagore and the Politics of Self* (1994); *The Tao of Cricket: On Games of Destiny and the Destiny of Games* (1989); *Science, Hegemony and Violence: A Requiem for Modernity*; and the crucial *The Intimate Enemy: Loss and Recovery of Self under Colonialism* (1983). In addition, Nandy has also edited several collections, including *The Multiverse of Democracy: Essays in Honour of Rajini Kothari* (1996); *Traditions, Tyranny, and Utopias: Essays in the Politics of Awareness* (1992); and *Barbaric Others: A Manifesto on Western Racism* along with Merryl Wyn Davies and Ziauddin Sardar (1990).

Nandy is known to be a strident critic of **modernity** and the "**neocolonial**" **nation** state. Key themes that repeatedly recur in his works are a reaffirmation of "tradition," "civilization," and the concept of a "total self," which has been traditionally denied fruition by the forceful imposition of Western thought. He remains keenly concerned with varied aspects of the political and public landscape of India and with finding modes of cultural expression other than those provided by the hegemonic West.

The Savage Freud, in particular, endeavors to locate the cultural structures that defy the domination of the West. In this collection of essays, in which he claims to critique the concept of a "quasi dominant global consciousness" (vii), Nandy seeks to expose the principles of control that structure the public domain; his controversial essay on widow burning argues that the debate around suttee—generated by the suttee of eighteen-year-old Roop Kanwar in 1987—has avoided the discussion of some basic issues such as dowry deaths and bride burnings.

Criticizing the middle-class response to suttee, Nandy asserts that it has been shaped by a "grand spectacle of evil" (34) in which the middle class sets itself up as the guardian of rational thought and action. Nandy thus emphasizes the role of the urban middle class (considered by many as the neocolonial elite) in shaping indigenous culture. Other essays in *The Savage Freud* take up contemporary issues pertaining to the new Indian nation, and many look at aspects of Indian public life that have been marginalized by the culture of the state, such as terrorism, mass culture, and the media. Nandy also pays detailed attention to Girindrasekhar Bose (1886–1953), the first non-Western psychoanalyst in colonial India.

The Intimate Enemy, a key work in Nandy's postcolonial theorizing, undertakes to analyze the mode and method by which India had opposed the discourse of the West during the period of British rule. Nandy argues that colonial Indians created an alternative language of **resistance**, a point that is further elaborated by an analytical critique of "father of the nation" Gandhi and the mystic Shri Aurobindo. He also reads the strongly nationalistic Gandhian movement as an effort to seek an independence that defied the logic, rationale, and discourse of Western paradigms. While *The Intimate Enemy* is largely an analysis of the cultural and psychological dimensions of colonialism, Nandy also argues that colonialism complicates issues, such as gender, that become inextricably linked with class and religion.

In much of his writing, Nandy consistently searches for a synthesis of insights drawn from Western psychology as well as from Indian culture, including the classics and recent historical experience. He argues that non-Western cultures have to rediscover and re-create traditions to allow for a new form of tradition that is more viable in our current historical circumstances and also create new traditions of resistance. An interdisciplinary scholar, Nandy is always concerned with making sure that the borders between cultures and fields of learning remain porous.

As a relentless opponent of the Western tendency to homogenize difference, Nandy views the West as "one civilization in many" and severely critiques Western metathought such as science, rationality, development, and the nation-state. In *Alternative Sciences*, he discards the hegemonic mode of Western science and argues for an alternative to be found beyond the standard East–West dichotomy. Equally censorious of the West as well as of the non-West, Nandy is always consistent as a rigorous critic of modern India. In "The Political Culture of the Indian State," published in *Daedalus* in 1989, Nandy argues that the polity of India has been altered since its conception by the architects of the new nation; in his view, "the state has now come to control, not serve, civil society." Democracy is the inevitable casualty in such a scenario.

Nandy continues to maintain his involvement in the study of democracy with his longtime association with the Centre for the Study of Developing Societies (CSDC) in New Delhi, where he is a senior fellow and chair. Founded in 1963 by scholar-activist Rajini Kothari, CSDS was set up to initiate both theoretical and empirical research in the study of social and political development in India from a cross-national perspective and to examine, observe, and rethink the structure and implementation of democracy. The center describes its current research program as having four main foci: "democratic politics and its future; politics of culture, including the new technologies of culture & communication; politics of alternatives and human futures; violence, ethnicity & diversity."

Further Reading: Group for the Study of Composite Cultures 1996; Z. Sardar 1997.

Pallavi Rastogi

Rasipuram Krishnaswami Ayyar Narayan Born in Madras in 1906, Narayan was reared by his grandmother. In 1930 he took a First in English at Maharajah's College (Mysore) and worked as a teacher before devoting himself to full-time writing. Narayan, who has spent almost all his life in India, has received the A. C. Benson Medal (Royal Society of Literature) and the National Prize of the Indian Academy, his country's highest literary honor, for *The Guide* (1958). In 1981 he was made an honorary member of the American Academy and Institute of Arts and Letters. From 1989 he has been a member of the *Rajya Sabha* (Upper House of the Indian Parliament).

Until 1993, when he gave up writing, Narayan produced an important amount of novels, articles, collections of short stories, travel books, an autobiography and shortened versions of two traditional Indian epics: *The Ramayana* (1972) and *The Mahabharata* (1978).

Though he has been defined as a traditional teller of tales, his writings show clearly the hybridization and complexity of postcolonial literatures. Most of his novels are located in Malgudi, a fictional city that provides him with a perfect tapestry where he can depict a myriad of Indian characters and attitudes. One recurrent theme in his works is the denunciation of havoc caused by outsiders to the local communities (e.g., the family-planning female worker in *The Painter of Signs*, 1976). Many characters feel threatened by the changes that take place while, at the same time, they would like to benefit from them. They suffer from a crisis of **identity** caused by the mixture of the ancient Indian traditions and the Western lifestyle. Nonetheless, in the end life goes on, and it neither returns to the former state nor changes to what had been dreamed of; the printer of *The Man-eater of Malgudi* (1961), despite all, keeps on printing.

Further Reading: G. Kain 1993; M. Pousse 1995.

Gabriel E. Abad-Fernández

Narration Within contemporary theory, narration is understood as a rhetorical mode established by a writer that presents the reader with the characters, dialogues, actions, settings, and events that constitute a fictional story or factual report. In *Narrative Discourse Revisited* (1988), Gerard Genette constructs narration as a productive act that translates knowledge about a subject to discourse about a subject. The production of discourse is an inherent power of narration because it reports worldviews and inscribes **identities**.

Narration has a number of implications for postcolonial theory when we look at who is in control of the act. During the early stages of imperialism, those who possessed the ability to narrate were invariably those who were in power. The monarchs, the colonial administrators, poets, writers, and even the explorers and sailors constructed images of the peoples and lands that they encountered or heard about through narration. As the empires grew, the unbalanced representation of such accounts and stories led to a variety of "counternarrations" in which writers and speakers from within the colonial system, especially colonial subjects, sought to offer subordinated or marginalized perspectives on the world that they experienced. In learning to adapt narration to their own needs, these writers and speakers appropriated the technique that had produced all of **colonial discourse**. In doing so, they discovered narration's perpetual malleability or, as **Homi Babha** calls it, its "ambivalence."

Many postcolonial theorists focus on narration because of its central role in all types of cultural representation. In *Orientalism* (1978), **Edward Said** emphasizes the normative effects of narration and the power that it has to construct and subsequently confine representations of the East into a series of stereotypes. **Gayatri Spivak**'s analysis of the **subaltern** (members of the nonruling class) reconsiders counternarrations. Within her study, Spivak explores the narrations by which the subaltern expresses his or her experience. Like Said's criticism of normative narration, Spivak articulates how narration can conceal identities by working to relegate subjects into subordinate positions. Homi Babha recognizes narration as the primary mode of representation in his colonial discourse theories. He also attributes one of his key concepts of ambivalence to narration, celebrating the ability of narration to foster ambivalence by opening sites of **agency** and **resistance** for the disfranchised.

Further Reading: H. Bhabha 1990b; G. Genette 1988; G. Spivak 1987.

Jason A. Clark

Nation/Nationalism   The importance of nationalism in the postcolonial world is attested to by the sheer scale of the political **decolonization**, especially that after 1945, that created so many new nations. In the fifteen years after 1955 the total membership of the United Nations (UN) nearly doubled to 126, the majority of the new member nations being the project of decolonization in Asia, Africa, and the Caribbean. As UN members, these nations were able to intervene in key world conflicts, such as those surrounding the wars in Vietnam and Algeria or the 1956 Suez crisis, thereby reinforcing the centrality of the nation-state as the normative unit of political power in a postempire world.

The crucial issue of political subjecthood within the new independent nation was not the only manifestation of the vital part that nationalism plays in any discussion of the postcolonial, however. Understanding and theorizing the national have been a seminal part of the development of postcolonial studies, whether seeking to understand the nature of nationalism within the new decolonizing states or looking at the ways in which the colonial project created changes within the expanding nation-states of Europe during the eighteenth and nineteenth centuries.

What both these analyses have in common is the recognition that nationalism is a fundamentally *modern* phenomenon. In Europe nationality emerged as a form of solidarity in response to the evolution of complex social relations in the eighteenth and nineteenth centuries in particular. Much study of the postcolonial has focused on how the period of modern colonial expansion worked to consolidate the emerging national identities of the European colonial powers. The Spain for which Columbus claimed the "Indies" in 1492 was essentially an idea of the monarch and an extension of monarchical power. But when Wallis became the first European to visit Tahiti in 1767, or when Cook journeyed round New Zealand and up the east coast of Australia in 1770, the issues of culture contact and the trade that followed carried a strong outline of national community, especially given the importance of Pacific exploration to the continuing power struggle between the British and the French. In the spatial locations outside of Europe, European **modernity** found peoples, objects, and narratives that altered its development of the idea of the nation-state. During the nineteenth and early twentieth centuries, as colonial activity became more systematized, the national was rendered the normative model in discussions of the legitimacy of having colonial possessions. In Britain thinkers such as John Stuart Mill and J. A. Hobson saw colonial expansion as a natural consequence of nationalism. From political economy to realist novels, ideas of the national recorded both the drive for imperial possession and an unease as to its consequences.

Those theorists of nationalism who see the nation as an imagined or constructed community, such as **Benedict Anderson** and Ernest Gellner, have proved especially useful to postcolonial studies, as have **Marxist** critics keen to stress the centrality of capitalism to the colonial project. In their differing ways, both point to the problematic inheritance of nationalism faced by the new decolonizing states in the twentieth century. Nationalism was one of the most powerful forces in the decolonizing era of African, Asian, and Caribbean states, yet it carried within it the clear evidence of its European heritage. This split sense of the national has been theorized by **Homi Bhabha** both in his study of the workings of **colonial discourse** in India in the nineteenth century and in his specific focus on the ways in which issues of migration complicate the idea of the postimperial nation. Bhabha's work as a whole is often indebted to the work of **Frantz Fanon**, though his account on the working of the national declines to engage with Fanon's forceful portrayal of the same subject, the consequences of which have been addressed by other writers. For Fanon, writing in *The Wretched of the Earth* (1965), nationalism in the postcolonial world was best understood as a process of action and not as a retreat to culture. The effort of the people to assert difference that counted, not the raiding of the past to produce representations that countered any colonial attempt to falsify. Nationalism needed to become social consciousness. Such a theory was entirely in tune with the processes of the 1960s and 1970s, where postcolonial nationalism was seen fundamentally as an anticolonial activity.

Fanon's model of the nation is relatively simplistic: the nation is a largely uninterrogated concept that asserts the difference of postcolonial society by its existence outside colonial dominance. Other writers of Fanon's generation, such as **Amílcar Cabral**, offered accounts of the national that drew more on the interplay of colonial and postcolonial histories. For Cabral, culture was a vital category in a way that it was not for Fanon. It existed and survived colonial domination and became a complex catalyst for postcolonial nationalism in the era of decolonization. Cabral's theory can be seen in the heated debates that surrounded the conceptualization of African literature and arts in the 1950s and 1960s, where some intellectuals advocated the return to precontact forms of narratives, while others argued for the necessity of using **European** models, given the interpenetration of cultures caused by colonial history. That it is not paradoxical to think about postcolonial nationalism within an idea of European history and especially within the paradigm of the modern state has been most forcefully shown by Partha Chatterjee's work on Indian nationalism. In both *Nationalist Thought and the Colonial World* (1986) and *The Nation and Its Fragments: Colonial and Post-Colonial Histories* (1993) Chatterjee extends Anderson's ideas about the "imagined community" of the nation to argue for the necessary understanding of the **agency** of nationalists within postcolonial cultures.

Nationalism in postcolonial **settler colonies** took different forms from those of the post-1945 decolonization era. In the case of Canada, Australia, and New Zealand, colonial status and a measure of self-government were achieved far earlier, and there was a greatly reduced amount of oppositional rhetoric surrounding the proclamation of political independence. Carl Berger has argued in *The Sense of Power: Studies in the Ideas of Canadian Imperialism 1867–1914* that those Canadians who argued for imperial unity after Canadian Confederation in 1867 were, in fact, proponents of a form of nationalism, basing their arguments on specific readings of Canadian history and society. Berger's elision of any duality between national and imperial belonging in Canada stands in differing ways for the other settler colonies, where the demographics and makeup of the settler population meant that strong ties to Europe were always likely to be maintained. In **Australia** and New Zealand, aspects of political nationalism did produce significant cultural movements advocating a sense of national literature or art. The political drive toward Australian Confederation in 1900 coincided with a distinct wave of literary nationalism. The establishment of the *Bulletin* magazine in Sydney in 1880, especially the work of writers such as Henry Lawson and Andrew Barton ("Banjo") Paterson, who were significant contributors, was a vital event in providing Australians with a home in thought. In **New Zealand**, the run-up to the 1940 centenary of the signing of the Treaty of Waitangi, the document that is the foundation of the modern nation, saw a similar set of processes. The 1940 Centennial was an event of clear political self-consciousness but also aided those writers and artists, such as Allen Curnow and Frank Sargeson, who made the 1930s the most important decade in New Zealand arts. Though lacking such explicit links with political processes, the early part of the twentieth century in **Canada** saw movements in the visual arts in particular that were distinctly national. The Group of Seven, painters based in Toronto and Montreal, demanded that Canadian painters concentrate on the local landscape to communicate an appropriate sense of national identity.

In the same way that the post-1945 nationalisms in Africa, Asia, and the Caribbean were necessarily a combination of local and imported models, settler colony nationalisms were often movements that asserted themselves as unique fidelities to experience but, in fact, were full of borrowings of previous models, especially those of Europe. This is, finally, a point about nationalism's false consciousness.

Further Reading: B. Anderson 1991; N. Lazarus 1999.

Stuart Murray

Nation Language. *See* Edward Kamau Braithwalte

Native American Literatures   The literatures of Native America comprise more than 30,000 years of history, as many as 300 individual cultural groups, and over 200 different languages, as well as dialects, derived from seven basic language families. The genre of American Indian writing incorporates both **oral** and written literary traditions and reflects the diverse forms that economic, social, and political organizations have taken within American Indian communities. Native American oral traditions reside as distinct forms of interaction among tribal peoples and include within their multiple genres ceremonial performance, liturgy, oratory, creation narratives, ritual drama, and "as-told-to" autobiographies. Native American written genres incorporate the influences of Euroamerican literary traditions and reflect an inheritance of continuity and cross-cultural encounter in a wide range of critical essays, histories, autobiographies, fiction, poetry, and drama. Contemporary Native American writing in English is distinct in form and language from oral and written tribal traditions, yet it continues to foster a series of worldviews and values that recall its origins in tribal practices. These include a deep reverence for the land, a strong sense of community, the importance of living in harmony with the spiritual and physical universe, and the recognition of the power of word and thought to maintain continuity and balance. The current popularity of American Indian writing may be attributed to its success in representing the cultural distinctiveness of American Indian literary traditions. Some of the best examples of this achievement include Andrew Wiget, *Native American Literature* (1985), A. LaVonne Brown Ruoff, *American Indian Literatures* (1990), and Kenneth M. Roemer, "Native

American Writers of the United States," *Dictionary of Literary Biography* (1997). Yet the literature remains imbricated in a history of colonial struggle to reassert the political, cultural, and intellectual integrity of American Indian peoples and to secure the recognition of Native American communities as sovereign **nations** within the geographical boundaries of the United States. Contemporary American Indian issues include treaty rights, land claims, sovereignty, religious freedom, language retention, and restoration of social and cultural community practices. Native American writers thematize these issues and participate in a process of cultural recovery and renewal by exploring the influences of American Indian colonial policy on the lives of American Indian peoples and by challenging a history of colonial occupation through their narrative interventions. Their strategies for reconstructing and restoring American Indian cultural traditions include examining the effects of American Indian assimilationist policy on Native American communities; assembling through creative and critical writing the innovative ways in which Native cultures have continued to survive and evolve; and recovering the historical and political interventions that American Indian cultural critics have made to preserve tribal traditions. The policy by European Crowns and the U.S. government of entering into government-to-government negotiations with American Indian peoples preserved the formal recognition of American Indian communities as sovereign nations within North America in spite of consecutive attempts by the federal government to disregard treaties and to erode Native American tribal sovereignty. Between 1778 and 1871, the U.S. government ratified more than 371 separate treaties with Native American communities and continued to seek treaty relationships with American Indian peoples until as late as 1903. Vine Deloria Jr. and Clifford M. Lytle have formulated the term "nations within" to describe the legal entitlement of American Indian peoples to retain distinct land bases and to conduct themselves as sovereign nations within the political and geographical ambit of the United States. Colonial legislation, however, has persistently sought to limit or extinguish the tribal–federal relationship by expropriating the lands of American Indian communities through policies of removal and assimilation and by intruding on tribal jurisdiction through a series of laws to undermine tribal authority. The formulation of the Indian Removal Act in 1830, which enabled the forced relocation of American Indian peoples east of the Mississippi to an "Indian Territory" in the West already occupied by indigenous communities, was followed in 1887 by the General Allotment Act, which undermined traditional practices of kinship and collective land tenure by allotting lands held in trust by the community to individual homesteads and by instituting a federal program for identifying American Indian peoples according to "blood quantum" codes. "Full-blood Indians" through the allotment system were deeded with "trust patents" over which the federal government exercised full control for twenty- five years; "mixed-blood Indians" were deeded with "patents in fee simple" over which they exercised rights but for which they forfeited tribal membership. Estimates suggest that during the allotment period alone, American Indian peoples were forced to relinquish some 86 million acres of land, with "surplus" reserve lands opened to European settlement, corporate utilization, and incorporation into national parks and forests.

The loss of American Indian tribal homelands and the ambiguity surrounding modern tribal identity represent two important themes for contemporary Native American writers who examine the effects of American Indian policy on modern tribal nations. Diane Glancy's *Pushing the Bear* (1996) explores the tensions that develop within a Cherokee family when their lives are disrupted by their forced removal from their traditional homelands in the southeastern United States to an "Indian Territory" in the Southwest. Glancy's novel imaginatively reconstructs the 1838 relocation of thousands of Cherokee, Creek, Chickasaw, and Choctaw peoples along the "Trail of Tears" to offer a more complex understanding of the intersections of American Indian identity with colonial policies of invasion and dislocation. Similarly, Louise Erdrich's *Tracks* (1988) examines the erosion of tribal values within a Chippewa community as a result of the breakdown of the extended family unit and the betrayal of Chippewa treaty rights through forced settlement on land allotments. The novel connects the issues of interfamily conflict, fear of abandonment, and destruction of community values to the systemic betrayal of the Chippewa peoples, whose trust in the treaty arrangements has been violated by the negligence of the Bureau of Indian Affairs and profiteering band members. A more pronounced treatment of the betrayal of community interests and the disregard for human life emerges in Linda Hogan's *Mean Spirit* (1990), a novel that documents the indifference of the federal government to a series of suspicious deaths within the Osage community. Hogan's narrative illustrates how the government's failure to protect the rights of Indian peoples in Indian Territory leads to their financial dispossession and murder when federal officials refuse to act on their behalf, and they become the targets of corrupt local officials. The themes of corruption and violence also emerge in James Welch's historical novel *Fool's Crow* (1986), which dramatizes the violation of American Indian treaty rights among the Plains Indian peoples in a moving portrayal of the final subjugation of the Blackfeet people by the U.S. cavalry. In an ironic comment on the legal status of treaty documents, Welch illustrates how the U.S. cavalry attacks and kills a peaceful gathering of Pikuni Blackfeet even as their leader attempts to shield the community behind the treaty's written guarantee of "peace and friendship." Both novels by Hogan and Welch critique the policies of a colonial government that insists on its right to intervene and reconstruct Native American communities yet fails to uphold the rights of American Indian peoples to legal protection. Simon Ortiz in *From Sand Creek* (1981) has also documented the legacy of injustice inherited by Native peoples in a series of poems that memorialize the betrayal of American Indian interests to colonial America's relentless westward expansion. Sand Creek, Marias River, and Wounded Knee represent paradigmatic sites within contemporary Native American literature as writers recast the dominant narrative of progressive westward expansion in a counternarrative that reclaims a history of dispossession as a historical context for reading contemporary Native American literatures. Though sometimes represented as "protest literature" for its narrative exploration of historical instances of massacre, genocide, and cultural disappearance, the novels and poetry of contemporary Native American writers resist containment as chronicles of victimization by asserting the continuity and strength of American Indian peoples in reconstructing and renewing their cultural traditions.

The publication in 1968 of N. Scott Momaday's *House Made of Dawn* marks a watershed moment in the development of the field of contemporary Native American literatures. In contrast to a range of historical and ethnographic texts that sought to predict the decline of American Indian peoples and that popularized images of American Indians as either "noble savages" or "uncivilized brutes," Momaday's novel asserted the integrity and strength of Native American cultural practices and offered a vision of their integration with contemporary storytelling traditions in literatures by American Indian authors. The renewal of interest in narratives by and about Native American peoples—prompted in part by Momaday's Pulitzer Prize-winning novel—inspired the publication of a range of texts that focused on the lives of American Indian peoples and that explored the complexities of their relationships with each other and with the ongoing effects of colonialism within Native American communities. Kenneth Lincoln has proposed the term "Native American renaissance" to describe the renewal of interest in literatures by Native American peoples and to define the practice by American Indian authors of transforming the disruptions of the colonial past into expressions of cultural revival in the present. Many of the dominant themes of this revival include explorations of **diaspora** and displacement, racism, cultural conflict, exile, mixed-blood identity, and cultural continuity.

At the forefront of this "renaissance" is a collection of writing that examines the intersections between conflicting cultural values and the legacy of colonial exploitation among Native American peoples. N. Scott Momaday's *House Made of Dawn* explores how the issues of cultural dislocation and spiritual exhaustion trouble a young man on his return from World War II. The story illustrates the protagonist's struggle to reconnect with his tribal community in the aftermath of his participation in the war, his relocation to Los Angeles following a homicide, and his journey to self-recovery through the cultural traditions of his people. The invocation of oral and written storytelling traditions in Momaday's narrative and his portrayal of the tension between traditional and assimilated lives represent two of the distinguishing features of the narrative, which asserts the importance of self-recovery and spiritual renewal through cultural connection with the community. Momaday's novel, in its treatment of the issue of cultural dislocation and loss of identity, recalls the earlier work of D'Arcy McNickle in *The Surrounded* (1936) and Zitkala–Ša in *American Indian Stories* (1921), both of whom explore the issue of cultural disconnection for American Indian people who have been forced to relocate to non-Native schools through government policies of compulsory assimilation and separatism. In contrast to the cultural barriers of racism and assimilation considered in writings by McNickle and Zitkala–Ša, Leslie Marmon Silko's *Ceremony* (1977) examines the relationship between contemporary moments of cultural imperialism and the federal government's policy of violating American Indian land sovereignty by mining Native American communities for their natural resources. In *Ceremony*, Silko illustrates how Tayo's recovery from his participation in the political and racial violence of the Vietnam War depends upon his recognition of the ongoing environmental exploitation of Native American communities by corporate America. The relationship that Silko proposes between economic colonialism and cultural violence has become an important topic in contemporary Native American writing, particularly for writers such as Joy Harjo, Wendy Rose, and Chrystos, whose poetry examines the intersections between racial and economic exploitation in the lives of working-class, lesbian, and mixed-blood American Indian people. The problem of economic exploitation is also a prominent theme in Linda Hogan's *Solar Storms* (1995), a novel that traces the widespread social, cultural, and environmental damage that occurs within a Native American community following the installation of a hydroelectric dam.

Geary Hobson in "The Rise of the White Shaman as a New Version of Cultural Imperialism" and Wendy Rose in "The Great Pretenders: Further Reflections on Whiteshamanism" have also argued that economic imperialism is a common feature of the appropriation movement in which many non-Native writers have adopted the traditions of American Indian peoples, not out of respect for the cultural distinctiveness of American Indian communities but in order to further their assumptions of cultural superiority and spiritual revival. In addition to exposing the issues of ethnocentrism and economic imperialism that underlie the appropriation movement, creative and critical writers such as Gerald Vizenor and Thomas King have devised an alternative aesthetic tradition that reconfigures the mythic trickster figure of tribal discourse from a multifaceted cultural hero to a contemporary symbol of contradiction and instability. In *The Trickster of Liberty* (1988) and *The Heirs of Columbus* (1991), Gerald Vizenor constructs a "cross-blood" figure that challenges popular notions about identity and knowledge and produces a postmodern liberatory space in which contradictory histories and languages can emerge. Thomas King in *One Good Story, That One* (1993) and *Green Grass, Running Water* (1993) deploys the trickster figure in narratives that illustrate the ethnocentrism within dominant Eurocentric cultural traditions while undermining the cultural arrogance on which they rely for their authority. Although the issue of cultural imperialism has been addressed by a number of Native American writers, the problem remains a significant one as it continues to work in tandem with the dominant misconception that American Indian communities are merely cultural enclaves passing through a stage of history rather than sovereign nations with distinct political, social, and cultural institutions and traditions.

Contemporary Native American critical practices encounter the difficulties of defining the field of Native American literatures when the constitutive features of the literature are constrained by questions of authenticity and **identity**. Rather than reinscribe structures of identification that originated in colonial policies based on blood quantum codes and in order to expand the range of creative and critical material beyond a narrow focus on the contemporary moment, Native American literary critics have sought a twofold "tribal-centered criticism" that, on the one hand, reconnects the values and worldviews of American Indian peoples with a contemporary critical framework and, on the other, undertakes recovery work to broaden rigid prescriptions on subject matter that overlook American Indian intellectual traditions. Paula Gunn Allen's *Grandmothers of the Light: A Medicine Woman's Source Book* (1991) proposes a "gynocratic" reading of Native American literature that emphasizes the concepts of balance and interconnectedness and that foregrounds the values of personal autonomy, communal harmony, and egalitarianism found within traditional oral narrative forms. Allen's critical practice contests the incorporation of Native American literatures within dominant Western perspectives and challenges paternalistic readings of Native literatures that have elided the role of women. In a similar manner, Robert Allen Warrior argues for the autonomy of American Indian intellectual traditions in his recovery of the work of Vine Deloria Jr. and John Joseph Matthews in *Tribal Secrets: Recovering American Indian Intellectual Traditions* (1995). Like Allen, Warrior politicizes literary aesthetics in his contention that Native American literary practices need to be assessed from a materialist perspective that considers both the historical circumstances from which it emerges and the political associations of its producers. His work has been instrumental in redefining the field of Native American literary studies from an emphasis on issues of identity to a consideration of the influences of earlier Native American cultural critics on contemporary writers. In contrast to Warrior's focus on the imbrication of historical forces with literary narratives, Jace Weaver's *That the People Might Live: Native American Literatures and Native American Community* (1997) suggests a contrapuntal reading that eschews distinctions between tribal and mixed-blood, rural and urban to argue for a conception of Native American literatures as "communitist" in its proactive representation of the values, worldviews, and intellectual traditions of Native American communities and in its restorative ability to advocate personhood and representational sovereignty for Native American peoples. Paula Gunn Allen, Robert Allen Warrior, and Jace Weaver articulate critical practices that recognize the historical, cultural, and political embeddedness of Native American literary traditions within contemporary America, yet they also articulate the distinctiveness of Native American critical practices through their formulation of discrete concepts and worldviews that emerge from the literature. Since "postcolonial" has long been resisted as a term for categorizing contemporary Native American literatures by Native American critics and American Indian writers, the challenge for postcolonial scholarship is to articulate a relationship between the literature and liberation struggle that can attend to the specificities of the historical and legal status of treaty relationships between American Indian peoples and the

U.S. government without overlooking contemporary forms of cultural and economic colonialism within Native American communities.

Further Reading: M. A. Jaimes 1992; A. Wiget 1994.

Cheryl Suzack

Nativism Because aboriginal rights are aligned with drives for independence in many regions, the concept of nativism is often associated with nationalism, anti-imperialism, and **negritude**. Early criticism of colonialism was accompanied by a resurgence in pride for **indigenous** arts and lifestyles. Such interest in traditional sources encouraged writers and critics like Léopold Senghor to argue for the reclamation of African traditions as a reversal of Europe's racist definition of blackness (1995, 48). Likewise, **Amílcar Cabral** speaks of a "national culture," one that recalls Africa's multiple civilizations, and promotes the "development of a *people's culture* and all aboriginal positive cultural values" (1979, 148, 153). **Ngũgĩ wa Thiong'o** insists that **African languages** are revolutionary, leading to the "inescapable conclusion" that since literature in Africa is an intrinsic part of antiimperialist struggles, writing must be done in African tongues (1986, 27, 28). Chinweizu, Onwuchekwa Jemie and Ihechukwu Madubuike similarly claim that decolonizing and liberating African literature involves looking to one's cultural roots rather than to Europe for inspiration (1983, 2). Haunani-Kay Trask, a Hawaiian activist, maintains that "Hawaiian literature," concomitant with the demand for Native sovereignty, is the specific right of the indigenous people, for whom only is the claim of Hawaii as nation legitimate (1999, 170). Collectively, these perspectives define nativism as a political platform because they utilize the empowered image of the "Native" as an opposition to European/Western colonialism.

Alternative definitions of nativism can be found in critiques of this position. **Frantz Fanon** warns against nationalism's exoticized worship of native culture and a blind discarding of Western ways (1965, 221). Fanon's arguments are further developed by Kwame Anthony Appiah, who notes the dangers in making the "Native" a kind of biological category in the same manner as race and how the concept of **nation** becomes closely aligned with "nativism" as many assume African independence requires an absolutely distinct literature of its own (1992, 56). Appiah further argues that, as a result, such beliefs encourage a fracturing of identity into contentious binaries—inside/outside, Western/traditional, indigene/alien; thus, "African literature" becomes caught up in the same ideological (colonial) framework that conceived of the "dark continent" as opposite to Europe (59). **Wole Soyinka** also maintains that the native image of Africa is prone to exploitation by demagogic opportunists who turn sentiment into a new aggression, if not rabid national consciousness (1988, 17). **Edward Said** observes similar problems in the **Rastafarian** movement, **Pan-Africanism**, Islamic fundamentalism (Islamism), and certain African and Latin American regimes (1993, 228). For Said, nativism constitutes an embracing of the "metaphysics

of **essences**"—as can be found in negritude, Irishness, Islam, and Catholicism—
and an "abandon[ment] of history for essentializations that have the power to
turn human beings against each other" (228–29).

Other scholars offer more complex definitions of the concept with the hope
of critically assessing the benefits that this problematic platform may offer. In
an analysis of **Derek Walcott**, Patrick Hogan identifies several different types
of nativism: reactionary nativism, the general inversion of colonial and racial
hierarchies; romantic nativism, the formation of **identity** via the values and
images ascribed to natives by their oppressors; opportunistic nativism, an idealization of the culture and history of the oppressed; sectarian nativism, or the
affirmation of tribal identities; and neocolonial nativism, a celebration of indigenous traditions by those who benefit as "junior partners" of former colonies.
All of these, in turn, are viewed by Hogan as impetus for movement and change
despite questionable, if not uncomfortable, results (1994, 113–114). Adéléke
Adé èk ó also gives multiple definitions: classical nativism, which supports an
"irreducible African aesthetic"; structural nativism, which seeks to combine the
indigenous with the modern; and linguistic nativism, which believes that African
literature must be written in native African languages (1998, ix). Like Hogan,
Adé èk ó promotes the employment of nativism by arguing that the popular
"rhetoric of difference and liberal **multiculturalism** are inspired by nativist discourses of self assertion" (23). This faith in the effectiveness of nativism is
shared by Benita Parry, who defends this concept by calling it a politicized
theory of history, race, and identity that urges and motivates writers to consciously work toward liberation (1994, 182, 186). Other critics seek a more
"natural" explanation for the popularity of nativism. Although his essay is primarily concerned with reading Chenjerai Hove's work, Matthew Engelke provides a bridge between proponents and critics by arguing that "Africanization,"
or the nativization of African literature, is "culturally natural, not naturally cultural" (1998, 34). This stance identifies the problems of nativism yet reads this
perspective as something that the oppressed, in their search for political empowerment, naturally adhere to. This is the argument proposed by E. N. Obiechina,
who finds that "[c]ultural nativism, or that aspect of it called literary nationalism,
is fundamentally a universal phenomenon" (1968, 25–26).

Further Reading: A. Appiah 1992; E. N. Obiechina 1968.

Seri Inthava Kau'ikealaula Luangphinith

Negritude   This is the Anglicized spelling and pronunciation of the French
word *négritude*, a term coined by Léopold Sédar Senghor and **Aimé Césaire**
between 1933 and 1935. The word itself derives from the French "*nègre*," which
many have translated into English as "nigger." Along with Léon-Gontran Damas
and other black poets from French colonies, Senghor and Césaire formed the
negritude movement in Paris in the 1930s in response to white racism and
imperialism. While "negritude" was coined during the negritude *movement*, it is

important to make a distinction between negritude as a literary movement and negritude as both a literary technique and a personal philosophy. Literary negritude is the poetic expression of a pride in the black experience, a literary theme that continues to be used today. The negritude movement, on the other hand, was a historical protest movement that lasted from the 1930s until the late 1950s and relied on French-language poetry as its medium. Its poets were among the first African writers, and its influence can be felt throughout later black political movements, such as Steve Biko's black consciousness movement in South Africa and the "black is beautiful" movement in the United States. The members of the negritude movement can be identified and, more often than not, are willing to identify themselves as negritude writers.

Césaire (b. 1913), one of the first negritude writers, is originally from Martinique, an island in the Caribbean that France colonized in 1635 and is still considered an overseas department of the French Republic. Damas (1912–1978) was from French Guiana, a French colony in South America since the late seventeenth century, also now an overseas department of France. Senghor (b. 1906), who worked closely with Césaire and Damas during the negritude movement, hails from Senegal. In 1960, when the French West African colony gained its independence, Senghor was elected its president, a position that he held until 1980.

Due to the assimilationist policies of French colonization, many blacks in French colonies grew up thinking of themselves as Frenchmen, an identity that was, for the educated elite like Senghor, Césaire, and Damas, harshly disrupted when they arrived at university in a racist Paris. For the first time, Césaire, Senghor, and Damas and other French-speaking black intellectuals began to develop a notion of shared blackness. In the mid-1930s, Césaire was studying under professors in Paris whose research on racial topologies encouraged his new orientation toward the idea of a universal blackness.

This idea of the black cultural archetype, or "the black personality," became a backbone of the negritude movement, especially as Senghor describes it. He defined the black personality as: "the sum total of those . . . values common to all Africans and permanent at the same time" and as "the symbiosis of the geography and history, of race and ethnic group" (Senghor 1971, 37, 40–41). The specific characteristics that he attributed to black people included a tendency toward imagination, a sensitivity to rhythm, and the ability to "think with their soul[s]" rather than with their heads. Many of these notions were similar to white stereotypes of black people, but the negritude poets gave them positive connotations rather than negative ones. Negritude set out to reverse the Western notions of Africa and blackness. Negritude poets made black a signifier for the positive and white an image of the negative. Jean-Paul Sartre called this idea Senghor's "anti-racist racism." The point, however, was not only to change Western perceptions of the black world but also to destroy the negative self-image held by blacks at that time due to mental colonization.

At the time that Senghor and Césaire coined the term "negritude," the word itself was seen as revolutionary. The negritude writers sought to shock their French audiences, for whom the words *"négritude"* or *"nègre"* would carry the connotations of racial epithets.

The goals of the negritude movement were to use poetry to assert the humanity of black people, the uniqueness of black culture, and the contribution of black culture to world history. Negritude writers promoted a return to the values of precolonial African cultures, especially African artistic forms. The negritude writers' discovery of African art's influence on "Western" modern art reinforced their commitment to rectifying the negative image of Africa in the West.

With the beginnings of a sense of shared blackness and influenced by the Harlem Renaissance writers of the United States, many of whom lived in or visited Paris in the 1930s, Senghor, Césaire, and Damas began writing poetry in French about being black. Some of the most famous African and Caribbean poetry stems from this period of the negritude movement in the 1930s and 1940s. Much of the early negritude poetry was published in *L'Edudiant noir* (The Black Student), a journal founded in Paris by Damas, Césaire, and Senghor. Damas was the first negritude poet to publish a book, *Pigments*, in 1937, although he never became as famous as Césaire or Senghor. In 1935 Césaire began his most famous poem, *Cahier d'un retour au pays natal* (Notebook of a Return to the Native Land, 1939). In both of these works one can find negritude's common themes, such as exaltation of blackness, conflation of women with the idea of "Mother Africa," references to African landscapes and animals as well as to the natural world in general, and the repeated visual and auditory image of the tom-tom, or drum. Other common themes in negritude poetry include exile; the black man in a white world; the dehumanizing effects of ill-employed technology; childhood; reconciliation of self with one's origins; traditional themes like love, death, solitude, suffering; and longing for the homeland, be that Africa or the Caribbean.

Césaire returned to Martinique in the 1940s and so was no longer in direct contact with Senghor but continued to write negritude poetry, publishing a number of books. These include *Les armes Miraculeuses* (the Miraculous Weapons, 1946), *Soleil cou-coupé* (Solar Throat Slashed, 1948), and *Corps perdu* (Lost Body, 1950).

In 1948 Senghor edited *Anthologie de la nouvelle poésie nègre et malgache de langue française* (Anthology of New Black and Malagasy Poetry in French), a text that became the key collection of negritude work, including Sartre's famous introduction "Orphee Noir" (Black Orpheus) and poetry by not only Césaire and Damas but also Martinican writers Gilbert Gratient and Étienne Lero, Guy Tirolien and Paul Niger of Guadeloupe, Haitian poets Jacques Romain, Jean-F. Brière, René Belance, and Léon Laleau, Senegalese writer Birago Diop, Cameroonian poet David Diop, and Jean-Joseph Rabárivelo, Jacques Rabémananjara, and Flavien Ranaivo from Madagascar. Senghor's other works include *Chants d'ombre* (Songs of Shadow, 1945), *Hosties noires* (Black Offerings, 1948), and *Ethiopiques* (1956).

Damas also made a number of contributions to negritude writing, including not only poetry but also short stories, in *Veillees noires* (1943). In 1947 he edited an anthology similar to the one that Senghor would publish a year later, which Damas titled *Poetes d'expression francaise d'Afrique Noire, Madagascar, Reunion, Guadeloupe, Martinique, Indochine, Guyane: 1900–1945* (Poets of French Expression from Black Africa, Madagascar, Reunion, Guadeloupe, Martinique, Indochina, Guiana: 1900–1945). Damas' anthology never received the same critical attention as Senghor's, but he continued writing, putting out *Poèmes nègres sur des airs africains* (1948), *Graffiti* (1952), and *Black Label* (1956).

All of the writing that came out of the negritude movement was written in French. In 1937, at a conference in Dakar, Senghor advocated a return to African languages yet never heeded this advice in his own poetry. However, he includes many African words in his poetry, which, according to some critics, indicates his love for his native languages, Serer and Wolof. Likewise, Césaire has tried to include African languages in his French poetry, though because he speaks no African language, he often settles for words that *sound* African. Unlike later English-speaking Africans, the negritude poets never felt the need to justify their use of a colonial language. However, the two groups of writers had similar reasons for using French and English, respectively: communication. One reason that French was chosen as the language of negritude is that it was seen as uniting black people colonized by the French who, dispersed throughout West Africa and the Caribbean, otherwise had no shared language. Despite this idealism, many critics have questioned whether African and Caribbean people who speak French choose to read French poetry, especially when it is filled with surrealistic images as many negritude poems are.

Beginning in the 1950s, many African writers began to reject the negritude movement. Some well-known writers who have criticized negritude include Ralph Ellison, **Ngũgĩ wa Thiong'o**, Ayi Kwei Armah, Taban lo Liyong, Ezekiel Mphahlele, and **Wole Soyinka**, none of whom were raised under French colonialism. In contrast to French assimilationist policies, English colonial policy, which was based on segregation, left the cultures and political organizations of its African "subjects" largely intact. Many have argued that this is the reason that the negritude movement never took hold in the English colonies and, in fact, that many English-speaking African poets have reacted negatively to the idea of negritude. Furthermore, in many English colonies, like Zimbabwe and South Africa, blacks and other nonwhite ethnic groups were constantly reminded of their "blackness" as a difference that was used to oppress them. Thus, many anglophone writers did not see negritude's return to "African roots" as positive.

Another aspect against which later writers reacted was the negritude writers' romantic view of Africa. Many felt that Senghor and Césaire had an unrealistic view of Africa because they had been so separated from their cultures by French colonialism and had lived in exile in Paris. South African writer Ezekiel Mphahale has voiced this concern the most strongly, arguing that Senghor and Césaire ignore the harsh realities of oppression and struggle in Africa in favor of what they perceived as positive in African societies.

A third major critique of the negritude movement has been its sexism. Outside of negritude poetry's subject matter, women have been largely ignored by the literary movement. Gender inequality in the education system during the period of the negritude movement was a major cause of women's absence in the movement. At the time that the negritude movement began, very few African women were even receiving primary school education. Moreover, though male black writers in French were publishing as early as 1920, francophone African women did not begin publishing literature until the mid-1970s. Few women had enough education to become writers, let alone to travel to Paris for university like the negritude men. Despite the glaring absence of women poets in the negritude movement, men have often treated women themselves as the subjects, even the themes, of negritude poetry. Negritude proclaimed, for the first time in writing, that blackness and black femaleness are beautiful; however it did so problematically. A prime example is Senghor's *"Femme Noir"* (Black Woman, 1945), his most famous poem. The poem is a direct address to an unnamed and therefore universalized "Naked woman, black woman" whose "form which is beauty" the speaker salutes. He simultaneously depicts the woman as mother and sex object. She nurtures the speaker, "making/lyrical [his] mouth" while remaining silent herself as "the Conqueror's fingers" explore her symbolic black body. Negritude's continued portrayal of African woman as mothers and sex objects, not dissimilar to the "matriarch" and "Jezebel" stereotypes of African American women by whites and black men in the United States, results in the entrapment of women into roles defined solely by their relationships to men and bearing little relationship to reality.

In locating the problems with negritude, criticisms of the concept often fail to make the distinction between the negritude movement and literary negritude. There are, however, a number of writers, in both Africa and in the diaspora, who use negritude themes but were not a part of the negritude movement itself— some because they came after it, some because they do not use French, and some because they are women. Writers whose work critics have connected to negritude include Cameroonian novelist **Mongo Beti**, Ghanaian poet and literary critic Abena Busia, Ghanaian novelist **Ayi Kwei Armah** (despite his own criticisms of negritude), South African poet and novelist Mongane Wally Serote, Senegalese poets Coumba Diakhâté and Mame Seck Mbacké, African American poet Sonia Sanchez, and Ugandan poet Okot p'Bitek. Such writers who produce negritude poetry or novels after the movement itself has petered out are in various ways taking on the responsibility of filling in the details of black life that Negritude left out: describing present black reality rather than glorifying the past, using African languages to fully reclaim their heritage in a way that is not possible through the French language, giving voices to women so as to defy male-conceived roles and stereotypes, and moving beyond a vision of race as the most important issue of black poetry.

Since the 1960s, critics have overtly and implicitly referred to negritude as a thing of the past. But like their supporters outside of the negritude movement, even after most African countries had achieved independence in the 1960s and the negritude movement had faded, the writers of the movement continued to publish work that utilizes negritude to varying degrees and in different forms. Césaire's own work has shown a movement from the black specificity of early negritude toward the universal **humanism** that was seen as the ultimate goal of negritude. In 1960 he published *Ferraments* (line fittings), followed much later by *Noria* (1976) and *moi, laminaire* (I, laminaire, a type of kelp, 1982). He also wrote plays, which some scholars see as more militant and political than was his negritude work. Much of his work has been collected in *Aime Césaire: The Collected Poetry* (1983; trans. and ed. by Clayton Eshleman and Annette Smith) and *Aime Césaire: Lyric and Dramatic Poetry 1946–1982* (1990; trans. and ed. by Eshleman and Smith). Senghor went on to write *Nocturnes* (1961), *Elegies majeures* (Major Elegies, 1979), and a number of essays about negritude and his fellow negritude writers. Damas published *Nevralgies* in 1965.

Further Reading: A. Berrian and R. Long 1967; B. Jack 1996.

Katrina Daly Thompson

Neocolonialism   Postcolonial theorists have expanded on the notion of imperialism after empire. This development is fueled by the fact that the hope for the end of empire opening up a new stage in the development of the Third World remains unfulfilled. Political independence brought an end neither to economic problems nor to economic dependency. On the contrary, some of the new states became more involved in, and dependent on, the Western-dominated world system than they had been under colonial rule. Neocolonialism and dependency became a word and theory, respectively, to explain this new state. The "neo" colonial represented the imposition of the metropolitan power' dominant cultural values through more effective technological, bureaucratic, and moralizing avenues.

The term is discussed at length by Kwame Nkrumah, the first president of independent Ghana and the leading exponent of **Pan-Africanism**, in his *Neocolonialism: The Last Stage of Imperialism* (1965). Neocolonialism is partly a planned policy maintained by advanced nations to influence developing countries but is also simply a continuation of past practices. Nkrumah's thesis followed that of Vladimir Lenin, who had described imperialism as the highest stage of capitalism. Nkrumah further added that neocolonialism was its *final* stage. By the late 1950s, it had become clear to the surviving empires that formal colonialism had to be liquidated. Only Portugal continued to resist its dissolution since the country's politically isolated and marginalized metropolitan economy could not afford neocolonialism. The Portuguese government needed to exploit its African resources and, since its economy was not competitive, could do so only through direct control. The British and French, on the other hand, saw a great need to modernize the relationship between themselves and their colonies and to bring that relationship into line with the requirements of the new multinational capitalism.

According to Nkrumah, the neocolonial stage is the most dangerous and the worst form of imperialism. He attributed this phenomenon to the fact that for those who practice it, the new order indicates power without responsibility. Those who suffer under it experience exploitation without visible means of redress. In the days of colonialism, the imperial power had to justify to its citizenry at home its actions abroad. By extension, those who served the ruling imperial power in the colonies could at least look to its protection against any violent move by local opponents. With a neocolonial order, that is not the case. The methods of neocolonialism, Nkrumah argued, are much more subtle and varied, operating not only in the economic realm but also in that of politics, religion, ideology, and culture. He outlined two principles that inspired early capitalism: the subjugation of the working classes and the exclusion of the state from having any voice in the control of capitalist enterprise. By abandoning these two principles and substituting for them "welfare states" based on high working-class living standards and a state-regulated capitalism at home, the developed countries succeeded in exporting their internal problem and transferring the conflict between rich and poor from the national to the international stage. Nkrumah envisaged a situation in which an economically free and politically united Africa would force the monopolists to come face-to-face with their own working class in their own countries, and a new struggle would arise within which the liquidation and collapse of imperialism would be complete.

In a neocolonial context, the state is, in theory, independent and has all the outward trappings of international sovereignty. In reality, however, its economic system and thus its political policy are directed from outside. Investment under neocolonialism increases, rather than decreases, the gap between the rich and the poor countries of the world. The system is based upon the principle of breaking up former large colonial territories into a number of small, nonviable states that are incapable of independent development and must rely upon the former imperial power for defense and even internal security. The economic and financial systems of the former colonies are thereby linked, as in colonial days, with those of the former colonial ruler.

In the neocolonialist territories, where the former colonial power has, in theory, relinquished political control, if the social conditions occasioned by neocolonialism cause a revolt, the local neocolonialist government can be sacrificed, and another equally subservient one can be substituted in its place. A revolt in a neocolonial state is often accompanied by threats to other underdeveloped nations that may have the potential of bucking the unequal relationship. Hence, the same social pressures that can produce revolts in neocolonial territories also affect those states that refused to accept the system. The imperial powers essentially have a ready-made weapon for continual dominance.

Under the guise of giving aid geared toward development, colonial objectives of imposing political and economic control are achieved by other formal means. Kwame Nkrumah had cited as examples of neocolonial regions Latin America, Asia, the Caribbean, and Africa. Nkrumah argued that with the help of Western counterintelligence and intelligence agencies, the setting up of military bases and stationing of troops, and the continual supply of "advisers" to these former territories, the self-determination of satellite states is continually undermined. He also indicted Labor in Europe for being an arm of imperialism, stressing that through the activities of the social democratic parties of Europe led by the British Labor Party and various intercontinental trade unions, European interests perpetuate big international monopolies in Africa, Asia, and Latin America.

The new order is usually marked by the request for a number of "rights" by the imperial power, including land concessions; prospecting rights for minerals and/or oil; and the right to collect customs, to carry out administration, to issue paper money, to be exempt from customs duties and/or taxes for expatriate enterprises, and, above all, to provide "aid." The growing conflict between the "West" and "East" (i.e., between the capitalist world bloc and the communist world bloc) was a major factor that determined the amount of independence that could be gained by former colonies; hence, there were demands and the granting of cultural privileges. Western information services in African states often operate as the exclusive preserve of the former colonial power and usually exclude the influx of information from socialist or even other African countries.

Nkrumah underscored the effectiveness of Western propaganda in the former colonies. He identified certain "Hollywood American movies" and other ideologically biased cultural products as influential in shaping the mind-set of Africans and other colonial territories. The success of such propaganda materials, he argued, is the only reason that Africans would cheer when their usually white heroes slaughter "red Indians" or Asiatics. In a similar vein, antisocialist propaganda usually cast trade union officers or revolutionary figures as villains. In other instances, this characterization is often placed upon the dark-skinned figure, while the white policeman or the federal agent is ever the hero. Nkrumah labeled Western propaganda as responsible for a unique ideological underbelly of political murders, which so often use local people as their instruments within the colonies. He blamed the monopoly press, newspapers and magazines, which operated under the auspices of foreign correspondence, and accused them of justifying Europe's political and economic imperial activities in international capitalist journalism. He also indicted Western radio stations, the Peace Corps, the United States Information Agency, and Moral Re-Armament for being part of the ideological plan for invading the so-called Third World. According to Nkrumah, the perpetuation of neocolonialism also encompassed the usage of the policy of divide-and-rule in African societies. He blamed modern-day religious evangelism as a phenomenon with a **pedagogy** that enhanced anticitizenship and oppositional behavioral tendencies among colonized **indigenous** communities. Postcolonial analysts emphasize the fact that indigenous educational patterns were repeatedly destroyed by the colonizer either by design or as the inadvertent result of policies that ignored local needs and traditions. Contemporary metropolitan traditions and publications that are exported to developing areas–such as textbooks that facilitate the developed world's policy goals–often arrive in forms below domestic standards and without much adaptation to local conditions. The use of foreign technical advisers on policy matters and the continuing foreign administrative models and curricular patterns for schools are cited as evidence of neocolonial practices. In addition, the dependence on expatriate teachers for secondary schools and colleges also leads to the inculcation of Western values and views in schools.

Nkrumah linked Africa's failure to make headway on the road to purposeful industrial development to the use of the continent's natural resources for the greater development of the Western world. He called for a union government on a Pan-African basis. He stated his conviction that for the first time in human history, the potential material resources of the world were so great that there was no need for rich and poor nations, emphasizing as the only drawback the organization needed to deploy these potential resources. He saw effective world pressure as a viable means to achieve redeployment but scorned civil rights movements based on appeals and moralizing arguments, claiming that only "deeds" can secure world realignment. Although he did not believe such counterpressures would lead to war and bloodshed, he suggested that often the absence of such initiatives constitutes a threat to world peace. Nkrumah highlighted the need for positive action as the remedy for neocolonialism. Failure to embark on these actions, he concluded, could eventually culminate in World War III. The Third World's cultural elite, many of whom live comfortably situated as expatriates in First World conditions, continues to contribute to the solidification of neocolonial global relationships. Critics accuse this intellectual class of deconstructing the language needed to articulate modern demands geared toward countering the U.S.–European hegemony. By extension, the conditions of people of African descent on the continent are also often linked with other "micro-African" experiences that dot urban centers around the world. Many such communities are defined by the way in which they suffer under the weight of material reconfigurations in the global economy.

Further Readings: M. Hardt and A. Negri 2000; K. Nkrumah 1965; W. J. Pomeroy 1970; M. K. Saini 1981; J. Woddis 1967.

Saheed Adeyinka Adejumobi

New Zealand/Maori Literature   New Zealand literature has traditionally been one of the most isolated of postcolonial literatures, seldom impinging on the world cultural stage. Writing from New Zealand first became noticed in an international context with the work of Katherine Mansfield (1888–1923). Many of Mansfield's short stories are set in a metropolitan milieu, but three in particular are prominent in their New Zealand setting: "Prelude" (1918) and "At the Bay" (1918), a diptych about the subtle relationships among the fictional Burnell family, and "The Voyage" (1924), a story of internal migration that ends on a note of startling optimism. These stories all concern childhood, which not only mirrors the biographical fact that Mansfield really spent only her childhood in New Zealand before moving to Europe but heralds the prominence of childhood as trope in New Zealand literature. The theme of childhood evokes both a sense of development out of the colonial dependence of a **settler colony** as well as the unique experience of a fresh landscape. Even though Mansfield's New Zealand origins were barely noticed in the celebration of her works in the United States and Europe, Mansfield's canonicity helped keep alive the very idea that there could be writers from places such as New Zealand. Work on Mansfield by New Zealand scholars (particularly the biographer Antony Alpers) has helped renationalize Mansfield, rescuing her from the maw of international **modernism**.

The real beginning of twentieth-century New Zealand literature, though, came with the fiction of Frank Sargeson (1903–1982) and the poetry of Allen Curnow (1911–   ). Both Sargeson and Curnow utterly eschewed any lingering Victorian inheritance and its attendant cultural ethos. Excelling in the brief narrative, Sargeson wrote colloquial stories featuring largely working-class characters. "Conversations with My Uncle" (collected in *Conversations with My Uncle and Other Stories*, 1936) though only a one-page sketch, gives a memorable glimpse of both bourgeois conformity and bohemian rebellion. New Zealand literature has always placed an unusual emphasis on exposing the limitations of middle-class normality, and this theme is nowhere more clearly expressed than in these early Sargeson stories. Sargeson's works allow the working class to enter the realm of letters with a thoroughness virtually unmatched in twentieth-century letters. In his later works, Sargeson wrote in longer forms and in more developed prose, as in *Memoirs of a Peon* (1965), whose satiric expansiveness is a far cry from the vernacular sketches of his early career. Sargeson's works were among the earliest in any postcolonial literature to take up homosexual themes.

Curnow's long poetic career stretched over seven decades; he is most famous for his early poems, written in the late 1930s and early 1940s, such as "House and Land" (1942) or "The Unhistoric Story" (1943), poems filled with wonderment and anxiety at the possibility of a truly New Zealand identity. The early Curnow poetic persona desperately wants to belong to his nation but knows his soul is not yet fully at home there, that it retains a settler mentality. Natural imagery, particularly that of the sea, is a motif throughout Curnow's work, though Curnow always looks at nature with an abstract eye. Curnow's work became less subjective and less strictly national in import as time went on, as seen in an austere later sequence, "Moro Assassinato," published in *An Incorrigible Music* (1979), about the murder by terrorists of the Italian politician Aldo Moro. The emergence of Sargeson and Curnow at midcentury paralleled more institutional developments in New Zealand literature such as the publication of the seminal journal *Landfall*, for many years the most prominent forum for New Zealand writers.

Pakeha (European-descended New Zealand) writing received an unexpected jolt from the unique genius of Janet Frame (1924–   ). Frame grew up in a middle-class North Island family; she had a bizarre early life in which two of her sisters drowned on separate occasions, and she herself was remanded to a mental institution, apparently without much justification, and almost lobotomized. The publication of a book of short stories by her is seen as the turning point in her life; Sargeson's recognition and support of her work were pivotal in enabling her artistic career. Frame might have been expected to write only autobiographical novels meditating on this trauma. But though many autobiographical themes are present in her writing (which includes three overtly autobiographical books), Frame's sense of marginal subjectivity is turned outward through quintessentially postmodern and postcolonial techniques. Frame's fiction is filled with sudden shifts in place, time, mode of **narration**, and levels of reality. *Owls Do Cry* (1957), her first novel, has a strong sense of social background as it chronicles a New Zealand family felled in various ways by forces of inauthenticity and disintegration. Frame does not monolithically focus on the character, Daphne Withers, whose plight is most like that of her own youth, "framing" her within a rich web of multiple meaning. In *Daughter Buffalo* (1972) as well as parts of other novels, Frame uses the United States as a setting, not only "writing back" against the neocolonial center but also writing about America in a way achievable by no American author. Frame's use of displaced and "re-placed" woman narrators makes her relevant to the idea of a postcolonial **feminism**. In the later novels *Living in the Maniototo* (1979) and *The Carpathians* (1988), the authorial perspective has become much more confident in its own disjunction, its decentered voices at once not yielding to any historical constraint yet retaining an undaunted eloquence of their own. In these books, Frame notes how much New Zealand may be filled with **mimicry** of America and Britain yet does not renounce the hope of a distinctive New Zealand identity.

The poems of Kendrick Smithyman (1922–1995) also have a postmodern aura that yet seems native to the author's sensibility; his characteristic themes such as mapping, landscape, and interchangeable signifier make him a participant in the postcolonial project. *Atua Wera* (1995) is Smithyman's final work and concerns a Maori prophet and his role in the Maori wars of the mid-nineteenth century. Bill Manhire (1946–   ), who served as New Zealand's first poet laureate in the late 1990s, developed an experimental poetic mode nimble in its juxtaposition of irony and sincerity. Feeling unconstrained by the traditional New Zealand poetic burden of writing the land, Manhire's poetry makes many international references, assuming a place in a global poetics of postmodernism. One major sequence, indicative of a greater New Zealand interest in Asia, narrates the life of the late Emperor Hirohito of Japan. Another poem, on the doomed racehorse Phar Lap, attempts to stake out a genuinely New Zealand cultural mythology without any kind of belabored evocation of landscape; a layer of salutary irony is added as the horse could equally as well be claimed as a national totem by Australia. Manhire has written wry, metafictive short stories; he has also been crucially important to New Zealand writing as a critic and teacher.

Although the majority of New Zealanders are descended from the British settlers who began to arrive in the early nineteenth century, the Maori population is a sizable and increasingly vocal minority, numbering roughly 600,000 as of the late 1990s. The Maori are people of Polynesian descent who arrived in what is now New Zealand around the thirteenth century, six centuries before any Europeans. The Maori at the time of European arrival comprised about forty to fifty *iwi*, each with a distinct tradition; the idea of a unified Maori people is, of course, a postconquest one, even though there are fundamental cultural similarities among Maori. Since modern Maori writing is written against a background of subordination and disinheritance, it can be seen as "postcolonial" in the general sense. But it must not be forgotten that Maori traditions, including poetic traditions, extend back well *before* the onset of European colonization. Maori writing in English began to develop from the 1960s, as the long-submerged culture and language of the **indigenous people** of New Zealand were revived and assumed a central role not only for Maori but for Pakeha New Zealanders. There was even movement for the name of the country to be changed to Aotearoa, a Maori name meaning "land of the long white cloud"; but this kind of politically inflected name change does not necessarily have currency in other contexts of **decolonization** (cf. the decision of Nelson Mandela and the African National Congress not to change the name of **South Africa** to "Azania" after the transition from apartheid in 1994). However, the hybrid term "Aotearoa/New Zealand" is increasingly used in contemporary discourse.

The poet Hone Tuwhare (1922–   ) was one of the first modern Maori writers to make a large-scale impact. Tuwhare worked as a manual laborer, and his poetry resonates as much upon the axis of class as on that of **race**. Plainspoken yet intensely multiple in meaning and stance, Tuwhare's poems are forceful, direct, and sometimes extremely funny. He is not ideologically prescriptive even when he protests against nuclear weapons, a cause central to New Zealand writers' political activities during the Cold War period. Witi Ihimaera (1944–   ) pioneered Maori fiction in English much as Tuwhare did for Maori lyric poetry. Though flamboyantly fictive, Ihimaera's novels, such as *The Matriarch* (1986), drew upon his own family and tribal background and especially exalted Maori female elders as keepers of their people's conscience and heritage. Ihimaera's often postmodern and metafictive works draw heavily upon Maori history and legend. His work often transcends binary oppositions, including the ostensibly ultimate opposition of life and death, both of which are seen as components of a cosmic continuum. Ihimaera has had the courage to advance beyond a positive critical stereotype of his work and write novels in the 1990s concerning issues of history and personal identity not necessarily confined to expectations of what "Maori fiction" should be. Patricia Grace (1937–   ), though possessing a less magniloquent voice than Ihimaera, may have the most consistent body of work in all of Maori **anglophone** writing. *Mutuwhenua* (1978) takes on the time-honored theme of interracial romance from a Maori perspective. The protagonist is an example of "double-consciousness" with an adult, Pakeha-centered identity of "Linda" that acts as a palimpsest on her genuine identity of "Ripeka." The book's conclusion stresses Ripeka's ability to juggle her personal independence and her ties to her Maori community. Although this sort of novel would usually revolve around plot, Grace is more interested in the overlay of cultural patterns than in indiscrete events or, indeed, fixed notions of what is "present," "past," and "future." The *whanau* (extended family) is the usual setting of Grace's works, although this does not entail domestic fiction in the customary sense. A characteristic preoccupation of Grace is what people, in both individual and collective terms, "value" in life. Grace's nonlinear mode of storytelling does not preclude depicting conflict, as in *Baby No-Eyes* (1998), but it does permit her vision to transcend the constraints of established fictional forms. By this time, Grace had declared that she would no longer use a glossary to define the Maori words that she used in her works because she saw this as pandering to Pakeha needs to have the Maori explained to them. In other words, the notion of a glossary, found in many New Zealand works going back to the nineteenth century, was as imperialistic as it was edifying. As New Zealand became more of a bicultural society, Maori words even appeared untranslated in works by Pakeha authors.

The bone people (1984), a novel by Keri Hulme (1947–), brought global visibility to New Zealand literature by winning the 1985 Booker Prize. This tale of a proud, isolated artist who becomes connected to the world outside her through taking responsibility for a small Maori boy, Simon, and also interacting with his violent Maori guardian, Joe, can be read as almost an allegory of an individualized, aesthetic modernism yielding to a more communitarian postmodernism. Hulme's alter ego, Kerewin Holmes, does, though, distance herself both from sexuality and from the kind of full-fledged extended family relationships characteristic of traditional Maori culture. This, as well as allegations made by the poet and critic C. K. Stead that Hulme's own claims to Maori ancestry are considerably overstated, prevent the novel from being used as a straightforward example of **subaltern** literature, as it is often deployed in North American universities. Also controversial is the fiction of Alan Duff (1950–), especially his unsentimental portrayal of the degradation and violence of urban Maori life in his depiction of the Heke family (the name meant to allude to a nineteenth-century Maori hero Hone Heke) in *Once Were Warriors* (1990). Although Duff's searing social realism was almost universally applauded, his critiques of the rhetoric of Maori victimization earned him a simultaneous celebrity and opprobrium not unreminiscent of the status of **V. S. Naipaul** in wider postcolonial circles. The young Maori poet Robert Sullivan (1967–), in *Star Waka* (1999), synthesizes traditional Maori themes within a matrix convergent with postcolonial concerns.

New Zealand society underwent a considerable shock in the 1980s as its traditionally socialist and protectionist economy was opened up to **globalization** and laissez-faire economics, ironically under the Labor government of David

Lange and his finance minister, Roger Douglas. The year 1990 saw the sesqui-centennial of the Treaty of Waitangi, the 1840 document by which the British had come into legal possession of New Zealand (and whose pledges to the Maori were largely breached). The commemoration was accompanied by a great deal of soul-searching about the disinheritance of the Maori from their land and the consequent need to reevaluate New Zealand identity, including a particular interest in the nineteenth-century land wars between Pakeha and Maori, a theme in recent fiction and historiography, as seen in the work of the novelist Maurice Shadbolt (1932–) and the historian James Belich (1956–).

There were also worries about emigration from New Zealand, particularly to Australia, although this was partially redressed by incoming populations from Polynesia and non-anglophone Europe, represented in the literary sphere by writers such as Sia Figiel (1967–) and Kapka Kassabova (1973–). On a more specific scale, the shift in the 1996 election and onward from the traditional Westminster system to a mode of proportional representation in the election of Parliament entailed a recalibration of the New Zealand political system. These kinds of changes perhaps had more immediate impact on literature than would be the case in other countries because of New Zealand's small population (3.5 million) and the fact that many of its intellectuals travel easily between literature, culture, and politics in their writing.

In the late 1990s, young writers such as Emily Perking (1970–) and Elizabeth Knox (1959–), who first surfaced in innovative journals such as *Sport*, attracted considerable attention in the wider English-speaking world, perhaps signaling that the era of the isolation of New Zealand literature is over.

Further Reading: T. Sturm 1998; M. Williams, 1990.

Nicholas Birns

Ngũgĩ wa Thiong'o   Ngũgĩ wa Thiong'o, who changed his name from "James Ngugi" in 1977, is one of the most influential African writers and theorists of postcolonial studies. Highly regarded as a novelist and playwright of the independence period of the late 1950s and early 1960s in Africa, Ngũgĩ is perhaps best known today for his injunction that the postcolonial African intellectual must write in African languages to actively resist the legacy of colonial and **neocolonial** political oppression.

Ngũgĩ was born in Limuru, Kenya, in 1938 to a family displaced from ancestral lands and directly involved in Kenya's rebellion against colonial rule, spearheaded by the Kenya Land and Freedom Army (Mau Mau). Ngũgĩ was educated at an independent Gĩkũyũ school and at mission-run and colonial schools, where he excelled because of his facility with the language of the colonizer. During study at Makerere University College in Uganda, Ngũgĩ contributed to various Nairobi newspapers, taking a surprisingly conservative stance on social and cultural issues, given his later political stridency. At Makerere, Ngũgĩ published short stories and worked on plays and his first-written, but second-published, novel, *The River Between* (1965), initially titled "The Black

Messiah." At Makerere he began extensive study of African and Caribbean literature, especially the writing of **George Lamming**, which continued during postgraduate study at Leeds University and formed part of his first volume of essays, *Homecoming* (1972). At Leeds, Ngũgĩ read Karl Marx, V. I. Lenin, and **Frantz Fanon** and developed an understanding of personal and cultural inferiority as one of colonialism's worst lingering wounds. Returning to Kenya to teach at the University of Nairobi, Ngũgĩ began working with the Kamĩrĩĩthũ Community Educational and Cultural Centre near his home. Between 1976 and 1977, with Ngũgĩ wa Mĩriĩ, who was influenced by **Paulo Freire**'s views on literacy for political change, Ngũgĩ wrote the Gĩkũyũ play *I Will Marry When I Want* (1982, trans. of *Ngaahika Ndeenda*, 1980). In September 1977 he published *Petals of Blood*, a novel attacking Kenyan neocolonialism, but probably his involvement in political consciousness-raising at Kamĩrĩĩthũ precipitated Ngũgĩ's yearlong detention without charge or trial. Detention, as he explains in his prison diary *Detained* (1981), confirmed Ngũgĩ's understanding of the neocolonial inheritance of colonial oppression, and he chose writing in national languages as his best method of active resistance, beginning his diary and a novel on the prison's rough toilet paper. Released in December 1978 after the death of President Jomo Kenyatta, Ngũgĩ was prohibited from lecturing, and he wrote the still-unpublished play *Mother, Sing for Me* (*Maitũ Njugĩra*) for Kamĩrĩĩthũ. In England, launching *Devil on the Cross* (1982; trans. of *Caitaani Mũtharaba-inĩ*, 1980), the novel he wrote in prison, Ngũgĩ was warned of his impending arrest in Kenya, and his exile began in London, where he wrote *Matigari* (1987; trans. of *Matigari ma Njirũũngi*, 1986). He taught at various American universities before assuming his present position as Erich Maria Remarque Professor of Comparative Literature at New York University. He edits the journal *Mũtiiri* at New York University, committed to Gĩkũyũ's survival as a language for cultural and technological communication. In 1998 he published *Penpoints, Gunpoints, and Dreams*, lectures on art and politics first delivered at Oxford University. He is presently completing the English translation of his anticipated Gĩkũyũ novel *Murogi wa Kagoogo*, which promises to be his longest.

Ngũgĩ's early plays often focus on the tension between tradition and modernity in Africa, a theme that reaches a critical impasse in the highly ambivalent play *The Black Hermit* (1968). Ngũgĩ's post-Makerere plays are concerned less with the alienated neocolonial elite than with the dispossessed. *The Trial of Dedan Kimathi* (1976), a Brechtian play written with Mĩcere Gĩthae Mũgo, blends Kimathi's life and trial, 400 years of Kenyan history, and the trial of collaborators. Kimathi denies the colonial court's authority, and the play becomes a trial of colonial law, African literature, and audience complacency. *I Will Marry When I Want* and *Mother, Sing for Me* are folk operas, mingling action, dialogue, mime, and song.

In some of his early short stories and his first two novels, *The River Between* and *Weep Not, Child* (1964), a hero combining the roles of Gĩkũyũ and Old

Testament prophet and nationalist politician is anticipated to save the country. Ngũgĩ's first two novels end in personal and collective failure, despite the glimmer of hope at the end of *Weep Not, Child*, a novel dealing with the sweeping destructiveness of the state of emergency declared to crush Mau Mau. In these novels, the benefits of Western education are ambiguously juxtaposed with the imperative of regaining stolen lands. *A Grain of Wheat* (1967), Ngũgĩ's third novel, partly based on Joseph Conrad's *Under Western Eyes*, eulogizes Christian reconciliation and national reconstruction.

There is a marked shift in Ngũgĩ's fiction, most of which was written outside Kenya, with the appearance of *Petals of Blood* (1977), which speaks from a politically engaged position. Like **Sembène Ousmane**'s *God's Bits of Wood* (1962), an example of African socialist realism, Ngũgĩ's novel includes representatives of different social classes whose activities allegorize national events. The short story "A Mercedes Funeral" from *Secret Lives* (1975) indicates a movement into the carnivalesque. A rural election becomes a fantastical display of candidates' bogus concern for the dispossessed by extravagantly scheming to bury a poor man, one candidate even producing a coffin shaped like a Mercedes-Benz. Ngũgĩ's last two Gĩkũyũ novels demand an active response from readers; in *Devil on the Cross*, cannibalistic capitalists seeking to consume the people mimic the typically overweight and sexually predatory white characters of the earlier fiction. Ngũgĩ's last novel, *Matigari*, blends disparate scenes from Kenyan history in a fluid time scheme. Matigari resembles the mythic Mau Mau general Stanley Mathenge, who disappeared in 1955, perhaps awaiting genuine independence before his return. Searching for truth and justice, he encounters poverty, disfranchisement, and alienation. Matigari takes up arms to reclaim his house and land, and, though killed, his spirit survives in Mĩriũki.

Ngũgĩ has also written in other genres, and *Penpoints, Gunpoints, and Dreams* touches on the connections between cyberspace and orality. In *Mũtiiri*, Ngũgĩ's love poems appear. He has collaborated on films, such as *Sembene: The Making of African Cinema* (1994), a series of interviews with the great Senegalese novelist and director who, like Ngũgĩ, was attracted by film's potential to reach a mass illiterate audience. Ngũgĩ has reached out to a younger audience in *The Adventures of Njamba Nene*: *Njamba Nene and the Flying Bus* (1986; trans. of *Njamba Nene na Mbaathi ĩ Mathagu*, 1982); *Njamba Nene's Pistol* (1986; trans. of *Bathitoora ya Njamba Nene*, 1984); and *Njamba Nene na Cibũ Kĩng'ang'i* (1986). These three stories write the child reader into Kenyan history, telling of a young boy, educated by his mother in traditional wisdom, who rescues a busload of children and transports a concealed pistol. In the third story, Njamba Nene avenges his mother's torture and murder by hunting down and killing the wounded perpetrator, Chief Kĩng'ang'i, in a hospital.

Despite his prolific production in different genres, Ngũgĩ is perhaps most widely cited today as a theorist of African and postcolonial literature and culture. Ngũgĩ's concerns, expressed in seven essay collections, have remained remarkably consistent over four decades, a consistency resulting in some repetition and a tendency toward didacticism. Ngũgĩ's most successful collections, *Decolonising the Mind* (1986), *Writers in Politics* (1981; 2d ed., 1997), and *Moving the Centre* (1993), contain the narrative drive of good autobiography.

Ngũgĩ remains controversial in his homeland for his historiography. Opposing what he terms official state-sanctioned historians, Ngũgĩ advances a Kenyan counterhistory, drawing particular attention to the Mau Mau period as the beginning of armed resistance against British colonialization in Africa. For Ngũgĩ, Mau Mau was a revolutionary, nationalist movement. His early novels, however, very differently represent Mau Mau as the product of tragic miscommunication, dividing families and communities. Ngũgĩ's last three novels elevate the spirit of Mau Mau, and, instead of anticipating a savior, they locate the political will for change within the community of workers and peasants. Ngũgĩ's last two novels clearly link neocolonialism with the forces of **globalization**. Increasingly, Ngũgĩ regards the Mau Mau period and the present struggle against international domination as stages in an unbroken, centuries-long history of **resistance**. Ngũgĩ's historiography has developed alongside his view of the postcolonial intellectual. His early faith in the transformative potential of Western education changed into a suspicion of the debilitating effects of a colonized mentality. Rejecting the African intellectual's Western orientation, Ngũgĩ asserts the intellectual's grounding in the people's collective wisdom and advances the model of the traditional oral intellectual, whose knowledge and ability are public property. While sometimes criticized for idealizing and even fetishizing traditional culture and for speaking on behalf of peasants and workers from a position of privilege, Ngũgĩ remains committed to the notion of the African postcolonial intellectual as a revolutionary activist who must not divorce culture from material realities. Ngũgĩ thus admires those who combine theory and praxis, such as **Amílcar Cabral** and Dedan Kimathi, and Ngũgĩ has sought to establish Kimathi in the pantheon of revolutionary intellectual activists.

Ngũgĩ is probably the best-known postcolonial exponent of **indigenous** languages, and he enjoins African writers to use African languages, convinced that only such writing constitutes true African literature. Language, for Ngũgĩ, is the repository of cultural and historical memory. Moreover, as he discovered in detention, writing in African languages is also a blow against the empire, and his Gĩkũyũ writings continue to be suppressed in his homeland. Ngũgĩ traces the promotion of English at the expense of African languages to a colonial strategy designed to create a class to whom to transfer power. Such a policy fosters linguistic inferiority, alienating English-speaking intellectuals from the people. Ngũgĩ acknowledges his own initially ambivalent reaction to Obiajunwa Wali's outrage over the 1962 Conference of African Writers of English Expression at Makerere. Wali believed that literature in the colonizer's language would bury African culture. Years later, Ngũgĩ accepted Wali's challenge, announcing in 1986's *Decolonising the Mind* his farewell to English. While most of Ngũgĩ's work since then has been first written in Gĩkũyũ, he laments the paucity of avenues for African-language publication.

Ngũgĩ's stance on African languages has elicited some criticism. He has been accused of overlooking the role that English played in uniting various African nationalities against the colonizer. His theory of language has been said to conceptualize language romantically and ahistorically as an archive of cultural purity. In addition, his injunction that African writers publish in African languages has been attacked as unrealistic for those less well known than Ngũgĩ himself.

Advocacy for African languages is a political act for Ngũgĩ, and a significant site for such advocacy is the teaching curriculum. During the debate about the future of literature teaching at the University of Nairobi in 1968, he argued that the core of an Afrocentric curriculum should be **orature**. The study of European literature should follow a primary focus on Kenyan, Pan-African, and African diasporan literatures and a secondary concentration on the literatures of Asia and South America. A countercanon of African and "Third World" literature should be studied to assert cultural integrity and slow the spread of global monoculture. Moreover, Kiswahili should replace English as a universal language because of the ideological baggage of linguistic imperialism.

Ngũgĩ's writing has further challenged the **Eurocentric** canon with his last two novels' formal hybridity. Drawing on traditional forms, **magic realism**, postcolonial allegory, and **film** techniques, this fiction is a type of Gĩkũyũ **postmodernism**. While suspicious of postmodernism's ahistoricism, Ngũgĩ has embraced its celebration of diversity and difference. To reflect and transform the seemingly fantastical nature of political reality for a mass audience, Ngũgĩ's last two novels introduce transformed biblical stories, familiar to his audience, to convey subversive messages. The novels imitate the Mau Mau practice of taking biblical parables and Christian hymns and changing the words to make these texts into tools for political consciousness-raising. Ngũgĩ's Mau Mau aesthetics thus exploits the forms of popular culture, showing, like Kimathi's Gichamu theater group, that a cultural revolution can foster political change.

All of Ngũgĩ's writings deal with Kenya's history, and most recently he has attempted to narrate the postneocolonial nation. Ngũgĩ's first novels convey the exuberant hope and uncertainty of independence, when he regarded **ethnic** nationalism as the major obstacle to harmonious **nationhood**. More recently, he has celebrated the difference of Kenya's nationalities, seeing attacks on "tribalism" as strategies of colonial and neocolonial suppression. Ngũgĩ regards the liberation struggle for true independence as incomplete, and he evokes the memory of the Mau Mau period to inspire the final struggle against neocolonialism. Ngũgĩ's sympathies are clearly Pan-Kenyan and Pan-African, and he welcomes regional unions in East Africa. His postneocolonial nation would maintain strong ties with Tanzania and Uganda and also with an alliance of "Third World" countries, united against the onslaught of globalization and the new world order and the threat of Africa's recolonization.

Further Reading: C. Cantalupo 1995; D. Cook and M. Okenimkpe 1997.

Oliver Lovesey

Kwame Nkrumah. *See* Decolonization

O

Orature   Orature is a notion used to describe African oral traditions. The term, first coined by Pio Zirmiru, Ugandan linguist and literary critic, stakes out space for the oral tradition in relationship to its written counterpart, literature. **Ngũgĩ wa Thiong'o** further developed the term in his work *Homecoming* (1972), in order to account for the ways that the local culture in Africa is predominantly transmitted through performance rather than through written literature. This performance of story, because of its base in the community and its participatory collective structure, provides help in maintaining precontact culture as well as creating sites of **resistance** to Western cultural traditions.

In 1962 a number of African writers at the Conference of Writers of English Expression at Makerere, including **Achebe**, Senghor, Okara, and Mphelele, expressed concern about the predominance of Western literature in the African universities, and they envisioned an academic program that emphasized orature. The discussion regarding the place of orature continued for a number of years and was finally resolved in 1973 when orature became the focal point of university departments. Since that, time orature has been developed in two primary directions: one, with regard to the oral folk traditions themselves and, second, as a way of melding with writing in order to create a hybrid form. In addition to the shift to an African language, the novel also drew from various oral narrative devices, especially the use of proverb, songs, and the fable. Orature has come to refer to the African oral tradition as well as the methodology for boundary-crossing between text and orality. Okot p'Bitek, who wrote the *Song of Lawino* (1966) and developed writing that used oral forms, also notes that the oral tradition is able to critique society because it is so immediately involved in it.

Ngaahika Ndeenda (I Will Marry When I Want, 1980) outlined by Ngũgĩ and Ngugi wa Mĩriĩ and staged in collaboration with the villagers of Kamĩrĩĩthũ, used Gĩkũyũ and drew from the folk traditions of song, dance, and mime in order to create a form with which the townspeople could identify. A later performance, *Maĩtu Njugĩra* (Mother Sing for Me, 1989) was closed down by the government, and Ngũgĩ was thrown in prison. In 1978 Ngũgĩ further developed the concept of orature by his shift to Gĩkũyũ, his native Kenyan language, in order to develop a writing approach that approximated orature in written form in his novel *Caitaani Mũtharabainî* (Devil on the Cross, 1982).

Ngũgĩ notes that there are three traditions in African literature. First, the oral tradition or orature has been kept alive since precolonial days and readily incorporates new elements. Some examples include the recording of Ozidi Saga by J. P. Clark, an epic regarding Ozidi and his grandmother. Among the Agĩkĩyũ there was a poetry festival that was stopped by the British because they saw it as threatening. When precolonial leader Harry Thuku was killed, a song emerged called "Kanyegenyĩu," which was primarily sung by women. It was deemed so threatening that it was banned by the authorities. *Mũthĩrĩgũ*, a combination of song, poetry, and dance, actually led to the arrest of a number of people. Orature has greatly assisted in keeping the African language alive, and the griot reflects the pinnacle of skill in working with the language.

Too often orature is couched within a discussion of the oral traditions from a Western perspective, and, as Adetokunbo F. Knowlese notes, the Western paradigm has three key components: speaker, speech, and audience. For classical African orature the paradigm entails a historical context, conforms to certain African expectations, follows standards as an art form, and is codified. Micere M. G. Mugo's book *African Orature and Human Rights* (1991) addresses the narrative arts by the Ndia people of the Kirinyaga District of Kenya. In particular she looks at how orature is imbricated in the social fabric of the precontact African community. The performances express a variety of social values and also indicate a concern with the clarification and transmission of the basic rights of the community members.

Mugo asserts that orature works by virtue of an "onion structure theory"— that life revolves around a central position and its layers of meaning. The orature artist addresses both the metaphysical concerns of the community as well as those having to do with questions about rights. The various orature forms provide the vehicle by which errors are pointed out or by which shared values can be passed along. Additionally, orature, as a collective, audience-oriented performance, facilitates considerable communication. So many people get involved that to interfere with the opportunity for the event would require that a large number of community members be arrested. Mugo, for example, is particularly emphatic that the study of orature provides a vital source for dealing with questions of social transformation. In addition to examining orature from a scholarly point of view, Mugo also applies forms of orature to her writing, for example, in her collection of poetry, *My Mother's Poem and Other Songs* (1994).

Oratures are a vital part of the cultural life of African communities; as performer, audience and context shift, the oratures also transform for a number of reasons. A story that is no longer considered useful is changed or discarded.

Scholars have noted that even the highly trained African storyteller, the griot, does not tell the same story twice. There is always a fluctuation between the preset text and improvisation. Through the use of a number of techniques the storyteller adapts his or her story to meet the needs and circumstances of the particular audience. In a number of these cultures, the griot spends a considerable amount of time in training, with particular attention given to the spiritual dimensions of storytelling, that is, the forces that are released in the process of the storytelling itself. These special powers or forces are called *nyama* by the Mande peoples of Western Africa. Their griots, or *jeli*, are a special group that the Mande identify as *nyamamkalaw*, or "nyama-handlers." This power of the spoken word has largely disappeared from the literate-based communities of the West.

Further Reading: M. Mugo 1991; Ngũgĩ 1993.

Kanta Kochhar-Lindgren

Fernando Ortiz (Fernández)   Ortiz (1881–1969, Havana, Cuba) is one of the outstanding Cuban intellectuals of the twentieth century. He had a law degree and was, in addition, a historian, ethnologist, musicologist, linguist, and literary critic. His work on Cuban and Afro-Cuban culture, and his contribution to research on sociology, anthropology, and what is called today cultural studies are without equal.

Articles written for newspapers and journals filled every stage of his existence. They appeared in *Azul y Rojo* (1902–1903). From 1904 onward he wrote for *Cuba y América*. After 1909, he published his work in *El Tiempo*. Using articles that he had published in newspapers, he compiled his books *La Reconquista de América* (The Reconquest of America, 1911) and *Entre Cubanos* (Among Cubans, 1913), both of which were published in Paris.

Without any doubt, the most famous work he produced is *Contrapunteo cubano del tabaco y el azúcar* (Cuban Counterpoint: Tobacco and Sugar, 1940). In this book Ortiz coined the term "transculturation" in relation to Afro-Cuban culture. Transculturation, in opposition to acculturation (a term in use by mostly North American anthropologists at the time that *Cuban Counterpoint* was published) refers to the way that subordinated groups select materials transmitted to them by the dominant culture. **Transculturation** does not suggest a loss of culture (like acculturation) but rather a transformation in culture in which both the dominant and dominated culture is changing. Ortiz recognized the intercultural dynamics and defined the process of transculturation in three steps: a partial loss of culture by the immigrant groups (European and African), the concurrent assimilation of cultural elements from other cultures, and thus the creation of a new Cuban culture with elements of all cultures involved. As Ortiz puts it: "[A] child always inherits something from both parents, but is also always different from each one of them" (*Cuban Counterpoint*, 103).

Ortiz's work was well known and appreciated by his contemporaries; in the 1950s his name was proposed for the Nobel Peace Prize. He wrote many books, among which only *Cuban Counterpoint* is available in English at the moment. The other books are *Los negros brujos* (Black Witches, 1906), *La identificación dactiloscópica* (Dactiloscopic Identification, 1913), *Los negros esclavos* (Black Slaves, 1916), *La fiesta afrocubana del Día de Reyes* (Afro-Cuban Fiesta, 1920), *Los cabildos afrocubanos* (Afro-Cuban Townships, 1921), *Historia de la arqueología indocubana* (History of the Indo-Cuban Archaeology, 1922), *Un catauro de cubanismos* (Dictionary of Cubanisms, 1923), *Glosario de afronegrismos* (Afro-Negrisms, a Glossary, 1924), *Proyecto de Código Criminal Cubano* (Project of the Cuban Criminal Code, 1926), *Los factores humanos de la cubanidad* (The Human Factors of Cubanity, 1949), *Martí y las razas* (Martí and the Races, 1942), *El engaño de las razas* (The Betrayal of Races, 1946), *El huracán, su mitología y sus símbolos* (The Hurricane, Its Mythology and Symbols, 1947), *La africanía de la música folklórica de Cuba* (Africanity in Cuban Music, 1950), *Wifredo Lam y su obra vista a través de significados críticos* (Wifredo Lam and His Work as Seen through Its Critical Meanings, 1950), *Los bailes y el teatro de los negros en el folklore cubano* (Black Dances and Theater in Cuban Folklore, 1951), *Los instrumentos de la música afrocubana* (The Instruments of Afro-Cuban Music, 1952, 5 vols.), and *Historia de une pelea cubana contra los demonios* (History of a Cuban Fight against Demons, 1959).

Further Reading: R. Ortiz 1997; S. Spitta 1997.

Silvia Nagy-Zekmi

Otherness.   *See* Alterity

Ferdinand Oyono   Ferdinand Oyono was born in Cameroon in 1929. He is known for his novels *Une vie de boy* (1956), *Le Vieux nègre et le médaille* (1956), *Chemin d'Europe* (1969; trans. as *Houseboy*, 1966), *The Old Man and the Medal* (1967), and *Road to Europe* (1989). In addition to writing, Oyono has had a successful career as a lawyer and a diplomat. Writing in the wake of the **negritude** movement, launched by **Aimé Césaire**, Léon-Gontran Damas, and Léopold Senghor and influenced by journals such as *La revue du monde noir*, *Légitime Defense*, and *L'Étudiant noir* of the 1920s and 1930s, Oyono has sought to counter the exotic-idealized myths of the colonial world by exposing the harsh and brutal reality of the everyday lives of black Africans. His works have aided in solidifying a new anticolonial African consciousness by exposing the hypocrisy and vapid manner of Europeans in Africa, while criticizing intense colonial exploitation of Africans and their native lands.

Oyono began writing in the 1950s during a sojourn in Paris as a student. In his work, he questions the moral and ethical validity of the French civilizing mission in Africa by recounting his stories through the voice of native narrators. In *Houseboy*, Toundi, the principal protagonist, is a young boy raised by a white priest and indoctrinated into the white colonial system, where he crawls up the ladder to become the "boy" of the French administration's local commandant. Dreaming of advancement to improve himself, he is brutally awakened by the realities of the colonial system in Africa. As Toundi exists on the fringes of two opposing worlds, one of the rich white colonial minority and the other of the squalid, exploited black African masses, Toundi slowly becomes more aware of the injustices of the colonial enterprise in Africa. As the novel concludes, he becomes entwined in a system from which there is no escape. Told as a parody, *Houseboy* symbolizes the struggle of an exploited nation to take hold of its own destiny as it slowly breaks the shackles of colonialism.

Since the 1960 publication of his third novel, *Road to Europe*, Oyono has concentrated on a career as a diplomat. Returning to independent Cameroon in the 1960s, he served as ambassador to Liberia. Subsequently, Oyono worked for the United Nations in New York City. After working for the United Nations Children's Fund for a period of time, he returned to Cameroon in 1985, where he has since served as a government cabinet minister.

Further Reading: B. Jack 1996a; L. Kesteloot 1991; F. Oyono 1966, 1967, 1989.

Valérie Orlando

P

Pacific Island Literatures   The 1960s and 1970s brought fundamental change to the Pacific. A number of entities claimed independence or semiautonomy, including Western Samoa (1962), the Cook Islands (1965), Tonga (1970), Fiji (1970), Papua New Guinea (1975), and the Solomon Islands (1978). In other places such as Tahiti, Aotearoa (**New Zealand**), and Hawaii, sovereignty movements became vocal and public. This push for political and cultural autonomy is evident in contemporary cultural and literary studies. The South Pacific Festival of the Arts, the South Pacific Creative Arts Society, the Institute of Pacific Studies (University of the South Pacific), and the South Pacific Association of **Commonwealth Literature** and Language Studies together fostered the collective creation and criticism of literature by Pacific peoples. Soon after, journals such as *Mana* (1974) and *SPAN* (1975) inaugurated the study of **indigenous** writers and led to numerous creative writing conferences that continue to encourage regionally oriented literary traditions. This enabled Albert Wendt of Western Samoa to produce two comprehensive anthologies, *Lali* (1980) and *Nuanua* (1995), both of which challenge A. Grove Day and Carl Stroven's compilation *The Spell of the Pacific* (1949), which is devoted almost entirely to white writers.

For Wendt, literature by islanders opposes colonial myths and critically analyzes colonialism (1995, 3). Such myths refer to the images of the noble savage and of the victimized brownskin. Wendt's *Leaves of the Banyan Tree* (1979) deconstructs such figures and explores the meaning of *fa'a Samoa* (the Samoan way) through three complex characters. Tauilopepe is the *aiga* patriarch and represents the "New Samoa": he transforms ancestral lands into a successful, Westernized plantation. His son, Pepe, for whom the ways of the *papalagi* (whites) are poor substitutes for *aitu* (guardian spirits and lions), rejects Tauilopepe as a "false god" but is killed off by disease. Gaupo is the illegitimate son of a woman whom Tauilo seduces in order to destroy her husband's business.

While educated and enthusiastic about the plantation, Gaupo values Samoan traditions and does not openly embrace "white" ways. But Gaupo is not an ideal "fusion": his ascent to power is based on cold calculation. Inevitably, all of these characters present a painful exploration of *fa'a Samoa*, complicated by a changing world.

Epeli Hau'ofa of Tonga offers a similar critique of colonial representation. Hau'ofa's novel *Kisses in the Nederends* (1987) uses biting satire to undermine the authority of everyone—white, **nativist**, and "mixed" alike. The story centers on the woes of Oilei Bomboki, an emerging political figure who drinks all night and comes home to flatulate in his wife's presence. As Bomboki's gastroenteritis becomes more pronounced, he seeks help from witch doctors (one of whom turns his face as pink as his rear); from the local, underfunded hospital, which prescribes expired painkillers; and from uncaring physicians who party at international conferences where no one manages to say anything about the sick. In the end, this poor man's experience leaves one feeling that life in Tonga, with its jumbled mix of traditional and modern, is literally a "pain in the arse."

Solomon Islander Jully Sipolo and Tongan Konai Helu Thaman are also concerned with changes in the traditional "family," but their work allows us to see through the eyes of women. Sipolo's *Praying Parents* (1986) portrays the cultural conflicts that erupt when Westernization challenges stagnant social expectations. The poems follow the narrator's departure, foreign education, and return—an experience which makes her unable to become a "traditional" parent like her mother, who, despite being underprivileged, "did not look on the dark side" (5). This unacceptable dark side is the oppression of village women abused by drunk and lazy husbands. Thaman's work also focuses on discord; however, her collection of poetry called *Kakala* (1993) also celebrates forgiveness and resolution. The desire to heal wounds allows Thaman to speak of fragrant garlands that once beckoned foreigners but also symbolize a "sacred oneness" that the narrator extends to her reader (24).

Given their "**feminist**" perspectives, Sipolo and Thaman represent a scholarly dilemma. They are championed by critics like Melissa Miller for exposing cultural constraints that perpetuate the gendered status quo (1989, 135–134). However, other scholars reject this reading. Specifically, Leialoha Apo Perkins cautions against a "feminist" reading of both Sipolo and Thaman because their elite status as educated, English-speaking professionals separates them from the masses of everyday village women (1989, 144). The image of the educated native feminist is actually satirized in Fijians Vilsoni Hereniko and Teresia Teaiwa's *Last Virgin in Paradise* (1993) in the figure of Temanu, who returns to her homeland (which she ironically never saw in her childhood) to argue that "Marawan culture has got to rid itself of all kinds of oppression. Marawan women must learn to fight for their rights" (25).

As *Last Virgin in Paradise* suggests, literature of the Pacific is suspicious of Western education and often reflects a desire to reaffirm the power of native traditions. The play itself utilizes untranslated dialogues and the traditional genre of "clowning" to reveal the ignorance of foreigners. Cook Islander Kauraka Kauraka's *Return to Havaiki: Fokihanga ki Havaiki* (1985) embraces Manihiki Māori and the myths of gods and warriors: the collection also features the poem "Darkness within the Light," which builds upon this traditional authority by challenging the "educated" reading of physical contact as sexual harassment (17). New Hebridean Albert Leomala, whose works include "Kros" (1975) and "Hom Belong Mi" (1975) also uses his people's language to dismiss Christianity and civilization as the harbingers of death. Hawaiian poet Diane Kahanu in "Ho. Just Cause I Speak Pidgin No Mean I Dumb" (1995) equates the local language to Pu'uhonua, the city of refuge that once harbored criminals and *kapu* (taboo) breakers from the law. The political argument of the play and these poems inevitably reveals the reclamation of cultural autonomy, a perspective used as the basis for much more oppositional texts such as *Voices of Independence* (Beier 1980), a collection of writing presented as an intrinsic part of Papua New Guinea's sovereignty movement.

The literary creation of "authority" is a popular nativist platform that some argue should not be used by non-natives. Poet and scholar Haunani-Kay Trask argues that Native Hawaiians (*nā kānaka maoli*) suffer from modern-day colonization perpetuated by nonindigenous ethnic groups that feel an affinity with the islands. She maintains that writers of Asian ancestry who claim the label of "local" support a "kind of **settler** assertion [that] is really a falsification of place and culture" (1999, 169). Trask further argues that the literary emergence of such individuals represents the usurpation of the native right to define what Hawaiian literature *is*. Given this political platform, it is clear why Trask and fellow *nā kānaka maoli* supported the creation of such literary collections as *Ho'omānoa Balaz* (1989) and the journal *Ōiwi* (1998), both of which are devoted to strictly native writers.

One of the most controversial writers of the Pacific is Lois-Ann Yamanaka, whose *Blu's Hanging* (1997) represents what Trask sees as racial colonization by Asians. Nominated in 1998 for a literary award from the Association for Asian American Studies, *Blu's Hanging* drew fire for lacking native characters and portraying **Filipinos** as sexual predators. But in all fairness to Japanese American Yamanaka, criticism should not overlook the novel's "honest" portrayal of rural Moloka'i's ugly history of plantation labor and its forced-exile community of lepers.

For other non-native Pacific Islanders, the conflation of race with the right to speak poses the converse problem of native xenophobia and disfranchisement. Fiji-born Indian writer Satendra Nandan in his novel *The Wounded Sea* (1991) claims that "indigenous racism, like local liquor, is worse than the imported kind" (139). Nandan specifically refers to the unfortunate events of Fiji, where, in 1987, a military coup deposed the Indian-dominated government, which prompted the imprisonment of various officials and scholars, the institutionalization of racial quotas in the Parliament, and a large exodus of Indians from the country. Nandan reminds us that native sovereignty comes at the expense of the disfranchisement of Indians, which is mirrored in the author's shattered sense of self and culture. For Nandan, the trauma of 1987 lingers in his memory in the image of Fiji as a perpetually "bleeding, unhealing wound" (168). Fellow Indian writer Subramani also depicts Fiji as a psychological wilderness in *The Fantasy Eaters* (1991). His short stories speak of Fiji as a land of narcosis where "99.8 percent of the people . . . are psychosomatic . . . running from the disorders of temperate wastelands" (26).

In contrast to both Nandan and Subramani, Sudesh Mishra explores a different "reading" of Fiji by seeking an alternative to racial difference as a signifier of place. His collection of poems *Tandava* (1992) depicts the nation as a mango tree with "stretched boughs like David's sling," which were bound to break at some point or another (15). By addressing the inevitability of conflict, the poet encounters madness, confusion, dispossession, and, later, a new season for the mango tree and a new diaspora, both of which move from static notions of geographical identity toward a more complex understanding of self as an intersection between history and racial memory.

The problem of defining the authority of the native and the place of the migrant continues to challenge many writers and critics alike. According to Rob Wilson, the complexity of history has made cultural (and by implication, racial) purity impossible. He further argues that this dilemma necessitates "a new kind of '**cosmopolitan**' knowledge . . . tracing unevenness, conscious of global/local discrepancies and movements" (1996, 9). As Mishra observes, such ambivalence makes for a dynamic flow of creativity. Assuredly, the future volatility of the Pacific will provide a plethora of subjects and sentiments for years to come.

Further Reading: V. Hereniko and R. Wilson 1999; Subramani 1985; A. Wendt 1995.
Seri Inthava Kau'ikealaula Luangphinith

Pan-Africanism   Pan-Africanism is an idea and a movement aiming to unite the Black people of Africa and the African **diaspora** in their struggles against oppression and exploitation of various forms, including imperialism, colonialism, and neocolonialism in Africa, and racial degradation and discrimination in America. It asserts the dignity and worth of the black Africans and their descendants across the world and seeks recognition of their contributions to civilization. It explodes the myth that black people had "no culture, no manifest heritage before they landed on the slave auction blocks" (Carmichael and Hamilton 1967, 38). It encompasses both political and cultural aspects. Broadly speaking, Pan-Africanism may be defined as the belief that all people of African descent should work together for the liberation and betterment of black people as a whole and for restoration of the dignity of the African motherland.

Pan-African sentiments emerged in the minds of oppressed African Americans, who entertained the idea of returning to Mother Africa to find a just place that would welcome them. Martin R. Delany, Alexander Crummel, and Edward W. Blyden were among the early Pan-Africanists. Delany in his "Official Report of the Niger Valley Exploring Party" (1861) propounded the idea of "Africa for the African race and black men to rule them" (110). In the aftermath of the Civil War, several thousand free African Americans left for Africa, the Caribbean, and Haiti to escape discriminatory treatment in America. Toward the end of the nineteenth century, black nationalist organizations emerged in America with the goal of establishing an autonomous black state within the United States, as fictionalized in Sutton Griggs' *Imperium in Imperio* (1889). Black nationalism also took firm root in the African colonies in a struggle to evict repressive white regimes.

Nationalism led to Pan-Africanism with its motto of "Africa for the Africans." In 1897 Mankayi Sontanga wrote the song "God Bless Africa," which became the unofficial anthem of the South African nationalists. Tanzania, Zambia, and Namibia have now adopted this song as a national anthem, in addition to the postapartheid South Africa (Ahmad et al. 1999, 106).

The term "Pan-Africanism" seems to have been coined by a Trinidadian lawyer, Henry Sylvester Williams, and was probably first used by him in a letter to a London associate in November 1899 (D. Lewis 1993, 248). Williams founded the African Association, which called a Pan-African Conference in 1900 in London. In a fervent appeal titled "To the Nations of the World," written by W.E.B. Du Bois, the conference declared that "[t]he problem of the twentieth century is the problem of the color line" (Lewis, 251). The 1900 conference focused on the issues of forced labor and segregation.

Though at the 1900 conference the African Association changed its name to the "Pan-African Association," that conference was not truly Pan-African in its representation, as there were only four African delegates in attendance. By the same definition, neither the 1958 Ghana conference nor the 1963 Ethiopia conference was Pan-African because participation was limited to African delegates.

In the early twentieth century, Pan-African ideas received an unexpected boost from Marcus Mosiah Garvey's "Back to Africa" movement. Garvey's United Negro Improvement Association sought the creation of "a central nation for the race," assistance in "civilizing the backward tribes of Africa," and a common "spiritual worship among the native tribes of Africa" (Lewis 214). Pan-Africanism is, on the other hand, secular, socialist, antisegregationist, and anticolonial. Both Garveyism and Pan-Africanism, however, inspired race pride and African unity by promoting the ideas of a common black culture and destiny. During the 1930s, the Martinican poet **Aimé Césaire** and Senegalese poets Leopold Sedar Senghor and Birago Diop in their **"negritude"** poems wrote romantic rhapsodies of life in Africa, often expressing revulsion of things European and embracing Pan-Africanism. As Jomo Kenyatta explains in his book titled *Facing Mount Kenya*, the European policy of "civilizing and uplifting poor savages" was "based on preconceived ideas that the African cultures are 'primitive,' " adding that the "European should realise that there is something to learn from the African" (1962, 120).

Four Pan-African conferences were held in the period between the two world wars, in 1919 (Paris), 1921 (London, Brussels, and Paris), 1923 (London and Lisbon), and 1927 (New York). The 1919 Paris conference is now regarded as the first Pan-African congress. Fifty-seven delegates from fifteen countries, including those from French and British colonies, attended. This congress repudiated the imperialist powers of the time—Belgium, Great Britain, Portugal, Spain, and France—for their exploitation of the natives and sought African participation in government. As a result of the Pan-African movement, the German colonies conquered by the Allies during World War I were designated as "mandates" by the League of Nations rather than returned to imperial rule (Du Bois, *The World and Africa* 1947, 11–12). The 1921 congress asserted the absolute equality of all races and the equality of rights between whites and blacks. According to the 10 November 1923 issue of *West Africa*, the 1923 congress, which met in London and Lisbon, spelled out the critical needs of Africans and their descendants. Most important of these were representation in government, land-ownership, trial by jury, free education, and development of Africa for the primary benefit of Africans (1377). With respect to black Americans, the conference demanded full civil rights and an end to lynching. With respect to the independent states of Liberia, Ethiopia, and Haiti, the conference forbade encroachment on their political integrity (1377; Esedebe 1994, 74). The 1927 congress in New York was attended by 208 delegates from twelve countries. It reiterated the demand for African representation in colonial administration and also asserted the right of the black people to Africa's land and resources.

With the fifth Pan-African conference, held in Manchester, England, in 1945, the leadership of the Pan-African movement passed from the hands of African Americans to those of Africans. As W.E.B. Du Bois points out in his autobiography, "American Negroes had too often assumed that their leadership in Africa was natural. With the rise of an educated group of Africans, this was increasingly unlikely" (1986a, 401). Led by Kwame Nkrumah and Jomo Kenyatta, the future presidents of Ghana and Kenya, respectively, the Manchester conference unequivocally claimed for the colonies the right to political self-determination.

With the dawn of independence in Africa, the venue of the Pan-African congresses was moved to African soil. A conference was held in Accra, the capital of Ghana, in 1958, but because only African states sent delegates, the conference cannot be called truly Pan-African. Delegates from eight self-governing states of Africa, namely, Egypt, Ethiopia, Ghana, Liberia, Libya, Morocco, Sudan, and Tunisia, attended. In his opening speech, Kwame Nkrumah, then prime minister of Ghana, declared that Africans must "assert our own African personality and . . . develop according to our ways of life, our own customs, traditions and cultures" (quoted in Esedebe 1994, 165). The conference demanded the speedy emancipation of all the colonies. The ailing W.E.B. Du Bois' address, titled "The Future of Africa," was given on his behalf by his wife, Shirley Graham. Du Bois asked for sacrifice for the sake of unity: "Give up individual rights for the needs of the nation; give up tribal independence for the needs of Mother Africa . . . Africa, awake! Put on the beautiful robes of Pan-African socialism" (1968a, 404).

The next congress was held in 1963 in Addis Ababa, Ethiopia. Representatives from thirty-two African states attended. Like the Accra conference, the Addis Ababa conference was not Pan-African because it did not include delegates from outside Africa, with the exception of W.E.B. Du Bois. Emperor Haile Selassie struck the note of African unity in his welcoming address, exhorting the delegates "to rouse the slumbering giant of Africa, not to the nationalism of Europe of the nineteenth century, not to the regional consciousness, but to the vision of a single African brotherhood" (cited in Esedebe 1994, 192). Emperor Selassie advocated "political union" of the continent, but he counseled gradualism toward that goal. Nkrumah, however, used the occasion to plead for the total liberation and immediate political unification of Africa into a Union of African States. Nkrumah's call for African union failed because the national delegations were unwilling to cede any part of their sovereignty. A compromise version that fell short of Nkrumah's Pan-African vision was adopted, and the Organization of African Unity (OAU) was launched. The OAU Charter puts forth the organization's purposes: to foster solidarity of the African states, to defend their sovereignty and territorial integrity, to make joint efforts to improve quality of life for the people of Africa, to eliminate all forms of colonialism from Africa, and to encourage international cooperation ("Appendix A," 232).

The Organization of African Unity is a concrete expression of Pan-African ideals. While the OAU has successfully fought colonialism, it has been less successful in tackling interstate and intrastate conflicts among the states of Pan-Africa, partly because of its rigid adherence to its principle of noninterference in the internal affairs of states. In border disputes between states, the OAU has generally sought to enforce existing borders. In 1986 the OAU formed a commission to deal with human rights violations within member nations.

Pan-Africanism has been promoted by major American civil rights leaders. During his May 1964 visit to Accra, Ghana, Malcolm X highlighted the importance of Pan-Africanism to African Americans, exhorting African Americans to " 'return' philosophically and culturally [to Africa] and develop a working unity in the framework of Pan-Africanism" (Malcolm X 63). Another black power leader, Stokely Carmichael, who immigrated to Guinea in 1969, argued that black Americans would win freedom from exploitation at home only with the creation of a free, united Africa. As he puts it the February 1976 issue of *Africa*: "What we must understand is that until Africa is free, the Black man all over the world is not free" (78; cited in Esedebe 1994, 229).

The resonance of Pan-Africanism through the century is apparent. The sixth Pan-African congress was held in Dar es Salaam, Tanzania, in 1974. With more than 500 delegates and observers from all over the world in attendance, President Julius Nyerere of Tanzania declared that the delegates must seek to "further the progress of opposition to racism, colonialism, oppression and exploitation everywhere" within "the context of a worldwide movement for human equality and national self-determination" (Nyerere 1976, 3–4).

John Henrik Clarke in "The Development in Pan-Africanist Ideas in the Americas and in Africa before 1900" (1977) alludes to the major themes of Pan-Africanism: "I consider any collective action of African people to restore or preserve their nationhood, culture, and manhood an act of Pan-Africanism" (1). Thus, Pan-Africanism includes the expression of black struggles against white racism, oppression, and exploitation, as well as positive assertions of black contributions and cultural values.

These Pan-African themes find expression in both art and literature. In art, the Harlem Renaissance sculptor Meta Warrick Fuller's *Ethiopia Awakens* (1914) and contemporary painter Mikelle Fletcher's *Guardian* (1971) exemplify Pan-African ideas. *Ethiopia Awakens* depicts Mother Africa awakening from a deathlike slumber. As she frees herself from the mummy bondage of colonialism, she begins to realize the glories of her ancient past and sees a vision of her future. *Guardian*, which depicts black Madonna and child, suggests that the black and white races must cooperate for mutual protection. The *aunkh*—the African emblem of life and prosperity—is the main protector, the other guardians being a jackal, the black Madonna liberation flag, and a miniature map of the continent of Africa. In poetry, W.E.B. Du Bois' "The Riddle of the Sphinx" (1921), Langston Hughes' "The Negro Speaks of Rivers" (1921), and Niger's contemporary poet Mamani Abdoulaye's "Chant negre" (1972) express Pan-African sensibilities. In Du Bois' "The Riddle of the Sphinx," the speaker holds the white man responsible for the black people's plight and prays for the rise of the "Black Christ" to right their wrongs. In "The Negro Speaks of Rivers," which is dedicated to Du Bois, Hughes takes pride in the history of black people and points to black contributions in building ancient and modern civilizations. In "Chant negre," the speaker hears African sounds ranging from victory shouts to love songs and from ferryman's songs to sorcerer's incantations, along with the plaintive cries of the black slave mothers, black men's spirituals, and blues from the New World. In fiction, black protest against racial oppression is exemplified in Sutton Griggs' *Imperium in Imperio* (1889), Claude McKay's *Home to Harlem* (1928), and Guinean writer Camara Laye's *The Dark Child* (1954). In Griggs' novel, Bernard Belgrave implicates whites for "the tears of the widows, the cries of the starving orphans, . . . and the gaping wounds of those unjustly slain" (217). In McKay's *Home to Harlem*, the Pan-Africanist Haitian intellectual Ray recounts stories of "black kings who struggled stoutly for the independence of their kingdoms: Prempreh of Ashanti, Behanzin of Dahomey, Ewari of Benin, Cetawayo of Zululand, Menelik of Abyssinia" (70). Camara Laye's *The Dark Child* restores dignity to the African past, culture, and civilization. These Pan-African works affirm the common heritage and destiny of people of African descent, as well as emphasize the need for black racial cooperation and solidarity.

Further Reading: P. O Esedebe 1994; J. Kenyatta 1962; J. Nyrere 1976; A. M. Sharakiya 1991–1992.

Harish Chander

Pedagogies   The rapid institutionalization of postcolonial studies in recent
years has brought to the fore the relationship of both students and teachers to
the disciplinary structure of the academy, prompting a reexamination of pedagogical methods. **Gayatri Spivak** has written of the dangers of "academic competition disguised as a politics of difference" (Spivak 1993, 53) that reinscribes
a discourse of marginality that finds ready validation by the **center** following a
principle of identification through separation. "Marginality" as a subject and
object is packaged for consumption following the dictates of standard course
requirements: the availability of textbooks, local teaching practices, consideration of suitable paper topics, and how best postcolonial studies might be
incorporated into the existing English literature or cultural studies syllabus.
"Value," argues Spivak, comes to reflect how far difference can be encoded as
an authorized form of knowledge. Both teachers and students reproduce the very
process of value coding that postcolonial studies takes as part of its critical
object.

To counter this process, Spivak advocates a process of constant critique within
the academy so that both teachers and students can occupy positions that systematically reverse, displace, and seize the apparatus of value coding, in essence,
a dialectical inquiry into the questions of **agency** predicated on a consciousness
of the interrelated triad of theory, pedagogy, and politics. A pedagogical theorist
who has proved empowering in advancing such a project is **Paolo Freire**. His
commitment is to an educational setting where exchange between teachers and
students is structured toward understanding how the learning experience takes
shape. Above all, it redefines the status of the teacher as student committed to
gaining knowledge from his or her students and being open to accommodating
this knowledge. In doing so, the historical context of the positions occupied by
both the students and the teacher is then visible to examination in relation to
the structure of the academy as a first step toward examining broader issues of
knowledge production by which the center defines the margin.

A historical awareness and a process of constant critique, while committed to
revealing the discursive inequality embedded within the process of value coding
within the academy, do not, of themselves, resolve the recapitulation of that
inequality within the teaching process. This requires a conceptualization that
both challenges and replaces the process of objectification. Here the work of
Mary Louise Pratt has proved instrumental. Pratt argues that Western forms of
representation "produce" the rest of the world for European consumption, which
is ultimately codified in the academy, as Spivak suggests. Yet the "other" of
this discourse is no passive recipient of this "production." Indeed, faced with
the unfamiliar culture of the colonizer, the other of Western discourse also develops ways of knowing and comprehending the unknown—although this coun-

terdiscourse is excluded from the "knowledge" recognized in the academy or, at best, admitted as material for anthropological study. Pratt describes these incidents of simultaneous knowledge production as "contact zones"—"social spaces where disparate cultures meet, clash, and grapple with each other, often in highly asymmetrical relations of domination and subordination" (Pratt 1992, 4). Despite such inequalities, the essence of the "contact zone" is a space where "ongoing relations" are established—an interaction and cultural exchange in which subjects are constituted by their relations with each other, an exchange that need not be as historically unequal as it may first seem.

The "contact zone" is a useful concept around which the classroom informed by postcolonial studies might be constituted. There are opportunities both to reread the "asymmetrical relations of domination" of which the academy has been a key repository and to reassess the roles of both student and teacher within this structure. As Freire proposed, such a classroom would be founded on interaction and exchange both pedagogically and culturally. As Spivak's strategy of constant critique within the academy implies, the disciplinary authority of the teacher not only needs to be the most visible of all roles both to his or her students but also needs to ensure the teacher's consciousness of his or her historical relation to "traditional" forms of knowledge codified and transmitted in the academy. To reconstitute the "contact zone" within the academy requires not just the inclusion of a few marginalized courses or texts with a "postcolonial" theme but an active engagement with the very structures of marginalization that the center, the academy, upholds. The ultimate goal of such a pedagogy is to address this historical asymmetry and to advance a politicized consciousness of the "margin" in the center (Spivak 1993, 63).

Further Reading: A. Collet, L. Jensen, and A. Rutherford 1997; M. Pratt 1992; G. Spivak 1993.

Lawrence Phillips

Performance   Postcolonial theater is performance staged as an act of **resistance** to colonialism and its consequences. In addition to critiquing cultural ambiguities and traumas of imperialism, postcolonial theater acts as a vehicle for precontact community maintenance and for cultural transformation. The theater has often been marginalized within the discussion of postcolonial studies— in part, because of the challenges of commenting on such a seemingly ephemeral discourse. However, in examples such as the work of Rendra in Indonesia and **Ngũgĩ wa Thiong'o** in Kenya, we see that postcolonial theater can exert tremendous power as a form of intervention in the public space.

Postcolonial theater takes a number of forms, ranging from the reworking of classics, ritual, history, storytelling, and the community-based performance work of Augusto Boal, to performance art by artists such as Guillermo Goméz-Peña and Coco Fusco. In the reworking of the classics, the classical story is threaded with the local story in order to create a more relevant, hybrid form. In India,

Utpal Dutt has used *Macbeth* in conjunction with *jatra*, a Bengalese folk theater. Trinidadian **Derek Walcott**'s *A Branch of the Blue Nile* (1986) revises the story of Antony and Cleopatra. *The Tempest* is revisited by **Aimé Césaire** as *Une tempéte* (1969), which portrays Prospero's magic as superior technology and Caliban as a rebel hero. David Malouf's *Blood Relations* (1988) moves *The Tempest* to Western Australia. **Wole Soyinka**'s *The Bacchae of Euripides* (1973) is infused with Yoruba cosmology; Antigone is revisited by **Edward Kamau Braithwaite** in *Odale's Choice* (1967) and set somewhere in Africa. *The Rez Sisters* (1986) by Tomson Highway reworks *Les Belles Souers* (1968) to shift the issue in the original regarding the unsettledness of seven Quebecois women to the parallel version at the reservation. Ritual, a vital element of precontact communities, can also be a focal point of a number of postcolonial plays. For example, Soyinka's *Death and the King's Horseman* (1975) is based on Elesin, the king's horseman's, unsuccessful efforts to prepare for his ritual death. *An Echo in the Bone* (1974) by Dennis Scott draws from a West Indian death ritual. Rituals can also be used to provide a backdrop, as in Mbongeni Ngena's *Township Fever* (1992 [1991]). *No'Xya'* (Our Footprints, 1990), put together by David Diamond, Headlines Theatre Company in Vancouver, and Gitksan and Wet'suwet'en Hereditary Chiefs, uses rituals to create a docudrama.

Finally, the category of history has gained particular importance in the development of postcolonial theater as a way of critiquing the hegemony of the Western interpretations. These plays often offer multiple perspectives regarding the retelling of the historical events and the surrounding cultural context. Two well-known examples include Michael Gow's *1841* (1988) and Stephen Sewell's *Hate* (1988)—plays that critique the story of the settlement of Australia and that were produced at Australia's bicentenary.

Postcolonial theater can also provide a format for the recuperation of lost heroes and their histories. For example, *The Trial of Dedan Kimathi* (1971) by Ngũgĩ wa Thiong'o and Micree Githal Mugo was considered so subversive that the play was closed down, and Ngũgĩ was thrown in prison. Women's histories have been recuperated through a number of plays such as *Parables for a Season* (1993) and *The Reign of Wazobia* (1993) by Tess Onwueme and *Have You Seen Zandile?* (1990) by Goina Mhlope, Tembi Mtshali, and Maralin Vanrenen.

The use of storytelling, an imaginative rendering of a cultural narrative often augmented by dance and song, is another way in which history is visited and reworked. In non-text-based cultures, the storyteller provides a particularly key way in which history is preserved. Some examples include Temi Osofian's *Once upon Four Robbers* (1991), Jack Davis' *The Dreamers* (1982), and Efua Sutherland's *Edufa* (1962), *Forwa* (1971), and *The Marriage of Anansewa* (1975).

In addition to script-based theater work, another strand of postcolonial theater has involved the implementation of Augusto Boal's Theatre of the Oppressed. This theater uses improvisational theater techniques to create community-based stories and audience participation in order to facilitate change within the community. Guillermo Goméz-Peña, a Mexican American performance artist, has also done a number of works that critique **colonial discourse**.

Further Reading: J. E. Gainor 1995; H. Gilbert and J. Tompkins 1996.

Kanta Kochhar-Lindgren

Periphery. *See* Center

Caryl Phillips (1958–)   Like many postcolonial artists, Caryl Phillips is a writer with a complex background. Born in St. Kitts (eastern Caribbean) in 1958, he moved to England only a few weeks later. He was brought up in Leeds and Birmingham, in a society that he felt both of and not of, and graduated from Oxford University in 1979. Since then, he has traveled extensively, keeping two "home" bases in London and New York.

A similar sense of displacement pervades his prolific output. His first two novels, *The Final Passage* (1985) and *A State of Independence* (1986), tackle the 1950s West Indian migration to Britain and the return to the native Caribbean. His later fictions, *Higher Ground* (1989), *Cambridge* (1991), and *Crossing the River* (1993), more specifically explore the **black Atlantic** world (theorized by Paul Gilroy) and the African diaspora, interwoven with the Jewish exile in his latest novel, *The Nature of Blood* (1997), a common experience already examined in *Higher Ground*.

Written in elegant and restrained prose, Phillips' fiction is neither plot-driven nor linear but rather relies on fragmented, sometimes labyrinthine narratives. Each novel explores the inner thoughts and existential states of several characters and thereby powerfully conveys their intense suffering but, above all, their formidable capacity for love and survival. Through individual lives, Phillips' purpose is to highlight the multiple ironies of history and redress its imbalances, which he does in an undogmatic way, as the open-endedness of his works testifes. So, his novels often give voice to those who were silenced in traditional historiographies, whether women, slaves, or victims of the Holocaust, a revisionary intent also expressed through a highly imaginative use of intertextuality. *The Nature of Blood*, to mention just one example, writes back to *Othello* and *The Merchant of Venice*, while echoing *The Diary of Anne Frank* as well.

If his plays and essays also deal with such issues as postcolonial identity, humans' natural tribalism, and the location of "home," they do so in ways that nicely complement the fiction. Unlike his novels, which are often historical, most of his dramatic works, among them *Strange Fruit* (1981) and *Playing Away* (1986), focus on the contemporary scene and address more directly than the novels what it means to be black and British today. Similarly, by showing how ethnocentrism undermines the complexity that people have inherited from history, his two book-length essays, *The European Tribe* (1987) and *The Atlantic Sound* (2000), provide his fiction with a clearer political subtext.

Further Reading: B. Ledent 2001; L. Yelin 1999.

Bénédicte Ledent

Post-Fordism   Post-Fordism refers, in narrow terms, to the modes of production, consumption, and finance regulation characteristic of capitalism since the early 1970s. More generally, it refers to the new configurations in social and international relations brought about by contemporary capitalism. The term is used to signal a change from Fordism, the era preceding it, which gets its name from the mass assembly methods adopted by Henry Ford in 1913 for his Ford Motor Company. These were part of a massive new mobilization of technology, capital, and management practices that had wide-ranging consequences for society, first in the developed nations of the West and, subsequently, in the rest of the world. Fordist methods followed principles of management associated with Frederick Winslow Taylor. Taylorism advocated principles of management that entailed a systematic division of labor and a separation of creativity from execution and of mental work from manual work. Fordism achieved efficient productivity for manufacturers and an immense accumulation of capital, but it also entailed a break with traditional modes of production typical of the cultures of craftsmen and artisans. Fordism met with initial resistance from organized labor, since its practice gave greater control over the production process to the management sector and alienated workers from mechanically repetitive activity. Fordism survived the depression with state intervention. After World War II, it resumed the accumulation of capital that gave the West a period of steady growth in productivity, improved living standards, and changed patterns of consumption. According to analysts, Fordism met with problems that came to a head in the early 1970s, partly due to changes in the field of production and partly due to contradictions inherent to capitalism.

Post-Fordism is described either as a radically new phase of transnational capitalism or as a redeployment of the financial, political, and management forces that characterized Fordism. Both descriptions acknowledge that capitalism has had to accommodate to a world affected by rapid growth in new technologies (such as microelectronics, information technology, service industries) and the impact of such growth on production and consumerist practices. Fordism brought about material prosperity and the accumulation of capital in the West through a balance between the interests of corporate management, organized labor, and the nation-state. From a fascist prison cell in 1929, the Italian Marxist **Antonio Gramsci** analyzed the rise of Fordism, prophetically, as a form of Americanism, which would impel all traditional societies based on individualism toward planned economies interlinked to global financial mechanisms and eventually affect not only workplaces but patterns of consumption, leisure, and social organization everywhere, while establishing a new conception of work and a new kind of civilization. The implications of his analysis can be extrapolated to all the postcolonial states, whose economies struggle belatedly to catch up with methods of mass production already established in the advanced capitalist coun-

tries, which also happen to be the states that practiced colonialism in the past
and are in a position currently to propagate various forms of deliberate and
involuntary economic and cultural **neocolonialism**. In this perspective, the consequence of post-Fordism for the formerly colonized peoples of the world is to
expose newly formed nations to the force of a global economy dominated by
nations that were the first to implement Fordist practices.

In a context where national boundaries have become increasingly porous to
the influence of corporate capitalism and financial markets controlled by the
most developed nations of the world, postcolonial nations experience post-
Fordism in at least four ways. Since they lag behind in terms of technology
and industrialization as well as in the maturation of their financial and political institutions, they must contend with economic and cultural domination and
exploitation. They are impelled to accelerate their rate of technological development. They experience direct and indirect pressures to assimilate into an increasingly global economy. As developing nations, they can provide new
locations, cheap labor forces, and massive new markets for corporate industries
based in the developed nations. The postcolonial nation-state has reacted to post-
Fordism either by adopting defensive-aggressive policies of protectionism (with
variable success) or by reconciling itself to trading off a gradual erasure of local
culture and indigenous modes of production and living for a stake in global
capitalism.

Further Reading: A. Gramsci 1971a; D. Harvey 1989.

Rajeev S. Patke

Postmodernism   As Jean-François Lyotard indicates in his essay "Note on the
Meaning of 'Post' " (1992), the word "postmodern" seems to denote a "coming
after the modern." However, rather than referring to a particular time, the "postmodern" can be understood as a way of thinking that erodes easy delimitation
between historical periods, past, present, and future, with the effect of throwing
time "out of joint." As a way of thinking that tests the limits of the centered
subject and our capacity to know, the postmodern paradoxically evades definition since it resists philosophies that rely upon totalization, grand **narratives**
that explain all, **essentialism**, and coherency.

Ihab Hassan's essay entitled "Towards a Concept of Postmodernism" (1987)
endeavors to explain postmodernism in terms of the disjunctive, antiform, play,
chance, anarchy, silence, performance, deconstruction, antithesis, absence, dis-
persal, misreading, antinarrative, the polymorphous, schizophrenia, difference,
irony, and indeterminacy. Attempting to define the postmodern in the face of
the conceptual cracks opened up by postmodernism, theorists tend to heap adjectives upon their readers. This in itself becomes a working example of the
way in which postmodernism draws attention not only to the limitations of
systems of knowledge but also to the limitations of language. If postmodernism
is understood in terms of the textual, it can be thought of in relation to Jacques

Derrida's theorization in *Writing and Difference* (1978), whereby language is understood as a system of *différance*, or infinite differences between signifiers and the infinite deferral of meaning.

The ghostly nature of "postmodernism" as it resists categorization and leaves its traces in many disciplines is addressed by Thomas Docherty in *Postmodernism: A Reader* (1993). Docherty outlines the tensions between understanding postmodernism as a period "after **modernity**," postmodernism as "an aesthetic style," and postmodernity as "a cultural reality." The cultural reality of postmodernism has been explored by Frederic Jameson, the Frankfurt school, and Lyotard, who understands postmodernism as a reaction against the totalizing philosophies of the Enlightenment. Strategically essentializing the Enlightenment in order to react against it, Lyotard questions Enlightened ideologies that claimed to master and emancipate. Noticing that monolithic assumptions are not only self-deceiving but also enslaving, Lyotard's essay "Answering the Question: What Is Postmodernism?" (1983) connects Enlightened thought and its need for a fixed politics with fascism. He concludes that we have already "paid a high enough price for the nostalgia of the one," and so Lyotard's answer to the Enlightenment is to "wage a war on totality," to "witness the unpresentable," and to "activate the differences and save the honor of the name." Undermining the closure of meaning, which is aligned with a totalitarian politics, noticing what evades representation and attending to difference rather than sameness, Lyotard's understanding of the postmodern demonstrates how attempts to assimilate **alterity** or otherness are undesirable and impossible. This leads him to an ethical demand to face the other that is problematized by Zygmunt Bauman in *Postmodern Ethics* (1993). Lyotard's work challenges not only the relationship between democracy and difference, which has been explored by Jürgen Habermas and Seyla Benhabib, but also our criterion of judgment, which is explored in Lyotard's *The Postmodern Condition* (1979) and "The Sublime and the Avant-Garde" (1989). Exploring the act of judgment in legal, ethical, political, and aesthetic terms, Lyotard's theorization investigates the limits of justice, ethics, politics, understanding, and representation.

Art forms also exploring such limits include the choreography of Merce Cunningham, the music of John Cage and Pierre Boulez, the writing of Thomas Pynchon and Samuel Beckett, and the poetry of John Ashbery. Theorists of the postmodern include Jean Baudrillard, Andreas Huyssen, Charles Jencks, Gianni Vattimo, and Hayden White.

Further Reading: T. Docherty 1993; J.-F. Lyotard 1989.

Sarah Fulford

Post-Postcolonial Theory   The genesis of postcolonial theory—or postcolonial studies, **colonial discourse** analysis, or simply postcolonialism—is usually dated to the publication of **Edward Said**'s *Orientalism* in 1978. The 1980s was a period of inception and exploration for this new "discipline," and the 1990s was

the period of its maturation and institutionalization. The latter decade ended
with a variety of books (Ania Loomba's *Colonialism/Postcolonialism*, 1998;
Leela Gandhi's *Postcolonial Theory: A Critical Introduction*, 1998; and Bart
Moore-Gilbert's *Postcolonial Theory: Contexts, Practices, Politics*, 1997) setting out to comprehensively introduce and review the field. Responding as well
as contributing to successful institutionalization, these three books present a
convenient codification of a field that had by then attained a certain visibility
and stability. At the same time, all three books also conclude by suggesting the
possibility that, in Moore-Gilbert's words, "the postcolonial 'moment' has been
and gone" (1997, 185). At the conclusions of these books an implicit question
is posed: after postcolonial theory, what? Though postcolonial theory might very
well have reached certain conceptual impasses, it would be inadequate to consider this question simply as a symptom of disciplinary exhaustion; a variety of
institutional and historical developments, too, contribute to the urgency of this
interrogative spirit.

Virtually from its inception, postcolonial theory has been confronted by spirited critiques from many quarters. The most effective of these have been made
from **Marxist** positions. Because of the significant valence of Marxism in a
variety of social movements in the Third World, there has been a particularly
contentious relationship between postcolonial theory and Marxist accounts of
the postcolonial world. Each has set out to explain the colonial and postcolonial
world from significantly divergent positions. Not without reason, certain Marxists have regarded "postcolonial theory" as the introduction of poststructuralist
positions into the theoretical consideration of the Third World. The earliest extended expression of this Marxist displeasure with postcolonial theory is Aijaz
Ahmad's *In Theory* (1992) which was soon followed by Arif Dirlik's *The Postcolonial Aura* (1997). Both these books argue that postcolonial theory as an
intellectual phenomenon is largely of Western provenance, that is, that it is part
and parcel of Western intellectual history. Were it not for the fact that, in many
ways, these books look back to theoretical positions that predate postcolonialism,
it would be accurate to describe them as explorations of post-postcolonial theory.
Both these books try to visualize something beyond postcolonial theory.

Beyond Postcolonial Theory (1998) is, indeed, the title of a third book, by E.
San Juan Jr., that sees itself as a conscious successor to the work of Aijaz Ahmad
and Arif Dirlik and aims to contest postcolonial theory on its own turf, so to
speak, by demonstrating the superior effectiveness of Marxism in dealing with
the cultural and social phenomena of the postcolonial world. Where Ahmad and
Dirlik set out mainly to critique postcolonial theory, San Juan's objective is to
render postcolonial theory obsolete by advancing alternative and more adequate
theoretical positions. San Juan does not deny the newness of the present historical conjuncture and therefore agrees with the need for theoretical innovation;
however, he regards Marxism as the best source of the principles according to
which such innovation might be attempted. San Juan inventories and contests
in his book many of the central theoretical innovations and contributions of

postcolonial theory: hybridity, **subalternity**, strategic **essentialism**. He finds in postcolonial theory a "liberal individualist ethos geared to the 'free play' of the market" (10) and observes that "the repudiation of foundations and objective validity . . . undermines any move to produce new forms of creative power and **resistance** against globalized inequalities and oppressions" (8).

Against the enthusiastic importation of notions of fragmentation and discontinuity from poststructuralism by postcolonial theory, San Juan unabashedly posits the totalizing analysis of Marxism. In pursuit of a holistic perspective on postcolonialism, he links notions of "postcoloniality" to "**globalization**" and "diaspora," suggesting that the condition of the postcolonial world cannot be adequately accounted for without reference to the latter two—mainly, but there are others as well—terms. It is in this trajectory of San Juan's argument that we might find some clues to a general answer to the question: after postcolonial theory, what? For, though he has given one of the most systematic articulations of the need to amend postcolonial theory by reference to new terms and historical events, the recognition of the relevance of "globalization" and "diaspora" to postcolonial theory is certainly not restricted to San Juan. It would be more representative of the mood of interrogation and disciplinary exhaustion gaining ground in postcolonial theory to present the journey beyond in more general terms than simply as a symptom of Marxist critiques.

For example, the three introductory texts presented at the outset all conclude by raising the question of globalization in the context of their presentation of postcolonial theory as a strategy of reading. All three note that the methodologies widely, if problematically, recognized as distinctive of postcolonial theory have been perfected over a textual terrain, the literary and historiographical archive of colonialism and its immediate aftermath. In this overwhelmingly textual context, it is not surprising that the most influential traditional disciplines contributing to postcolonial theory thus far have been literary criticism and history. If the distinctive methodologies of postcolonial theory require an already existing archive, how will they respond to the still-unfolding challenges of globalization? The textual accounts of globalization, understood as the increasing interpenetration of regional economies in the wake of "free-market" policies of "liberalization" or "structural adjustment programs" across the world, are only now being produced; it might very well be the case that the most interesting work with regard to formerly colonized societies might now come to be done in the social sciences. Certainly, the most widely cited critical works on the cultural dimensions of globalization have been produced thus far by anthropologists and sociologists, by such figures as **Arjun Appadurai** (e.g., in his book *Modernity at Large*, 1996). Will the challenges of globalization overwhelm the methodologies of postcolonial theory? Will these methodologies be rendered obsolete as globalization takes on a more and more urgent character? Or will globalization force fresh methodological innovations within postcolonial theory? Whatever might be the answers to these questions, globalization poses a serious challenge to postcolonial theory as it is presently constituted.

A similar challenge emanates from the set of issues cohering around the term "diaspora." As a critical term, diaspora works in a complementary manner to globalization. The postcolonial period has been marked by a steady flow of immigrants from the former colonies into Europe and North America, so that there are now substantial "minority" populations there, constituting an increasingly significant postcolonial diaspora. That these immigrants, too, represent a dimension of the postcolonial condition is readily apparent, for example, in the literary example of **Salman Rushdie**, a writer who can at one and the same time be described as a postcolonial writer from India and a diasporic writer from Britain. While some of this immigration predates the period of globalization, the presence of such immigrants has become especially visible only more recently, and the continuation of this flow of bodies from the former colonies may be linked now to the expanding effects of globalization.

Postcolonial theory has certainly not ignored the question of diaspora. A critic as central to the field as **Homi Bhabha**, for example, has written on various diasporic issues. Still, by and large, the critical division of labor between, for example, the field of Asian American literature—the literature of the Asian diaspora in North America—and postcolonial literature remains largely in place, obscuring the salience of the one for the other. The social and historical processes that brought, and continue to bring, many of the more recent immigrant communities of color to North America and Europe are postcolonial in the strictest sense of the term: they are a direct result of European and North American colonialism during earlier periods. How, then, will postcolonial theory respond to the issues brought to the foreground by "diaspora"? Will it accept the challenge of linking diaspora in a substantive way to what is referred to as postcoloniality? Such questions represent another avenue for the evolution of postcolonial theory, as presently constituted, beyond itself.

The most signal contribution made by postcolonial theory to contemporary criticism might very well in the future come to be regarded as the exploration of the salience of race in an international context. Postcolonial theory has enriched considerably our understanding of the functioning of racial categories in colonial as well as postcolonial contexts. Will postcolonial theory now take the lessons of this exploration to an interrogation of globalization and diasporic phenomena? Will it remain recognizably postcolonial in doing so? As the colonial period, strictly defined, recedes further and further into the past, *post*colonialism itself begins to appear dated as a term. Its significance begins to take on a purely historical character. It remains to be seen what explorations of globalization and diaspora retain from postcolonial theory.

Finally, discussions of post-postcolonial theory should also recognize the particular structure of intellectual work in the North American academy, which in many ways remains the primary venue of postcolonial theory. The thoroughly commodified nature of this work produces its own dynamic of obsolescence and restless innovation. If there is something called postcolonial theory, the North American academy ordains, sooner or later it must be succeeded by something called post-postcolonial theory. Without gainsaying the validity of the historical and theoretical reasons, reviewed earlier, behind the various desires to move beyond postcolonial theory, this dynamic, too, should be acknowledged in discussions of post-postcolonial theory.

Further Reading: A. Ahmad 1992; E. San Juan Jr. 1998.

S. Shankar

Post-Soviet Literature. *See* Eastern European Literatures

Poststructuralism. *See* Post-Postcolonial Theory

Primitivism Though they have often been used in the context of art and art history, the term and concept of primitivism are useful in postcolonial studies as they imply a hierarchy between cultural modes. As Gill Perry notes, the term "primitive" was generally used in the nineteenth century and after to "distinguish contemporary European societies and their cultures from other societies and cultures that were considered less civilized" (Hiller 1991, 5). This concept was used in art history to describe the work of artists like Pablo Picasso and Paul Gauguin, whose visual experimentations with shape and form depart from Western artistic conventions.

Yet when these Western artists adopted these untraditional painting styles, they were considered to be engaging in a modern primitivism. In this way, an East–West binary was enforced so that Western "modern primitive" art could be distinguished from **Third World** "primitive" art. This binary necessarily sets up an inclusive/exclusive power relationship within culture that empowers **Eurocentrism** and allows language to act as a discourse that asserts cultural imperialism without force.

If it is problematic to deem a work of art "primitive" for not conforming to Western painting conventions, it is perhaps equally so when some art has been called primitive for the *subject* that it depicts. For example, Pablo Picasso's *Les Demoiselles d'Avignon* (1907) features five distorted nude women, three of whom are wearing African masks. Because African masks symbolize African culture, which has in the past been labeled "primitive" by the West, the painting is deemed by Western critics to contain primitive aspects, while it is simultaneously hailed as modern because it is by a European artist. Here we must question if this particular work would be considered modern in any way if the geography within which it was created was positioned in the Third World. This dilemma faced by the concept in the context of art history reflects the ambivalence felt by the colonial/postcolonial subject.

Not only are the art and culture of most Third World nations considered primitive, but this sweeping generalization is also made about its natives. In other words, Third World culture is primitive; hence, those who engage with it are savages. We may here recall Thomas Macaulay's infamous "Minute on Indian Education" (1835), in which his belief that indigenous Indian culture is subordinate to Western culture called for a missionary-like quest to forge "a class of persons, Indian in blood and colour, but English in taste, opinions, in morals, and in intellect." Here, Macaulay proposes a plan for the de-primitivization of India as an extension of the British Crown.

Macaulay's assertion leads us to ask a couple of troubling questions. Does the moment of colonization for a Third World nation free it from the derogatory confines of being labeled primitive? Is culture more refined when it is manufactured by white Westerners? Though there could be a myriad of answers to these questions, it is important to view the concept of primitivism itself as an ideological discourse (that manifests through language) that operates in the same way that racism and sexism do. By implanting the notion of better than and less than at the site of a culture's expression, one attempts at once to invalidate it while claiming to possess the authority to speak for it. In this way, the concept of primitivism is important in postcolonial studies, for it draws attention to the loaded implications of a single word and how that word can become an ideological tool for exerting hegemony around the world. Many postcolonial fiction writers, including **Chinua Achebe**, **Salman Rushdie**, and Shyam Selvadurai, combat institutionalized notions of primitivism by using dialects and other languages in their English writing that may disorient Western readers. This strategy in postcolonial writing in English illustrates that what may once have demarcated the primitive during the colonial age must be viewed as difference in the postcolonial age—difference that is regarded neither as better than nor as less than.

Further Reading: S. Hiller 1991; M. Torgovnick 1990.

Rahul Krishna Gairola

Psychoanalysis Psychoanalysis arguably provides the most comprehensive discursive construal of subjectivity and subjected identities. Of particular significance to the postcolonial project are Jacques Lacan's structuralist-psychoanalytic models. Bringing together structuralism, Freudian psychoanalysis, and Hegelian **Marxism**, Lacan's psychoanalytic operations have been instrumental in simultaneously describing the importance of language/linguistic structures in the formation or interpellation of the subject as well as the interdiction or repudiation of otherness. Despite important differences in the ideological and dialectical positions between **Frantz Fanon** and the Tunisian Jewish writer Albert Memmi, both maintain the importance of language as a crucial index and instrument of racial othering (see Pellegrini 1997, 128). Dissimilar—although not wholly incommensurable—to the ethnopsychoanalytic work on language structures of Memmi and Fanon, Lacan's emphasis upon language as the means through which subjective **identity**, social reality, and, more radically, the Freudian unconscious are structured and negotiated attests to the fundamental ambivalence of these material and psychical mechanisms.

Moreover, although "classical" psychoanalytic discourse tends to emphasize sexual difference over and above other varieties of difference or dialectics of "otherness," it maintains a significant, if equivocal, relation to postcolonial theory and practice. Indeed, it is not surprising that most extant modes of postcolonial theory either employ psychoanalytic heuristic procedures or formulate (counter) discursive applications that oppose them. From Freud to Memmi, from Fanon to Lacan and Octave Mannoni, from Rey Chow to **Homi Bhabha**, psychoanalysis may be specified in terms either of the machinery of the colonial enterprise or as the instrumental **agency** against forces of imperialism. Regarding more recent implications concerning psychoanalysis and postcolonialism, Emily Apter observes that it provides "indispensable paradigms for rethinking colonial paternalism, transference, fetishism, negation, sadism, masochism, unconscious drives, and those inversionary structures of identification that give racist shame and guilt psychic form and performative visibility" (1999, 79).

Apropos, Frantz Fanon may be considered one of the most transmissibly prominent exponents of the intractable coalition between psychoanalysis and postcolonial theory/practice. Although greatly influenced by Jean-Paul Sartre's phenomenological existentialism and the writings of **Aimé Césaire**, Fanon's theses may also be soundly associated with the works of Freud and Lacan. Supplementing, while problematizing, Freud's various studies on group and individual psychosocial operations, Fanon appropriated psychoanalytic models to (re)articulate identities and issues pertaining to the colonial situation. For example, the terms *epidermalization* (designating a situation of internalized racism) and *sociogeny* (a supplemental development of Freud's much-discussed couple "ontogeny" and "phylogeny") index Fanon's "postcolonial" (or, in his words, *sociodiagnostic*) (re)vision of Freudian psychoanalytic codes and discursive structures.

In *Black Skin, White Masks* (1967), Fanon attacks Lacan's colleague Mannoni, whose seminal "psychology of colonialism" (elaborated in the text *Prospero and Caliban*) propelled both ethnopsychoanalysts into fame and infamy. Tenably occupying politically and ideologically antithetical positions, Fanon and Mannoni may be held to demonstrate the means by which psychoanalytic heuristics may be employed according to wholly dissonant ideological paradigms. Their respective engagements with ethnography and psychoanalysis enabled both Fanon and Mannoni to radically repudiate the (false) promise of equality and rhetoric of *le semblable* (the similar one) in Enlightenment liberalism. Further, both maintained the deeply pathological nature of the colonial encounter. However, while Mannoni posited of particular **subalterned** peoples (he nominated the Malagasy as an example) a "natural" predilection for being colonized, Fanon sought to develop a global ethicopsychical politics of antiracism.

Fanon's own work has been, and continues to be, influential in postcolonial theory and cultural studies. For example, not only do the writings of Homi Bhabha, Kobena Mercer, Samira Kawash, Rey Chow, and bell hooks (Gloria

Watkins) feature expositions of the Fanon oeuvre, but their own discursive modes may be perceived to be indebted to Fanon's prodigious theoretical legacy.

As the project of underpinning designations or categories of discourse becomes increasingly problematized, psychoanalytic rubrics (not necessarily or simply Fanon's) have exhibited a dialectical flexibility and enduringness amid and against a horizon of multifarious discursive operations. Not only has psychoanalysis played an increasingly significant role in postcolonial counterdiscourse, but ethical and politicotheoretical objectives have become increasingly shared by a diversity of scholars from putatively disparate discursive milieus. Employing Lacanian, phenomenological, **queer**, Marxist, and/or feminist versions of psychoanalysis, a diversity of critics such as Alphonso Lingis, Emily Apter, Judith Butler, Stokely Carmichael, Slavoj Žižek, and Rey Chow has conjectured upon numerous articles of postcolonial significance. For example, Lacanian Marxist Žižek has published variously on the racial other in relation to the hegemonic white symbolic (or phallic) social structures. His work has also explored fundamentalist or totalitarian **nationalism** as a form of superego-evil and skinhead intolerance against other(ed) ethnoracial groups as a mode of id-evil. In *The Metastases of Enjoyment* (1994), Žižek has even applied the Lacanian matrix of "courtly love" to surmise upon interracial, nonheterosexual love. Similarly, Chow's work on diasporic Asians utilizes much of Lacan in describing the mechanisms of fetishism, naming, power, and knowledge as they pertain to nonwhite and nonheterosexist identities.

Further Reading: E. Apter 1999; R. Chow 1994, 1996; F. Fanon 1967; A. Pellegrini 1997; S. Žižek 1994.

Matthew Cleveland

Q

Quebec and Postcolonialism   The 1991 Canadian census documents that 85 percent of Quebec's citizens are French Canadian (les Québécois de vieille souche, "of old roots"), claiming inheritance to a common culture, language, and history, although such parameters—culture, language, history—have been increasingly debated in framing Quebec sovereignty and nationalism, particularly as Quebecois migrants (de nouvelle souche, "of new roots") contest such foundations. This heritage, though contested, has marked Quebec's history, its sense of national belonging, and its cultural alienation. Despite the linguistic and cultural dominance of French, the relationships of Quebec to France, Québécois français (pejoratively called *joual, choual*) to French français, and francophone Canadians to their **anglophone** neighbors (from Canada and the United States) have been historically vexed. The colonial history of North America and the subjugation of "New France" to the British "rest of Canada" mark the provincial history and cultural identity of Quebec. The geographical proximity and spatial contiguity with the United States, as well as importation of American culture, have also penetrated Quebec's territorial borders, making it a space of linguistic/cultural translation, especially since the *Révolution tranquille* (Quiet Revolution).

The "Quiet Revolution" was a period of urbanization, secularization, and a rise in nationalist, sovereigntist fervor in Quebec, marking radical political and cultural shifts in the territory. In 1963 the radical separatist group Front de Libération du Québec (FLQ) began bombings to protest Canadian colonization of Quebec. In the 1970 provincial elections, the Liberal Party (under Robert Bourasa) gained a majority of parliamentary seats; however, the Parti Québécois (PQ), formed in 1968 as a separatist party, also gained prominence. The extremist measures of the FLQ escalated during the bleak period of Quebec's history known as the "October Crisis," when members of the FLQ kidnapped British diplomat James Richard Cross and, five days later, Quebec politician

Pierre Laporte, who was later murdered by the sovereigntist activists. In retaliation, the Trudeau administration authorized the military occupation of Quebec under the War Measure Act and the arrest of over 300 members of the FLQ, including nationalist intellectuals and poets—such as Gaston Miron, cofounder with Gilles Carle and Olivier Marchand of the publishing house Les Editions de L'Hexagone and a leading proponent of nationalism and "decolonization" of Quebec. This period led to censorship and suppression of political, if not artistic, freedom in Quebec. Despite his arrest and political suppression, Miron was awarded several prizes for *L'Homme rapaillé* in 1971. In an editorial called "Document Miron," the editors of *La Barre* du jour protested Miron's arrest, with Nicole Brossard and Roger Soublière writing a separate essay calling for nouvelle écriture, "new writing." Miron and other poets—notably, Michèle Lalonde, whose "Speak White" contested the political, cultural, and linguistic subordination of "French Canada" to its dominant anglophone provinces—advocated ideological forms of poetry, or *non-poèmes*, as Miron called them. Influenced by anti-colonial theorists such as Albert Memmi, **Frantz Fanon**, and Jean-Paul Sartre, Miron published an influential article, "Décoloniser la langue" (1950), asserting the need for a decolonized Quebec and Québécois language. For Miron, poetry is political and must decolonize language (or the "colonial bilingualism" of English/French), writing new and revolutionary refrains.

Post-1970 writers such as Brossard, Jacques Godbout, Jacques Ferron, and Michel Tremblay charted new ground in *la littérature québécois*, refusing the appellation "French Canadian" and redeploying *joual* (Canadian French, or "Quebeckish") from a nationalist, anticolonialist perspective. These writers broke with literary and linguistic traditions, forging a poetics of revolution. Works such as Godbout's *Salut Galarneau*! and Tremblay's play *Les Belles-Sœurs* politically, dialectically, and innovatively revalued the once-devalued *joual*. Brossard's innovations are less dialectic, more stylistic: through blanks spaces, typography, holographic images, and neologisms, she infuses writing with desire. Brossard's later poetry—allied with feminist and lesbian francophone writers Louky Bersianik, Louise Cotnoir, Louise Dupré, and France Théoret and anglophone writers Gail Scott and Daphne Marlatt—mapped novel trajectories within *une écriture au féminin*, "a writing in the feminine." Corporeality preoccupied writers *au féminin*. Quebecois women writers, as Dupré explained, are "doubly alienated"—in language and in body. Théoret's graphically disturbing *Bloody Mary* (1991) dismantles masculinist logic through feminist self-expression. Brossard, writing from the sites of woman, lesbian, and French Canadian, textually spirals these points into horizons of becoming.

Nationalist sentiments, though, however complicated through race, gender, and sexuality, remain woven through Quebec's cultural imagination. Under Rene Levesque's leadership, the PQ held a referendum on sovereignty in 1980, resulting in a 60 percent NON (no) vote. Although reelected in 1981, the Liberal Party regained control of the provincial government in 1985. When Jacques Parizeau became premier in 1994, the PQ regained power and held another referendum in 1995 (50.6 percent NON vote, 49.4 percent OUI [yes] vote). Parizeau, once boasting that sovereignty would be won without anglophone and allophone (see later) support, ultimately blamed the "ethnic vote and money" for its defeat. Post-1995 discourses of national identity heatedly debate ethnicity, migration, and language.

Another compelling reason for examining Quebec in relation to postcolonialism is the number of successful Quebecois migrant writers (most from formerly colonized areas). Migrant francophone writers—moving from Southeast Asia, East Asia, North Africa, Latin America, and the Caribbean, primarily Haiti—sought refuge, economic stability, and exilic creativity in Quebec, primarily in Montreal. Contemporary migrant literatures have created shifts in conceptions of *la littérature québécois*, mapping distinctions between being/ becoming Quebecois, though definitions of "Québécois" and "Québécitude" remain contested. Moving from discourses of *modernité/modernisme/décoloniser* in the 1960s to *postmodernité/postmodernisme/postcolonialisme* in contemporary scholarship, critics ask who and what are signified by "Quebecois"? Does it include or exclude Haitian-, Maghrebian-, Italian-, Vietnamese-, Latin American-, and other migrants in Quebec? (Even the triangulation of francophone-anglophone-allophone does not address the pluriphonic, polysemic variations within contemporary *littérature québécois*, *allo-*, denoting "other," designating liminality between anglo-/franco-, and reducing multilingualism to singularity.)

The largest group of migrant writers, having fled Duvalierism and the Macoutes, is Haitian-Quebecois and includes writers such as Émile Ollivier, Joël Des Rosiers, Dany Laferrière, Anthony Phelps, Jean Jonaissant, Stanley Péan, Liliane Devieux, Jan J. Dominique, Ghyslaine Charlier, and Nadine Magloire. A journalist in Duvalier's Haiti in the 1970s, Laferrière fled Port-au-Prince for Montreal in 1976 after two colleagues were found dead, yet even exile is treated with cool, dispassionate humor in his writings. A Haitian diasporic writer in Ottawa, Gérard Étienne adds to *la littérature canadienne francophone*, if not *la littérature québécois*. Maghrebian writers and artists, such as Michka Saäl (Jewish Tunisian) and Flora Balzano (part Italian, Spanish, Polish, and Corsican who grew up in Algeria during the revolution) have also thrived in Quebec. Several Egyptian-Quebecois writers have published in Quebec, notably Anne Marie Alonzo but also Andrée Dahan and Mona Ltaiff Ghattas. Alonzo, the most prolific of these, has published many volumes of poetry exploring feminist, lesbian, and migrant consciousness. Nadine Ltaif—born in Egypt, raised in Lebanon, emigrated to Quebec—has written fictional texts on migration and exile. Pascale Rafie (born in Quebec to a Quebecois mother and a Lebanese father) textually explores second-generation children of migrant parents. Algerian-Quebecois writers Flora Balzano and Nadia Ghalem write from different migratory spaces—the first of Muslim, the latter of Christian heritage.

Other migrant writers have published in Quebec, increasing the diversity and pluriphonism of *la littérature québécoise*. Writers Fulvio Caccia, Marco Micone,

Tiziana Beccarelli Saad, and Bianca Zagolin are important Italian-Quebecois voices. Diasporic Jewish writers in Quebec are also important. A. M. Klein, of Jewish Ukrainian descent, wrote many important volumes of poetry exploring Judaism and Judaic identity historically and in the shadows of the Holocaust. Régine Robin, also Jewish Ukrainian-Quebecois born of French migrant parents, has written literary and theoretical texts exploring *métissage* (mixed blood) and hybridity. Latino/a writers—notably, the Uruguayan-Quebecois lesbian writer Gloria Escomel—have further contributed to the diversity of contemporary Quebecois literatures. Asian-Canadian writers—Bach Mai (Vietnamese) and Ying Chen (Chinese-Quebecois)—are also important new francophone voices. Mai explores exile in *D'Ivoire et d'opium* (1996), a semiautobiographical text recounting the return of a Eurasian journalist to her native country in order to make a documentary film; while on site, she experiences the double dislocations of origin as a Eurasian in Vietnam.

Artists, scholars, and activists continue to debate issues of nationality, culture, and language, as well as notions of *l'étranger* (foreigners in relation to dominant culture). Important scholars and theorists—Louis Balthazar, Robert Berrouët-Oriol, Joël Des Rosiers, Robert Fournier, Simon Harel, Diane Lamoureux, Lucie Lequin, Maïr Verthuy, Pierre Nepveu, Gilles Marcotte, Régine Robin, Sherry Simon, Robert Schwartzwald, Pierre L'Hérault, Daniel Salée, and Alexis Nouss—have interrogated and continue to examine the imbrications of civic, ethnic, sexual, and gendered forms of citizenship and nationality within Quebec.

Further Reading: R. Schwartzwald 1985; S. Simon 1994.

Jana Evans Braziel

Queer Theory   One of the more recent signifiers among the constitutive discourses of (homo)sexuality developed in the last 150 years, "queer" confounds the categories that license sexual normativity through its demonstration that sexuality is a discursive effect. Perhaps better understood as a zone of possibilities than as a theory, the rubric of "queer" designates the different political and theoretical work carried out under it as always inflected by a sense of potential and future possibilities that it cannot as yet quite articulate. Its effects are variously threatening and exhilarating, not least because of its determined indeterminacy of specification and radical potential.

Until its reincarnation at the beginning of the 1990s, "queer" had been a term of derogation used about men classified by heterosexist societies as "homosexual" and of identification used by men who identified themselves primarily on the basis of their homosexual interest. Given this history, it is unsurprising that the term's resurrection and new signification in the last decade was both welcomed and attacked or that resistances to "queer" came most insistently from advocates of lesbian and gay identity politics: they were, after all, precisely the politics brought most acutely under interrogation by "queer." Unsurprisingly, too, reservations about "queer" bore numerous similarities to the discourses by which the term "gay" as an inclusive signifier of homosexual-identified men had been resisted in the 1970s and 1980s. As the shift from "homosexual" to "gay" had pointed to a changing reality, both in the ways a hostile society labeled homosexuality and in the way those stigmatized saw themselves, in distinguishing itself from those terms that form its semantic history, "queer" equally foregrounds a changing reality. Nevertheless, the path traced by "homosexual," "gay," "lesbian," and "queer" provides an accurate history of the terms and identificatory categories commonly used to frame same-sex desire in the twentieth century. As sexual liberationists had from the 1960s annexed the word "gay" to mark a clean break with the pathologizing discourses of medicine that had classified homosexuality as a deviation for the previous 100 years, so by the second half of the 1980s the notion of a unitary lesbian and gay identity and the assumptions that structured the core of the ethnic model of lesbian and gay identity were challenged and critiqued by lesbians and gays of color and members of non-normative sexualities. Ironically enough, the very characteristics that made possible the civil rights achievements of the gay and lesbian movement of the 1970s also generated a substantial and irrecuperable dissatisfaction with the assumptions that underpinned its construction of a unified gay and lesbian identity. The suspicion that normative models of identity could no longer suffice for the representational work demanded of them was strengthened by influential poststructuralist and **postmodernist** understandings of identity, gender, sexuality, power, and **resistance**; these provide the context in which "queer" becomes an intelligible—perhaps even an inevitable—phenomenon.

Jean-François Lyotard's 1983 declaration that the impulse of this fin-de-siècle is the end of rational politics, in the sense of the concept, and his embrace of the libidinal economy (and rejection of the conceptual economy) opened a space in which queer theory could be conceptualized. Where, as we have seen, the lesbian and gay movements were committed fundamentally to the notion of **identity politics** in assuming identity as the necessary prerequisite for effective political intervention, "queer," on the other hand, exemplifies a more mediated response to categories of identification. The growing awareness of the limitations of identity categories in terms of political representation and the increasing engagement with poststructuralist theories of identity as provisional and contingent enabled the emergence of "queer" as a new form of personal identification and political organization. From Althusser's thesis that the subject is constituted by ideology, to Freud's theory of the unconscious, or from Lacan's emphasis on subjectivity as something originating outside the subject, to Saussure's conclusion that we are constituted through language preexistent of any individual, the twentieth century produced a powerful body of texts requiring us to realize— as Roland Barthes does in his *Mythologies* (1978)—that our understanding of ourselves as coherent, unified, and self-determining subjects is nothing more or less than an effect of those commonly circulating codes of representation that society used to describe the self and through which, consequently, identity comes to be understood. Consequently, identity has been reconceptualized as nothing more or less than a sustaining cultural fantasy or myth.

Of special significance to this profound late twentieth-century cultural shift in the theorization of the subject in Western culture, especially where the emergence of queer scholarship and activism from gay and lesbian understandings of identity politics is concerned, is the work of the cultural historian **Michel Foucault.** More explicitly engaged in the denaturalization of dominant understandings of sexual identity than the French poststructuralists who preceded him, Foucault emphasized that sexuality is not an essentially personal attribute but an available cultural category. Further, he argued that sexuality is the effect of power rather than simply its object. Because it conceived of modern subjectivity as an effect of networks of power not in themselves fundamentally repressive and of sexuality as a discursive production of a power endlessly prolific and multivalent rather than a natural condition, Foucault's work on power, knowledge, and sexuality had the effect of undermining liberationist arguments for, and strategies of resistance to, power.

The social constructivist writer who has been most influential in the development of "queer" has been Judith Butler. Her 1990 monograph, *Gender Trouble: Feminism and the Subversion of Identity*, elaborates on Foucault's argument about the ways in which marginalized identities are complicit with those identificatory regimes that they seek to counter. Butler's major argument has been that there is nothing authentic about gender, no hidden "core" that produces the reassuring signs of gender. Gender is, rather, a cultural fiction, a performative effect of a set of acts repeated within a regulatory frame that is in itself highly rigid. The consequent reiterative stylization of the body produces, over time, the appearance of substance, of a natural sort of being (1990, 33). Gender is thus reframed as an *effect* of the sex/gender system which purports merely to describe it, that is, as no more or less than an ongoing discursive practice that is open to intervention and resignification.

The regulatory fiction signified by the term "woman" reproduces those normative relations between sex, gender, and desire that naturalize heterosexuality. The cultural matrix through which gender identity has become intelligible requires, further, that identities in which gender does not "follow" from sex and those in which the practices of desire do not "follow" from either sex or gender are unable to exist. Attempts to "naturalize" same-sex desire—the usual strategy of lesbian and gay movements—or any commitment to gender identity works ultimately against the legitimation of homosexual subjects.

Butler's argument that the performative repetition of normative gender identities naturalizes heterosexuality has been very productive for the development of queer studies in the 1990s because of the attention that it draws to the consolidation of the subject through the reiterative performance of gender. Productive, too, has been her insistence that gender is more than the mere cultural inscription of meaning on a pregiven sex. Rather, it follows that gender also designates the very apparatus of production whereby the sexes themselves are established. Sex, too, is a gendered category, Butler argues; and gender designates the very apparatus of production by which the sexes themselves are established (7).

The debates about performativity initiated by the work of Butler caused a denaturalizing pressure to be exerted on sex, gender, sexuality, bodies, and identities, a pressure felt most strongly in lesbian and gay studies' crisis about "gay" identity. The cognition that, like "woman," "homosexual" is a name that refers not to a "natural kind" of thing but to a homophobic, discursive construction that has come to be (mis)recognized as an object has profoundly destabilized that version of identity politics that is advocated in both liberationist and ethnic models of homosexuality. It has also, productively, generated a more sophisticated understanding of the interworkings of identity and power by leading to what David Halperin in *Saint Foucault* (1995) characterized as "a deepened understanding of the discursive structures and representational systems that determine the production of sexual meanings, and that micromanage individual perceptions, in ways which serve to maintain and reproduce the underpinnings of heterosexist privilege" (32). The result has been the adoption of analytical models that question the authenticity of identity, particularly those that critique the putatively causal relation between a secure identity and an effective politics.

The theory of performativity largely underwrites the "queer" project. Like it, "queer" opts for denaturalization as its primary strategy. "Queer" rejects the minoritizing logic of toleration or simple political interest-representation in favor of a more thorough resistance to normative regimes, thus demonstrating its understanding that sexuality is a discursive effect. Assuming for itself no specific materiality or positivity, "queer" 's resistance to what it differs from is necessarily relational rather than oppositional. Because of the extent to which it is committed to denaturalization, "queer" itself can have neither a foundational logic nor a consistent set of characteristics ("There is nothing in particular to which it necessarily refers," as Halperin puts it [62]). Fundamentally—because necessarily—indeterminate, always ambiguous, always relational, "queer" is a largely intuitive and half-articulate theory. But by deconstructing the categories, oppositions, and equations that sustain conventional understandings of sexual identity, "queer" calls them into question as it demarcates a flexible space for the expression of all aspects of cultural production and reception. "Queer" is, then, less an identity than a critique of identity. Itself always an identity under construction, a site of permanent becoming, "queer" is best represented as endlessly interrogating both the preconditions of identity and its effects.

"Queer" has typically occupied a predominantly sexual register, but its denaturalizing project has been productively brought to bear on other axes of identification than those of sex and gender. Because it is both antiassimilationist and antiseparatist, the queer project marks an attempt to speak from and to the differences and silences that have been suppressed by the homo–hetero binary, an effort to unpack the monolithic identities "lesbian" and "gay," including the intricate ways that lesbian and gay sexualities are inflected by heterosexuality, race, gender, and ethnicity. While some have argued that "queer" encodes a **Eurocentric** bias that makes it insensitive to the largely identity-based policies of ethnic communities, the denaturalizing impulse of "queer" can be articulated within precisely those contexts to which it has been judged indifferent. In *Tendencies* (1993, 9), Eve Kosofsky Sedgwick observed the potential for "queer" to be spun outward in ways and along paths unsubsumable under categories of gender and sexuality. The processes of denaturalization initiated by the queer project have enormous potential in the exploration of the ways that race, ethnicity, and postcolonial **nationality** crisscross with sex, gender, sexuality and other identity-constituting, identity-fracturing discourses.

"Queer" 's denaturalizing impulse is consistent with the wider interrogation of epistemological categories that has animated much informed critical discourse during the last decade. The significations of the terms "race," "whiteness," "hybridity," and "masculinity" have all, for example, been the subject of intensive scrutiny, analysis, and deconstruction (much as the term "woman" had been and continues to be). As Sedgwick predicted, the leverage of "queer" has been employed by "[i]ntellectuals and artists of color whose sexual self-identification includes 'queer' to do a new kind of justice to the fractal intricacies of language, skin, migration, state" (9). Anthologies of the 1980s, such as *This Bridge Called My Back: Writings by Radical Women of Color* (Cherrie Moraga and Gloria Anzaldoúa, 1983), *Twice Blessed: On Being Lesbian, Gay and Jewish* (Christie Balka and Andy Rose, 1989), and *In the Life* (Joseph Beam, 1986), focused on the meshings of racial and sexual identities, for example. But by problematizing normative consolidations of sex, gender, and sexuality, "queer" is most productive in its critique and disruption of all those versions of identity, community, and politics that are popularly believed to evolve "naturally" from such consolidations, and, for these reasons, it has been, and is, indispensable for the present and future of postcolonial studies.

Further Reading: R. Barthes 1978; J. Butler 1990; M. Foucault 1981, 1988; D. Halperin 1995; E. Sedgwick 1993.

James N. Brown

R

Race. *See* Ethnicity

Angel Rama   Rama (Montevideo, 1926–Madrid, 1983) is considered one of the Latin American critics most influential in his time. He also wrote narrative works and plays; however, his major contributions were in the area of literary criticism. Having started his career as a literature professor rather early, he taught in Latin American and U.S. universities for over thirty years, until his untimely death in a tragic airplane accident together with his wife, Marta Traba, herself a renowned critic of Latin American literature and art.

Rama's work concerns mostly the literary history of Latin America, which he perceives as a continuum linked by intertextual references and characterized by a resistance to existing power structures. In *La novela en América Latiña: Panoramas 1920–1980* (The Latin American Novel, 1982) Rama is concerned with the ideological roots of literary production and states that literature in the 1960s and 1970s in Latin America is often inspired by "a lack of trust in schools, discourses, groups, and, above all, a spontaneous refusal of the current rhetoric of power" (467).

In one of his most recognized books, *Transculturación narrativa en América Latina* (Narrative Transculturation in Latin America, 1982) Rama reviews Fernando Ortiz's concept of **transculturation** and applies it to the literary works of the twentieth century, particularly those of **José María Arguedas**.

La ciudad letrada (1984; *The Lettered City*, 1996), which was published posthumously, is Rama's best-known and most influential work, thanks, in part, to a recent translation in English by John Charles Chasteen, and it is sadly the only book by Rama translated into English to this day. This book is a wide-ranging study of the intricate relationships between the colonial and neocolonial processes, the "civilizing mission" of the *polis*, and the emergence of the Latin American societies. So the links start to emerge in the book that hold together the lettered culture, state power, and urban location that are what Angel Rama calls *la ciudad letrada* (the lettered city). According to Chasteen (1996), Rama's discussion of the lettered city of the colonial period "brings post-colonial continuities and contrasts into clear focus" (ix) and offers us a "basic key to the understanding of the literature and history of an entire world region" (xiv).

Rama's major works include *Rubén Darío y el modernismo* (Rubén Darió and Modernism, 1970); *Diez problemas para el narrador latinoamericano* (Ten Problems for a Latin American Narrator, 1972); *La novela latinoamericana. Panoramas 1920–1980* (The Latin American Novel, Survey 1920–1980, 1980); *Transculturación narrativa en América Latina* (Narrative Transculturation in Latin America, 1982); *La ciudad letrada* (1984; (*The Lettered City*, 1996) *La crítica de la cultura en América Latina* (Critique of Latin American Culture, 1985).

Further Reading: J. Chasteen 1996; J. Kubayanda 1986.

Silvia Nagy-Zekmi

Rastafarianism   This is a Jamaican spiritual-political movement. Growing out of the confluence of Marcus Garvey's **Pan-Africanism** and indigenous Jamaican religious traditions, Rastafarianism took form after Ras Tafari was crowned Emperor Haile Selassie I of Ethiopia in 1930. This event was seen as a "fulfillment of biblical prophecy; the emperor was and is hailed as the living incarnation of God." Millennial in character, Rastafarianism anticipates the destruction of Western culture and the repatriation of all blacks to Africa. Consequently, many Rastafari have embraced poverty and oppression rather than compromise with a capitalist world that they see as doomed. Their rejection of Western culture is profound; Western accounts of history, the King James version of the Bible, even the English language are dismissed as distortions designed to keep Africans in a state of economic and spiritual slavery. In their place Rastafarianism fashions a history and a language ("Dreadtalk" or "Iyaric") that affirm **black power** and black liberation. At the heart of their worldview is a reading of the Bible that identifies the Western world as Babylon, the Rastafari themselves as Israel, and Ethiopia as Zion. Nevertheless, since the 1960s the focus of Rastafarianism has shifted from African repatriation to the struggle against oppression in the black diaspora. Through the medium of reggae, *and* especially through the music of Bob Marley, the movement's emancipatory message has influenced black power movements in Europe, North America, Australia, and even Africa. Its message of spiritual uplift has also crossed racial lines, making Rastafarianism a truly global movement away from the divisiveness of racism. In Jamaica itself, Rastafarianism, once suppressed as a dangerous cult, is now recognized as a vital cultural movement and has adherents both within and without the mainstream of Jamaican society.

Further Reading: B. Chevannes 1994; N. S. Murrel et al. 1998.

Hugh Hodges

Resistance Literature   Resistance literature is an art form that responds to oppression using the written word as a weapon against aggression and geographical displacement. Many resistance writers began as journalists before turning to literature, which does not have the emotional constraints of journalism. The purpose of their literature is to educate and to elicit sympathy for their communities. Distinguishing itself from propaganda, resistance literature is always conscious of its honesty and artistic integrity, which are integral to the collective values of the resisting community. These values include a commitment to others and the preservation of their identity, dignity, and homeland, all of which are threatened by colonialism. Without any pretense of being objective and by providing a rewriting and rereading of history, resistance literature presents an alternative historical narrative that gives voice to the disfranchised. In her *Resistance Literature* (1987) and *After Lives, Legacies of Revolutionary Writing* (1996), literary critic Barbara Harlow highlights the relationship between a vital and meaningful culture and the armed struggle for independence. Resistance literature is always concerned with a specific historical and political crisis, rather than the story of one individual. Instead, the individual characters or authors become a microcosm for an entire group, and, through the extension, the problems of injustice and inhumanity become a universal concern. The innovations in the literary form of these works reflect the current reality of the respective society while rejecting both a linear or Western perspective of history and the impossible temptation to return to the past. The literary texts are influenced by, and pay tribute to, ancestral values that have been devalued or absorbed by the colonizer. Yet resistance writers refuse to lapse into a simplified **nativism** of the past that reinforces the stereotype of the group as an authentic or backward civilization.

Resistance or commitment literature includes a diverse body of prose, essays, poetry, and diaries, often blurring the Western distinction between genres. These literary texts are always informed by the author's political agendas against the colonial forces and/or a military regime. They frequently include stories within a story to reveal the complications of the political conditions and the results of these complications on the daily life of otherwise ordinary citizens who have been forced into reclaiming their freedom and homeland. Many of these works have been written while the authors were in prison, in hiding, in forced exile, or facing death sentences for their political activities and ideologies. Resistance literature both critiques the repressive outsider and articulates the author's criticism of his or her own community while simultaneously showing solidarity with the group. Although European writers of the French resistance and the authors writing against Franco during the Spanish civil war could be considered resistance writers, the term "resistance literature" has come to denote those writers disfranchised by colonialism and the subsequent struggle for independence and the problems of establishing a new political order that does not merely repeat the power structures of the colonizers. Although influenced by European writers who often used literature to denounce injustice, resistance literature faces the debates over the choice of language, the target choice of criticism, and the validity of those writers safely, but forcibly, living in exile while many of their comrades are in prison or living in fear in their home countries. Resistance literature has its roots in **nationalism** and **Marxism**. While some writers are committed pacifists, and others are strong supporters of the armed struggle, the more than 100 volumes of diaries, essays, verse, and prose left by India's Mohandas Gandhi (1869–1948) set an example of the pen as a weapon and teacher.

In South America *I, Rigoberta Menchú, an Indian Woman in Guatemala* (1984) and *Crossing Borders* (1998) typify resistance literature. Menchú's autobiographies not only tell the story of her life as an activist and her rise from an illiterate peasant to the recipient of the Nobel Peace Prize in 1992 but also recount the story of her family and the struggle faced by the twenty-two indigenous ethnic groups in Guatemala in the aftermath of the Spanish colonization. Her autobiographies can be read as both coming-of-age stories and the history of the United Nations' recognition of indigenous rights. Similar to other works of commitment, she shares a profound tie to the land and a respect for her ancestors. Her explanation of Mayan culture is an effort to preserve a particular way of life, to draw attention to the plight of the Indian in Guatemala, and also to explain the complicated social structures to the outsider in order to promote understanding. Born in the province of El Quiché in a small village founded by her father, Menchú, who never attended school, learns Spanish to respond legally to the military authorities. Subsequently, as a young woman, she discovers the Bible as an educational tool and weapon. Her spirituality is a blend of Catholicism and ancient Mayan traditional beliefs. Despite the tragedies of having a younger brother and a father burned alive, her mother kidnapped, raped, tortured, and killed, and her two younger sisters becoming guerrillas, Menchú retains her faith in justice and humanity.

The choice of language between the colonizer's language or the maternal language is a major debate for resistance writers, for the choice of language implies the choice of audience. The pressure of this question has occasionally had unfortunate consequences. The Algerian writer Kateb Yacine's poems, plays, and novels are considered landmarks by Maghreb literary critics and have influenced young North African writers as well as the French writer Albert Camus. In 1948 he published his poem "Nedjma, or the Poem or the Knife," and later he published the lyrical novel *Nedjma* (1975), whose beauty and unknown parentage wreak havoc in the lives of the young men who fall in love with her. *Nedjma* can be read as a political allegory for Algeria. Like many resistance writers, Yacine faced prison for his military resistance but continued to write. With the Arabization of North Africa after independence, however, and the continued attacks of his patriots, Yacine stopped writing entirely. The more recent Moroccan novelist Mohammed Khaïr-Eddine chose to write in the language of the colonizer to defamiliarize the French reader in his own language and thereby to reproduce the alienation of colonization. A more pragmatic reason for his choice of French reflects his French education. Another Moroccan writer, Tahar Ben Jelloun, often expresses exasperation when questioned on his choice of language, implying that the medium is more important than the content. He explains that he can express his ideas more easily in French than in Arabic, the sacred language of the Qur'an. Other writers, like the Moroccan novelist and essayist Abdelkebir Khatibi, chose to publish their works simultaneously in both Arabic and French to avoid prioritizing one reading public over another.

These later Moroccan writers came to be known as the "Souffles" generation with the publication of their journal by the same name in 1966. Their manifesto called upon artists and writers to create new art forms that would bring back their cultural life ravished by colonization into artifacts sold as souvenirs. Critic Marc Gontard refers to Khaïr-Eddine's writing as "guerrilla linguistics." During Morocco's independence, many of the Souffles writers were imprisoned or forced into exile. Like many resistance writers, Khaïr-Eddine returned to Morocco to work on the preservation of Berber culture, and upon his recent death in 1996 he was mourned as a national hero.

Because resistance literature is a response to a particular political situation, its thematic focus changes with the political shifts. Second, the number of writers who have gone into exile has raised more complications in classifying literature by national boundaries, as with the *Beur* **literature** in France. In Algeria resistance literature first recounted the brutality of the French forces that colonized Algeria in 1830 and their brutality during the Algeria War of 1954 until Algerian independence in 1962, as in **Assia Djebar**'s *Algerian Quartet* (*L'amour, la fantasia* [1985], *Ombre sultane* [1987], *Loin de Médine* [1991], *Vaste est la prison* [1995]). Marxist novelist and essayist Rachid Boudjedra's change of focus and sympathies in his novels reflect the changing trends of resistance literature. His novel *Le vainqueur de coupe* (1981) is an empathic portrait of a young Algeria villager who becomes a terrorist in Paris. Since 1981, over 100,000 Algerian civilians have been killed during the fighting between the military and the Islamic Fundamentalists. Boudjedra's most recent novel, *La vie à l'endroit* (1997), a condemnation of terrorism, focuses on the effects of terrorism on the daily life of a photographer and his French lover. Boudjedra, himself the target of numerous death threats, urges intellectuals and artists not to flee Algeria in despair.

This change of sympathies following political changes can also be found in Middle Eastern literature, particularly Palestinian and Lebanese. From 1975 until 1992, the Lebanese Christians and Muslims and the displaced Palestinians and the Israelis who invaded Lebanon in 1978 and again in 1982 waged a war that killed over 150,000 people and displaced even more. Meanwhile, a group of women, which Miriam Cooke in her *War's Other Voices: The Centering of the Beirut Decentrists* (1987) identifies as the Beirut Decentrists, were busy writing novels, unbeknownst to each other (see also Evelyn Accad's *Sexuality and War, Literary Masks of the Middle East*, 1990). In their works, each of these women witnesses the horrible war in Lebanon from a **feminist** perspective that condemns the violence that erupted around them in a country previously characterized by its diversity and religious tolerance. Although the plots of their novels differ, and the writers worked as individuals rather than as a cohesive literary movement, their works explore the same themes. Their fiction charts the disintegration of the noble ideas of religion, nationalism, and freedom into the tragic consequences on civilians as the violence grew on the streets of Beirut.

Two of the Beirut Decentrists, Etel Adnan and Hanan al-Sheikh, were journalists when the war broke out, and later they went into exile. Like the Souffles writers, their work blurs the boundaries between truth and fiction. Etel Adnan's *Sitt Marie Rose* (1982) is based on the true story of Marie Rose Boulos, a Lebanese divorced teacher who taught mentally disabled children and was murdered for her Palestinian sympathies. Reminiscent of Faulkner, the novel's narrative moves from one character's consciousness to another, giving the reader the perspective of all the participants. The novel closes with a haunting image of the deaf children dancing while Sitt Marie Rose is dismembered by her male schoolmates, now her enemies. After the novel's publication, Etel Adnan was forced to leave the country, yet she was recently invited back to Lebanon in 1999 to celebrate the novel's translation into Arabic.

Hanan al-Sheikh's novels and short stories are also set during the war. In *The Story of Zahra*, she recounts the fatal sexual relationship between one of Lebanon's snipers and a young woman. Through the young woman's family history, al-Sheikh, like other Lebanese female writers, dismantles the illusion of an idealistic Lebanon before the war. Liana Badr, although born in Jerusalem, has since returned to Palestine and is considered by some critics to be one of the Beirut Decentrists. Active with the Palestine Liberation Organization (PLO) and the Palestinian woman's movement, her novels *The Eye of the Mirror* (1994) and *A Balcony over Fakihani* (1993) capture the plight of women's struggle for freedom within the larger Palestinian resistance from the refugee camps of Beirut, the setting of several massacres during the war.

Like Egyptian feminist, physician, and writer **Nawal El Saadawi** and the Moroccan novelist and feminist **Fatima Mernissi**, women writers throughout the Middle East have often been vocal critics of the hypocrisy, sectarianism, and chauvinism that lead to aggression from both within and outside their societies. The Iraqi painter and sculptor Nuha al-Radi's *Baghdad Diaries* (1998) documents the devastation caused by the Iraqi War and the embargo by the United States on Iraqi civilians.

With the creation of Israel, Palestinian literature is more aligned with the armed struggle to regain the rights and the land of the indigenous Palestinians. Born in 1936, Ghassan Kanafani was one of the first to coin the phrase "resistance literature." When his family was displaced from Acre in 1948, they became refugees in Damascus. As a journalist and writer, Kanafani revealed the effects of the state of Israel on the Palestinians, a perspective largely overlooked and silenced by the support of Israel after the tragedy of World War II. A member of the Popular Front for the Liberation of Palestine, Kanafani was killed with his niece in 1972 by a car bomb planted by the Israeli Secret Police in Beirut. Always concerned with child welfare, as shown in his collection of short stories *Palestine's Children* (1984), the proceeds from his book sales still provide financial support for the education of refugee children. Kanafani's controversial *Men in the Sun* (1978), the story of three Palestinians who die by suffocation while being smuggled out of Iraq in a water truck, can be read as a criticism of Arab leadership. The touches of surrealism and the multiple narrators of *All That's Left to You* (1990) demonstrate his diverse talents as a writer and the ethical problems faced by the young Palestinians living in Gaza.

Another Palestinian writer who left Israel in 1948 is the novelist Jabra I. Jabra, whose novels, poetry, and autobiography express the collective pain felt by all classes of Palestinian society both inside the occupied territory and in exile. While Kanafani's work tends toward the tragic, Emile Habiby's *The Secret Life of Saeed, the Pessoptimist* (1985) uses satire and fantasy to describe the difficulties for Palestinians living inside Israel. Anton Shammas' *Arabesque* (1988), the first Palestinian novel to be written in Hebrew, also deals with the problems of identity and individual relationships between Israelis and Palestinians faced by young people.

Today's most popular Palestinian poet, revered as a national hero, is Mahmoud Darwish. Born in Palestine in 1942, Darwish was a journalist imprisoned by the Israelis; he left for Beirut in 1971 until he moved to Paris. Now, when he makes one of his frequent returns to Palestine, he is greeted as a national icon. His poetry is characterized by his sophisticated use of the Arabic language and is filled with nostalgic images of the natural landscape of Palestine. His poems express the loneliness of exile, and many are dedicated to other resistance writers or victims of the fighting in the Middle East. Much of his poetry has been put to music. He remains a controversial figure, as shown in the recent Lebanese court case over the accusation that some of his poems, which were set to music by Marcel Khalife, were sacrilegious and the recent uproar in Israel over the suggestion to include several of his poems within the Israeli school curriculum. The present controversies generated by Darwish's work attest to the continued power of resistance literature.

Women writers also figure predominantly in Palestinian resistance literature. Sahar Khalifah's *Wild Thorns* (1985), set in her native Nabluus in the West Bank, tells the story of a family living under occupation. Her novel shows the tensions created by an outdated patriarchal society within the Palestinian community and the tensions between those who chose to work for the Israelis building Israeli housing on occupied land, those who choose to resist the occupation, and those in exile who have lost touch with the realities within the occupied territories. Her realistic novel tell a simple story that illuminates the many complications of daily survival under occupation. While the men join the armed struggle in Khalifah's novel, Leila Khaled's autobiography, *My People Shall Live: The Autobiography of a Revolutionary* (1973), traces the early roots of the resistance of the Popular Front for the Liberation of Palestine and her later disenchantment with the party leadership. Leila Khaled, a Marxist and guerrilla fighter, was one of the first resistors to hijack a TWA plane in 1969 and made a failed second attempt in 1970 in an effort to draw international attention to the Palestinian plight. Her story has also been the inspiration for *The Homeland* (1995) by the Syrian writer Hamida Na'na. *The Homeland* fictionalizes the later life of Leila Khaled to show the deterioration of the resistance into empty bourgeois slogans. With the reported corruption within the PLO and the Oslo Peace Accord, some Palestinian writers are expressing a sense of betrayal and new hopelessness. At the International Palestinian Writer's Conference in 1997, when asked what direction Palestinian literature would look to in the future, Ahmad Harb, a prizewinning Palestinian novelist, responded with a depressed, "I don't know" and compared the question to asking him to stand naked. Nevertheless, he, like other resistant writers, continues to write to help outsiders understand the reasons for their resistance and to critique those on the inside, to remind them of the need to continue to fight for communal justice rather than individual gain, and to demonstrate to others that they are not struggling alone.

Further Reading: B. Harlow 1987; S. Jayyusi 1992.

Lynne Rogers

Roberto Fernández Retamar   Retamar is a poet, essayist, and professor of philology who is known for his meticulous efforts to dismantle **Eurocentric** colonial and **neocolonial** thought. "Caliban" (1971) become a kind of manifesto for Latin American and Caribbean writers; its central figure, the savage of Shakespeare's *Tempest*, becomes in Retamar's hands a powerful metaphor of their cultural situation—both in its marginality and in its revolutionary potential. The Caliban theme has already emerged in postcolonial cultural discourse addressed by José Enrique Rodó (1872–1917) in his essay *Ariel*, whereby Rodó claims Latin America as the land of Ariel the playful fairy, as opposed to North America with its Calibanesque pragmatism. Ernest Renan in *Caliban* (1878) offers, according to **Aimé Césaire**, a "scientific" rambling about "inferior, or bastard races" that "did not come from Hitler's pen, but from Renan's" (qtd. in Retamar's "Caliban" [10]). Jean Guéhenno published in 1928 *Caliban parle* (Caliban Speaks), an "autobiographic"account of Caliban himself that contests Renan's vision of him. Octave Mannoni published in 1950 *Psychologie de la colonization* (in English, *Prospero and Caliban: The Psychology of Colonization*, 1964). In this book Mannoni talks about the Prospero complex, which is subsequently rejected by **Frantz Fanon** in *Black Skin, White Masks* (1967). George Lamming (*The Pleasure of Exile*, 1960) picks up on this theme, focusing his inquiry on the question of language. Propero has supposedly *given* the language to Caliban. Just two years before Fernández Retamar's essay, Aimé

Césaire wrote *Une tempête* (1969), a play in which the characters are the same as in Shakespeare's; however, they are slaves on the brink of a rebellion. Retamar's essay counters Rodó's idea of Latin America's being the land of Ariel: "Our symbol," writes Retamar, "is not Ariel, as Rodó thought, but rather Caliban" (14).

Retamar worked on another idea that is related to that of Caliban and was long part of Latin American consciousness (although it is not to be found only in Latin America), the dichotomy between civilization and barbarism. Domingo Faustino Sarmiento's iconic book *Civilización y barbarie* (1845) has laid the foundation for this debate in Latin American cultural history. Retamar wrote another book of counterdiscourse: *Algunos usos de civilizacón y barbarie* (Some Uses of Civilization and Barbarism, 1988), in which he criticizes Sarmiento's Eurocentric racist approach to Latin America, described as "bands of abject races, a great continent abandoned to savages incapable of progress" (23).

In 1986 Retamar concluded his Caliban project with the essay "Caliban revisitado" (Caliban Revisited) by saying, "I will not spend an inordinate amount of time on Caliban's anagrammatic history" (53). However, he clarifies some of the ideas that he proposed in "Caliban" and responds to some critics (Borges, Fuentes, Rodríguez Monegal) who wrote (not always kindly) about this essay, which, admittedly, represented a crossroads in Retamar's oeuvre.

Further Reading: N. Lie 1997; J. Saldívar 1990.

Silvia Nagy-Zekmi

Salman Rushdie   Salman Rushdie, probably the most controversial postcolonial writer, is also probably the most "postcolonial." While he is negotiating the interstices of metropolitaneity and of hybridity, he remains rooted in his postcolonial context, India after independence, and in his quintessential self. Because of his criticisms of postcolonial peoples in *Satanic Verses* (1988) and his subsequent "banishment" into an enforced metropolitan exile in London, Rushdie is often depicted as an alienated expatriate. However, the pattern in all of his works is of a young man growing up into his sense of Indianness, after what seems to be an interminable series of tests and trials. It is important to read the Indian context in Rushdie's work to understand where self-awareness really lies for his characters.

Edward Said first posed Salman Rushdie as an example of a **postmodern**, postcolonial, metropolitan intellectual. Rushdie's defense of the Third World in his essay "Outside the Whale" (1986) was juxtaposed by Said against **Naipaul**'s indictment of the Third World's "present barbarities, tyrannies and degradations" as resultant from "innately native histories" ("Intellectuals in the Post-colonial World," 1986, 47). But then Said wrote, "One way of getting hold of the commonest post-colonial debate is to analyze not its content, but its form." Rushdie's form thus became a major factor in defining him as a postmodern postcolonial. *Midnight's Children* is said to have birthed a new postmodern **magic-realist**

novel with vast sweeps of rewritten, reinvented histories. In 1983 in one of his first interviews, in talking to Michael Kaufman, Rushdie said that he wrote in the tradition of Garcia-Marquez and Günter Grass. When Indian critics saw *Midnight's Children* (1981) as following G. V. Desani's *All about H. Haterr*, Rushdie was offended. However, in the *New Yorker*'s special issue on "Indian Writing in English" (23 and 30 June 1997), celebrating the fiftieth anniversary of Indian independence, Rushdie acknowledged his debt to Desani. But Indian writers, from Desani through Raja Rao and Rushdie, were also following consciously in the traditions of Joyce and Kafka while incorporating, as Raja Rao did in *Kanthapura* (1938), Indian storytelling traditions. In an article entitled "The National Longing for Form" (1990) and in his book *Salman Rushdie and the Third World* (1989), Timothy Brennan felt that the novel form was foreign to Rushdie, "creating [the] crippling subaltern status" of working in an "oppressive cultural form." Rushdie's father read him bedtime stories from the *Thousand and One Nights*, familiarizing him with Islamic storytelling. But Rushdie also went to Rugby from age thirteen onward, where he must have read many novels. **Homi Bhabha** claimed that Rushdie was denied poetic license by the Muslims (*Location of Culture*, 1994, 226) because the novel form was foreign to them, though they, too, as a result of many years of colonial education, whether in Iran or India, knew the novel form *and* their storytelling tradition. All of Rushdie's novels follow an Indian/Islamic storytelling style, a stream-of-consciousness narrative told by a loquacious young Indian man that Rushdie himself must have been.

Similarly, there is much debate about whether in any of his narratives, again from *Midnight's Children* to *Satanic Verses*, Rushdie was (re)creating history "postmodernly" and therefore "postcolonially" by breaking the colonial mold of history. **Gayatri Spivak** argued his postcoloniality, based on "his citation, re-inscription, re-routing [of] the historical" ("Reading *The Satanic Verses*," 1989b, 79). For Sara Suleri, Rushdie was consciously creating "contraband histories" and was therefore postmodernly blaspheming (1989, 604–24). Two recent student guidebooks to Rushdie are D.C.R.A. Goonetilleke's (1998) and Catherine Cundy's (1996) books simply titled *Salman Rushdie*. Keith Booker's *Critical Essays on Salman Rushdie* (1999) collects the important U.S. essays on Rushdie.

Rushdie's works are not those of a disembodied voice inhabiting a postmodern and shifting space, playing "post-Joycean, sub-Joycean" (Rushdie to Kaufman) tricks with language and history. Though living in an enforced condition of migrancy, Rushdie in his works—even the newer ones—remains very Indian. They are bildungsromans, where the main characters, whether Saleem Sinai in *Midnight's Children* or Gibreel Farishta in *Satanic Verses* or Ormazd Cama in the *Ground beneath Her Feet* (1999), if not grow, are shocked, into an awareness of themselves as "Indian."

"But first," as Rushdie would say, "a little bit of history." With *Midnight's Children* Salman Rushdie broke on the literary scene with a bang. *Grimus* (1975) had gone virtually unnoticed, as had *Shame* (1983), a work about Pakistani dictatorships. Not until the grand controversy over *Satanic Verses* and the *fatwa* declaration of heresy by the Ayatollah Khomeini was any serious interest taken in Rushdie's work by the nonacademic readers in this country. While interest remained in the U.S.–Iranian relations over "the Satanic Verses issue," *Haroun and the Sea of Stories* (1991) did well. Neither *The Moor's Last Sigh* (1995) nor *The Ground beneath Her Feet* has generated much interest among U.S. readership, despite the fact that the latter deals with a rock music culture that should interest younger American readers. But most of its popular culture scene is set in Bombay, an unfamiliar context for Americans. In fact, Bombay is the backdrop of most of his novels. Salman Rushdie said in his talk on 4 July 1996 at the Oxford University Union that Bombay is "the most Indian of cities" and seemed to concede that "if you're not a Bombaywallah, you can't understand all these shenanigans."

Roland Barthes' notion of the "death of the author" became actuality for Rushdie, with the ayatollah's *fatwa* on *The Satanic Verses*. Meaning was wrenched from his hands, and Islamic fundamentalists chose to read the work as blasphemous instead of revisionary. Therefore, this "most visible writer in hiding," as an Associated Press (AP) report called him, has, in his effort to have the "meaning" of his work rest with him, taken to giving many interviews to ensure that the meaning that he writes into his texts is understood as he wishes it to be understood. Upon the occasion of the fiftieth anniversary of India's independence, in explaining his contexts and talking about *Mirrorwork* (1997), this "midnight's child" almost became the spokesperson for India. Salman Rushdie "resurrected" himself, seemingly coming back from the dead to tell all about the meaning of the work, India, Hindi hobson-jobson (Anglo-Indian corruptions of the language)—in other words, the "location of [his] culture." In *Grimus* Rushdie wrote, "how terrible to see a meaning or a great import in everything around one, everything that one does, everything that happens to one" (149). After "the Satanic verses affair," the terribleness of making meaning seems to have struck him all the more. Contextual research, therefore, is important to any interpretation of Rushdie's work.

Like the later *Haroun and the Sea of Stories*, *Grimus* was rooted in Rushdie's early reading of the *Arabian Nights* and of his familiarity with such Islamic works as Farid-ud-din Attar's *The Conference of the Birds* (1177). While Flapping Eagle (a character in *Grimus*) is supposed to have been a postmodern mixture of science fiction, Amerindian legend, and J.R.R. Tolkien, he reaches his Muslim self in Calf Island, after 740 years of wandering. There he "feels inner multiplicities seizing him" (222). Calf is the esoteric Sufi concept of Qaf, a still point in a turning world. Rushdie's quintessential self is always aspiring to reach this mountain of Kâf, rather than be "chameleon, adaptable, confused" (293). In *The Satanic Verses*, for example, Gibreel Farishta, after all his wanderings in metropolitan London and India, eventually finds *himself* not in the discos of Eloween Deoween (L-O-N-D-O-N) but in the Shandar café, the focal point of the Muslim community in the London of Rushdie's book. It is there that the hideous horns and penis of the hybridized migrant fall off. It is in the Islamic self, the way in which Rushdie and Gibreel Farishta were raised Muslim in Bombay, that identity and comfort lie. Each one of his books seems to be a journey toward reaffirming that selfhood located in the Muslim childhood of Bombay, India.

In *Midnight's Children* Saleem Sinai's long journey from Bombay to Delhi, from independence through "Ladakh," "Naxalite fire," "Indira emergency," and Sanjay sterilizations, with some backward looks over the shoulder to the 1857 mutiny and the Amritsar massacre, is not just a journey of **subalternity** but a "pickling process of chunteyfication" (442–43), to "give immortality after all" (444) to one's quintessential self. "The art is to change the flavour in degree, but not in kind." Rushdie, through his character Saleem Sinai, despite exploring his Muslim roots, his grandfather's Kashmiri antecedents, and living among the Methwolds and the Parsis of Bombay, finds himself one with the "multiheaded [Shiva] multitudes" of independence day. Baby Saleem, who has been born as a "midnight's child" at the moment of India's independence, finds that despite his minority Muslim upbringing and his character's alienation and teasing-distancing from things Indian, is really one with his ayah, Padma, the "dung goddess," as Rushdie calls her, one with baby Shiva, with whom he could have possibly been exchanged. Shiva is not just the god but a possible descendant of Shivaji, an ancestor of the Shiv Sena. Yet it is he, Saleem or Salman, who "alone of all the more-than-five-hundred-million" is "to bear the burden of history" (*Midnight's Children*, 370).

The controversy of *The Satanic Verses* centered around a small section of the book. In the section entitled "The Return to Jahilia," Salman, the Farsi Scribe, while jotting down the dictates of the angel Gabriel to Mahound (the Dantesque name for Mohammed), alters some of the *Qur'an*, thus casting aspersions on the holy book. The main character of the novel is a modern-day individual whose name is Gibreel Farishta or, translated literally, Gabriel Angel. Gibreel seems to be dreaming the suppressed story of Islamic mythology where three "satanic" verses were supposedly dictated to the Prophet Mohammed. Mahound wants Salman killed, an ironic harkening to Salman Rushdie's own situation. Like Salman Rushdie, Salman, the Farsi, the character in the novel, lives a life on the run, hiding out here and there, until Khalid finds him and takes him to Mahound. Just as he is about to have his throat cut, Salman "fingers" Baal, the poet, the supposed lover of Mahound's favorite wife, Ayesha, as being the enemy of the prophet. Salman, the Farsi, escapes with a north-bound camel train. The book itself, however, is Gibreel Farishta's bildungsroman, a journey from the immaturity of wanting to be "Western" in clothing and manner to a coming to a knowledge of himself as Indian, and not just Indian, but Muslim, in, of all places, London. Gibreel has a veritable Homeresque journey of flying to England and dropping from an exploding plane, to questioning his religious upbringing (a sort of natural questioning process where he sees the religious leaders as hypocrites), to a realization that he doesn't belong anywhere except with his own people. Much of the questioning in this novel caused true believers a great deal of distress.

The Moor's Last Sigh is a work that can be seen as quite anti-Semitic and antagonistic to the current Indian regime in the creation of the character Raman Fielding, who represents Bal Thackeray, the individual behind the Hindu Nationalist Party. Rushdie attempted to retain interpretive authority in his own author's hands by providing readings, lectures, and interviews explaining his intent. The story centers around a Keralite spice merchant's family that, because of its mixture of Jewish and Indian Christian roots, doesn't quite belong in India. Moraes Zogoiby eventually escapes to Spain, where his uncle Vasco has gone, by renewing a "passage," an airline ticket, that his mother had saved for him because of what she knew would be the ultimate unbelonging. He wants to go to Israel, but his father, Abraham, reminds him of the racism toward the darker Jews (*Moor's*, 341). Eventually, not even belonging in Spain, Zogoiby nails his story to a door and leaves. The story ends and begins as the ending of a story of another man, who could be Rushdie, on the run with death on his heels, nailing his story anywhere he can. This bildungsroman with a typical journey of self-awareness defies postcolonial criticism, which despite claims of migrations and hybridity, does not allow for the changing identities and nationalities that typify such a story of diasporas and of Rushdie's own recent years. There are also odd echoes of guilt—maybe not for blasphemy but perhaps for the innocents killed in the foray over the *Satanic Verses*. Moraes, "the Moor," is certainly a metaphor for Rushdie himself, if not a conflation of his authorial condition with that of his character, apologetic for "murder most foul," that "had slipped so quickly to the back of my brain" (*Moor*, 404). Like Macbeth seeing Banquo's ghost, Rushdie writes, "If murder can be committed by inaction, then yes" (64). He was, and is, a man on the run with many name changes: " 'Adam Zogoiby.' Known before that as Adam 'Braganza.' And before that as 'Aadam Sinai'." Hybrid? No. " 'Mufto' 'Mutto' " (358, 359)—in camouflage, yes.

Naming and playing upon names are Rushdie's way of dealing with issues of **identity**. But Elaichipillai Kalonjees (an actual Keralite name meaning a trader in cardamom and black pepper), the Mirchandanis (a Sindhi name meaning a tradesperson in chillies) or the Parsis, named by the British for their trades, the Sodawaterwallas, the Sodawaterbottleopenerwallas, have actual rooted identities. His puns include the slightest hint of racism. "Kalonjee" in *The Moor's Last Sigh* is "black skinned" (Kala). The same Parsi names are played upon from *Midnight's Children* to *The Ground beneath Her Feet*. Rushdie makes fun of the hybrid mixture of these peoples: "Peppercorns, whole cumin, cinnamon sticks, cardamoms, mingled with the imported flora (Parsis) and birdlife, dancing rat-a-tat on the roads (the Parsis) and sidewalks perfumed with hail" (375). Like Raja Rao, Rushdie carries "his" India with him, witnessed by his insistent writing about this mélange in which he remains a rooted, Bombayite Muslim. With *The Moor's Last Sigh* we see that the postcolonial is not a geographical site, an existential condition, or a political reality. It is a lived experience of connection with one's homeland, despite not being from there—one's place of birth and upbringing in the cross-cultural colonial situation.

In *The Ground beneath Her Feet* this feature of rooted postcoloniality takes on an odd poignancy. The Parsis, the most hybridized and Westernized of the Indians, are an unhappy lot. The book asks its protagonist, Ormazd Cama, the question, "Do you know who you are? Do you know what you want?" (447). Ormus Cama's brother finally answers this for us. When Madonna Sangria comes to see him at the Tihar jail and offers to marry him so he can have a U.S. passport, he refuses because he says he sees in the eyes of his successful rock star that the latter is already dead and in hell in his successful New York life (566). Rushdie definitely believes that the culturally disembodied might as well be dead. Because of Rushdie's need to remain connected to *his* India, I posit that Rushdie is the most postcolonial of all the writers. Unlike that of **Narayan** or **Anita Desai**, his writing takes us through migrations and metropoles to arrive back in India, most particularly in Bombay. This is the lesson of Rushdie's own bildung, that he is not a hybrid postmodern postcolonial but a postcolonial whose lived experience is a longing for the country of his birth.

Further Reading: D.C.R.A. Goonetilleke 1998; K. Booker 1999.

Feroza Jussawalla

S

Nawal el Saadawi   Nawal el Saadawi is an Egyptian writer and **feminist**. She was born in 1932 in Kafir Tahla. Her father, Egyptian minister of education, made sure that his nine children all had university educations. In 1955 Nawal earned a medical degree in Cairo. While working as a doctor, she published twenty-four books in Arabic. These have been translated and are widely popular with English-speaking audiences. Although world-renowned, she has been repeatedly punished by Egyptian authorities because of her writings on female sexuality, a taboo in ultra-Islamic circles.

In 1972 el Saadawi was dismissed from her position as director of public health because of her work *Woman and Sex* (1969). These memoirs significantly angered political and theological authorities, who succeeded in also forcing her to step down from her position as chief editor of a health journal and as assistant secretary of the Medical Association in Egypt. Nevertheless, from 1973 to 1976 Nawal was able to conduct research on women and neurosis in the Faculty of Medicine at Ain Shams University. From 1979 to 1980 she served as the United Nations adviser for the Women's Program in Africa and the Middle East.

Under Anwar Sadat, she was imprisoned in 1981. Upon his death, she was released. Shortly after her liberation, el-Saadawi founded the Arab Women's Solidarity Association (AWSA), an international organization dedicated to assisting women in the Arab world. In 1985 this organization was granted consultant status by the United Nations and considered as a nongovernmental association (NGO). Despite this international recognition, the Egyptian government succeeded in closing down AWSA in 1991 in order to divert its funds to a religious women's association. Although el-Saadawi took the Egyptian government to court, she lost the case. El- Saadawi has sought to teach the world that women are usually the first to die in war and the first to be dismissed when there is an economic crisis. She seeks to give women who are silenced a voice in order to struggle for change in the Arab world. Nawal el-Saadawi's best-known books in English translation include *Two Women in One* (1975), *Woman at Point Zero* (1983), *The Hidden Face of Eve* (1980), and *God Dies by the Nile* (1985).

Saadawi's novels insist on the urgency of studying a wide spectrum of women's lives in order to promote change in Egypt and the Middle East. *Two Women in One* is set in contemporary Egypt. Eighteen-year-old Bahiah Shaheen struggles to gain independence as she fights family tradition. Like the author who creates her, Bahiah is a medical student who yearns for freedom. She finds it impossible to cope with the falseness of traditional women's lives. She rebukes tradition by wearing pants instead of the stiff skirts that women in her culture are compelled to wear. She is often accused of being a man. This accusation, due to her outspoken manner, is one that Nawal el-Saadawi has had to refute herself on numerous occasions. Like Nawal, Bahiah seeks a life different from the one that has been handed her and is willing to confront opposition at any cost. *Woman at Point Zero* is the story of Firdaus, a prostitute who is executed because she killed her pimp. The novel is based on real conversations that Nawal had with Firdaus while incarcerated in the 1970s. This work first appeared in Arabic and then was published in English in 1982. During the 1980s Nawal wrote *Memoirs from the Women's Prison* about her own, firsthand experience in prison. This novel is considered one of her most important books.

Nawal el-Saadawi's works are testaments to women's survival not only in the Middle East but across the globe. She handles not only sexual issues relating to women (particularly the phenomenon of female circumcision, widely practiced in Egypt today) but also how patriarchy and class shape what women do, say, and think as well as how they must act in society. In much of her work, the central message most evident is that women's sexual lives and their relationships with men are inextricably connected within larger political contexts.

Further Reading: F. Malti-Douglas 1995; M. Matthes 1999; A. Mazrui and J. Abdala 1997.

Valérie Orlando

Nayantara (Pandit) Sahgal (1927–)   Daughter of Vijayalakshmi and Ranjit Sitaram Pandit and niece of Jawaharlal Nehru, Nayantara Sahgal was born in Allahabad. She and her two sisters were, as children, repeatedly subjected to loneliness and suffering as the British incarcerated adult family members. In the preface to her autobiography *Prison and Chocolate Cake* (1954) Sahgal tells us about the death of her father soon after a period of internment. The tragedy also revealed for her a face of her community that she had not yet seen: a patriarchal one whose "justice" deprived the wife and the daughters of the dead man's inheritance. Later, she experienced at firsthand the harsh patriarchal setup of a government that legalized unfair divorce settlements. Sahgal's novels as well as her journalism consistently reflect these colonial, national, and patriarchal tensions.

For Sahgal, colonialism was a fiction destined to end whose effects were real and long-term. She captures this destiny in representations that are down-to-earth, neither exotic nor ethnic. In the article "The Myth Reincarnated" (1995), she says that she fears the return of this fiction or myth in the guise of **globalization**, in the unequal meeting of India with the West. Sahgal has no use for the term "postcolonial," and yet her novels are ingrained in the theoretical and historical concerns of this field. In *A Time to Be Happy* (1958) the narrator is a man who, like the author's uncle, has forsaken the lucrative profession of his family to join the Congress. This character, a pro-Gandhian idealist, has a counterpart in all of Sahgal's novels and serves to foreground the inadequacies of many British and Indian officials.

On the national front Sahgal is like **Kushwant Singh** in her criticism of the home government. Her articles with titles such as "Murder of Gandhi Continues" (1969) or "Nehruism in Retreat" (1973) announce her disillusionment with the Congress after independence. While *A Voice for Freedom* (1977) and *Indira Gandhi: Her Road to Power* (1978) are works of nonfiction that criticize the Emergency, *A Situation in New Delhi* (1977) and *Rich like Us* (1985) capture that grim political situation in fiction. Sahgal's insight into national and international political practices has occasioned prophetic novels such as *Storm in Chandigarh* (1969) that predicted a second partition of the Punjab and *A Day in Shadow* (1971), anticipating the Indo-Soviet Treaty of 1975.

All of Sahgal's novels, including *This Time of Morning* (1965), represent the situation of women in India. The main female characters in these novels belong to the Hindu upper class, while lower-class females appear in the margins. Her novels are doubly political in that they bring together the public and the private: government corruptions are revealed even as certain marital relationships are shown to be conducive to the mistreatment of women. Her female characters who seek freedom do not subscribe to the death of the traditional family. Many feminists consider this a betrayal of their cause. Sahgal's **feminism** collides with her Gandhism in the (Gandhian) belief that women are better sufferers and that the suffering somehow benefits the nation. The feminist conflict within a Gandhian ideology can be traced in the other autobiographical work, *From Fear Set Free* (1962). The search for feminist freedom is figured in the Danish protagonist Anna of *Plans for Departure* (1985), a novel also on the departure of the colonizers. The search for identity that accompanies a feminist vision continues in *Mistaken Identity* (1988), where the identity of the nation as well as the individual is reexamined. Sahgal's quest for identity, her discovery of "dividedness," has created in this novel a memorable character, Bhushan, who wittily parts with labels of class and creed to declare himself a "human being" during trial by a colonial court.

Sahgal's more recent publications, *Relationship: Extracts from a Correspondence* (1994) and *Point of View: A Personal Response to Life, Literature and Politics* (1996), provide valuable insights into the aesthetics and politics of this prolific writer.

Sahgal is winner of the Sinclair Fiction Prize and the Commonwealth Literary Prize (Eurasia region). She has been a writer in residence and fellow at several universities in the United States. She was awarded a D.Litt. by the University of Leeds in 1997.

Further Reading: J. Jain 1994; C. Joseph 1998.

Clara A. B. Joseph

Edward Said   Few intellectuals have reached the stature, visibility, and pre-eminence of Edward Said. Professor of comparative literature, cultural critic, political activist, and accomplished pianist, Said's work fundamentally initiated what would become known as postcolonial studies. Edward Wadi'a Said was born in Jerusalem Palestine, in 1935. While his mother, Hilda, was of Lebanese descent but from Nazareth, Edward's father, Wadi'a, was an affluent Palestinian stationery and book merchant from Jerusalem who eventually established his business in Cairo. The consummate Palestinian Christian bourgeoisie, the Said family frequented their residences in Palestine and Egypt as well as their summer home in Lebanon.

Said was a student in an elite English school in Cairo in 1948 when the Zionists successfully dispossessed 80 percent of the Palestinian population. Not until 1990 did Said return, not uncontroversially, to Jerusalem. Despite the magnitude of the trauma, Said was an awkward and sheltered boy with little concern for the tribulations of Palestine, isolated in a "gigantic cocoon." Said's education was one of refinement but also in a multiethnic and multireligious Middle Eastern community.

However, in 1951 he was expelled from Victoria College in Cairo for poor behavior. Since Wadi'a had acquired American citizenship some years earlier, Edward was an American citizen and finished his secondary education at the ironically named Mount Hermon School, a Protestant boarding school in New England. He entered Princeton University and studied history and English literature and pursued his Ph.D. at Harvard, writing his dissertation on Joseph Conrad, a figure who would remain central in his academic research.

While the Suez Crisis would have an impact on his self-view as an Arab Palestinian, he remained out of politics. Emblematic of the shift in the Palestinian struggle itself, the decisive 1967 defeat of the Arab forces and, consequently, the Israeli occupation of the remaining Palestinian territories were the catalyst that compelled Said to a political commitment for the liberation of Palestine. In 1968 he wrote his first article related to the Arab and Palestinian causes, entitled "The Arab Portrayed," which appeared in a book edited by another Palestinian activist-scholar, Ibrahim Abu Lughod, whom he had befriended at Princeton.

In 1970 Said went to Beirut, where his family had relocated some years before. This sojourn was formative not only because it is there that he met his second wife, Miriam, with whom he would have two children, but also because in Beirut he became directly involved in the struggle for the liberation of Pal-

estine, meeting intellectuals, activists, and writers involved in liberation struggles throughout the colonized world. By the early 1970s, Said translated
speeches of Yassir Arafat into English for press releases, for example, while
maintaining his position at Columbia University. Although he always remained
independent and never was affiliated with a political party, Said was elected to
the Palestinian National Congress in 1977. By this time, Said had been transformed into the most articulate, charismatic, and dynamic voice for the Palestinian cause in the West.

Also during the 1970s Said, a scholar of comparative literature, wrote for the
first time on Arab cultural productions, including the Nobel laureate Naguib
Mahfouz, Lebanese novelist Elias Khouri, and Palestinian poet Mahmoud Darwish. While Said never claimed to be a scholar of Arabic culture or literature,
his work in the field displayed his ability to cross boundaries but also his skill
in critically unpacking Arabic texts as well.

In 1975–1976, Said was a fellow at the Center for Advanced Study at Stanford
University, where he wrote his groundbreaking and seminal book *Orientalism*
(1978). While he had reached academic acclaim some years before this date,
particularly with his theoretical treatise *Beginnings* (1975), *Orientalism* was the
definitive work of his lifetime. Over the next three years, he published *Covering
Islam* (1981) and *The Question of Palestine* (1979), which were called, in conjunction with *Orientalism*, his trilogy. The success of these books not only in
the academy but also in the mainstream public catapulted Said to a level of
prestige and visibility that few scholars ever reach.

In the 1980s and 1990s Said, with unrelenting energy, exploited this unique
level of prominence and fame not only in the cause of Palestine but also by
remaining a sustained critic of tyranny in the Arab world and the often arbitrary
policies of the West, as well as a fierce advocate for human rights. In the 1980s
Said actively lobbied the Palestine Liberation Organization (PLO) to reevaluate
the strategy of armed struggle in the pursuit of national liberation, urged Palestinians and other Arabs to understand the importance of mutual respect and
coexistence with Israelis, was an articulate advocate of a two-state solution, and,
in doing so, established innumerable meaningful political and personal relationships with peace-minded Israelis. He also became a leading unofficial spokesperson in the West for the *Intifada*, which started in 1988.

During this period, Said became the most visible and sustained target of vociferous attacks by right-wing Jewish and Christian Zionists, who rarely dared
to assail him on an intellectual or scholarly level but, more often than not, on
the most base and unfounded personal level. Inflammatory articles not only
appeared in reactionary rags such as the *Daily Telegram* and the *Commentary*
but also "reputable" venues such as the *New York Times*, the *Wall Street Journal*,
and the *Times Literary Supplement*. The demonization of Said confirmed the
inherent racism in Zionist ideology and demonstrated how deeply it is en-
trenched within the Anglo-American worldview of the Middle East. That is, as
an articulate Arab intellectual, he still is seen as a dangerous "terrorist" whose

articulate and "rational" demeanor is used to subvert the image of the intelligent and "objective" Western scholar. In 1985, in fact, the Jewish Defense League called him a "Nazi," and, soon after, his office at Columbia University was torched.

Despite his critical support for the PLO and the leadership of Yassir Arafat, Said became one of the most outspoken opponents of the secretly negotiated Oslo Accords, which effectively signed away the Palestinian right to armed struggle without receiving any assurances for statehood or the repatriation of hundreds of thousands of refugees. After the establishment of the "Palestinian Authority" in the 1990s, Said, remaining a staunch advocate of human rights and democratic principles, was a critic of the abuses and corruption of the Yassir Arafat regime. Consequently and ironically, the very books that brought an unprecedented awareness of the Palestinian cause to the West were banned by Palestinian authority.

The 1990s was a politically and personally wrenching period for Said. Soon after his mother's death, he was diagnosed with leukemia in 1991. The disease was virtually debilitating, hospitalizing Said. This experience compelled Said to write his memoirs, entitled *Out of Place*, relating the experience of his youth and sense of exile. After aggressive treatment, Said's illness went into remission, while still taking a toll on his health. During this time, he returned to Palestine, the first time since before 1948, and continues to be a frequent visitor of Palestine as well as Lebanon.

In 1993 Said published his most comprehensive work on postcoloniality, entitled *Culture and Imperialism*. That same year, he was invited, not uncontroversially, to give the BBC's prestigious Reith Lectures, which were published the following year under the title, *Representations of the Intellectual*. With these two publications, Said reasserted, for the first time since the publication of his brilliant *The World, the Text, and the Critic* (1983), his mastery of not only political issues but his chosen field of comparative literature and intellectual history. In the meantime, he reconfirmed his political commitment with the publication of *The Politics of Dispossession* and *Peace and Its Discontents* in 1995. Further demonstrating the connection between politics and scholarship, Said became the president of the Modern Language Association in 1998 against a backdrop of some dissent.

Despite his illness, Said remains the most tireless, forceful, and insightful activist in the continued struggle for peace, equity, and social justice, just as he remains perhaps the most esteemed scholar alive in the academy. He travels throughout the world endlessly giving talks and participating in key cultural-political forums, writes a regular editorial column for the Egyptian *al-Ahram*, which appears in English and Arabic, and continues to be prolific in his literary and political output, taking a leading role in the many arenas in which he has placed himself.

Few living intellectuals can claim to have written a text that has revolutionized several fields in both social sciences and humanities, and fewer are responsible for the genesis of a whole field of inquiry. Aided by the admittedly **Eurocentric**, but brilliant, works of the theorists **Michel Foucault**, **Antonio Gramsci**, and Raymond Williams, Said's *Orientalism* reveals the connections between the process of the production of knowledge and colonial domination, otherwise stated as knowledge and power.

More precisely, Said asserts in *Orientalism* that the Orient is a creation of the West. That is, the "Orient" was created as an object of scholarly knowledge in the West that, necessarily, coincided with the rise of the age of Western imperialism. As an object (as opposed to subject) of knowledge, the Orient is configured as passive, reified, unchanging, and stagnant. Likewise, the "Orient" is a psychic creation where fantasy and feelings of mastery take on geographic and racial principles. In both cases, the discourse of the Orient, Orientalism itself, facilitates a relationship of power between the Occident and Orient that is unequal and based on the domination of the latter by the former. Orientalism, however, Said states, is not merely "an airy European fantasy about the Orient but a created body of theory and practice in which, for many generations, there has been a considerable material investment" (1978, 6).

Said meticulously discusses the development and transformation of Orientalism from its pre-Romantic resonances to its post–World War II manifestations. Often overlooked in the discussion of *Orientalism* are the manner and method in which the author scrupulously reveals the various pedigrees of the discourse or discourses of Orientalism. Contrary to his detractors' misreadings, Said specifically demonstrates that Orientalism is not monolithic but, in fact, maintained different political, intellectual, and discursive forms since its inception in the late eighteenth century. In other words, Mozart's image of the "Orient" differed from Verdi's image. The former's vision looked East to find a humanity lost in the scientific age, while the latter's image clearly corresponds to a vision of imperial domination, Asiatic despotism, and racist stereotypes. The same can ironically be said about the views of Napoleon and the colonialist Balfour. Said adroitly shows us the discursive, political, historical, and ideological differences between early racist Orientalists such as Ernest Renan, Sylvestre De Sacy, and Edward Lane; later "scholarly" and even sympathetic icons such as H.A.R. Gibb and Louis Massignon; and post–World War II anti-Muslim and/or pro-Zionist Orientalists such as Gustave von Grunebaum and Bernard Lewis.

This brilliant study shows us that the representation of the Orient was created and codified to facilitate in the mind and policies of the Western imperialist apparatus control of conquered peoples and territories. Through representation there could be containment, Said states. The fact that the discourse of Orientalism is elastic and that—as the production of knowledge regarding "the Orient"—it finds its reproduction in "voluntary" and "noncoercive" institutions (e.g., higher education and journalism) ensured its longevity and ability to change as the needs for colonial and imperialist control changed.

Understanding this, then, Said's masterpiece reveals that colonial control as well as indigenous resistance are a question of narrative. That is, to challenge colonialism is to challenge the representation and narrative that designate the native as an inferior, backward, irrational, or passive figure. The struggle for colonized peoples, in particular, the role of the intellectual in the colonial struggle, is to make the history of the oppressed, otherwise erased or displaced, visible and viable again. This is the foundation for postcolonial studies.

Undoubtedly, while Palestine is little mentioned in *Orientalism*, we understand the ethical, intellectual, and political project that Said puts before us. That is, Said's work is dedicated to making visible the narrative, history, culture, and **identity** of colonized and oppressed people, such as the Palestinians themselves. Said followed the publication of *Orientalism* with his first extended scholarly work on Palestine and the Palestinians, *The Question of Palestine*, which was followed by studies such as *Covering Islam* (1981), *The Politics of Dispossession, Peace and Its Discontents*, and his coedited *Blaming the Victim* (1988). This diverse set of texts has in common not only that they discuss critically the stereotyping of Arabs and/or the erasure of the victimization of the Palestinians but also that they all discuss the relationship between politics, power, and narrative; they all discuss the ability and right to represent and speak for oneself and make visible one's own suppressed and displaced history and identity.

Said's landmark *Culture and Imperialism* picks up and continues this project of making visible the invisible and suppressed. The study demonstrates the impressive breadth of Said as a literary scholar and intellectual, discussing an array of topics such as nineteenth-century English literature, Operation Desert Storm, late twentieth-century political analysis, Third World liberation theory, and opera and **film**. The research reveals how the colonized world exists in, and has penetrated, the most pristine circumstances in European literature. The foremost example is Said's well-cited reading of Jane Austen's *Mansfield Park* in his *Culture and Imperialism* (1993), where the leisure of Sir Thomas Bertrams' family, for example, is sustained by his plantations in the West Indies. That is, while little mentioned in the narrative, the existence of slave plantations in Antigua facilitates the reproduction of the Bertram's lifestyle and, therefore, is central to the reproduction of the novel itself.

On the other hand, *Culture and Imperialism* is a forceful platform to address issues of importance that he was unable to discuss in his earlier work—foremost of which is the question of how indigenous peoples resist colonial discourse and domination. Said does not reinscribe notions of native authenticity in his discussion. To the contrary, he follows **Frantz Fanon**'s admonitions of the role of cultural producers in colonized societies to dynamically form national identities that are both authentically native and without fantasy or nostalgia. Three fine examples are the author's discussion of **al-Tayib Salih**'s *Season of Migration to the North* (1969), **Ngũgĩ wa Thiong'o**'s *The River Between* (1965), and **Aimé Césaire**'s *Une Tempête* (1969), all of which struggle with native identity in the wake of colonialism, but not by rejecting all things foreign. Rather, Said shows us that these authors claim Western literary tradition as their own, while recognizing themselves, their cultures, and their histories as victims to it. In doing so, *Culture and Imperialism* shows us how innumerable authors and intellectuals of the colonized world make their suppressed histories and identities visible and viable again and strive for "the invention of new souls," as Fanon and Césaire said, without romantically harking back to an undefiled time before colonialism.

Undoubtedly, most of his scholarship since and including *Orientalism* revealed the centrality of discourse and culture in the reproduction of power and domination. Said's chapters on **resistance** to colonial domination in *Cultural and Imperialism*, whether through direct and crude political coercion or through the nuanced apparatus of Western scholarship, resonate with Said's own life and work. His works can be read as allegorical statements on the condition of the dispossessed, the colonized, the exiled, and, specifically but not exclusively, the Palestinian people. His autobiography, *Out of Place* (1999), in fact, demonstrates how much of his oeuvre, his love and vast knowledge of the high Western literary and cultural tradition, his commitment to the Palestinian cause and human rights are an allegorical statement of his own exile and personal position between (or sharing) several cultures. This is clearly and eloquently reflected in "Intellectual Exile: Expatriates and Marginals," one of the most powerful essays in *Representations of the Intellectual* (1994).

Despite his tenacious illness, Said continues to write on literary and political topics. He remains an indefatigable scholar and political intellectual, publishing, teaching, and giving talks worldwide. He has demonstrated not only his ability to cross over into many disciplines and fields but also his remarkable ability to grow and change, as his advocacy of a one-state, binational solution indicates. He is most representative of the postcolonial condition himself, a hybrid intellectual of many talents, commitments, and cultures.

Further Reading: E. Said 1978.

Stephen P. Sheehi

Tayeb Salih (1929–) Born in the village of Debba in the Marawi region of northern Sudan, Tayeb Salih received an Arab Islamic early education in a traditional *khalwa*, or religious school. During the 1940s he received colonial education at an intermediate school in Port of Sudan, then secondary school in Umm Durman. Afterward, he studied biology at Khartoum University and taught at an intermediate school in Rafa'a, a small town south of Khartoum, then at a teacher training college in Bakht al-Rida. In 1953 he went to London to work for the Arabic section of the BBC and later on for the United Nations Educational, Scientific, and Cultural Organization (UNESCO). Since then, Salih has lived in London, except for the period 1974–1980 when he was a high-ranking official in Qatar's Ministry of Information.

Salih, who writes in Arabic, is the author of a number of short stories and three novels: *The Wedding of Zein* (1964; trans., 1969), *Season of Migration to the North* (1966; trans. 1969), and *Bandarshah* in two parts: *Dau al-Bayt* (1972) and *Maryud* (1976; both trans. 1996). After the 1989 coup that brought the

National Islamic Front to power in the Sudan, Salih wrote a series of articles in the London-based weekly *Al-Majallah* criticizing that regime's repressive policies.

The majority of Salih's narratives are set in the fictional village of Wad Hamid in northern Sudan and form a narrative cycle stretching from the mid-nineteenth century to the present. The main narrator of the Wad Hamid cycle, Meheimeed, appears as a child in one of Salih's earliest short stories, "A Handful of Dates"; Meheimeed reappears in *Season of Migration to the North* as a young man returning from England with a Ph.D. in English literature, shortly after Sudanese independence in 1956. He then reappears as a middle-aged man in Salih's last short story to date, "The Cypriot Man" (1976), and as a disenchanted, wistful retiree in *Bandarshah*, where he represents the failures of the first generation of postcolonial Sudanese intellectuals.

The overarching concern of Salih's fiction is with the impact of colonialism and Western **modernity** on rural Sudanese society in particular and Arab culture and **identity** in general. In his highly acclaimed short story "The Doum Tree of Wad Hamid," the attempts of both colonial and postcolonial governments to impose modernization programs threaten to sever the villagers' ties to their spiritual world, represented by a sacred tree that the authorities wish to cut in order to build a steamer dock. Set a few years after Sudanese independence and told from the viewpoint of an elderly villager, the story registers the bitterness and resignation of the elders who find themselves unable to preserve their way of life as their children, educated in modern colonial schools, eagerly set the village on an irreversible course of modernization. This younger generation, contemporaries of Meheimeed, is brought to the foreground in *The Wedding of Zein*, a novella set also in the wake of independence. They are the village leaders who both orchestrate the introduction of modern schools, hospitals, and irrigation schemes into the village and oversee most other affairs of the village. They befriend and protect the protagonist, Zein, a village idiot who is regarded as a saintly fool in the tradition of Sufi dervishes and whose unthinkable wedding to the most desirable girl in the village they organize. This group of young men (who like to be called "Mahjoub's gang") present themselves as benign and responsible—albeit at times Machiavellian—politicians who are capable of harmoniously integrating (represented by Zein's wedding) traditional culture and religious beliefs with "progress," as they conceive it. Zein's wedding represents both the leaders' ability to bring together the sometimes contentious factions within the village community as well as its spiritual unification through the agency of Zein's creative mysticism. As such, the novel constructs a **utopian** world in which the material and spiritual resources of the newly independent **nation** realize their full potential.

Such idealism is shattered in Salih's best-known novel, *Season of Migration to the North*, which depicts the violent history of colonialism and racism as shaping the reality of contemporary Arab societies. A naively optimistic, Western-educated Meheimeed confronts his double, Mustafa Sa'eed, a Kurtz-like figure who reverses the trajectory of Joseph Conrad's characters by journeying to the heart of darkness in the north, London, where he commits heinous acts of (psychological and physical) sexual revenge that literalize the violence of **colonial discourse**. The story continues in Wad Hamid, where Sa'eed settles, marries a young Sudanese, then disappears after a few years and is presumed dead. As her father forces her into a traditional, arranged marriage to an aged womanizer, Sa'eed's widow kills her new husband when he tries to rape her, then takes her own life. This murder-suicide, an indirect result of Sa'eed's influence on his young wife, shocks and enrages the villagers but unveils the violence of traditional patriarchy, linking it in kind to sexualized colonial violence. In this way, the novel shows that the synthesis of traditional culture and modern ideas (in this case on the status of women) that is envisioned by the liberal Arab ideology and to which *The Wedding of Zein* gave such poetic expression can never be fruitful or successful in the shadow of colonialism.

The crisis of Arab consciousness, ideology, and leadership that crystallized in the Arab defeat in the 1967 war with Israel is the subtext in Salih's last novel, *Bandarshah*, which centers around the relationship between past, present, and future or, in the allegorical scheme of the novel, grandfathers, fathers, and grandsons. This problematic relationship is depicted as a vicious cycle in which the past repeats itself: grandsons are ever in conspiracy with grandfathers (of whom they are the split image and whose first name they always bear) against fathers. The novel ends by suggesting that the vicious cycle can be broken only when the rigid patriarchal order reflected in the novel's central allegory and governing traditional society is broken.

Further Reading: M. Amyuni 1985; W. Hassan 1998.

Waïl S. Hassan

Science Fiction. *See* Utopian Writing

Samuel Selvon Samuel Dickson Selvon (1923–1994) was born in Trinidad's San Fernando, the largest town in the southern port. As in his fiction, Selvon grew up in a culturally diverse and racially mixed world; his father was an East Indian dry goods merchant, and his mother was Anglo-Scottish. Selvon began as a wireless operator for the Royal Navy Reserve during World War II. In 1945 he began his literary career by becoming a journalist with the *Trinidad Guardian* and fiction editor of the *Guardian Weekly*. Between 1945 and 1950 several of Selvon's earliest short stories and poems were published locally or broadcast in London by the BBC program *Caribbean Voices*. Selvon left his native island for London in 1950.

Two years later he published his first novel, *A Brighter Sun*, set among the East Indian rural peasantry in Trinidad; this novel gained him an international reputation as a significant new voice among a wave of West Indian writers such as **George Lamming** (with whom he migrated to England), Andrew Salkey,

V. S. Naipaul, and **Derek Walcott**. The success of this first novel allowed Selvon to dedicate his time to writing, and over the next three decades he published nine more novels, many short stories, and poems, as well as plays for broadcast on the BBC.

While Selvon is better-known for his novels, in particular, his London trilogy *The Lonely Londoners* (1956), *Moses Ascending* (1975), and *Moses Migrating* (1983), his work includes several plays written for radio and television. He is the author of a stage play, *Switch*, and coauthor with Horace Ové of the filmscript for *Pressure* (1978), one of the first black feature films to be released in Britain. Furthermore, Selvon contributed a number of poems, short stories, and articles to Caribbean literary magazines like the Barbadian journal *BIM*. During the early 1950s, Selvon survived London by taking on various part-time jobs and working as a freelance writer. His stories and reviews could be found in British journals and newspapers such as *The London Magazine*, *The Evergreen Review*, the *Evening Standard*, and the *Sunday Times*. With the publication of his second novel, *An Island Is a World* (1955) and being awarded his first Guggenheim Fellowship in that same year, Selvon decided to become a full-time writer.

The decade from 1950 to 1960 proved to be Selvon's most prolific. He followed the publication of *The Lonely Londoners* with a collection of short stories set in both Trinidad and London entitled *Ways of Sunlight* (1957). He published *Turn Again Tiger* (1958), marking the conclusion of his first sojourn in London. Selvon returned to his native island on a rather infrequent and relatively brief basis. After being awarded a Trinidad Government Scholarship, he returned home in the same year as the publication of *I Hear Thunder* (1963). His next novel, *The Housing Lark*, appeared in 1965. In 1968, he was awarded another Guggenheim Fellowship. Selvon's longest stay in Trinidad came in 1969, when he composed the novel *The Plains of Caroni* (1970), while visiting the village of Tacarigua for several months. During this time, Selvon was awarded the Trinidadian literary prize the Humming Bird Medal for Literature. His later novel, *Those Who Eat the Cascadura* (1972), recounts his experiences in Tacarigua.

Selvon's most famous novel, *The Lonely Londoners*, introduces the character of Moses Aloetta. Moses appears twenty years later in Selvon's other two London novels as the primary narrator. In these stories, Selvon "colonizes England in reverse and liberates his black characters from standard English and the entrapping stereotypes that surrounded them" (Nasta and Rutherford 1995, viii–ix). Like Moses, Selvon, too, left London, however, not for Trinidad. In 1978 Selvon left London for Canada, where he taught creative writing courses and has lectured at numerous educational institutions in the Caribbean, the United States, Britain, and Canada. He has been awarded an honorary doctorate by the University of the West Indies. In a postcolonial context, Selvon creates voices for the voiceless West Indians, while at the same time he celebrates the diversity and complexity of what it means to be West Indian during a time when England wished to narrow such definitions.

Further Reading: S. Nasta 1998; S. Nasta and A. Rutherford 1995.

James M. Ivory

Sembène Ousmane (1923–) Senegalese writer and filmmaker, Ousmane Sembène was born 1 January 1923 in Ziguinchor in the southern Casamance region of Senegal, French West Africa. (Though often referred to as "Sembène Ousmane," Sembène is his family name, and Ousmane is his given name.) His family was of the Lebou branch of the Muslim Wolof people. As a boy Sembène was influenced by his maternal uncle, an Islamic scholar, and attended Qur'anic schools. At age twelve he traveled to Dakar to attend French schools but dropped out after two years, turning to a masonry apprenticeship, further Islamic study, traditional culture, union activity, and theater. In 1942 Sembène joined the French colonial military and fought in Europe and Africa during World War II. Demobilized in 1946, he participated in the landmark 1947–1948 Dakar-Niger railway strike against the French. In 1948 he left again for Europe for thirteen years. Though principally resident in France, he also traveled to Denmark, the USSR, China, North Vietnam, and elsewhere.

Sembène's artistic career began in the early 1950s with poetry in French working-class periodicals. His first, semiautobiographical novel, *Le Docker noir* (The Black Docker) appeared in 1956: it relates the difficult life of African workers in the French port city Marseilles. His next novel, *O pays, mon beau peuple*, followed in 1957, telling a classic "been-to" story of a young man who returns to Senegal after a stay in France and meets with great difficulty. Sembène's next novel, *Les bouts de bois de Dieu* (God's Bits of Wood, 1960), gained him international fame as one of Africa's most important writers. A sweeping, realist historical novel with resonance in Émile Zola, *Les bouts* offers a fictionalized, heroic account of the 1947–1948 railworkers' strike in which Sembène had taken part. Sembène returned to Africa soon after its publication, but it struck him how little impact European-language literature could have on the African populace, only rarely literate in European languages. From there he moved to **film**. Following a year of study at Moscow's Gorky studios, Sembène released his first two films—*L'Empire Sonhrai* and *Borom Sarret* (The Cart Driver)—in 1964, inaugurating more than three decades of literary and cinematic productivity. By 1999 Sembène had produced some ten novels or novella collections and twelve films, the most important of which include *Mandaabi* (The Money Order, 1968), *Xala* (1974), and *Camp de Thiaroye* (1989).

Sembène's works show both range and focus. On the one hand, he shifts easily from epics of nineteenth-century Islamic intrigue (the film *Ceddo*, 1976), to brutal exposés of French colonial history (*Camp de Thiaroye*; the 1976 film *Emitai*), to tragic or savage depictions of postcolonial life (*Xala*; the 1981 novel *Le Dernier de l'Empire* [The Last of Empire]). Despite this range, Sembène's work unwaveringly commits to justice and social critique. Most often in his works, ordinary men (and notably, throughout Sembène's works, women) are depicted as dignified or heroic, while the neo-African bourgeoisie, the former French colonial administration, and religious hypocrites are attacked. Stylistically, Sembène generally prefers straightforward narration and is not a formal experimentalist. His films are, importantly, typically shot in the Wolof or Diola languages, with subtitles in French.

Sembène's works have received much critical attention and are widely taught in both English and French. Among his novels, *God's Bits of Wood* stands out in the eyes of critics, widely regarded as one of the great rallying **resistance** novels of Africa's late colonial era. There and in his other novels, Sembène is seen as a narrator of the people, an inheritor of the griots, or traditional storytellers whom he strives explicitly to honor. His cinematic output has been equally richly treated by critics, with many films deemed highly important.

Perhaps along with Kenya's **Ngũgĩ wa Thiong'o**, Sembène has become one of the most honored and most consistently, unwaveringly radical of Africa's major postcolonial cultural producers. His commitments to social justice, to resistance against both colonialism and **neocolonialism**, to African popular audiences, and to high artistic and narrative standards have made him one of the most important figures in African culture in the second half of the twentieth century.

Further Reading: F. Pfaff 1984; S. Gadjigo et al. 1993.

David Chioni Moore

Léopold Senghor. *See* Nativism

Settler Colony   While the origin of settler nations as colonies is clear, what is less so is the constant ambivalence of these outposts of empire to their own histories as colonies. On the one hand, they avow a nationalist identity separate from the imperium; on the other, they fail to come to terms with **indigenes** and such others as Chinese cosettlers. In the late nineteenth and early twentieth centuries, after decades of ethnicide, European settlers thought that they had established their own nationalistic identity in the discourse of white male settler egalitarianism, or settlerism. Yet, settlers also experienced anxieties about an identity separate from the imperium. The settlers were unable to close off or resolve—when such questions were supposed to be nonexistent—their relations to the unsettling figures of, for example, indigenes, Chinese cosettlers, and women.

All along, part of settlerism's coherence and stability was its flexible incorporation of imperialist ideologies—primarily racism, patriarchy, and attitudes of cultural superiority toward indigenes and Asians. As a narrative of successful European-style national self-creation, it is an effective discourse of successful colonization—displacing and erasing the antagonism between settlers and the indigenous and ethnic other in the mythical coherence of a superficial class politics. It is the same (bourgeois) settler **nationalism**, in a liberal guise, that today celebrates the "postcolonialism" of settler colonies. Increasing ethnic diversity in Australia, biculturalism in New Zealand, and the importance of Asian economies are evaporating the exclusive relationship with England. These factors, plus gender critiques of the trope of settler male camaraderie above class, have left a need for another more localized, less **Eurocentric** definition of national identity (on gender, see K. Schaffer 1988). One outcome of these forces is the description of settler colonies as multicultural societies. Multiculturalism in settler colonies is both a practice of various new arrivals and an ideology of governments.

Among the calls for a republic and multiculturalism is the rhetorical inclusion of settler nations in the discourse of postcolonialism. A discourse of postcolonialism has a different implication in the context of settler nations than in nations that fought for independence from the colonizer. Postcolonialism is a faceted term. There are various positions to rehearse: there is the anticolonial discourse analysis of **Edward Said** and **Homi Bhabha**, which is linked to work on political **resistance** within the Third and Fourth Worlds (Barbara Harlow, for instance); there is a culturalist position, which celebrates terms like hybridity, heterogeneity, **Creolization** (the one that is closest to a **postmodern** position), (eg. **Edouard Glissant**); there are claims for inclusion of the settler colonies (Stephen Slemon, Bill Ashcroft, Gareth Griffiths, and Helen Tiffin). None of these are particularly invested in the nation-state except the last. A conception of settler postcoloniality that posits and appropriates an interrelationship between indigenous cultures, the culture of a hegemonic nation, and **decolonizing** discourse concerns us here.

The claim that settler colonies and Third World colonies "share" (Slemon 1988, 165) postcolonialism has been made most publicly in a text that presents itself as an introduction to the postcolonial field. The Australian critics Bill Ashcroft, Gareth Griffiths, and Helen Tiffin, in *The Empire Writes Back*, state that "we use the term 'post-colonial' . . . to cover all the culture affected by the imperial process from the moment of colonization to the present day" (1989, 2). This assimilationist and homogenizing move has been criticized by Arun Mukherjee for overlooking questions of race: that is, there are crucial differences between the experiences of white settlers and non-white postcolonials. The whites were treated as cousins, while the nonwhites were treated as subjects. Furthermore, the model of *The Empire Writes Back* relies heavily on a model of **center and periphery**, where postcolonialism is defined by a relation to the center, and the subjectivity of the postcolonial is essentially linked to the colonizer.

Vijay Mishra and Bob Hodge problematize the totalizing project of *The Empire Writes Back* further by calling attention to the fact that settler colonies don't have a prolonged independence struggle, "[t]hus making strategic moves of these settler colonies towards greater political and economic autonomy within a capitalist world economy appear as heroic and revolutionary ruptures" (1991 409). While Mishra and Hodge offer "fused postcolonialism" (of indigenous opposition and settler imperial complicity) as an adequate settler category, it is difficult, given the minority status of Kooris in Australia (just under 2 percent of the population) and Maoris in New Zealand (9 percent), for example, to tell whether this articulation between the settler and the indigene is not still a relation of appropriative dominance.

Stephen Slemon takes another tack in the question of the status of what he calls the Second World settler colonies within the discourse of postcolonialism. He says that the project of "anti-colonialist resistance in writing has been mistaken (as synonymous) for the project of . . . articulating the literary nature of Third- and Fourth-World cultural groups" (32). This ignores the possibility that interesting anticolonialist writing comes from the settler colonies, produced by their ambivalent relation to the colonizer. He makes some effort to mark a "*genuine* difference," based on the lack of a stable self/other division between settler/colonized and colonizer, between Second and Third World writings.

While his argument is persuasive and useful in terms of theories of the fragmentary nature of the subject, Slemon overstates the "genuine difference." First, his position relies on a formal conception of the settler self divided inwardly, whereas the most forceful act of foundation for the settler has, and is, the division between the white self and the indigene. His argument seems (unintentionally) predicated on a division between Third World resistance carried out by a unified subject of a unified culture fighting something "purely external to the self" and a split subject of the Western settler cultures carrying on a battle with explicitly internal, psychological overtones. Yet hasn't the burden of "decolonizing the mind," to utilize **Ngũgĩ wa Thiong'o**, always been an integral part of Third World resistance? "The physical violence of the battlefield was followed by the psychological violence of the classroom" (Ngũgĩ 1986, 9). Struggle over hearts and minds, whether the "villainous complicity" of local feudal lords with the colonizers (Césaire 1972, 24) or whether in the ideology of **negritude**'s imbrications with Western primitivism or any page of **Frantz Fanon**'s *Black Skin, White Masks* (1967), indicates that Third World resistance was never with an object or discourse "purely external to the self."

What is striking about Slemon's article is its entanglement within **colonialist discourse**. The "genuine difference" reproduces a neoimperialist schema, (unintentionally) attributing a depth psychology exclusively to the settler countries. It is difficult to tell the difference between Slemon's ambiguity and a more (post)modernist use of ironies of identity to discuss settler nations; both rely on a notion of doubleness. Settler countries—with Western bureaucratic states, more or less advanced capitalist economies, democratic institutions, a liberal bourgeois public sphere for whites—are not concerned with the intertwined effects of the discourses of racism, underdevelopment, and sometime military rule, as are Third World postcolonial countries. What settler colonies are concerned with is not colonialism per se but cultural imperialism, specifically, the imperialism of the United States for a Canadian like Slemon. Hence, Slemon's discourse could be read as a revamped nationalism, rather than a postcolonialism.

Settler colonies' "dominion nationalism" (Serle 1973, 143) strives for cultural independence, while reproducing in broad outlines the sociopolitical formations of Euroamerica. But unproblematic identification with the postcolonial, in an apparent attempt at cultural decolonization from the imperium, elides both the internal colonization of racial, ethnic, gender, and class minorities and the differences that separate them from Third World postcolonial societies.

An exclusive emphasis on culture—specifically, literature—in settler appropriations of postcolonialism overlooks the role of their hegemonic Western institutions and modern economy (see Lata Mani's suspicion of cultural explanations of social phenomena [1989, 64]). From this angle, settler postcolonialism also serves to reformat all political and territorial issues into cultural ones. Settler postcolonialism is grasped as the projection of an ideal point of departure rather than the result of a troubled history (to paraphrase **Marx**). It assumes that there is a realm of innocent representational origin free of the imperium (like settler egalitarianism), on which the nation is founded.

Today the nation space can no longer be read as a homogeneous culture; we prefer to see it as a nation system—a matrix of various interests, ethnicities, classes, and genders that demand a postcultural (in which there is no single authentic culture or group) interpretation of national identity. But settler postcolonialism is another name for an anxiously renovated European nationalism (which in another period was called bush egalitarianism: pluralism for the white man). This troubled and troubling "bush postcolonialism" confers a new and positive meaning on the indigene in a period when Australia suddenly perceives that its best interests lie in seeing itself as more Asian, New Zealand perceives itself as bicultural, and both nations perceive themselves as more plural "in the nice sense." Now that these two settler nations have lost predominant material ties to Britain and see symbolic connections to the old imperium as increasingly irrelevant, anxiety over identity seems to be neatly solved by claiming a new postcolonial (bureaucratic) multicultural status. But this attempt to deal with the present neglects the past. The white "postcolonial" now elevates indigenous culture to forge new feelings of homeliness with very little regard for questions of indigenous sovereignty: demands by the indigene for territorial sovereignty contradict the assumed harmony of the postcolonial moniker. In this vector settler postcolonialism is not a rupture with, but a continuation of, expropriative "settlerist" history.

Further Reading: S. Slemon 1988, 1990.

Phillip R. O'Neill

Sex Tourism. *See* Travel Writing

Short Story Cycle   A short story cycle is a collection of stories that blend into a coherent whole through a dynamic of recurrence and development. The fundamental structure of a cycle emerges from the interaction of diverse elements in the independent stories: connective patterns in the development of character, themes, leitmotifs, settings, and structures draw the separate **narratives** together into a totality strengthened by varying types of internal cohesion. The cycle must assert the individuality and autonomy of each of the component parts while creating a necessary interdependence that emphasizes the essential unity of the work. In this intratextual process, each story develops its specific action, but meaning accumulates from one story to the next as each new story expands or modifies earlier ones. Individual stories tend to have titles, a manifestation of the independence that enables them to function dynamically within and outside the whole. Short story cycle theory has been developed by Forest Ingram, J. Gerald Kennedy, Susan Garland Mann, Maggie Dunn, and Anne Morris, among others.

The specificities of the form make the short story cycle an especially suitable vehicle for the distinctive characteristics of postcolonial fiction. The cycle illustrates the process of postcolonial literature toward plurality, multiplicity, polyphony, and fragmentation, as it tends to favor the multivoiced text. Because postcolonial cycles challenge generic boundaries and oblige toward new manners of apprehending literature and theory, they occupy a renewed position as empowered narratives of **resistance**. The cycle itself is a hybrid, occupying an indeterminate place within the field of narrative, resembling the novel in its totality yet composed of distinct stories. Its elliptical form invites the reader to participate in the process of signification, placing him or her in a strategic position, charged with determining meanings—historical, racial, or cultural—in the cyclic scheme by imaginatively bridging textual insularity. The form is also more demanding on the reader in certain ways, obliging him or her to abandon the self-contained world or situation of one story before entering the next independent story. A cycle intensifies the normally participatory act of reading by insisting that we "fill in the blanks" as we go along, the discovery of connections becoming essential to the reader's experience through a greater awareness of alternative formal, rhythmic, and thematic possibilities.

On different levels, postcolonial short story cycles may project a desire to come to terms with both a personal and collective past: this type of fiction often explores the character and history of communities as reflections of personal odysseys of displacement and search for self—a process rather than a structure. This process is not different from that involved in the appreciation of a story cycle, in which the evolution and gradual unfolding of themes, a discovery of unity in disunity, integrate the essence of the form. The short story cycle may also serve as an analogy for the coexisting conjunction of centripetal and centrifugal forces in postcolonial societies and character. Also, story cycles enable writers to work, often with subversive irony, in a form that is not the dominant genre in the overwhelming cultures, demanding consideration as a formal manifestation of the pluralistic cultures in which they are created and nourished.

Character development in a cycle tends to be an accumulative rather than a continuous process. The gradual revelation of character through apparently random glimpses serves to emphasize the idea of a personal and cultural identity as a collective self, shared by people with a common history and ancestry and providing a consistent frame of reference and meaning. **R. K. Narayan**'s *Swami and Friends* (1944), **V. S. Naipaul**'s *Miguel Street* (1959), Alice Munro's *The Lives of Girls and Women* or *Who Do You Think You Are?* (1971), Margaret Laurence's *A Bird in the House* (1970), Isabel Huggan's *The Elizabeth Stories* (1984), Sara Suleri's *Meatless Days* (1989), and Shyam Selvadurai's *Funny Boy* (1994) center on the development of a specific character throughout the stories. Other short story cycles have collective protagonists and create composite portraits of the postcolonial world through polyvocality. The passage from appreciation of individual stories to the whole presented in the cycle also sets individuals against the social group to which they belong. The narrated accounts link individual lives to a larger scheme of belonging, making the analogy between communities and story cycles obvious. Places represented in cycles tend to be distinctly plural phenomena constructed out of the interpenetration of past and present, of colonizations and immigration, and the cohabitation of different races and cultures. Each place has its individual history, embodied in the characters that live there or that visit, and the descriptions of the landscape, for instance, encode stories about its origins, its inhabitants, and the broader society in which it is set. Place acquires centrality, often emerging as a character, in cycles such as Narayan's *Malgudi Days* (1982), Stephen Leacock's *Sunshine Sketches of a Little Town* (1912), Linda Svendsen's *Marine Life* (1992), Rosemary Nixon's *Mostly Country* (1991), M. G. Vassanji's *Uhuru Street* (1992), and Rohinton Mistry's *Tales from Firozsha Baag* (1987). Other cycles, such as Rajiva Wijesinha's *Servants* (1995), and Yasmine Gooneratne's *The Pleasures of Conquest* (1995), center on themes of immigration and **transculturality** and the features specific to the postcolonial milieu.

Short story cycles typically conclude with a section or sections that summarize the themes, symbolism, and the patterned action that the cycle possesses, frequently demanding a reinterpretation of what has come before. Often, no temporal relationship exists among the various stories of a cycle: central concern is for a psychological time or a symbolic time of seasons and the cyclical nature of human experience. In this manner, through the drawing together in a final story or series of stories the themes and motifs, symbols, or the characters and their communities that have been developing throughout, the author places the finishing touches on the portrait being created. In some cases, cycles deliberately evade a sense of finality and refuse to fulfill the reader's expectation of closure, providing open-ended or cyclical conclusions that may further heighten stuctural analogy to the thematic presentation of the postcolonial condition.

Further Reading: F. Ingram 1971; S. Mann 1989.

Rocío G. Davis

Bapsi Sidhwa Bapsi Sidhwa, born in 1938, is Pakistan's best-known writer of fiction in English, perhaps the only one since Ahmed Ali to have gained recognition abroad. It is noteworthy, however, that she is a Parsi and has, indeed, spent much of the last couple of decades abroad.

Her first novel, *The Crow Eaters* (1981), was about a Parsi family and was hilarious in its account of a budding patriarch dealing with the vagaries of strong women in what is arguably the most idiosyncratic community in the world. The next novel, *The Bride* (1983), moved on to a vital social issue, namely, the male chauvinism that seems to dominate much of Pakistan society. Sidhwa sets this novel in the northern mountains, however, and suggests that the obsession with his honor that governs the Pathan protagonist is essentially an aberration. *Ice Candy Man* (1991; *Cracking India* in America) was Sidhwa's partition novel. It is her best known and her best and has recently been filmed. Set in Lahore, a multicultural center for many centuries, it charts the growing awareness of its child protagonist of the forces tearing people apart during the process of partition. The interplay of sexual and racial passions is tellingly portrayed, concluding with the conversion to Islam of the Hindu ayah abducted by the Ice Candy Man of the title, who had earlier murdered his more broad-minded (also Muslim) rival, the masseur. Sidhwa's most recent novel, *An American Brat* (1993), is based on her time in America and, while it deals with problems of growing up in the context of migration, indicates a transition from indigenous postcolonial writing to what is more concerned with transcontinental hybridity.

Further Reading: H. Mann 1994; C. Abrioux 1990.

Rajiva Wijesinha

Khushwant Singh (1915–   ) Singh is one of India's most prolific writers and is among the nation's most prominent voices. Novelist, short story writer, essayist, translator, editor, columnist, professor, historian, lawyer, and politician, Singh's subjects and talents are wide-ranging, but he often focuses his artistic energy on, and directs his criticism toward, situations and issues that have arisen during or since independence from Britain and the subsequent partition of the subcontinent. Singh is best known in the West for his novel on partition, *Train to Pakistan* (1956), in which a love affair between a Sikh peasant and a Muslim girl in a border village is tragically impacted by the eruption of religious violence. In *I Shall Not Hear the Nightingale* (1959), Singh explores the conflict between loyalty to the British and loyalty to the independence movement. As editor of the *Hindustan Times* and while serving as a member of Parliament, Singh (a Punjabi Sikh) straightforwardly and often emotionally expressed his opinion on political struggle and violence in the Punjab and in Jammu and Kashmir, harshly inveighing against the policies of the central government and the tactics of militant splinter groups. A number of his editorials and addresses to Parliament can be found in his *My Bleeding Punjab* (1992).

Further Reading: M. Lal and V. K. Sharma 1998; V. Shashane 1972.

Geoffrey Kain

South African Literature The question of when exactly South Africa first entered "postcolonial" status is a disputed one. The Afrikaner (descendants of Dutch settlers, also known as "Boer") republics and British colonies joined to form the Union of South Africa in 1910, only eight years after England reasserted imperial rule in the bloody Anglo-Boer War of 1899–1902. The country voted to leave British Dominion and became the independent Republic of South Africa in 1961. So if colonialism is narrowly defined as rule imposed by a foreign power, that practice ended in South Africa early in the twentieth century.

But for most of the century, the government was elected by a white **settler** minority, while the overwhelming majority of black, "colored" (mixed race), and Asian peoples were increasingly disfranchised, dispossessed, and violently oppressed. The Land Act of 1913 appropriated all but the most arid 13 percent of the country's land for whites, leaving blacks to starve or to work in the white-owned mines and fields. In 1948 the Afrikaner-led right-wing National Party (NP) was elected to power on a platform of apartheid (literally, "separateness"), or "separate development," in which strict racial segregation was legislated at every level of society, from the Parliament to the bedroom. The NP remained in power until 1994, when the first countrywide democratic elections were held, and a coalition government led by the African National Congress (ANC) was elected to power. In this sense, then, South Africa has only recently attained postcolonial status.

Most importantly, the literature of South Africa shares many thematic and stylistic features with that of colonial and postcolonial literature from Africa and other formerly colonized lands. Writers of every race were preoccupied with the struggle against oppression and apartheid, and literature became an important vehicle for opposing the system. While this preoccupation is especially evident in literature from the apartheid era, one can see these concerns manifesting themselves as early as the establishment of the first British colonies in the 1820s. For example, Thomas Pringle's poem "The Caffer Commando" (1827; "kaffir" is a term, now considered highly derogatory, for black Africans) is an indictment of the "tyrannous mood" of England, whose "edict is written in African blood." The first South African novel, *The Story of an African Farm* (1883) by Olive Schreiner, portrays, albeit indirectly, the rigid social and racial hierarchies that were in place even then. Sol Plaatje, journalist, linguist, folklorist, historian, and founding member of the South African Native National Congress (which later became the ANC), wrote *Native Life in South Africa* (1916), which is both a sociological survey of black conditions in South Africa and a resounding political critique of the Land Act. Plaatje also authored *Mhudi* (published 1930, but probably written between 1917 and 1919), the first novel in English published by a black South African, which revisits the turbulent history of the 1830s and describes the interactions between black Africans, Boer settlers, and English missionaries from the Africans' point of view.

Two landmark novels in South Africa's literary history were produced in the period between World War II and the election of the National Party in 1948. Peter Abraham's *Mine Boy* (1946) tells the story of Xuma, a naive young African man who goes to Johannesburg looking for work. He finds a world of poverty, crime, and violence but also a new kind of community in a shebeen (illegal drinking establishment) whose owner befriends him. He manages to secure a job as a "boss boy" overseeing other black workers in the mines and eventually leads his men in a strike against unsafe working conditions. *Cry the Beloved Country* (1948) by Alan Paton also tells of a man's journey to Johannesburg: the Reverend Kumalo goes in search of his missing son Absalom. He finds that Absalom has been arrested for murdering the son of his white neighbor Mr. Jarvis, with whom the preacher forms an unlikely and tentative friendship. Other notable preapartheid writers in English include Herman Charles Bosman, R.R.R. Dhlomo, Pauline Smith, Roy Campbell, Eugène Marais, and William Plomer.

The themes of racial oppression, exploitation, and anticolonial resistance were already present in much of South African literature before 1948. But during the apartheid era and especially after the infamous police massacre of unarmed protesters at Sharpeville in 1960, these themes became the inevitable subtexts of virtually any work of fiction. Alex La Guma's *A Walk in the Night* (1962) portrays a cast of lost souls and criminals wandering through the ghetto, their walks periodically interrupted by encounters with the racist white police. Richard Rive's *Emergency* (1964) is set in Cape Town in the aftermath of the Sharpeville incident and concerns one young man's decision to join in the struggle against apartheid. Bessie Head went into permanent exile in Botswana in 1964, and most of her fiction was set there, but the fact of growing up as an English-speaking orphan of mixed race alienated from a predominantly Afrikaans-speaking colored community informs all of her writing, especially the semiautobiographical *A Question of Power* (1974). In Njabulo Ndebele's novella *Fools* (1983), a black schoolteacher who has been disgraced in his community for raping a female student regains his self-respect through a small, but significant, act of defiance against the brutality of a white man. Zoë Wicomb's *You Can't Get Lost in Cape Town* (1987) is a series of loosely connected short stories that together describe a young colored woman's coming-of-age under apartheid and the self-loathing and inferiority complex that result from a lifetime's immersion in hateful racial ideologies. Similar themes are present in the work of Ezekiel Mphahlele, Miriam Tlali, Lewis Nkosi, Mongane Serote, Ahmed Essop, Christopher van Wyk, Farida Karodia, Mbulelo Mzamane, Achmat Dangor, Mandla Langa, and others, many of them writing from exile.

While the novel and the short story are probably the South African genres most widely read in Europe and the United States, poetry was a crucial literary form in the struggle against apartheid. A manuscript for a novel was difficult to duplicate and keep hidden from police and censors, but a poem could be easily duplicated and distributed, committed to memory, and performed at meetings and demonstrations. Thus, a whole school of resistance poetry by black and colored writers sprang up in the 1960s and thereafter. Some critics complain that this poetry is too didactic and polemical, elevating politics above aesthetics. Such critiques do an injustice to the formal sophistication of some of the poetry of Tatamkhulu Afrika, Dennis Brutus, Oswald Mtshali, Don Mattera, Arthur Nortje, Sipho Sepamla, James Matthews, Mzwakhe Mbuli, Mongane Serote, and Mafika Gwala. More importantly, these critics neglect the main point of protest literature: in the hands of these writers poetry becomes an invaluable tool for consciousness-raising and rallying resistance against the apartheid regime.

Drama played a similarly important role in the struggle. In the 1970s and 1980s black resistance and liberation plays were performed at venues and events ranging from weddings and township churches to upmarket locales like the Market Theatre in Johannesburg and the Baxter Theatre in Cape Town. Financial constraints and the need for mobility resulted in minimalist, but resourceful, stage sets and costumes, such as black actors using pink rubber clown noses to take on white roles. These resistance plays are characterized by rapid scene and character changes, frequent singing and chanting, and heavy linguistic code-switching between English, Afrikaans, Zulu, and other **African languages**. Perhaps the best-known playwright in this tradition is Mbongeni Ngema, whose *Sarafina* (1988) toured around the world to great commercial success. Ngema also coauthored, with Percy Mtwa and Barney Simon, *Woza Albert!* (1983), in which the Second Coming takes place in South Africa: predictably, Jesus is arrested as a terrorist and sent to Robben Island. Maishe Maponya's *Gangsters* (1984) rewrites Samuel Beckett's *Catastrophe* (1982) as the interrogation and torture of a black liberation poet by the Security Police. Another of Maponya's plays, *The Hungry Earth* (1979), depicts the hardships faced by migrant laborers in the gold mines, a theme also taken up in Matsemela Manaka's *Egoli: City of Gold* (1980). While most of these plays are concerned with the struggle against apartheid, much of Zakes Mda's work seems to anticipate problems of corruption and the unequal distribution of wealth that continue to plague many nations long after independence from direct colonial domination; *We Shall Sing for the Fatherland* (1979), for instance, is set in an imaginary, postrevolutionary future in which veteran freedom fighters are left homeless, forced to sell blood and rummage through dustbins for food while the bankers and politicians grow rich. Similarly, *And the Girls in Their Sunday Dresses* (1988) portrays a group of women waiting all day in the hot sun for food intended for hunger relief, while the workers in the storeroom sell the rice to buy expensive clothes and other luxuries.

The writers best known outside South Africa are whites writing in English. While many of the same political themes are present in their work, white literature frequently employs a more oblique style than the more didactic black **resistance literature**. Indeed, many critics have noted that whereas black South African literature tends to articulate clear political positions and to conform to the conventions of social realism, white South African writing frequently exhibits the ambiguity, fragmentation, disorientation, and self-consciousness characteristic of European and American **postmodernism**. Critic and fiction writer Lewis Nkosi attributes this dichotomy between black and white literature to the colonized black subject's "urgent need to document and to bear witness," on the one hand, and, on the other hand, to "the capacity to go on furlough, to loiter, and to experiment" that arises from the socioeconomic and educational privilege of white South Africans (Attridge and Jolly 1998, 75).

Despite these differences, the injustices and divisions of apartheid do frequently impose themselves on white literature as well as that of black, colored, and Indian writers. Much of playwright Athol Fugard's work concerns the sometimes insurmountable obstacles to forming close human relationships across racial lines under apartheid. *Master Harold and the Boys* (1982), for example, portrays a white schoolboy, Hally, who is trapped between his affection for his family's longtime servant Sam and the role of "master" that the power dynamics of apartheid force him to adopt. As the title suggests, *Statements after an Arrest under the Immorality Act* (1974) depicts an illegal affair between a white woman and a colored man in a small, conservative rural town. In Nobel laureate Nadine Gordimer's *Burger's Daughter* (1979), the only child of infamous communist agitator Lionel Burger tries to distance herself from the struggle after her father dies in prison, only to find herself drawn ineluctably into the political turbulence surrounding the student uprisings of 1976 and 1977. In *July's People* (1981), set in an imaginary future following the eruption of a race war, a wealthy white family flees its suburban home and hides from the revolutionary army at the familial homestead of their servant, whom they know only as "July" and whom they soon realize they know little about. *Age of Iron* (1990), by two-time Booker Prize-winner J. M. Coetzee, is narrated by an elderly white woman, a retired schoolteacher dying of cancer in the midst of the national state of emergency in the mid-to-late 1980s. Through encounters with a homeless man who takes up residence in her yard and with the Security Police who search her house for evidence against her maid's young son, she is forced to confront apartheid's crimes against humanity and her complicity in that system.

This process of overcoming denial to face the horrors of apartheid is a very common theme in white South African writing; another notable example is André Brink's *A Dry White Season* (1979), in which a white schoolteacher reluctantly investigates the death of a black friend in police custody, only to find himself the subject of a police conspiracy against him. Other important white writers include Stephen Gray, Sheila Roberts, Ingrid de Kok, C. J. Driver, Menán du Plessis, Anthony Akerman, Paul Slabolepszy, Pieter-Dirk Uys, Sheila Fugard, Jeremy Cronin, Douglas Livingstone, Breyten Breytenbach, Christopher

Hope, Lionel Abrahams, Kelwyn Sole, Karen Press, Dorothy Driver, and Guy Butler.

Two other very important genres in South African letters are the autobiography and the prison memoir. Some of the key autobiographical works are written by some of South Africa's most famous figures—Nelson Mandela's *A Long Walk to Freedom* (1994), for example—or by their family members, such as *Every Secret Thing* (1997) by Gillian Slovo, daughter of political militants Joe Slovo and Ruth First. Others works are written by well-known novelists and poets, such as Don Mattera's *Memory Is the Weapon* (1987) and Ezekiel Mphahlele's *Afrika My Music* (1984). But equally important are the autobiographies of persons less internationally famous: *Call Me Woman* (1985) portrays the life of Ellen Kuzwayo, a black woman who grew up in the countryside but lived most of her adult life in Johannesburg, working as a teacher and social worker. In *Strikes Have Followed Me All My Life* (1991), Emma Mashinini describes her life as a trade union activist. Other important autobiographies include Trevor Huddleston's *Naught for Your Comfort* (1956), Bloke Modisane's *Blame Me on History* (1963), Helen Joseph's *Side by Side* (1986), Albie Sachs' *Soft Vengeance of a Freedom Fighter* (1990), Helen Suzman's *In No Uncertain Terms* (1993), Ronnie Kasril's *Armed and Dangerous* (1993), AnnMarie Wolpe's *The Long Way Home* (1994), and Mamphela Ramphele's *A Life* (1995).

Many of the autobiographies just mentioned describe the authors' experiences in South African jails and prisons; not surprisingly, in a country where political imprisonment was used systematically as a tool of social control, the prison memoir itself has also become an important literary genre. Such memoirs became especially common after 1963, when the South African legislature passed the so-called 90 Day law, under which Security Police were authorized to detain suspects in solitary confinement without trial for virtually indefinite periods. In many cases such detainees were released without ever being charged with a crime or were acquitted of the charges for lack of evidence, a fact that reveals the arbitrary and flagrant abuse of the so-called preventive detention laws. The memoirs by those detainees tend to concentrate on the experiences of solitary confinement and torture and the interrogation-duels that took place between the detainees and the police: notable examples include Ruth First's *117 Days* (1965), Albie Sachs' *Jail Diary* (1966), Molefe Pheto's *And Night Fell* (1983), and Tshenuwani Simon Farisani's *Diary from a South African Prison* (1987). Other prisoners were convicted under the apartheid security laws, and their memoirs go on to describe the ordeal of extended sentences served in South Africa's brutal prisons. The most famous of these texts include James Kantor's *A Healthy Grave* (1967), *Robben Island* (1982), as told by Indres Naidoo to Albie Sachs, *The True Confessions of an Albino Terrorist* (1984) by Afrikaner poet Breyten Breytenbach, *Hell-Hole Robben Island* (1984) by Moses Dlamini, and *No Child's Play* (1988) by Caesarina Kona Makhoere. Some political prisoners chose to write about their experiences in the form of thinly veiled autobiographical novels—most notably, Alex La Guma's *The Stone Country* (1967) and D. M. Zwelonke's *Robben Island* (1973)—or plays, such as *The Island* (1973) by Athol Fugard, Winston Ntshona, and John Kani. Moreover, prison poetry— by Dennis Brutus, Jeremy Cronin, Dikobé wa Mogale, and David Evans, for example—constitutes an important subgenre of its own. Many poems, stories, and essays by women prisoners are compiled in the anthology *A Snake with Ice Water* (1992), edited by Barbara Schreiner.

With the official end of apartheid in 1994, many critics have speculated about the directions that South African literature will take. That question remains to be definitively answered, but certain patterns seem to be emerging. The Truth and Reconciliation Commission (TRC), established to investigate human rights violations and conduct amnesty hearings for perpetrators, preoccupied South Africans for two and a half years and also seems to have captured the nation's literary and artistic imagination. For example, Afrikaans poet and radio journalist Antjie Krog covered the TRC for the South African Broadcasting Company. In *Country of My Skull* (1998) she combines the memoir form with elements of poetry and fiction. In *Ubu and the Truth Commission* (1998), Jane Taylor juxtaposes Alfred Jarry's protosurrealist *Ubu Roi* with actual testimony from the amnesty and human rights violation hearings. The Khulumani Theatre Group provides a further opportunity for the victims of state violence under apartheid who testified before the TRC to tell their stories.

Other writers have chosen to take on the very real social problems that continue to haunt the new South Africa. Zakes Mda's *Ways of Dying* (1995) portrays poverty and violence within the black townships; Gordimer's *The House Gun* (1998) concerns a burglary turned murder; Coetzee's *Disgrace* (1999) involves a rape and accusations of sexual harrassment; and Sindiwe Magona's *Mother to Mother* (1998) centers around the murder of white American scholar Amy Biehl in a Cape Town township and is written in the form of a letter from the mother of one of the murderers to Biehl's mother. Still other writers are turning to the preapartheid past: Anne Landsman's *The Devil's Chimney* (1997) is narrated by a contemporary, alcoholic Afrikaner housewife who tells the story of a woman who lived on the same semidesert ostrich farm almost a century earlier. Ann Harries' *Manly Pursuits* (1999) is a historical satire set in Cape Town on the eve of the Anglo-Boer War, taking Cecil Rhodes, Olive Schreiner, Rudyard Kipling, and other famous figures as characters. Rayda Jacobs' *The Slave Book* (1998) takes as its subject slavery in the Western Cape in the 1830s. These and other contemporary writers are engaged in a process of salvaging and rewriting the past, a process that is perhaps necessary to the larger ongoing project of decolonization.

Further Reading: D. Attridge and R. Jolly 1998; M. Trump 1990.

Shane D. Graham

Wole Soyinka An African writer from the Yoruba community, Wole Soyinka was born in 1934 and has been active on the literary scene since the late 1950s.

He is an accomplished poet, essayist, novelist, playwright, actor, producer, director, and Nobel laureate in literature (1986). An eloquent public speaker, he has also made his contribution in the academic world as a professor of comparative literature. Well known in Africa as one of its leading playwrights, Soyinka has attracted both admiration and aspersion. The vilification has tended to subside in recent times as many of his ideas come to be recognized as prophetic, especially when considering the direction that modern politics has taken in Africa.

Soyinka has lived through some of the most exciting moments not just of Nigerian history but of the African continent as a whole. He has witnessed the transformation of the continent from a colonial sphere into a neocolonial playground. Growing up in a society where *litterature engagée* is the norm, Soyinka always provides a social dimension for his plays, a dimension that anchors his work in our moral responsibility. Yet his concern is not expressed from a patronizing and elitist angle. Soyinka has always placed at his creative center the social, cultural, and political concerns of the people who constitute the majority of the population. Inevitably, he has fallen foul of those who would wish him to portray more sympathetically the newly crowned political elite of this continent.

Even though Soyinka's career begins at the twilight of the colonial process in Africa, his earliest works do not ignore imperialism's negative impact on the people. His critique of colonialism demonstrates a continental awareness: from condemning the British massacre of Kenyans at Hola, to his tenacious fight against the apartheid regime and its nefarious Portuguese colleagues, this writer's acerbic pen communicates with understanding the pain of an entire continent.

Soyinka's work has had a considerable impact on African literature in the last forty years. He has traveled extensively to introduce the world to African theater specifically and African literature in general. His performances and productions illustrate the work of a political activist who believes that artistic activity should be integrated in, and committed to, social issues. Because the culture of the colonized is usually the primary target of imperial process, this author believes that the only way to eradicate the destructive tendencies of imperialism is by creating works that emphasize the humanity of the colonized. Thus, his work mercilessly exposes the hypocrisies of those who would colonize humanity in the name of their imagined civilization and profit. At the same time it also attacks the negative self-image of the African. This author warns against mindless self-praise and unquestioning acceptance of all **indigenous** traditions in the name of **negritude**, black pride, or whatever. Even as he does this he can be seen, at the same time, to nurture symbols of indigenous growth that are under constant assault from various "**modern**"—Western—cultural forces. Consequently, the strategy that Soyinka has assumed is to marginalize metropoles in the cultural programs of the ex-colonized. As he put it succinctly in *Death and the King's Horseman* (1975), the period of modern colonization is not the first time that black people have had to confront and overcome hostile, devastating forces. They overcame them in the past; they will rebuild again. His work illustrates the philosophy that he articulated very early against negritude when he said that "tigritude" is demonstrated, not talked about. The vitality of African culture and ideas can be seen only in its robust growth, a growth that does not wait to react to external stimulation. Protest literature, literature that sharpens its teeth on revelations of new grievances, is an art form that encourages the continued psychological dependence of the deracinated on the colonizer. This type of literature cannot form the foundation of a new society. From this position we see a sharp contrast between the theoretical assumptions in postcolonial thought and writers such as Soyinka who do not view themselves as part of a clique tied to knee-jerk reactions directed against the ever-dominant metropoles. Whereas it is true that recent African history is fraught with hostile contacts between Africa and the West, the continued bewailing of this contact with constant diatribes from African artists is a form of flattery that acknowledges and entrenches the **centrality** of the metropole and its history in African life. Soyinka has long recognized this, and his adoption of satire, among other techniques, is one way of marginalizing the metropoles in his work.

One of the earliest steps that Soyinka took in an attempt to develop a unique voice was to train himself in native forms of theater. For two years he traveled all over Nigeria, researching forms of indigenous African drama. The result can be seen in an invigorated awareness of myth and its central role in the literary imagination of the African, Nigerian people. Since then, Soyinka has always drawn freely on Yoruba myths as part of his creative impulse. By electing to let his creative predisposition be linked to the turbulent Ogun, Soyinka has legitimated the adoption of African religious thought into modern literary imagination. His essay "The Fourth Stage" (1969) is a unique infusion of Yoruba metaphysical thought into the theory of tragedy.

Soyinka's major concern that manifests itself from his earliest work is the social-political corruption in especially the African neocolonies and its disastrous impact on institutions that hardly had time to take root in the postcolonial era. Soyinka's works focus on the amazing speed with which the new African rulers took to destructive tendencies, looting the people whom they were supposed to guide and protect. He eloquently expresses his disappointment in the indigenous political and religious rulers, a disappointment that arises out of the vast hope that the **decolonization** process had first created. As such, Soyinka returns again and again to his favorite themes: political and economic corruption, the misuse of military power to entrench unjust dictatorships on a defenseless people, the general struggle in recent history of the African people in the face of insurmountable odds. These are some of Soyinka's themes that have constantly appeared in his works ever since the late 1950s.

From the earliest times, Soyinka has always had some skepticism about any political myths, "isms" imported from alien cultures. These "isms," as he parodied them in *Kongi's Harvest* (1967), are nothing but an excuse by corrupt opportunists to create the illusion of being intelligent when all they are doing is mouthing irrelevant "ideologies" as they subject the countries that they rule to their rapacious appetites. When Soyinka first articulated this, he seemed to be an iconoclast who just wanted to rock the boat of modern African political thought by discarding "theory" that had already been tested elsewhere. More disturbing to his critics was Soyinka's rejection of a servile attitude toward "correct" theory generated from the outside on the continent. His celebration of the fall of the Berlin Wall, that it came to free the African mind from blind apemanship, is to be understood in this context. If the African must worship political myths, let these be at least of a homegrown variety.

That is not to say that Soyinka avoids criticizing Africa's own institutions. On the contrary, he constantly berates the African army and the military dictatorship that it establishes on a helpless people. Lampooning Idi Amin, Bokassa, and Abacha, among other infamous military figures, Soyinka has never shied away from exposing their atrocities. Instead, this author successfully links the army's atrocities to the deprivation of the African people of their human rights and the attendant destruction of any democratic tendencies.

Some of his greatest and most artistically interesting works are *The Road* (1965), *Death and the King's Horseman* (1975), *Idanre* (1967), and his autobiographies. At times Soyinka has a complex style that requires close reading for proper understanding of what he is saying. In these works in particular merge his greatest concerns: hatred for corruption and parasitic military regimes with the introduction of Yoruba poetics into English. As the reader moves from Soyinka's plays to his essays and autobiographies, he or she is amazed at the sheer breadth of his ideas and the range of his commitment. This author's ideas range from a discussion of history and its impact on the present, to the role of indigenous myth in modern society in transition, to the individual and his or her social responsibility, to art and its function in a society, and to his embracing understanding of women. Madame Tortoise, Sidi, Omae, Sunma, Segi, and Iyaloja remain some of the most remarkable characters in African literature, memorable for their strength and intelligence. From the market women and their precocious daughters to lovers, mothers, wives, courtesans, these women have a wide range of roles that they play in the articulation of the author's ideas. His work is a constant experimentation with new forms that might make especially his playwriting a unique experience.

Further Reading: J. Gibbs 1980; J. Gibbs, K. H. Ketu, and H. L. Gates, 1986; O. Tanure 1994.

Ramenga Mtaali Osotsi

Gayatri Chakravorty Spivak   Born in Calcutta on 24 February 1942, Gayatri Spivak graduated from Presidency College in 1959 with a first-class honors degree in English, and gold medals for English and Bengali literature. After a master's degree in English at Cornell, Spivak took a year's fellowship at Girton

College, Cambridge. Arriving in the United States in 1961, she later married a white American whose surname she kept. While teaching at the University of Iowa, Spivak completed her doctoral dissertation on William Butler Yeats under the supervision of Paul de Man at Cornell. Born five years before the independence of India from British colonial rule, it is perhaps fitting that Spivak's doctoral thesis should examine an Irish poet who wrote of **decolonizing** politics in **Ireland** at the time of civil war. Initially known for her translation of Jacques Derrida's *Of Grammatology* (1976), Spivak's main work includes *Myself Must I Remake: The Life and Poetry of W. B.Yeats* (1974), *In Other Worlds: Essays in Cultural Politics* (1987), *Selected Subaltern Studies*, with Ranajit Guha (1998), *The Post-Colonial Critic: Interviews, Strategies and Dialogues* (1990), *Thinking Academic Freedom in Gendered Postcoloniality* (1992), *Outside in the Teaching Machine* (1993), *Imaginary Maps* (1995) and *A Critique of Postcolonial Reason: Toward a History of the Vanishing Present* (1999). Well known among international audiences, Spivak has held appointments in France, India, and Saudi Arabia. She has also lectured in Belgium, Finland, France, Germany, Hong Kong, Ireland, Italy, Singapore, South Africa, Strasbourg, Sweden, Taiwan, and the former Yugoslavia. Spivak currently holds the Avalon Foundation Professorship of the Humanities at Columbia University.

Engaging with the writings of Jacques Derrida, **Michel Foucault**, Sigmund Freud, Jacques Lacan, and Karl **Marx**, Spivak's work has developed poststructuralist, Marxist, and **psychoanalytic** thought. Exploring deconstruction in terms of an ethical responsibility to the Other, Spivak's concern with **alterity** also demonstrates how postcolonial criticism pays a ghostly debt to the philosopher Emmanuel Levinas. However, as Donna Landry and Gerald Maclean notice in their introduction to *The Spivak Reader* (1996), scholars of Derrida and Levinas have tended to ignore Spivak's contributions to the post-Enlightenment ethical movements associated with these thinkers. In spite of Spivak's positioning and dispositioning within the European academy, Landry and Maclean outline her popular appeal in North America. Her 1991 lecture "War and Cultures" at the Institute of Arts in Detroit gained popular appeal as she addressed questions of **multiculturalism** to an ethnically mixed metropolitan audience from the Detroit community. Concerned with the international division of labor, the status of the migrant, the epistemic violence of colonialism, and the **agency** of the gendered "**subaltern**," Spivak has addressed a variety of different audiences within and without the academy.

The Post-Colonial Critic problematizes both the relationship between the intellectual and the community and Spivak's engagement with European critical thinkers. In so doing, Spivak considers the difficulty of representation, selfrepresentation, and representing others. In an interview with Elizabeth Grosz (1984), which is included in *The Post-Colonial Critic* under the title "Criticism, Feminism and the Institution," Spivak outlines the relationship between textuality and politics, theory and practice, the universal and the specific, and the academy and a practical politics. Spivak argues for the textuality of the social as she notices how textuality should be related to the notion of the "**worlding**" of the world (i.e., the ways in which we choose to represent the world to our- selves) on a supposedly uninscribed territory; she connects this with the impe- rialist project, which has to assume that the earth that it had territorialized was previously uninscribed. Using Derrida's philosophy of the world as a text, Spi- vak argues that textuality sees that what is defined against or over the text as "fact," "life," or "practice" is "worlded" in a certain way so that practice can take place. Disbanding easy distinctions between world and text, theory and practice, Spivak draws on Louis Althusser and Foucault's analysis of the intel- lectual to argue that there is no noninstitutional environment and that the insti- tution does not exist in isolation. This leads to her conclusion that the definition of the institution as a place of pure learning is misguided. In turn, Spivak cri- tiques the definition of the **universal** against which to become specific. For example, as the Western intellectual defines the universal so as to say: "I am specific as opposed to that universal," he fails to acknowledge that the definition of the universal is itself contaminated by nonrecognition of a specific production.

As she draws on Derrida, whose work focuses specifically on the situation of the intellectual who questions his or her own disciplinary action, Spivak ad- dresses the connections and disconnections between postcolonial criticism and European critical theory. In response to charges that she uses First World elite theory that is contaminated by Western structures of knowledge, Spivak resists the desire to construct herself as a "true native" of the "pure East" who is "para- institutional." She asks, "What is an **indigenous** theory?" and claims not to defend the dependence of the postcolonial intellectual upon Western models. Acknowledging her complicity with, or production within, a European con- sciousness, Spivak seeks to deconstruct and expose such a positioning. In this way, she develops the Foucauldian project to struggle against the forms of power that produce and transform her. Resisting the seduction of a cultural politics "beyond the institution," Spivak asks, How can cultural minorities achieve a practical politics?

In answering such a question, Spivak seeks to preserve the discontinuities between **feminism**, Marxism, and deconstruction in the hope of identifying the limits of our **narratives** rather than establishing narratives as solutions. In this way, she is skeptical of grand narratives of social justice that cannot be wholly trusted or applied universally. Critiquing Western metaphysics, she discusses the need for the critic to unlearn her or his privilege so as to see the itinerary of silencing. Of course, here Spivak strategically reduces Western metaphysics to an essence so as to attack it. Attempting to forge a politics from what the text does not say and to work within the limits of saying, Spivak aligns herself with the thinking of Pierre Macherey so as to ask how far others are silenced and to explore the complicity between violence and discourse.

In an interview in Canberra in August 1986, which is included in *The Post- Colonial Critic* under the title "Strategy, Identity and Writing" (1986), Spivak acknowledges that there are structures of violence in the world that cannot be reduced to the violence of writing. Her essay "Can the Subaltern Speak?" (1989a) examines physical, textual, ideological, and epistemic violence so as to draw attention to the strategic exclusions of history. Spivak asks how one avoids a politics of representation that speaks on behalf of other women and thus silences them. Related to this is the question of how minority groups are to retain their specificity and difference while forging a practical politics of **resistance**. The essay argues that the gendered "subaltern" will always be represented rather than represent herself. Use of **Antonio Gramsci**'s term "the subaltern" as a general label with which to represent the dispossessed subject is itself a working example of this tendency. In this way, "the subaltern" remains trapped within signification and the representation of herself as a victim. Hence, there is little chance of the subaltern's effectively answering back because that subject has been constituted as a subject through the "planned violence of the imperialist project." With this conclusion, Spivak notices how decolonizing endeavors run the risk of repeating the structures of colonialism. Moreover, as Spivak explains in her interview with *Polygraph*, "Negotiating the Structures of Violence" (1987), if you make the subaltern conscious of her own history or her-story, she is no longer a "subaltern," and so the "subaltern" disappears.

In Part Four of "Can the Subaltern Speak?" Spivak analyzes the case of *suttee* to discover a different discursive capacity for the female "subaltern" in the "contentious traditions" to which Lata Mani (1987) refers in her essay of this title where she discusses the self-immolating Hindu woman who throws herself onto the funeral pyre of her dead husband. Mani explains how the *suttee*-widow appears nowhere as subject. For instance, if she resists the act of *suttee*, she is viewed as a victim of Hindu men, whereas if she concedes to the act, she is considered victimized by religion. Mani concludes that women in this discourse remain eternal victims. Yet Spivak is interested in how the *suttee*-widow escapes definition because of the conflicting representations of patriarchy and imperialism. She outlines how in their understanding of *suttee*, Eurocentric and phallocentric discursive fields have the effect of occluding the woman's subjectivity but also of contradicting one another. Spivak argues that *suttee* provides an example of the violent aporia that opens up as the woman falls between subject and object status. Considering **Homi Bhabha**'s use of **psychoanalytic** and deconstructive theorization in *The Location of Culture* (1994), this aporetic gap in representation can be viewed as a potentially subversive space for the dispossessed. However, this appears to be a nondiscursive space, whereby the *suttee*-widow has intervention only to the extent that the contentious master texts of patriarchy and imperialism deconstruct one another with reference to the case of self-immolation, with the effect that the "gendered subaltern" disappears into a violent aporia. If the extent of the *suttee*-widow's intervention is her self-immolation or an ultimate self-silencing, then what kind of **agency** is provided by her disappearance?

In answer to this question, "Can the Subaltern Speak?" demonstrates how in their contentious readings or understandings of *suttee*, the masterful discourses of imperialism and patriarchy disrupt one another, resulting in a *différend*, or irresolvable difference, between two discourses. For Spivak, the case of *suttee* marks the place of "disappearance" with something more than erasure or silence. Spivak's analysis leads to recognition that the subaltern is not always represented, in the same way that the conflicting discourses of imperialism and patriarchy position the *suttee*-widow differently. Using this contradiction, Spivak seeks to deconstruct the ideologies of patriarchy and colonialism so as to expose their lack of unity in an effort to see the specificity of the marginalized figure caught between tradition and modernization. In this way, she argues that the imposed order, discursive teleology, and political hegemony of the master–slave dialectic can be readdressed, and so an awareness of the disjunctions of imperialist and patriarchal discourses constitutes the agency of the gendered subaltern.

In "Can the Subaltern Speak?" Spivak aims to theorize a provisional, antiessentialist, and historically contingent **humanism** that sets humanism apart from an imperialist project or Enlightenment rationale, so as to problematize assertions of the individual agency of the subaltern. Such a critical project is anticipated in *The Post-Colonial Critic*, where Spivak posits a "practical politics of an open end," which admittedly cannot be "some kind of massive ideological act" bringing "about a drastic change" since this implies a closure whereby oppression is solved. This would deny Spivak's notion of an "everyday maintenance politics" whereby the political repression and **essentialism** of masterful ideologies are put under pressure with vigilant attention to who is held captive by such narratives.

Of course, such a strategy relies on the reader's/agent's cooperation or her or his capability to look to the emancipation of the oppressed term/subject. Such a reading is demonstrated earlier in Spivak's essay "Three Women's Texts and a Critique of Imperialism" (1985b), where she rereads the "master text" or canonical text of Charlotte Brontë's *Jane Eyre* (1847) alongside Jean Rhys' *Wide Sargasso Sea* (1968). Spivak takes up the issue of how the figure of the madwoman, Bertha Antoinette Mason, in *Jane Eyre* converges with the colonial image of the Other who is dehumanized into an object or "it." In this representation, Spivak argues that the Creole woman from the colonies is portrayed as a beast for the greater glory of the British woman, Jane Eyre. This is explicitly compared with India's being represented as barbaric, as in the British assessment of *suttee*, in order to justify the intervention of Christianity and English law in India, which has the effect of disguising the hidden agenda of European exploitation of the former colonies. Spivak notices how the unquestioned ideology of imperialist axiomatics or the accepted principles of imperialism allow Jane to be loved by Rochester, since his West Indian first wife is represented as a lunatic who is unworthy of his love. At the end of *Jane Eyre* the self-immolation of Bertha leads to the legal rights of Bertha being silenced in the fire at Thornfield. Hence, Bertha must immolate herself as a madwoman, in order to reappropriate Jane Eyre as the "feminist individualist heroine of British fiction (1985b, 251)."

In her reading of *Jane Eyre*, Spivak attacks the silences of First World feminism whereby Sandra Gilbert and Susan Gubar view the novel as "Plain Jane's Progress." Applauding *Wide Sargasso Sea*, since Rhys does not allow a woman from the colonies to be sacrificed for her sister's consolidation, Spivak demonstrates the importance of rereading narratives or histories that are taken for granted. Spivak's analysis goes beyond the field of literary criticism as she undermines the representative dynamics of texts under study in the field of "English literature" and thus not only questions institutional texts within the canon but also reexamines the ideological and historical circumstances in which these texts have been produced. Such a project has been undertaken by a number of postcolonial critics, including **Edward Said** in his essay "Jane Austen and Empire" (1993), where he rereads the occluded spaces of Jane Austen's *Mansfield Park* (1814).

However, in revising the textual, Spivak is keen not to forget the reader's own positioning or to imagine that the critic can in some way gain a purity beyond oppression. In her 1986 interview with Walter Adamson, which is included in *The Post-Colonial Critic* under the title "The Problem of Cultural Self Representation," Spivak's interest is in "who is the reader?" and what political element comes out in the transaction between the reader and texts. For Spivak, the critic's hands cannot remain clean. Arguing that there is a danger of essentialism when the reader translates all of the elements within a larger structure into a kind of continuous configuration that the knowing subject can control, Spivak begins to identify the relationship between knowledge, criticism, and mastery, that is, a situation whereby the critic gains cultural capital over a particular field that she or he claims to control or master. Spivak's theorization forces her reader to consider the complicity of criticism with mastery as the critic risks delimiting the diversity of cultural expression by claiming an authentic reading of a representative field in order to gain cultural capital and so demonstrate her or his cultivation. The critic must therefore remember that she or he is caught within structural production so that it is not truth but the routinization of cultural authority, masquerading as authentic, that is called into question. In view of this, it is not surprising that Spivak interrogates the liberal tendencies behind literary criticism as it attempts "to save the masses, speak for the masses, describe the masses." Using the example of Foucault, Spivak asks what the intellectual can do toward the texts of the oppressed. How does the critic undermine constructing the Other simply as the object of knowledge and thus avoid speaking "in the name of"? Her answer in interview is concise: "Represent and analyse them, disclosing one's own positionality for other communities in power" (Spivak and Harogym, 56). In her 1986 interview with Sneja Gunew, which is entitled "Questions of Multi-Culturalism" and included in *The Post-Colonial Critic*, Spivak discusses her notion of earning the right to criticize.

Taking the example of the student who says of his critical position: "I am only a white bourgeois male, I can't speak," Spivak asks, Why does he not develop a certain rage against the history that has written such an abject script that he is silenced? Through a historical critique of his own position, she argues, he will see that he has earned his right to criticize, and he will be heard. In her 1987 interview with Rashmi Bhatnagar, Lola Chatterjee, and Rajeshwari Sunder Rajan, Spivak continues with this debate by arguing that those in the position of being constituted by Western liberalism must negotiate so as to see what positive role can be played from within the constraints of Western liberalism. Spivak acknowledges that "Western liberalism" is a very broad term that needs to be broken open, and she argues that such an act of deconstruction would lead one to change something that one is obliged to inhabit since one cannot work from the outside.

Retaining a self-consciousness regarding her own positioning as a postcolonial intellectual, "Postmarked Calcutta" (1987) recalls Spivak's discussion about Third Worldism in Calcutta that provoked questions from the audience regarding domestic First Worldism, which was at the basis of how and why she was lecturing in India. Examining the postcolonial diasporic and the position of the First World Indian diasporic in North America, Spivak acknowledges that this is very different from that of Indians elsewhere. Spivak explains how she was initially reluctant to take up American citizenship not because she wanted to remain Indian but because she did not wish to be identified with a superpower and thus move from having been a British subject into the **neocolonialism** of the United States. Nevertheless, in 1966 she got her green card and became a "resident alien." Outlining her dispositioning within India and her unhomeliness as an "alien" in the United States, Spivak continues to forge a practical politics out of her disjunctive status as a postcolonial intellectual educated in "the British way" and lecturing French theory in the United States. Problematizing the notion of being at home and investigating how the subject centers itself, Spivak continues to critique the sovereign subject and the representative spaces that you, she, and I occupy.

Further Reading: S. Harasym 1990; D. Landry and G. Maclean 1996.

Sarah Fulford

Sri Lankan Literature   Sri Lanka has three languages, Sinhala, Tamil, and English. Each has its own literature with, regrettably, little translation into the others. For postcolonial purposes the literature in English is most important, though it should be noted that this reaches a very small proportion of the Sri Lankan population. Writing in Tamil has generally followed trends in Tamilnadu, the Tamil state in India, though recently there has been a spate of creativity roused by the ethnic conflict. Writers in Sinhala largely followed European trends, some years after they had been superseded elsewhere. Thus, Martin Wickremesinghe, widely considered the father of modern Sinhala writing, followed Edwardian and Russian models, while the more innovative Gunadasa Amerasekera was seen as Lawrentian in his most significant work.

The most innovative was Ediriweera Sarachchandra, who established himself initially as a dramatist. Eschewing Western models, he turned to folk traditions, interweaving aspects of Japanese theater to produce stunning poetic dramas such as *Maname* (1965). He also experimented with novels, the most famous of which was written after the 1971 insurgency in which many university students were killed. His anguished, largely autobiographical account of a professor torn by conscience, published as *Curfew and a Full Moon* (1978) in his own translation, helped to restore writing in English to respectability—especially because he wrote his next novel in English straightaway.

Previously, since independence, writing in English had been thought an almost despicable occupation. Such attitudes perhaps sprang from diffidence caused by a developing **nationalism** that celebrated the indigenous languages. An English professor claimed that a Lankan "would surely write in Sinhala or Tamil if he could; if he does not it is because he cannot" (Halpe, 1976, 1). while the poet Lakdasa Wikkramasinha vowed to stop writing in the language of colonial masters whom he deplored.

So there was little writing in English at the time, in marked contrast, say, to India. Only two writers of fiction manifested a sustained commitment to the art, namely, Punyakante Wijenaike and James Goonewardene. Yet they, too, felt obliged to write what might be termed "village well" fiction. The impression that this created was that writers in English, being "unable" to write in Sinhala or Tamil, nevertheless accepted that genuine Lankan experiences could be only those of the village, not those of their own urban upper-class society. With Sarachchandra's English novel, however, the situation changed, and writing in English began more seriously also to explore the responses of the urban elite to social change in the country.

The pioneering work of the 1980s, however, has now yielded pride of place to a recent phenomenon, namely, the publication of books about the country by expatriates. Rienzie Crusz, the poet now in Canada, was not, for instance, seen in Sri Lanka as especially Lankan, but with Michael Ondaatje's *Running in the Family* (1982) the situation changed. That was recognized as a brilliant evocation of the now-lost lifestyle of an earlier generation. Later writers were able to portray current Lankan experience, since the dramatic political developments in the country seemed to cry out for literary analysis that appealed universally.

Most prominent among these expatriates were Shyam Selvadurai and Romesh Gunesekera. The former, now in Canada, dealt in *Funny Boy* (1994), with the racial tensions that developed over a decade into the riots of 1983. He depicted this in juxtaposition with the growing self-awareness of a homosexual in a society that demands conformity. The intertwining of themes that deal critically with questions of tolerance and individuality was brilliantly done for a first novel. Selvadurai's second, *Cinnamon Gardens* (1999), which explores similar themes in a less tense colonial period, had a quieter reception but also shows involvement with what seems still his home country.

Romesh Gunesekera, on the other hand, clearly sees himself as a British writer and deals mainly with emigrant perceptions. His work has been less well received among Sri Lankan critics, who see it as "Orientalization" of a classic sort. That, however, is due to his publicists, who claim he portrays the anguish of a fractured land. Though what he describes, both in *Reef* and in his very strange second novel, *The Sandglass*, is not easily recognizable by Lankans, the presentation of expatriate outlooks cannot be faulted. His work then raises questions of what constitutes postcolonialism in a context in which the discourse is still dominated by the colonial power.

Of the writers resident in Sri Lanka, the most prominent are Carl Muller and Jean Arasanayagam. The former writes about the Burgher community in a manner that has irritated its more socially prominent members. The Burghers saw themselves as descendants of Europeans and therefore more civilized than Sinhalese or Tamils, but Muller presents a working-class element that has absorbed all aspects of Lankan culture with great gusto.

A more searching account of multiculturalism occurs in the work of Jean Arasanayagam, also Burgher but married to a Tamil and so caught up as a victim of race riots during the 1980s. Her poetry, anodyne before, moved into a strident political phase and has since explored various aspects of identity that have been fractured by recent problems. Her work is the best example today of Lankan writing engaging at a profound level with the hybridity with which the politicians cannot deal.

Further Reading: N. De Mel 1995; R. Wijesinha 1997.

Rajiva Wijesinha

Subaltern Studies The term "subaltern" is taken from **Antonio Gramsci**'s *Prison Notebooks* (1971), where "subalterno" euphemistically stands for the proletariat. The Subaltern Studies Collective, a group of revisionary historians in South Asian studies, has extended it to include all oppressed groups such as the peasantry, millworkers, women, "tribal" people. Subaltern history is thus "history from below," giving voice to those who have been written out of history. It begins as a challenge to the established historiography of Indian **nationalism** wherein official and elitist accounts have no place for the struggles of the poor and the outcast. In its methods it makes use of neglected documents of colonial governance, oral discourse, and disregarded sources in popular memory. It is exemplarily self-reflective and constantly aware of the vast problems involved in accessing the sources of subaltern history.

The collective's work is directed against two dominant modes of thinking: elite and radical historiography. Ranajit Guha, the founder-editor, sets out the agenda clearly in the manifesto contained in the first volume. "On Some Aspects of the Historiography of Colonial India" takes issue with both colonial as well as bourgeois-nationalist versions of elitism that suggest that the making of the Indian nation and anticolonialism were "exclusively or predominantly elite achievements" (I, 1982–1989, 1). The relationship to radical historiography is less confrontational in that a tactical silence is usually maintained. But some members are more outspoken: Dipesh Chakraborty concedes that **Marxist** historiography did turn to popular movements but was economistic in erasing subaltern initiative from history and was guilty of elitist prejudices "in the garb of scientism, enlightened consciousness or historical inevitability" (V, 235). Rejecting Europe as the sovereign theoretical subject of history wherein all national histories are extensions of this European metanarrative, the subaltern project not only is concerned with producing histories from Europe's "periphery" but also emphasizes the need to focus on the dispossessed of that periphery. Thus, the epistemic violence of **neocolonialist** and neonationalist modes of history writing is continually scrutinized. A critical detachment from its own class origin and sometimes metropolitan location is integral to the subalternists' self-description of their program of recovering suppressed native voices.

The subaltern corpus so far comprises ten volumes, published between 1982 and 1999, Guha's *Elementary Aspects of Peasant Insurgency in Colonial India* (1983), and arguably some other monographs by major contributors. Attempts to define how much of a cohesive school they represent and what benefits accrue to an academic coterie that claims a common objective are highly controversial. In this context it can be said that one obvious gain to the subaltern project was the inclusion of "outside" discussants in the later volumes. Such inclusion can be read in the spirit of an auto-critique. For instance, **Gayatri Spivak**'s against-the-grain appreciation of the first four volumes and her questioning of whether the subaltern can speak are, at the same time, a defense of the subalternist's "*strategic* use of positivist **essentialism**."

The immediate context of the rise of subaltern studies can be traced to the failure of twenty years of central planning and state intervention in poverty alleviation. The impact of peasant rebellions like the Naxalbari movement, the consequent mobilization of left-wing students, and the political associations of intellectuals amplified the conviction in the nation-state's and historians' imbrication in elitist and neocolonialist practices. This is reiterated in Guha's valedictory statement in the Preface to volume VI, along with his indictment of the "bad faith" and neocolonialism of the Cambridge school of historiography, which, in tending to view British rule as based on the collaboration of its subjects and discerning radical continuities between the precolonial and the postcolonial periods, thereby suggests that contemporary problems in India are a function of inadequate and incomplete modernization.

Apart from Gramsci, the many other influences (necessarily uneven and always a function of the individual historian's preferences) include E. P. Thompson's "unsung voices of history," **Michel Foucault**'s notion of history as discourse and the constitution of the subject in power–knowledge relations, **Edward Said**'s critique of "Orientalism," Roland Barthes' semiology, and Jacques

Derrida's "deconstructionism" and its implied demystification of the workings of capital. In the course of the ten volumes produced so far, the initial emphasis on visible revolt has shifted toward an interest in pervasive power. This Foucauldian turn has resulted in a redefinition of the "subaltern" as the locus of their project. Initially, the term "subaltern" modified the Gramscian idea of peasant subordination in that it argued for, and invested, autonomy in subaltern groups. Recovering the small voice of history thus yielded studies of peasant consciousness in grain riots, forest rights, communal disturbances, insurgencies, and so on. This consciousness was generally found to be rooted in religiosity, rumor, and myth rather than in hegemonic cultural forms. In the later volumes, where colonial power is understood as a diffuse force circulating through the entire body politic, the subaltern is not an independent entity and is located only within elite discourses. The subaltern cannot, therefore, simply speak. This understanding of power has encouraged some scholars to join the collective and others to leave it.

The essay that best captures the current subalternist preoccupation with the constitutive power of elite discourses is David Hardiman's "Power in the Forest: The Dangs, 1820–1940" (1994). Describing Bhil chieftains as subalterns seeking to capture the repressed tongue of Dangi subalternity, Hardiman meticulously traces the putative subalternity of an elite circle (the Bhil chieftains) within a subaltern community (the Dangs). Critics have, in fact, observed that the focus has increasingly shifted away from the "subaltern" toward "community" as the critique of the nationalist project has proceeded. For Partha Chatterjee, because the "fragments" that constitute Indian society are centralized under the rubric of the colonial and postcolonial state, the investigation must be widened to include a critique of Enlightenment rationalism and secularism.

The bourgeois fabrication of the nation-state and its attempts to frame communities lead Gyan Pandey to consider "The Prose of Otherness" (1994), the historiography of partition, which, although arguably the single most significant event in twentieth-century India, has been relegated to a minor motif in the final eventuality of independence. Pandey sees this historiography as lying within one of three modes: for Ian Talbot (*Punjab and the Raj, 1849–1947*; 1988), history is a chronicle of the British administration in India; for Ayesha Jalal (*The Sole Spokesman: Jinnah, the Muslim League and the Demand for Pakistan*; 1985), it is the actions of Jinnah and other "rational" political leaders; for Sumit Sarkar (*Critique of Colonial India*; 1985) and others like C. A. Bayly, history is the "signs of deepening class-contradiction and the growing anti-imperialist movement." According to Pandey, such imperialist, nationalist, and unreconstructedly Marxist historiographies banish events such as "communal riots" to the realm of "an Other history," that of primitive India threatening civilization. Pandey also uses Anees Qidwai's recollections as a volunteer among refugees, *Azadi ki Chhaon Mein* (1990), and Saadat Hasan Manto's story "Toba Tek Singh" (1948; where the refusal of poggles, or lunatics, to be repatriated is the only sane response to the project of partition, and the central protagonist dies occupying the borderless no-man's land). This turn to autobiography and fiction is productive but remains untheorized in this essay as it does in much later work inspired by this move. Spivak's sophisticated reading, though, of a contemporary Bengali short story, **Mahasweta Devi**'s "Stanadayani," is meant to reveal some of the limitations of current Western **feminist** theories, while retrieving the voiceless agent.

One of the cooperative's strengths lies in its aggregation of case studies. Shahid Amin, for example, moves from his earlier contextual ordering of the subaltern's (i.e., the sugarcane cultivator's) space, time, and resources in a complex of relationships to read the judicial discourse around the famous Chauri Chaura episode. He demonstrates how the power of the colonial state operates to produce the event merely as "a series of criminal acts rather than violent instance of mass peasant politics" (V, 198). Although he emphasizes that it must be the construction of this event "rather than its particularistic truth or falsity that deserves recognition" (186–87), he still argues that it must be read as an instance of mass peasant politics, not a criminal act.

As another outside voice, Bernard Cohn's paper "The Command of Language and the Language of Command" (IV) narrates the efforts of the British in learning Indian languages in the eighteenth and nineteenth centuries. What could have easily been a simple history soon becomes an inquiry into the beginnings of the European production of knowledge about India. He detects an ambivalence around these representations of India, which, because of the incommensurability of translation, introduce an element of indeterminacy. This awareness of the problematic of cultural **translation** would suggest an alignment of the collective with the work of **Homi Bhabha**. Gyan Prakash, who appears in volume 9 with an essay on the coming of science to the colonies as a form of translation between the lines, has earlier made clear another alignment that the collective has in Edward Said's and Ronald Inden's work. Published elsewhere, his "Writing Post-Orientalist histories of the Third World: Perspectives from Indian Historiography" (1990) is a critique of postnational foundational histories and of "objectivist bias." It is, instead, necessary to attain "blurred genres and off-centred identities" along with a commitment to a politics of difference based on a convergence of Marxist, poststructuralist, and feminist thought. Not all subalternists, however, would support his endorsement of a jostling inclusion of scholars and writers as varied as Romila Thapar, Bernard Cohn, Nicholas Dirks, **Ashis Nandy**, and **Salman Rushdie**.

The power of history in explaining current processes like the rise of Hindu fundamentalism in India is evident in Partha Chatterjee's rich essay in volume VIII. Historical claims of *Hindutva* (or Hindu-ness), were generated only through modern forms of historiography, a "historiography which is necessarily constructed around the complex identity of a people-nation-state" (VIII, 2). Reviewing the genealogy of historiography in nineteenth-century Bengal, he shows that the contemporary rhetoric of Hindu fundamentalist politics is inextricably tied to the imagining of India as a nation in the nineteenth century. The "gods and kings" approach of Mrityunjay Vidyalankar's *Rajabali* (1808), to the "secular" *Bharatbarsher Itihas* by Tarinicharan Chattopadhyaya (1858), and on to Bankim Chandra's writings all mark the movements in Bengali (and, by extension, Indian) historiography toward the building of a Hindu national past. The schema, sanctioned by European scholarship, of a dark age of medievalism falling between the periods of classical glory and modern Renaissance was in congruence with the nationalist agenda. Invested with the historical agency to realize the project of **modernity**, the Indian nation could then look to ancient India as a classical source of modernity while banishing the "Muslim period," with the help of British historians, to medieval gloom. In contrast to this unitary history of India, Chatterjee gestures toward a future of alternative *histories* for different regions, a confederal notion that de-premises the sovereignty of a single state. The location of a "truer" history in the everyday world of popular life with its inherent tolerance and Gandhian resonances is, of course, limited by its vulnerability to the technologies of the state.

This move toward critiquing elite texts and practices is enhanced in the last volume (X), which in its Preface clarifies that very little is independent of the subaltern effect: "nothing—not elite practices, state policies, academic disciplines, literary texts, archival sources, language—was exempt from the effect of subalternity" (v). This mobilizing statement is clearly intended to set free the "school of thought" manacles under which the substantial and varied body of work by eclectic contributors has been subsumed. The volume thus presents myriad modes and varying themes in an effort to demonstrate the widening ambit of the project. This becomes clear if we consider just a few essays from the collection. Sudesh Mishra's piece, which mixes history with hyperbole in an act of intense remembering, articulates the world of the indentured Indian emigrant to Fiji. Reminiscent of **Derek Walcott**'s writing, migrancy entails enunciation and making sense of the new: "it was as if *machli* (fish in Hindi) as a word and culture had never existed prior to *ika*. . . . And yet the one was forever inside the other" (X, 3). The success (or failure) of narrating such dislocated and dispossessed subjects challenges the traditional modes of history writing. Moving to the Middle East, the troubled relationship between nationalism and feminism is the focus of Rosemary Sayigh's consideration of women's life stories in Palestinian camps. In a vastly different mood, exploring popular visual culture, Christopher Pinney teases out the "mythopolitics" of **magic realism**, the threatening hybridity at work in nineteenth-century Indian art. The eleventh volume, now under preparation, further indicates the increasingly crossdisciplinary orientation of the project as it purports to make a difference in the politics of knowledge.

Marxist critic Sumit Sarkar has called the later work of a section of the subaltern group a kind of "academic 'common sense.' " Apart from the now-common and somewhat simplistic criticism that their approach denies **agency/autonomy** to Indians, Sarkar echoes Bhabha's well-known arguments about **mimicry** when he contends that the metamorphosis in "two generations of Macaulay's dream-child into Kipling's *bunderlog* [literally, monkey-folk] is sufficient evidence that the earlier expectations had not been entirely realized." For critics like Sarkar, arguments that show how communal divisions were constructed by colonialism (through census categories, etc.), although well-intentioned, are at best double-edged. The subalternist's tendency to explain the contours of the future nation-state in terms of the nineteenth-century colonial moment is vigorously disputed by their peers who advocate the view that the nineteenth century discourses derived much of their sustenance from already present historical/philosophical traditions within Indian society.

That the collective has made worldwide waves among historians is indisputable. Following a survey of Indian history writing, Terence Ranger concludes that it "would be most valuable for Southern Africanists to keep in constant touch with this self-confident, subtle, radical, indigenous school of social history" (1990, 10). Whether these historians deserve quite such generous praise might be debated, not least among Indian historians themselves. But Ranger's call for dialogue remains legitimate and, in fact, has spawned spirited enthusiasm among revisionary historians in places as far apart as Latin America and Ireland in their efforts to continue the tentative South–South conversations now becoming increasingly popular. The subalternist project sees postcoloniality as a strategy that demands, in Spivak's terms, not only the erection of local narratives to Europe's long story but a "tampering with the authority of storylines."

Further Reading: G. Bhadra, G. Prakash, and S. Tharu 1999; J. Didur 1997; R. Guha, 1982–1989; R. Guha and G. Spivak, 1988.

Prem Poddar

T

Testimonio   *Testimonio* is generally defined as a **narrative** told in first person by a narrator who is also the actual protagonist, or witness, of the events that he or she recounts. This extraliterary or, by some critics, even postliterary genre has been introduced to the literary canon motivated by both political and aesthetic reasons. The fundamental agenda of the **postmodernists** is to object to monolithic elitism and to create a bridge over the river that divides the elite from the masses, where the various ways of life confront, enjoy, juxtapose, represent, dramatize, and legitimate each other mutually. This strategy of affirming and negating the existing structures of power places the various types of discourses in opposition. In spite of their general conception as narratives, testimonies may appear in many genres. For example, in Latin America in the 1980s an important corpus of testimonial poems appeared chronicling the tortures that occurred during the 1970s under military dictatorships in the Southern Cone. However, such testimonial poems or plays have not really been studied by critics as profoundly as have testimonial narratives.

The word "testimony" suggests bearing witness in a legal or religious sense, which distinguishes the *testimonio* from autobiographical or other types of memorial discourse. The testimonial narrative consists of a narration of lived or witnessed experiences that is published in printed form and that, for the moment, is found in the center of discussion about what constitutes the literary. Frequently, the testimonial narrative is offered by (various) marginalized person(s) whose individual and/or group rights have been violated. As such, they live to represent that group (like the Holocaust victims: to tell the story is the only thing that may ease the guilt of surviving). They introduce themselves into the academic realm, sometimes—especially, if the narrator of a *testimonio* is functionally illiterate—through their relation to an intellectual (anthropologist, writer, etc.) who appears as the author (!) of the book that results from this collaboration (cf. Elizabeth Burgos, I, *Rigoberta Menchú, an Indian Woman in*

Guatemala [1983; in English, 1984], or Moema Viezzer, *Domitila: Let Me Speak!* [1977; in English, 1978]).

Mostly anonymous *testimonio*-like texts have existed at the margins of literature—long before *testimonio* was introduced in the literary canon—representing, for example, the woman, the insane, the slave, the criminal, the proletarian: figures that were excluded from authorized representations.

Generally speaking, the testimonial voice parts from the individual experience, that is, from the private, and there is an explicit reason for these individual experiences to enter into the public domain. The most frequent reason is the desire to denounce the injustices committed by representatives of public institutions (police, military, bureaucrats, etc.) against individuals (who represent the private sector). From the disappearance of the limits between the public and the private emerges a hybrid space from which the subject offers its testimony. John Beverly was one of the first ones to point out that, in fact, the testimonial narrative is an appropriate space for a creative collaboration of the intellectual and the marginalized where real solidarity between the two can emerge.

The two principal types of discussions regarding testimonial narrative in academic circles in general and in North American academic circles in particular concentrate on two issues: a notion of **subalterity** offered by the person giving the *testimonio* and the presence (or absence) of fictionalization of the events. As to the notion of subalterity manifested in the *testimonio*, we may recall **Gayatri Spivak**'s famous question: "Can the subaltern speak?" to which she herself had answered no, mainly because no methodology for determining who or what might constitute this group can avoid a certain **essentialism**; that is, the subaltern group is generally defined by its difference from the elite. Neil Larsen warns about the risks of believing that we have easy access to the subaltern's way of thinking just because we have the opportunity of observing and listening to a particular person belonging to this group. Robert Carr also points out the danger in believing that in the testimonial narrative we are facing a transparent subject that can be studied from the academic realm. To all this, John Beverly suggests a type of solution, a compromise: to consider the person who offers the *testimonio* not as a subaltern but rather as an "organic intellectual of the subaltern class" (1991, 12). This suggestion is interesting, particularly because it implies, according to Beverly himself, that the intellectual is capable of not only transcending national barriers (a postmodernist characteristic) but also penetrating into other cultures. Considering subalterity as a class, of course, can be criticized as an unnecessary and unfair homogenization of subaltern groups.

The other topic of great interest in academic circles is the question of veridiction in the testimonial narrative. George Yúdice says that it is not appropriate to address this issue because "the truth" as such is irrelevant for the testimonial narrative, which is a testimony regardless of the truthfulness of the narrated events as long as it complies with the condition of generating a transforming praxis. Yúdice also states that the use of the "*meraviglia*" is licit, as it was during the era of the epic, for the narration to create more effect. However, speaking of Randall, Barnet, and others, Beverly points out that the core of the *testimonio* is found in its ethical/aesthetical function, which may be fulfilled only if the narration is truthful and real. The publication of David Stoll's book *Rigoberta Menchu and the Story of All Poor Guatemalans* (1999) is a good example of how important it is, for some, for the person offering the testimony to be truthful in order to maintain moral authority. Finding questionable passages in *I, Rigoberta Menchú*, Stoll disputes the merit of Menchú's testimony because, in his view, it cannot be the eyewitness account that it purports to be.

When the *testimonio* is not written directly by the subject and is mediated, the mediator should limit intervention in the edition of the testimony in order to avoid influencing, if at all possible, the narration in order to reduce doubts with regard to the authenticity of the text. Burgos and Viezzer, respectively the mediators of Rigoberta and Domitila's testimonies, in their prologues emphasize the difficulty in transposing the testimony from oral to written form. The result is a text devoid of questions and of *verba dicendi*, a monologized text, in both its form and ideology. The difference between the voice of the *testimoniante* and the underlying voice of the mediator preserves the personal voice of the *testimoniante* as well as that of the Other. Hugo Achugar believes that the voice of the other appears as a voice different from that of the mediator, which, in its turn, appears in footnotes and other paratexts.

In addition to testimonial narratives and mediated testimonies, testimonial novels should also be included in the discussion of this genre: Miguel Barnet's *The Autobiography of a Runaway Slave* (1966) or Elena Poniatowska's *Hasta no verte, Jesús mío* (Until We Meet Again, My Jesus; in Spanish, 1969). In these cases the original account is silenced and not accessible to the reader, for the author *admittedly* acts as an editor reordering the sometimes rambling and repetitive stories of the person offering the account. This is different from the mediator's role, who insists upon the faithful recording of the testimony.

The stance taken by academics such as Sylvia Molloy and Elzbieta Sklo-dowska, inasmuch as it questions the fictional aspects of the testimonial narration, also allows for its entry into the canon at the expense of sacrificing the ethical/aesthetical function. Testimonial narrative may be considered, especially in its mediated form, as one of the hybrid postmodernist discursive forms that express sociopolitical positions in addition to aesthetical/ideological aspirations of the progressive postcolonial elites. At the same time, the *testimonio* is an important manifestation of **resistance literature**, for its contents often question or even attack the "official story" written by the victorious, the European colonizer, the white man manifesting, not surprisingly, a **Eurocentric** colonialist perspective based on the Cartesian concept of an existing truth. However, parallel to the official story there is a resistance literature, a manifestation of the subaltern versions of history that fills the voids and silences of the official story by offering another point of view, that of the defeated, a sort of a counterhistory that includes events, provides contexts, and describes historical figures that, in conjunction with the version on official documents (and at times in contrast to them), present a very different reality from that which is to be found in the official archives. As a result, the counterhistory is a type of resistance writing (or it may appear in oral form, thereby counterbalancing the European supremacy of the written form); its function is to contradict or correct certain aspects of the official story or to reveal other aspects not included. If the principal recourse of the official story is writing, the counterhistory tends to be of an oral nature, since it is frequently based on memories, testimonies, interviews, and so on. According to Emma Sepúlveda, *testimonio* has gained a reputation as a discourse of resistance that gives voice to the marginalized, the colonized, and the oppressed, whose goal is to offer a different perspective that frequently comes from sources lacking power and active means of resistance to the official story written by those who have power. This it does by, for example, revealing certain aspects of the events that are either omitted or distorted in the official version of history. The existence of the *testimonio* in a space between speaking and writing, once again, questions the primacy of writing in our conception of history, as do other characteristics of this genre, such as the indeterminable wavering between autobiography and communal record or between a personal and a political statement. The testimonial narrative of the marginalized offers the possibility of influencing the reader's thinking, and, in this manner, it operates as a discourse of resistance. In sum, *testimonio* is an effective form of appropriating dominant forms of discourse in order to create powerful subaltern voices.

Further Reading: A. Dingwaney 1995; D. Sommer 1998.

Silvia Nagy-Zekmi

Thailand.   *See* Benedict Anderson; Travel Writing

Theater.   *See* Performance

Third World.   *See* Decolonization; Dependency Thesis

Pramoedya Ananta Toer   The life of Indonesian novelist Pramoedya Ananta Toer mirrors his country's tumultuous progress through the twentieth century. Javanese, like three-fifths of his countrymen, he was born in the summer of 1925. His Dutch-trained schoolteacher father left a position in the colonial system for native education to teach in independent schools organized by the nationalist movement *Budi Utomo* (Beautiful Endeavor). After *Budi Utomo* was proscribed in 1935, Pramoedya's disillusioned father eventually abandoned the family, at which time Pramoedya left his secondary-school training as a radio and telegraph operator to support his mother and younger siblings. In 1943 the Japanese invaded Java. Their almost effortless defeat of the Dutch inspired Indonesian nationalists: the Japanese slogan of occupation, *Nipon Abang* (Japanese Are Your Elder Brothers) neatly summed up the notion of Asian self-rule. Pramoedya and other young nationalists flocked to Jakarta to participate in the government of the Japanese occupation. Pramoedya was trained as a journalist for a position at the Japanese press agency Domei in 1943 but soon realized that Japanese occupation was to be as brutal and exploitative as colonization by the Netherlands had been. He left Domei and, when independence was declared by future-president Sukarno, enlisted in one of the many noncentralized armies of independence then forming to oppose the Japanese. He eventually served as an information officer and worked at the Voice of Free Indonesia, an underground radio station. In 1948 he was imprisoned and tortured by the Dutch.

The next few years were a bloody and chaotic time in Indonesia as Japan surrendered to the British, who were to occupy the region until the Dutch could return to reclaim their extremely profitable colony. It was the era of the *pemuda*, the fervent revolutionary youth, who fought guerrilla and terrorist actions against successive occupational governments. Their fervor inspired Pramoedya and other figures of *Angkatan '45* (Generation of 1945), the first generation of truly Indonesian writers. While imprisoned by the Dutch, Pramoedya wrote *Keluarga Gerilya* (Guerrilla Family; 1989) and *Perburuan* (The Fugitive). Both novels use elements from the *wayang* (traditional Javanese shadow plays where stories from Hindu-Javanese epics are retold) and involve poor freedom fighters who draw on the mystic traditions of Java for strength in the struggle against the colonizer.

Pramoedya was released as independence was declared in 1949, and President Sukarno's fifteen-year administration marks the most public and prominent period of Pramoedya's life. As a leader of *Lekra* (Institute for People's Culture), the cultural wing of the revolutionary government, Pramoedya participated wholeheartedly in the outspoken, Chinese-style rhetoric of the era, to the extent that when Sukarno fell from power after Indonesia's "year of living dangerously" (1965), Pramoedya was jailed as a political prisoner by General Suharto, Indonesia's second president. He spent the next fourteen years as a political prisoner in the camp on remote Buru Island, and possession of his books was made illegal.

Once again prison stimulated Pramoedya to write, or rather (denied writing materials) to compose and perform stories for fellow prisoners. The four novels of the *Buru Quartet* (*This Earth of Mankind* [1991], *Child of All Nations* [1993], *House of Glass* [1992], and *Footsteps* [1994]) date from this period. More complex in structure than Pramoedya's earlier work, they weave together the experiences of dozens of Indonesians to tell the story of **nation formation**. To a Western reader, these tales of the early twentieth-century independence movement, the war for independence, and the birth of the Indonesian nation seem entirely patriotic, but like his earlier novels they, too, were banned by Suharto's government. The fervor (positive and negative) that his work inspires in Indonesia clearly depends upon a frame of reference shared by Pramoedya and his local readers.

In 1979 Pramoedya was released to house arrest. He settled in Jakarta and saw the *Buru Quartet* and *The Fugitive* translated into English but did little new writing. In the late 1990s, with the end of the increasingly corrupt administrations of Presidents Suharto and Habibie, the beginning of Indonesia's recovery from the financial calamity of 1997, and the new presidency of the widely respected Abdurrahman Wahid, the political climate became more open, and Pramoedya resumed his role as activist, writer, and national conscience.

Postcolonial literature has come to be known as that which is written by formerly colonized people in forms and (often) languages acquired from the colonizer and that treats the experiences of the colonized and in some sense "writes back" to the **center**, the colonizer. Pramoedya's work fits this model only partially, both stylistically and in terms of content. Though he acknowledges a debt to Westerners like William Saroyan and John Steinbeck for certain narrative techniques, even more in evidence are local literary influences: the forms, values, and motifs from Javanese *wayang* and those of what he has called *sastra assimilitiv* (assimilitive literature), the productions of the burgeoning independent press in the early twentieth century. Though he writes of independence, Pramoedya's project is not to "write back" but to write inward, addressing his countrymen. Instead of his native Javanese, he writes in the Indonesian langague, a regional lingua franca whose adoption by the new republic was a strong force for unification of the tremendously diverse new nation. In his novels, especially *Keluarga Gerilya* and the *Buru Quartet* novels, his characters come together from all over the archipelago to struggle together for independence. The colonizer and the colonizer's language are almost totally absent in Pramoedya's novels. Thus, perhaps the third state of the development of a national literature, as explicated by Frantz Fanon in his *The Wretched of the Earth* (1965), provides a better theoretical model than postcoloniality per se: just as Fanon posits, Pramoedya's work can be characterized as a local hybrid that uses local tools to address a local audience to further a local cause, in this case, the building of the Indonesian nation from its constituent parts.

Further Readings: P. Toer 1990.

Elizabeth B. Fitzpatrick

Transculturation   In the 1940s the Cuban ethnologist **Fernando de Ortiz** wanted to describe how a hybrid Afro-Cuban culture emerged from the colonial contact between **indigenous** and imperial cultures. No vocabulary was available to discuss this process from a postcolonial writer's perspective; Ortiz coined the neologism "transculturation" to replace such terms as "deculturation" or "acculturation," which replicated the logic of empire by explaining cultural contact from the perspective of the metropolis. Instead of thinking about culture in terms of a one-sided transfer from a civilized metropolis to a primitive periphery, Ortiz drew attention to the complex process by which subordinated groups select what to absorb from the dominant culture. His concept has proved very influential for postcolonial discourse in Latin America and was incorporated into literary studies by Uruguayan critic **Angel Rama** in the 1970s.

Some disagreement exists over the political implications of transculturation. As Sabine Hofmann has demonstrated, in Caribbean theory two understandings of transculturation's political consequences compete. Miguel Barnet discusses transculturation as a process that fuses elements from different origins into a unified, national culture. Antonio Benítez-Rojo and Gustavo Pérez Firmat reject the notion that transculturation resolves its contradictory elements and produces a synthetic culture. They argue that "transculturation" describes a promiscuous culture that proliferates the interplay between competing cultural discourses and perpetuates their irresolvable contradictions. This emphasis on culture as a promiscuous staging of differences has also proved influential for the term's use in theater studies. For Pérez Firmat, transculturation operates linguistically through a particular practice of **translation**: he argues that verbal restatements and paraphrases make cultural displacements visible and enact shifts in meaning that ultimately fail to reproduce hegemonic culture. As an open-ended process of mutual influence, "transculturation" designates a new, hybrid culture that can no longer be traced to separable native and metropolitan origins. Recognizing the complexity of culture in the former colonies necessitates new models for postcolonial subjectivity. Theories of transculturation undercut the ideology of political movements that claim to erase the history of empire and to recover a precolonial, (ab)original culture. Transculturation challenges us to examine what it means to think of culture as transimperial and transnational.

Ortiz's concept has only recently appeared in English-language criticism, primarily as a result of Mary Louise Pratt's work. For Pratt, "transculturation" is a dual process: she uses the term in Ortiz's sense to discuss the encounter between different cultures in what she calls "contact zones," that is, spaces where different cultures influence one another. But for her, these contact zones are not limited to the colonies: she also discusses the effects of colonial cultures on and in the metropolis. This twofold understanding makes transculturation a concept central to discussions of cosmopolitan culture and of **globalization**.

Further Reading: S. Hofmann 1997; M. Pratt 1992.

Colleen Glenney Boggs

Translation Studies In a concerted effort to bring practice and theory together, as well as to formalize the discipline, translators and translation scholars created the field of translation studies in the early 1970s. It has since established itself as an important empirical science, comprising a plurality of approaches. Translation research has always drawn from related disciplines, such as linguistics and literature, a practice that makes for a remarkably heterogeneous field. The "cultural" turn that translation studies took in the 1980s, however, influenced the field as a whole and even attracted the interest of several postcolonial scholars from outside. The most notable of these, Niranjana, is discussed later.

This development can be traced back to the process of self-criticism engaged in by the field of anthropology under the influence of poststructuralist thought. Anthropologists are not innocent observers of the cultures that they study but interfere with them by their very presence and biases, an insight that postcolonial critics have applied to the study of colonization. The success of the colonial enterprise depended in part, on the skills of interpreters and translators who facilitated the advance into conquered territory, the establishment of trading posts, and the conversion of natives to Christianity. Postcolonial critics are therefore interested in the politics of translation and analyze interpreting and translating practices in given historical contexts; they also use translation as a metaphor to explain processes of colonization and **decolonization**. This kind of research reveals that, in colonial encounters, translation could be both at the service of imperialism and a site of **resistance**. One famous historical example of this contradictory nature is the controversial figure of La Malinche, interpreter and mistress of Hernán Cortés during the conquest of Mexico. She was expected not only to translate but also to persuade her own people not to resist the invasion. Although history has largely vilified her for selling out to the Spanish conquerors, she is being reappropriated and reinterpreted by contemporary scholars as an ambiguous and tragic figure of intercultural contact, of the clash between cultures, and of asymmetrical power relations. As a colonized subject, she can be viewed as a subject in translation, caught between misrepresentation and cultural survival. Thus, the metaphor of translation is useful in gaining a better understanding of colonial power relations, of the limits of cultural transfer, and of the problematic of difference and **alterity**.

Tejaswini Niranjana was one of the first to explain translation as an instrument of colonization. Her poststructuralist standpoint is informed by Walter Benjamin, Jacques Derrida, and Paul de Man, and her book entitled *Siting Translation* (1992) creates a bridge between traditional scholarship in translation studies and postcolonial theory. She starts by demonstrating how colonized India was represented by colonial translators as the "non-Western other" and how, through the imposed English system of education, these representations have come to be accepted as reality. Niranjana shows that, in a colonial context, the practice of translation is supported by the tenets of Western metaphysics and that it needs to be studied and understood in that perspective. She calls for the need to question the innocence of representation, as ethnography has done, and to reveal the colonial translator's complicity with hegemonic power. On the other hand, her rereading of Benjamin's work on history leads her to point out that both Derrida and de Man did not give sufficient importance to the use of translation as a metaphor for displacement as well as refiguring. Based on that analysis, she advocates the use of translation and retranslation as a postcolonial tool of liberation.

One of the most positive aspects of the relationship between the fields of translation studies and postcolonial studies is the emphasis that it places on history, and Niranjana's scholarship attests to it. Several other scholars have since published research done in specific colonial contexts, and their work is reviewed and explained by Douglas Robinson in *Translation and Empire* (1997), which is one volume in a series aimed at giving an account of the field of translation. Robinson notes that translation scholars themselves have been rather slow to embrace postcolonial theories and that the field of translation studies in this area has evolved in a parallel way to that of **cultural studies**. All the studies discussed by Robinson concern the history of translation within a problematic of "power differentials." The strength of this book is to never lose sight of the problems facing the practicing translator and to present theories in a pragmatic perspective. Robinson is, indeed, careful to point out the pitfalls of either demonizing translation or glorifying it as an instrument of liberation since the real value in postcolonial translation research is in being able to explain both sides of the colonial cultural encounter and to show degrees of appropriation or misappropriation, understanding or misunderstanding from both perspectives. This position points the way to future research into the politics of translation and, in particular, into the role played by the person of the translator involved in the cultural life of a specific area or particular era.

Both practitioners and critics know that translation always presents an irreducible element of resistance. In focusing on that surplus element and in using it as a metaphor for cultural resistance, postcolonial translation critics are reexamining cultural history and explaining the necessary conditions and limits of cultural exchange. This new perspective is paving the way for exciting future scholarship in the area of intercultural negotiation and contributes to a deeper understanding of how difference is maintained and preserved even in a situation of cultural hybridity. By the same token, awareness is being raised among practicing translators of the difficult issues associated with cultural transfer. Translated texts are being analyzed more often from a postcolonial perspective, and research is growing to include previously neglected areas such as the politics of publication. Translation studies and postcolonial studies have everything to gain from this association, which also promises to aid in bringing translation studies out of the relative obscurity that has always characterized it.

Further Reading: T. Niranjana 1992; D. Robinson 1997.

Anne Malena

Travel Writing The return of Hong Kong to Chinese sovereignty in 1997 marked the death of the system of colonies, protectorates, and territories through which Britain in the nineteenth century encircled the globe. This examination of postcolonial travel writing begins in 1947, when Britain granted India independence and the terminal illness of the empire became apparent. Postcolonial travel writers no longer had an empire to serve. They no longer had to encourage their readers to take up the burden of bringing British political, religious, and cultural order to the dark and mysterious parts of the world and of carrying away its natural resources to enrich their lives. They were no longer charged with classifying the world's flora and fauna or of mapping its rivers and mountains in the name of civilization.

This same period saw the development of postcolonial theory, which **Edward Said** may be said to have defined in *Orientalism* (1978). He emphasizes the reductive rhetoric of the imperialist and points to the portrayal of the East in Western **art** and discourse as always and at the same time exotic and inferior, remarkable and decaying, spiritual and violent. In *Imperial Eyes* (1992) Mary Louise Pratt characterizes the practice of pre-mid-nineteenth-century European men and women writers as assuming a masculine superiority in their encounters with place and people. Said would seem to imply that postcolonial travel writing continues to embody the attitudes expressed in the writing of their predecessors. Others, such as Susan Morgan in *Place Matters* (1996), perceive the narrative voices of both male and female colonial- and imperialist-era travel writers as more varied. Her examination of Victorian women travel writing about Southeast Asia produces evidence to dispute the univocal claims of Said and Pratt.

The particular blind spots developed by our cultures have been exposed so widely that it is safe to say that the **narrative** voices of postcolonial travel writing are rarely naive even when infected by the superior tone of the West. Writers' voices are further complicated by the commingled identities of self emanating from a mixed heritage of place, race, and class. Books written in English are published in Singapore, Delhi, Harare, and Auckland and read by people who live in the United States, Australia, England, and Canada. These English-speaking readers frequently identify with varied places and peoples because of where they have lived and worked and because of their own mixed ancestry. Homelessness is often a theme in the work of such mixed-identity writers, but the theme also appears importantly in the work of travel writers born in England. Graham Greene, for instance, reveals that his faith is responsible for his lack of belonging to a place, but others identify the sense as having come from the physical circumstances of their lives. Bruce Chatwin, who is known for his works on Patagonia, traces his affinity for travel to the nomadic life that he experienced as a child of a navy officer growing up in World War II England.

A number of English travel writers whose work is associated with Africa were raised in colonial Africa. Laurens van der Post was born and raised in South Africa. Elspeth Huxley and Beryl Markham grew up in East Africa. Christina Dodwell was born in and returned to the British colony of Nigeria and chose Africa for her first travel adventure. In fact and fiction, van der Post and Huxley romanticize and critique the colonial and postcolonial world that they experienced. Rejecting the language as well as the racial beliefs of his Afrikaans family, van der Post exposes the devastation that the **indigenous people** of Africa have experienced at the hands of Europeans, while he celebrates nostalgically the poetic beauty of Africa. Australian-born Alan Moorehead protests the devastation of African wildlife and calls for preservation programs.

Postcolonial Africa is more likely to be the destination of the photographer, anthropologist, zoologist, Peace Corps worker, cyclist, amateur adventurist, or the newspaper correspondent assigned to troubled spots of the world than of the explorer or geographer. Few postcolonialists set out to transform Africa. British expatriates, American Peace Corps workers, Muslims, and tribespeople mingle in the village life that Daisy Waugh describes in East Africa in *A Small Town in Africa* (1994). Waugh and Mark Hudson, who writes about West Africa in the award-winning *Our Grandmother's Drums* (1989), find the distance between their culture and African culture much greater than they anticipate. Yet their narratives do not become tales of them and us. Both Waugh and Hudson live among the people, not apart from the natives, as was the British colonial tradition. They find hypocrisy, kindness, cruelty, naïveté, and wisdom in the Africans and in those individuals who have come to work and live for a time in Africa. The narrative voices of Waugh and Hudson are neither reverent nor superior.

Like Hudson, Nigel Barley traveled to Africa for anthropological fieldwork. In his travel writings in which he presents the work that he has done among the Dowayo tribe in Cameroon, Barley mocks the godlike pose of the anthropologist come to peer at the rituals of human subjects. Instead he finds the personal, the serendipitous, and the unexpected in his travels to Africa and later to Indonesia. His narratives, like those of Waugh and Hudson, accept both cultural and individual differences.

Patrick Marnham, who was born in Israel, takes as his explicit subject the postcolonial world of India, Iran, Afghanistan, Pakistan, and India. He has written about Africa as well. While he concluded that British institutions, including the practice of anthropology and paleontology, were absolutely destructive to Africa, he believes them to have been helpful to India. He is one of many who find meaning in the East. On the other hand, Geoffrey Moorhouse searches for meaning in India but does not find it. Instead, he finds the place an abandoned mine—much of its wealth carried off and its people left to struggle with its poverty and lack of adequate infrastructure. His is not a positive view of colonialization whether he casts his gaze at the Arab world or at Africa. The only positive contribution of the missionaries and their work in colonial countries is the desire for freedom that they instilled in those whom they came to convert, as Moorhouse views the situation.

Other travel writers well known for their observations on postcolonial life in India are Eric Newby, who also writes about the Middle East, and William Dalrymple, who observes that nostalgia for the Raj era was rampant in Britain in the 1980s but not in contemporary India. For the British such as Jonathan Raban, who travels to the Arab world to satisfy his curiosity aroused by its postcolonial presence in London, the past is very much with those in Britain. Alexander Frater is drawn to revisiting the region of his birth in *Chasing the Monsoon* (1990). **V. S. Naipaul**'s journeys to India are to satisfy his curiosity about his own heritage. His grandparents were from the north of India. A Hindu, he grew up in colonial British Trinidad and moved from the postcolonial decadence he knew there to England, where he completed his education and has enjoyed a successful career as a writer. Some have accused him of blindness to the faults of the West. Perhaps it is best to say that he is not blind to the faults of the East.

Sarah Hobson moves about the lands that were Britain, masquerading as a boy in Iran and living with a family in India. Her travel books are works of cultural exploration. So, too, are those of inveterate travelers Bettina Selby and Dervla Murphy, who take the globe as their home. Unlike the perspective of the colonial/imperialist travel writer, the Third World in their works is a place to be experienced and explored, not to be cultured and conquered. Jan Morris, one of the most prolific travel writers of the postcolonial age, travels the world in her books as well as exploring the British empire as it was.

In the nineteenth century the Netherlands, France, and Britain contended for dominance in the area that we now refer to as Southeast Asia. Siam, never a colony but very much under the imperial dominance of Britain, became Thailand in 1939. In postcolonial travel writing, as in news stories, the country's prostitutes are featured. The nineteenth-century harem of King Monghut has become the whorehouse of the tourist. Contemporary travel writers do not examine the historical circumstances behind the myth and the reality of the sex industry in Thailand. The image of exotic women sexual slaves, who differ from those of other lands in their beauty and in their supposed naive search for love, is highlighted in the title—"Love in a Duty-free Zone"—that contemporary British travel writer Pico Iyer gives his essay on Thailand in *Video Night in Kathmandu and Other Reports from the Not-so-far East* (1988).

While contemporary portraits of Thailand continue to emphasize the exotic and the romantic in its people, its women, and its temples and ceremonies, they are set amid the Western landscape of shopping malls and hotels. The Westernization of Southeast Asia is documented by postcolonial travel writers from Norman Lewis to Pico Iyer. Through what Iyer calls "America's pop-cultural imperialism" (1988, 5), he and other travel writers of the second half of the twentieth century depict the peoples of the world being stripped of their culture by the invasion of peoples, goods, and entertainment from abroad. The unsaved and uncultured world depicted in the writing of earlier journeyers has become Paradise Lost in the writings of many of those who have traveled to the East since World War II.

This is true not just in the depiction of Bali and the islands of the South Pacific but also in travelers' representations of Burma and Indochina. Norman Lewis, for example, in both *A Dragon Apparent: Travels in Indo-China* (1951) and *Golden Earth: Travels in Burma* (1952) depicts the simplicity and virtues of Buddhist nonmaterialism. Poverty and illiteracy are glossed over in the idealization of living in harmony with the earth and its people. He does not note the inherent contradiction between much of the violence that he experiences and learns of and the picture that he has of the Burmese as possessing a kind of purity unknown to those of the West. If education and the ability to read and write carry with them freedom from ignorance and a loss of naïveté, he seems to prefer freedom from the greed that he associates with Western progress and civilization.

Gavin Young is another like Lewis who semi-idolizes the people of the East, writing extensively about the Marshlands and Marsh Arabs of Mesopotamia as well as about Southeast Asia. His works project the virtues of the life of the solitary and rugged individualist to be found in the offbeat places of the former colonized world that he describes in his solitary, ship-hopping journeys from Europe to China and back to England, recorded in *Slow Boats to China* (1981) and *Slow Boats Home* (1985). In his view, civilization brings mass culture and bureaucrats and a loss of individualism. He sees the West not as the purveyor of peace, progress, and prosperity but as the destroyer of people's spirits. He acknowledges his debt to Wilfred Thesiger, the last explorer of the Arab world, who made Arabia his spiritual home.

As World War II brought on a new wave of travel writers, so, too, did the revolutions in French Indochina. Jon Swain in *River of Time* (1996) tells of the "violence as well as sensuous pleasure" that he found to be "intrinsic" to the people of Indochina (5). While paradise was certainly lost, in Swain's writing it is not through the impact of the West that the Armageddon descends, even though Europe and America played their role. Paradise is lost through internal struggles that unfortunately the West was not able to contain. Swain's book, like so many others on the East, continues to picture it in the extremes, as if those extremes were inherent in the people rather than in the interplay between their history and culture.

One strategy used by postcolonial writers who are self-conscious about their journeys and the distorting lenses through which they view foreign lands is to narrate their journey through recounting individual encounters. They figure as the hero in their episodic travel adventures that sometimes, as in the case of Australian Murray Laurence, become picaresque tales. Laurence has lived and worked in Asia, Europe, and South America. As his title, *High Times in the Middle of Nowhere* (1986), suggests, this book is about the experience of traveling and the linguistic encounters that he has with people whom he meets on the way to somewhere in airplanes, trains, and buses and waiting lounges and stations. Another device is to pose as an amateur, though the majority of postcolonial travel writers are professional travelers and writers. Andrew Eames, who is a journalist and editor, narrates an admittedly prototype adventure of the twenty-year-old setting out to see the world armed with the Lonely Planet Guide, in *Crossing the Shadow Line: Travels in South-East Asia* (1986).

If earlier travelers made themselves out to be heroes and heroines by going where no man or woman had gone before, those at the end of the twentieth century and beginning of the twenty-first portray the places as safe for anyone of an adventurous spirit and a sense of humor. Redmond O'Hanlon, an armchair naturalist and writer, undertakes adventure travel to some of the remaining wild spots of the earth—the Amazon and Borneo. Some of his journeys are taken with his friend James Fenton, poet and journalist turned travel writer. They, like Australian Tim Flannery, who is both a mammologist and paleontologist, depict the discomfort and dangers as comic incidents, better overcome through an indomitable spirit than manufactured arms. Another whose travels take her to politically and socially threatening locales is Sheila Paine. She travels alone to remote places in the Muslim world of Pakistan, Afghanistan, Iran, and Iraq. Paul Theroux, too, travels alone and in discomfort, almost as if he seeks it. These lone travelers beckon readers to venture forth from their armchairs to see the world.

Further Reading: S. Morgan 1996; E. Said 1978.

Barbara Brothers

U

Universalism In postcolonial studies, as in other areas of the humanities, universalism is a contentious concept. Once a central criterion for judging the worth of a literary text, it is now discredited by postcolonialists as a strategy of European imperialism. Some dismiss it as "a myth" (Ashcroft, Griffiths, and Tiffin 1995, 55). Others censure its imperial function but contend that to reject altogether the concept of commonality in human nature is a questionable proposition. They agree that the imperial conception of universalism was designed to impose on the colonial native the values and morals of European culture that were promoted as universals (Viswanathan 1989). Ironically, though Victorian England fostered the idea of a universal human nature, it never embraced a commonness with colonial natives (Bhabha 1985). James Frazer's *The Golden Bough* (1940), for instance, which sought to establish through a comparative study of myths and cultures the affinities of humankind, was considered "a dangerous . . . forbidden text." His thesis that all humans possessed an essential similarity was "at one level threatening to the Victorian mind" (ix–x).

Many postcolonial scholars who denounce the European conception of universalism reject *any* concept of universalism, insisting that there are only cultural and historical particulars; for them, the responsibility of the postcolonialist is to retrieve and revalidate distinct identities once suppressed by imperial notions of human **essentialism**. Others, such as **Chinua Achebe**, spurn the European conception of universalism but not the idea of human commonality: "I should like to see the word 'universal' banned altogether from discussions of African literature *until* such a time as people cease to use it as a synonym for the narrow, self-serving parochialism of Europe" (1995, 60; emphasis added). He advises the postcolonial writer not "to run after universality," noting that if writers are faithful to their particular experiences and perspectives, "there is enough that is in common between peoples, between one people and another, for what he says to be appreciated" (qtd. in Turkington 1977, 10). Several postcolonial writers have insisted that their texts operate simultaneously on regional, national, ethnic, *and* human levels. **Timothy Mo**, the Hong Kong British novelist, in *An Insular Possession* (1986) observes through his protagonist that under "the different veneers of varying laws, institutions, and civilizations . . . the Old Adam is the same. His nature contains the same admixture of bad and good . . . whether . . . subsumed under an integument which is yellow, black, red, white, coffee, or any combination of fleshly tints" (257). The West Indian poet **Edward Kamau Brathwaite** believes that there is "a shared common humanity. . . . Scholars compartmentalize their concepts of literature into various canons—African, Afro-American, Caribbean, etc. Very few look for commonalities" (1989, 11).

Arguing for universalism (in a general, not just a postcolonial, context), Northrop Frye distinguishes between primary and secondary concerns: primary concerns are shared by all peoples of all times and include the "essential passions of the heart" and the desire to live comfortably with food, shelter, and companionship; secondary concerns include "loyalty to one's place in the class structure, and in short to everything that comes under the heading of ideology" (1990, 21). The anthropologist Bronislaw Malinowski makes a similar point: he contends that there are "cultural universals because there are universal human needs, biological, derived, and integrative. But the actual empirical content of a culture varies with the social context in relation to a given geographical environment" (1944, 448–49).

Another cultural anthropologist, Renato Rosaldo, makes a similar distinction between common human experience and cultural specifics, the domain of anti-universalists. When his wife fell to her death from a treacherous mountain trail while doing fieldwork in the Philippines, he examined his own grief in relation to the natives' and made a telling comparison between anthropology and literature, as he perceives them: "Unlike novelists, anthropologists seemed to ignore the actual experience of mourning and to pay attention just to the rules of mourning" (qtd. in Sass 1986, 54). Rosaldo argues that the *experience* of grieving is human; the *ritual* of grieving is ethnic, national, or regional.

Those who endorse these arguments for human commonality contend further that to deny the concept of universalism in postcolonial literature is to succumb to the reductive view that postcolonial texts cannot appeal to any common element in readers (inside and outside particular cultures), cannot echo or awaken in them any thoughts or feelings of human commonality, cannot alert them to aspects of themselves. "In a way, this is to diminish the worth of postcolonial writings, relegating them to being distinct sociopolitical artifacts that point up cultural and historical specificities; . . . it constitutes a retrogressive step from such acknowledgments of the power of literature wherever it originates to touch on commonalities despite differences in cultures and histories as W. B. Yeats's recognition that there is something ancestral in the *Upanishads*" (Ramraj 1999, 261).

Recent human genome studies have confirmed that the genetic differentiation between people of different "races" *is* minuscule and that there *is* an inherent human commonality. This research guarantees that the debate between essentialism and **constructivism**, universalists and disparatists will be ongoing.

Further Reading: B. Ashcroft, G. Griffiths, and H. Tiffin 1995; 55–82; W. Siemerling and K. Schwenk 1996.

Victor J. Ramraj

Utopian Writing and Science Fiction In order to understand the significance of utopian writing in a postcolonial context, it is first necessary to establish what works belong to it. Although the established genre boundaries are by no means clear-cut, it can be argued that while (e)utopias project a society considerably better than the one against which it is set and while dystopias extrapolate from the imperfect present into an even more wretched future, antiutopias generally call into question the very possibility or even desirability of a utopian society. With the exception of a few sporadic excursions into the eutopian genre (Lora Mountjoy, *Deep Breathing*, 1984; John Elder, *The Hidden Mask*, 1995), a great deal of postcolonial speculative writing is overtly dystopian, depicting scenarios reminiscent of the menacing worlds of Kafka or Beckett. Many novels, however, tend to de-emphasize the finality of their alternative historical hypothesis. Spatially and temporally indeterminate, they seek to interrogate the assumptions underlying dystopian assertions of the future from a postcolonial point of view; instead of revealing symptoms of crisis, they explore social and political causes and envisage cultural alternatives challenging the totalizing attitudes of Western dystopianism. The preoccupation of many writers with defamiliarizing Orwellian notions of utopia as a closed system of manipulative structures beyond human agency or remedy indicates a close alliance between the operations of textual deconstruction and those of cultural decolonization—operations that do not seek to reappropriate the classical utopia of social perfection in a postcolonial context but engage, instead in a kind of a contestatory heterodoxy, an agenda of disparate utopias and the particular projects that they pursue. For all their cultural differences, writers of utopian fiction thus share a common concern, namely, the relocation of the utopian text from a classical to a postcolonial setting and the interrogation and dialectical transformation of the narrative patterns associated with the genre.

More recent writings from countries as diverse as **New Zealand**, Samoa, **Australia**, **Canada**, **South Africa**, India, Ghana, and Nigeria reveal that the thematic and linguistic scope of utopian literature has been widened over the last thirty years to admit perceptions derived from non-Western cultural contexts, to create new plot possibilities, and to increase interpretive plurality. One of the earliest texts is Janet Frame's dystopia *Intensive Care* (1970), which presents a nightmarish portrait of future New Zealand: the country's leading role in social legislation and experiment has turned into unrivaled expertise in the extermination of people considered imperfect in the eyes of the new regime, a global superpower from North America. With its idiosyncratic language and ingenious blend of different literary forms, *Intensive Care* is the first postcolonial novel to stand out against the classical dystopian narrative á la Orwell's *1984* (1949) with its bias on mimetic representation and formal coherence. Another major text of the 1970s addressing the dangers of **globalization** and institution-alized dehumanization is David Ireland's *The Unknown Industrial Prisoner* (1971). Set in the indeterminate future, it depicts a large group of workers in an Australian oil refinery operated by foreign investment. Capturing the sick-ening reality of life in this horrid enclave in a series of disconnected passages and narrative units, the novel's rejection of neocolonial exploitation in the guise of laissez-faire capitalism flames forth in a manner unmatched in ferocity and violence by any other dystopia of the 1970s. Afrikaans writer Karel Schoeman's *Na die geliefde land* (Promised Land, 1972), by contrast, is a rather timid ren-dering of future South Africa after the demise of apartheid that embarrasses the reader with its method of deliberately holding back details about the circum-stances of change.

Intensive Care, *The Unknown Industrial Prisoner*, and *Promised Land* may all be seen as "watershed" novels in the history of utopian fiction from formerly colonized countries or "dependent cultures" (John Hirst). They are marked off against their classical precursors by the elaboration of narrative techniques an-ticipating the more radically open-ended forms of writing of the 1980s and of postmodernism. In the 1980s and 1990s their tentative intervention in the generic specificities of literary utopianism was followed by a downright explosion of forms and figurations aspiring toward a dynamic transformation of the genre in order to render it more receptive to the strategies of cross-cultural exchange. Of particular significance are responses stressing the relevance of regional, **ethnic**, or **feminist** attitudes in the process of creating a different society. Antiutopian novels such as the Canadian Matt Cohen's *The Colours of War* (1977) or the Australian Gerald Murnane's *The Plains* (1982) focus on the relation between utopianism and regionalism and explore as well as confront the belief in a separate regional identity. Their political awareness is what they share with writers such as the Australian Banumbir Wongar (*Walg*, 1983; *Karan*, 1985), the Canadian Charles de Lint (*Svaha*, 1989), and the Samoan Albert Wendt (*Black Rainbow*, 1992), who emphasize the significance of native perceptions in the struggle for an improved society. Culturally more diverse is the response of feminist writers. The lines of demarcation between the confident progressiv-ism of feminist utopianism in the 1970s and its critique voiced in the dystopian projections of Margaret Atwood (*The Handmaid's Tale*, 1985; "Freeforall," 1986), and the Afro-American science fiction writer Octavia Butler (*Adulthood Rites*, 1988; *Parable of the Sower*, 1994) have been blurred by the cultural and topical heterogeneity of utopian issues derived from different backgrounds. The complex writings of Glenda Adams from Australia (*Games of the Strong*, 1982), Sandi Hall from New Zealand (*The Godmothers*, 1982), Nadine Gordimer from South Africa (*A Sport of Nature*, 1986), and Hélène Holden from **Quebec** (*After the Fact*, 1986) no longer espouse **essentialist** notions of female self-empowerment as promoted in many role-reversal utopias of the 1970s; rather, they pursue notions of female solidarity beyond previously constructed traditions of womanhood. The different assumptions underlying them are due to the different sociopolitical contexts and historical circumstances in which they originate as well as to the growing concern with asserting the cross-cultural dimension of the future at stake. In Buchi Emecheta's *The Rape of Shavi* (1983), for instance, the role of women in the shaping of a just society is explored not so much with regard to a predominantly Western ideal of female emancipation but rather with regard to the enrichment that this process receives from the contributions made by women rooted in African cultures.

A more recent phenomenon is the use of **magical realist** techniques in utopian fiction by women writers. Rachel McAlpine (*The Limits of Green*, 1985; *Running Away from Home*, 1987) and Fiona Farrell (*The Skinny Louie Book*, 1992) from New Zealand and Suniti Namjoshi (*The Mothers of Maya Diip*, 1989) and Nalo Hopkinson (*Brown Girl in the Ring*, 1998) from Canada have explored the potential of a narrative form based on the sustained opposition of two ontologically discrete systems of reference and tried to render it more suitable for their own purposes. Their novels are concerned with the creation of a future or alternative world governed by the copresence of the marvelous and the real, the supernatural and the factual, a world in which no one formation or value system can be superimposed upon the other, and patriarchal representations of futurity are replaced by a whole (not necessarily feminist) diversity of incommensurable views and perceptions.

The most radical challenge to received forms of utopian narration is represented by a growing number of writings subverting the cognitive constraints of genre utopian and science fiction by their playful use of widely different literary idioms and patterns. The postmodernist explorations of writers such as Mike Johnson from New Zealand (*Lear: The Shakespeare Company Plays Lear at Babylon*, 1986; *Anti Body Positive*, 1988), Amanda Lohrey (*The Reading Group*, 1988), and Rodney Hall (*Kisses of the Enemy*, 1987) from Australia, Ivan Vladislavic (*Missing Persons*, 1992; *The Folly*, 1993) from South Africa, Timothy Findley (*Headhunter*, 1993) from Canada, Ben Okri (*Astonishing the Gods*, 1995) from Nigeria, and Kojo Laing (*Major Gentl and the Achimota Wars*, 1992) from Ghana can be conceived of as "utopographic metafictions" in the sense that they expose as well as challenge the signifying practices employed to create and sustain the illusion of a closed narrative world. They seek to disrupt the hierarchized relation between reality and fiction enacted in Western utopian writing with its bias toward realism and the epistemological closure to which it ministers: the fictionality self-consciously foregrounded in these novels lays bare the deliberation with which cultural tensions are erased, fragmentations concealed and differences bypassed through the formal device of realist verisimilitude in traditional utopian discourse. In their revisionist project utopographic metafictions are joined by a further group of writings more explicitly concerned with exploring the relation between utopian ideals and the conceptual legacy of the colonial past. Peter Carey's parahistorical novel *The Unusual Life of Tristan Smith* (1994), Ian Wedde's alternatively performed account of New Zealand's past, present, and future in *Symme's Hole* (1986), and Scottish writer Alasdair Gray's mock-historical antiutopia *The History Maker* (1994) resemble each other not only in the radical manner in which they destabilize traditional notions of the past as a set of established truths but also in the ways in which they envision a future open to culturally different inscriptions of the present. The facts of a "commonly shared" past are elbowed out of center stage by a fantastic and often hilarious reassessment of ancient systems of belief and local lore confronting the officially sanctioned records of national and imperial historiography. Amitav Ghosh's near-future dystopia *The Calcutta Chromosome: A Novel of Fevers, Delirium and Discovery* (1996) is peculiar for the manner in which it confronts established modes of knowledge construction in Western science with premodern and native discourses of history, medicine, and theology. Not unlike many other recent productions, it combines the tactics of historiographic metafiction with the speculative freedom of utopian projection in order to fabricate a universe of the miraculous and the numinous, challenging the very nature of reality as we understand it.

The most recent explorations in the genre are significant for their preoccupation with a poetics of cross-cultural exchange that seeks to account for the interaction of codes and attitudes in postcolonial cultures and acknowledges their important function in the process of creating new perceptual possibilities. Australian writer James Cowan's metafictional fantasy *A Mapmaker's Dream* (1996) introduces a beckoning array of culturally divergent utopian ideals and aspirations seen from the point of view of a medieval Venetian monk. Mike Nicol's magical future history *This Day and Age* (1992) evokes a violent portrait of postapartheid South Africa, challenging the tenets both of a nonracial nationalism that sublimates regional differences and of an unquestioned **multiculturalism** that can be misappropriated for the purposes of enforced assimilation rather than for the promulgation of cultural diversity. His preoccupation with getting to the root of the current despair of a loss of history prevailing among many white liberals is what Nicol shares with John Cranna (*Arena*, 1992), who dismantles the widespread belief in a magnificent past as a colonial myth designed to ensure the supremacy of European traditions in New Zealand. The novels of Craig Harrison from New Zealand (*The Quiet Earth*, 1981; *Days of Starlight*, 1988) and Damien Broderick from Australia (*The Dreaming Dragons*, 1980; *The Dark between the Stars*, 1991) represent the most sophisticated attempts at enriching genre science fiction by a sharpened political awareness of the marginalization involved in being a writer from the "periphery." Unequivocally dystopian novels such as Peter Wilhelm's *The Mask of Freedom* (1994) and Edward Lurie's *Jacob with a 'C'* (1993) from South Africa or the New Zealand writer Joan Rosier-Jones' *Mother Tongue* (1996) explore the political anxieties of many whites in the former settler colonies where Western cultural hegemony is challenged by **indigenous peoples** and their rightful claim to power.

Further Reading: N. B. Albinski 1987; A. Weiss 1998.

Ralph Pordzik

V

Vietnam. *See* Francophone Literatures

W

Derek Walcott   There is little doubt that Derek Walcott is the most highly acclaimed and internationally renowned **anglophone** Caribbean poet and playwright of his generation, having received the Nobel Prize in literature in 1992. Frequently described as "the best poet the English language has today," Walcott can claim a rightful place among the major poets of the Western literary tradition from Homer onward, but, more than that, Walcott demands to be read first as a Caribbean poet who has consistently sought to honor his people and their islands.

One of the keys to understanding Walcott's Caribbean aesthetic can be found in his acceptance speech delivered to the Swedish academy. In "The Antilles: Fragments of Epic Memory" (1993) Walcott describes the disparate cultures of the Caribbean region (European, African, Asian, Indian, and American) as the shattered fragments of a broken vase. He declares that Caribbean art must be seen as the product of an act of restoration or remaking in which the object newly made has a power and meaning that were unrecognized in the original. An English-speaking Methodist from the French-speaking Catholic island of St. Lucia, Walcott's poetry and plays respond to the cultural and historical legacies of empire and slavery. With both white and black ancestry, Walcott seeks to answer the conundrum of Caribbeanness in the current era of independence and incipient **neocolonialism**.

To date Walcott has produced fourteen volumes of poetry over a period of about fifty years, from *25 Poems* in 1948 to *Tiepolo's Hound* in 2000. As evidenced in his 1962 collection *In a Green Night*, Walcott's early poetry is characterized by a willingness to imitate and assimilate the voices of a number of Western poets. *In a Green Night* does, though, contain some of Walcott's most arresting short poems. "A Far Cry from Africa" is notable for its vitriolic political tone and its closing expression of the unfathomable division at the heart of the Caribbean psyche. This volume is followed by a number of others—*The*

Castaway (1965), *The Gulf* (1969), *Sea Grapes* (1976), and *The Star Apple Kingdom* (1979)—in which Walcott continues to struggle with the multiple divisions and tensions caused by a history of dispossession and forgetting in the region. His determination to answer that feeling of rootlessness and historylessness is seen in his adoption of the story of Robinson Crusoe as a metaphor for the Caribbean condition (see "The Castaway" [1965], "Crusoe's Journal" [1970] and "Crusoe's Island" [1965], and his essay "The Figure of Crusoe" [1969]). Walcott's concerns in this period also center upon the notions of alienation and exile, which, in turn, necessitate an increased intimacy between the poet and his craft. Shabine, the disaffected narrator of "The Schooner *Flight*," an early poetic odyssey, declares that his poetry will be his gift to the Caribbean people. This dialectic of alienation and identification, movement and stasis is explored further in *The Fortunate Traveller* (1982), *Midsummer* (1984), and *The Arkansas Testament* (1988). The travels and travails of the former and latter volumes frame the moment of stasis contained in the middle volume. *The Bounty* (1997) reveals the inward and outward concerns of his poetry. The first section presents a moving eulogy to his mother, Alix, who back in 1948 provided the money for him to privately publish his first volume. The second section covers European, African, and Caribbean ground in its examination of the transcendent and transient power of **art**.

A brief survey of Walcott's career indicates that his major preoccupations concentrate around questions of language, history, identity, and tradition. These questions are central to Walcott's two long poems, *Another Life* (1973) and *Omeros* (1989), both of which stand alone as major contributions to postcolonial literature. A portrait of the Caribbean artist as a young man, *Another Life* records the elation of the poet waking to the possibility of naming the Caribbean in its own terms. Best read in relation to his essays "What the Twilight Says: An Overture" (1972) and "The Muse of History" (1974), Walcott's poem is autobiographical and historical, individual and communal, and personal and political. In *Another Life*, having assimilated the features of its ancestors, Walcott's Caribbean voice most conclusively emerges. If *Another Life* is a poem of the Caribbean mind, *Omeros* is a poem of the Caribbean body, a poem of the **nation** of the dispossessed. Part fact, fiction, and metafiction, *Omeros* pivots on a formal and thematic comparison between the modern Caribbean and the ancient Aegean. Inviting his readers to see St. Lucia as a modern-day Troy in which a battle is fought to possess the island and a woman, Walcott closes the poem by suggesting that there is no need for the Homeric metaphor. The Caribbean people, whether they are black, white, or brown, ennoble themselves in their daily lives.

In addition to his poetic achievements, Walcott has also made a significant contribution to Caribbean theater. He has written numerous plays (twelve of which have been published in five volumes), and between 1959 and 1976 he was the founder and director of the Trinidad Theatre Workshop. In his plays Walcott has consistently attempted to fuse a classical poetic discipline with the physicality of folk movement and expression. His most recent play, *The Odys-*

sey, provides another revision of the Homeric epic that illustrates the links to be found between his poetic and dramatic agendas.

Part of the generation of Caribbean writers that produced such figures as **V. S. Naipaul, Edward Kamau Brathwaite, Wilson Harris, Sam Selvon**, and **George Lamming**, Walcott is a writer who now works on an international stage. Yet, his work is still characterized by his commitment to the Caribbean. Not afraid to be critical of politicians, tourists, and neocolonial prospectors, Walcott argues that, as a region, the Caribbean will prosper only once its people accept, appropriate, and assimilate the painful legacies of its past. Employing a variety of poetic forms, registers, rhythms, and languages to considerable effect, Derek Walcott is truly "the mulatto of style" (Walcott 1998, 9).

Further Reading: E. Baugh 1978; R. Hanmer 1997; D. Walcott 1998.

Simon Beecroft

Albert Wendt. *See* Pacific Island Literatures

Worlding   Gayatri Chakravorty Spivak coined the term "worlding" to describe the process by which the native's perception of himself or herself and the space that he or she inhabits is translated into the episteme of the Enlightenment by contact with the colonizer who assumes that his worldview is universal and thus supreme. This radical relational reinscription of European and native subjectivities is tracked by Spivak through the correspondence between Captain Geoffrey Birch (an assistant agent of the British governor in India) and the British colonial authorities in 1815. In his letter, Birch describes how, as a result of the recent British expansion of their polticial control over the Simla Hills, he was prompted to set out on a journey through the hills to, as he states: "acquaint the people who they are subject to, for as I suspected they were not properly informed of it and seem only to have heard of our existence from conquering Goorkah and from having seen a few Europeans passing thro' the country" (1985, 254). Prior to this time, the representation of authority and control exercised by a combination of indigenous emperors and kings over the region is described by Spivak as "not taking anyone in as the representation of truth" (252). After this point, however, the implementation of European rule through actions like Birch's is carried out by "effectively and violently sliding one **discourse** under another" so that the European "stranger" becomes taken for granted as "Master," and the native comes to see himself or herself as "other" (254). Soldiers/colonizers like Birch, therefore, engage in "worlding" when they imagine the colonized territory as "uninscribed earth" (253), perceive themselves as "informing" the native subjects of Britain's inscription of its sovereign authority over it, and oblige the native subjects to reflect back to them this construction as "truth."

Further Reading: G. Spivak 1985, 1999.

Jill Didur

Z

Zimbabwean Literature   Considering its much smaller population, the **settler** literature of the former Rhodesia can hold its own with that of its **South African** neighbor. This is mainly due to the work of Doris Lessing (1919–   ), whose early work reflects her maturation in an African landscape. Lessing's *The Grass Is Singing* (1950) and the early portions of her Martha Quest series record the political tensions of the late colonial period.

The white minority in Rhodesia refused to relinquish control after the onset of **decolonization** and in 1965 unilaterally declared independence from Britain, declaring Rhodesia a republic. The black African population, comprising largely the Shona and Ndebele peoples, waged a "Chimurenga," or war of liberation, which resulted in the establishment of the majority-rule state of Zimbabwe in 1980 with Robert Mugabe as prime minister and later president.

Literature by black Africans begins to emerge with the stories and novels of Charles Mungoshi (1947–   ), whose work records the tension between personal ambition and community memory in a clear, elevated language reminiscent of **Chinua Achebe**. A wild card in the Zimbabwean canon is the work of Dambudzo Marechera (1952–1987). Marechera lived a short, but tumultuous, life, and, though active in the resistance to white supremacy, he dissented from the pieties of postindependence nationalism. His writing, as in *Black Sunlight* (1980), is more reminiscent of Western existential and countercultural writers than anything in African literature. Kristine Rungano (1963–   ) writes poetry animated by the tension between her philosophical pacifism and her political commitment to armed struggle.

Tsitsi Dangarembga (1959–   ) is the Zimbabwean novelist most frequently read in a postcolonial context. Her novel *Nervous Conditions* (1987) is a prominent example of postcolonial **feminism**. *Nervous Conditions* is a Zimbabwean variation on the female bildungsroman that recounts the dual struggle of a young Shona woman, Tambudzai, against colonialism and patriarchy. Tambudzai successfully achieves her own identity, but her cousin Nyasha is a victim of excessive Europeanization as well as the arrogance of her father, Babamakuru, almost an allegorical figure for a postcolonial complacency that, in fact, **mimics** colonial patterns of domination. Dangarembga's use of Shona words interspersed with her English narrative shows that she is conscious of African and international readership.

By the late 1990s, discontent with the Mugabe regime was growing, and Zimbabwe seemed set for a period of transition that may well signal a new era in the nation's literature.

Further Reading: P. H. Parekh and S. F. Jagne 1998; F. Veit-Wild and A. Chennells 1999.

Nicholas Birns

Bibliography

'Abd al-Ghani, Mustafa. 1994. *Al-ittijah al-qawmi fi al-riwayya*. Kuwait: 'Alam al-ma'rifa.

Abdoulaye, Mamani. 1972. "Chant negre." In *Poemerides*. Paris: J. P. Oswald.

Abrioux, Cynthia. 1990. "A Study of the Stepfather and the Stranger in the Pakistani Novel *The Bride* by Bapsi Sidhwa." *Commonwealth Essays and Studies* 13:1.

Achebe, Chinua. 1995. "Colonialist Criticism." In *The Post-Colonial Studies Reader*. Ed. Bill Ashcroft, Gareth Griffiths, and Helen Tiffin. London: Routledge. 57–61.

———. 2000. *Home and Exile*. New York: Oxford University Press.

Adam, Ian, and Helen Tiffin, eds. 1991. *Past the Last Post: Theorizing Post-Colonialism and Post-Modernism*. Hemel Hempstead: Harvester Wheatsheaf.

Adé èk ó, Adéléke. 1998. *Proverbs, Textuality, and Nativism in African Literature*. Gainesville: University Press of Florida.

Afshar, Haleh. 1996. *Women and Politics in the Third World*. New York: Routledge.

Afzal-Khan, Fawzia, and Kalpana Seshadri-Crooks, eds. 2000. *Pre-occupation of Post-colonial Studies*. Durham, NC: Duke University Press.

Ahmad, Aijaz. 1987. "Jameson's Rhetoric of Otherness and the 'National Allegory'." *Social Text* 17.

———. 1992. *In Theory: Classes, Nations, Literatures*. London: Verso.

———. 1995. "The Politics of Literary Postcoloniality." *Race and Class* 36.3: 1–20.

Ahmad, Iftikhar, et al., eds. 1999. *World Cultures: A Global Mosaic*. Englewood, NJ: Prentice-Hall.

Ahmed, Leila. 1992. *Women and Gender in Islam*. New Haven, CT: Yale University Press.

Ajayi, J.F.A. 1965. *Christian Missions in Nigeria 1841–1891: The Making of a New Elite*. London: Longmans.

Alarcón, Norma. 1993. *Sexuality of Latinas*. Berkeley, CA: Third Woman Press.

Alatas, S. H. 1977. *The Myth of the Lazy Native: A Study of the Image of the Malays, Filipinos and Javanese from the 16th to the 20th Century and Its Function in the Ideology of Colonial Capitalism*. London: Frank Cass.

Albinski, Nan B. 1987. "A Survey of Australian Utopian and Dystopian Fiction." *Australian Literary Studies* 13: 15–28.

Alden, Patricia, and Louis Tremaine. 1999. *Nuruddin Farah.* New York: Twayne.

Alessandrini, A. C., ed. 1999. *Frantz Fanon: Critical Perspectives.* London and New York: Routledge.

Allen, Chadwick. 2000. "Postcolonial Theory and the Discourse of Treaties." *American Quarterly* 52.1: 59–89.

Allen, Roger 1995. *The Arabic Novel: An Historical and Critical Introduction.* 2d ed. Syracuse: Syracuse University Press.

———. 1998. *The Arabic Literary Heritage.* Cambridge: Cambridge University Press.

Almeida, Irène Assiba d'. 1994. *Francophone African Women Writers: Destroying the Emptiness of Silence.* Gainesville: University Press of Florida.

Amin, Samir. 1989. *Eurocentrism.* New York: Monthly Review Press.

Amireh, Amal, and Lisa Suhair Majaj, eds. 2000. *Going Global: The Transnational Reception of Third World Women Writers.* New York and London: Garland.

Amyuni, Mona Takieddine. 1985. *Tayeb Salih's Season of Migration to the North: A Casebook.* Beirut: American University of Beirut Press.

Anderson, Benedict. 1983 (rev. 1991). *Imagined Communities: Reflections on the Origin and Spread of Nationalism.* London: Verso.

———. 1990. *Language and Power: Exploring Political Cultures in Indonesia.* Ithaca, NY: Cornell University Press.

———. 1998. *The Spectre of Comparisons: Nationalism, Southeast Asia and the World.* London: Verso.

Anderson, Debra. 1995. *Decolonizing the Text: Glissantian Readings in Caribbean and African-American Literatures, Francophone Cultures and Literatures.* New York: Lang.

Ang, Ien. 1985. *Watching Dallas: Soap Opera and the Melodramatic Imagination.* London: Methuen.

Ansell-Pearson, Keith, Benita Parry, and Judith Squires, eds. 1997. *Cultural Readings of Imperialism: Edward Said and the Gravity of History.* New York: St. Martin's.

Anzaldúa, Gloria. 1987. *Borderlands: La Frontera.* San Francisco: Aunt Lute.

Appadurai, Arjun. 1996. *Modernity at Large: Cultural Dimensions of Globalization.* Minneapolis: University of Minnesota Press.

Appadurai, Arjun, and Carol A. Breckenridge. 1995. "Public Modernity in India." In *Consuming Modernity: Public Culture in a South Asian World* Ed. Carol A. Breckenridge. Minneapolis: University of Minnesota Press. 1–20.

Appiah, Anthony Kwame. 1992. *In My Father's House: Africa in the Philosophy of Culture.* New York: Oxford University Press.

Appiah, Anthony Kwame, and Henry Louis Gates Jr., eds. 1999. *Africana: The Encyclopedia of the African and African American Experience.* New York: Basic Civitas Books.

Apter, Emily. 1999. *Continental Drift: From National Characters to Virtual Subjects.* Chicago: University of Chicago Press.

Arnold, A. James. 1981. *Modernism and Negritude: The Poetry and Poetics of Aimé Césaire.* Cambridge: Harvard University Press.

———, ed. 1997. *A History of Literature in the Caribbean.* Vol. 2: *English- and Dutch-Speaking Regions.* Amsterdam and Philadelphia: John Benjamins.

————, ed. 2000. *A History of Literature in the Caribbean. Vol. 3: Cross-Cultural Studies.* Amsterdam and Philadelphia: John Benjamins.

Arnold, Stephen H., ed. 1998. *Critical Perspectives on Mongo Beti.* Boulder, CO: Lynne Rienner.

Arteaga, Alfred. 1997. *Chicano Poetics: Heterotexts and Hybridities.* Cambridge: Cambridge University Press.

————, ed. 1994. *An Other Tongue: Nation and Ethnicity in the Linguistic Borderlands.* Durham, NC: Duke University Press.

Ashcroft, Bill, Gareth Griffiths, and Helen Tiffin. 1989. *The Empire Writes Back: Theory and Practice in Post-Colonial Literatures.* London: Routledge.

————, eds. 1995. *The Post-Colonial Studies Reader.* London and New York: Routledge.

————. 1998. *Key Concepts in Post-Colonial Studies.* London and New York: Routledge.

Attar, Farid ud-din. 1984. *The Conference of the Birds.* Trans. Afkham Darbandi and Dick Davis. New York: Penguin.

Attridge, Derek, and Rosemary Jolly, eds. 1998. *Writing South Africa: Literature, Apartheid, and Democracy, 1970–1995.* Cambridge: Cambridge University Press.

August, Raymond. 1974. "Babeling Beaver Hunts for Home Fire: The Place of Ethnic Literature in Canada Culture." *Canadian Forum* 8: 8–11.

Azodo, Ada Uzoamaka, and Gay Wilentz, eds. 1999. *Emerging Perspectives on Ama Ata Aidoo.* Trenton, NJ: African World Press.

Babeti, Adriana, and Cornel Ungureanu, eds. 1997. *Europa Centrală. Nevroze, dileme, utopii.* Iasi: Polirom.

Bacchetta, Paola. 1999. "When the (Hindu) Nation Exiles Its Queers." *Social Text* 17.4: 141–166.

Badawi, M. M. 1988. *Early Arabic Drama.* Cambridge: Cambridge University Press.

————. 1993. *A Short History of Modern Arabic Literature.* Oxford: Oxford University Press.

Bahri, Deepika, and Mary Vasudeva. 1996. *Between the Lines: South Asians and Post-Coloniality.* Philadelphia: Temple University Press.

Balaz, Joseph P., ed. 1989. *Hoʻomānoa.* Honolulu, HI: Ku Paʻa.

Balutansky, Kathleen M., and Marie-Agnès Sourieau, eds. 1998. *Caribbean Creolization. Reflections on the Cultural Dynamics of Language, Literature, and Identity, Barbados, Jamaica, Trinidad/Tobago.* Gainesville, FL: University Press of Florida.

Bande, Usha. 1988. *The Novels of Anita Desai: A Study in Character and Conflict.* New Delhi: Prestige.

Bandypadhyay, Samik. 1986. "Introduction." *Five Plays.* Calcutta: Seagull. v–xxx.

Baran, Paul A. 1957. *The Political Economy of Growth.* New York: Monthly Review.

Barlow, Tani. 1997. *Formations of Colonial Modernity in East Asia.* Durham, NC: Duke University Press.

Barratt, Harold. 1984. "Metaphor and Symbol in *The Dragon Can't Dance.*" *World Literature Written in English* 23: 405–13.

Barratt Brown, Michael. 1974. *The Economics of Imperialism.* Harmondsworth: Penguin.

Barrett, Michele. 1992. *Destabilizing Theory: Contemporary Feminist Debates.* Stanford, CA: Stanford University Press.

Barthes, Roland. 1978. *Mythologies.* Trans. Annette Lavers. New York: Hill and Wang.

————. 1994. "The Death of the Author." In *Falling into Theory: Conflicting Views on Reading Literature.* Ed. David H. Richter. Boston: Bedford Books. 222–26.

Basadre, Jorge. 1971. Introduction to *Seven Interpretative Essays of Peruvian Reality.*

By José Carlos Mariátegui. Trans. Marjory Urquidi. Austin: University of Texas Press.

Basu, Amrita. 1998. *Community Conflicts and the State in India*. New York: Oxford University Press.

Baugh, Edward. 1978. *Derek Walcott, Memory as Vision: Another Life*. London: Longman.

Beck, Ulrich. 1992. *Risk Society: Towards a New Modernity*. London: Sage.

Becker, Marc. 1993. *Mariátegui and Latin American Marxist Theory*. Athens: Ohio University Center for International Studies.

Beer, George Lewis. 1923. *African Questions at the Paris Peace Conference*. New York: Macmillan.

Beidelman, T. O. 1982. *Colonial Evangelism*. Bloomington: Indiana University Press.

Beier, Ulli, ed. 1980. *Voices of Independence: New Black Writing from Papua New Guinea*. New York: St. Martin's.

Benítez-Rojo, Antonio. 1996. *The Repeating Island. The Caribbean and the Postmodern Perspective*. Durham, NC, and London: Duke University Press.

———. 1998. "Three Words toward Creolization." In *Caribbean Creolization. Reflections on the Cultural Dynamics of Language, Literature, and Identity, Barbados, Jamiaca, Trinidad/Tobago*. Ed. Kathleen M. Balutansky and Marie-Agnès Sourieau. Gainesville, FL: University Press of Florida. 53–61.

Bennett, Bruce, and Jennifer Strauss, eds. 1998. *The Oxford Literary History of Australia*. Melbourne: Oxford University Press.

Benson, Eugene, and L. W. Conolly, eds. 1994. *Encyclopedia of Post-Colonial Literatures in English*. London and New York: Routledge.

Berrian, Albert H., and Richard A. Long, eds. 1967. *Negritude: Essays and Studies*. Hampton, VA: Hampton University Press.

Betts, Raymond F. 1998. *Decolonization*. London: Routledge.

Beverly, John. 1991. "Through All Things Modern: Second Thoughts on Testimonio." *Boundary 2* 18.2: 1–21.

Bhabha, Homi. 1984. "Representation and the Colonial Text: A Critical Exploration of Some Forms of Mimeticism." *The Theory of Reading*. Ed. Frank Gloversmith. Brighton: Harvester Press.

———. 1985. "Of Mimicry and Man: The Ambivalence of Colonial Discourse." *October* 28: 125–33.

———. 1986. "Foreword: Remembering Fanon." In *Black Skin, White Masks*. By Frantz Fanon. London: Pluto Press.

———. 1989. "The Commitment to Theory." In *Questions of Third Cinema*. Ed. James Pines and Paul Willemen. London: British Film Institute. 111–132.

———. 1990a. "DissemiNation: Time, Narrative and the Margins of the Modern Nation." In *Nation and Narration*. Ed. Homi K. Bhabha. London: Routledge. 291–322.

———. 1990b. *Nation and Narration*. London: Routledge.

———. 1990c. "The Other Question: Difference, Discrimination, and the Discourse of Colonialism." In *Out There: Marginalization and Contemporary Culture*. Ed. Russell Ferguson et al. Cambridge: New Museum of Contemporary Art and Massachusetts Institute of Technology. 71–87.

———. 1994. *The Location of Culture*. London: Routledge.

———. 1997. "Minority Culture and Creative Anxiety." Keynote at the *Re-Inventing Britain Conference*. http://old.britcoun.org/studies/stdshb1.htm

Bhadra, Gautam, Gyan Prakash, and Susie Tharu, eds. 1999. *Subaltern Studies X*. Delhi: Oxford University Press.

Bickerton, Derek. 1981. *Roots of Language*. Ann Arbor, MI: Karoma Publishers.

Birbalsingh, Frank, ed. 1996. *Frontiers of Caribbean Literature in English*. New York: St. Martin's.

Birkle, Carmen. 1996. *Women's Stories of the Looking Glass: Autobiographical Reflections and Self-Representations in the Poetry of Sylvia Plath, Adrienne Rich, and Audre Lorde*. München: Wilhelm Fink Verlag.

Bissoondath, Neil. 1994. *Selling Illusions. The Cult of Multiculturalism in Canada*. Toronto: Penguin.

Bivona, Daniel. 1998. *British Imperial Literature, 1870–1940: Writing and the Administration of Empire*. Cambridge: Cambridge University Press.

Bjornson, Richard. 1991. *The African Quest for Freedom and Identity*. Bloomington: Indiana University Press.

Blaut, J. M. 1992. *The Colonizer's Model of the World: Geographical Diffusionism and Eurocentric History*. New York: The Guilford Press.

Bloom, Harold, ed. 1998. *Jamaica Kincaid*. Philadelphia: Chelsea House.

Bongie, Chris. 1998. *Islands and Exiles: The Creole Identities of Post/colonial Literature*. Stanford, CA: Stanford University Press.

Bonn, Moritz Julius. 1948. "Imperialism." In *Encyclopedia of the Social Sciences*. Ed. Edwin Seligman. Vol. 7. [1932.] New York: Macmillan. 536–545.

Booker, Keith, ed. 1999. *Critical Essays on Salman Rushdie*. New York : G. K. Hall.

Brathwaite, Edward Kamau. 1971. *The Development of Creole Society in Jamaica, 1770–1820*. Oxford: Clarendon Press.

———. 1974. *Contradictory Omens: Cultural Diversity and Integration in the Caribbean*. Mona, Jamaica: Savacon Publications.

———. 1984. *History of the Voice: The Development of Nation-Language in Anglophone Caribbean Poetry*. London: New Beacon Books.

———. 1989. "History in E. K. Brathwaite and Derek Walcott: Panel Discussion." *The Common Wealth of Letters Newsletter (Yale)* 1.1: 3–14.

Breckenridge, Carol A., ed. 1995. *Consuming Modernity: Public Culture in South Asia*. Minneapolis: University of Minnesota Press.

Breitman, George, ed. 1965. *Malcolm X Speaks*. New York: Grove.

Brennan, Timothy. 1989. *Salman Rushdie and the Third World: Myths of the Nation*. New York: St. Martin's.

———. 1990. "The National Longing for Form." In *Nation and Narration*. Ed. Homi Bhabha. London: Routledge. 44–70.

———. 1997. *At Home in the World: Cosmopolitanism Now*. Cambridge: Harvard University Press.

Breton, André. 1971. "Un grande poère noir." Preface to Aimé Césaire's *Cahier d'un retour au pays natal*, 3rd ed. Paris: Présence Africaine.

Brewer, Anthony. 1980. *Marxist Theories of Imperialism: A Critical Survey*. London: Routledge and Kegan Paul.

Brinker-Gabler, Gisela, ed. 1995. *Encountering the Other(s): Studies in Literature, History and Culture*. Albany: SUNY Press.

Briton, Celia M. 1999. *Edouard Glissant and Postcolonial Theory: Strategies of Language and Resistance*. Charlottesville and London: University Press of Virginia.

Brown, Stewart, ed. 1995. *The Art of Kamau Brathwaite*. Bridgend, Wales: Seren.

Brydon, Diana, ed. 1995. *Testing the Limits: Postcolonial Theories and Canadian Literatures*. Special issue of *Essays on Canadian Writing* 56.

———. 2000. *Postcolonialism: Critical Concepts in Literary and Cultural Studies*. New York and London: Routledge.

Buck, David D. 1999. "Was It Pluck or Luck That Made the West Grow Rich?" *Journal of World History* 10, 2: 413–430.

Bunch, Charlotte. 1987. *Passionate Politics: Feminist Theory in Action*. New York: St. Martin's.

Burke, Peter. 1997. *Varieties of Cultural History*. Ithaca, NY: Cornell University Press.

Busby, Margaret, ed. 1993. *Daughters of Africa: An International Anthology of Words and Writings by Women of African Descent from the Ancient Egyptian to the Present*. London: Vintage.

Butalia, Urvashi, and Ritu Menon. 1998. *The Other Side of Silence*. New Delhi: Penguin.

Butler, Judith. 1990. *Gender Trouble: Feminism and the Subversion of Idenity*. New York: Routledge.

Cabral, Amilcar. 1969. *Revolution in Guinea: Selected Texts*. Trans. and ed. Richard Handyside. New York: Monthly Review Press.

———. 1979. *Unity and Struggle*. New York: Monthly Review Press.

Caldeira, Teresa Pires de Rio. 1990. "Women, Daily Life, and Politics." In *Women and Social Change in Latin America*. Ed. Elizabeth Jelin. London: Zed Books.

Cantalupo, Charles, ed. 1995. *The World of Ngũgĩ wa Thiong'o*. Trenton, NJ: Africa World Press.

Carby, Hazel. 1995. *Oil on the Waters* [sound recording]: *The Back Diaspora: Panel Discussions and Readings Exploring the African Diaspora through the Eyes of its Artists*. Washington DC: Library of Congress Archive of Recorded Poetry and Literature.

———. 1997. " 'White Woman, Listen!': Black Feminism and the Boundaries of Sisterhood." In *Black British Feminism: A Reader*. Ed. Heidi Safia Mirza. London: Routledge.

Carmichael, Stokely. 1969a. *Black Power*. Harmondsworth, England: Penguin.

———. 1969b. "Pan-Africanism—Land and Power." *The Black Scholar* 1.1: 36–43.

———. 1971. *Stokely Speaks: Black Power Back to Pan-Africanism*. New York: Vintage.

Carmichael, Stokely, and Charles V. Hamilton. 1967. *Black Power: The Politics of Liberation in America*. New York: Vintage-Random.

Cartey, Wilfred, and Martin Kilson, eds. 1970. *The Africa Reader: Independent Africa*. New York: Vintage-Random.

Casper, Leonard T. 1991. *In Burning Ambush: Essays 1985–90*. Manila: New Day.

Certeau, Míchel de. 1998. *The Capture of Speech and Other Political Writings*. Edited and with an introduction by Luce Giard; trans. Tom Conley. Minneapolis: University of Minnesota Press.

Césaire, Aimé. 1972. *Discourse on Colonialism*. New York: Monthly Review Press.

Chabal, Patrick, Moema Parente Augel, David Brookshaw, Ana Mafalda Leite, and Caroline Shaw, eds. 1996. *Postcolonial Lusophone Africa Literature*. London: Hurst.

Chakrabarty, Dipesh. 2000. *Provincializing Europe: Postcolonial Thought and Historical Difference*. Princeton, NJ: Princeton University Press.

Chanady, Amaryll. 1985. *Magical Realism and the Fantastic: Resolved versus Unresolved Antimony*. New York: Garland.

Charef, Mehdi. 1983. *Le Thé au harem d'Archi Ahmed*. Paris: Mercure de France.

"Charter of the Organization of African Unity." 1994. In *Pan-Africanism: The Idea and Movement, 1776–1991*, 2nd ed. Ed. P. Olisanwuche Esedebe. Washington, DC: Howard University Press. 249–57.

Chasteen, John. 1996. *The Lettered City*. Durham, NC: Duke University Press.

Chatterjee, Partha. 1986. *Nationalist Thought and the Colonial World: A Derivative Discourse*. Minneapolis: University of Minnesota Press.

Chaudhuri, Rosinka. 2000. *"That Which They Found Good and Like Best": Orientalist Themes, English Verse and Identity Formation in Nineteenth Century India*. Calcutta: Seagull Books.

Chevannes, Barry. 1994. *Rastafari: Roots and Ideology*. Syracuse, NY: Syracuse University Press.

Chew, Sing C., and Robert A. Denemark. 1996. *The Underdevelopment of Development: Essays in Honor of Andre Gunder Frank*. Thousand Oaks, CA: Sage.

Chideya, Farai. 1995. *Don't Believe the Hype: Fighting Cultural Misinformation about African-Americans*. New York: Plume.

Chilcote, R. H. 1991. *Amílcar Cabral's Revolutionary Theory and Practice: A Critical Guide*. Boulder, CO: Lynne Rienner.

Chinweizu, Onwucheka Jemie, and Ihechukwu Madubuike. 1983. *Toward the Decolonization of African Literature*. Washington, DC: Howard University Press.

Chow, Rey. 1991. *Woman and Chinese Modernity*. Minneapolis: University of Minnesota Press.

———. 1994. "Where Have All the Natives Gone?" In *Displacements*. Ed. Angelika Bammer. Bloomington: Indiana University Press. 128–151.

———. 1996. "The Dream of a Butterfly." In *Human, All Too Human*. Ed. Diana Fuss. New York: Routledge. 45–67.

Clarke, John Henrik. 1977. "The Development in Pan-Africanist Ideas in the Americas and in Africa before 1900." *FESTAC '77 Colloquium*. Lagos: International Secretariat.

Clarke, John Henrik, and Amy Jacques Garvey, eds. 1974. *Marcus Garvey and the Vision of Africa*. New York: Vintage-Random.

Clifford, James, and George E. Marcus, eds. 1986. *Writing Culture: The Poetics of Politics and Ethnography*. Berkeley: University of California Press.

Cohen, Anthony P. 1994. *Self Consciousness: An Alternative Anthropology of Identity*. London: Routledge.

Cohen, Robin. 1997. *Global Diasporas: An Introduction*. London: UCL Press.

Colin, Legum. 1976. *Pan-Africanism: A Short Political Guide*. Westport, CT: Greenwood.

Collet, Anne, Lars Jensen, and Anna Rutherford, eds. 1997. *Teaching Post-Colonialism and Post-Colonial Literatures*. Aarhus and Oxford: Aarhus University Press.

Conlon, Frank. 1995. "Dining Out in Bombay." In *Consuming Modernity: Public Culture in South Asia*. Ed. Carol A. Breckenridge. Minneapolis: University of Minnesota Press. 90–127.

Connell, Liam. 1998. "Discarding Magic Realism: Modernity, Anthropology and Critical Practice." *ARIEL* 29.2: 95–110.

Cook, David, and Michael Okenimkpe. 1997. *Ngũgĩ wa Thiong'o: An Exploration of His Writings*. 2d ed. Oxford: James Currey.

Coulson, Anthony, ed. 1997. *Exiles and Migrants: Crossing Thresholds in European Culture and Society*. Brighton: Sussex Academic.

Cowasjee, Saros. 1977. *So Many Freedoms: A Study of the Major Fiction of Mulk Raj Anand*. Delhi: Oxford University Press.

Craveirinha, José. 1993. "Poetry Is Playing with Words." In *Echoes of the Sunbird: An Anthology of Contemporary African Poetry*. Ed. Don Burness. Athens, OH: Ohio University Press, African Series, No. 62. 58–59,

Crenshaw, Kimberlé, Neil Gotanda, Gary Peller, and Kendall Thomas, eds. 1995. *Critical Race Theory: The Key Writings That Formed a Movement*. New York: The New Press.

Croly, David. 1864. *Miscegenation: The Theory of the Blending of the Races, Applied to the American White Man and Negro*. New York: H. Dexter, Hamilton.

Crow, Brian. 1996. *An Introduction to Post-Colonial Theatre*. Cambridge: Cambridge University Press.

Cudjoe, Selwyn. 1980. *Resistance and Caribbean Literature*. Athens: Ohio University Press.

———. 1989. "Jamaica Kincaid and the Modernist Project: An Interview." *Callaloo* 12: 396–411.

Cvetkovich, Ann, and Douglas Kellner, eds. 1997. *Articulating the Global and the Local: Globalization and Cultural Studies*. Boulder, CO: Westview.

D'Almeida, Irène Assiba. 1994. *Francophone African Women Writers: Destroying the Emptiness of Silence*. Gainesville: Florida University Press.

Das, Sisir Kumar. 1991, 1995. *A History of Indian Literature*. Vol. 8: *1800–1910: Western Impact, Indian Response*. Vol. 9: *1911–1956: Struggle for Freedom: Triumph and Tragedy*. New Delhi. Sahitya Akademi [National Academy of Letters].

Dash, J. Michael. 1988. *The Other America: Caribbean Literature in a New World Context*. Charlottesville: University Press of Virginia.

———. 1995. *Edouard Glissant*. New York: Cambridge University Press.

Dash, Julie, dir. and prod. 1992. *Daughters of the Dust*. 113 min. film.

Davidson, Basil. 1992. *The Black Man's Burden: Africa and the Curse of the Nation-State*. London: James Currey.

Davies, Meryl Wyn, Ashis Nandy, and Zianddin Sardar, eds. 1993. *Barbaric Others: A Manifesto on Western Racism*. Boulder, CO: Pluto Press.

de Certeau, Michel. 1998. *The Practices of Everyday Life*. Vol. 2. Minneapolis: University of Minnesota Press.

Delany, Martin R. 1966. "Official Report of the Niger Valley Exploration Party" (1861). In *Negro Social and Political Thought 1850–1920: Representative Texts*. Ed. H. Brotz. New York: Basic Books. 101–107.

de Lauretis, Teresa. 1993. "Upping the Anti [*sic*] in Feminist Theory." In *The Cultural Studies Reader*. Ed. Simon During. New York: Routledge. 74–89.

Deleuze, Gilles. 1988. *Foucault*. Trans. Seán Hand. Minneapolis: University of Minnesota Press.

De Mel, Neloufer. 1995. *Essays on Sri Lankan Poetry in English*. Colombo, Sri Lanka: English Association of Sri Lanka.

Denzin, Norman K. 1992. *Symbolic Interactionism and Cultural Studies: The Politics of Interpretation*. Oxford: Blackwell.

Derrida, Jacques. 1976. *Of Grammatology*. Baltimore: Johns Hopkins University Press.

———. 1978. "Violence and Metaphysics." In *Writing and Difference*. Trans. Alan Bass. Chicago: University of Chicago Press. 79–153.

DeYoung, Terri. 1998. *Placing the Poet: Badr Shakir al-Sayyab and Postcolonial Iraq.* Albany: SUNY Press.

Dhairyam, Sagri. 1992. " 'Artifacts for Survival': Remapping the Contours of Poetry with Audre Lorde." *Feminist Studies* 18.2: 229–56.

Dhareshwar, Vivek, P. Sudhir, and Tejaswini Niranjana. 1993. *Interrogating Modernity: Culture and Colonialism in India.* Calcutta: Seagull.

Dhawan, R. K., ed. 1989. *The Fiction of Anita Desai.* New Delhi: Bahri.

———. 1992. *The Novels of Mulk Raj Anand.* New York: Prestige.

Diawara, Manthia, ed. 1991. "V. Y. Mudimbe: A Special Section." *Callaloo: A Journal of African-American and African Arts and Letters* 14.4: 929–1035.

Dickason, Olive Patricia. 1992. *Canada's First Nations: A History of Founding Peoples from Earliest Times.* Toronto, Oxford, and New York: Oxford University Press.

Didur, Jill. 1997. "Fragments of Imagination: Re-thinking the Literary in Historiography through Narratives of India's Partition." On-line journal *Jouvert* http://152.1.96.5/jouvert/v1:2/Didur.htm

Dingwaney, Anuradha, ed. 1995. *Between Languages and Cultures: Translation and Cross-Cultural Texts.* Pittsburgh: University of Pittsburgh Press.

Dirlik, Arif. 1997. *The Postcolonial Aura.* Boulder, CO: Westview.

Docherty, Thomas, ed. 1993. *Postmodernism: A Reader.* London: Harvester.

Donnell, Alison, and Sarah Lawson Welsh, eds. 1996. *The Routledge Reader in Caribbean Literature.* New York: Routledge.

Du Bois, W.E.B. 1947. *The World and Africa: An Inquiry into the Part Which Africa Has Played in World History.* New York: Viking.

———. 1968a. *The Autobiography of W.E.B. Du Bois: A Soliloquy on Viewing My Life from the Last Decade of Its First Century.* New York: International, 1968.

———. 1968b. *Dusk of Dawn: An Essay toward an Autobiography of a Race Concept.* New York: Schocken.

———. 1969. "The Riddle of the Sphinx." In *Darkwater: Voices from Within the Veil.* [1921]. Millwood, NY: Kraus-Thomson. 53–55.

Duncan, Erika. 1999. "A Portrait of Meena Alexander." *World Literature Today* 73.1: 23–28.

During, Simon. 1998. "Postcolonialism and Globalisation: A Dialectical Relation After All?" *Postcolonial Studies* 1.1: 31–47.

Durix, Jean-Pierre. 1998. *Mimesis, Genres and Post-Colonial Discourse: Deconstructing Magic Realism.* New York: St. Martin's.

Eagleton, Terry. 1994. "Goodbye to Enlightenment." *Guardian Weekly* 6 (March): 28.

Eagleton, Terry, Fredric Jameson, Edward W. Said, and Seamus Deane. 1990. *Nationalism, Colonialism, and Literature.* Minneapolis: University of Minnesota Press.

Elam, Harry J., and Alice Rayner. 1998. "Between Story and Spectacle in *Venus* by Suzan-Lori Parks." In *Staging Resistance: Essays on Political Theater.* Ed. Jeanne Colleran and Jenny S. Spence. Ann Arbor: University of Michigan Press. 283–300.

El-Enany, Rasheed. 1993. *Naguib Mahfouz: The Pursuit of Meaning.* London: Routledge.

Emenyonu, Ernest. 1994. "Literatures in Indigenous Nigerian Languages." In *The Gong and the Flute: African Literary Development and Celebration.* Ed. Kalu Ogbaa. Westport, CT: Greenwood Press. 89–103.

Engelke, Matthew. 1998. "Thinking about Nativism in Chenjerai Hove's Work." *Research in African Literatures* 29.2: 23–43.

Erickson, John D. 1993. "Veiled Woman and Veiled Narrative in Tahar ben Jelloun's *The Sand Child.*" *Boundary 2* 20.1: 47–64.

Eschle, Catherine. 2000. *Democracy, Social Movements, and Feminism.* Boulder, CO: Westview.

Esedebe, P. Olisanwuche. 1994. *Pan-Africanism: The Idea and Movement, 1776–1991.* 2d ed. Washington, DC: Howard University Press.

Ewen, Alexander, ed. 1994. *Voice of Indigenous Peoples: Native People Address the United Nations.* Santa Fe, NM: Clear Light.

Eze, Emmanuel Chukwudi, ed. 1997. *Postcolonial African Philosophy: A Critical Reader.* Cambridge, MA, and Oxford: Blackwell.

Fanon, Frantz. 1965 (c. 1963). *The Wretched of the Earth.* Trans. Constance Farrington. New York: Grove.

———. 1967. *Black Skin, White Masks.* Trans. Charles Lam Markmann. New York: Grove.

———. 1980. *A Dying Colonialism.* Trans. Haakon Chevalier. London: Writers and Readers.

Farred, Grant, ed. 1996. *Rethinking C.L.R. James.* Oxford: Blackwell.

Ferguson, Moira. 1994. "A Lot of Memory: An Interview with Jamaica Kincaid." *Kenyon Review* 16: 163–88.

Feuerwerker, Yi-Tsi Mei. 1998. *Ideology, Power, Text: Self-Representation and the Peasant "Other" in Modern Chinese Literature."* Stanford, CA: Stanford University Press.

Focus on Maryse Condé. 1993. Special issue of *World Literature Today* 67.4: 693–768.

Forgacs, D., ed. 1988. *An Antonio Gramsci Reader: Selected Writings, 1916–1935.* London: Lawrence and Wishart; New York: Schocken.

Foucault, Michel. 1972. *The Archaeology of Knowledge.* Trans. A. M. Sheridan Smith. New York: Pantheon.

———. 1981. *The History of Sexuality. Vol. 1: An Introduction.* Trans. Robert Hurley. Harmondsworth: Penguin.

———. 1986. "What Is an Author?" In *Critical Theory since 1965.* Ed. Hazard Adams and Leroy Searle. Tallahassee: Florida State University Press. 138–48.

———. 1988. "Power and Sex." In *Politics, Philosophy, Culture: Interviews and Other Writings, 1977–84.* Trans. David J. Parent. Ed. Lawrence D. Kritzman. New York: Routledge. 110–24.

———. 1991. "Governmentality." In *The Foucault Effect: Studies in Governmentality.* Ed. Graham Burchell, Colin Gordon, and Peter Miller. Chicago: University of Chicago Press. 87–104.

Fowlkes, Diane L. 1997. "Moving from Feminist Identity Politics to Coalition Politics through a Feminist Materialist Standpoint of Intersubjectivity in Gloria Anzaldúa's *Borderlands/La Frontera: The New Mestiza.*" *Hypatia* 12.2: 105–24.

Fox, James R. 1992. *Dictionary of International and Comparative Law.* Dobbs Ferry, NY: Oceana.

Fraser, Nancy, and Linda Gordon, eds. 1994. *Critical Politics: From the Personal to the Global.* Melbourne: Monash University Press.

Fraser, Robert. 1980. *The Novels of Ayi Kwei Armah: A Study in Polemical Fiction.* London: Heinemann.

Frazer, Robert, ed. 1994 (1890). "Introduction." In *The Golden Bough.* By James Frazer. London: Oxford University Press. i–xlii.

Freire, Paulo. 1997a. *The Paulo Freire Reader*. Ed. and intro. by Ana Maria Araújo Freire and Donaldo Macedo. New York: Continuum.

———. 1997b. *Pedagogy of the Oppressed*. New, rev. 20th anniversary ed. Trans. Myra Bergman Ramos. New York: Continuum.

Frutkin, Susan. 1973. *Aimé Césaire: Black between Worlds*. Miami, FL: University of Miami Press.

Frye, Northrop. 1990. "Literary and Linguistic Scholarship in a Postliterate World." In *Myth and Metaphor: Selected Essays 1974–1988*. Ed. Robert Denham. Charlottesville: University of Virginia Press. 18–27.

Gadjigo, Samba, et al., eds. 1993. *Ousmane Sembène: Dialogues with Critics and Writers*. Amherst: University of Massachusetts Press.

Gafaiti, Hafid. 1997. "Between God and the President: Literature and Censorship in North Africa." *diacritics* 27.2: 59–84.

Gainor, J. Ellen, ed. 1995. *Imperialism and Theatre: Essays on World Theatre, Drama, and Performance*. London: Routledge.

Gandhi, Leela. 1998. *Postcolonial Theory: A Critical Introduction*. New York: Columbia University Press.

García Canclini, Néstor. 1989/1995. *Hybrid Cultures. Strategies for Entering and Leaving Modernity*. Minneapolis and London: University of Minnesota Press.

Geertz, Clifford. 1973. *The Interpretation of Cultures: Selected Essays*. New York: Basic Books.

———. 1988. *Works and Lives: The Anthropologist as Author*. Stanford, CA: Stanford University Press.

Geiss, Immanuel. 1974. *The Pan-African Movement: A History of Pan-Africanism in America, Europe and Africa*. Trans. A. Keep. New York: Africana.

Genette, Gerard. 1988. *Narrative Discourse Revisited*. Trans. Jane E. Lewin. Ithaca, NY: Cornell University Press.

Gérard, Albert. 1971. *Four African Literatures: Xhosa, Sotho, Zulu, Amharic*. Berkeley: University of California Press.

Ghosh, Bishnupriya, and Brinda Bose, eds. 1997. *Interventions: Feminist Dialogues on Third World Women's Literature and Film*. New York: Garland.

Gibbs, James, ed. 1980. *Critical Perspectives on Wole Soyinka*. Washington, DC: Three Continents.

Gibbs, James, Ketu H. Katrak, and Henry Louis Gates Jr. 1986. *Wole Soyinka: A Bibliography of Primary and Secondary Sources*. Westport, CT: Greenwood.

Giddens, Anthony. 1990. *The Consequences of Modernity*. Stanford, CA: Stanford University Press.

Gikandi, Simon. 1991. *Reading Chinua Achebe: Language and Ideology in Fiction*. Portsmouth, NH: Heinemann.

———. 1992. *Writing in Limbo: Modernism and Caribbean Literature*. Ithaca: Cornell University Press.

Gilbert, Helen, and Joanne Tompkins. 1996. *Postcolonial Drama: Theory, Practice and Politics*. London: Routledge.

Gilroy, Paul. 1987. *There Ain't No Black in the Union Jack: The Cultural Politics of Race and Nation*. Chicago: University of Chicago Press.

———. 1993. *The Black Atlantic: Modernity and Double Consciousness*. Cambridge: Harvard University Press.

Glazer, Nathan, and Daniel P. Moynihan, eds. 1975. *Ethnicity. Theory and Experience.* Cambridge: Harvard University Press.

Glissant, Edouard. 1989. *Caribbean Discourse: Selected Essays.* Trans. Michael J. Dash. Charlottesville: University Press of Virginia.

———. 1997. *Traité du Tout-Monde.* Paris: Gallimard.

———. 1997. *Poétique de la Relation.* Paris: Gallimard.

Gomes, Aldónio Gomes, and Fernanda Cavacas. 1997. *Dicionário de Autores de Literaturas Africanas de Língua Portuguesa.* Lisboa: Editorial Caminho.

Goodison, Lorna. "Not Exile, but Making a Life." 1999. In *Defining Ourselves: Black Writers in the 90s.* Ed. E. Nunez. New York: Peter Lang.

Goonetilleke, D.C.R.A. 1998. *Salman Rushdie.* London: Macmillan.

Gordon, Avery F., and Christopher Newfield, eds. 1996. *Mapping Multiculturalism.* Minneapolis and London: University of Minnesota Press.

Gordon, L. R., T. D. Sharpley-Whiting, and R. T. White, eds. 1996. *Fanon: A Critical Reader.* Oxford, U.K., and Cambridge, MA: Blackwell.

Gramsci, Antonio. 1971a. "Americanism and Fordism." In *Selections from the Prison Notebooks.* Ed. and trans. Quintin Hoare and Geoffrey Nowell Smith. New York: International. 277–318.

———. 1971b. "Notes on Italian History." In *Selections From the Prison Notebooks.* Ed. and trans. Quintin Hoare and Geoffrey Nowell Smith. New York: International. 52.

———. 1999. *Classics in Politics: Antonio Gramsci.* (CD-ROM). London: Elecbook (eb 0006, ISBN 1 901843 05X). URL: http://www.elecbook.com/gramsci.htm.

Green, Mary Jean, et al., eds. 1996. *Postcolonial Subjects: Francophone Women Writers.* Minneapolis: University of Minnesota Press.

Greenblatt, Stephen. 1989. "Towards a Poetics of Culture." In *The New Historicism.* Ed. H. A. Veeser. New York: Routledge. 1–14.

———. 1990. *Learning to Curse: Essays in Early Modern Culture.* New York: Routledge.

Gregory, Derek. 1994. *Geographical Imaginations.* Cambridge, MA: Blackwell.

Grewal, Inderpal, and Caren Kaplan. 1994. *Scattered Hegemonies: Postmodernity and Transnational Feminist Practices.* Minneapolis: University of Minnesota Press.

Griffin, Keith. 1973. "Underdevelopment in History." In *The Political Economy of Development and Underdevelopment.* Ed. Charles K. Wilber. New York: Random House. 77–90.

Griggs, Sutton Elbert. 1969. *Imperium in Imperio.* 1889. Miami, FL: Mnemosyne.

Grimshaw, Anne, ed. 1992. *The C.L.R. James Reader.* Oxford: Blackwell.

Group for the Study of Composite Cultures. 1996. *Plural Worlds, Multiple Selves: Ashis Nandy and the Post-Columbian Future.* Los Angeles: University of California Press.

Guha, Ranajit, ed. 1982–1989. *Subaltern Studies I-VI.* Delhi: Oxford University Press.

Guha, Ranajit, and Gayatri Chakravarty Spivak, eds. 1988. *Selected Subaltern Studies.* New York: Oxford University Press.

Gunn, Giles, ed. 2001. "Special Topic: Globalizing Literary Studies." *PMLA* 16.1: 9–197.

Gutierrez, Gustavo. 1973 (1974). *A Theology of Liberation.* Maryknoll, NY: Orbis; London: SCM.

Habermas, Jürgen. 1981. *Knowledge and Human Interests.* London: Heinemann.

Hadjor, Kofi Buenor. 1992. *Dictionary of Third World Terms*. London: I. B. Tauris.

Hall, Stuart. 1980. "Cultural Studies: Two Paradigms." *Media, Culture and Society* 2: 57–72.

———. 1990. *The Hard Road to Renewal*. London: Verso.

———. 1997. "The Question of Cultural Identity." In *Modernity: Introduction to Modern Societies*. Ed. Stuart Hall, David Held, Don Hubert, and Kenneth Thompson. Malden, MA: Blackwell. 273–325.

Halpe, Ashley. 1976. "Editorial." *Navasilu* 1:1. (Journal of the English Association of Sri Lanka in Colombo.)

Halperin, David. 1995. *Saint Foucault: Towards a Gay Hagiography*. New York: Oxford University Press.

Hamilton, Russell. 1993. "Portuguese Language Literature." In *A History of Twentieth-century African Literatures*. Ed. Oyekan Owomoyela. Lincoln, NE and London: University of Nebraska Press. 240–84.

———. 1995. "The Audacious Young Poets of Angola and Mozambique." *Research in African Literatures* 26.1: 85–96.

Handyside, Richard, ed. 1970. *Revolution in Guinea: Selected Texts*. New York: Monthly Review Press.

Hanmer, Robert. 1997. *Epic of the Dispossessed: Derek Walcott's Omeros*. Columbia: University of Missouri Press.

Hannerz, Ulf. 1992. *Cultural Complexity. Studies in the Social Organization of Meaning*. New York: Columbia University Press.

———. 1996. *Transnational Connections*. London and New York: Routledge.

Harasym, Sarah, ed. 1990. *The Post-Colonial Critic: Interviews, Strategies, Dialogues*. London: Routledge.

Hardt, Michael, and Antonio Negri. 2000. *Empire*. Cambridge: Harvard University Press.

Hargreaves, Alec. 1989. "Beur Fiction: Voices from the Immigrant Community in France." *The French Review* 62.4: 661–68.

———. 1990a. "In Search of a Third Way: Beur Writers between France and North Africa." *New Comparison* (Autumn): 72–83.

———. 1990b. "Language and Identity in Beur Culture." *French Cultural Studies* 1: 47–58.

Harlow, Barbara. 1987. *Resistance Literature*. New York: Methuen.

Harlow, Barbara, and Mia Carter, eds. 1999. *Imperialism and Orientalism: A Documentary Sourcebook*. Malden, MA: Blackwell.

Harvey, David. 1989. *The Condition of Postmodernity: An Enquiry into the Origins of Cultural Change*. Cambridge, MA, and Oxford: Blackwell.

Hashmi, Alamgir. 1983. *Commonwealth Literature: An Essay towards the Re-Definition of a Popular/Counter Culture*. London: Vision.

———. 1988. *The Commonwealth, Comparative Literature, and the World*. Islamabad: Gulmohar.

Hassan, Waïl S. 1998. "Tayeb Salih: Culture, History, Memory." Diss., University of Illinois at Urbana-Champaign.

Hau'ofa, Epeli. 1987. *Kisses in the Nederends*. Honolulu: University of Hawaii Press.

Hawley, John C., ed. 1996a. *Cross-Addressing: Resistance Literature and Cultural Borders*. Albany: SUNY Press.

———. 1996b. *Writing the Nation: Self and Country in Post-Colonial Imagination*. Amsterdam: Rodopi.

———. 1998. *The Postcolonial Crescent: Islam's Impact on Contemporary Literature.* New York: Peter Lang.

Haynes, Douglas, and Gyan Prakash, eds. 1992. *Contested Power: Resistance and Everyday Social Relations in South Asia.* Berkeley: University of California Press.

Henighan, Stephen. 1999. "Two Paths to the Boom: Carpentier, Asturias, and the Performative Split." *Modern Language Review* 94.4: 1009–24.

Henry, Paget, and Paul Buhle, eds. 1992. *C.L.R. James's Caribbean.* Durham, NC: Duke University Press.

Hereniko, Vilsoni, and Teresia Teaiwa. 1993. *Last Virgin in Paradise.* Suva, Fiji: Mana.

Hereniko, Vilsoni, and Rob Wilson. 1999. *Inside Out: Literature, Cultural Politics, and Identity in the New Pacific.* Lanham, MD: Rowman and Littlefield.

Hergenhan, Laurie, ed. 1988. *The Penguin New Literary History of Australia.* Melbourne: Penguin Books.

Hidalgo, Cristina Pantoja. 1998. *A Gentle Subversion: Essays on Philippine Fiction.* Quezon City: University of the Philippines Press.

Hiller, Susan, ed. 1991. *The Myth of Primitivism: Perspectives on Art.* London: Routledge.

Hirst, Paul, and Grahame Thompson. 1996. *Globalization in Question: The International Economy and the Possibility of Governance.* Cambridge: Polity.

Ho, Elaine. 2000. *Timothy Mo.* Manchester: Manchester University Press.

Hofmann, Sabine. 1997. "Transculturación and Creolization: Concepts of Caribbean Cultural Theory." In *Latin American Postmodernisms.* Ed. Richard A. Young. Atlanta, GA: Rodopi. 77–86.

Hogan, Patrick Colm. 1994. "Mimeticism, Reactionary Nativism, and the Possibility of Postcolonial Identity in Derek Walcott's *Dream on Monkey Mountain.*" *Research in African Literatures* 25.2: 103–20.

———. 2000. *Colonialism and Cultural Identity: Crises of Tradition in the Anglophone Literatures of India, Africa, and the Caribbean.* Albany: SUNY Press.

Holland, R. F. 1985. *European Decolonization, 1918–1981: An Introductory Survey.* New York: St. Martin's.

Hollinger, David. 1995. *Postethnic America: Beyond Multiculturalism.* New York: Basic Books.

Holstein, James A., and Gale Miller, eds. 1993. *Reconsidering Social Constructionism: Debates in Social Problems Theory.* New York: de Gruyter.

hooks, bell. 1984. *Feminist Theory from Margin to Center.* Boston: South End Press.

———. 1995. *Killing Rage: Ending Racism.* New York: Penguin.

Houari, Leïla. 1985. *Zeida de nulle part.* Paris: L'Harmattan.

Houaria, Kadra-Hadjadji. 1986. *Contestation et révolte dans l'œuvre de Driss Chraïbi.* Paris: Editions Publisud.

Hurtado, Aída. 1996. *The Color of Privilege: Three Blasphemies on Race and Feminism.* Ann Arbor: University of Michigan Press.

———. 1988. "Relating to Privilege: Seduction and Rejection in the Subordination of White Women and Women of Color." *Signs* 14.4: 833–55.

Ingram, Forrest L. 1971. *Representative Short Story Cycles of the Twentieth Century: Studies in a Literary Genre.* The Hague: Mouton.

Innis, Hugh R. 1973. "The Cultural Contributions of the Other Ethnic Groups." In *Bilingualism and Biculturalism: An Abridged Version of the Royal Commission Report.* By Hugh R. Innis. Toronto: McClelland and Stewart. 129–59.

International Gramsci Society: http://www.italnet.nd.edu/gramsci.

Iser, Wolfgang. 1993. *The Fictive and the Imaginary. Charting Literary Anthropology.* Baltimore: Johns Hopkins University Press.

Jack, Belinda Elizabeth. 1996a. *Francophone Literatures: An Introductory Survey.* New York: Oxford University Press.

———. 1996b. *Negritude and Literary Criticism: The History and Theory of "Negro-African" Literature in French.* Westport, CT: Greenwood.

Jaimes, M. Annette, ed. 1992. *The State of Native America: Genocide, Colonization, and Resistance.* Boston: South End Press.

Jain, Jasbir. 1994. *Nayantara Sahgal.* Rev. ed. Jaipur: Printwell.

James, C.L.R. 1963. *The Black Jacobins: Toussaint L'Ouverture and the Santo Domingo Revolution.* New York: Vintage-Random.

———. 1977. *Nkrumah and the Ghana Revolution.* Westport, CT: Lawrence Hill.

Jameson, Fredric. 1981. *The Political Unconscious.* Ithaca, NY: Cornell University Press.

———. 1986. "Third World Literature in the Era of Multinational Capitalism." *Social Text* 15.

Jameson, Fredric, and Masao Miyoshi, eds. 1998. *The Cultures of Globalization.* Durham, NC: Duke University Press.

JanMohamed, Abdul. 1983. *Manichean Aesthetics: The Politics of Literature in Colonial Africa.* Amherst: University of Massachusetts Press.

JanMohamed, Abdul, and David Lloyd. 1990. *The Nature and Context of Minority Discourse.* New York: Oxford University Press.

Jayyusi, Salma Khadra. 1977. *Trends and Movements in Modern Arabic Literature.* 2 vols. Leiden: E. J. Brill.

———, ed. 1992. *Anthology of Modern Palestinian Literature.* New York: Columbia University Press.

Johnson, James Weldon. 1965 (1912). *Autobiography of an Ex-Coloured Man.* In *Three Negro Classics.* Comp. John Hope Franklin. New York: Avon-Hearst Corporation. 391–511.

Johnson, Richard. 1986–1987. "What Is Cultural Studies Anyway?" *Social Text* 16: 38–80.

Johnson-Odim, Cheryl. 1992. *Expanding the Boundaries of Women's History: Essays on Women in the Third World.* Bloomington: Indiana University Press for the *Journal of Women's History.*

Jonas, Joyce. 1996. *Anancy in the Great House: Ways of Reading West Indian Fiction.* Westport, CT: Greenwood Press.

Joseph, Clara. 1998. "Nayantara Sahgal's Novels: Gandhian Ideology and a Female Subject." Diss., York University. ⟨http://wwwlib.umi.com/cr/yorku/fullcit?pNQ 33536⟩.

Jussawalla, Feroza. 1989. "Resurrecting the Prophet: The Case of Salman, the Otherwise." *Public Culture* 2.1: 106–17.

———. 1996. "Rushdie's *Dastan-e-Dilruba: The Satanic Verses* as Rushdie's Love Letter to Islam." *Diacritics* 26.1: 50–73.

Kahanu, Diane. 1995. "Ho. Just Cause I Speak Pidgin No Mean I Dumb." *Bamboo Ridge: The Hawaiian Writers' Quarterly* 25: 36.

Kain, Geoffrey. 1999. "An Interview with Prafulla Mohanti." *Journal of Commonwealth and Post-Colonial Studies* 6.2: 1–18.

———, ed. 1993. *R. K. Narayan: Contemporary Critical Perspectives*. East Lansing: Michigan State University Press.

Kalouaz, Ahmed. 1986. *Point kilométrique 190*. Paris: L'Harmattan.

Kandiyoti, Deniz, ed. 1991. *Woman, Islam, and the State*. Philadelphia: Temple University Press.

———. 1996. *Gendering the Middle East: Emerging Perspectives*. New York: Syracuse University Press.

Kaufman, Michael T. 1983. "Author from Three Countries." *The New York Times Book Review* 13 (November): 3, 22–23.

Kauraka Kauraka. 1985. *Return to Havaiki: Fokihanga ki Havaiki*. Suva, Fiji: Institute of Pacific Studies.

Kearns, Francis E., ed. 1970. *The Black Experience*. New York: Viking.

Keating, AnaLouise. 1996. *Women Reading Women Writing: Self-Invention in Paula Gunn Allen, Gloria Anzaldúa, and Audre Lorde*. Philadelphia: Temple University Press.

Kent, George. 1973. "A Conversation with George Lamming." *Black World* 22.5: 92.

Kenyatta, Jomo. 1962. *Facing Mount Kenya*. New York: Random.

Kesteloot, Lilyan. 1991. *Black Writers in French: A Literary History of Negritude*. Washington, DC: Howard University Press.

Kettane, Nacer. 1985. *Le Sourire de Brahim*. Paris: Denoël.

Khalidi, Rashid, Lisa Anderson, Muhammad Muslih, and Reeva Simon, eds. 1991. *The Origins of Arab Nationalism*. New York: Columbia University Press.

Khatibi, Abdelkebir. 1983. *Maghreb pluriel*. Paris: Denoël, 1983.

Kiberd, Declan. 1995. *Inventing Ireland: The Literature of the Modern Nation*. Cambridge: Harvard University Press.

King, Adele. 1980. *The Writings of Camara Laye*. Oxford: Heinemann.

King, Bruce. 1993. *V. S. Naipaul*. Basingstoke: Macmillan.

King, Ursula, ed. 1994. *Feminist Theology from the Third World—A Reader*. Maryknoll, NY: Orbis.

Kirk, John M. 1983. *José Martí, Mentor of the Cuban Nation*. Gainesville: University of South Florida.

Klinck, Carl F., ed. 1976, 1990. *Literary History of Canada: Canadian Literature in English*. 2d. ed. vols. 1–3. Toronto: University of Toronto Press (vol. 4 ed. William H. New).

Kom, Ambroise. 2000. *La malédiction francophone: défis culturels et condition postcoloniale en Afrique*. Hamburg: LIT; Yaoudé: CLE.

Kom, Ambroise, ed. 1993. "Mongo Beti: 40 ans d'écriture, 60 ans de dissidence." *Présence Francophone* 42.

Kotei, S.I.A. 1981. *The Book Today in Africa*. Paris: UNESCO.

Krishna, Sankaran. 1999. *Postcolonial Insecurities: India, Sri Lanka, and the Question of Nationhood*. Minneapolis: University of Minnesota Press.

Kroetsch, Robert. 1989. "Unhiding the Hidden: Recent Canadian Fiction." In *The Lovely Treachury of Words. Essays Selected and New*. By Robert Kroetsch. Toronto: Oxford University Press. 58–63.

Kubayanda, Josaphat. 1986. "Order and Conflict." In *The Historic Novel in Latin America*. Ed. Daniel Balderston. Gaithersburg, MD: Hispamerica. 23–44.

Kuwabong, Dannabang. 1999. *Echoes from Dusty Rivers*. Hamilton, Ont.: Capricornus.

Lal, Malashri, and Vijay K. Sharma. 1998. "An Interview with Khushwant Singh." *ARIEL* 29.1: 137–42.

Landry, Donna, and Gerald Maclean, eds. 1996. *The Spivak Reader*. London: Routledge.

Lane, Christopher. 1995. *The Ruling Passion: British Colonial Allegory and the Paradox of Homosexual Desire*. Durham, NC, and London: Duke University Press.

Laronde, Michel. 1993. *Autour du roman beur*. Paris: L'Harmattan.

Larsen, Nella. 1928. *Quicksand*. In *An Intimation of Things Distant: The Collected Fiction of Nella Larsen*. Ed. and intro. Charles R. Larson. New York: Anchor-Doubleday, 1992. 29–162.

Laye, Camara, 1954. *The Dark Child*. New York: Noonday Press.

Lazarus, Neil. 1999. *Nationalism and Cultural Practice in the Postcolonial World*. Cambridge: Cambridge University Press.

Lazreg, Marnia. 1994. *The Eloquence of Silence: Algerian Women in Question*. New York: Routledge.

———. 1988. "Feminism and Difference: The Perils of Writing as a Woman on Women in Algeria." *Feminist Issues* 14.1: 81–107.

Ledent, Bénédicte. 2001. *Caryl Phillips*. Manchester: Manchester University Press.

Lee, Sonia. 1984. *Camara Laye*. Boston: Twayne.

Lee, Spike, dir. and prod. 1990. *Jungle Fever*. Forty Acres and a Mule Filmworks.

Lefebvre, Henri. 1991. *The Production of Space*. Trans. Donald Nicholson-Smith. Oxford: Blackwell Trans. of *Production de l'espace*, 1974.

Lenin, V. I. 1933. (1916). *Imperialism, the Highest Stage of Capitalism*. New York: International.

Leomala, Albert. 1975. "Hom Belong Mi." In *Some Modern Poetry from the New Hebrides*. Ed. Albert Wendt. Suva, Fiji: Mana. 14–15.

———. 1975. "Kros." In *Some Modern Poetry from the New Hebrides*. Ed. Albert Wendt. Suva, Fiji: Mana. 18–19.

Levinson, Marjorie. 1993. "News from Nowhere: The Discontents of Aijaz Ahmad." *Public Culture* (Fall) 6.1: 97–131.

Lewis, David Levering. 1993. *W.E.B. Du Bois: Biography of a Race, 1868–1919*. New York: Henry Holt.

Lewis, Samella. 1990. *African American Art and Artists*. Berkeley: University of California Press.

Lie, Nadia. 1997. "Countering Caliban: Fernandez Retamar and the Postcolonial Debate." In *Constellation Caliban: Figurations of a Character*. Ed. Nadia Lie. Amsterdam: Rodopi. 245–270.

Lim, Shirley Geok-lin. 1995. *Life's Mysteries: The Best of Shirley Lim*. Singapore: Times Books International.

———. 1996. *Among the White Moon Faces: An Asian-American Memoir of Homelands*. New York: Feminist Press.

Lionnet, Françoise. 1992. "Logiques metisses: Cultural Appropriation and Postcolonial Representations." *College Literature* 9: 100–20.

———. 1992. "Of Mangoes and Maroons: Language, History, and the Multicultural Subject of Michelle Cliff's *Abeng*." In *Decolonizing the Subject: The Politics of Gender in Women's Autobiography*. Ed. Sidonie Smith and Julia Watson. Minneapolis: University of Minnesota Press. 321–34.

Lipsitz, George. 1994. *Dangerous Crossroads: Popular Music, Postmodernism and the Politics of Race*. London: Verso.

Lloyd, David. 1987. *Nationalism and Minor Literature: James Clarence Mangan and the Emergence of Irish Cultural Nationalism*. Berkeley: University of California Press.

———. 1997. *Writing on the Edge: Interviews with Writers and Editors of Wales*. Amsterdam: Rodopi B.V.

Loomba, Ania. 1998. *Colonialism/Postcolonialism*. New York: Routledge.

Loomba, Ania, and Martin Orkin, eds. 1998. *Post Colonial Shakespeares*. New York: Routledge.

López, Alfred J. 2001. *Post and Pasts: A Theory of Postcolonialism*. Albany: State University of New York Press.

Lotman, Yuri M. 1990. *Universe of the Mind: A Semiotic Theory of Culture*. Bloomington: Indiana University Press.

Lowe, Lisa. 1996. *Immigrant Acts: On Asian American Cultural Politics*. Durham, NC: Duke University Press.

Lowe, Lisa, and David Lloyd, eds. 1997. *The Politics of Culture in the Shadow of Capital*. Durham: Duke University Press.

Lupke, Christopher. 1998a. *Politics of Culture in the Shadow of Capital*. Durham, NC: Duke University Press.

———. 1998b. "Wang Wenxing and the 'Loss' of China." *Boundary 2* 25.3: 97–128.

Lyotard, Jean-François. 1989. *The Lyotard Reader*. Ed. Andrew Benjamin. Oxford: Blackwell.

Macleod, Christine. 1997. "Black American Literature and the Postcolonial Debate." *Yearbook of English Studies* 27: 51–56.

MacQueen, Norrie. 1997. *The Decolonization of Portuguese Africa: Metropolitan Revolution and the Dissolution of the Empire*. London and New York: Longman.

Maes-Jelinek, Hena, ed. 1991. *Wilson Harris: The Uncompromising Imagination*. Sydney and Mundelstrup: Dangaroo.

———. 2000. Special Wilson Harris issue of *Journal of Caribbean Literatures* 1.2.

Maes-Jelinek, Hena, Kirsten Holst Petersen, and Anna Rutherford, eds. 1989. *A Shaping of Connections: Commonwealth Literature Studies—Then and Now*. Sydney, Mundelstrup, and Coventry: Dangaroo Press.

Makdisi, Saree. 1998. *Romantic Imperialism: Universal Empire and the Culture of Modernity*. Cambridge: Cambridge University Press.

Malcolm X, with the assistance of Alex Haley. 1965. *The Autobiography of Malcolm X*. New York: Grove Press.

Malinowski, Bronislaw. 1944. *A Scientific Theory of Culture and Other Essays*. Chapel Hill: University of North Carolina Press.

Malti-Douglas, Fedwa. 1995. "Writing Nawal El Saadawi." In *Feminism Beside Itself*. Ed. Diane Elam. New York: Routledge. 271–292.

Mani, Lata. 1989. "Multiple Mediations: Feminist Scholarship in the Age of Multinational Reception." *Inscriptions* 5: 1–23.

Mann, Harveen Sachdeva. 1994. "*Cracking India*: Minority Women Writers and the Contentious Margins of Indian Nationalist Discourse." *The Journal of Commonwealth Literature* 30: 2.

Mann, Susan Garland. 1989. *The Short Story Cycle: A Genre Companion and Reference Guide*. Westport, CT: Greenwood.

Mannoni, Octave. 1964. *Prospero and Caliban: The Psychology of Colonization*. Trans. Pamela Powesland. New York: Praeger.

Mariátegui, José Carlos. 1971. *Seven Interpretative Essays of Peruvian Reality*. Trans. Marjory Urquidi. Intro. Jorge Basadre. Austin: University of Texas Press.

———. 1996. *The Heroic and Creative Meaning of Socialism: Selected Essays of José Carlos Mariátegui*. Ed. and trans. Michael Pearlman. Atlantic Highlands, NJ: Humanities Press.

Martin, Lewis W., and Karen W. Wigen. 1997. *The Myth of Continents: A Critique of Metageography*. Berkeley: University of California Press.

Marx, Karl. 1973. *Grundisse*. New York: Vintage.

Marx, Karl, and Friedrich Engels. 1976. *Collected Works*. New York: International.

Marx-Scouras, Danielle. 1992. "A Literature of Departure: The Cross-Cultural Writing of Driss Chraïbi." *Research in African Literatures* 23.2: 131–44.

Massad, Joseph. 1997. "Political Realists or Comprador Intelligentsia: Palestinian Intellectuals and the National Struggle." *Critique* 11: 14–26.

Massey, Doreen. 1997. "Problems with Globalization." *Soundings* 7: 34–50.

Matthes, Melissa. 1999. "Shahrazad's Sisters: Storytelling and Politics in the Memoirs of Mernissi, El Saadawi, and Ashrawi." *Alif* 19: 68–96.

Maturana, Humberto, and Francisco J. Varela. 1984. *The Tree of Knowledge: The Biological Roots of Human Understanding*. Boston: Shambala.

Mazrui, Alamin, and Judith Abdala. 1997. "Sex and Patriarchy: Gender Relations in *God Dies by the Nile*." *Research in African Literature* 28.3: 17–32.

Mazrui, Ali A., and Toby Kleban Levine. 1986. *The Africans: A Reader*. New York: Praeger.

McClintock, Anne. 1995. *Imperial Leather: Race, Gender, and Sexuality in the Colonial Context*. New York: Routledge.

McClintock, Anne, Aamir Mufti, and Ella Shohat, eds. 1997. *Dangerous Liaisons: Gender, Nation, and Postcolonial Perspectives*. Minneapolis: University of Minnesota Press.

McKay, Claude. 1928. *Home to Harlem*. New York: Harper.

McNeill, Pearlie, and Pratibha Parmar, eds. 1986. *Women in the Break: Women in Personal Crisis*. London: Sheba Feminist Publishers.

Merini, Rafika. 1999. *Two Major Francophone Women Writers, Assia Djebar and Leila Sebbar*. New York: Peter Lang.

Meyer, Jean, et al. 1991. *Histoire de la France coloniale: Des origines à 1914*. Paris: Armand Colin.

Mignolo, Walter D. 1995. *The Darker Side of the Renaissance: Literacy, Territoriality, and Colonization*. Ann Arbor: University of Michigan Press.

———. 1999. "Linguistic Maps, Literary Geographies, and Cultural Landscapes: Langues, Languaging, and (Trans)nationalism." In *The Places of History: Regionalism Revisited in Latin America*. Ed. Doris Sommer. Durham, NC: Duke University Press. 49–65.

Miller, Christopher L. 1998. *Nations and Nomads: Essays on Francophone African Literature and Culture*. Chicago: University of Chicago Press.

Miller, Melissa. 1989. "Pacific Lives in Poetry: Questions of Representation." *Literary Studies East & West* 3: 134–40.

Mishra, Ganeswar. 1985. "How Does an Indian Village Speak? A Study of the Form of Prafulla Mohanti's *My Village, My Life*." In *Autobiographical and Biographical Writing in the Commonwealth*. Ed. Doreen MacDermott. Barcelona: University of Barcelona Press. 25–38.

Mishra, Sudesh. 1992. *Tandava*. Melbourne: Meanjin.

Mishra, Vijay, and Bob Hodge. 1991. "What Is Post(-)colonialism?" *Textual Practice* 5.3: 399–414.

Mo, Timothy. 1986. *An Insular Possession*. London: Chatto and Windus.

Mohanty, Chandra. 1991. "Under Western Eyes: Feminist Scholarship and Colonial Discourses." In *Third World Women and the Politics of Feminism*. Ed. Chandra Mohanty et al. Bloomington: Indiana University Press. 51–80.

Mohanty, Chandra, and Jacqui Alexander, eds. 1995. *Feminist Genealogies, Colonial Legacies, Democratic Futures*. New York: Routledge.

Monego, Joan. 1984. *Maghrebian Literature in French*. Boston: Twayne.

Moore-Gilbert, Bart. 1997. *Postcolonial Theory: Contexts, Practices, Politics*. New York: Verso.

Moraga, Cherrie, and Gloria Anzaldua. 1983. *Cuentos: Stories by Latinas*. New York: Kitchen Table, Women of Color Press.

Moran, Albert, ed. 1996. *Film Policy: International, National and Regional Perspectives*. London: Routledge.

Morgan, Susan. 1996. *Place Matters: Gendered Geography in Victorian Women's Travel Books about Southeast Asia*. New Brunswick, NJ: Rutgers University Press.

Morley, David, and Kuan-Hsing Chen, eds. 1996. *Stuart Hall: Critical Dialogues in Cultural Studies*. London: Routledge.

Mudimbe, V. Y. 1988. *The Invention of Africa: Gnosis, Philosophy and the Order of Knowledge*. Bloomington: Indiana University Press.

———. 1991. *Between Tides* [*Entre les eaux*, 1973]. Trans. Stephen Becker. New York: Simon and Schuster.

———. 1993. *The Rift* [*L'Écart*, 1979]. Trans. Marjolin de Jaeger. Minneapolis: University of Minnesota Press.

Mufti, Aamir, and Ella Shohat. 1997. "Introduction." In *Dangerous Liaisons: Gender, Nation and Postcolonial Perspectives*. Ed. Anne McClintock, Aamir Mufti, and Ella Shohat. Minneapolis: University of Minnesota Press. 1–12.

Mugo, Micere M. G. 1991. *African Orature and Human Rights*. Lesotho: Institute of Southern African University of Lesotho.

Muhkerjee, Arun P. 1990. "Whose Post-Colonialism and Whose Postmodernism?" *World Literature Written in English* 30.2: 1–9.

Müller, Klaus-Peter. 1999. "Constructionism in the Sciences, in Literature and in Literary Theory." In: *Lost Worlds and Mad Elephants. Literature, Science and Technology 1700–1990*. Ed. Elmar Schenkel and Stefan Welz. Berlin and Cambridge, MA: Galda and Wilch. 305–30.

Murrel, Nathaniel Samuel, et al., eds. 1998. *Chanting Down Babylon: The Rastafari Reader*. Philadelphia: Temple University Press.

Muthu, Mircea. 1995. *Cântecul lui Leonardo*. Bucuresti: Editura Didactica si Pedagogica.

Naficy, Hamid. 1996. "Theorizing 'Third World' Film Spectatorship." Special issue of *Wide Angle* 18.4: 3–26.

Nair, Supriya. 1996. *Caliban's Curse: George Lamming and the Revisioning of History*. Ann Arbor: University of Michigan Press.

Nandan, Satendra. 1991. *The Wounded Sea*. Sydney: Simon and Schuster.

Nandy, Ashis. 1983. *The Intimate Enemy: Loss and Recovery of Self Under Colonialism*. Delhi: Oxford University Press.

Narasimhaiah, C. D. 1987. *The Swan and the Eagle*. Delhi: Motilal.

Nash, Christopher, ed. 1990. *Narrative in Culture. The Uses of Storytelling in the Sciences, Philosophy, and Literature.* London: Routledge.

Nasta, Susheila, ed. 1988. *Critical Perspectives on Sam Selvon.* Washington, DC: Three Continents Press.

Nasta, Susheila, and Anna Rutherford, eds. 1995. *Tiger's Triumph: Celebrating Sam Selvon.* London: Dangaroo Press.

Nehru, Jawaharlal. 1946. *The Discovery of India.* New York: John Day.

Ngũgĩ wa Thiong'o. 1986. *Decolonizing the Mind: The Politics of Language in African Literature.* London: James Currey.

———. 1993. *Moving the Centre: The Struggle for Cultural Freedoms.* London: James Currey Heinemann.

———. 1998. *Penpoints, Gunpoints, and Dreams: Toward a Critical Theory of Art and the State in Africa.* Oxford: Clarendon Press.

Niranjana, Tejaswini. 1992. *Siting Translation: History, Post-Structuralism and the Colonial Context.* Berkeley, Los Angeles, and Oxford: University of California Press.

Nkrumah, Kwame. 1963. *Africa Must Unite.* New York: Frederick A. Praeger.

———. 1965. *Neo-colonialism: The Last Stage of Imperialism.* London: Nelson.

Ntuli, D. C., and C. F. Swanepoel. 1993. *Southern African Literature in African Languages: A Concise Historical Perspective.* Pretoria, South Africa: Acacia.

Nyerere, Julius. 1976. "Opening Address." In *Resolutions and Selected Speeches from the Sixth Pan-African Congress.* Dar es Salaam, Tanzania: Open University Press. 7–13.

Obiechina, E. N. 1968. "Cultural Nationalism in Modern African Creative Literature." *African Literature Today* 1: 24–35.

O'Callaghan, Evelyn. 1989. "The Modernization of the Trinidadian Landscape in the Novels of Earl Lovelace." *Ariel* 20: 41–54.

Odamtten, Vincent O. 1994. *The Art of Ama Ata Aidoo: Polylectics and Reading against Neocolonialism.* Gainesville: University Press of Florida.

Ogungbesan, Kolawole, ed. 1979. *New West African Literature.* London: Heinemann.

O'Hanlon, Rosalind. 1988. "Recovering the Subject: *Subaltern Studies* and Histories of Resistance in Colonial South Asia." *Modern Asian Studies* 22.1: 189–224.

'Ōiwi: A Native Hawaiian Journal. 1998. Honolulu, HI: Kuleana 'Ōiwi.

Ong, Aihwa. 1987. *Spirits of Resistance and Capitalist Discipline: Factory Women in Malaysia.* Albany: SUNY Press.

Orlando, Valérie. 1999. *Nomadic Voices of Exile: Feminine Identity in Francophone Literature of the Maghreb.* Athens: Ohio University Press.

Ortiz, Ricardo L. 1997. "Café, Culpa and Capital: Nostalgic Addictions of Cuban Exile." *Yale Journal of Criticism: Interpretation in the Humanities* 10.1: 63–84.

Osundare, Niyi. 1993. *African Literature and the Crisis of Post-Structuralist Theorising.* Ibadan: Options Book and Information Service.

Ouzgane, Lahoucine. 1997. "Masculinity as Virility in Tahar ben Jelloun's Work." *Contagion* 4: 1–13.

Oyono, Ferdinand. 1966. *Houseboy.* London: Heinemann Press.

———. 1967. *The Old Man and the Medal.* London: Heinemann Press.

———. 1989. *Road to Europe.* London: Heinemann Press.

Padilla, Genaro. 1993. *My History, Not Yours: The Formation of Mexican American Autobiography.* Madison: University of Wisconsin Press.

Padmore, George. 1972. *Pan-Africanism or Communism*. Garden City, NY: Doubleday.

Pakenham, Thomas. 1991. *The Scramble for Africa: 1876–1912*. New York: Random House.

Parameswaran, Uma. 1988. *The Perforated Sheet: Essays on Salman Rushdie's Art*. New Delhi: Affiliated East-West Press.

Paravisin-Gebert, Lizabeth. 1999. *Jamaica Kincaid: A Critical Companion*. Westport, CT: Greenwood.

Parekh, Pushpa H., and Siga Fatima Jagne. 1998. *Postcolonial African Writers*. London and Chicago: Fitzroy Dearborn.

Parks, Suzan-Lori. 1990. *Venus*. New York: Theatre Communications Group.

Parry, Benita. 1994. "Resistance Theory/Theorising Resistance, or Two Cheers for Nativism." In *Colonial Discourse/Postcolonial Theory*. Ed. Francis Barker, Peter Hulme, and Margaret Iversen. Manchester: Manchester University Press. 172–96.

Patton, Sharon F. 1998. *African-American Art*. New York: Open University Press.

Pearlman, Michael, ed. and trans. 1996. *The Heroic and Creative Meaning of Socialism: Selected Essays of José Carlos Mariátegui*. Atlantic Highlands, NJ: Humanities Press.

Pellegrini, Ann. 1997. *Performance Anxiety: Staging Psychoanalysis, Staging Race*. New York: Routledge.

Perez-Torres, Rafael. 1995. *Movements in Chicano Poetry: Against Myths, against Margins*. Cambridge: Cambridge University Press.

Perkins, Leialoha Apo. 1989. "Women Writers as Women and as Writers." *Literary Studies East & West* 3: 141–47.

Perret, Delphine, and Marie-Denise Shelton, eds. 1995. *Maryse Condé*. Special Issue of *Callaloo* 18.3: 535–711.

Pfaff, Françoise. 1984. *The Cinema of Ousmane Sembène, a Pioneer of African Film*. Westport, CT: Greenwood.

Pines, James, and Paul Willemen, eds. 1989. *Questions of Third Cinema*. London: British Film Institute. 111–13.

Pomeroy, W. J. 1970. *American Neo-colonialism: Its Emergence in the Philippines and Asia*. New York: International.

Pouchet-Paquet, Sandra. 1992. Foreword to George Lamming's *The Pleasures of Exile*. London: Heinemann.

Pousse, Michel. 1995. *R. K. Narayan: A Painter of Modern India*. New York: Peter Lang.

Prakash, Gyan. 1995. *After Colonialism: Imperial Histories and Postcolonial Displacements*. Princeton: Princeton University Press.

Pratt, Mary Louise. 1992. *Imperial Eyes: Travel Writing and Transculturation*. London and New York: Routledge.

Press, John. 1965. *Commonwealth Literature: Unity and Diversity in a Common Culture*. London: Heinemann.

Provost, Kara. 1995. "Becoming Afrekete: The Trickster in the Work of Audre Lorde." *MELUS* 20.4: 45–59.

Quine, Willard van Orman. 1953. *From a Logical Point of View: 9 Logico-Philosophical Essays*. Cambridge: Harvard University Press.

Rabinow, Paul, ed. 1984. *The Foucault Reader*. New York: Random House.

Radhakrishnan, R. 1993. *Postcoloniality and the Boundaries of Identity*. Special issue of *Callaloo* 16.4: 750–71.

———. 1996. *Diasporic Mediations: Between Home and Location.* Minneapolis: University of Minnesota Press.

Rajan, Gita, and Radhika Mohanram, eds. 1995. *Postcolonial Discourse and Changing Cultural Contexts: Theory and Criticism.* Westport, CT: Greenwood.

Ramraj, Victor. 1999. "Afterword: Merits and Demerits of the Postcolonial Approach to Writings in English." In *Voices of the Other: Children's Literature and the Postcolonial Context.* Ed. Roderick McGillis. New York: Garland. 253–68.

Ranger, Terence. 1990. " 'Subaltern Studies' and Social History." *Southern African Review of Books* 3.3–4: 8–10.

"Rediff Interview/ Mahasweta Devi." December 24, 1997. http://www.rediff.com/news/dec/24devi.html

Reid, Mark A. 1997. *PostNegritude Visual and Literary Culture.* Albany: SUNY Press.

Resources on Antonio Gramsci: http://www.soc.qc.edu/gramsci/

Rhodes, Colin. 1994. *Primitivism and Modern Art.* London: Thames and Hudson.

Rich, Adrienne. 1977. *The Meaning of our Love for Women Is What We Have Constantly to Expand.* New York: Out and Out Books.

———. 1984. *Blood, Bread, and Poetry: Selected Poems, 1979–1985.* New York: W. W. Books.

Riley, Denise. 1988. *"Am I That Name?": Feminism and the Category of "Woman" in History.* Houndmills, U.K.: Macmillan.

Rivera Cusicanqui, Silvia. 1997. "La nocion de 'derecho' o las paradojas de la modernidad postcolonial: Indigenas y mujeres en Bolivia." *Temas Sociales* 19: 56–75.

Robertson, Roland. 1992. *Globalization: Social Theory and Global Culture.* London: Sage.

Robinson, Douglas. 1997. *Translation and Empire: Postcolonial Theories Explained.* Manchester, U.K.: St. Jerome.

Rodney, Walter. 1982. *How Europe Underdeveloped Africa.* Washington, DC: Howard University Press.

Rohlehr, Gordon. 1981. *Pathfinder: Black Awakening in the Arrivants of Edward Kamau Brathwaite.* Port of Spain, Trinidad: Private publication.

Ross, Andrew. 1993. "The Popularity of Pornography." In *The Cultural Studies Reader.* Ed. Simon During. New York: Routledge. 221–242.

Ross, Robert L., ed. 1991. *International Literature in English: Essays on the Major Writers.* New York and London: Garland.

Ruiz, Vicki. 1998. *From Out of the Shadows: Mexican Women in Twentieth Century America.* New York: Oxford University Press.

Russell, Kathy, Midge Wilson, and Ronald Hall. 1992. *The Color Complex: The Politics of Skin Color among African Americans.* New York: Anchor.

Said, Edward. 1978. *Orientalism.* New York: Pantheon.

———. 1986. "Intellectuals in the Post-Colonial World." *Salmagundi* 70–71: 44–64.

———. 1990. "Embargoed Literature." *The Nation.* 251.8: 278–280.

———. 1993. *Culture and Imperialism.* New York: Alfred A. Knopf.

Saini, M. K. 1981. *Politics of Multinationals: A Pattern in Neo-colonialism.* New Delhi: Gitanjali Prakashan.

Saks, Eva. 1988. "Representing Miscegenation Law." *Raritan* 8.2: 39–69.

Saldívar, José David. 1990. "The Dialectics of Our America." In *Do the Americas Have a Common Literature?* Ed. Gustavo Perez-Firmat. Durham, NC: Duke University Press. 62–84.

———. 1997. *Border Matters: Remapping American Cultural Studies.* Berkeley: University of California Press.

Saldívar, Ramón. 1990. *Chicano Narrative: Dialectics of Difference.* Madison: University of Wisconsin Press.

Sandoval, Ciro A., and Sandra M. Boschetta, eds. 1998. *Jose Maria Arguedas: Reconsiderations for Latin American Cultural Studies.* Athens: Ohio University Center for International Studies.

San Juan, E., Jr. 1998. *Beyond Postcolonial Theory.* New York: St. Martin's.

Sardar, Ziauddin. 1997. "A Futurist beyond Futurists: The a, b, c, d (and e) of Ashis Nandy." *Futures* 29.7 (September): 649–60.

Sarkar, Sumit. 1983. *Modern India: 1885–1947.* Madras: Macmillan.

Sarkar, Tanika. 1995. *Women and the Hindu Right.* New Delhi: Kali for Women.

Sass, Louis A. 1986. "Anthropology's Native Problems: Revisionism in the Field." *Harper's*: 49–57.

Sassen, Saskia. 1998. *Cities in a World Economy.* Thousand Oaks, CA: Pine Forge Press.

Saunders, Walter. 1994. "The Owning of Images and the Right to Represent." *Film news* 5: 6–7.

Schaffer, Kay. 1988. *Women and the Bush: Forces of Desire in the Australian Cultural Tradition.* Sydney: Cambridge University Press.

Schuchhardt, Hugo. 1882–1891. *Kreolische Studien.* Vols. 1–9. Vienna: Commissioned by C. Gerold's son from classnotes from the History of Philosophy course at the Viennese Academy of Science.

Schwartz, Meryl F. 1996. "Imagined Communities in the Novels of Michelle Cliff." In *Homemaking: Women Writers and the Politics and Poetics of Home.* Ed. Catherine Wiley and Fiona R. Barnes. New York: Garland. 287–311.

Schwartzwald, Robert. 1985. "Literature and Intellectual Realignments in Québec." *Québec Studies* 3: 32–56.

Scott, Joan. 1988. *Gender and the Politics of History.* New York: Columbia University Press.

Sebbar, Leila. 1982. *Shérazade: 17 ans, brune, frisée, yeux verts.* Paris: Stock.

———. 1985. *Les carnets de Shérazade.* Paris: Stock.

———. 1991. *Le fou de Shérazade.* Paris: Stock.

Sedgwick, Eve Kosofsky. 1993. *Tendencies.* Durham, NC: Duke University Press.

Segy, Ladislas. 1958. *African Sculpture.* New York: Dover.

Senghor, Léopold Sédar. 1971. *The Foundations of "Africanité" or "Négritude" and "Arabité."* Trans. Mercer Cook. Paris: Presence Africaine.

———. 1995. "Negritude: A Humanism of the Twentieth Century." In *I Am Because We Are: Readings in Black Philosophy.* Ed. Fred Lee Hord and Jonathan Scott Lee. Amherst: University of Massachusetts Press. 45–54.

Serequeberhan, Tsenay. 1997. In *Postcolonial African Philosophy.* Ed. Emmanuel Chukwudi Eze. Cambridge, MA: Blackwell. 141–61.

Serle, Geoffrey. 1973. *From Deserts the Prophets Come.* Melbourne: Heinemann.

Shahane, Vasant Anant. 1972. *Khushwant Singh.* Boston: Twayne.

Shankar, Subramanian. 2001. *Textual Traffic: Colonialism, Modernity, and the Economy of the Text.* Albany: State University of New York Press.

Shapiro, Michael J. 1997. *Violent Cartographies: Mapping Cultures of War.* Minneapolis: University of Minnesota Press.

Sharakiya, A. M. 1991–1992. "Pan-Africanism: A Critical Assessment." *Trans Africa Forum* 8.4: 39–52.

Sherzer, Dina, ed. 1996. *Cinema, Colonialism, Postcolonialism: Perspectives from the French and Francophone World.* Austin: University of Texas Press.

Shnookal, Deborah, and Mirta Muñiz, eds. 1999. *José Martí Reader: Writings on the Americas.* Hoboken, NJ: Ocean Press.

Shohat, Ella. 1991. "Imagining Terra Incognita: The Disciplinary Gaze of Empire." *Public Culture* 3.2: 41–70.

Siemerling, Winfried, and Katrin Schwenk, eds. 1996. *Cultural Difference and the Literary Text; Pluralism and the Limits of Authenticity in North American Literatures.* Iowa City: University of Iowa Press.

Simoes da Silva, A. J. 2000. *The Luxury of Nationalist Despair.* Amsterdam and Atlanta, GA: Rodopi.

Simon, Sherry. 1994. *Le trafic des langues: Traduction et culture dans la littérature québécoise.* Montreal: Boréal.

Sinfield, Alan. 1992. *Faultlines. Cultural Materialism and the Politics of Dissident Reading.* Oxford: Clarendon.

Sipolo, Jully. 1986. *Praying Parents.* Honiara, Solomon Islands: Aruligo.

Sivanandan, Ambalavaner. 1990. *Communities of Resistance: Black Struggles for Socialism.* London: Verso.

Slaymaker, William. 1996. "Agents and Actors in African Antifoundational Aesthetics: Theory and Narrative in Appiah and Mudimbe." *Research in African Literatures* 27.1: 119–28.

Slemon, Stephen. 1988. "Post-Colonial Allegory and the Transformation of History." *Journal of Commonwealth Literature* 23: 157–68.

———. 1990. "Unsettling the Empire: Resistance Theory for the Second World." *World Literature Written in English* 30.2: 30–41.

———. 1995. "The Scramble for Postcolonialism." In *The Post-Colonial Studies Reader.* Ed. Bill Asheroft, Gareth, Griffiths, Helen Tiffin. London: Routledge. 45–52.

———. 1996. "Post-Colonial Critical Theories." In *New National and Post-Colonial Literatures: An Introduction.* Ed. Bruce King. Oxford: Clarendon. 178–97.

Smith, Adam. 1961. *An Inquiry into the Nature and Causes of the Wealth of Nations.* 2 vols. London: Methuen.

Smith, Dorothy. 1987. *Everyday World as Problematic: A Feminist Sociology.* Boston: Northeastern University Press.

Smith, Linda Tuhiwai. 1999. *Decolonizing Methodologies: Research and Indigenous Peoples.* London: Zed Books.

Snell, Marilyn. 1997. "Jamaica Kincaid." *Mother Jones* 22.5: 28–32.

Sollors, Werner. 1986. *Beyond Ethnicity: Consent and Descent in American Culture.* New York: Oxford University Press.

———. 1997. *Neither Black nor White. Neither Black nor White Yet Both: Thematic Explorations of Interracial Literature.* New York: Oxford University Press.

———, ed. 1996. *Theories of Ethnicity: A Classical Reader.* Basingstoke and London: Macmillan.

Sommer, Doris. 1998. "Sacred Secrets: A Strategy for Survival." In *Women, Autobiography, Theory: A Reader.* Ed. Sidonie Smith. Madison: University of Wisconsin Press. 197–207.

Soyinka, Wole. 1988. *Art, Dialogue & Outrage: Essays on Literature and Culture.* Oxford: New Horn.

Spitta, Silvia. 1995. *Between Two Waters: Narratives of Transculturation in Latin America.* Houston: Rice University Press.

———. 1997. "Transculturalism, the Caribbean, and the Cuban-American Imaginary." In *Tropicalizations: Transcultural Representations of Latinidad.* Ed. Frances Aparicio. Hanover, NH: University Press of New England. 98–115.

Spivak, Gayatri Chakravorty. 1985a. "The Rani of Sirmur: An Essay in Reading the Archives." *History & Theory: Studies in the Philosophy of History* 24.1: 247–72.

———. 1985b. "Three Women's Texts and a Critique of Imperialism." *Critical Inquiry* 12: 243–62.

———. 1987. *In Other Worlds: Essays in Cultural Politics.* New York: Methuen.

———. 1989a. "Can the Subaltern Speak?" In *Marxism and the Interpretation of Culture.* Ed. Cary Nelson and Lawrence Grossberg. Urbana: University of Illinois Press. 271–313.

———. 1989b. "Reading *The Satanic Verses.*" *Public Culture* 2.1: 79–99.

———. 1993. *Outside in the Teaching Machine.* New York and London: Routledge.

———. 1995. *Imaginary Maps.* New York: Routledge.

———. 1999. *A Critique of Postcolonial Reason: Toward a History of the Vanishing Present.* Cambridge: Harvard University Press.

Spivak, Gayatri C., and Sarah Harasym, ed. 1991. *The Post-Colonial Critic: Interviews, Strategies, Dialogues.* New York: Routledge.

Sprinker, Michael. 1993. "The National Question: Said, Ahmad, Jameson." *Public Culture* 6.1(Fall): 3–29.

Sprouse, Keith Allan. 2000. "Chaos and Rhizome: Introduction to a Carribean Poetics." In *A History of Literature in the Caribbean. Vol. 3. Cross-Cultural Studies.* Ed. A. James Arnold. Amsterdam and Philadelphia: John Benjamins. 79–86.

Stadtler-Djedji, Katherina. 1995. "Une archeologie du discours africain: V. Y. Mudimbe." *Matatu: Journal for African Culture and Societies* 13–14: 257–65.

Steele, Cassie Premo. 2000. *We Heal from Memory: Sexton, Lorde, Anzaldúa, and the Poetry of Witness.* New York: St. Martin's.

Stein, William W. 1997. *Dance in the Cemetery: José Carlos Mariátegui and the Lima Scandal of 1917.* Lanham, MD: University Press of America.

Stoler, Ann Laura. 1995. *Race and the Education of Desire: Foucault's History of Sexuality and the Colonial Order of Things.* Durham, NC: Duke University Press.

Stoll, David. 1999. *Rigoberta Menchu and the Story of All Poor Guatemalans.* Boulder, CO: Westview.

Stratton, Florence. 1994. *Contemporary African Literature and the Politics of Gender.* London and New York: Routledge.

Stroven, Carl, and A. Grove Day, eds. 1949. *The Spell of the Pacific: An Anthology of Its Literature.* New York: Macmillan.

Sturm, Terry. 1998. *The Oxford History of New Zealand Literature in English.* 2d ed. Auckland: Oxford University Press.

Subramani. 1985. *South Pacific Literature: From Myth to Fabulation.* Suva, Fiji: University of the South Pacific.

———. 1988. *The Fantasy Eaters: Stories from Fiji.* Washington, DC: Three Continents Press.

Suleri, Sara. 1989. "Contraband Histories: Salman Rushdie and the Embodiment of Blasphemy." *Yale Review* 78.4: 604–24.

Tagg, Philip. 1996. "Popular Music Studies versus the 'Other.' " Online essay at: http://www.theblackbook.net/acad/tagg/articles/cascais.pdf

Tanure, Ojaide. 1994. *The Poetry of Wole Soyinka*. Lagos: Malthouse.

Taussig, Michael. 1993. *Mimesis and Alterity: A Particular History of the Senses*. New York: Routledge.

Taylor, Lucien. 1998. "Creolite Bites: A Conversation with Patrick Chamoiseau, Raphael Confiant, and Jean Bernabe." *Transition: An International Review* 74: 124–61.

Thaman, Konai Helu. 1993. *Kakala*. Suva, Fiji: Mana.

Third Text. 1987. London: Kala.

Thomas, Nicholas. 1994. *Colonialism's Culture: Anthropology, Travel and Government*. Princeton: Princeton University Press.

Tlhagale, B., and I. Mosala, eds. 1986. *Hammering Swords into Ploughshares: Essays in Honour of Archbishop Mpilo Desmond Tutu*. Johannesburg: Skotaville.

Todorov, Tzvetan. 1984. *Mikhail Bakhtin: Dialogical Principle*. Trans. Wlad Godzich. Minneapolis: University of Minnesota Press.

Toer, Pramoedya Ananta. 1990. *The Fugutive*. Trans. Willem Samuels. New York: Morrow.

Tomlinson, John. 1999. *Globalization and Culture*. Chicago: University of Chicago Press.

Torgovnick, Marianna. 1990. *Gone Primitive: Savage Intellects, Modern Lives*. Chicago: University of Chicago Press.

Touabti, Hocine. 1981. *L'Amour quand même*. Paris: Belfond.

Trask, Haunani-Kay. 1999. "Decolonizing Hawaiian Literature." In *Inside Out: Literature, Cultural Politics, and Identity in the New Pacific*. Ed. Vilsoni Hereniko and Rob Wilson. Lanham, MD: Rowman and Littlefield. 167–82.

Trinh, T. Minh-ha. 1989. *Woman, Native, Other*. Bloomington: Indiana University Press.

Trivedi, Harish, and Meenakshi Mukherjee, eds. 1996. *Interrogating Post-colonialism: Theory, Text and Context*. Shimla: Indian Institute of Advanced Study.

Trump, Martin, ed. 1990. *Rendering Things Visible: Essays on South African Literary Culture*. Athens: Ohio University Press.

Turkington, Kate. 1977. *Chinua Achebe: "Things Fall Apart."* London: Edward Arnold.

Turner, Bryan S., ed. 1990. *Theories of Modernity and Postmodernity*. London: Sage.

Turner, Graeme. 1996. *British Cultural Studies: An Introduction*. 2d ed. Boston: Unwin Hyman.

Umeh, Marie, ed. 1996. *Emerging Perspectives on Buchi Emecheta*. Trenton, NJ: Africa World Press.

United Nations. 2000. *United Nations Treaty Collection*. http://untreaty.un.org/.

Varela, Francisco J., Evan Thompson, and Eleanor Rosch. 1991. *The Embodied Mind: Cognitive Science and Human Experience*. Cambridge: MIT Press.

Veit-Wild, Flora, and Anthony Chennells, eds. 1999. *Emerging Perspectives on Dambudzo Marechera*. Trenton, NJ: Africa World Press.

Verma, K. D. 2000. *The Indian Imagination: Critical Essays on Indian Writing in English*. New York: Palgrave.

Viswanathan, Gauri. 1989. *The Masks of Conquest: Literary Study and British Rule in India*. New York: Columbia University Press.

Walcott, Derek. 1998. *What the Twilight Says: Essays*. London: Faber and Faber.

Walder, Dennis. 1998. *Post-Colonial Literatures in English*. Cambridge: Blackwell.

Walker, Keith. 1999. *Countermodernism and Francophone Literary Culture: The Game of Slipnot*. Durham, NC: Duke University Press.

Waters, Malcolm. 1995. *Globalization*. London and New York: Routledge.

Watson, C. W. 1996. "The Construction of the Post-Colonial Subject in Malaysia." In *Asian Forms of the Nation*. Ed. Stein Tønnesson and Hans Antlöv. Richmond, Surrey: Curzon. 297–322.

Weeks, Jeffrey. 1997. "The Body and Sexuality." In *Modernity: An Introduction to Modern Societies*. Ed. Stuart Hall, David Held, Don Hubert and Kenneth Thompson. Malden, MA: Blackwell. 363–394.

Weiss, Allan. 1998. "Separations and Unities: Approaches to Québec Separatism in English- and French-Canadian Fantastic Literature." *Science Fiction Studies* 25: 53–61.

Weiss, Linda. 1998. *The Myth of the Powerless State*. Ithaca: Cornell University Press.

Weiss, Timothy F. 1992. *On the Margins. The Art of Exile in V. S. Naipaul*. Amherst: University of Massachusetts Press.

Wendt, Albert. 1995. "Introduction." In *Nuanua: Pacific Writing in English since 1980*. Ed. Albert Wendt. Honolulu: University of Hawaii Press. 1–8.

———. 1979. *Leaves of the Banyan Tree*. Honolulu: University of Hawaii Press.

Werbner, Richard, and Terence Ranger, eds. 1996. *Postcolonial Identities in Africa*. Atlantic Highlands, NJ: Zed.

Wiget, Andrew. 1985. *Native American Literature*. Boston: Twayne Publishers.

Wiget, Andrew, ed. 1994. *Dictionary of Native American Literature*. New York and London: Garland.

Wijesinha, Rajiva. 1993. "Timothy Mo's *The Redundancy of Courage*: An Outsider's View of Identity." *The Journal of Commonwealth Literature* 29: 2.

———. 1997. *Breaking Bounds: Essays on Sri Lankan Writers in English*. Belihuloya, Sri Lanka: Sabaragamuwa University Press.

Willett, Cynthia, ed. 1998. *Theorizing Multiculturalism. A Guide to the Current Debate*. Malden, MA, and London: Blackwell.

Williams, Mark. 1990. *Leaving the Highway: Six Contemporary New Zealand Novelists*. Auckland: Auckland University Press.

Williams, Patrick, and Laura Chrisman, eds. 1994. *Colonial Discourse and Post-Colonial Theory: A Reader*. New York: Columbia University Press.

Williams, Raymond. 1958. *Culture and Society: Coleridge to Orwell*. London: Hogarth Press.

Willinsky, John. 1998. *Learning to Divide the World: Education at Empire's End*. Minneapolis: University of Minnesota Press.

Wilson, Rob. 1996. "Towards an 'Asia/Pacific Cultural Studies': Literature, Cultural Identity, and Struggle in the American Pacific." *Studies in Language and Literature* 7: 1–18.

Woddis, J. 1967. *Introduction to Neocolonialism*. New York: International.

Woodward, Jack. 1989. *Native Law*. Toronto: Carswell.

Wren, Robert M. 1981. *Achebe's World: The Historical and Cultural Context of the Novels of Chinua Achebe*. Harlow: Longman.

Wright, Derek. 1994. *The Novels of Nuruddin Farah*. Bayreuth: Bayreuth African Studies.

————, ed. 1992. *Critical Perspectives on Ayi Kwei Armah*. Washington, DC: Three Continents.

Writing Diasporas—Transnational Imagination Conference, 2000. www.swansea.ac.uk. uk/conferences/transcomm

Yadav, Alok. 1993–1994. "Nationalism and Contemporaneity: Political Economy of a Discourse." *Cultural Critique* 26: 191–229.

Yamanaka, Lois-Ann. 1997. *Blu's Hanging*. New York: Avon.

Yarbro-Bejarano, Yvonne. 1994. "Gloria Anzaldúa's *Borderlands/La Frontera*: Cultural Studies, 'Difference,' and the Non-Unitary Subject." *Cultural Critique* 28: 5–28.

Ybarra-Frausto, Tomas. 1991. "Rasquachismo: A Chicano Sensibility." In *Chicano Art: Resistance and Affirmation, 1965–1985*. Ed. Richard Griswold del Castilo, Teresa McKenna, and Yvonne Yarbro-Bejarno. Los Angeles: Wright Art Gallery.

Yeğenoğlu, Meyda. 1998. *Colonial Fantasies: Towards a Feminist Reading of Orientalism*. Cambridge: Cambridge University Press.

Yelin, Louise. 1999. "Caryl Phillips." In *British Writers*. Ed. George Stade and Sarah Hannah Goldstein. New York: Charles Scribner's Sons. 379–94.

Yoder-Neck, Hilda van, ed. 1998. Special issue of *Callaloo* on Caribbean literature. 21.3.

Young, Robert. 1990. *White Mythologies: Writing, History and the West*. London: Routledge.

————. 1995. *Colonial Desire: Hybridity in Theory, Culture and Race*. London and New York: Routledge.

————. 1999. *Postcolonialism: An Historical Introduction*. Malden: Blackwell.

Yuval-Davis, Nira, and Ruth Lister. 1997. *Gender and Nation*. London: Sage.

Zamora, Lois Parkinson. 1997. "Magical Ruins / Magical Realism: Alejo Carpentier, François de Nome, and the New World Baroque." In *Poetics of the Americas: Race, Founding, and Textuality*. Ed. Bainard Cowan and Jefferson Humphries. Baton Rouge: Louisiana State University Press. 63–103.

Zamora, Lois Parkinson, and Wendy B. Faris, eds. 1995. *Magical Realism: Theory, History, Community*. Durham, NC: Duke University Press.

Zell, Hans, Carol Bundy, and Virginia Coulon, eds. 1983. *A New Reader's Guide to African Literature*. London: Heinemann.

Žižek, Slavoj. 1994. *The Metastases of Enjoyment: Six Essays on Woman and Causality*. London: Verso.

Index

Page numbers in **bold** indicate main entries.

About the Editor and Contributors

GABRIEL E. ABAD-FERNÁNDEZ is part-time Lecturer in the Department of Modern Languages at the University of Málaga, Spain. He formerly worked at the University of Northumbria at Newcastle (U.K.).

BELLA ADAMS works as a part-time lecturer at the Universities of Sunderland and Northumbria (U.K.).

SAHEED ADEYINKA ADEJUMOBI is a doctoral candidate in African history at the University of Texas at Austin.

FREDERICK LUIS ALDAMA is Assistant Professor at the University of Colorado and the author of a biography of Arturo Islas.

PAUL ALLATSON lectures in Spanish studies at the University of Technology, Sydney.

CHADWICK ALLEN is Assistant Professor in the Department of English at Ohio State University and the author of *Blood as Narrative/Narrative as Blood: Constructing Indigenous Identity in Contemporary American Indian and New Zealand Maori Literary and Activist Texts* (2001).

HAROLD BARRATT is a graduate student at the University College of Cape Breton (Canada).

SIMON BEECROFT has published in the *Journal of Commonwealth Literature*.

NICHOLAS BIRNS teaches American and postcolonial literature at New School University in New York. He edits *Antipodes*, a journal of Australian literature.

COLLEEN GLENNEY BOGGS is a graduate student in English at the University of Chicago.

JANA EVANS BRAZIEL is Assistant Professor of English at the University of Wisconsin at La Crosse; she researches migrant literatures and is the coeditor of *Bodies Out of Bounds: Being Fat in America* (2001).

ROGER J. JIANG BRESNAHAN teaches writing and cultural studies at Michigan State University and has published two volumes of interviews: *Conversations with Filipino Writers* (1992) and *Angles of Vision: Conversations on Philippine Literature* (1992).

ELOISE A. BRIÈRE teaches the literatures of Francophone Africa and the Americas at the State University of New York at Albany. She has been president of the International Council for Francophone Studies and published *Le Roman Camerounais et ses Discours* (1993).

BARBARA BROTHERS, Professor of English and Dean of the College of Arts and Sciences at Youngstown State University (Ohio), has edited four volumes on British travel writing from 1837 to 1997 for the *Dictionary of Literary Biography*.

JAMES N. BROWN is currently an Honorary Associate in the Department of Cultural Studies at Macquarie University (Sydney).

HARISH CHANDER teaches in the Department of Humanities at Shaw University in North Carolina.

BALASUBRAMANYAM CHANDRAMOHAN is Senior Lecturer and the Field Manager of Post-Colonial Studies at the University of Luton (U.K.) and the author of *A Study in Trans-Ethnicity in Modern South Africa: The Writings of Alex La Guma (1925–1985)* (1992).

JASON A. CLARK is in graduate studies in English at the University of Vermont.

MATTHEW CLEVELAND teaches in the School of English at the University of New South Wales (Australia).

ROCÍO G. DAVIS is Professor of American and Postcolonial Literature at the University of Navarre (Spain).

JILL DIDUR is Assistant Professor of English at Concordia University in Montreal and has published articles on nationalist discourse and other postcolonial topics.

GRACE EBRON has published in the *Literature of Travel and Exploration*, the *Encyclopedia of American Immigration*, the *Handbook of African History*, and the *Encyclopedia of Life Writing*.

NADA ELIA is Scholar in Residence in the Afro-American Studies Program at Brown University and is author of *Trances, Dances and Vociferations: Agency and Resistance in Africana Women's Narratives* (2000).

ANDREA FEESER is Assistant Professor of twentieth-century art and theory at the University of Hawaii at Manoa. She recently completed a book on French art, politics, and masculinity in the context of World War II.

ELIZABETH B. FITZPATRICK is Reference Librarian at the University of Massachusetts at Amherst.

SARAH FULFORD is a Lecturer in literature at the University of Durham (U.K.).

RAHUL KRISHNA GAIROLA has taught at Rhode Island College.

SAMIR GANDESHA teaches sociology and philosophy at Centennial College in Toronto.

S. M. GHAZANFAR is Professor and Chair of the Department of Economics at the University of Idaho. He has published in the *History of Political Economy* and the *Journal of Social, Political, and Economic Studies.*

BISHNUPRIYA GHOSH is Associate Professor in postcolonial, cultural, and women's studies in the English Department, Utah State University. She has edited and introduced the feminist collection *Interventions* (1997) and is currently completing revisions to her book *The "Renaissance" in Indian Writing under Globalization.*

DEVARAKSHANAM BETTY GOVINDEN is in the Faculty of Education at the University of Durban at Westville (South Africa).

SHANE D. GRAHAM is a doctoral candidate in English and African Studies at Indiana University at Bloomington.

LYNDA HALL, a Sessional Instructor at the University of Calgary (Canada), has edited *Lesbian Self-Writing: The Embodiment of Experience* (2000) and *Converging Terrains: Gender, Environment, Technology and the Body* (2000).

DORIS HAMBUCH is Assistant Professor in the English Department at King Saud University in Riyadh, Saudi Arabia.

GRAEME HARPER is Director of the Development Centre for the Creative and Performing Arts at the University of Wales, Bangor. His publications include *Black Cat, Green Field* (1988), which won the Australian National Book Council Award for New Fiction, *Unruly Pleasures: The Cult Film and Its Critics* (2000), and *Captive and Free: Colonial and Postcolonial Incarceration* (2001).

WAÏL S. HASSAN is Assistant Professor of English at Illinois State University; he has completed a book manuscript on Tayeb Salih.

JOHN C. HAWLEY is Associate Professor of English at Santa Clara University (California) and editor of nine other books, including *Postcolonial and Queer Theories: Intersections and Essays* (Greenwood 2001), *Cross-Addressing: Re-*

sistance Literature and Cultural Borders (1996), and *Historicizing Christian Encounters with the Other* (1996).

ERICH HERTZ is a graduate student in the Department of English at the University of Notre Dame.

KEVIN HICKEY is Visiting Assistant Professor of English at Western Connecticut State University at Danbury.

ANDREA SCHWIEGER HIEPKO is a doctoral candidate at the Latin American Institute at the Free University of Berlin.

HUGH HODGES is a doctoral candidate in English studies at the University of Toronto.

NIKOLAS HUOT is a graduate student in the Department of English at Georgia State University.

JAMES M. IVORY is an Assistant Professor of English at Appalachian State University in Boone, North Carolina, and the author of *Identity and Narrative Metamorphoses in Twentieth-Century British Literature* (2000).

NALINI IYER is Associate Professor of English at Seattle University and has published articles in *ARIEL* and *The Doris Lessing Newsletter.*

CLARA A. B. JOSEPH teaches in the Department of English at York University (Canada).

FEROZA JUSSAWALLA is Professor of English at the University of Texas at El Paso and editor of *Interviews with Writers of the Postcolonial World* and *Interviews with V. S. Naipaul.*

GEOFFREY KAIN is Professor of Humanities at Embry-Riddle University, Florida, and the editor of *R. K. Narayan: Critical Essays* and *Ideas of Home: Literature of Asian Migration.*

KATHRYN L. KLEYPAS lectures at the University of Southern California.

KANTA KOCHHAR-LINDGREN teaches in the M.A. program in humanities at Central Michigan University.

BÉNÉDICTE LEDENT is Senior Lecturer in Caribbean literature and English at the University of Liège (Belgium).

OLIVER LOVESEY is Professor of English at Okanagan University College in Kelowna, British Columbia (Canada) and the author of *Ngũgĩ wa Thiong'o* (2000).

SERI INTHAVA KAU'IKEALAULA LUANGPHINITH is Assistant Professor of English at the University of Hawaii at Hilo. She has contributed to *Updating the Literary West* (1997) and *Asian American Novelists* (Greenwood 2000).

CHRISTOPHER LUPKE is Assistant Professor of Chinese language and culture at Washington State University.

HENA MAES-JELINEK, Honorary Professor of the University of Liège (Belgium), has published extensively on Wilson Harris and coedits the series Cross/Cultures for Rodopi Press.

ANNE MALENA is Assistant Professor of translation and Francophone literature at the University of Alberta and the author of *The Negotiated Self: The Dynamics of Identity in Francophone Caribbean Narrative* (1999).

ANITA MANNUR is a Visiting Lecturer of Asian American studies at the Massachusetts Institute of Technology.

DAVID CHIONI MOORE is Acting Director of International Studies at Macalester College and author of articles in *PMLA, Transition, Diaspora, Research in African Literatures,* and others.

SALAH M. MOUKHLIS is Assistant Professor of English at Holyoke Community College (Massachusetts).

MIHAELA MUDURE teaches in the English Department at Babes-Bolyai University in Cluj-Napoca, Romania. She has published several books and articles on comparative multiculturalisms.

KATWIWA MULE is Assistant Professor of African and comparative literature at Smith College and has published on various African authors.

KLAUS-PETER MÜLLER has been Associate Professor of English at the University of Stuttgart (Germany) and is the author of many books, including *Epiphanie: Begriff und Gestaltungsprinzip im Frühwerk von James Joyce* (1984) and *Wertstrukturen und Wertewandel im englischen Drama der Gegenwart* (2000).

STUART MURRAY is Senior Lecturer in Commonwealth and postcolonial literature in the School of English at the University of Leeds (U.K.). He is the author of *Never a Soul at Home: New Zealand Literary Nationalism and the 1930s* (1998) and editor of *Not on Any Map: Essays on Postcoloniality and Cultural Nationalism* (1997).

NIMA NAGHIBI has published in *Interventions: International Journal of Postcolonial Studies* and elsewhere.

SILVIA NAGY-ZEKMI is Associate Professor of Latin American and Caribbean studies at State University of New York at Albany. She has published four books, including *Paralelismos transatlánticos: Postcolonialismo y narrativa femenina en América Latina y Africa del Norte* (1996) and *Historia de la canción folklórica en los Andes* (1989).

PHILLIP R. O'NEILL, a Lecturer in English at Santa Clara University, has published in *New Literatures Review* and elsewhere.

VALÉRIE ORLANDO is an Assistant Professor of French and Francophone studies at Illinois Wesleyan University and the author of *Nomadic Voices of Exile: Feminine Identity in Francophone Literature of the Maghreb* (1999).

RAMENGA MTAALI OSOTSI has worked extensively in African literatures and currently teaches at James Madison University (Virginia).

RAJEEV S. PATKE is Associate Professor of English at the National University of Singapore; he is the author of *The Long Poems of Wallace Stevens* (1985), and coedited *Institutions in Cultures: Theory and Practice* (1996).

DIANA REBEKKAH PAULIN is Assistant Professor of American studies and English at Yale University. She has published in *Cultural Critique* and elsewhere.

RANJINI PHILIP is Assistant Professor of English at Zayed University (United Arab Emirates), and is the Chair of the TESOL Arabia Literature Special Interest Group.

LAWRENCE PHILLIPS teaches English and American literature at Goldsmiths College, University of London, and has most recently published articles in *Race & Class*, *Scrutiny2*, and *Henry Street*.

PREM PODDAR is Lektor in postcolonial studies at Aarhus Universitet (Denmark); he is the author of *Translating Nations* and recently completed *Articulating India*.

RALPH PORDZIK teaches English literature at the Universities of Munich and Essen (Germany) and is the author of books on postmodernist poetry, South African poetry, and the utopian novel in the new English literatures.

RITA RALEY is Assistant Professor of English at the University of Minnesota. She is writing a book on global English and has published in *ARIEL*, *Diaspora*, and elsewhere.

LUZ ELENA RAMIREZ is Assistant Professor of English at California State University at San Bernardino. She has published in *Texas Studies in Literature and Language* and elsewhere.

VICTOR J. RAMRAJ is editor of *ARIEL: A Review of International English Literature*. His publications include a book on the Canadian writer Mordecai Richler and an anthology, *Concert of Voices: An Anthology of World Writing in English* (1995).

PALLAVI RASTOGI is completing his dissertation at Tufts University (Boston) on colonial and postcolonial Indo-British travel narratives.

SUSANNE REICHL is Assistant Professor in the Department of English and American studies at the University of Vienna, Austria.

JENNIFER C. RODGERS is a teaching assistant in comparative Literature at the University of Massachusetts, Amherst.

LYNNE ROGERS teaches at Bir Zeit University in the West Bank.

ROBERT L. ROSS is Research Associate at the Edward A. Clark Center for Australian Studies at the University of Texas and editor of *Antipodes: A North American Journal of Australian Literature.*

SIMON RYAN is a Senior Lecturer in literature at the Australian Catholic University (Brisbane) and is the author of *The Cartographic Eye: How Explorers Saw Australia* (1996).

ANNEDITH M. SCHNEIDER, Assistant Professor of cultural studies at Sabanci University in Istanbul, Turkey, is currently working on a book manuscript entitled *Remembering Hybridity: Nation, Community and Identity in Narratives of the Algerian Conflict.*

S. SHANKAR is Assistant Professor of English at Rutgers University. He is the author of the novel *A Map of Where I Live* and the volume of criticism *Textual Traffic: Colonialism, Modernity and the Economy of the Text*; he is the translator of Komal Swminathan's acclaimed Tamil play *Thaneer, Thaneer!* ("Water!").

STEPHEN P. SHEEHI is Assistant Professor of the practice of Arabic in the Department of Asian and African Languages and Literature at Duke University. He has published in *The British Journal of Middle Eastern Studies, The Journal of Arabic Literature,* and *Critique.*

DANIEL L. SILVERSTONE is completing a doctorate in literature at Boston University.

TONY SIMOES DA SILVA lectures at the University of Exeter (U.K.), and is the author of *The Luxury of Nationalist Despair: The Novels of George Lamming* (2000).

JOSEPH SLAUGHTER is an Assistant Professor of English and comparative literature at Columbia University.

CHERYL SUZACK has published a chapter in *Postcolonizing the Commonwealth: Studies in Literature and Culture,* edited by Rowland Smith (2000).

IMRE SZEMAN is Assistant Professor of English and cultural studies at McMaster University (Canada) and coeditor of both *Pierre Bourdieu: Fieldwork in Culture* and the second edition of *The Johns Hopkins Guide to Literary Theory and Criticism.*

KATRINA DALY THOMPSON specializes in Shona and Swahili languages, literatures, and film.

SHAWKAT M. TOORAWA is in the Department of Humanities at the University of Mauritius and is an affiliate at the W.E.B. Du Bois Center for Afro-American Studies at Harvard University.

HARISH TRIVEDI, Professor of English at the University of Delhi (India), is the author of *Colonial Transactions: English Literature and India* (1993, 1995), and co-editor of *Interrogating Post-colonialism* (1996) and *Postcolonial Translation* (1999).

JESÚS VARELA-ZAPATA is Dean of Humanities at Santiago de Compostela University (Lugo, Spain) and the author of *V. S. Naipaul: Sociedad Post-Colonial* (1998).

REBECCA WEAVER is Assistant Editor of *American Literary History*.

RAJIVA WIJESINHA, Professor of languages at Sabaragamuwa University (Sri Lanka), is the author of several works of fiction as well as literary criticism in *The Journal of Commonwealth Literature* and elsewhere.

DEREK WRIGHT, who recently retired from the University of Queensland (Brisbane, Australia) and returned to Tasmania, has published ten books and over 100 essays and articles on world literatures in English.